Third Edition

BUSINESS

STRATEGY, DEVELOPMENT, APPLICATION

Gary J. Bissonette

Queen's University

Mc
Graw
Hill

Business: Strategy, Development, Application
Third Edition

The Internet addresses listed in the text were accurate at the time of publication. The inclusion of a website does not indicate an endorsement by the authors or McGraw-Hill Ryerson, and McGraw-Hill Ryerson does not guarantee the accuracy of information presented at these sites.

ISBN-13: 978-1-25-965491-6
ISBN-10: 1-25-965491-5

1 2 3 4 5 6 7 8 9 M 23 22 21 20

Printed and bound in Canada.

Care has been taken to trace ownership of copyright material contained in this text; however, the publisher will welcome any information that enables it to rectify any reference or credit for subsequent editions.

Product Director: *Rhondda McNabb*
Portfolio Managers: *Amy Clarke-Spencley & Mark Grzeskowiak*
Marketing Manager: *Emily Park*
Senior Content Developer: *Amy Rydzanicz*
Photo/Permissions Research: *Karen Hunter*
Portfolio Associate: *Christine Albert*
Senior Supervising Editor: *Jessica Barnoski*
Copy Editor: *Kelli Howey*
Plant Production Coordinator: *Heitor Moura*
Manufacturing Production Coordinator: *Jason Stubner*
Cover Design: *Katherine Strain*
Cover Image: © *voyata/Shutterstock*
Interior Design: *Katherine Strain*
Page Layout: *MPS Limited*
Printer: *Marquis*

About the Author

Gary Bissonette is an Assistant Professor at Queen's University School of Business, and is the former Chief Executive Officer (CEO) of the YMCA of Kingston, Ontario. Gary also possesses considerable product/territorial management expertise in the private sector and has 20+ years of teaching experience at both the graduate and undergraduate levels in both Canada and the United States. A successful entrepreneur, Gary has operated his own consulting business (insurance brokerage firm specializing in employee benefits programs), as well as participated in a number of turnaround initiatives within the private sector. Gary holds an MBA from Clarkson University and a Bachelor of Administration from the State University of New York at Plattsburgh. In addition to his teaching responsibilities at Queen's University, Gary also served as the Director of the Queen's School of Business "Living Case" initiative and oversaw the creation of this innovative teaching initiative.

Courtesy of Queen's University

Brief Contents

Contents

PART 3

Managing the Value Chain

CHAPTER 10
The Marketing Challenge 356

CHAPTER 11
Understanding the Marketing Effort 389

CHAPTER 12

Technology, Analytics, and Operations Management *440*

PART 4

Financial Management

CHAPTER 13

Understanding Business Finances *485*

CHAPTER 14

Financial Statements Structure and Interpretation 539

CHAPTER 15

Analyzing New Business Ventures 590

Preface

An Innovative Approach to Teaching Business Management Fundamentals

In a marketplace full of introductory business textbooks, what makes this one different? Why does it make sense to choose this textbook versus others available to you? The response to these questions can be best described by the analogy of Blue Ocean versus Red Ocean thinking.

In creating the first edition of this textbook for the Canadian marketplace, the choice that presented itself was the following: create a textbook in a similar vein to the many books that already populate the marketplace and seek to convince you to try an alternate version of already existing products (Red Ocean), or create a new, unique, and thought-leading approach that supports the teaching of core concepts and models in a manner that generates a true understanding of business and communicates an excitement and appreciation for its role in today's society (Blue Ocean).

Business: Strategy, Development, Application third edition builds upon and continues to reinforce this latter approach. Created from the ground up for the Canadian market by an author with considerable middle and senior management expertise and many years of teaching experience at both the university and college levels, this textbook delivers a unique interpretation of the practical application of business in a way that ensures a true understanding of today's complex—yet exciting—business environment. Fundamental to its delivery is the communication of chapter content in a manner that students can easily grasp, and that ensures core learning takes place. Rich in examples, Web-based interaction, and practical-application illustration, the textbook delivers to the instructor and students a sound base for future business management learning and action.

Yes, this textbook is truly different in its approach—"Blue Ocean" different. It is uniquely positioned: focusing on knowledge and skill development in a usable format that students can immediately transfer to current employment situations, or use to leverage in managerial or self-employment opportunities that will challenge them in the future. It is also significantly more interactive, challenging students to participate in the current global marketplace via active, Web-based searches and references.

Why Choose This Textbook?

Many of us have been challenged throughout our careers with trying to find the perfect textbook that would enable an instructor to deliver an entry-level business management course in a way that was creative, thought provoking, and of interest to students. Essential to this search was the desire to have a textbook that goes beyond the typical template, definition-focused approach common to entry-level textbooks, and deliver content that results in a true understanding of business fundamentals. This textbook responds to this challenge and desired outcome. Specifically, *Business: Strategy, Development, Application* delivers the following:

- chapter content that explains the use of key business concepts and models via a writing style that encourages understanding and generates interest in the topic being discussed;
- extensive use of Canadian-based examples from a wide spectrum of business scenarios within the for-profit, not-for-profit, and SME (small and medium-size enterprise) business environments;

- a full understanding and appreciation of the globalization taking place today and the unique positioning that Canada and its economic base currently have—and will continue to benefit from—due to this globalization process;
- an emphasis on identifying and defining current business trends occurring within the Canadian marketplace, including but not limited to multicultural diversification, sustainable business thinking and practices, and regulatory trends and shifts; and
- delivery of key business concepts and models from the viewpoint of the C-level or general manager, thus ensuring not only a base-level understanding of such core business requirements, but also an understanding of how and why such concepts and models are used in managing a business entity.

A Special Note to Students

Regardless of the occupation that you enter into, you will come in direct contact with the world of business and, ultimately, the global marketplace. Whether you enter into the field of marketing, engineering, nursing, programming, or social services, or consider a business opportunity as an entrepreneur, many aspects of your job responsibilities will be framed around the business concepts and models discussed within this textbook. In writing this textbook, it is my hope that you will come to fully understand how businesses and the marketplace operate, and how you can use this information to your advantage as you pursue your chosen career. Also unique to this textbook is the writing style that is focused on defining and describing the role of the general manager in overseeing a business entity and how business fundamentals come into play within their decision-making process. The textbook's intent is to deliver a variety of business and management tools illustrated in a manner that will help to ensure easy application in the future.

Organization of the Textbook

Business: Strategy, Development, Application has been designed to be as flexible and modular as possible with each chapter possessing the ability to stand on its own. The textbook is built around four themes:

- Macro Business Environment
- Managing and Guiding Your Team
- Managing the Value Chain
- Financial Management

Although presented within the textbook as noted above, each section (theme) has been developed independently of the other sections so that instructors can feel comfortable in rearranging sections to fit their teaching style and/or course emphasis. A special focus has also been placed on ensuring that the textbook responds not only to the operational framework of corporate Canada, but also to the needs of students and instructors interested in SMEs and not-for-profit organizations.

Specific areas of focus within the four theme sections are as follows:

Part		Chapter Topics
Part 1: Macro Business Environment	Chapter 1	What Is Business?
	Chapter 2	The Canadian Economic Environment
	Chapter 3	The Global Marketplace
	Chapter 4	The Environment and Sustainable Business Practices

Part		Chapter Topics
Part 2: Managing and Guiding Your Team	Chapter 5 Chapter 6 Chapter 7 Chapter 8 Chapter 9	Ethics and Corporate Social Responsibility Developing a Business Strategy Entrepreneurship and Forms of Business Ownership Developing Your Business Structure and Culture Managing and Leading the Organization's Talent
Part 3: Managing the Value Chain	Chapter 10 Chapter 11 Chapter 12	The Marketing Challenge Understanding the Marketing Effort Technology, Analytics, and Operations Management
Part 4: Financial Management	Chapter 13 Chapter 14 Chapter 15	Understanding Business Finances Financial Statements Structure and Interpretation Analyzing New Business Ventures

In-Chapter Learning Features

A fundamental feature of this textbook is its turnkey approach to supporting student learning. Each chapter has been carefully crafted in a manner that will ensure that students fully understand the material being presented, and that they are directed to supplemental resource locations to update and enhance their competencies of critical concepts and models. In-chapter learning features include the following:

Learning Objectives
Help students preview what they should know after reading the chapter.

LEARNING OBJECTIVES

This chapter is designed to provide students with:

LO1	The ability to identify the major contributing factors that impact overall economic development
LO2	Exposure to the core economic model that shapes Canada's economic growth and development
LO3	A base-level understanding of what constitutes economic activity and how economies grow and contract
LO4	The ability to recognize trends that will influence the future composition of economic development in Canada
LO5	Guidance on how managers use information on economic trends in today's marketplace to better manage their organizations and respond to the competitive challenges confronting them

Snapshot—What to Expect in This Chapter
Outlines the key topics covered within the chapter.

Snapshot

What to Expect in This Chapter

This chapter provides students with a broad introductory overview of the fundamentals behind how our economy works and how we as managers can use our understanding of it to better manage our organizations. The content emphasized in this chapter includes the following:

- Canada and Its Economic System
- Key Economic Influencers
  - Contributing Factors to Economic Development
  - The Underlying Economic Model
  - Canada: A Mixed Economic System
- The Economy in Simple Terms
- The Economic Growth Cycle
- Managing the Movement in the Economy
- Trends Impacting the Canadian Market
- Managing in Challenging Times
  - Understanding Competitive Models
  - Sensing Market Change
- Management Reflection—Analyzing Market Trends

Business in Action Vignettes

Spread throughout each chapter; provide practical, marketplace applications of business situations and business best practices.

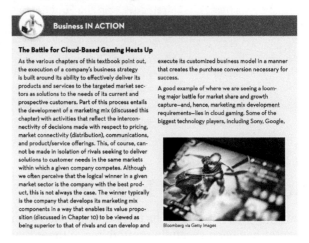

Business IN ACTION

The Battle for Cloud-Based Gaming Heats Up

As the various chapters of this textbook point out, the execution of a company's business strategy is built around its ability to effectively deliver its products and services to the targeted market sectors as solutions to the needs of its current and prospective customers. Part of this process entails the development of a marketing mix (discussed this chapter) with activities that reflect the interconnectivity of decisions made with respect to pricing, market connectivity (distribution), communications, and product/service offerings. This, of course, cannot be made in isolation of rivals seeking to deliver solutions to customer needs in the same markets within which a given company competes. Although we often perceive that the logical winner in a given market sector is the company with the best product, this is not always the case. The winner typically is the company that develops its marketing mix components in a way that enables its value proposition (discussed in Chapter 10) to be viewed as being superior to that of rivals and can develop and execute its customized business model in a manner that creates the purchase conversion necessary for success.

A good example of where we are seeing a looming major battle for market share and growth capture—and, hence, marketing mix development requirements—lies in cloud gaming. Some of the biggest technology players, including Sony, Google,

Bloomberg via Getty Images

Web Integration

Refer students to specific Web sites where they can continue to analyze the success of a business or the challenge highlighted within a Business in Action vignette.

Web Integration

Want a great place to track the movement in the TSX, the value of the Canadian dollar, and the price changes to oil and commodities? Visit www.financialpost.com. Click on "Markets > Futures."

Highlighted Key Takeaways

Presented throughout each chapter; reinforce the key learning fundamentals that students should understand as they read through and comprehend the information offered within a chapter's various sections.

Productivity gains, strong business investment, technological innovation, moderate wage increases, and a favourable currency exchange rate are all key factors that are deemed to be critical in ensuring that our economy remains resilient and competitive now and in the future.

Management Reflection

Provides a closing commentary on how managers use the key models and concepts discussed within a chapter and, in some cases, how small businesses or not-for-profits respond to the themes/challenges posed in the material presented.

LO6 **Management Reflection—The Business Decision-Making Landscape**

Being in business goes beyond simply developing your value proposition and understanding its asset base and cost structure. It is about being able to understand the macro environment around you; the resources, capability, and capacity that you possess; and the ability to communicate to the marketplace the uniqueness and importance of the products/services you offer. At its core base, developing and managing a business requires its owners/managers to:

- create a vision of the opportunity in the marketplace
- confirm that the market size of customers is large enough that, once commercialized, the opportunity can enable the organization to make a profit and sustain this profitability for the anticipated planning cycle and beyond
- confirm that a position within the market is feasible, which will enable the company to compete in a manner that is superior to its direct competition
- confirm that the market situation will stay constant long enough for the business plan to be developed and executed
- confirm that the business has the resource base and the capability to execute the strategy
- execute the strategy in an efficient and effective manner, achieving the objectives set forth within the business plan created

End-of-Chapter Support: Developing Business Knowledge and Skills

In addition to the above, the end-of-chapter support within *Business: Strategy, Development, Application* has been designed to provide instructors and students with an effective review and with additional learning materials focused on reinforcing the critical takeaways from within each chapter. Key ingredients of this end-of-chapter support include the following:

- **Chapter Summary:** An overview of the content of a chapter and the key models and concepts that were presented;
- **Key Terms:** Identification of the key business terms used in a chapter;
- **Questions for Discussion:** A set of chapter-related questions and points of reflection that ensure students fully understand the key components of chapter material presented;
- **Question for Individual Action:** A chapter-specific assignment suitable for assigning to an individual student;
- **Team Exercise:** A chapter-specific assignment that instructors can assign to groups or teams of students for analytical and/or presentation purposes; and
- **Case for Discussion:** A pertinent and to-the-point application/illustration of the chapter theme designed to complement both the reading material presented and the in-class discussions that will take place. Case discussions have been designed for use within a single instructional session.

Award-Winning Technology

Mc Graw Hill connect®

McGraw-Hill Connect® is an award-winning digital teaching and learning solution that empowers students to achieve better outcomes and enables instructors to improve efficiency with course management. Within Connect, students have access to SmartBook®, McGraw-Hill's adaptive learning and reading resource. SmartBook prompts students with questions based on the material they are studying. By assessing individual answers, SmartBook learns what each student knows and identifies which topics they need to practise, giving each student a personalized learning experience and path to success.

Connect's key features also include analytics and reporting, simple assignment management, smart grading, the opportunity to post your own resources, and the Connect Instructor Library, a repository for additional resources to improve student engagement in and out of the classroom.

MANAGER'S HOT SEAT VIDEOS

This resource allows students to watch real managers apply their years of experience to management and organizational behaviour issues. Students assume the role of the manager as they watch the video and then answer multiple-choice questions following the segment. The Manager's Hot Seat videos are ideal for group or classroom discussions.

APPLICATION-BASED ACTIVITIES

The Connect Application-Based Activities are highly interactive and automatically graded application- and analysis-based exercises wherein students immerse themselves in a business environment, analyze the situation, and apply their knowledge of business strategies. Students progress from understanding basic concepts to assessing and solving complex real-world scenarios.

ISEEIT! VIDEOS

These brief, contemporary videos offer dynamic student-centred introductions, illustrations, and animations to guide students through challenging concepts. Ideal for before class as an introduction, during class to launch or clarify a topic, or after class for formative assessment.

Instructor Resources

- **Instructor's Manual:** Prepared by the text author, Gary Bissonette, this manual contains a short topic outline of the chapter and a listing of learning objectives and key terms, a resource checklist with supplements that correspond to each chapter, a detailed lecture outline including marginal notes recommending where to use supplementary cases, lecture enhancers, and critical thinking exercises.
- **Computerized Test Bank:** Written by Greg Libitz, Queen's University, contains a variety of true/false, multiple-choice, and short and long essay questions. True/false questions test three levels of learning: (1) knowledge of key terms, (2) understanding of concepts and principles, and (3) application of principles. We've tagged each question according to its knowledge and skills areas. Designations align questions with the text's Learning Objectives, topics, and difficulty levels as well. Multiple versions of the test can be created and printed.
- **Microsoft® PowerPoint® Presentation:** Prepared by Sandra Wellman, Seneca College, the slideshow for each chapter is based around the learning objectives and includes many of the figures and tables from the textbook, as well as some additional slides that support and expand the text discussions. Slides can be modified by instructors with PowerPoint®.

Acknowledgements

Although the cover of this textbook lists me as the sole author, this is somewhat of a misnomer. The completion of what is now the third edition of this textbook could not have been accomplished without considerable contribution by many others. First and foremost, I would like to thank my wife, Lynda. Not only has she been an ongoing supporter of this initiative, but she spent countless hours proofing, editing, and questioning the communication approach within it. It was truly a joint initiative. Her commitment to enabling me to succeed will never be forgotten. She is truly the best life partner one could ever hope for.

Much of what I have learned over the course of my career has been the result of a combination of my own experiences, both positive and negative. Equally as important has been my advantage to work at Queen's University with some of the brightest minds in Canada. The work of Drs. Ken Wong, Peter Richardson, and Elspeth Murray has had a real influence on both my teaching style and conceptual emphasis. David McConomy has been a true mentor, both in reviewing and commenting on this textbook as it unfolded and in demonstrating best practices in the classroom. Additional thanks goes to Queen's professors Greg Libitz and Darren McCaugherty, who, in using the first two editions of this textbook, provided insight and commentary into the enhancements and adjustments found in both the second and, now, this third edition. In addition to his constructive feedback, it should be noted that Greg Libitz has also contributed to this third edition via the preparation of a number of the new cases found at the end of many of its chapters. I would also like to acknowledge the Smith School of Business of Queen's University, which has also been an invaluable part of my professional development, offering an academic environment second to none.

With respect to my publisher, I would like to recognize and thank the editorial and marketing team at McGraw-Hill, including Amy Clarke-Spencley, Portfolio Manager; Amy Rydzanicz, Senior Content Developer; Jessica Barnoski, Senior Supervising Editor; and Kelli Howey, Copy Editor, for their patience, commitment, and support to this undertaking. Their guidance and professional interaction is truly appreciated.

Finally, I extend sincere thanks to the reviewers who provided insightful feedback that helped to shape this book over these three editions.

PART 1

CHAPTER 1

What Is Business?

LEARNING OBJECTIVES

This chapter is designed to provide students with:

LO1	A macro-level understanding of what business is
LO2	An overview of the major components of a business model and how their successful development and execution determines business performance
LO3	An awareness of the overarching role of the business owner or "C-suite" management team
LO4	An understanding of how businesses plan
LO5	Exposure to the concept of visionary leadership
LO6	Via a Management Reflection, an overview of the relationship between business strategy and business model development, and the importance of successfully executing both for a business to achieve its identified objectives
LO7	Via an Appendix, an introduction to the difference between profit and profitability

Snapshot

What to Expect in This Chapter

This chapter provides students with a broad introductory overview of what a business owner or a senior management team needs to understand to successfully manage a business organization. The content emphasized in this chapter includes the following:

- The Big Picture
- What Is Business?
  - The Full Business Model
- The Role of the Business Owner or "C-Suite" Manager
  - Putting Plans into Action
  - Thinking across Multiple Horizons
  - Corporate Social Responsibility
- The Concept of Visionary Leadership
- Management Reflection—The Business Decision-Making Landscape
- Appendix—The Business Model and Profitability
  - The Difference between Profit and Profitability
  - Improving Profitability

Business IN ACTION

Microsoft—Reinventing the Business Model

Over the past 5⁺ years, a quiet renaissance has been occurring at Microsoft. After years of relying on operating system sales (Windows) and its Office suite of products (Word, Excel, PowerPoint, etc.), Microsoft made a critical change in 2014. It was during this year that Microsoft brought in its new CEO, Satya Nadella, to take the helm of one of the world's largest software and technology companies. Disruptions within the marketplace, driven largely by market and technology forces, required Microsoft to redefine where and how it would do business. Looking long-term, Nadella and his management team redefined Microsoft's approach to business from that of a proprietary, closed-technology system organization to one that embraced open-sourced systems and cooperative ventures and partnerships with rivals, and looked to the cloud versus maintaining a dependency focus on singular PC-based software sales and a consumer-faced mobile (cellular) market presence.

Fast-forwarding to 2018, Nadella's visionary leadership has propelled Microsoft from that of what many considered to be an aging dinosaur in 2014 to, on November 30, 2018, briefly stealing (from Apple) the title of the world's most valued company, a position it had not held since 2002.

Recognizing that the new market model evolving was one of an open ecosystem, whose software development

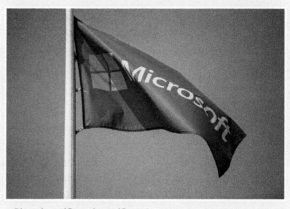
© Bloomberg/Contributor/Getty Images

roots had shifted to a broad technology design community for application creation and support, Nadella and his team abandoned the previous fixed notion that Microsoft software was to be available only on Microsoft devices and embraced a market-driven mandate requiring Microsoft products to be available across an increasingly broad business ecosystem. Today, Microsoft Office products operate across a variety of operating systems including Apple's iOS (iPad, etc.) and Linux-based applications. Microsoft has also executed on the necessary steps to ensure that its Windows operating system would work as an open-style software in the smartphone sector, thereby improving its presence in a market in which up to this point it had been a marginal player.

So why the change? The PC-centric world of doing business is being disrupted by a variety of key factors. Mobile services are changing the way that people work and communicate. Cloud technologies are redefining how data are collected, managed, and stored. New entrants such as Amazon and Google have disrupted traditionally strong profit streams within the storage and computing sector via lower prices.

So just what is Microsoft's focus today? Microsoft has refocused its business model to one that looks to support its customers whose own business models require the need for a variety of diverse approaches to business and technology management. This requires the creation and maintenance of a strong network of application development and delivery capabilities, supported by a flexible platform in a way that will remain central to customer needs, thereby accelerating Microsoft's growth.

For Nadella, the go-forward risk lies in in two critical areas. First, rivals that possess service capabilities comparable to Microsoft (Amazon and Google, for example) will continue to actively compete for customers. Amazon in particular has demonstrated significant strength and success in the delivery of cloud-based services. Second, the intensification of competition has exerted significant downward pressure on price, thereby impacting operating margins and overall profitability. To put this in simple terms, the old business model, where Microsoft delivered 100% of a business's core services with little to no competition, thereby enabling it to generate significant profit margins from its core product base (Office, Windows, etc.), is no longer sustainable in today's technology-diverse and hypercompetitive market. To compete with competitors in this environment (content and application marketplace), Microsoft faces the risk of higher costs and lower operating margins.

So far, the investment community is demonstrating its support for the new vision Nadella and his team have communicated for Microsoft. Share value for Microsoft stock has risen from $36.89 in January 2014 to a high of $115.62 on October 1, 2018. With the initial renaissance complete, Nadella and his team must continue to focus on keeping Microsoft relevant in today's rapidly changing technology sector. Businesses as well are shifting key aspects of their business models faster than ever before. This means that standing still at Microsoft is not an option. The company must continue to innovate in a way that enables it to maintain a leadership position in the market segments it chooses to compete in.

The Big Picture

Perhaps the best way to begin thinking about business, in its broadest context, is to view it as a system of integrated actions designed to

a. ensure that an organization develops and grows a market for its goods and/or services and, in doing so,

b. create organizational value (wealth) on behalf of its stakeholders

To accomplish both facets of this definition organizations must succeed in properly identifying solutions to needs that the marketplace desires, and create the right business model for delivering such solutions to the right customer, at the right place, at the right time, for the right price. Critical to this is the ability to accomplish the above-mentioned objectives in a manner that offers its customers superior value when compared against its rivals. This process results in the development of a series of integrated actions that are often departmentalized into cross-functional areas such as technology application, product engineering and design, manufacturing and operations, marketing and sales, distribution, and service.

How a business operates can initially be assessed against three fundamental characteristics (see Figure 1.1):

a. the commercial endeavours it undertakes

b. its employee interaction model, and

c. its organizational culture and formalized decision-making structure

Commercial Endeavours refers to the markets the organization serves, the products and services it offers, and the needs it professes to meet in the marketplace.

Commercial endeavours refers to the markets the organization serves, the products and services it offers, and the needs it professes to meet in the marketplace. It reflects the results of understanding the demand/supply relationships that exist in the marketplace at large, as well as within the customer segments it chooses to pursue. It also, as part of its ongoing assessment process, recognizes the capacities and capabilities of competitors within such selected markets to deliver products/services to similar buyers. Understanding this relationship, coupled with an understanding of the cost requirements needed to produce goods and services, along with the price sensitivities of targeted customers, is what enables the creation of a business model—the successful execution of which ideally results in delivering a profitable outcome to the organization.

Employee Interaction refers to the value-creating skills an organization's employees bring to the marketplace. The success of many businesses lies with the specialized skills that exist within its labour force.

Employee interaction refers to the value-creating skills that an organization's employees bring to the marketplace. The success of many businesses lies with the specialized skills that exist within its labour force. The leveraging of these skills in the production of goods and/or the delivery of services is what enables a business to create value and enables transactions to occur that will allow the firm to make a profit. A great way of understanding the importance of the talent (people) component of an organization is the viewpoint expressed via the following statement: A successful business strategy results from 5% planning and 95% execution, and successful execution of a company's strategy is the result of the leveraging of

FIGURE 1.1   **Business: The Big Picture**

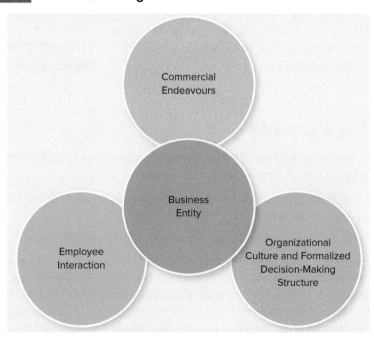

5% technical competencies and 95% people capabilities. Again, it is the people who make a difference in a business's overall success. As an example, a company can have superior technology and/or financial capital when compared to rivals, but if its management team and its employees cannot leverage such advantages then overall results most likely will be compromised.

Organizational culture and decision-making structure is a reflection of the framework of business activities and decision-making ecosystem that exists within an organization. It comprises the underlying business system and its related culture, which an organization creates, and the transaction processes that it develops to service the marketplace it targets.

These three characteristics, when assessed jointly, result in a macro-level understanding of a business entity whose objective is the development, communication, and delivery of goods and/or services that are sought after by the marketplace, in response to a defined need, in a manner that is valued by the customers being targeted.

As an example of this assessment process, think of the industry-leading search engine company Google (Alphabet Inc.). Google's business system can be assessed against the three characteristics identified above. For Google, the "commercial endeavour" objective is the generation of revenue and profits resulting from such market offerings as its "point and click" and mobile-based advertising services, its pursuit of new business opportunities through acquisitions (YouTube, Dropcam, Skybox Imaging, Nest Labs, Inc., and DoubleClick, to name a few), and its business activities related to markets such as mobile phone services (voice, applications, and software), mapping and navigation, security services, aerospace (drones and UAVs), artificial intelligence (Google Home, etc.), and gaming. Its "employee interaction" relates to the many developers, engineers, and system designers with specialized skills whom Google employs to develop and support the products and services the company offers. Google's "organizational culture and decision-making structure" refers to the formal framework it has put into place to manage and deliver its products and services. It refers to Google's server farms and related infrastructure, managerial hierarchy, operating processes, and decision-making and communication processes.

> The efficiency and effectiveness of a business entity can be assessed against three fundamental characteristics: the commercial endeavours it undertakes, its human resource (employee) interaction model, and its organizational culture and decision-making structure.

What Is Business?

LO1, LO2

"Business" is a challenging word to define and understand because it has several different but related meanings. For some, it is simply a mechanism from which to drive profit via the sales of goods/services. For others, it is the ability to create and develop an organization whose primary mission is to satisfy an identified customer or society-based need. Recognizing that the definition will be personalized by each of us involved in a business operation, let's try to provide a broad-based definition of what business is all about.

Business can most easily be thought of as a set of mission-focused actions aimed at identifying the needs of a particular market, or markets, and the development of a solution to such needs through the acquisition or transformation of goods and services that can be delivered to the marketplace at a profit. Through

Organizational Culture and Decision-Making Structure is a reflection of the framework of the business activities and decision-making ecosystem that exists within an organization.

Business refers to the mission-focused activities aimed at identifying the needs of a particular market or markets, and the development of a solution to such needs through the acquisition and transformation of resources into goods and services that can be delivered to the marketplace at a profit.

the development of a business model, managers will attempt to initiate and control these actions in a manner that results in the most efficient and effective profit maximization approach.

Business models can be best visualized as the underlying operational platform or structure a business uses to position its approach to a given market and thereby to generate its revenue and, most importantly, derive its profit. An easy way to think of this is to visualize an "ecosystem" comprising a number of integrated parts, which interact and are codependent on each other. When visualizing a business model, think of it as having two primary parts:

- the company-centric side, which we will call the business system, that reflects the underlying mechanics as to how our business is structured, and

- the market-centric side, which refers to how we connect our business to the marketplace.[1] This market-centric side takes into consideration two important requirements. First, our ability to properly assess potential market opportunities and determine where and how we want to compete, and second, our ability to effectively develop and communicate a market position around which to build a value proposition, and its accompanying revenue model, in a way that outperforms rivals focused on the same set of customers.

The company-centric side (business system) comprises five key areas (see Figure 1.2):

1. Activities
2. Resources
3. Partners
4. Cost Structure
5. Portfolio of Products and Services

Activities refer to key processes an organization undertakes in order to deliver products and services to the marketplace. Examples of activities would be research and development, materials procurement, manufacturing processes, marketing and sales, and customer service. It would also include support activities such as finance and accounting, information technology, and so on.

> **Business Models** can be best visualized as the underlying operational platform or structure which a business uses to position its approach to a given market and thereby generate its revenue and, most importantly, derive its profit.

> **Activities** refer to key processes an organization undertakes in order to deliver products and services to the marketplace.

FIGURE 1.2   **Company-Centric Side (Business System)**

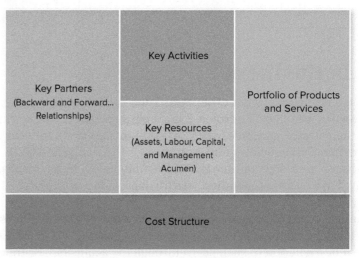

Source: Adapted from *Business Model Generation*, Osterwalder, Pigneur, John Wiley & Sons, Inc., 2010.

Resources refer to four core areas—*assets, labour, capital,* and *managerial acumen.* **Assets**, in simplistic terms, represent the infrastructure and resource base of the organization. This includes (but is not limited to) an organization's land, buildings, process and infrastructure base (bricks and mortar, ecommerce, etc.), equipment and technology framework, raw materials, and brand power. **Labour** refers to the human resource (talent) requirements of the business, while **capital** refers to the money needed by an organization to support asset-based expenditures, meet operating cash requirements, and invest in the development of the new products or services that the organization desires to introduce into the marketplace. **Managerial acumen** refers to the foresight, drive, knowledge, ability, decision-making competency, and ingenuity of the organization's key individuals—its owners or top-level managers.[2] A key component of managerial acumen is the visionary leadership that a senior management team or business owner provides to the organization. Visionary leadership refers to the ability of managers to establish a direction for the organization based on the needs identified in the marketplace and the mission (reason for being) of the organization. This is then translated into a strategic plan designed to guide the organization to fulfilling such needs while meeting its mission (purpose or reason for the organization's existence).

Partners refers to complementary dependencies and/or collaborative relationships a business has with other organizations that are deemed essential to the design, development, and delivery of its products and services to the marketplace. Examples of partners would be retailers and wholesalers that are distributing our products, suppliers and subcontractors that are manufacturing our products and/or product components on our behalf, service companies that provide after-sale service and support to our customers (e.g., call centres), and joint ventures we have undertaken with other organizations. To illustrate partner relationships, let's take a quick look at Microsoft Corporation. Examples of Microsoft partners[3] are suppliers such as Intergen Ltd. (marketing), Infosys Ltd. (business consulting), Accenture (business consulting), Beyondsoft Corp. (product development and testing), Assembly/Edelman (social media), Flextronics International Ltd. (manufacturing), Hitachi (components and logistics), Qualcomm Inc. (chips—Surface), and AMD (chips—Xbox). Authorized distributors include such organizations as SYNNEX Corporation, Tech Data, D&H Distributing, MA Labs, Inc., and ASI Corp., to mention a few. And, as per the Business in Action relating to Microsoft, market development joint ventures exist with a variety of companies such as Salesforce.com and Dropbox.

A key component of managing any business is understanding the expenses that will be incurred as a result of offering products and/or delivering services to the marketplace. This is referred to as an organization's **cost structure**. These costs must be recognized within an organization's business plans and pricing strategies to ensure the costs of the operation and other related financial obligations are fully offset by the revenue generated by the business and that acceptable levels of profit are realized. Examples of common operating expense categories that many organizations experience and that make up a company's cost structure are cost of revenue (manufacturing and distribution costs), sales and marketing expenses, general and administrative expenses, research and development expenses, and interest expense. Again using Microsoft Corporation as an example, Figure 1.3 shows major category expenses incurred during the fiscal year ending June 30, 2018, along with the dollar amounts (USD in millions) spent within each of these areas.

Product/service portfolio refers to the different items, products, and/or services a company offers for sale. An easy way to think of this portfolio is to think of it as being made up of an organization's various product lines. Microsoft's product portfolio is organized around three major business segments: Productivity and Business Processes, Intelligent Cloud, and More Personal Computing. Commercial cloud revenue (part of Intelligent Cloud), as an example, consists of products such

Resources refers to four core areas: assets, labour, capital, and managerial acumen.

Assets refers to (1) the infrastructure and resource base of the organization; (2) the resources that the organization has at its disposal and that it can utilize in the generation of business activity and, ultimately, profit.

Labour refers to the human resource (talent) requirements of the business.

Capital refers to the money needed by an organization to support asset-based expenditures, meet operating cash requirements, and invest in the development of new products and/or services which the organization desires to introduce into the marketplace.

Managerial Acumen refers to the foresight, drive, knowledge, ability, decision-making competency, and ingenuity of the organization's key individuals—its owners or top-level managers.

Partners refers to complementary dependencies and/or relationships we have with other organizations that are deemed essential to the design, development, and delivery of products and services to the marketplace.

Cost Structure the expenses that will be incurred as a result of offering products and/or delivering services to the marketplace.

Product/Service Portfolio refers to the different items, products, and/or services that a company offers for sale.

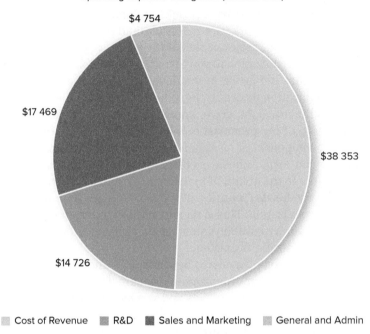

FIGURE 1.3   **Microsoft Corporation—10-K Filing, 2018**

Operating Expense Categories (Millions USD)

$4 754

$17 469

$38 353

$14 726

■ Cost of Revenue   ■ R&D   ■ Sales and Marketing   ■ General and Admin

Source: Based on data from Microsoft Corporation, 10-K Filing, August 2018.

as Microsoft Office 365, Microsoft Azure, and Microsoft Dynamics 365, while More Personal Computing would include Windows, Microsoft Surface, and Xbox software and services, and Productivity and Business Processes includes products and services such as the recently acquired LinkedIn and the Office suite of products.[4]

> A key component of managing any business is understanding the expenses (costs) that must be considered when setting the price of a product/service offering.

 Business IN ACTION

Canadian Tire—Building Out the Business Model

Established in 1922, Canadian Tire is one of Canada's most recognized retail brands. With more than 490 coast-to-coast retail locations, backed by a strong entrepreneurial-based dealer network, Canadian Tire sells more products, in more places, than any other Canadian retailer. With more than 90% of the Canadian population living within 15 minutes of a Canadian Tire store, and with more than 80% of Canadians shopping at its retail locations every year, the company markets itself as Canada's store.

With such a stellar history and such a well-recognized brand in Canada, individuals may question why Canadian Tire's management team feels a pressing need to make core, fundamental changes to its current business model. The answer is that the competitive landscape has changed dramatically over the last 15 years, and how you and I shop for the products and services we purchase has changed even more. In the past, Canadian Tire's response to changes in the retail market has been sluggish versus a nimble

Brad Calkins/Dreamstime.com

market leader. This inertia has resulted in more than one iconic brand (Eaton's, Zellers, Sears, etc.) disappearing from the marketplace, as new and more nimble retail specialists, along with well-established U.S.-based brands (Amazon, Walmart, Home Depot, Lowe's, Marshalls, etc.), create an even more congested market space. Decision making at Canadian Tire, often tied to length of time in getting its 400+ independent dealers to agree on change, has been slow and its business model has, in the past, been fixated on trying to be all things to all people.

So have things changed at Canadian Tire? The response to this question is a definitive yes. The retailer gained traction with the appointment of Stephen Wetmore as President and CEO of Canadian Tire Corporation, Limited in 2009. Creating an underlying sense of urgency within the company, Wetmore acquired The Forzani Group in 2011 (Sport Chek, Hockey Experts, Sports Experts, National Sports, Intersport, and Atmosphere), and restructured Canadian Tire and its family of companies—which also includes Canadian Tire retail stores, Mark's (acquired in 2002), Canadian Tire Financial Services, PartSource, Gas+, CT REIT, Canadian Tire Jumpstart Charities, and the renamed FGL Sports. Although Canadian Tire Retail (independently owned and operated by Dealers) still represented 66% of

revenue at the end of 2017 (down from 72% in 2014), the diversification undertaken under Wetmore's management tenure repositioned the company's focus and permanently redefined the organization's makeup in a big way. For Wetmore and his management team at that time, the future of Canadian Tire lay in the selection of key products and services and in the targeting of key customers. This meant shifting away from the broader generalist mass-market merchandiser position the company had initially pursued. Canadian Tire Retail would focus its new customer-centric enterprise business model and product offerings around five key groupings: automotive, living, fixing, playing/sporting goods, and apparel (Mark's). Key anchors would be sporting goods and automotive. Facilitation meant strengthening the automotive presence and developing Canadian Tire into Canada's leading sporting goods retailer. Supporting this push was a renewed emphasis on technology, omnichannel marketing initiatives, rebuilding of the Canadian Tire loyalty program, refocusing on the male-gender core customer, and the execution of some business-savvy acquisitions.

Fast forward to 2018 and we see Canadian Tire continuing to evolve in the face of heightened bricks and mortar competition, along with the continual evolution of online retail and the growing presence of Amazon. Retiring from Canadian Tire in 2014, Stephen Wetmore returned in 2016 as CEO of one of Canada's most iconic brands. The challenge then and now is how to continue to evolve and grow Canadian Tire in today's disruptive market environment. This means a continual focus on advancing Canadian Tire's operational capabilities in in-store, digital, and ecommerce methodologies, strengthening its overall digital marketing abilities, and increasing its focus on owned brands beyond FGL Sports and Mark's. In support of this, one of Wetmore's more recent moves was the acquisition of Norway-based Helly Hansen for just under $1 billion (CAD) in July 2018.

For Wetmore and his team, standing still is not an option. Customers demand best-of-breed service delivery more today then ever before. The iconic Canadian Tire money of yesterday has been replaced by its Triangle Rewards program (April 2018), allowing seamless collection and use of rewards across all of its banners. The key is to continue to drive traffic and ultimately derive "share of wallet" from its 11+ million customer base, of which 2.1 million hold Canadian Tire credit cards. To do this, Canadian Tire must continue to present a relevant and meaningful product selection to its customers that is perceived by such customers to represent the best value in the marketplace.

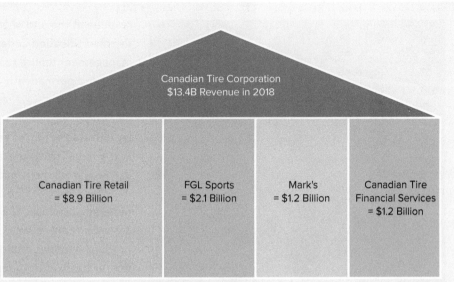

Canadian Tire Corporation $13.4B Revenue in 2018

Canadian Tire Retail = $8.9 Billion

FGL Sports = $2.1 Billion

Mark's = $1.2 Billion

Canadian Tire Financial Services = $1.2 Billion

Adapted from Canadian Tire Corporation's Investor Presentation, September 2014. Updated June 2019.

The market-centric side (see Figure 1.4) of business model development focuses the business's efforts on the external factors required for success. Market-centric decisions look to draw conclusions relating to properly assessing potential market opportunities in order to determine where and how we want to compete. An easy way to think of this is to view it in terms of a narrative or story. This is what the company or business is communicating to the marketplace. Creation of the market-centric side means focusing our analysis on the following areas:

1. Available Customer Segments and Opportunity Assessment
2. Positioning
3. Value Proposition Development
4. Revenue Model Development

Available customer segments Businesses recognize that they cannot be all things to all people. Markets by their very nature are made up of various segments possessing

FIGURE 1.4   Market-Centric Business Model

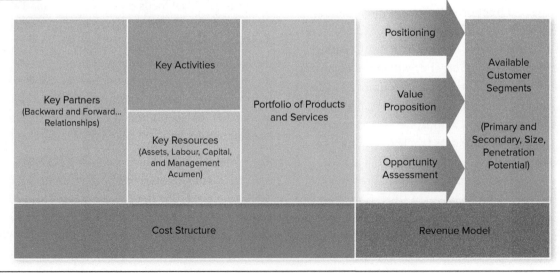

Source: Adapted from *Business Model Generation*, Osterwalder, Pigneur, John Wiley & Sons, Inc., 2010.

different needs, wants, and desires. Differences in demographic factors such as age, gender, and income will result in different segments requiring different products and services. The same holds true for lifestyle and behavioural factors that influence purchase decisions. Thrill seekers, for example, desire different products and services from risk-aversive individuals. These concepts will be discussed in more detail in later chapters in this textbook. The important takeaway here is that businesses need to decide what customer segments will most likely respond to their efforts and be most receptive to their product and/or service offerings; this is what is meant by the term *opportunity assessment*. **Opportunity assessment** involves analyzing the marketplace in such a way (via marketing research and data analytics) that enables the organization to determine which segments are most likely to respond to its communication messages and purchase its products and/or services. We refer to these as *primary segments*. We also look to identify *secondary segments*—which, although not as lucrative as primary segments, offer additional sales opportunities.

Positioning **Positioning**, which also will be discussed in greater detail in later chapters, refers to our ability to develop a unique, credible, sustainable, and valued place in the minds of our customers for our brand, products, and/or services. Think of positioning as the outcome of the communication strategy we initiate in support of our products and/or services that results in customers formulating an opinion as to what our brand stands for. Tim Hortons, for example, positions a significant portion of its communication efforts around the message of being "truly Canadian." This enables it to create an emotional link between its products and being Canadian, a message its U.S.-based rivals cannot match.

Value proposition development A **value proposition** is a statement that summarizes to whom a product or service is geared toward and the benefits the purchaser will realize as a result of using the product or service. Recognizing the conclusions reached as a result of an organization's positioning analysis, it communicates to potential purchasers how the product or service differs from competing products or services offered in the marketplace. For example, suppose you decide to purchase a smartphone. The question for you is which product to purchase; the marketplace offers a number of competing choices. You could purchase an Apple iPhone or a Samsung phone (two industry leaders), or one of the models offered by other major players such as Huawei, Lenovo, or Google. Or, depending on where you live, you might look to purchase from global and regional players such as LG, OPPO (China), Wiko (France), Micromax (India), Telenor (Norway), Xiaomi (China), or Vivo (China), to name a few.[5] Your decision will be influenced by the benefits the products offer and the price you are willing to pay. In order to position themselves in the marketplace, companies develop value propositions for the purpose of communicating to customers how their products or services are different and the important benefits they offer. It is important to understand that value propositions are not driven strictly by tangible or functional product benefits. In fact, many of the reasons why products or services are purchased have little to do with the actual product itself, but more with the perceived benefits the product or service offers. As was noted with respect to the other market-centric elements identified above, the concept of a value proposition will be more fully discussed in later chapters. What is important to understand at this stage is that the value proposition defines what makes you unique and how this uniqueness translates into meaningful value to the customer. Fundamental to this is to ensure we have correctly concluded that what we think adds value is viewed by the customer as equally important.

> Companies develop value propositions for the purpose of communicating to customers how their products/services are different and the important benefits that they offer.

Opportunity Assessment is analyzing the marketplace in such a way (via marketing research and data analytics) that enables the organization to determine which segments are most likely to respond to its communication messages and purchase its products and/or services.

Positioning refers to our ability to develop a unique, credible, sustainable, and valued place in the minds of our customers for our brand, products, and/or services.

Value Proposition is a statement that summarizes whom a product or service is geared toward and the benefits the purchaser will realize as a result of using the product or service.

Revenue model development A **revenue model** focuses on the relationship between the prices organizations are able to charge for their services, the volume of purchases they are able to generate, and the profitability derived from such activity. Revenue could potentially come from a single source (one product within a business's product portfolio), or from a number of products, product lines, and/or divisions within an organization. Going back to our Microsoft Corporation example, Figure 1.5 shows the sources that make up Microsoft's 2018 fiscal-year revenue of $110+ billion (USD).[6] In reviewing Microsoft's 10-K filing, we can see that the More Personal Computing division, largely driven by Windows sales, continues to make up the largest percentage of the company's revenue. Having said this, although larger than the other two operating divisions, More Personal Computing experienced the slowest year-over-year growth (compared to 2017), achieving +8% in 2018. Productivity and Business Processes led the way with +20% growth in year-over-year revenue (compared to 2017), while the Intelligent Cloud division experienced year-over-year revenue growth of +18%.

The revenue model, however, is not just about generating sales. It also takes into consideration the relationship between price and expenses (costs) and the underlying operating margins and profit margins organizations realize as a result of doing business. Referring back to Microsoft Corporation's 2018 fiscal-year performance, the company generated operating income of $35 058 billion (USD) and net income (profits) of $16 571 billion (USD) from revenue of $110 360 billion (USD).[7] The concepts of profit and profitability are discussed more fully in the appendix provided at the end of this chapter, while the concept of margins and margin management, along with a more detailed discussion relating to the realization of operating income and of net income (profits), occurs in later chapters.

The Full Business Model

Figure 1.6 provides the concept of the business model in its entirety. On the business-centric side we have the core components of an organization's business

FIGURE 1.5   **Microsoft Corporation, 10-K Filing, 2018**

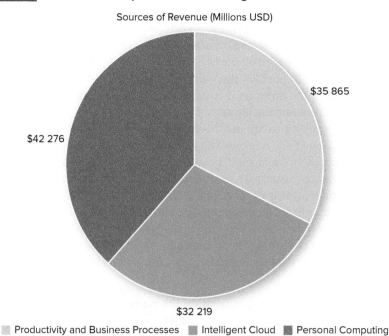

Sources of Revenue (Millions USD)

$35 865

$42 276

$32 219

Productivity and Business Processes   Intelligent Cloud   Personal Computing

Source: Based on data from Microsoft Corporation 10-K Filing, August 2018.

FIGURE 1.6	**Full Business Model**

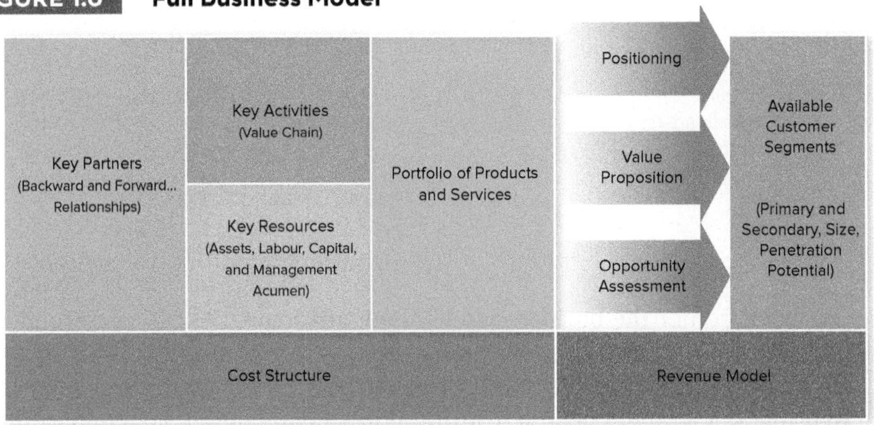

Source: Adapted from Business Model Generation, Osterwalder, Pigneur, John Wiley & Sons, Inc., 2010.

system. This incorporates the products and/or services it intends to offer to the marketplace, the key activities required to develop and deliver such products and/or services, the key resources that will be needed, and the partners the organization is dependent on for its overall success. It also, in conducting actions across these various areas, needs to fully identify and manage the costs that will be incurred along the way.

The market-centric side is all about targeting and communicating the reasons why customers should purchase our product and/or service versus that of alternate solutions in the marketplace. Customer selection is as important as the communication of what are perceived to be key benefits that customers can expect. Attached to this is the need to determine at what price such products and/or services will be offered and, given the costs incurred, what profit can be expected.

Business models are, as a result of the analysis provided above, the unique manner and structure by which we conduct business on a day-to-day basis, and reflect conscious decisions relating to resource deployment in route to developing revenue and driving profit. No two companies are alike, and it is their deployment of assets and capabilities, via their business model, that determines which companies are more profitable.

> Business models are, as a result of the analysis provided above, the manner and structure by which we conduct business on a day-to-day basis, and reflect conscious decisions relating to resource deployment in route to developing revenue and driving profit.

The Role of the Business Owner or "C-Suite" Manager*   LO3, LO4

As was concluded above, the role of the business owner or top-level management team is to anticipate, recognize, and act upon opportunities that then drive the creation of products and/or delivery of services believed to offer solutions to problems in a unique, important, and valued (meaningful) way to a targeted customer or customers. This leveraging of a market opportunity is realized via the efficient and

---

*The term "C-suite manager" refers to an organization's top-level management team. Examples of C-suite managers include the CEO (Chief Executive Officer), COO (Chief Operating Officer), CFO (Chief Financial Officer), CIO (Chief Information Officer), and CMO (Chief Marketing Officer).

FIGURE 1.7   **Role of the General Manager**

effective execution of the business model the management team creates, and the deployment of the productive resources the organization possesses.

Fundamental to this challenge is for the business owner and their management team to develop a strategy geared toward taking advantage of such opportunities and recognizing the required capabilities, competencies, and capacity the company must possess in order to successfully execute such a strategy. Commonly referred to as the strategic planning process, the focus of developing strategy (discussed in more detail in Chapter 6) is to draw conclusions relating to where a company will compete, what will be its competitive scope, and how it will execute in a way that outperforms rivals. Once strategic direction is determined, it then becomes the role of the management team to develop and execute the business model in pursuit of the objectives identified. The effectiveness of this execution is what, ultimately, determines the level of growth and profitability realized (performance) by the organization (see Figure 1.7).

Putting Plans into Action

So exactly how do managers put a business model into motion? Understanding its strategic opportunities and its capabilities, competencies, and overall capacity, the business management team develops a business plan via a process called the business planning cycle (see Figure 1.8). The business planning cycle outlines the focus and methodology for setting the business model in motion. In an ideal situation, this plan would be built around the leveraging of a competitive advantage. A company has a **competitive advantage** when it possesses capabilities that enable the company to perform critical activities better than its rivals. The performance of these activities is then leveraged in a manner that offers customers a product or service at a lower cost, greater perceived value, or a combination of the two versus that which competitors are able to deliver. If the business plan is competitive and executed properly, and customers are attracted to the company's product/service offering(s), the company generates money, or revenue, from the sale of the product. Assuming that the plan is executed in an efficient and effective manner, this revenue will exceed the expenses associated with producing or delivering the product/service, thereby generating a profit for the firm. This then enables the company to grow through reinvestment of these profits (along with capital from other sources, if required) into the business and the expansion of the business opportunities that the organization undertakes.

Competitive Advantage occurs when a company possesses capabilities that enable it to perform critical activities better than its rivals; this advantage enables it to generate greater sales and/or margins and creates preference for its products and services in the minds of its customers.

The role of the business owner or management team is to anticipate, recognize, or sense an opportunity to create a product or to deliver a service that is felt to be unique, important, and of value (meaningful) to a targeted customer or customers.

In fact, businesses grow by executing a series of planning cycles over time (see Figure 1.9). Each planning cycle is designed to direct the positioning of the company

FIGURE 1.8   Business Planning Cycle

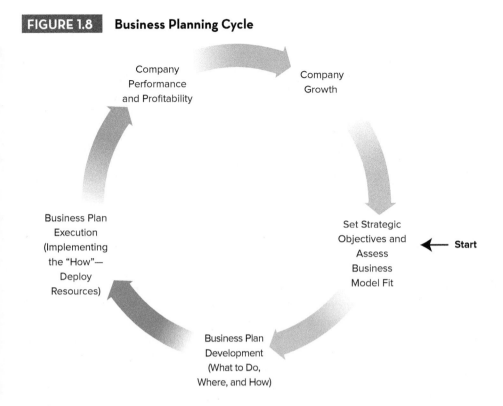

within the marketplace, orchestrate the creation of a business plan that will achieve the objectives formulated for the planning period, ensure linkage with the vision and mission of the organization, and implement the required adjustments to the business model that will ensure the plan is executed in a fashion that leads to growth and profitability. The management team must then allocate the resources and leverage the company's capabilities in a manner that ensures the tactics designed to achieve the objectives identified actually work and produce the desired results. Finally, the management team needs to assess the success of the company in achieving the desired objectives, and determine adjustments required in order to further grow the company via future planning cycles (see Figure 1.10).

If an organization does not achieve its objectives as a result of either poor positioning or poor execution of the strategies initiated, then the company will most

FIGURE 1.9   Growth via Planning Cycle Execution

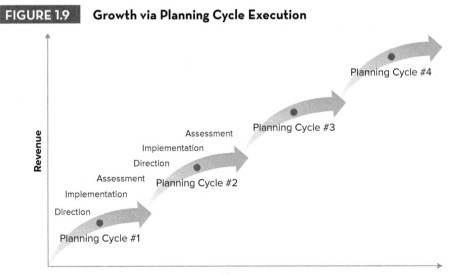

FIGURE 1.10   Planning Cycle Staging

Planning Cycle Staging

Direction/Positioning	Implementation	Assessment
• What do we want to do? • Why do we want to do it? • Can we do it?	• How will we do it? • What needs to be changed in order to succeed? • Where will resources be allocated?	• Did we meet our goal? • What needs to be changed or improved? • What systems require fine-tuning? • What further capacity adjustments are required?

likely not achieve the results anticipated and will need to redirect the current organizational effort in order to get back on track and achieve its revenue and profitability targets. A flattening, or declining, of revenue or a reduction in overall profitability are key identifiers as to whether a given plan is working. Figure 1.11 illustrates a failure to grow the company to the desired position and meet its objectives during a planning cycle. It should be noted that this failure to meet the objectives of a planning cycle can be the result of poor positioning, poor operational execution, or a combination of the two.

> The failure to meet the objectives of a planning cycle can be the result of poor positioning, poor operational execution, or a combination of the two.

The following example illustrates the planning cycle concept. When most of us hear the company name Amazon, our attention is immediately focused toward its presence in the ecommerce and online shopping market sector. Planning cycles today have Amazon continuing its presence and current dominance in this sector. What many of us do not realize, however, is that Amazon's business model is fluid and is expanding in the direction of a stronger bricks and mortar presence. Current planning at Amazon structured within its planning cycle development is the creation

FIGURE 1.11   Planning Cycle Outcome

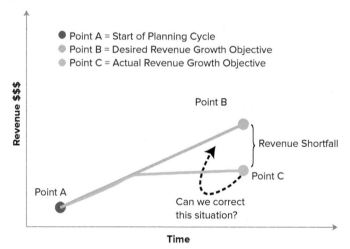

of a physical presence in the marketplace as well. Amazon Go, its cashierless, technology-savvy convenience store chain, with 10 locations in 2018, is targeting the opening of up to 50 additional locations in 2019 and, assuming market acceptance, is considering a plan to open as many as 3,000 new locations by 2021. In addition, Amazon also is planning on a significant expansion of its Whole Foods operation (acquired in 2017), with a long-term vision of moving Whole Foods from a current regional player to a national player in the United States and beyond. Planning cycles relating to Whole Foods not only detail the store footprint expansion noted above, but also focus on the integration of operational efficiencies and synergies between Amazon and Whole Foods. Whole Foods offers Amazon a bricks and mortar platform that enables it to create opportunities for minimizing the cost of returns, provide lockers for delivery, centralize purchasing, and offer an additional outlet for the products and services it sells (for example, the Amazon Echo and the Kindle are now available for purchase at Whole Foods). In addition, Amazon continues to provide additional discounts and opportunities to its Prime membership holders, thereby reinforcing their relationship and loyalty as Amazon customers.[8]

Before we go on, we should recognize that while **for-profit companies** need competitive business models, so do **not-for-profit organizations (NFPs)**, such as hospitals, school boards, YMCAs, social service agencies, educational institutions, and registered charities. By definition, not-for-profit organizations are those that are not in business to make a profit, but rather seek to deliver services to the people, groups, and communities they serve. Nevertheless, not-for-profits still need a business plan, operating model, and business system that will enable them to cover their operating costs and to employ strategies to fund the ongoing delivery of meaningful services. Small businesses, as well, need to recognize the need for a well-thought-out business plan and business model in order to determine just how, where, and when to compete.

> **For-Profit Companies** are organizations whose overarching objective is profitability and wealth creation on behalf of their shareholders and stakeholders.
>
> **Not-for-Profit Organizations (NFPs)** are organizations whose overarching objective is not profitability and wealth creation but to deliver services to the people, groups, and communities that they serve via a model of collective interest and social goal achievement.

Business IN ACTION

BlackBerry—Reinventing the Business Model

John Chen, Executive Chairman and CEO of Waterloo, Ontario-based BlackBerry (formerly Research In Motion), has reinvented the organization from that of a smartphone hardware company to an IoT (Internet of things) software market leader. When Chen took the helm at BlackBerry the company—the inventor of the smartphone and once one of Canada's highest-valued technology-based operations—was bleeding customers, employees, revenue, cash, and share value (declining from $138.87 in May 2008 to $6.33 in November 2013 when Chen arrived). The company had formally placed itself on the selling block and was attempting to overcome disappointing results with its recently launched BlackBerry 10 operating system. For Chen, however, all was not lost at BlackBerry. A turnaround specialist with a number of successful tenures under his belt

(such as his turnaround of Sybase Inc. back in the late 1990s), Chen set a new strategy for BlackBerry on the basis of its strengths (security, connectivity, privacy, trusted in regulated verticals).

Fast forward to 2019, and one sees a company that is financially stable with a strategy and product portfolio that positions it well for future growth. Today, BlackBerry presents to the marketplace a software and services company possessing a technology platform designed to bring trust to the IoT. That trust is built on three core pillars—security, privacy, and control—that have been the foundation of BlackBerry since its beginnings. This focus and trust is what has enabled the company to remain at the front end of the innovation curve.

Turnarounds require identifying key ingredients around which a redefined business model can be created. A fundamental associated with this is to "know thyself." In business, this means understanding

a company's core underlying strength and value, sticking to this, and rebuilding around it. Chen recognized BlackBerry's leadership in security, privacy, and connectivity and built a relevant and innovative strategy around this foundation. A turnaround often means making some hard decisions about where a company should enhance and maintain its resource commitment and where it should reduce or divest itself of resources. When Chen took over at BlackBerry, he did just that. Moving quickly, but with a defined strategy in mind, Chen divested the company of a number of nonessential assets. He also looked to reduce operating expenses via a number of initiatives, such as the outsourcing of smartphone manufacturing. This move served an additional purpose as Chen envisioned the technology market shifting its focus from hardware to software. He believed product differentiation—and therefore value—would not continue to be found in hardware, but had a future in software. Actions such as these freed up much-needed cash for BlackBerry and reduced its operating losses. Although a vital first step, cutting expenses was the easiest part of Chen's turnaround plan. The more challenging task was to deliver revenue growth. Since the turnaround, BlackBerry has delivered records in gross margin and software and services revenue. The company also

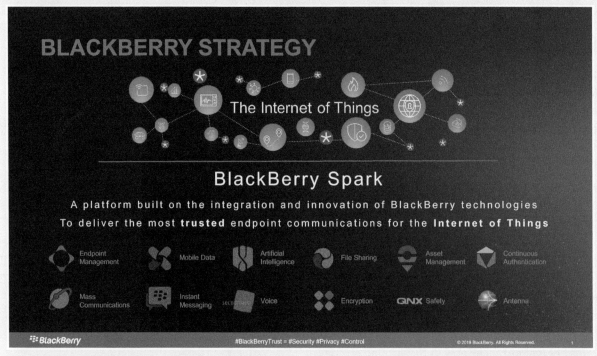

recently announced that its software now connects and protects over half a billion endpoints, including over 150 million cars.

For its next chapter—a growth chapter—BlackBerry has all the right components: an IoT platform with BlackBerry Spark, which offers artificial intelligence-based cybersecurity as one of its USPs; a strong IP portfolio; and a customer base that includes NATO, the United Nations, all of the G7 governments, all of the Fortune 100 largest banks, and more.

Chen is without doubt that BlackBerry will survive, and he is optimistic that the company will grow to be as iconic as it once was. Whether it remains a niche player with specialized focus or a broader player competing across a number of markets and products remains to be seen. A potential sale of the company down the road has not been ruled out. The focus at this time, however, is to maintain and grow Black-Berry's position as a key player in cybersecurity and the IoT.

Web Integration

Want to learn more about BlackBerry's products, services, and future plans? Visit **www.blackberry.com**.

Thinking across Multiple Horizons

As discussed above, businesses, via decisions made by their management team, utilize resources with the idea of transforming them into products and services. These products and services are then sold to other businesses or to consumers (such as you and me) to achieve a *profit* for the firm. Profit is necessary in the immediate term for the business to pay its bills and reinvest in the future. Making a profit on a monthly, quarterly, and annual basis is fundamental to ensuring the immediate survival of the firm. In reflecting on this commentary one might be inclined to think that planning cycle decisions and underlying adjustments to the business model are all geared toward short-term performance. Short-term performance (the need to drive immediate profit) is, however, just one of three fundamental objectives that business owners and their management teams must consider as they look to draw conclusions on the strategic direction of the organization.

As managers consider current and future business direction, an equally important objective to short-term profit must be considered. This second objective is to set in motion the ability of the organization to achieve *long-term growth and profitability*. Businesses recognize that the demand for the products and services they currently offer will change, and could in fact disappear over time. Given this, businesses are constantly searching for new markets and new opportunities to further grow the scope and focus of their organizations. Although immediate-term operating performance is based on the products and services a business offers today, new products and services will need to be developed to ensure the organization remains healthy and continues to grow. Apple Inc. has driven significant profits over the past 18 years from its iPod (2001), iPhone (2007), and iPad (2010) products, iTunes, and its App Store. It recognizes, however, that it must continue to look beyond this current success and seek new opportunities for future growth, thus ensuring its ongoing profitability. Ongoing enhancements to these products and services, as well as continuous improvements to its iMac lineup, will carry Apple through the next few years (mid-term), but it will be current investments in Apple Pay, Apple Watch, and Apple TV (to name a few), along with new market opportunities created organically (internally) or through acquisitions, that will fuel future growth and profitability at Apple (Figure 1.12). It is this ability of management teams to look forward across multiple horizons, investing in and nurturing new growth opportunities, that is critical to creating a sustainable, long-term growth and profitability trajectory for an organization.

FIGURE 1.12   **Apple—Thinking across Multiple Horizons**

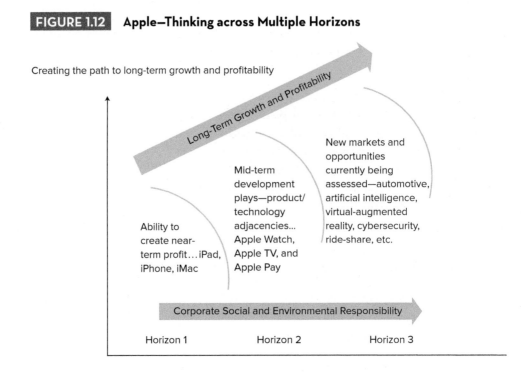

Creating the path to long-term growth and profitability

Corporate Social Responsibility

An additional objective, and one that is becoming increasingly important as part of the business decision-making process, is that of *social and environmental responsibility*. On a global basis, consumers are encouraging—and, in some industries, demanding—that businesses operate and act in a manner that demonstrates social responsibility with respect to product development, resource consumption, and operating processes. Green initiatives, truth in advertising, environmentally sustainable resource practices, and other environmental and social codes of conduct are challenging businesses to position themselves as good corporate citizens in order to acquire and retain customers. Individual managers are also challenged to make decisions and implement actions that conform to the highest ethical standards. Managers are expected to place society, the organization, and the organization's broader **stakeholder** community ahead of personal and/or shareholder gain when making decisions and when interacting with the marketplace. This increasing realization of social responsibility and environmental obligation will impact managerial decision-making across all horizons and will require the deployment of resources in ways that ensure society, as well as companies, prospers going forward. Social responsibility, including ethics and environmentally sustainable business concepts and practices, is discussed more fully in Chapters 4 and 5.

These same fundamentals also hold true for the not-for-profit sector. Although NFPs do not strive for a profit, they do need to create operational surpluses and/or acquire external capital funding commitments that enable reinvestment in the organization to ensure it remains vibrant and responsive to community needs. NFPs also need to assess their services on a regular basis to ensure they remain meaningful to the customers they serve and to expand such services where demand exists and where they have the capabilities to do so. Also, NFPs are held to a high level of social responsibility in that their core existence is based on their ability to meet societal needs that are not responded to by the for-profit sector. Referring back to prior comments relating to not-for-profits and registered charities (such as the YMCA), a fundamental requirement of planning is that these organizations earn or

Stakeholder refers to individuals, groups, or organizations that have a direct or indirect relationship with an organization, and that can be impacted by its policies, actions, and decisions. Stakeholders could include customers, suppliers, government, employees, and so on.

maintain an operating surplus on an annual basis to ensure that future building, equipment, technology, and programming financial needs are met for both today and tomorrow. They also need to continually review the programs and services they offer to ensure they remain meaningful to their respective members and program and service users. Add to this the need to develop programs and services that respond to new and emerging community needs. Finally, these organizations must ensure that they do all of these things in accordance with their charitable missions, and must be willing to accept responsibility for the delivery of socially required programs and services that for-profit entities would choose not to deliver due to an absence of a profit opportunity.

In closing, organizations and their management teams must learn to make decisions that enable all three of these responsibilities to be considered equally. Too much emphasis on short-term profitability, for example, may result in decisions that are detrimental to long-term market opportunities and fall short of social responsibility expectations.

© Mattz90/Dreamstime.com/GetStock.com

Many analysts have concluded that the current overemphasis on short-term profits was fundamental to the collapse of the financial services sector in 2008, and continues to constrain long-term opportunity development within a number of companies. Investment banks and other financial services companies are still feeling the fallout relating to the overleveraging of their organizations in high-risk investments, which provided some very positive short-term results (pre-2008) but exposed the organizations to significant losses and asset devaluation when the global marketplace found itself in a prolonged recession during the period 2010–12. Likewise, too much emphasis on developing future products or services—versus responding to customer needs today—may result in liquidity issues for the business if it is unable to cover its expenses in the short term. Managers and management teams therefore must, as part of their planning process, manage the balance between short-term profit requirements and aspirations with longer-term objectives and risk management techniques in a manner that ensures optimal market position and sustainable operating performance.

Business IN ACTION

Toyota Builds for a Greener Future

Toyota's commitment to the environment, and its status as one of the greenest automakers, is symbolized by its famous Prius—to date, the world's best-selling hybrid vehicle. While the Prius is the most visible symbol of Toyota's approach to protecting the environment, the company continues to seek approaches to meeting the world's growing transportation needs in ways that are less harmful to the planet. To achieve this balance, Toyota continually re-examines its products, business strategies, and daily operations, and

sets goals for environmental improvement. Although being a good corporate citizen has been embedded into its business values (dating back to 1935), Toyota fundamentally placed environmental sustainability and corporate social responsibility as core to its business strategy with the release of the Toyota Earth Charter and Global Vision in 2010. These two value drivers formally defined Toyota's commitment to the environment and to the communities where it does business. Environmental initiatives and programs

© Diego Azubel/epa/CORBIS

are core to the Toyota organization and its Canadian operations. These programs range from the development of the Hybrid Synergy Drive systems, to partnerships in Canada with organizations such as Evergreen and Earth Day, as well as a conscious effort to reduce its environmental footprint from manufacturing operations. Toyota's Earth Charter consists of four pillars: growth in harmony with the environment with the challenge to achieve zero carbon emissions through all areas of business activity; pursuit of all possible environmental technologies and the development of those technologies; the creation of a voluntary improvement plan based on preventive measures and compliance with laws to address environmental issues; and the building of close relationships with individuals and organizations involved in environmental preservation. For Toyota, the integration of its commitment to the environment is a conscious part of its business decision and implementation process. This commitment has resulted in the development of one of the most comprehensive waste-reduction

and recycling programs in North America, significant energy reduction initiatives, and global leader status in its efforts to achieve an optimal balance between fuel consumption and emissions reduction.

Toyota's commitment, however, does not merely start and stop with environmental sensitivity relating to its own manufacturing footprint. In January 2016, the company fully aligned its commitment with the 17 Goals to Transform Our World (Sustainable Development Goals) as defined by the United Nations. The company also has formally endorsed and is actively striving to meet the "under 2 degrees C scenario" and accompanying objectives agreed to under the Paris Agreement, adopted in 2015 and reaffirmed in October 2018. A founding member of the World Business Council for Sustainable Development (WBCSD), Toyota is working cooperatively with other automotive and technology-based partners to develop and incorporate environmental changes in the areas of autonomous driving, future mobility systems, and ride-sharing, to name a few.

Highlighted in its newly released Toyota Environmental Challenge 2050, the company is dedicated to the commitment to reduce the environmental burden attributed to automobiles to as close to zero as possible, and to continue to drive its decision-making process via values that ensure a positive contribution to our Earth and its societies. Criteria relating to this commitment include minimizing GHG emissions, reducing overall air pollution, water-usage reduction strategies, reversing biodiversity degradation, and respecting and adhering to ecosystem responsibilities as the organization continues to develop its operational footprint.

Web Integration

Want to know more about Toyota's sustainability initiatives? Visit **www.toyota.com** and type *sustainability initiatives* or *Toyota's Earth Charter* in the search browser.

LO5   The Concept of Visionary Leadership

Up to this point, we have been discussing the task-related responsibilities of business owners and C-suite managers. This discussion has focused on the development and implementation of a business model. The planning for such implementation occurs through the concept of a planning cycle(s) and recognizing the need to think about the organization's ongoing evolution across multiple horizons. The discussion also brought forward the requirement to balance the need for short-term profit with longer-term growth and profitability objectives, and to frame such responsibilities around recognition of the corporate and business social responsibility obligations we have to stakeholders, to the society at large, and to our planet.

An equally important responsibility that we, as managers, have for our organization is to provide our employees and related stakeholders with the visionary leadership required to successfully plan, organize, develop, and execute our strategy and its underlying business model. **Visionary leadership** is all about inspiring your workforce (talent) to pursue a shared goal beyond ordinary expectations. It is about creating a clear statement as to the direction in which the organization is heading, and then creating a culture within the company that encourages and supports employees in a way where they become motivated to achieve the organization's vision because they fully identify with it, find it meaningful, and believe that the company has the competencies, capabilities, and capacity to achieve it. It is fundamental to note that visionary leadership is not driven by, nor is the domain of, any particular gender, race, or creed. Visionary leadership is, as described above, the ability to effectively motivate and harness the collective capabilities of others to the achievement of specified goals and/or objectives. Whether you are male, female, or of a specific ethnic origin is immaterial to this definition and capability.[9]

Visionary leaders understand the driving forces that will influence market direction going forward, as well as the constraining forces that must be overcome in pursuit of the identified vision (Figure 1.13). This in-depth understanding applies to both what is happening outside the company (customers, competitors, government, etc.) as well as what is happening inside the company. A core innate skill of a visionary leader is the ability to articulate and communicate the vision of the organization such that employees fully understand how the responsibilities assigned to them assist in meeting this vision as well as the underlying importance of the work they are being asked to do.

In their book *Fast Forward: Organizational Change in 100 Days* Drs. Elspeth Murray and Peter Richardson point toward the importance of visionary leadership skills in effectively managing organizational change. Where visionary leaders excel is in their ability to:

1 Create a shared understanding among managers and employees of the organization's vision for the future.

2 Build support and critical mass among employees for the vision and the desire to obtain it.

Visionary Leadership involves inspiring your workforce (talent) to pursue a shared goal, beyond ordinary expectations.

FIGURE 1.13   **Key Abilities of Visionary Leaders**

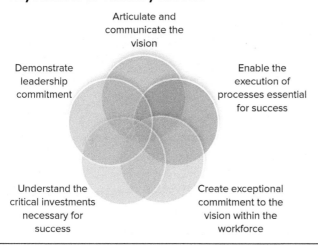

Source: Adapted from *Fast Forward: Organizational Change in 100 Days*, Murray & Richardson, Oxford University Press.

(3) Respond to, and effectively deal with, opposition to the vision and the strategy. This implies ensuring that opposing viewpoints are heard, considered, and responded to in a constructive manner. The intent here is not to challenge opposing views, but to embrace them and enable them to be part of the decision-making process.

(4) Ensure that accountability for the various strategic objectives identified as being essential to vision obtainment is fully communicated and appropriately embedded into the organization's performance and reward programs.

(5) Free up resources, particularly human resources, required to successfully complete the initiatives identified as critical to strategic and operating plan success.

(6) Make the tough decisions, where and when required, in order to keep the plan on track.

For visionary leaders it is all about creating "intelligent momentum," which Murray and Richardson identify as the creation of "winning conditions" within the organization. This means that visionary leaders are able to correctly identify the direction and nature of change required for the organization to create a long-term sustainable path for growth and profitability, and then demonstrate the leadership commitment to effectively follow through on such changes, work through the sources of resistance, and obtain heightened levels of commitment from a predominant number of their employees (the critical mass).[10] In many cases visionary leaders are viewed as "transformational" leaders, passionate individuals possessing a unique charismatic ability to transform others, thereby creating valuable and positive change to the organization.

So, what makes visionary leaders so successful? Visionary leaders understand that vision enables strategy, which provides the guidelines for the tactics and activities to be implemented within the business model. In addition, they are able to communicate the key metrics to be used to measure the success of the organization as it pursues the identified vision.

> Visionary leaders understand that vision enables strategy, which provides the guidelines for the tactics and activities to be implemented within the business model. In addition, they are able to communicate the key metrics to be used to measure the success of the organization as it pursues the identified vision.

 Business IN ACTION

Women—Visionary Leaders In Their Own Right

It has been reported that Margaret Thatcher, former Prime Minister of the United Kingdom, once said that "If you want something said, ask a man; if you want something done, ask a woman." Although one could debate the accuracy of this statement, it needs to be reinforced that the capabilities to lead and grow a business or organization are not limited to the male species. Successful female entrepreneurs and political and business leaders abound today more than ever before. In 2018, for example, there were approximately 22 female presidents and/or prime ministers in the world, and over a dozen women holding the CEO title of a Fortune 500 organization.

Some of the more prominent women currently leading major organizations include the following:

Indra Nooyi—who, in joining the C-suite in 2001 (as CFO) and taking over the helm at PepsiCo in 2007, guided the organization to revenue growth of over 70% via a series of acquisitions and organic-growth initiatives. Indra stepped down as CEO of PepsiCo in October 2018.

Carol Meyrowitz, President and CEO of TJX Companies—TJ Maxx (USA), HomeGoods (USA), Marshalls, Winners (Canada), and HomeSense (Canada). Since becoming CEO in 2007, Meyrowitz has grown TJX Companies into a $43-billion (USD) business that continues to lead and shape the women's retail apparel, home fashion, and accessory sector. The company now has 4070 stores in nine countries and positions itself as a unique offline experience.

Mary Barra, Chairman and CEO of General Motors. Barra has been largely responsible for reshaping what was perceived to be a slow-to-change automotive manufacturer into a savvy player in the automotive sector, particularly in the areas of electric and autonomous-driving vehicles. Although revenue has declined, Barra has expertly redefined the markets within which GM will compete and has improved its overall financial performance.

Ginni Rometty, Chairman, President, and CEO of IBM. Faced with significant market disruption and shrinking sales, Rometty reignited IBM and it turned around the company, which repositioned itself as a key business player in the cloud computing, artificial intelligence, and data management sectors.

It is not just American women who are making these inroads: Canadian women are achieving significant success in the C-suite as well. Women CEOs of Canadian companies include Helena Foulkes of Hudson's Bay Company (shown below); Linda Hasenfratz of Linamar Corporation, the second largest car parts manufacturer in Canada; Dawn Farrell, President and CEO of TransAlta Corporation since 2012; Nancy Southern, CEO of ATCO Ltd.; Gillian Riley, President and CEO of Tangerine, a subsidiary of Scotiabank; Laurie Schultz, President and

WENN Rights Ltd/Alamy Stock Photo

CEO of ACL, a software tech company considered to be one of the best Canadian companies to work for; and Mandy Rennehan, CEO of Freshco.

What makes each of these women so successful? Each has demonstrated solid competencies in managing their companies. They also have successfully articulated and communicated their vision for their respective companies to internal and external stakeholders. Each can also be credited with demonstrating exceptional commitment to the vision, through demonstrated leadership and the execution of processes and activities essential for success.

Recognizing that the past is not always a predictor of future performance, these women, like all business leaders regardless of gender, race, or creed, will be challenged in the market space they desire to have their companies compete within. Strategically, they, along with their respective teams, will need to determine what to do and where to compete. Then they will need to execute in a way that makes the vision that they create for their companies a reality.

LO6
Management Reflection—The Business Decision-Making Landscape

Being in business goes beyond simply developing your value proposition and understanding its asset base and cost structure. It is about being able to understand the macro environment around you; the resources, capability, and capacity that you possess; and the ability to communicate to the marketplace the uniqueness and importance of the products/services you offer. At its core base, developing and managing a business requires its owners/managers to:

- create a vision of the opportunity in the marketplace
- confirm that the market size of customers is large enough that, once commercialized, the opportunity can enable the organization to make a profit and sustain this profitability for the anticipated planning cycle and beyond
- confirm that a position within the market is feasible, which will enable the company to compete in a manner that is superior to its direct competition
- confirm that the market situation will stay constant long enough for the business plan to be developed and executed
- confirm that the business has the resource base and the capability to execute the strategy
- execute the strategy in an efficient and effective manner, achieving the objectives set forth within the business plan created

As this process demonstrates (see Figure 1.14), being in business is really a question of developing strategy and executing tactics across your business model. **Strategy** is the development of plans and decisions that will guide the direction of the firm and determine its long-term performance. Strategy focuses on the vision of the firm and the opportunity it believes exists in the marketplace. It also checks that the life expectancy of the product or service is long enough to ensure that the initial investment can be recovered and that the firm can make a profit. Finally, strategy development assesses whether the firm has the competencies and resources to compete in this targeted market. **Tactics** are the immediate-term actions that a firm executes to meet the short-term objectives set forth in

Strategy refers to the development of plans and decisions that will guide the direction of the firm and determine its long-term performance.

Tactics refers to the immediate-term actions which a firm executes in order to meet the short-term objectives set forth in the current planning cycle.

FIGURE 1.14   **Business Decision-Making Model**

| Visualize and Assess the Business Opportunity | Confirm Market Size and Profitability Potential | Determine Market Position, Approach, and Continuity | Assess Company Resources and Capabilities | Determine the Tactics Required to Achieve Objectives | Adjust, Build Out, or Reinvent the Business Model |

the current planning cycle. Tactics can be thought of as the action items a firm undertakes to ensure that it is successful in achieving its strategic objectives. Tactics could involve the expenditure of money for new equipment, the hiring of new staff with specialized skills, or the manufacturing processes undertaken to develop a product or service. To successfully grow a company, the management team has to be successful in both planning strategy and executing tactics. Strategically, managers need to understand where the market is going and how their products and services will fit into the market and meet customer needs. Tactically, they need to ensure that the right product reaches the right customer at the right time, and at the right place for the right price. As noted earlier, Chapter 6 outlines in more detail the strategic planning process and the relationship between strategy and tactics. The intent here is just to introduce these concepts so that you get a sense as to their overall importance in managing a business. Their introduction now also will make them easier for you to understand as you move through this course and textbook.

As managers, in conducting business we need to avoid the temptation to become predominantly focused on short-term results. Managers need to make decisions in recognition of both immediate needs and longer-term requirements in order to protect and grow the general health of the organization. A key aspect of this process is to understand that business (and the marketplace) is not static, but dynamic. It is changing all the time. What has worked in the past may not necessarily work in the future. As an example, Blockbuster Inc. built its market leader position in the movie rental marketplace on the basis of a bricks and mortar (physical store locations) business model. Successful in the 1970s, 80s, and 90s, this model gave way to video streaming, downloading, and competitive intensity from market entrants such as Netflix, Redbox, Amazon, cable companies, and mobile device and content distributors (Rogers, Bell, Telus, etc.). The end result is that, by failing to change, Blockbuster went from market leader valued at more than $500 million (USD) to a financially challenged organization in little over four years, with $900+ million (USD) in debt and $1.1 billion (USD) in losses. It ultimately was forced to liquidate its assets due to its inability to meet its debt obligations in 2010.[11]

For managers, Blockbuster and other examples like it (Target Canada, Toys R Us USA, Sears Canada, Aeropostale, Bon Ton) provide a constant reminder that we must continually assess and reassess market conditions and the customers they serve. Innovation and reinvention of how to conduct business and where to compete are becoming more fundamental to business planning than ever before. Visionary leadership and the ability to anticipate new market space and new market opportunities are necessary skills of today's managers. Managers must also recognize that the decisions they make impact both internal and external stakeholders. These stakeholders expect managers to conduct business in a manner that is ethical, socially responsible, and mindful of the sustainability requirements of our world.

Having said all of this, building, growing, and managing a company is one of the most rewarding experiences an individual will ever have. The feeling of accomplishment of a job well done is second to none. Welcome to the world of business—it's a career choice filled with excitement and never-ending challenge.

Business is not only about producing and distributing goods and services; it is about delivering value to customers in a manner that meets their needs and desires.

LO7 # Appendix—The Business Model and Profitability

The Difference between Profit and Profitability

Profit is the "bottom line" result an organization has realized for an identified, immediate period of time. In simple terms, Total Revenue − Total Expenses = Profit.

Profitability measures how well a company is using its resources over a specific period of time to generate earnings relative to its competitors.

Stockholders refers to any person, company, or organization that owns at least one share of stock in a specific company.

Individuals often confuse the concepts of profit and profitability. **Profit** is strictly the "bottom line" results that an organization has realized for a given period of time. In simple terms, Total Revenue − Total Expenses = Profit. If a firm had total current-year revenue from the sale of its products and services of $10 million, and the organization had total current-year expenses of $7 million (costs of developing, manufacturing, and selling such products and services), then it would realize a current-year profit (excluding tax considerations) of $3 million ($10 million − $7 million = $3 million). **Profitability**, on the other hand, corresponds to the efficiency and effectiveness of an organization to use its assets and its capital to generate profits for the organization over a period of time. Profitability analysis takes into consideration such factors as return on the capital invested, return on equity, the financial leverage the organization undertook to finance its assets and operations, the level of pre-tax income it earned, and so on. Profitability analysis is generally assessed over a period of time so that efficiency and effectiveness results, as noted above, can be compared on a period-over-period basis. This enables a management team to determine whether the operation has improved in its effective utilization of its assets and capital. Profitability analysis also focuses on comparisons among competitors within an industry to determine which organizations are the most effective in their utilization of resources. Competitors who are the most profitable over a period of time are generally the most attractive to investors for investment purposes. The benefit of profitability analysis is that it levels the playing field between competitors, recognizing that some may be significantly larger than others.

Let's look at an example to illustrate the importance of profitability analysis as one metric for assessing the overall value of a company. Assume that we have three companies within a given industry, companies X, Y, and Z. For the current year, Company X achieved a profit of $60 million, Company Y achieved a profit of $15 million, and Company Z achieved a profit of $7.5 million. On the surface, without any additional information, one could conclude that Company X was the most profitable company. Profitability analysis, however, goes beyond the absolute monetary value of the current-year profit. Referring to the data in Table 1.1, let's draw additional conclusions relating to the performance of these three companies. In other words, let's conduct a simplified profitability analysis. Table 1.1 provides us with the level of sales that occurred in the current year, as well as identifying the size of the asset base of each company and the value of the equity stake that **stockholders** have within each firm. Table 1.2 takes this information and, based on the profit earned by each company, calculates the return on each of the categories noted (sales, assets, and equity). As you can see from the results identified in Table 1.2, Company Y is the most profitable company, earning a healthy 15% return on

TABLE 1.1	Company X	Company Y	Company Z
Profit	$60 million	$15 million	$7.5 million
Sales	$600 million	$100 million	$250 million
Assets (total)	$240 million	$30 million	$200 million
Equity (total)	$100 million	$10 million	$140 million

TABLE 1.2

	Company X	Company Y	Company Z
Return on Sales (profit/sales)	10%	15%	3%
Return on Assets (profit/assets)	25%	50%	4%
Return on Equity (profit/equity)	60%	150%	5%

sales, a 50% return on the assets utilized to drive these sales, and $1.50 in profit for each $1.00 of equity invested in the company. The profitability analysis shows that Company X, despite having the largest absolute profit, would rank second in profitability, followed by Company Z in a distant third position. Let's further extend this analysis to Figure 1.15, as a company's profitability is usually assessed over time, and this historical track record can be thought of as a good baseline reflection of its ability to generate future profits and raise additional capital. Assume that this chart reflects the profitability level of each company over the past several years. As you can see, Company Y has consistently outperformed both companies X and Z for the period shown. For an investor, the returns being realized from Company Y are superior to those of X and Z—and, therefore, all other things being equal, Company Y would be the preferred company to invest in.

Although Company X is making a decent return, its management team will be challenged to further improve its efficiencies and processes to drive profitability more closely in line with the profitability growth of Company Y. Company Z's performance clearly is significantly below that of X and Y. Its lower returns would be cause for concern—particularly if the demand for its goods and services softens, as this could cause further erosion to its earnings and, therefore, its return on sales, assets, and equity. Further erosion of its sales levels or its cost base could result in it moving from a position of a small profit to that of an operating loss. At this point, it is important just to understand the value of assessing companies in terms of profitability versus absolute profits. The analytical process associated with assessing an organization's financial capacity and profitability is covered in more detail in Chapters 12 through 14.

FIGURE 1.15   **Profitability Analysis: Return on Sales**

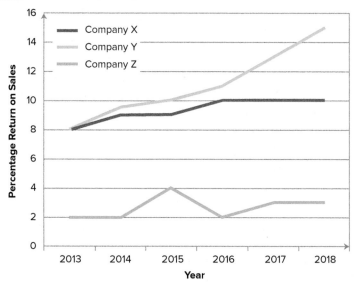

Improving Profitability

Like Company X above, companies in the marketplace are continually being challenged to develop new product opportunities, meet evolving needs in emerging markets, and streamline operations, all in an effort to improve immediate and longer-term profitability. Competition from Amazon, TJX Companies banners Winners and Marshalls, and other specialty-based retailers, as well as up-and-coming Canadian players—for example, Simons Inc.—has challenged NRDC Equity Partners, the owner of the Hudson's Bay Company and its banner stores The Bay, Home Outfitters (being liquidated as of this writing), Lord & Taylor, and Saks Fifth Avenue, to try to find better ways to use their assets, human resources, and capital to improve current profitability levels or attract additional capital to fund their operations. In Canada, for example, The Bay has been investing heavily into renovating and repositioning its stores, as well as installing new kinds of information technology to lower overall operating costs. The intent of these investments is to position The Bay as more of an upscale retailer, using high-end designers such as Chanel and Juicy Couture to attract a wealthier and more "trendy" customer base. The anticipated outcome of these investments and business strategy adjustments will be a stronger profitability position going forward. Although satisfied with the progress being made with respect to improved operational efficiencies, considerable soft spots still exist in the HBC product portfolio. European operations continue to be a challenge, resulting in HBC selling off 50% of its interest in its European Galeria Kaufhof business to a German rival. Sales in 2018 also weakened with its Lord & Taylor and Saks Off 5th banners; on a positive note, luxury Saks sales were up in 2018. The challenge for newly appointed CEO Helena Foulkes (February 2018) will be to continue to simplify the business and improve operational efficiencies and reach via investments in digital and ecommerce initiatives, while right-directing the downward trends at Lord & Taylor and Saks Off 5th. All of this, of course, requires money. Activities centred around divesting HBC of real estate in an effort to raise capital lie on her list of things to consider as well. As we will discuss in more detail in later chapters in this book, managing the asset and capital structure while building sales growth all influences the profit and profitability of an organization.[12]

The challenge to improve profitability faces companies large and small. Assume that Backyard Pools is a small business specializing in the installation and servicing of residential pools. The operation includes a retail location that sells the chemicals necessary for ongoing swimming pool maintenance and use, and also sells related summer seasonal products such as patio furniture, BBQ grills, and pool toys. Backyard Pools is very busy during the months of April through September, and enjoys an annual operating profit. However, there is not tremendous demand for swimming-pool products and related services in Canada from October to March. In an effort to improve its overall profitability and keep its assets (building, employees, etc.) functional and revenue-producing during the off-season, Backyard Pools could look to broaden its offerings. This could include (as many similar operations have found) expanding their product line to include spas (which have year-round demand) and branching out into opposite-season lines, such as fitness equipment, billiard tables, and products whose demand and sales peak during the winter months.

Web Integration

Visit the Web site of a local swimming pool retailer in your town, and see what products they have added to maximize the use of their asset base during the swimming pool off-season. Need an example? Visit **www.stlawrencepools.ca** to see what this company has done.

Chapter Summary

In this chapter, we have described the nature of business and discussed the ways in which businesses create profits and interact with the marketplace in order to meet the needs, wants, and desires of targeted customers. Our discussion focused on the interaction of business as a commercial endeavour, guided by employee interaction and supported by organizational efficiency and structure, which results in the development of a business system and, ultimately, a business model designed to deliver desired goods and services to the marketplace. Utilizing productive resources at their disposal (assets, labour, capital, and managerial acumen), businesses seek to drive a profit from the sale of such goods and services and ensure long-term profitability and growth by continually seeking to make the most efficient use of their resources. While striving for profitability, businesses are being increasingly challenged by customers, and the marketplace at large, to be good corporate citizens, acknowledging their responsibility to act in a socially acceptable manner and respecting the finite nature and scarcity of resources. This new requirement of businesses is resulting in a significant emphasis on resource sustainability and environmental initiatives. To help you to understand why some companies are more successful than others, this chapter's focus emphasizes the importance of positioning, and developing and communicating a value proposition to the customer group that a business is trying to attract in a manner that differentiates the business's products and services from those of its direct competitors, and that attempts to develop and sustain a competitive advantage in the marketplace. The creation of this value proposition takes into consideration both tangible and intangible benefits that the product or service offers, and looks to determine the extent at which price will become a key decision criterion within the customer's purchase decision. The chapter closes with a discussion associated with the importance and interrelationship between strategy and tactics and the need for managers to recognize that in order to be successful, businesses not only have to properly develop a plan for attacking the marketplace, but also must be effective in the implementation of this plan.

Developing Business Knowledge and Skills

Key Terms

commercial endeavours *p. 4*

employee interaction *p. 4*

organizational culture and
   decision-making structure *p. 5*

business *p. 5*

business models *p. 6*

activities *p. 6*

resources *p. 7*

assets *p. 7*

labour *p. 7*

capital *p. 7*

managerial acumen *p. 7*

partners *p. 7*

cost structure *p. 7*

product/service portfolio *p. 7*

opportunity assessment *p. 11*

positioning *p. 11*

value proposition *p. 11*

revenue model *p. 12*

competitive advantage *p. 14*

for-profit companies *p. 17*

not-for-profit organizations (NFPs) *p. 17*

stakeholder *p. 20*

visionary leadership *p. 23*

strategy *p. 26*

tactics *p. 26*

profit *p. 28*

profitability *p. 28*

stockholders *p. 28*

Questions for Discussion

1. In your opinion, based on the concepts presented within this chapter, what key fundamentals do managers need to understand to successfully manage a business? (LO1, LO2, LO3, LO4)

2. What are the major components of a business model? How are the two parts of a business model (company-centric and market-centric) interrelated? (LO2)

3. What are the overarching responsibilities of managers? Is any single responsibility more important than the others? (LO3)

4. What are the three fundamental objectives managers need to consider as they manage the ongoing evolution of a business entity? What importance does each bring to the resource allocation process? (LO3, LO4)

5. Why is it important for managers to think beyond the immediate horizon? How does doing so change the emphasis among managerial responsibilities? (LO4)

6. Define what is meant by a business planning cycle. What are its key components? (LO4)

7. What is meant by the term "visionary leadership"? (LO5)

8. Provide an overview of the relationship between business strategy and business model development, and the importance of successfully executing both in order for a business to achieve its identified objectives. (LO6)

9. What is the difference between profit and profitability? How are the two interrelated? (LO7)

Question for Individual Action

Research one of the outstanding business leaders of our time—for example, Steve Jobs (Apple), Jeff Bezos (Amazon), Elon Musk (Tesla), Daniel Ek (Spotify), Mary Barra (GM), Ginni Rometty (IBM), Sheryl Sandberg (Facebook). Highlight their leadership success. Were they considered a visionary leader? If so, what made them so visionary? What allowed them to be successful in profitably growing the companies they worked for?

Team Exercise

Twitter and Facebook are two of the largest social networking engines in today's Internet-based marketplace. A key to their long-term survival and success will be their ability to shift from solely providing social networking services to incorporating revenue generation and profitable business opportunities into their sites. At this stage of their evolution, what have each of these sites recently done to evolve their Web services to more of a revenue-generating and profitable business model?

Case for Discussion

Sylvie DeShane, CEO of Cruiser Laptops Inc., has just returned from the annual Computer and Electronics Show held in Las Vegas, Nevada. This one-week show provides computer and electronics companies with the opportunity to showcase new and upcoming products and services. It also provides CEOs and other senior managers of global suppliers an opportunity to discuss and assess the status of the marketplace and trends occurring within it. Sylvie spent a great deal of time meeting with other North American and global–based CEOs (Dell, Hewlett-Packard, Acer, MDG) discussing the increasing trend by buyers to select which laptop they were going to purchase predominantly on the basis of price. As one customer put it, "What difference does it make which brand I buy? All manufacturers use the same components anyway." With razor-thin margins to begin with, Sylvie and others are concerned that this continual emphasis on pushing the price down will cause serious profitability problems down the road. Add to this the influx into the North American market—one in which Cruiser Laptops has been able to maintain a strong market share—of low-priced Chinese and Asian products, it would appear to indicate that prices could go even lower. Lenovo, as an example, has promised to ramp up its presence in North America. Already the #1 laptop producer worldwide (unit sales), their expansion into the U.S. means even more "Windows-based" operating system alternatives for customers to choose from. But it does not stop there. New, emerging country–based manufacturers such as Grundig (Turkey), Meebox (Mexico), Positivo Informatica (Brazil), and Siragon (Venezuela) are threatening to cut into Cruiser's international sales volumes as well. It would appear that unless you are Apple, the ability to hold and/or increase price going forward, in the face of this increasing competition, will become even more of a challenge.

Sylvie's dilemma: To determine just how manufacturers like Cruiser Laptops Inc. allowed price to become such an important part of the decision-making process and, given this, what changes to the current business model need to be made if Cruiser Laptops Inc. is to remain competitive and profitable.

Questions

1. What does this trend in the laptop industry imply about the way Windows-based operating system manufacturers have been positioning their products to customers? What have they failed to do?

2. If Sylvie decided to position Cruiser Laptops Inc. as a premium-price laptop manufacturer, what sort of things must she do to be successful? How would this impact the current business model?

3. If positioning as a premium-price manufacturer is not possible, what other options does Sylvie have? What sort of things must she do in order to be successful with this alternate position? Again, what does this mean for her management team in terms of where and how the current business model needs to be adjusted?

4. If you were Sylvie, what type of analysis would you conduct prior to determining a strategic direction? What key questions would you ask?

CHAPTER 2

The Canadian Economic Environment

LEARNING OBJECTIVES

This chapter is designed to provide students with:

LO1	The ability to identify the major contributing factors that impact overall economic development
LO2	Exposure to the core economic model that shapes Canada's economic growth and development
LO3	A base-level understanding of what constitutes economic activity and how economies grow and contract
LO4	The ability to recognize trends that will influence the future composition of economic development in Canada
LO5	Guidance on how managers use information on economic trends in today's marketplace to better manage their organizations and respond to the competitive challenges confronting them

Snapshot

What to Expect in This Chapter

This chapter provides students with a broad introductory overview of the fundamentals behind how our economy works and how we as managers can use our understanding of it to better manage our organizations. The content emphasized in this chapter includes the following:

- Canada and Its Economic System
- Key Economic Influencers
  - Contributing Factors to Economic Development
  - The Underlying Economic Model
  - Canada: A Mixed Economic System
- The Economy in Simple Terms
- The Economic Growth Cycle
- Managing the Movement in the Economy
- Trends Impacting the Canadian Market
- Managing in Challenging Times
  - Understanding Competitive Models
  - Sensing Market Change
- Management Reflection—Analyzing Market Trends

Business IN ACTION

Canada—A "Petro Economy"

Over the past several years, more and more has been written about Canada's ongoing dependency on its energy and commodity (mining, natural resources, agriculture) sectors to drive overall economic growth. One just has to look at the "market watch" section of any of our major newspapers or business-focused Web sites to recognize that movements in the price of crude oil and commodities will have immediate, and in many cases significant, impact on both the TSX composite (Toronto Stock Exchange) and the value of the Canadian dollar (as compared to the U.S. dollar and other major currencies). As the price of crude oil and commodities goes up, so too does the value of the TSX and the value of the Canadian dollar. Should the price of oil fall, this change often negatively impacts the value of the TSX and the Canadian dollar. This aligned movement occurs because Canada earns much of its revenue from the sale of oil in U.S. dollars and because crude oil sales represent the largest category of foreign exchange contribution to the Canadian economy. Canada, as the fourth largest supplier of crude oil in the world, ships 99% of its crude oil to the United States.

When oil prices are high, the amount of money, in U.S. dollars, that Canada earns on each barrel of oil goes up. Conversely, when prices drop the amount of money goes down. A good example of this was the

The Canadian Press/Darryl Dyck

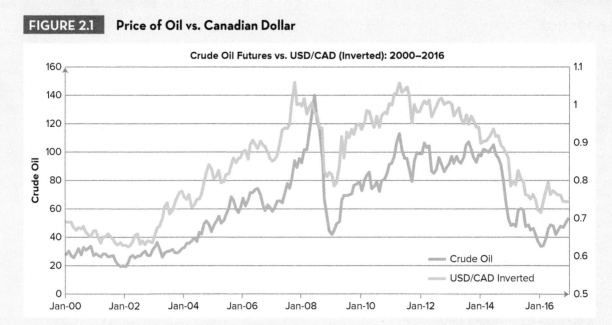

FIGURE 2.1   **Price of Oil vs. Canadian Dollar**

Crude Oil Futures vs. USD/CAD (Inverted): 2000–2016

Source: Based on and adapted from "Beginner's Guide to FX Trading," https://www.babypips.com/learn/forex/black-crack.

downward pressure on the price of oil from July 2014 to January 2015 (see Figure 2.1). During this period the price of crude oil fell from over $100 per barrel to below $46.39 per barrel, a price not seen since 2009. This downward price of oil is matched by a similar cascading of the value of our Canadian dollar. During the first week of July 2014, the Canadian dollar was worth $0.94 USD. On January 27, 2015, the value of the Canadian dollar (relative to the U.S. dollar) had fallen to $0.8062.

Prices for crude oil as of January 2019 remain low relative to the price point noted above in 2014 ($100 USD per barrel). Although crude oil prices did top $70 per barrel (USD) briefly in late 2017, the price of crude oil has remained largely in the $50 to $60 range (USD) over the past five years, with crude oil at $54 (USD) per barrel in January 2019. In response, the Canadian dollar saw a brief climb to $0.81 (USD) in late 2017, but has since found itself in the $0.74 to $0.76 range as the price of oil has dropped, as noted, during this same time period.

This growing dependency on the energy sector to drive our economy forward results in Canada often being referred to as a "petro economy." Energy continues to be one of our largest export sectors and our dependency on it to fuel our balance of trade relationships continues to increase. As shown in Figure 2.2, during periods of strong

global demand for energy and the corresponding higher prices resulting from it Canada benefits from strong trade surpluses. A balance of trade surplus is the difference between the value of imports (goods flowing into the country) versus exports (goods flowing out of the country). A surplus results when exports exceed imports. In looking at the chart, we can see that in the first six months of 2014 Canada recorded a strong balance of trade surplus, largely driven by high oil prices. As oil prices collapsed in the latter half of 2014 and have remained relatively low since then, we can see that this balance of trade surplus actually turned into deficits.

It should be noted that energy is not the sole determining factor in whether Canada has a balance of trade surplus or deficit. It is, however, a key influencer in such outcomes—energy accounts for 23% of the companies that make up the TSX index, with approximately another 20% (materials, utilities, and industrials) of companies comprising the TSX being directly prone to oil price disturbances.

During this course, take the time to visit the market watch section of a business newspaper or business-focused Web site and track the movement of the TSX and the Canadian dollar based on the price changes occurring in the price of a barrel of oil or base commodities such as gold, copper, zinc, and potash.

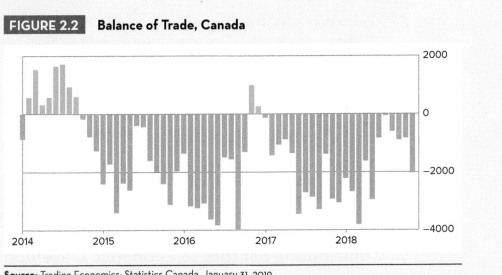

FIGURE 2.2   **Balance of Trade, Canada**

Source: Trading Economics; Statistics Canada, January 31, 2019.

Web Integration

Want a great place to track the movement in the TSX, the value of the Canadian dollar, and the price changes to oil and commodities? Visit **www.financialpost.com**. Click on "Markets > Futures."

Canada and Its Economic System

As a current member of the **G7/8**,[1] Canada possesses one of the most fully developed and diversified economic systems in the world. Our abundance of natural resources, the skills of our labour force, and the sophistication of our technology-based businesses have enabled our economy to grow and prosper over the past 200-plus years. During this time, we have seen our economy move from being primarily agricultural to a diversified system with products and services sought by consumers and businesses around the world. Productivity gains, strong business investment, technological innovation, moderate wage increases, and a favourable currency exchange rate are all key factors that are deemed critical to ensuring our economy remains resilient and competitive now and in the future. Specific products driving Canada's current economic and trade performance include crude oil and other petroleum gases; gems; machinery; wheat, canola, and other agricultural-based products; metals such as gold and nickel; and minerals such as sulphur and potash. On the manufacturing side, although impacted by the economic downturn of 2008–09, the renegotiation of NAFTA (now called USMCA), and the imposition of tariffs by the United States in 2018, areas such as telecommunications, aerospace, IT services support, energy support products (e.g., gas turbines), forestry-related products, and the automotive sector continue to demonstrate Canada's ability to develop world-class competitive products.[2]

As indicated above, core to our economic activity is our trading relationship with the United States of America. The U.S. remains by far our largest trading partner, accounting for approximately 73% of our external trade volume and just over 50% of our import volume. Although we anticipate this will change going forward—as the global marketplace continues to evolve, trade relationships with developing countries mature, and the relationship with the United States changes— at least for the foreseeable future the U.S.A. will continue to be a key linchpin in our economic prosperity.[3]

G7/8 is a quasi-organization comprising the world's major fully developed economies. The G7 consists of the United States, Japan, Germany, Great Britain, France, Italy, and Canada. In 2006, the G7 transitioned to the G7/8 with the inclusion of Russia into its membership. Heads of the G7/8 countries meet at least once annually to discuss major economic, political, and societal issues challenging the global marketplace. Recent meeting trends have also resulted in representatives of major developing economies (such as China) attending at least part or all of such summit meetings. Although still relevant, the G7/8 is seeing its overall global economic influence diminishing, as the larger G20, consisting of the G7/8 countries as well as representatives from developing economies, is anticipated to become the more policy-influencing organization with respect to economic decisions globally.

Productivity gains, strong business investment, technological innovation, moderate wage increases, and a favourable currency exchange rate are all key factors that are deemed to be critical in ensuring that our economy remains resilient and competitive now and in the future.

LO1, LO2   Key Economic Influencers

What enables some economies and nations to prosper, while others struggle? The response to this question is twofold. The first part has to do with the contributing factors for economic development that are in place within a particular economy. The second part focuses on the economic model that governs overall activity.

Contributing Factors to Economic Development

A core requirement to the stability and growth of any economic system lies in its ability to support and promote both the current and future economic activity taking place. This encompasses both the ability to provide a stable environment for economic growth and to ensure that the required business and economic management systems are in place to support an organized approach to economic development. In assessing the potential for current and future economic growth, the factors identified in Figure 2.3, although not all-inclusive, are generally viewed as being essential to economic vitality.[4]

In assessing Canada with regard to these factors, it can be quickly determined that Canada is fortunate to possess, within its economic fabric, the elements critical to supporting and growing an economic system. Our political system is stable. Our economy contains the necessary factors of production, such as roads, ports, utility systems, educated workforce, and technology-based business management systems,

FIGURE 2.3   **Contributing Factors to Economic Development**

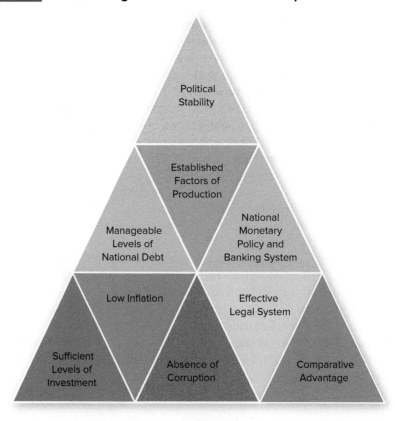

FIGURE 2.4   **Canada Government Debt**

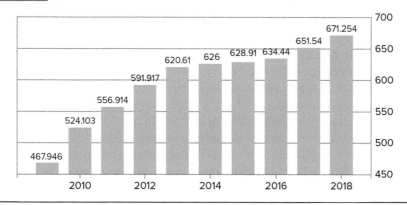

Source: Adapted from "Untangling Public Debt in Canada," IFSD, University of Ottawa, http://www.ifsd.ca/en
/blog/last-page-blog/untangling-public-debt; Government of Canada; Statistics Canada.

that are essential to the efficient and effective development and delivery of goods
and services throughout our economy. Our national and provincial debt levels,
although having grown considerably over the past several decades, are within
acceptable limits, with both our federal and provincial governments working to effectively manage debt loads as they balance the desire to stimulate growth with the
need to be fiscally responsible to both current and future generations (see Figure 2.4).

A key indicator of fiscal responsibility, Canada's debt-to-GDP ratio is showing
upward tendencies, although vastly improved over where it stood in the 1960s (see
Figure 2.5). The federal government will need to effectively manage its cash consumption tendencies going forward with this in mind, as further upward movement
of this key indicator will impact our ability to borrow as well as the cost of borrowing (e.g., interest payments).

Our banking system is considered to be one of the most efficient and technology-
savvy in the world, and our inflation levels have been well managed in recent years
by the monetary policies and actions put in place by our central bank, the Bank of

FIGURE 2.5   **Canada's Debt-to-GDP Ratio**

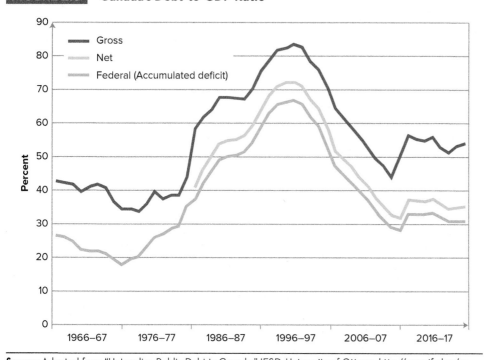

Source: Adapted from "Untangling Public Debt in Canada," IFSD, University of Ottawa, http://www.ifsd.ca/en
/blog/last-page-blog/untangling-public-debt; Government of Canada; Statistics Canada.

Comparative Advantage refers to the ability of a country
to produce or supply goods or
services at a lower cost than
other countries or to possess
resources or unique services
that are unavailable elsewhere.

**Foreign Direct Investment
(FDI)** occurs when a company
or individual from one country
makes an investment into a
business within another
country. This investment can
reflect the physical ownership
of productive assets or the
purchase of a significant
interest in the operations
of a business.

Canada. Our country is considered to possess a strong, fair, and equitable legal system, and the existence of corruption is viewed as being minimal in both our public and private sectors. In addition, our possession of a strong natural resource base results in our having a **comparative advantage** when it comes to the commodities and energy market sectors.

Foreign direct investment (FDI) is another key barometer of a country's long-term health. FDI is an important long-term source of capital for a country that aids in its economic development and the underlying technical and working asset structure supporting its various industry sectors. In 2017, FDI into Canada totalled $33 billion. Although down significantly from levels seen in the 2013 to 2015 range, stability in our country's economy and political systems continues to keep Canada attractive in an increasingly complex global environment. The reduction that did occur in 2017, and is anticipated to carry forward in the near term, is largely due to the downward investment trends relating to energy (see the Business in Action, Canada: A "Petro Economy"), along with the uncertainty associated at the time with changes to NAFTA (the North American Free Trade Agreement), now renamed USMCA (the U.S.–Mexico–Canada Agreement) and the increasing protectionist policies and attitudes being exhibited with our largest trading partner, the United States. Still, investment in Canada remains active, with the largest investment dollars coming from the U.S. Both Europe and Asia/Oceania also are active investors in Canada, with Europe representing approximately one-third of the overall inflow of investment and Asia/Oceania representing approximately 13%.[5]

The end result is that many domestic and foreign companies and investors have historically viewed Canada as a safe and lucrative place to do business, and should continue to do so looking forward.

> A core requirement to the stability and growth of any economic system lies in its ability to service and promote both the current and future economic activity taking place.

The Underlying Economic Model

In addition to these contributing factors to economic development, in order for an economic system to develop and grow and to encourage and foster a climate that promotes and rewards economic risk, a balanced relationship also needs to be established among three fundamental market composition principles:

1. The law of supply and demand
2. Allowance for private ownership, entrepreneurship, and wealth creation
3. Extent of government involvement in influencing economic activity and direction

Law of Supply and Demand
refers to the ability of the
market, independent of
external influences, to
determine the price for which
a product or service will be
bought and sold.

Law of supply and demand A core fundamental of an open economic environment, the **law of supply and demand** refers to the ability of the market, independent of external influences, to determine the price for which a product or service will be bought and sold. Demand reflects the number of purchasers who are willing to pay for a product or service at various price points. Demand can be perceived to be elastic or inelastic, depending on the movement in the quantity demanded for the various price points at which producers are considering offering a product or service to the marketplace. Inelastic demand results when movement in price does not result in significant changes in demand. Figure 2.6 illustrates an inelastic demand situation; the demand for gasoline changes little even though the price of gasoline rises. This

FIGURE 2.6   Demand for Gasoline in Canada, 2013–17

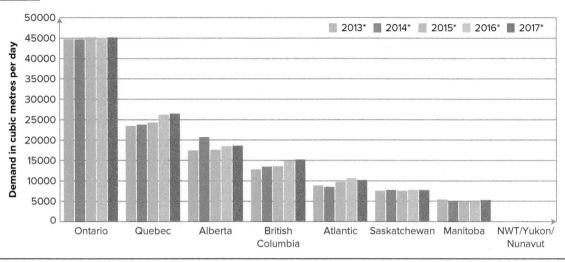

Sources: Adapted from data of the Canadian Association of Petroleum Producers.

is due to purchasers' need for gasoline to operate their vehicles and the lack of sub-stitutes for gasoline in the marketplace. Average gasoline prices in Canada rose from a low of $0.965 per litre in 2009 to over $1.30 per litre in 2012 and 2013. They then fell dramatically in 2014 and 2015 (under $1.00 per litre) and then steadily moved up again in 2016 through 2017, reaching $1.20+ per litre before dropping back down again toward the end of 2018 and into 2019 (hovering around the $1.00 per litre range).[6] Despite this significant increase in price, the overall demand for gasoline remained relatively stable across Canada, as shown in Figure 2.6.[7]

Elastic demand, however, reflects a situation where the quantity demanded does change significantly due to a change in price. Assume that buyers are interested in purchasing a wearable device from manufacturers such as Apple, Google, LG, Lenovo, etc. If offered at an initial price point of $699, demand for such a wearable device may be relatively low. As the price drops, however, more and more buyers are likely to become attracted to the opportunity of owning such a wearable device (see Figure 2.7).

FIGURE 2.7   Elastic Demand: Wearable Devices

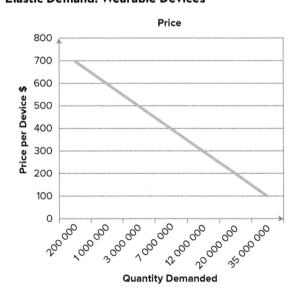

FIGURE 2.8   **Supply Curve: Wearable Devices**

While "demand" reflects the buyer's position toward a product, "supply" reflects how much of a product or service producers are willing to provide the market at various price points. The easiest way to think of this is as a supply schedule (see Figure 2.8) representing the amount of product or service a producer is willing to offer at a particular price point. Suppliers need to think about the cost of production versus the revenue that will be received from selling their product, and the change in profit that will be realized at different points on the schedule. Using our wearable device example, suppliers may be willing to offer only a limited number of such devices at $99, as their ability to make a profit at this price point is very suspect. Conversely, they are willing to provide a large quantity of such devices at the price of $699, as this would maximize their profit potential.

Together, these concepts (demand and supply) form the basis for the law of supply and demand, which, again, defines the relationship between quantity demanded and quantity supplied. In pure economic terms, it refers to the point where the quantity supplied equals the quantity demanded, with the price point set by this equalization (see Figure 2.9). At this point, the market is in perfect equilibrium with there

FIGURE 2.9   **Supply and Demand: Wearable Devices**

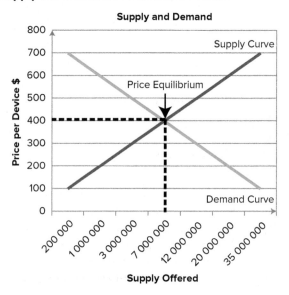

being no shortage or surplus of goods at the agreed-upon price point. When prices fall too low, a shortage may occur due to demand exceeding supply or the willingness to supply. When prices move higher, surpluses within the market may occur due to purchasers becoming unwilling to pay the higher price. When such events occur, in the absence of other external factors the market will correct itself back to an equilibrium price.

Our focus on this law with respect to economic activity and development looks at the freedom within the market to allow prices to be set in such a fashion. In some situations, price may be influenced or controlled by external mechanisms such as duties, tariffs, subsidies, or regulatory practices. In other economic settings, the law of supply and demand is provided with a much freer rein and, as such, plays a much bigger role in the actual price being charged for a particular product or service. Keep in mind that the example above has been kept simple to illustrate the theory behind the law of supply and demand. Influences such as consumer income, consumer preference, the number of product or service substitutes, and cost base reductions due to technology and productivity improvements have been removed from our analysis. Such factors, when considered, can result in significant influence on the relationship between supply and demand, particularly in the long run.

Allowance for private ownership, entrepreneurship, and wealth creation This principle refers to the openness of the market to support, encourage, and promote the concepts of private enterprise, personal ownership, entrepreneurship, and wealth creation. To a varying degree, economies around the world allow individuals and corporations these rights. Some economies, such as the United States and Canada, fully support these concepts in a climate of risk versus return. Developing economies such as the People's Republic of China and India are allowing greater access to these fundamentals, whereas others, such as North Korea, are less willing to provide strong support of these capitalistic principles.

Government involvement in influencing economic activity and direction Government involvement in the economy relates to the varying roles government can play within ongoing day-to-day economic activities. Some of these activities include:

- Acting as a customer via the purchasing of goods and services
- Acting as a regulator, restricting access or defining competitive boundaries within particular economic sectors
- Acting as a manager via powers granted to Crown organizations, such as the Bank of Canada
- Acting as a taxation agent
- Acting as an economic stimulation agent via grant and subsidy programs, infrastructure development programs, and specific industry or company bailout programs, and
- Acting as a competitor (providing services in direct competition for private-sector businesses)

These three market composition principles will come together to provide the overall framework for economic activity within a given nation or economy. With each nation developing its own economic equilibrium, and with government policies shifting on an ongoing basis, it is best to view the relationship among these three market composition principles as being on a continuum. This is illustrated in Figure 2.10. At one end of the continuum is a fully **open system**, which is

Open System refers to an economic system that adheres to the principles of economic freedom: the law of supply and demand, full and open access to the principles of private ownership, entrepreneurship, and wealth creation, and an absence of regulation on the part of government.

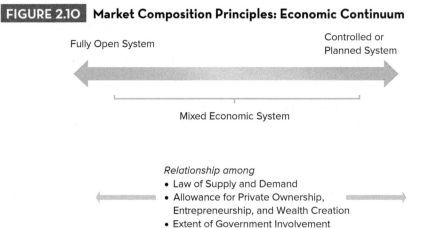

FIGURE 2.10 **Market Composition Principles: Economic Continuum**

Fully Open System

Controlled or
Planned System

Mixed Economic System

Relationship among
- Law of Supply and Demand
- Allowance for Private Ownership,
  Entrepreneurship, and Wealth Creation
- Extent of Government Involvement

Controlled Systems refers to economic systems where the fundamentals of the law of supply and demand, private ownership, entrepreneurship, and wealth creation are largely restricted or absent, and the government fully controls the economic direction and activity.

Mixed Economic System refers to an economic system that contains components of both open and controlled systems. It includes the core principles of economic freedom, with some degree of centralized economic planning and government regulation and involvement.

governed largely by the law of supply and demand, provides full and open access to the principles of private ownership, entrepreneurship, and wealth creation, and possesses an absence of regulation on the part of a government. Open systems are also interpreted as being systems where foreign trade and movements in labour and capital are largely unrestricted. At the opposite end of the continuum is an economic system that is considered to be planned or controlled, in that the fundamentals of the law of supply and demand, private ownership, entrepreneurship, and wealth creation are largely restricted or absent, and the government fully controls the economic direction and activity on behalf of all (state authorities making decisions relating to domestic prices, output, and production). **Controlled systems** are also defined as economies that operate without or experience minimal external trade.[8]

Within today's global economy no system can be considered completely open, although the economy of the United States historically has been considered to be the closest example of an open system given its significant emphasis on the law of supply and demand, private ownership, entrepreneurship, and wealth creation. However, as a result of the financial services and economic crisis of 2008, the growing disparity between classes, the shifting global attitudes among the world's larger economies toward protectionism, and the increasing disruptions taking place within our evolving global markets, we have seen an increasingly active economic management role being undertaken by governments (particularly in the United States), which have moved economies in the direction of a more **mixed economic system**. As indicated earlier, North Korea is currently one of the most-referred-to planned or controlled economic systems. Again, keep in mind that the openness or restrictiveness of a system can change over time (as noted with the U.S. above) as regulatory policies, development strategies, and external influences will impact overall economic governance. The evolution of the economies of the People's Republic of China and India, Great Britain's decision to leave the European Union (Brexit), and protectionist tendencies within the United States, along with the variety of actions taken by the governments of various countries (tariff imposition, election tampering, technology rights infringements, etc.), coupled with economic actions by their central banks in managing the globalization of the world's trade environments, are good examples of this.

Canada: A Mixed Economic System

Canada, like most fully developed economies, is considered to be a mixed economic system. By this, we mean that our economy allows the law of supply and

Business IN ACTION

2019 Index of Economic Freedom

According to the 2019 Index of Economic Freedom, Canada is ranked as one of the world's most attractive investment destinations. Created by the Heritage Foundation in partnership with the *Wall Street Journal*, the Index of Economic Freedom assesses a country and its underlying economy on the basis of four fundamental categories: Rule of Law (property rights freedom and freedom from corruption), Limited Government (fiscal freedom and freedom from government spending), Regulatory Efficiency (business freedom, labour freedom, and monetary freedom), and Open Markets (trade freedom, investment freedom, and financial freedom). Each of these 10 freedoms, as they are referred to, are evaluated by a series of underlying metrics and are weighted equally in the overall final score composition.

According to the Heritage Foundation, economic freedom is the fundamental right of every individual to control their own labour and property in an economically free society. This means that individuals have the right to work, produce, consume, and

Used by permission of The Heritage Foundation

invest in an open market environment. As part of this freedom, governments endorse and support the principles of free movement of labour, capital, and trade. In assessing companies on this basis, the index's intent is to recognize that the relationship among economic freedom and healthy societies, cleaner environments, and overall economic growth is one of mutual benefit.

So, how did Canada fare? Our country's overall score was 77.7 out of 100, which placed us 8th in the world overall (unchanged from 2018, but down from 6th in 2014). As a country, however, we have improved our score by just under 10 points since 1995. This compares well to the world average of 60.8, and a regional average of 73.06 (which includes the United States at 76.8 and Mexico at 64.7). Figure 2.11 shows

FIGURE 2.11   **2019 Index of Economic Freedom, Canada**

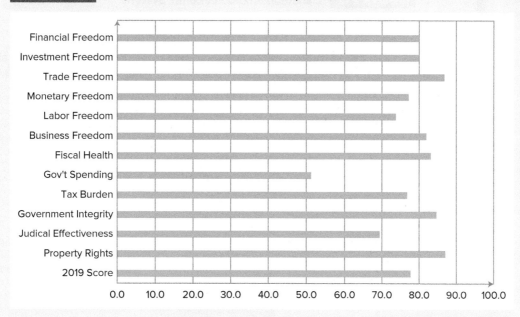

Source: Adapted from 2014 Index of Economic Freedom. Updated with 2019 data, The Heritage Foundation.

our rankings within each of the 10 freedoms identified above.

According to the Heritage Foundation, Canada possesses a transparent and stable business climate, a system of commerce and global trading that is firmly institutionalized as fundamental to the way we do business, and a stable and responsible banking system backed by prudent and well-managed regulations. As Canadians, we have a reputation of an honest, responsible, and responsive government that exhibits prudent fiscal responsibility. Although our score on government spending is low compared to our other scores, the Heritage Foundation does credit our governments, federal and provincial, with initiating significant efforts to reduce government spending and balance our overall budgets. Tax reforms have also been put into place to further improve our global competitiveness and reduce the overall tax burden relative to GDP. In the eyes of the Heritage Foundation, Canada continues to be the freest economy in the North America region.

demand to significantly influence the market. The principles of private ownership, entrepreneurship, and wealth creation, and their corresponding risk and return opportunities, are present and supported within our economic fundamentals. Our government, although an active participant in our economy, attempts to manage and influence economic activity through a cooperative/competitive model, participating where and how it feels it is of benefit to the market as a whole. Our government will become more or less engaged when it believes that, in doing so, it would be in the best interest of our nation in order to protect and regulate industries or guide economic initiatives. It also manages the economy via its powers of taxation, regulation, national debt targets, provincial transfers, and monetary policy control (see Figure 2.12).

Canada, like most fully developed economies, is considered to be a mixed economic system.

FIGURE 2.12   **Canadian Mixed Economic System**

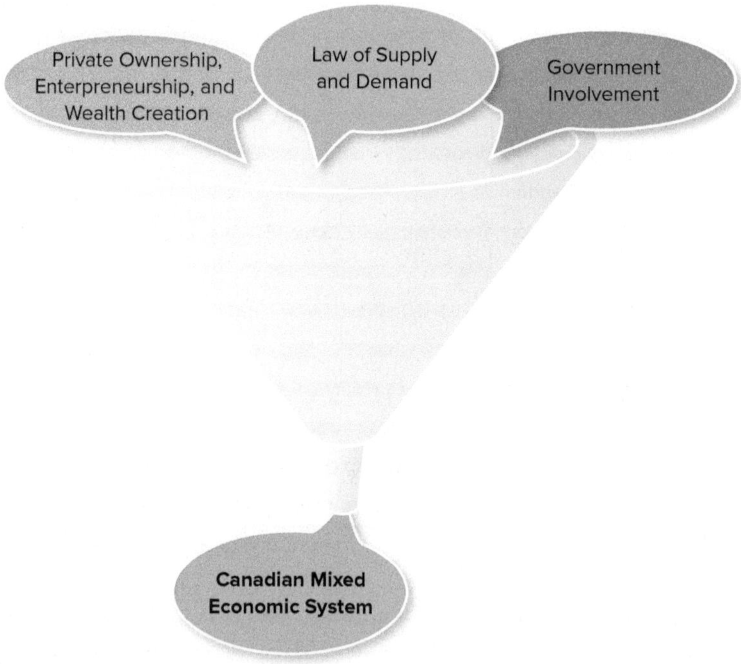

Business IN ACTION

Role of the Bank of Canada

The Bank of Canada is Canada's central bank. Created in 1934, the Bank of Canada became a Crown corporation in 1938. The fundamental responsibility of the Bank of Canada is to develop and manage the monetary policies and financial systems associated with Canada's economic activity. Specifically, the Bank of Canada has the following core areas of responsibility: influencing the economic activity within Canada via actions focused on managing inflation and currency supply; developing and managing the financial systems in place within Canada to ensure that sound fundamental practices are followed and safeguards are in place to protect the interests of Canadians; providing fund management services to our **chartered banks** and other financial institutions; and providing ongoing research and leadership in the development of corporate administration practices focused on ensuring that efficient and effective systems and practices are followed within the financial services sector. Over the past several years, increasing emphasis has been placed by the media on actions taken by the Bank of Canada with respect to its efforts to balance growth in economic activity and the resulting inflationary pressures. This media attention is most often associated with the benchmarks developed with respect to targeted inflation rates and with its setting of the base lending

The Canadian Press Images/Bayne Stanley

rate (the rate at which money is lent to our chartered banks), which, ultimately, impacts the borrowing and the savings rate you and I experience in the marketplace. Interest rate adjustment is the primary weapon the Bank of Canada uses in controlling inflationary pressures in the short term. Monetary managers and economists within the Bank of Canada typically meet eight times per year to assess the status of our economy and related inflationary pressures, and may or may not take action to influence the growth rate or the direction of economic activity depending on the outcomes derived from their analysis. With the continual evolution of the global economy, their management of this important part of the Bank of Canada's mandate will become increasingly apparent. The current Governor of the Bank of Canada is Stephen S. Poloz (appointed in June 2013).

Web Integration

Want to learn more about the role of the Bank of Canada and the methods it uses to influence economic activity? Visit www.bankofcanada.ca.

The Economy in Simple Terms

Perhaps the easiest way to understand the economy is to look at yourself as a self-contained economic unit. Your individual productivity will generate X number of dollars as a result of the economic activity you engage in. This productivity and its resulting economic activity will be predicated on the basis of four fundamental factors:

1 Expenditures: the purchases you make in support of your day-to-day economic activity that are deemed to be of value in meeting sustenance needs

Chartered Banks are financial institutions regulated under the Canada Bank Act. Their primary responsibility is to bring together borrowers and lenders by accepting deposits and lending out money—all in a manner that safeguards the interests of their customers.

and in improving your overall quality of life. Clothing, food, housing, and transportation would be examples of such expenditures.

2 **Savings:** dollars you set aside today that will support economic activity and wealth creation in/for the future. Placing money in an RRSP (Registered Retirement Savings Plan) or purchasing GICs (guaranteed investment certificates) are examples. Your savings are then lent to others with the intent of stimulating their economic activity in the hopes of enhancing their wealth and private ownership levels.

3 **Capital asset investments:** investments you are making today to further expand your capacity to conduct and expand your productivity and overall economic capacity. If your business requires an additional truck in order to expand, the purchase of this truck would be considered an investment focused on expanding your productivity and economic activity. Investments in real estate with the purpose of building future equity via wealth appreciation are an additional example.

4 **Credit:** the borrowing of dollars to support expenditures or investments being made. You may have needed to borrow money to purchase the above-mentioned truck, which you deem necessary to expand your business's capacity and capabilities, or to finance the real estate purchase you made.

$$\text{Economic Activity} = \text{Expenditures} + \text{Savings} + \text{Investment} + \text{Credit}$$

The economy, as a whole, operates on these same principles. Economies move and grow as a result of the activities of everyone (consumers, businesses, and government) in these same areas (expenditures, savings, investments, credit). This is done on a continuous basis, quarter after quarter, year after year. As is illustrated above, interdependency among these four areas develops, with each one acting as a pillar in support of the overall economic activity (see Figure 2.13). It should be noted that economic growth relies as well on an equilibrium-based relationship among these factors. Too much credit (debt) will, ultimately, hinder economic growth, as larger and larger amounts of economic productivity must be used to repay this debt versus generating new economic growth opportunities. Savings, while necessary, also cannot be overemphasized, as too much emphasis on savings versus spending will similarly result in a tendency to reduce economic growth due to such expenditure reductions.

FIGURE 2.13   **Four Pillars of Economic Activity and Growth**

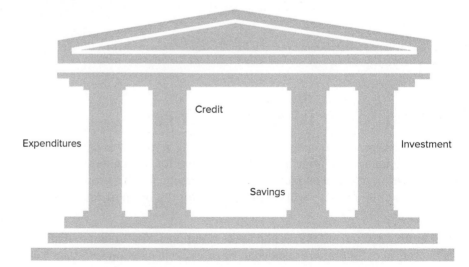

The Economic Growth Cycle

So, how do economies grow? The answer to this question varies depending upon the development stage of the economy and what is interpreted as its key GDP driver. The total value of a nation's economy is measured by its **gross domestic product, or GDP**. Think of GDP as being all the economic activity generated by individuals, businesses, and government for the economy as a whole. GDP is the total market value of the goods and services a nation produces domestically over a defined period of time (usually one year). Examples of factors that contribute to economic growth and, therefore, the total value of GDP are:

GDP (Gross Domestic Product) refers to the total market value of the goods and services (economic output) a nation produces domestically over a period of time (generally one calendar year).

- goods and services produced and purchased domestically for consumption
- business investments within the economy
- net value of goods produced for export vs. received
- government spending

Economists track the movement of GDP (upward or downward) over a period of time to determine whether an economy is growing or contracting. Figure 2.14 shows the overall movement in the Canadian economy between 2009 and 2017. As you can see in Figure 2.14, overall our economy experienced both growth and contraction (as measured by GDP) through 2009 to 2017. As noted in the Business in Action, Canada: A "Petro Economy," downward pressure on oil prices and the energy/commodity sector in 2015 and going forward has had a negative impact on the overall value of our GDP. The end result is that we have seen a decline in the overall value of our economic output, when measured in U.S. dollars, through the period up to the end of 2017. GDP growth for the first three quarters of 2018 was comparable to that experienced in 2017, resulting in an anticipated small growth rate year-over-year of just under 2%.[9] Projected GDP through 2019 and 2022 is expected to stay in the 2% range annually (slightly above or below). Economic growth will vary not only from year to year, but also quarter to quarter. As shown in Figure 2.15, quarterly growth in Canada between December 2015 and October 2018 varied between –0.5% and 1.1% on a quarter-by-quarter basis.[10]

> Economists track the movement of GDP (upward or downward) over a period of time to determine whether an economy is growing or contracting.

FIGURE 2.14 **Canada's GDP Output, 2009–17**

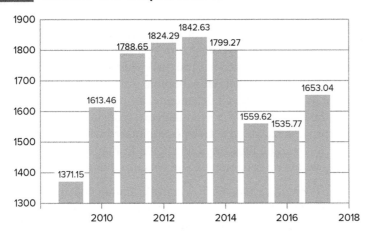

Sources: www.tradingeconomics.com; Statistics Canada.

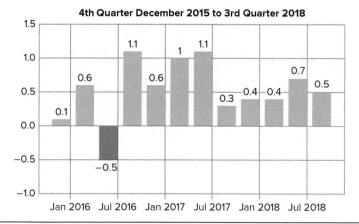

FIGURE 2.15   Canada's GDP Output by Quarter, 2015–18

Sources: www.tradingeconomics.com; Statistics Canada.

Key economic drivers of GDP vary from country to country. Personal consumption, fixed asset investments, export and domestic production, service sector development, and government spending, to mention a few, all impact the enhancement or retrenchment of economic growth. Think of the global marketplace as a world full of buyers and sellers. For some economies, for example the People's Republic of China, the current key economic driver lies with government spending, and the production of goods and services and the underlying capital investments associated with it. This production can be either import or export focused. In China's case, a predominant portion of the production activity currently taking place is still for the purpose of exporting these products and services to other countries (although this is changing as the Chinese domestic economy further develops). For others, such as the United States, the key GDP driver is that of consumer spending. The United States is one of the leading purchasers of goods and services (see Figure 2.16). Its GDP, supported by a robust growth rate of 3%+, topped $20 trillion in the 3rd quarter of 2018 ($17 trillion at the end of 2014), keeping it the largest in the world; the United States, because of its consumer-purchase-based economy, is considered by many to be the engine that drives the current global economy. Approximately 79% of U.S. economic activity is driven by consumer spending on goods and services,[11] many of which are imported from other countries (as noted earlier, approximately 79% of Canada's exports go to the United States).

Canada is also largely driven by consumer spending as its key economic driver; however, our dependency on consumer spending is not as great as that in the United States. Approximately 70% of GDP activity in Canada is driven by consumer spending and services.[12] Other activities that influence GDP movement include our natural resource sector (mining, forestry, potash, agriculture, etc.), technology sector, and energy-producing industries (oil and natural gas). This broad base of economic activity enables our economy to withstand economic downturns in one sector, thereby preventing it from having significant detrimental influence on economic activity as a whole. Although the key economic driver may vary (consumer spending, production, etc.), the overall process by which activity is stimulated within an economic cycle is largely the same and can be illustrated as shown in Figure 2.17. The movement of economic activity within an economy can be visualized or sequenced as follows:

1 Growth in the economy via its GDP driver(s) (mainly consumer spending in the United States and Canada) results in an increase in corporate revenue and profits and government tax revenue (increased tax revenue, GST revenue, provincial tax revenue, etc.).

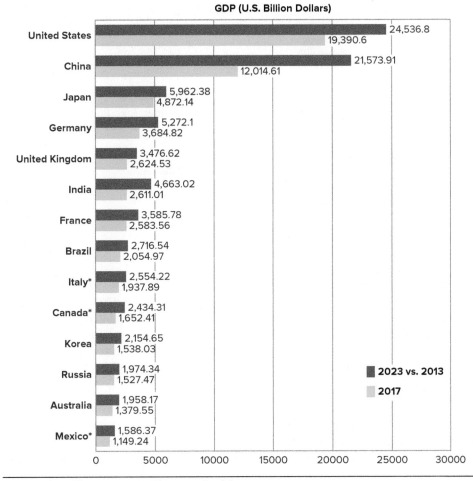

FIGURE 2.16   **Gross Domestic Product of G20 Countries, 2017, and Projections for 2023 (in billions USD)**

GDP (U.S. Billion Dollars)

Country	2023 vs. 2013	2017
United States	24,536.8	19,390.6
China	21,573.91	12,014.61
Japan	5,962.38	4,872.14
Germany	5,272.1	3,684.82
United Kingdom	3,476.62	2,624.53
India	4,663.02	2,611.01
France	3,585.78	2,583.56
Brazil	2,716.54	2,054.97
Italy*	2,554.22	1,937.89
Canada*	2,434.31	1,652.41
Korea	2,154.65	1,538.03
Russia	1,974.34	1,527.47
Australia	1,958.17	1,379.55
Mexico*	1,586.37	1,149.24

Source: Adapted from International Monetary Fund data.

2 As a result of this increase in profits and tax revenue, both business and government will possess increased capacity to invest in new infrastructure and new product/service offerings for consumers. These investments expand the economic infrastructure to meet the growing needs of the economy and the people within it, and add further stimulation to economic activity.

3 Increased business activity has historically resulted in a need for more employees, resulting in an expansion of employment opportunities. In Canada, as an example, between 2005 and 2008 we realized some of the lowest unemployment numbers ever as a result of strong economic growth and the need for an expanded workforce. With the recovery of our economy following the financial crisis of 2008–09, where unemployment rates moved up significantly (above 8.5%), renewed economic activity has again resulted in downward pressure on unemployment rates, with rates at the end of 2018 falling back into the 6.25% range (although this does vary by province and region).

4 With an increase in the need for workers, employers historically have been forced to pay higher wages to attract and retain employees. These higher wages result in additional dollars for workers (consumers) to spend and, therefore, contribute to economic growth (via further spending and/or expanded credit capabilities). As long as this real wage growth outpaces

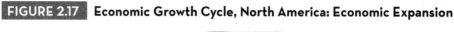

FIGURE 2.17   **Economic Growth Cycle, North America: Economic Expansion**

inflationary pressures, true economic growth will occur. With prolonged periods of economic growth, the cycle continues to repeat itself and overall economic activity continues to expand. During the period from 2001 through 2006, for example, Canada's GDP growth averaged between 2.5% and 3.5% annually. Although not quite as robust, annualized growth rates over the five years 2013–18 have been in the 2.0% to 2.50% range, although in 2017 GDP growth did hit 3.0%.[13]

The reason for the emphasis on "historical" implications in the commentary above lies with the accelerating disruption of technology impacting the labour market combined with an aging workforce. This is truly a wild card, so to speak, for Canada going forward. The implementation of automation via artificial intelligence, robotics, and machine-based learning methodologies, to name a few, will impact labour requirements in the years to come. This impact will be in terms of both the number of workers required and the skill set associated with the positions available. The impact of the effects of technology may result in a continued excess supply of workers in some market sectors resulting in offsetting pressures for wage increases, even as further economic growth occurs. We are seeing some of the impact of this "technology effect" now, as although we have seen economic growth over the last decade, market pressures associated with scarcity of labour and the upward impact on wages are becoming more noticeable (2018–19).

> Our broad base of economic activity enables our Canadian economy to withstand an economic downturn in one sector, thereby preventing it from having a detrimental influence on economic activity as a whole.

In periods of economic contraction, the reverse holds true. For example, a softening of consumer spending will place downward pressure on corporate profits and government tax revenues (see Figure 2.18). With this reduction to profits and tax revenue, businesses and government will reduce spending. This in turn will reduce investment in economic expansion–based activities. With this reduced spending and lower levels of consumer spending, fewer workers will be needed because the

FIGURE 2.18   Economic Growth Cycle, North America: Economic Contraction

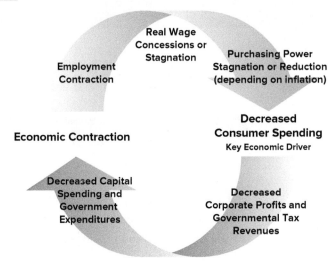

amount of goods and services being produced will be reduced. This will have a negative impact on employment requirements, resulting in an increasing supply of available workers (due to downsizing, retrenchment, and business closings) that, ultimately, will be reflected in higher unemployment rates. With more workers available, the supply of workers will exceed the demand, which will result in a downward pressure on wages and wage increases. This results in fewer dollars for consumers to spend and therefore contributes to a further slowing of economic activity (the cycle continues). A number of analysts and economists view this as what took place in the global economy commencing in the fall of 2008, and peaking in the fourth quarter of 2009 and into the first half of 2010. This was further accelerated by the financial crisis that was a compounding catalyst to this recessionary period. It should be noted that this recent economic crisis resulted in significant capital infusion by governments and central banks (including the Government of Canada and the Bank of Canada). Much of this infusion was the result of the need to ensure liquidity in the financial services sector, as well as the need to develop mechanisms for job creation. This significant capital infusion should be considered an abnormal response by governments to general recessionary periods (not driven by catastrophic events, such as the financial sector meltdown), with this liquidity infusion largely debt-based (money has been borrowed) versus being revenue-driven as a result of economic activity.

It should also be noted that market uncertainties and/or business inertia, often driven by government interaction (tariffs, trade barriers, etc.), can also have a negative impact on economic output domestically (and globally). Diminished productivity, immigration policies that do not allow for adequate replacement of an aging workforce, and interest rate management by a central bank (relative to the broader global market) can all impact the economic growth cycle. Companies themselves can also contribute to this by failing to invest in innovation and emerging opportunities. With some exceptions, Canadian companies in particular are broadly thought of being guilty of business inertia with respect to the investment in capital stock (tangible working assets: equipment, machinery, and intellectual property development), resulting in a lag in our productivity relative to other countries. Canada, as an example, lags the United States in worker productivity by an estimated 30%, and by as much as 50% in sectors heavily dependent on STEM workers (science, technology, engineering, and mathematics).[14]

Business IN ACTION

GDP—Shifting the GDP Emphasis

GDP represents the total market value of the goods and services a specified area (nation, province, etc.) produces domestically over a period of time. It is a reflection of the overall economic output of such a country, or province, or region. What makes up GDP? Well, take the province of Alberta as an example. In 2013, the total value of Alberta's GDP was $331.9 billion. This means the total value of goods and services produced by economic manufacturers, suppliers, and buyers in Alberta equalled this amount. Where did it come from? The first pie chart within Figure 2.19 illustrates the various sectors of Alberta's economy whose contribution to economic activity stimulated Alberta's 2013 GDP to the $331.9-billion level. Most notable in 2013 is Alberta's heavy dependency on energy, which at the time made up 24.6% of the province's GDP.

Fast forward to 2017 and we can see that the underlying economic activity that drives Alberta's GDP composition has changed a bit. Although

Government of Alberta ■

© Government of Alberta

still important, energy now makes up only 16% of Alberta's GDP. Real estate, rentals, and leasing now account for 12% of the province's GDP. Alberta's overall GDP, which fell slightly between 2013 and 2017 ($327 billion in 2017) due to a fairly significant recessionary period in 2015 and 2016, is now growing again with 2018 generating $335 billion in economic activity. Keep in mind, however, that Alberta's GDP remains heavily dependent on the energy sector, and that as oil prices move up or down its overall economic activity, which is closely tied to this core metric, will move with it. Looking forward in the near term, overall economic activity in Alberta is anticipated to remain relatively modest with respect to overall growth potential.

FIGURE 2.19   **Alberta's GDP, 2013 and 2017**

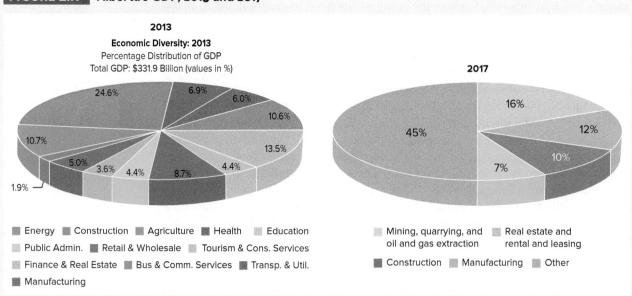

Source: Statistics Canada and Alberta Innovation and Advanced Education.

Business IN ACTION

The Canadian Banking System

The World Economic Forum annually identifies the most sound banking systems in the world. For the past 10 years years (2008–2018), Canada's banking system has been at the top of the list (either #1 or #2). Why do we have such a high status worldwide? Canada's banks are considered to be some of the best managed and well-capitalized banking operations. Add to this a consistent and well-developed and organized regulatory system governed by a carefully crafted Bank Act, a strong track record for risk assessment and control, and a

The Canadian Press/Mario Beauregard

stable and secure operational environment, and one understands quickly why our major banking institutions are given the highest ratings globally. As noted above, Canada possesses a simple but well-thought-out regulatory system. This regulatory system, with its two primary regulators—the Financial Consumer Agency of Canada (FCAC) and the Office of the Superintendent of Financial Institutions (OSFI)—has resulted in a consistent and prudent process toward risk, heightened reserve requirements to ensure liquidity, and a national banking system approach that enables our banking institutions to operate at the scale essential to maintain a high level of services in a secure and stable financial environment. This simple but effective approach is what enabled Canada to weather the financial crisis of 2008–09 the best of any fully developed economy. Unlike

The Canadian Press/Kevin Frayer

the United States, whose banking system consists of a complex network of different regulators resulting in a state-level banking system, our national banking system ensures that our chartered and member banks can respond quickly and efficiently to shifts in both national and global economic conditions, required adjustments to capital reserves, international liquidity rules, and systemic risk management initiatives. Again referring back to the financial crisis of 2008–09, Canadians can be proud that our banking system required no taxpayer-funded bailouts, there were no bank failures, and our banks continued to lend money during this period. No other fully developed economy in the world can make this same claim.

Equally important to the risk and operational management requirements of banks is their ability to meet the expectations of the people they serve and to contribute positively to the economic prosperity of our country. Canadian banks are highly regarded in this key competency as well. A recent survey by the Canadian Bankers Association reported that 81% of Canadians see their banking system as among the best in the world, and over 90% believe that Canadian banks do a good job at bringing forward banking innovations into the Canadian market. The banking sector contributed an estimated 3.3% to Canada's GDP ($54 billion of GDP in 2018), paying $12.2 billion in taxes, paying out $18.3 billion in dividend income, spending $13.3 billion on technology, and employing 270 000 Canadians and paying $27.5 billion in salaries and benefits to its Canadian workforce. Canadian banks are also international players on the global stage. Our big five charter banks (RBC, BMO, TD, CIBC, and Scotiabank), all of which are Canadian owned, have all been active regarding acquisitions globally and compete domestically and internationally in a variety of financial service sectors. The big five noted above, along with our sixth big Canadian bank, the National Bank of Canada, are defined as Schedule 1 banks under the Bank Act, and when combined handle more than 80% of the banking activity in Canada.

Web Integration

Want to learn more about the Canadian banking system? Visit **bankingcanada.net**, the Canadian Bankers Association Web site at **cba.ca**, or any of the chartered member bank Web sites.

Managing the Movement in the Economy

Inflation is a rise in the level of prices of goods and services within an economy over a period of time.

Managing the movement in the economy is no easy task. In general, growth in overall economic activity is desired; however, this growth needs to be managed in a way that stimulates investment yet maintains control of **inflation** and other inefficient economic influencers. This balance is critical to ensure the growth that is taking place is real growth and not masked by inflation. The Government of Canada, in conjunction with its affiliated regulatory agencies, provincial governments, and Crown corporations such as the Bank of Canada, seeks to maintain equilibrium between growth and inflation in order to provide an environment that makes the best use of the capacity and capabilities of our economic platform without allowing it to overheat. It must also take into consideration that, given the geographic distribution of Canada's economic clusters (Halifax, Montreal, Toronto, Winnipeg, Edmonton, Calgary, and Vancouver), regional disparity will exist in terms of growth rates and future economic potential. As an example, the last few years (2014 to 2017) have not been particularly kind to the provinces of Alberta, Saskatchewan, and Manitoba. The drop in energy prices has resulted in these provinces experiencing regional recessions, each to a varying degree. With this behind them, these provinces have seen a return to growth and are expected to lead overall Canadian GDP growth for the upcoming few years (through 2021) (Figure 2.20). Having said this,

FIGURE 2.20   **Provincial Projected GDP Growth**

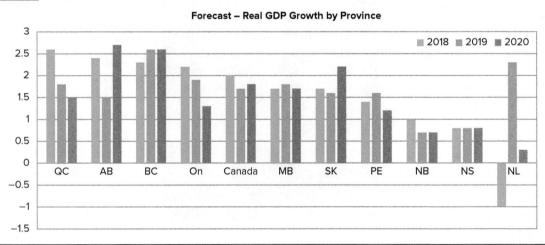

Source: Adapted from RBC Economic Research data: Provincial Outlook, December 12, 2018.

however, pipeline construction delays and softer than anticipated prices for oil and gas, along with a further softening in the mining sector, could dampen this anticipated growth.

The current downward pressure on global energy prices will continue to impact Newfoundland and Labrador, where the economy is less diversified and where energy predominantly is the engine of their economic growth. British Columbia (which has led the country in growth over the past couple of years), Ontario, and Quebec should also see some continued economic growth given the diminishing uncertainty created by the renegotiation of NAFTA, now referred to as USMCA, where a deal was reached in September 2018. This growth could be hampered, however, by manufacturing and service capacity constraints as a number of capital investment projects were put on hold due to global market uncertainty. British Columbia, as an example, should see significant short-term growth driven by the construction of LNG Canada's Kitimat project (liquefied natural gas export).[15] Similarly, economic growth in the Maritime provinces has been relatively weak over the past several years and, although some improvement is expected, will lag behind the other areas of our country. The end result is that Canada's GDP should continue to grow, but that this growth will most likely lag slightly behind other fully developed economies. The challenge for our government and the Bank of Canada, given this relatively mild growth forecast, the potential long-term exposure to downward energy prices, and a general slowing of global economic growth, will be how to create fiscal and regulatory policies that will stimulate economic activity in the weaker sectors of our economy without negatively impacting economic growth elsewhere.

> Economic growth needs to be managed in a way that stimulates investment yet maintains control of inflation and other inefficient economic influencers.

Trends Impacting the Canadian Market LO4

As we have seen in this chapter, the Canadian economic market is a complex entity that continues to change and evolve as internal and external influences impact both its direction and its composition. Looking forward, we continue to view our economic market as being stable and expected to continue in importance within the global community. As managers, it is important that we understand the trends occurring within this economic market, as they pose opportunities and challenges to the livelihood of our individual businesses and for Canadians as a whole. Recognizing that a multitude of factors influence the economy at any given time, the following are some prominent trends we will need to continue to monitor in order to plan appropriately for our business operations and for the goods and services that will be demanded by Canadians as a whole.

- consumer debt loads
- inflation
- geographic clustering and economic imbalance
- currency exchange rate impact
- branch market impact
- sustainability and green initiatives
- aging workforce, immigration, and multiculturalism

- long-term competitiveness
- small business emphasis
- globalization and potential geopolitical instability
- increased threat of cyber attacks

Consumer debt Both the Bank of Canada and the Canadian government have expressed ongoing concerns associated with the rising levels of personal debt that Canadians have taken on over the past several years. Unprecedented record low interest rates, coupled with a consistent rise in home values, have fuelled the increase in household credit debt (mortgages, credit card debt, and student loans).[16]

The concern has to do with the relationship between income and debt. In third-quarter 2018, the debt-to-income ratio had risen to 177.5%, up from 164% in 2014 (see Figure 2.21). This means that for every dollar of income Canadians earn, they owe their mortgage holders, credit card holders, and other personal debt holders (student loans, etc.) approximately $1.78. Keep in mind that this is an average, which includes individuals with little or no debt. Twenty percent of household debt is owed by approximately 8% of Canadians whose debt-to-income level exceeds 350%. Having said this, it would appear (perhaps hoped) that the acceleration of debt has peaked, at least in the short run. This is largely due to the actions taken by the Bank of Canada to cool overheated housing markets (largely in Vancouver and Toronto), as well as implementing a "stress test" that validates a mortgage applicant's ability to meet their mortgage payments at the conventional five-year mortgage rate and heightens the required down payment needed to purchase a home.

So why the emphasis on debt by the Bank of Canada, if things appear to be stabilizing? Taking on excessive debt at today's low interest rates is one thing, but holding this debt during periods where the rate of interest associated with such debt is on the rise could cripple many Canadians financially. Adding to this is the fact that, from a valuation perspective, the housing market has been quite

FIGURE 2.21   **Canadian Household Debt-to-Income Ratios**

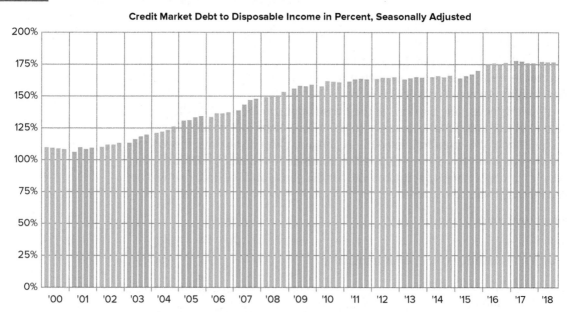

Credit Market Debt to Disposable Income in Percent, Seasonally Adjusted

Source: Statistics Canada. Table 36-10-0435-01. Household sector, selected indicators.

"heated" for the past several years, resulting in Canadians, particularly first-time buyers, paying record high prices for homes. Both the government and the Bank of Canada have consistently communicated concerns that interest rate increases are on the horizon. The Bank of Canada has also expressed concern that the housing market is "stretched" with respect to prices.[17] Should interest rates rise, and home values stagnate or fall, many Canadians could find themselves having to pay a greater portion of their income in support of interest on their debt, resulting in fewer dollars being available for other necessity-based and luxury-based purchases. In a worst-case scenario, such as a significant drop in home values, the amount of debt owned on their mortgages could exceed the market value of their homes, resulting in the mortgages becoming "underwater" and possibly tipping these mortgage holders into insolvency. High debt levels coupled with higher interest rates would, in the minds of many analysts, create considerable drag on the economy. Here lies the catch-22: a strengthening in the economy has a tendency to see interest rates rise as a measure to offset inflation. The high debt situation may inhibit the Bank of Canada's ability to manage economic growth in this way, however, as higher interest rates will impact borrowers resulting in an economic slowdown. To add a further layer of complexity, credit card providers continue to increase the supply of credit to the market and the retail sector continues to drive growth via leveraged purchase arrangements with consumers (i.e., buying on credit). If this credit-leveraging purchase pattern continues, sooner or later the ability to take on more debt becomes overly burdensome. Consumers, at this point, will be forced to reduce their spending. With roughly 70% of our economic activity dependent on spending, the economic growth cycle will stagnate, resulting in an economic downturn—and, as we discussed earlier, the cycle will continue until a new equilibrium is reached and the downward pressure is relieved.

Inflation As mentioned above, significant inflationary pressures will have a negative impact on the growth of economic activity in Canada. Inflation robs an economy of true growth and psychologically negatively impacts the confidence levels of consumers and business operators alike. Near-term inflationary pressures, although relatively stable in the 1.8% to 1.9% range, are building at this time (quarter 1, 2019) in Canada. This is particularly true with respect to food staples (fruit, vegetables, meat), along with the drop in the value of the Canadian dollar relative to the U.S. dollar. What is keeping inflation at bay overall are expenses relating to energy, and natural-resource base commodities. Lower oil prices, as well as low prices for copper, nickel, and other mining-centric commodities, should help to keep the overall inflation rate in check. The December 2018 RBC Economics long-term inflation forecast is for inflation to remain within the Bank of Canada's acceptable range of 1% to 3% for the upcoming five-year period. Although this number is relatively low, keep in mind that the anticipated GDP growth rate for the period is expected to lie within the same range, thereby yielding little real economic growth.[18] It is also important to recognize that although levels of inflation are anticipated to be stable in the near term, this is a macro-level conclusion; inflation in some business sectors may be significantly greater. As an example, business sectors experiencing tight labour market availability may see upward pressure on wages. Higher interest rates on debt may result in upward pressure on prices in capital-intensive industries, where borrowing is an important part of their business model. Prices associated with grains, coffee, and rice, due to an ever-growing demand for these commodities globally, have been on the rise and are expected to continue. Weather conditions, such as droughts and excessive rainfall, as well as crop disease, all can impact harvest levels resulting in sharp short-term increases in prices. According to the Food Institute of the University of Guelph, food prices are expected to rise 1.5% to 3.5% annually for the near future, with prices of vegetables rising as much at 4.5% to 6% or more.[19] As many of these food types are imported into Canada seasonally, the downward pressure on the Canadian dollar relative to the U.S. dollar will add to this upward pressure on price.

Geographic clustering and economic imbalance As already mentioned, the Canadian economy has been transitioning to one predicated on the concept of geographic clustering. Geographic clustering occurs when regional economies develop into what are considered distinct from one another and separated by significant geographic space where interdependency is minimized. In essence, a variety of distinct regional economic platforms occur. Although this occurs frequently at the local level, enough interdependency exists at the regional and national levels to mitigate any negative consequences on the economy. The danger occurs when such distinctness occurs at the broader macro level, resulting in the inability of governments to effectively implement national-based economic management actions to effectively control economic expansion or contraction via monetary policy or inflation-control mechanisms. With the current economic distinctness between our western provinces and central and eastern Canada, our management of the economy is being somewhat hampered. As an example, weakening energy and commodity prices are the result of weak demand and a supply glut in the global market. This is impacting the growth and profitability of our mining, natural resource, and energy sectors, which make up a substantial slice of our economic pie and are regionally clustered in our western provinces. Add to this the growing opposition to oil and gas pipeline initiatives, along with anticipated further tightening of carbon emission allowances, and one can quickly see that these sectors of our economy, and the provinces where they are concentrated, will face increasing challenges going forward. Having said this, low energy and commodity prices benefit our manufacturers and service providers, many of which are concentrated in Ontario and Quebec. Lower prices for energy and commodities enable them to reduce costs and improve their competitiveness and profitability. As one can see, this growing economic distinctiveness creates regions of conflicting economic values, where gains on one side are offset by losses on the other. Continued emphasis must be placed on maintaining the interdependency of our regions, and creating diversified economic platforms within these clusters to ensure the negative impact of geographic clustering can be minimized. The challenge for our Canadian government and the Bank of Canada is how to do just that.

Currency exchange rate impact The overall movement in the value of the Canadian dollar, when benchmarked against the U.S. dollar, has both positive and negative effects for the Canadian economy. On the positive side, a strengthening of the Canadian dollar assists in reducing the price of goods and services being imported into the country from other countries. It also makes trips and vacations, for example to the United States, less expensive for Canadians. In addition, upward appreciation in the dollar would also result in the revenue received from exports—such as energy (oil and natural gas), natural resources, and other commodities, which are largely traded in U.S. dollars—to grow, leading to stronger profits within these sectors. On the negative side, a stronger Canadian dollar impacts our tourism and manufacturing export sectors, as the price of Canadian goods and services being exported to other countries rises, making these goods and services more expensive when compared to their domestically produced counterparts, and the cost of visiting Canada by residents of the U.S. (who account for a large percentage of our tourism trade) becomes more expensive than before. Having said this, a weakening of our dollar relative to the U.S. dollar favours our export manufacturing sector as they derive a competitive cost advantage over their U.S. rivals, all other things being equal. Assume the Canadian dollar fell to $0.75 USD. This would provide manufacturers with an approximately $0.25 cost advantage over their U.S. competitors. A weaker dollar, however, increases the costs of imports into Canada. To illustrate this, assume that a case of Florida oranges costing $9.00 when the Canadian dollar was at **parity** with the U.S. dollar would now cost $0.25 more per dollar, or $11.25 (all things being equal). So, which is better? Again, this is the challenge for our government and our Bank of Canada. In general, the Bank of Canada has historically stated that it would ideally like to see our dollar stay around $0.77 to $0.80 USD. This is felt to be an appropriate level to maintain our competitiveness in the global market and balance the geographic clustering tendencies noted above. It is the global marketplace, and not the Bank of Canada, however, that determines the relationship between our dollar and that of the U.S. dollar and other currencies worldwide.

Parity means being equal or equivalent to; specifically, the value of one currency being equal to that of another.

Branch market impact Although Canada is a $1.6-trillion-plus economy **PPP (purchasing power parity)**, the overall size of our economy is small when compared to other countries. This includes both fully developed economies such as the U.S. ($19+ trillion) and Germany ($3.8+ trillion), and developing economies such as the People's Republic of China ($12+ trillion PPP) and India ($2.6+ trillion PPP).[20] In addition, with our wealth of natural resources, energy, and commodity-based goods and services, many global organizations have looked to actively purchase Canadian-owned companies in order to ensure long-term access to such reserves. In the past decade, the number of Canadian-owned companies purchased by foreign firms in this critical economic sector has alarmed a number of analysts and government-sector managers and elected officials. The acquisitions of Inco by Vale of Brazil (formerly CVRD) and Falconbridge by Xstrata of Switzerland in 2006 are just two of many examples of the trend occurring within this valuable business sector. More recent examples include the acquisition of Vancouver-based Norstat International Inc. (developer of satellite systems) by Hytera Communications (China), ITF Technologies (Montreal) by One-Net Communications (China), and the Airbus acquisition of Bombardier's aerospace division. For some, the fundamental concern is that Canada, in seeing its major businesses being acquired by foreign entities, is in danger of losing control of its economic base and runs the risk of simply becoming a branch market economy. The Canadian government has been challenged over the past few years to revamp the Investment Canada Act and include a stronger national security test for assessing the impact of foreign ownership in Canadian corporations as a mechanism for controlling the economic and cultural impact of such acquisitions.[21] This issue continues to resurface each time a major Canadian operation becomes a target for acquisition, as occurred in the fall of 2010 when Australia-based BHP Billiton attempted a **hostile takeover** of Saskatchewan-based Potash Corporation. This deal was blocked by the Canadian government on the grounds that it was not in the interest of Canada to see this Canadian-based organization become owned by a foreign entity. The first quarter of 2011 saw these concerns arise once more when the London Stock Exchange (LSE) announced its intention to acquire the Toronto Stock Exchange (TSX), as well as in 2012 and 2013 with discussions associated with potential acquisitions of Rona by Lowe's (USA), BlackBerry by Lenovo (China), and Manitoba Telecom Services business unit Allstream

PPP (Purchasing Power Parity) a measure that takes into account the relative cost of living and the inflation rates of each country, and adjusts the total value of economic activity accordingly.

Hostile Takeover refers to an attempt by a company to take over another company whose management and board of directors are unwilling to agree to the merger or takeover.

to Accelereo Capital Holdings (Egypt). Both the Norstat International and ITF Technologies deals identified above were closely scrutinized with respect to domestic and broader global concerns prior to their approval.[22] With globalization continuing, the debate associated with foreign ownership is only expected to become louder, and it is anticipated that additional modifications to the Investment Canada Act will occur in the near future. Having said this, one should not conclude that the acquisition of companies is all one-way (foreign companies acquiring Canadian firms). Canadian companies themselves have been active purchasers of companies outside of Canada. This is especially true of our banks and large pension plan managers (e.g., Ontario Teachers' Pension Plan and British Columbia Investment Management Corporation), as well as major Canadian-based international players such as Enbridge Inc., TransCanada Corp., Fortis, Brookfield Partners, and Manulife Financial, all which have made significant acquisitions over the past decade. In 2018, as an example, Canadian acquisitions abroad totalled 807, worth over $102 billion.[23]

Web Integration

Want to learn more about changes to Canada's Investment Act and Competition Act? Google "Canada's Investment Act" or "Canada's anti-trust legislation."

Sustainability and green initiatives Sustainability and green initiatives will have an increasing emphasis across the business spectrum. Companies will find it necessary to seek to achieve both market positioning advantages and cost advantages through the execution of green-based strategies as part of their overall business plan. This will include an increased emphasis on green products, more environmentally friendly packaging, reduced carbon emissions, and greater sensitivity to the use of finite resources in the development, production, and distribution of goods and services to the global community at large. To date, Canada's performance with respect to environmental sustainability has been mixed. According to the Conference Board of Canada, our country and its underlying economic infrastructure has scored particularly well in some areas (water quality, use of forest resources, threatened species management, and low-emitting electricity production), while lagging considerably behind peer countries in areas such as nitrogen oxides and other greenhouse gas emissions reduction, municipal waste generation, and overall energy utilization versus conservation,[24] to name a few. This conclusion is further supported by a December 2016 EKOS-CBC poll, which indicated that just under 72% of Canadians think that governments should take action to protect the environment even if it increases energy costs and hurts some industries.[25] As a country our focus needs to be not just on improving quality of life, but doing so in a way that is sustainable. As Canadians, we will be increasingly challenged (at all levels of economic activity) to ensure that future GDP growth is not accomplished at the expense of the global environment and/or the exhaustion of our finite resource base. To improve our overall performance, our government and businesses have to commit to operating in a manner that does not further degrade our environment (in fact, we should focus on seeking to restore it) and encourages a significant shift toward more sustainable consumption practices. This will require fundamental shifts to the way we do business at all levels of government and across all boardrooms. This shift can no longer be thought of as tomorrow's problem, but now must be viewed as today's challenge.

Aging workforce, immigration, and multiculturalism Similar to many other fully developed economies, Canada's workforce is aging. As an example, in March 2011 the Petroleum Human Resources Council of Canada issued a report that indicated Canada's aging workforce is poised to impact the employment needs of Canada's energy sector. The report indicates that over 30% of this workforce is expected to retire within the next decade, resulting in a need to hire and train at least 39 000 workers.[26] As baby boomers slide into retirement, analysts are becoming increasingly concerned about intellectual capital shortages in fields such as information technology, health care, education, and skilled trades in a number of market sectors, including the petroleum sector as noted above.

With an aging population and one of the lowest birth rates of any fully developed country, Canada's strategy for replacing retiring workers and for continuing to grow our economic base is closely tied to immigration. The need for skilled and well-educated workers will continue to rise, resulting in our need to import such skills due to a shortage domestically. Reliance on immigration brings both challenges and opportunities. The challenges are focused on ensuring that immigrants in Canada find a country that is welcoming to them and respectful of their ethnic backgrounds and traditions. Assimilation into society in a manner that enables them to actively contribute to social and cultural growth is a key to ensuring that Canada remains a preferred choice for the highly technical employee base that a knowledge-based economy will need. Recognition of skill and degrees earned abroad will be a fundamental component of this process in order to ensure that upon their arrival to Canada immigrants are able to positively contribute to Canadian society with minimal barriers. Having said this, a fundamental requirement of this assimilation process will be the challenge of ensuring that this immigrant population possesses, or quickly develops, the required language and critical thinking competency skills necessary for functioning in today's highly technical marketplace. With immigration and multiculturalism comes the emergence of new ethnic markets that represent business opportunities for the delivery of goods and services to these growing market segments. Toronto and Vancouver, as examples, are two of the most culturally diversified cities in North America. Within these two cities, and across Canada as a whole, we are seeing a growing shift within the retail and service sectors, in particular, to actively market to ethnic neighbourhoods and segments goods and services specific to their cultural and social preferences. This trend will continue to grow stronger as the percentage of our population that comprises immigrants to Canada continues to grow.

Web Integration

Want to learn more about the impact of immigration and multiculturalism in Canada? Google "Unlikely Utopia, the Surprising Triumph of Canadian Pluralism," by Michael Adams, or go to **www.environicsinstitute.org/michael-adams**.

Long-term competitiveness With the rise of the developing economies of Asia, Eastern Europe, and South America, Canada will be challenged to maintain its competitive advantages in the marketplace. As one of the world's largest exporters of natural resources, commodities, and energy, these market segments should, in the long run, continue to grow and enable sections of the country to realize ongoing GDP growth. For other parts of Canada, the drive to retain competitive advantages may not be so easy. The challenge to improve productivity levels, the increased cost base associated with our strong currency, and the ability of businesses within developing countries to operate with lower overall costs (largely due to savings in the labour sector) mean that Canadian manufacturers and the economy as a whole will need a shift in emphasis to remain competitive. Where technology advantages have historically been one mechanism for achieving overall competitive advantage, businesses within developing countries now possess the same level of sophistication in this area. For Canada, in addition to our energy and resource sector, our future lies in the ongoing development of knowledge-based industries, where our business acumen will enable us to continue to show global leadership. Education, banking and financial services, and sophisticated operational process development are areas where we must continue to excel in order to ensure our economic platform and our quality of life are protected and enhanced.

Small business emphasis Although our larger corporations (e.g., Royal Bank, Manulife, Enbridge, Magna International, Power Corporation, George Weston) tend to dominate the business headlines, it is small business that makes up the most significant portion of the fabric of our marketplace. Companies in Canada that have more than 500 employees make up less than 1% (.003) of Canadian businesses. Businesses that are largely owned and operated by sole proprietors and possess no employees make up over 56% of our country's businesses. In fact, businesses with fewer than 20 employees represent over 99% of our approximately 2.4 million business establishments, of which 1.2 million have employees.[27] Entrepreneurship continues to drive small business creation in Canada and this trend is not anticipated to subside going forward. Domestic ethnic market development, global niche market opportunities, and specialty goods and services offerings are just a few examples of where continuous small business growth will be driven. With technological advances occurring at lightning speed, opportunities for Internet-based companies and techno-savvy start-ups both at home and abroad will accelerate in both urban and rural environments.

Globalization and potential geopolitical instability Globalization refers to the growing interconnectivity of the world and the heightened interdependence we are seeing among its various economic regions. The advent of social networking tools—Facebook, Instagram, Snapchat, and Twitter, for example—has enabled us to transmit information to as many as one billion people across the globe with simply the tap of a finger. The Internet has enabled the development of business models that are able to reach potential buyers with few boundaries or restrictions. As the global economy becomes more connected and emerging economies—such as the BRIC countries (Brazil, Russia, India, China) and CIVETS countries (Colombia, Indonesia, Vietnam, Egypt, Turkey, South Africa)—continue to develop their domestic and export-based economies, new business opportunities will arise as never before. At the same time, so will increased competitive pressures. Canadian businesses will need to adapt to remain competitive. Adapting means becoming more efficient and effective in our operational processes, improving the productivity of our workforces, reinventing our businesses as global market needs change, and becoming increasingly innovative and entrepreneurial as product and market life cycles become shorter.

Unfortunately, one also needs to place on the table the near- to mid-term impact that terrorism and political instability and differing geopolitical ideologies bring to markets. Threats from factional organizations such as ISIS and other terror organizations could potentially evolve into broader conflicts and/or destabilize our increasingly interconnected global markets. Ideological differences between global regions over the Ukraine, Syria, Iran, and North Korea, as an example, can also lead to sanctions and other economic-restriction policies. Chapter 3 provides a more detailed look at the global marketplace, the concept of globalization, and the emerging trends and risk factors influencing this macro-market environment.

Increased threat of cyber attacks (cyber security) Behind the United States, Canada is viewed as one of the most attractive countries for potential cyber attack activities. Our high levels of Internet and ecommerce development and utilization, coupled with a large well-developed financial system, large natural resource sector, and increasing online dependency for management of our critical infrastructure, place us in an attractive position with respect to criminal and hacking cyber activity. Analysts feel we are targeted as a result of the diversified nature of our economy as well as the view of Canada as a back-door opportunity into the U.S. market due to our close economic ties. Canada also has been seen as slightly behind the times in terms of cyber attack readiness and prevention. Recent data breaches, such as those that have occurred at Desjardins Group (credit union clients) in 2019, Aetna and Marriott Inc. (Starwood) in 2018, Equifax in 2017, and eBay in 2014, to name a few, have impacted millions of consumers/customers and demonstrate the ongoing concern given the potential damage that can be inflicted upon economies, corporations (large and small), and individuals. Ottawa has vowed to continue to increase spending and create stronger reporting and monitoring regulations relating to cyber security management and data privacy, to guard against hacker attacks (and their consequences) and privacy breaches, but the battle—or war, as many people call it—has only just begun. A major first step in this direction was the enactment of PIPEDA (Personal Information and Electronic Documents Act) in November 2018; this legislation outlines a company's obligations with respect to the reporting of a data breach and establishes regulatory guidance for data security safeguards.[28]

In addition to large multinational organizations, smaller organizations are particularly vulnerable given their limited cyber security resources. Malware, RATs (Remote Access Trojans, which use employee access privileges to obtain and steal business and personal data), organized crime, and government-based hacking activities are all becoming increasingly sophisticated in their approach and methodologies. As managers it is fundamental that we establish cyber security policies and actively manage our data systems, intellectual property, and other critical assets in a way that protects them from exposure in this increasingly hostile environment.

Managing in Challenging Times   LO5

As managers, it is fundamentally important that we understand what is happening in both our domestic economy and within those global economies that influence our overall economic activity and prosperity. With heightened global activity comes an increased interdependency on national, regional, and even local economies. In this regard, as managers we must be in tune not only with the general directions that are occurring, but also with the opportunities and threats that will develop as a result of such increased economic activity and interdependency. In order to fully understand where the market is going, managers look to generally answer three fundamental questions:

1. What are the general indicators saying about the current economy and about the current relationships among the key variables governing our mixed

economic system (law of supply and demand; support for the concepts of entrepreneurship, wealth creation, and private ownership)?

2 What broad-level changes (political, economic, social, technological, environmental, and legal) are occurring within the sectors of the economy that directly impact my organization's future growth and market position?

3 What specific current competitive actions and/or market forces may disrupt the way in which business is done within my organization's particular market sector?

> As managers, it is fundamentally important that we understand what is happening in both our domestic economy and within those global economies that influence our overall economic activity and prosperity.

In terms of the first question, managers will generally look to monitor a number of key economic indicators that reflect the general movement in the economy. Some of the primary economic indicators that we assess on the basis of movement within them are:

- unemployment rate
- inflation rate
- Consumer Price Index (CPI)
- new housing starts
- manufacturing inventory
- Consumer Confidence Index
- price of crude oil (per-barrel basis)
- stock market indexes (TSX, S&P 500, Dow Jones)
- currency exchange rate
- monthly retail sales

In addition, many industry-specific indexes can be used to further assess the health and stability of particular market sectors. As an example, manufacturing firms will also look at productivity indexes, inventory and manufacturing-level indexes, and export and producer price indexes. Information relating to each of these indicators can be picked up via government releases, media reports, industry trade and analyst reports, and Web-based searches. Ongoing monitoring of these indicators enables us to assess whether the economy is expanding rapidly, beginning to slow, or moving into a potential market contraction or **recession**. To illustrate this, Figure 2.22 shows the movement in monthly retail sales in Canada for the period January 2018 to October 2018. Looking at 2018, we can see that the movement from month to month has demonstrated some volatility, with changes from month to month in the 1% to 3% range.[29] Trending this relatively uneven performance forward for the near term, we can assume that the overall growth in the retail sector will most likely be modest as we complete the end of 2018 and roll into 2019. When we add to this the overall historical trends relating to retail sales, as shown in Figure 2.23, we can further validate the largely downward trend of retail sales growth year over year for the period 2014 through third-quarter 2018. Given this trend of very modest growth, businesses may be reluctant to initiate significant retail-sector investment projects as it may be questionable whether such initiatives would yield the desired return on investment results. Such investments may be put on hold until indicators and forecasts signal stronger upward growth potential.

Recession is a period of time that marks a contraction in the overall economic activity within an economy. A recession is typically believed to occur when an economy experiences two or more quarters of negative GDP movement.

FIGURE 2.22 Canadian Retail Sales, Month-over-Month (MOM) Change, 2018

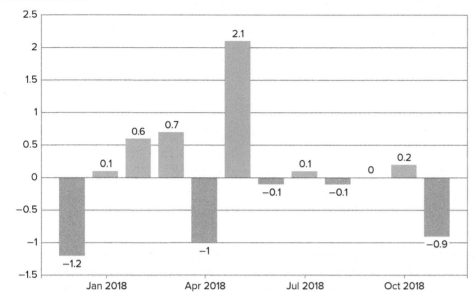

Source: Statistics Canada, Tradingeconomics.com/canada/retail-sales.

FIGURE 2.23 Canadian Retail Sales, 2014–18

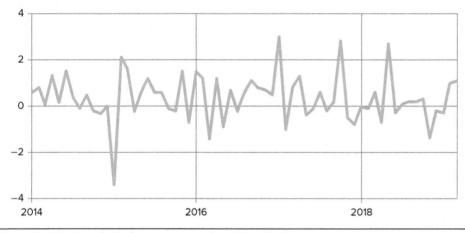

Source: Statistics Canada, Tradingeconomics.com/canada/retail-sales.

Web Integration

Want to know Canada's current unemployment rate and get a good understanding of the "pulse of the economy" at this time? Go to http://www.thecanadaguide.com/basics/the-economy/.

In addition to the economic factors discussed above, managers will also assess at the macro level the political, social, technological, environmental, and legal changes that are occurring, commonly referred to as a **PESTEL analysis** (see Figure 2.24). Politically, the assessment will be looking for trends in government legislation or activity that may signal a change to the management of the economy and, therefore, the equilibrium relationship within the mixed economic system. This could include mild intervention in the form of interest rate adjustments, or more significant intervention such as direct government investment in particular

PESTEL Analysis refers to a macro-level assessment of the political, economic, social, technology, environmental, and legal trends that can or will impact the markets within which an organization competes.

FIGURE 2.24 **PESTEL Analysis**

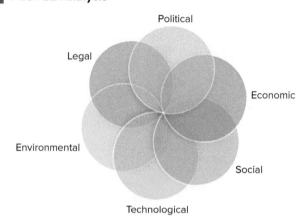

market segments or consideration of anti-trust legislation or changes to Canada's Investment and Competition Act in order to protect Canadian companies or market sectors potentially at risk. Increasing tendencies toward **protectionism**, as we have seen recently in the United States, could also form part of this high-level political assessment. Socially, managers will look for trends that may fundamentally change how consumers want, need, or use products/services, as well as the changing composition of the marketplace. This can include demographic shifts and cultural shifts, as well as behavioural changes. Managers also need to pay attention to change occurring in the legal sector and its potential impact on the overall business risk. This can include changes to employment law, product liability risk exposure, contract law, and consumer rights, to name a few. Changes associated with environmental compliance regulations (such as cap and trade and/or carbon tax initiatives) and other environmental sustainability obligations must also be reviewed and brought into the decision-making process. Finally, managers must constantly assess the speed and direction of technology shifts that could potentially render current products, services, and operational processes obsolete. Telecommunications, automation, machine-based learning, and other AI (artificial intelligence) and analytics-based methodologies, along with digitization and ecommerce-based business models, are dramatically changing the way in which business is done today, with the rate of change continuing to accelerate as we move forward in the current and upcoming decade.

With respect to the third question posed at the beginning of this section, managers are constantly looking to see where and how their markets are changing in light of competitive influences. In evaluating the current market within which a business is competing, managers need to understand the composition of the competitive model that currently governs the marketplace and the potential for disruption to this model moving forward.

Managers must constantly look to see where and how their markets are changing in light of competitive influences.

Understanding Competitive Models

An important consideration for any business owner or manager has to do with understanding the nature of competition with respect to the products or services the business is offering and the markets that are being served by these products and

FIGURE 2.25 **Competitive Models**

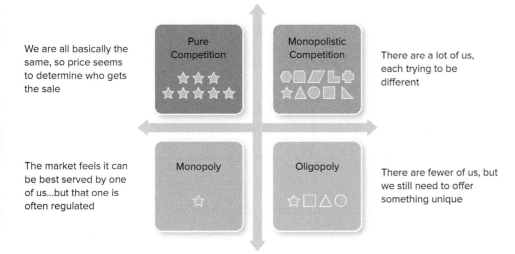

We are all basically the same, so price seems to determine who gets the sale

Pure Competition

Monopolistic Competition

There are a lot of us, each trying to be different

The market feels it can be best served by one of us...but that one is often regulated

Monopoly

Oligopoly

There are fewer of us, but we still need to offer something unique

services. Understanding the type of competitive environment a business is facing is fundamental to creating a strategy for competing and understanding where and how to allocate resources in support of product/service positioning and overall marketing effort. For simplicity, we tend to categorize markets as fitting into one of four definitive quadrants (see Figure 2.25): purely competitive markets, monopolistic markets, oligopoly-based markets, or a monopoly-controlled market.

> Understanding the type of competitive environment a business is facing is fundamental to creating a strategy for competing and understanding where and how to allocate resources in support of product/service positioning and overall marketing effort.

Purely competitive markets Purely competitive markets are markets that are characterized by a number of similar products or services and where no single competitor has a dominant market leader position. A key fundamental characteristic of this market is the absence of differentiation among the products or services being offered. These markets generally are characterized as possessing few barriers to new market entrants. Think back to our discussion in Chapter 1 regarding value propositions: purely competitive markets are markets where suppliers of products and services are largely unable to create distinctions between the products and services being offered to the target audience. Commodity-based markets and agricultural markets (absent of agricultural-based subsidies that artificially regulate price) offer a number of good examples of purely competitive markets. In the mining sector, allowing for some variation in quality grades, copper is copper, nickel is nickel, and potash is potash, with price being a heavily weighted decision criterion within the purchase decision of where to buy, with the relationship between supply and demand impacting the price level at which customers are willing to purchase the product. Figure 2.26, as an example, illustrates the recent historical price movement for potash (2005 through 2017), which has been predominantly influenced by the relationship between supply and demand.[30]

Purely Competitive Markets are markets that are characterized by a number of similar (undifferentiated) products or services, the absence of a dominant market leader, and few barriers to entry.

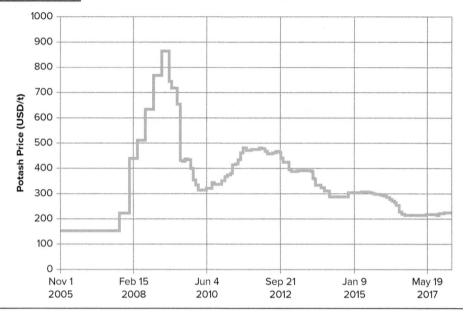

FIGURE 2.26 Historical Price Movement—Potash

Source: infomine.com.

Monopolistic Markets are markets that possess a number of different suppliers of products and services, but the nature of the product or service, along with the marketing effort initiated by businesses within the sector, has enabled true differentiation to set in.

Monopolistic markets In contrast to purely competitive markets, **monopolistic markets** are markets that possess a number of different suppliers of products and services but where the nature of the product or service, along with the marketing effort initiated by businesses within the sector, has enabled true differentiation to set in. Products and services are viewed by customers as being somewhat different and unique, resulting in a significant shift in the development and marketing of value propositions. The manufacturing of cell phones is a good example of a market that exhibits monopolistic market tendencies. Suppliers such as Huawei, Samsung, Lenovo, Apple, and Xiaomi, to name a few, all compete for customers on the basis of product differences, value, and overall price/quality perceptions.

Oligopoly-based Markets are markets that contain a small number of suppliers that control a large percentage of market share within the market, and that compete on the basis of products and/or services that have achieved success in distinguishing themselves from their competitors.

Oligopoly-based markets **Oligopoly-based markets** are markets that contain a small number of suppliers that control a large percentage of market share within the market and that compete on the basis of products or services that have achieved success in distinguishing themselves from their competitors. The emergence of oligopolies often is the result of the significant capital investment required to enter an industry and the significant economies of scale and scope necessary to be competitive. In addition to the difference in the number of product/service suppliers from that of monopolistic competitive markets, oligopolies will generally have greater control over the price being charged for a product or service due to the limited competition within this marketplace. An example of a current industry where an oligopoly-style marketplace exists is the commercial passenger airline manufacturing business, where Boeing and Airbus are the two major players, with Bombardier Inc. (whose aerospace division is now part of Airbus) and Embraer existing as smaller-niche marketers.

Monopoly-based Markets are markets that are served by a single product/service supplier.

Monopoly-based markets **Monopoly-based markets** are markets that are served by a single product/service supplier. In monopoly-based markets, many of which are government regulated, the belief is that a single entity can provide the product or service more efficiently and at a better price point than an open-market concept could. Again, similar to oligopolies, the extent of capital investment needed, as well as the infrastructure requirements necessary to maintain the flow of goods or services, makes the monopoly competition model the best solution. The delivery of utilities such as electricity and natural gas is supplied in a monopoly-based market setting in many areas, although we are seeing tendencies in the marketplace today to minimize such a regulated approach to industry and allow alternative mechanisms for product/service delivery to become enabled (i.e., a deregulated market).

As we mentioned in the opening comments to this section (Understanding Competitive Models), a key fundamental in competing in the marketplace is to know which type of market environment you are operating in. This will assist in understanding the role that differentiation plays in the market, the number and type of competitors that are challenging a business, and the emphasis that will be placed on price as a key factor within the delivery of products or services to the marketplace. As an example, purely competitive markets, where there is an absence of product differentiation, tend to experience a market where the product is viewed largely as a commodity and where price is a key determinant in the buying process. Conversely, monopolistic markets (many competitors), where differentiation is a significant weapon of competitive rivalry, can minimize price as a major customer decision criterion and, in fact, attract higher prices by delivering great products or services combined with great marketing.

In addition to recognizing the current status of the competitive market (environment), managers must also recognize that market configuration and composition are not static. Markets change and evolve as new competitors and innovations come into play. One only has to look at the automobile industry as an example of this evolutionary migration. In the 1970s, the North American automobile industry operated in a largely oligopoly-based market environment with three major players: General Motors, Ford Motor Company, and Chrysler Motors (a fourth, American Motors, also existed, but was acquired by Chrysler). As the 1970s progressed into the 80s and 90s, the market configuration changed dramatically, with Japanese and European automobile manufacturers capturing significant market share in North America through the marketing and delivery of quality-based, well-differentiated products. This entry of additional competitors fundamentally shifted the market from one that operated under oligopoly-based strategies to one that acted significantly more like a monopolistic market. The market today continues to shift even more toward one of monopolistic tendencies with the addition of Korean, Chinese, Indian, and Russian producers (see Figure 2.27). In general, the ongoing

FIGURE 2.27 **Market Evolution: Competitive Models**

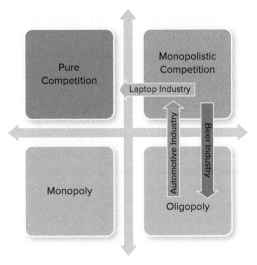

Commoditization is the process by which products and/or services that have been considered unique and/or distinguishable in the past become similar, or non-differentiated in the eyes of the consumer.

growth of the global marketplace and the emergence of companies within the world's developing nations will continue to trigger such shifts. Laptop manufacturers are facing increasing downward pressure on price, and the perception of commoditization, as the differences between laptops, particularly those that utilize the same operating system (e.g., Windows), become less and less distinctive. This increasing trend toward **commoditization**, due to a similarity of components and system capabilities, results in customers increasingly looking at price as key decision criteria. In such situations, the ability to outperform rivals solely on the basis of lower costs (and thereby offer lower prices) becomes the major factor in determining who gains and/or holds market share in this increasingly competitive sector, which more and more reflects the underlying fundamentals of a purely competitive market. Not all shifts will, however, be toward increasingly competitive situations. Some shifts can be in opposite directions. As an example, the current decade has brought about a massive consolidation within the beer industry, as major players have merged in order to take advantage of production and distribution economies of scale and acquire greater market share. Consolidations of this nature have a tendency to reduce the number of broad market competitors, thereby enabling the remaining industry players to gain greater control of prices and/or implement scale or scope-related cost-reduction tactics, thereby improving profitability. It should be recognized that such movements may not be in a single direction only over the long term, as market structure is fluid by the nature of competitive rivalry. Although the major beer producers have consolidated, the reduction in options, coupled with the perceived standardization of taste and largely similar production approaches, has given rise to the craft-beer industry, which, as players grow in size and market share strength, could send the market back toward stronger monopolistic-competitive characteristics and business modelling.

> In addition to recognizing the current status of the competitive market (environment), managers must recognize that market configuration and composition are not static.

Sensing Market Change

So, how do we sense whether the market within which we are operating is changing? What tools are available to assist in the assessment process? These are two fundamental questions that keep managers up at night as they seek to maintain the competitiveness of their organizations. One of the most-often-used business tools for this purpose is a business model called Porter's Five Forces (see Figure 2.28), created by Michael Porter of the Harvard Business School.[31] Within this model, Porter suggests that there are five overarching long-term forces that managers and business owners can use to keep their finger on the pulse of the industry within which they operate. These forces, in Porter's opinion, are the underlying factors that influence an industry's long-term attractiveness and profitability. By assessing movements and trends within these five key areas—the intensity of competitive rivalry; the potential for new entrants into the industry; the probability of new products or services that will act as substitutes to the current products and services being offered; the power that suppliers have over manufacturers of goods and services; and the power of buyers within the industry—managers can assess potential risks and disruptions to their markets and the relative strength of their position, as measured against their current rivals and the longer-term changes anticipated.

FIGURE 2.28 **Porter's Five Forces**

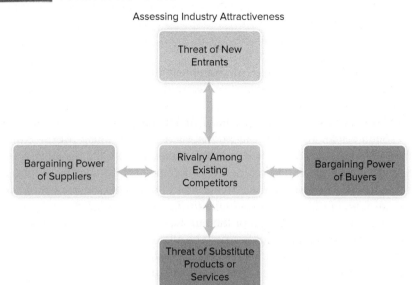

Source: Adapted from Porter's Five Forces, Michael Porter.

In simple terms, by using Porter's Five Forces as a basis for analysis, we are trying to ascertain the following:

① **Rivalry among existing competitors:** How many competitors are currently challenging us for customers in our industry and markets? How strong are they? In general, the more competitors there are, the more intense the rivalry is to acquire customers and grow market share.

② **Threat of new entrants:** What is the probability that new entrants will enter our industry and markets? Where will they come from? How will their products and services impact our growth and our ability to retain our market share?

③ **Threat of substitute products or services:** What is the probability that our product or service offering could be rendered obsolete, or its overall sales potential significantly impacted by a substitute offering? Do we see such substitute products emerging on the distant horizon?

④ **Bargaining power of suppliers:** What is our relationship with our suppliers? How much control do they have in influencing our operations and our overall cost structure? Are we able to extract concessions from them, if required? Is it easy for them to shift their efforts to supporting one of our competitors? Are we significantly dependent upon them for critical aspects of our product/ service offering?

⑤ **Bargaining power of buyers:** How much choice do buyers have in the purchase of products and services within our industry? Is it easy for them to switch from one product to another? What substitute products/services are currently available to buyers, and what potential substitutes are threatening to attack our industry and market?

By analyzing these five forces, our objective is to draw conclusions as to whether the collective impact of those forces, which are impacting the marketplace, will increase demand, decrease demand, redefine the basis for competition, and/or require us to rethink the way that our business model is currently geared toward driving profitability.

Web Integration

Want to learn more about Porter's Five Forces? Go to **www.quickmba.com** and search Porter's Five Forces.

Let's use the music industry as an example to illustrate the value of Porter's Five Forces. In the 1980s and even into the 90s, the music industry was largely an oligopoly-based market controlled by the music companies (Sony, Warner, etc.). Music companies would sign artists (suppliers) to a label, and then market that label and the artist's music through bricks and mortar locations, such as HMV, Music World, Sam the Record Man, Walmart, and so on. The music companies also largely managed the price of the music (CDs), suggesting to retailers the price point to be charged to you and me, the buyers. There also existed the requirement to purchase the full CD of an artist's music, regardless of our desire to actually own and listen to all the songs on the CD. With little choice (except location of the purchase), as buyers we paid the expected price. Artists, as well, found it necessary to be aligned with a music company in order to break into the market and sell their music. For many, a significant portion of the revenue from the sale of their music remained with the music company versus flowing directly to them. What's changed? The answer, of course, is the advent of the Internet and the creation of both new entrants and substitute products. The control the music companies had over the market has largely eroded. With the emergence of Napster and Kazaa in the early years, followed by iTunes and other downloading sites, the delivery of music to the buyer was dramatically changed. No longer were we forced to purchase the entire CD. We could now pick and choose the individual songs we desired to purchase. No longer did we need to visit bricks and mortar locations to purchase music. It could simply be purchased (or, in some cases, downloaded free) via Internet-based sites. Artists technically no longer needed recording studios and labels to market their music. Direct sales to customers, via sites such as Apple's iTunes, UndergroundHipHop, or GhostTunes, to name a few, enabled artists to reap a much larger percentage of the revenue benefits of their work (70% to 80%). This market continues to evolve and change, as customer tastes and choice options have now migrated toward music streaming. This evolution has created a whole host of new competitors such as Spotify, Amazon, Pandora, SoundCloud, iHeartRadio, Tencent, and Deezer (along with Apple and Google). Like CD sales, which experienced rapid declines in sales with the advent of single-title purchases via download, so too are single-purchase sales declining: 2018 saw single-purchase sales (downloads) in North America decline by just under 30%.[32] In essence, the industry has been fundamentally changed forever. Buyers have greater choice on where and how to buy and/or listen to their music, and artists have greater choice on where and how to sell their music. Bricks and mortar locations have to compete not only with each other, but also with Internet-based competitors (download and music-streaming). Recording studios must now demonstrate to artists the value of their services, provide greater incentives to artists to maintain their recording studio relations, and communicate to artists the benefits that will accrue by signing with a particular label.

The music industry is not the only industry in flux at this time. A quick review of the impact of technology demonstrates how forces of change can quickly reorder the competitive landscape in market sectors. The publishing industry is facing tremendous change brought on by the advent of ereaders, tablets, and a variety of mobile devices. The need for physical, hard copies of books is being challenged by electronic versions of texts (ebooks) sold through online retailers (Amazon, Google, Apple, etc.). For bricks and mortar–based operations such as Indigo/Chapters and Barnes & Noble, revenues are impacted by the lower revenue streams resulting from lower prices attached to ebooks, as well as from loss of market share to seasoned, online, and well-capitalized competitors. The mobile device market sector is also facing significant turbulence. Market leaders Samsung and Apple are continuing to see their market share decrease

FIGURE 2.29   Smartphone Market Share Worldwide by Vendor, 2009-2018

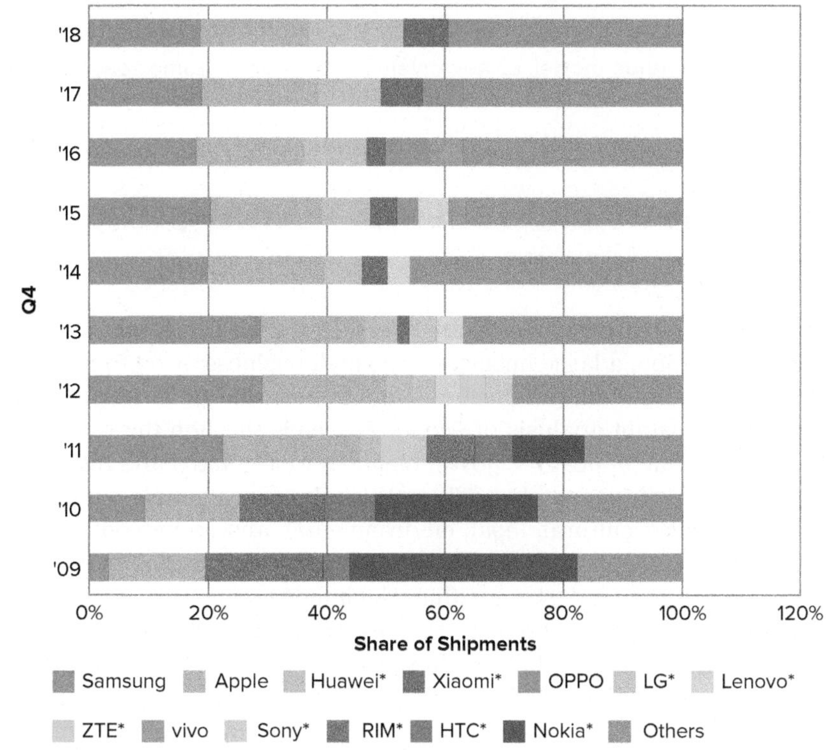

Source: Data provided by and adapted from Statista.com.

as rivals such as Huawei, Xiaomi, LG, OPPO, and others continue to grow in global reach and improve the quality of their product offerings (see Figure 2.29).

Samsung possessed 32% of overall global market share in 2013. Its market share has now fallen to just under 18%. Meanwhile, Huawei's global market share has grown from 4.5% to just over 15% during this same time period. Yes, overall unit sales have increased globally, resulting in higher sales volumes for both companies, but the dynamics of who is getting the larger percentage of new customers going forward is changing. As mobile phone sales mature and unit sales flatten, repurchase rates, driven largely by reselling to a company's existing customer base, which is reflected in market share, will become all the more important. This places Samsung, as an example, at risk. Unlike Apple, which possesses a privatized operating system that enables it to lock in users (supported with strong brand identification and marketing), Samsung competes on the basis of a similar set of features, operating system (Android), and overall user experience. This makes it much more vulnerable to the growing list of competitors challenging its market position. Lenovo, Xiaomi, LG, and Huawei, for example, all have proven very adept at offering similarly featured phones at lower prices. This increase in competition has resulted in both market share loss and required reductions in selling price by Samsung. Apple, as noted above, has been largely immune to the competitive pressures of rivals who all share the same operating system. This too, however, is changing, as Apple is finding increasing price pressures outside of North America as it seeks to extend its reach into Asia and other developing global regions.

For managers, the lesson learned is that we must constantly assess our industry and its markets for potential disruptive changes that will render our products obsolete, force changes to our revenue model, and/or negatively impact our customer base. This requires continual vigilance and market research and an understanding we must recognize that the status quo is not static and that competitive positions will be, and are, constantly under attack.

The lesson learned is that we must constantly assess our industry and its markets for potential disruptive changes that will render our products obsolete, force changes to our revenue model, or negatively impact our customer base.

Management Reflection—Analyzing Market Trends

Managers, regardless of whether we are overseeing a for-profit business or a not-for-profit organization, a large business or a small business, need to recognize the importance of understanding the economic platform that governs our economy. This requires a constant analysis of economic trends through the review and assessment of economic indicators, governmental actions, and shifts that are occurring in global competitiveness. In addition to analyzing economic data, managers need to assess social, cultural, legal, environmental, and technological trends as well, and seek to recognize and respond to disruptive innovations that will impact the specific markets and industries within which they compete. The marketplace is not static. The situation changes daily. These changes are influenced by both controllable and non-controllable factors. In some cases, these changes can be the result of broader macroeconomic forces beyond a specific industry. In others it can be a gradual or sudden shift in industry-specific forces that totally disrupts the status quo. As managers, we need to continuously assess what is happening at the macro and industry levels via business models such as PESTEL analysis and Porter's Five Forces. Our focus is on sensing trends, both positive and negative, which will enable us to redirect our business efforts in order to ensure our long-term business success. To be successful we not only have to develop viable business models, but also must actively assess their ongoing relevance as markets evolve and consumer wants, desires, and behaviours change. This requires knowing the underlying fundamentals of economic growth, as well as the key critical influences driving future demand and our overall relevance.

Chapter Summary

In this chapter, we have described the current composition of the Canadian economy and the key contributing factors that influence its growth and overall direction. In addition to identifying the core fundamentals necessary for economic development, we also focus on describing the market composition principles that govern our economic activity and the nature of Canada's mixed economic system. A considerable emphasis is placed on describing how economic activity is generated and how economies are stimulated or contracted on the basis of movement in their key economic drivers. The discussion associated with the economic growth cycle is fundamental to this overall process. With the basics of the economy having been identified, we shift our focus toward understanding how we attempt to manage our overall economic activity and some of the key trends that will influence our marketplace evolution going forward. We close off our chapter discussing how managers use this information to better understand how changes within the economy and the marketplace in which they operate will impact their organizations. We also provide a brief glimpse as to how the nature of competition within markets can change, and how managers, via such models as Porter's Five Forces, can seek to better understand and respond to trends and market changes through proactive analysis.

Developing Business Knowledge and Skills

Key Terms

G7/8 *p. 37*

comparative advantage *p. 40*

foreign direct investment (FDI) *p. 40*

law of supply and demand *p. 40*

open system *p. 43*

controlled systems *p. 44*

mixed economic system *p. 44*

chartered banks *p. 47*

GDP (gross domestic product) *p. 49*

inflation *p. 56*

parity *p. 61*

PPP (purchasing power parity) *p. 61*

hostile takeover *p. 61*

recession *p. 66*

PESTEL analysis *p. 67*

protectionism *p. 68*

purely competitive markets *p. 69*

monopolistic markets *p. 70*

oligopoly-based markets *p. 70*

monopoly-based markets *p. 70*

commoditization *p. 72*

Questions for Discussion

1. Identify the major contributing factors that influence the economic development of a region or nation. Are there any additional factors not mentioned that you feel are significant contributors to whether a country's economy develops? (LO1)

2. What are the three fundamental principles that influence a mixed economic system? Discuss the differences between the relationship of these three principles with respect to the current structure of the Canadian economy and that of a developing nation such as China or India. (LO2)

3. Describe the economic growth cycle. How does the cycle change between an expanding and contracting economy? (LO3)

4. Do you think the Canadian government should modify the Canadian Investment Act and/or the Competition Act to incorporate a national security test to assess the impact a potential acquisition of a Canadian company by a foreign entity could have on our economy? Why? (LO4)

5. What is a PESTEL analysis? How does it assist managers in better understanding changes that are occurring within the market sector in which their companies compete? (LO5)

Question for Individual Action

Conduct an analysis of recent acquisitions of Canadian firms that have occurred over the past few years. Do you think there is legitimate concern that Canada's economy runs the risk of becoming a branch market to other foreign economies, given the dynamics and evolution of today's global market?

Team Exercise

Can Canada's manufacturing sector survive in today's global economy? Conduct preliminary research on the current status of Canada's manufacturing sector. On the basis of this research, form an opinion as to what Canada's manufacturing sector will need to do to survive in today's global marketplace. Is it possible for our manufacturers to compete with the lower labour costs in Asia and abroad? What about productivity levels—are we as productive as other global manufacturers? Prepare a presentation that formulates the pros and cons of this situation and then look to validate your position on this subject matter.

Case for Discussion

McDonald's Corporation—How to Restore the Golden Arches
(All $$$ figures quoted in USD)

As this chapter points out, business is fluid with both internal and external influences constantly impacting an organization's market position and its business model. Immediate-term impact factors and longer-term forces continue to shape and influence individual market sectors and the broader economy at large.

As an example, it is a different ball game for the Quick Service Restaurant (QSR) sector, and nowhere is it more noticeable than at the McDonald's Corporation. Since 2014, when McDonald's Corporation recorded its first decline in global same-store sales in over a decade, McDonald's has been searching for a "market fit" approach that will restore the lustre in a brand which once dominated the fast-food industry. Since 2014, annual revenue has continued to decline, dropping from peak sales of just over $28 billion (USD) in 2014, to just over $21 billion (USD) in 2018. Year-over-year sales declines for the past two years have been between 7% and 8% per year.[33] To be fair to McDonald's, part of the reason for the revenue decline is an intentional shift to its business model. As part of its new strategic approach, McDonald's is re-franchising company-owned stores. In selling these stores to franchisees McDonald's replaces the full revenue from these stores for the royalty and licensing revenue it receives in supporting franchise operations. This does translate into a decline in revenue, but one which, if handled properly, should result in a stronger bottom line.

The problem, however, is deeper than just a loss of revenue due to re-franchising initiatives. McDonald's same-store sales, particularly in North America, continue to be a concern. Although same-store sales (sales from restaurant locations open for more than one year) did increase by 2.6% in 2018, this fell short of market expectations. Add to this the fact that same-store sales had decreased in prior years, so McDonald's operations open for at least one year are just getting back to the revenue levels they experienced in 2013.[34] Compounding the drive to grow revenue further is a downward trend with respect to number of customers visiting these locations, and a market perception of lagging quality of the product served relative to rivals. A review of the customer satisfaction scores for the QSR sector shows McDonald's scores lag behind rivals such as KFC, Burger King, Taco Bell, Wendy's, Papa John's, and Domino's Pizza, to name a few.[35] It is estimated that McDonald's has experienced a drop in visits of as much as 500 million customers globally since 2012. This customer erosion has continued into 2018 despite McDonald's aggressively working to update its menu, install enhanced ordering technology (kiosks) and mobile platforms, and partnering with Uber Eats to test delivery options.

Upward pressure on costs has forced McDonald's to increase its prices (up by 2%), and to look toward higher-priced menu items to drive stronger revenue from its business operations. Significant capital investment is also being made to revitalize aging storefront locations and modernize restaurant interiors in the hopes of capturing and retaining customers. McDonald's 2017 growth plan emphasizes enhancing its digital and artificial intelligence methodologies capabilities to improve its customer experience and reduce expenses.

The good news for McDonald's is that, despite the challenges identified above, it still remains the anchor player in the QSR sector. Its customer base contains some of the most loyal customers of any QSR competitor. The problem, however, is that it just can't seem to attract new customers or increase the frequency of visits of its existing customers beyond its core customer base.

For McDonald's, the solution to getting back on track is not an easy one. Considerable headwinds will challenge the company going forward. Pending minimum wage legislation in the U.S. and elsewhere will impact one of its biggest cost lines (wages). Price sensitivity, particularly relating to higher-ticket items such as the Big Mac, its Quarter Pounder line of burgers, and its new Bacon-Smokehouse Burger lines will continue to challenge its average revenue per customer, as many customers could opt to trade down to its lower-priced value menu options (2 for $4), which generate lower profit margin, or visit new and emerging competitive options whose price points are no longer significantly different. Over the past few years value menu items have increased their overall percentage of revenue to 15%. But is competing on price really something that McDonald's wants to do? Then there are changing customer preferences and demographic shifts occurring in the broader market environment. As an example, in the U.S., McDonald's share of the "family with kids under 12" market fell from 18.6% in 2012 to 14.6% in 2014. The organization also continues to slide in terms of its quality perception. A 2014 customer survey by Nation's Restaurant News ranked McDonald's at 104 out of 105 restaurants without table service, while a Consumer Reports survey had McDonald's burgers ranked considerably below those of 20 competitors.[36] Add to this the absence of a truly "big hit" menu item in the last few years, product failures such as Mighty Wings, and marginal contributors such as McWraps, and the organization finds itself facing a tough position to be in just when competition is heating up in both the burger segment and across the broader "fast casual" restaurant sector. As McDonald's woes heightened over the past few years, competitors such as Panera, Five Guys, Noodles & Company, Shake Shack, and Potbelly Sandwich Shop, to name a few, were grabbing an increasingly larger slice of the fast casual pie. Chipotle Mexican Grill, as an example, saw its same-store sales spike by 6.1% in 2018.

All of this does not mean to imply that McDonald's is on the skids. It is still the largest QSR player in the marketplace and still lures significantly more customers than its competitors. As an example, an average McDonald's pulls in about $2.6 million in revenue, versus Burger King's average of $1.2 million per storefront location. Also, 30% of McDonald's revenue continues to flow from its key mainstay menu items: the Big Mac, hamburgers, cheeseburgers, McNuggets, and fries.[37] McDonald's net income was a respectable $5.92 billion in 2018, up 14% over 2017, although just 6% above the $5.585 billion in 2013.[38]

What these current results do imply, however, is that, although improved over the last few years (2016–18), the status quo of relying on product line extensions and the convenience of fast food may no longer be acceptable and the business model could appear to need some fairly significant tweaking. As part of his initial assessment in this regard, current CEO Steve Easterbrook needs to draw some hard conclusions about McDonald's current competitive positioning, particularly in North America, its largest market. In this regard, he has asked you to assist with the initial macro-level analysis, the results of which will aid in a better understanding of just what is happening with respect to industry structure and customer behaviour—the core outcome of which will be how to enable McDonald's to remain attractive in an increasingly crowded market segment.

Questions

Conduct some additional initial research on McDonald's to further familiarize yourself with the organization. Once you have done this, then look to respond to the following three questions:

1. Using the PESTEL and market structure business models, identify what you feel are the key macro-level shifts/changes that Easterbrook and McDonald's will need to respond to as they seek to reestablish McDonald's position in the North American marketplace.

2. Now focus on the industry and the QSR and fast casual sectors. Using Porter's Five Forces model, what issues/challenges must Easterbrook and McDonald's recognize and respond to?

3. Where to start? If you were advising Steve Easterbrook and his team based on your analysis in questions 1 and 2, what are the three high-priority items you would recommend they tackle first?

CHAPTER 3

The Global Marketplace

LEARNING OBJECTIVES

This chapter is designed to provide students with:

LO1	An overview of the rapidity and extent of change occurring in the global marketplace
LO2	An understanding of the reasons why businesses expand their operations into international markets
LO3	Exposure to the interconnectivity of the political and economic influences impacting the global marketplace
LO4	An understanding of the macro-level trends that will impact the global marketplace going forward
LO5	An understanding of the fundamental process associated with the development of international trade
LO6	An understanding of the challenges managers face in considering expansion into the global arena

Snapshot

What to Expect in This Chapter

This chapter provides students with a broad introductory overview of the globalization process currently underway around the world, and the trends and challenges that we as managers will face in guiding our organizations through this economic transformation. The content emphasized in this chapter includes the following:

- Quick Facts—The Global Landscape
- Our Changing World
- The Global Marketplace
- Why Go Global?
  - New Market Opportunities
  - Cost Reduction Opportunity
  - Resource Base Control
  - Closeness to Markets
  - Economies of Scale
- Global Market Stability: The Role of Government
  - Ongoing Commitment to International Trade System
  - Market Openness
  - Absence of Protectionism
  - Adherence to the Fundamentals of Fair Trade
  - Balanced Economic Development
  - Responsible Sovereign Debt Management
- Global Market Trends
- The Concept of International Trade
  - Evolution of a Global Presence
  - A Note on Currency Exchange Rates: How Are They Influenced?
- Management Reflection—Challenges of Managing in Today's Global Environment

Business IN ACTION

Can Canada Compete in Today's Global Marketplace?

A key question often asked by business students is, "Can Canada compete in today's emerging, dynamic marketplace, against economies significantly larger than ours?" The answer to this question is yes, although where and how effectively we compete will ultimately be the determinant of our overall success. Canada's economy possesses current operational and strategic advantages. Operationally, our

economy has a solid private-sector domestic demand component to it. As the main driver of our economy, our broad base of economic activity results in us creating an ongoing demand for goods and services. This demand results in the continuous evolution of domestic-based businesses that focus on both supplying this demand internally and/or filling this demand externally via the development of import

© Author's Image/PunchStock

operations and infrastructure. How we choose to compete is where the true challenge lies. Recognizing the competitive intensity of the global marketplace and the underlying skill sets required for survival, Canadian businesses will continue to be challenged to become more efficient and productive than ever before.

The critical comment above lies with the term "productive." By "productive" we are looking at the efficiency of a country's workforce to transform inputs into outputs. Think of it as a measure of GDP on a per hour of work basis. We often view productivity from the perspective of three key components: the availability of capital and our willingness to make investments to improve workforce capabilities; the use of technology from a connectivity and advanced, leading-edge application; and our ability to drive competitive advantage via workforce motivation, drive, and skill-based competencies.

The path on which the Canadian economy has been trending with respect to our "productive" competitiveness points toward concerns relating to our continued long-term economic success. As an example, a recent study by the Washington-based Brookings Institution and the Martin Prosperity Institute at the University of Toronto's Rotman School of Business indicated that Canadian worker productivity has slipped significantly over the past

decade. Comparing our worker productivity to that of U.S. workers, as an example, saw Canadian workers in 1996 lagging behind their U.S. counterparts by approximately 17%. By 2018 that gap had widened significantly, as our productivity lag behind U.S. workers is as much as 100% depending on the particular industry sector (advanced industries) being assessed. What this means for Canada is that lags in productivity have historically been directly correlated with slower growth and downward pressure on the overall standard of living, as competitive pressures force companies to look for the ability to compete via lower wages and/or other cost-saving initiatives. The risk here, of course, lies in the downward spiral that such actions create and that reinforce the further erosion of an economy's competitiveness as time goes on.

So, how do we respond to this productivity challenge and reverse the current trend that could significantly impact our ability to compete now and into the future? Strategically, Canada possesses three key advantages. First, our natural resource base offers us the ability to supply emerging nations with key products and services. Although we anticipate a temporary slowdown in this demand due to the near-term cooling of the global economy, emerging nations will continue to look to Canada as a key provider in the energy, mining, and agricultural sectors. Second, a key but somewhat quiet strength lies in our expertise associated with health, education, and financial services. Canadian companies and the products and services they offer, and the intellectual capabilities that are core to these areas, offer us tremendous opportunity in the global marketplace as developing economies move toward maturity. Third, Canada's highly educated population and closeness to the U.S. market coupled with our strong trade ties with the U.S. make us an attractive place to do business. Recognizing this, the critical link lies in our ability to reinforce our commitment to innovation. This will require higher levels of incubator investment in homegrown technology-based and STEM-based business opportunities, active attraction of foreign companies in these fields seeking to invest in Canada as a footprint to their overall global operation, "kickstart" innovation programs underwritten by our federal and provincial governments, particularly in technology, digital, and analytics-based market sectors, and a further assessment in the deregulation of technology-related industries, of which such actions would ignite the required capital investments to improve production efficiencies and effectiveness.

It needs to be more aggressively acknowledged that, as a country, we will face challenges going forward as globalization continues to drive overall worldwide economic development. Slower global growth coupled with a near-term uncertainty relating to commodity prices remain a threat to our energy, mining, and agricultural sectors. Lower prices in this key export driver can lead to trade deficits that will put downward pressure on our economy.

Our elevated levels of household debt, as mentioned in Chapter 2, also remain a cause of concern. We also face potential labour market shortages, particularly with respect to skilled trades and science-based occupations. Our aging population and increasing reliance on immigration will present policy challenges to the underlying fabric of our universal benefits approach to economic structure.

Recognizing these challenges, continual improvements in productivity will become more important than ever. As a small exporting nation we simply need to be better than others in those areas where we choose to compete. As tomorrow's managers it is important for you to recognize that the critical building blocks for the future lie in innovation, education, technology investment, and training. It will be these investments, and our ability to leverage them, that will determine our ability to maintain and enhance our current level of competitiveness.

Quick Facts—The Global Landscape

The following figures are presented as quick facts that are designed to offer an overview of the current and projected growth in the global marketplace, and Canada's position within it. This information is intended to serve as a base point from which the discussion within this chapter can be better understood.

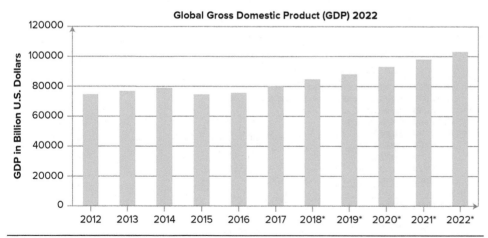

Source: Adapted from IMF World Economic Outlook. "World Economic Update, Legacies, Clouds and Uncertainties," January 2015.

Real GDP Growth, by Country Group
(Year over year)

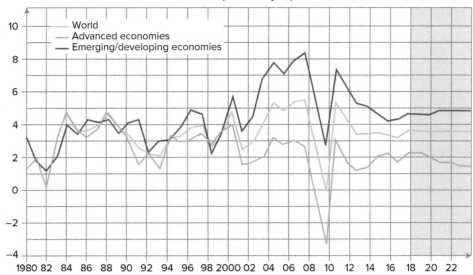

Source: Adapted from IMF World Economic Outlook. "World Economic Update, Legacies, Clouds and Uncertainties," January 2015.

Trade tensions
Major trade actions have raised trade policy uncertainty.
(billion us dollars)

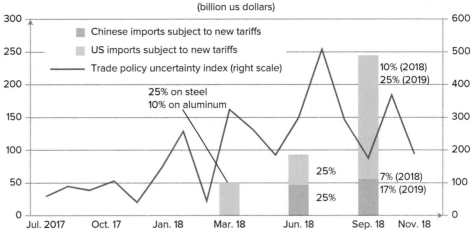

Source: Adapted from IMF World Economic Outlook. "World Economic Update, Legacies, Clouds and Uncertainties," January 2015.

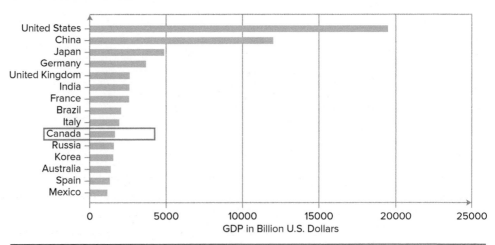

Source: Adapted from IMF World Economic Outlook. "World Economic Update, Legacies, Clouds and Uncertainties," January 2015.

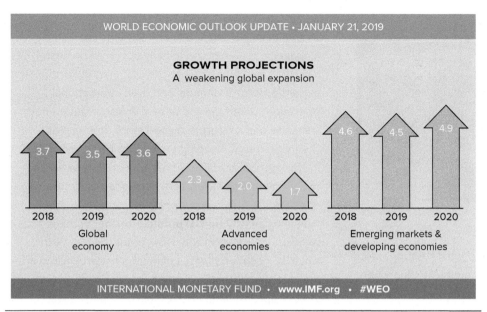

Source: Adapted from IMF World Economic Outlook. "World Economic Update, Legacies, Clouds and Uncertainties," January 2015.

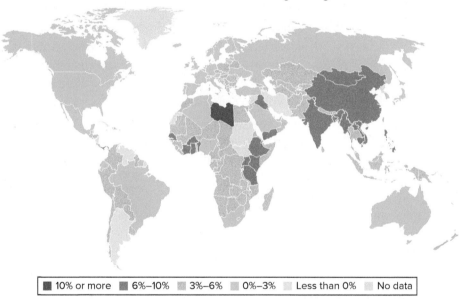

Real GDP Growth—Annual Percentage Change

■ 10% or more ■ 6%–10% ▩ 3%–6% ▢ 0%–3% Less than 0% No data

Source: Adapted from IMF World Economic Outlook. "World Economic Update, Legacies, Clouds and Uncertainties," January 2015.

 Business IN ACTION

Lululemon Athletica—From a Small Business to a Global Player

Founded by Dennis (Chip) Wilson in 1998, Lululemon Athletica started with its first store in Vancouver's trendy beach area known as Kitsilano. Following an initial exposure to yoga through classes he was attending, Chip recognized the re-emergence of the practice as a growing trend in the marketplace. Experienced in the retail sector through his many years of work in the skate and snowboard business, and with an understanding of the technical side of athletic fabric development, Chip set out on his new venture to

© Christopher Morris/Corbis

create not just a retail operation that sold yoga clothing and affiliated products, but a community hub where people could become educated in the physical aspects of healthy living and the mental strength that could be generated from such interaction. Another critical component of Chip's strategy was to create his clothing around feedback received from yoga instructors who were asked to wear it and comment on it. Gone were the days of participating in yoga, dance, running, or general fitness in sweaty and constricting cotton-based athletic wear. Lululemon offered the marketplace an innovative, unique, and distinctive clothing line that enabled participants to stay dry and move freely while keeping in style with the latest in sportswear trends.

Success did not come all at once for Chip. The transition from a small, single-location sole proprietor to an international player competing with the likes of Nike, Adidas, and Under Armour was the result of

careful planning and sound financial and market risk management. Expansion initially occurred domestically, followed by entry into the U.S. market, further expansion across Canada, and then international operations (Australia and Japan). It also included both franchise and corporate-owned store approaches to the marketplace. Funding the expansion required the involvement of traditional financing options as well as the use of equity-based cash infusions via venture capital firms. Lululemon went public in July 2007, launching an **IPO (initial public offering)** with the goal to raise US$200+ million. Now, more than 20 years since its inception (1998), Lululemon has grown into an international business with annual sales in fiscal year 2018 of approximately US$2.6 billion (up from $711 million in 2007), and net income of $258 million (see Figure 3.1). Although somewhat tarnished by the 2013 sheer pants scandal and the February 2018 resignation of former CEO Laurent Potdevin for "code of conduct violation reasons," Lululemon has rebounded and investors view the company's growth potential as full steam ahead. The company at the end of the third quarter 2018 had recorded +10% same-store sales growth and online sales growth of 48% (revenue was up 13% overall in 2018). Revenue in 2019 is expected to top US$3 billion. According to Target Research (2015), in the all-important 25- to 35-year-old demographic Lululemon remains the athleisure brand of

IPO (Initial Public Offering) refers to the initial sale of stock, by a corporation, through a public exchange.

FIGURE 3.1   Lululemon Athletica Growth

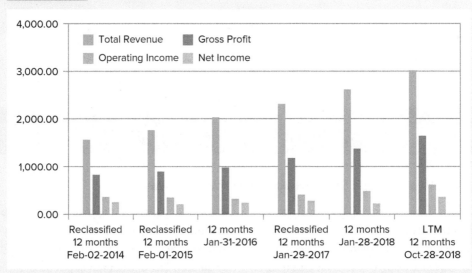

Sources: Googlefinance.com; yahoofinance.com.

choice, outdistancing such heavy hitters as Nike, Under Armour, Athleta, Gap, and Adidas. Of these current purchasers, in the U.S. 55% rate Lululemon as their favourite brand, while an impressive 70% of Canadian purchasers favour Lululemon over the competition.

Lululemon's product line includes clothing for men and women as well as a full line of fitness-related accessories including bags, socks, underwear, and yoga mats. The company also provides an extensive offering of yoga and lifestyle-related educational DVDs, and prides itself on the education and support it gives its customers concerning fabric care and proper garment sizing and fitting. New to the portfolio is its "office, travel, commute" assortment, featuring trench coats, shirts and pants, and looks to combine the best of both worlds—comfortable athleisure wear with the fashion required for the office environment.

Analysts estimate that the current value (market capitalization) of Lululemon Athletica, now traded on the NASDAQ stock exchange under the symbol LULU and the TSX (Toronto Stock Exchange) under the symbol LLL, is in excess of US$19.7 billion (compared to US$9.58 billion in 2015). As of the end of fiscal year 2018, the company had 57 stores in Canada, 270 in the United States, and 70 international showrooms and/or retail outlets in Australia, the United Kingdom, China, Germany, Netherlands, Switzerland, New Zealand, Japan, South Korea, and Singapore. Merchandise is also available for purchase online.

The Canadian Press/Bayne Stanley

Web Integration

Want to learn more about Lululemon? Visit their Web site at www.lululemon.com, or go to Google Finance or Yahoo Finance and search LULU.

Our Changing World

LO1

What a great time to be studying business! The dynamics of the global marketplace have never been more challenging than they are today. The growth of developing economies in Asia, Eastern Europe, the Middle East, and Central and South America present both opportunities and challenges to Canadian businesses looking to maintain and grow their market share in the global arena. The development of these new markets has resulted in a resurgence of the demand worldwide for Canadian natural resources, resulting in significant recent growth within these economic sectors (mining, agriculture, energy), and a perception that such growth, although slower going forward, will still offer expansion opportunities. At the same time, manufacturing sectors within Canada continue to be challenged to improve their overall competitiveness in the face of new, emerging competitors from China, India, Vietnam, Brazil, and Romania, to name a few. What was once a North America–centric view of the global marketplace, largely resulting from the dominant position the United States economy held globally, is rapidly changing to a more global-centric, interconnective model, as strong, well-capitalized economic growth continues throughout the world. Although today's growth continues to rely on U.S. economic capacity, the next few decades will see a significant shift in this regard as China, India, Brazil, and other economies mature and benefit from the significant foreign direct investment (FDI) currently underway within these countries and from the overall development of their monetary banking systems, legal systems, transportation and production systems, and competitive business models and operating platforms. The end result will be a tremendous growth in these economic regions as 3+ billion people experience an improved standard of living and a heightened desire to buy products and services and benefit from enhanced levels of personal wealth. As the old saying goes, the world is your oyster—view it as an opportunity to experience and benefit from the immense market opportunities that are presenting themselves across its surface.

> Although today's growth continues to rely on significant U.S. economic capacity, the next few decades will see a significant shift in this regard as China, India, Brazil, and other economies mature and benefit from the significant foreign direct investment (FDI) currently underway within these countries, and from the overall development of their monetary banking systems, intermodal transportation facilities, and competitive business models and operating platforms.

The Global Marketplace

Today, the global marketplace is home to some of the largest international-focused business organizations in many sectors. Several of these international companies, such as Royal Dutch Shell (Netherlands), ExxonMobil (U.S.), Walmart (U.S.), BP (Britain), and Total (France), generate revenues that exceed the total GDP of some countries. For example, Walmart's $500+ billion (USD) in sales in the 12-month period ending January 31, 2018[1] is equal to almost 30% of Canada's total GDP ($1.6 trillion USD). In addition, we are also seeing a number of companies from developing countries compete on the international stage as they seek access to the global marketplace. Sinopec, Alibaba Group Holding, Xiamen C&D, China National Petroleum (China), Pemex (Mexico), Gazprom (Russia), PDVSA (Venezuela), PTT (Thailand), and Tata Steel (India) are but a few of these rapidly emerging global players, with a scale and global reach to rival the many North American and European companies whose brands form part of our daily lives. In addition, many small and medium-size businesses are also expanding beyond local, regional, and national borders to become players in the global market. With the ongoing technological revolution these companies are able to actively compete beyond their domestic markets, buying and selling products and services on a worldwide basis. As noted in the Business in Action vignette, the successful Canadian business Lululemon Athletica started out as a small local player and has evolved into an international organization with retail store locations (in addition to Canada) in the U.S. and Australia, China, Germany, Netherlands, New Zealand, Singapore, and the United Kingdom.[2] Auto parts producer Magna International Inc. (287 on the Fortune Global 500) is another example of a Canadian international organization: it possesses more than 312 manufacturing operations and over 83 development and engineering centres spread out over more than 29 countries.[3] Toronto-based Brookfield Asset Management has moved from 441 to 272 on the Fortune Global 500, with revenues in excess of

$40 billion (USD) and an employee count exceeding 80 000.[4] Whether it is through operational growth, strategic alliances, formal partnerships, mergers, or acquisitions, the global marketplace is becoming home to an increasing number of businesses seeking to operate via an international-based business model. With operations becoming increasingly distributed across the globe, managers are more than ever challenged to maintain control and direction over their organizations and to ensure that strategies and operational tactics are being executed in a manner in which the organization's products and services remain relevant and that operational activities continue to meet the growing challenge of an increasingly competitive marketplace.

Business IN ACTION

Fortune Global 500

Each year, U.S.-based *Fortune* magazine publishes the Fortune 500 list of the 500 largest (by sales revenue) global companies. In 2017, combined revenue among these 500 totalled $30 trillion (USD), with profits in excess of $1.9 trillion (USD). Over the past several decades, this list (in particular the top 100) has been dominated by internationally focused companies whose headquarters are largely located within the G7 nations (United States, Japan, Germany, Great Britain, France, Italy, and Canada). In fact, in 2004 more than 40% of these organizations were headquartered in North America. While the G7 nations still make up a sizeable number of top 500 global companies (e.g., in 2018 the U.S. had 121 companies, while Japan had 52), developing-nation economies have made great strides in entering this prestigious ranking. Reflecting back to 1998, at that time there were six Chinese companies listed in the Fortune Global 500; in 2014, this number had grown to 95. The 2018 Global 500 now has 110 Chinese

companies, with three Chinese companies in the top 10 (State Grid Corp. of China, #2; Sinopec Group, #3; and China National Petroleum, #4) and 21 companies in the top 100. Walmart remains the largest company in the world by revenue (now six years in a row), and 2018 saw Apple credited with being the world's most profitable company. A review of the 2018 Top 100 Fortune Global 500 companies identifies 22 (up from 10 in 2008) of these companies as having headquarters in developing economies (nations). As these economies continue to grow, it is anticipated that representation on this list will grow as well, with companies from the BRIC countries (Brazil, Russia, India, China) leading the way. Newcomers to the 2018 list of the Global 500 were 33 in total, with China leading with 12 companies joining the list. Other countries adding newcomers to the list were India, Poland, Taiwan, Mexico, South Korea, and Germany, to name a few. Canada had 12 companies in the Global 500 in 2018. Leading our representation

© Iain Masterton/Alamy

© Alex Segre/Alamy

was Manulife Financial (#241). The other Canadian companies achieving this unique global status were Brookfield Asset Management (#272), Power Corp. of Canada (#282), Magna International (#287), Royal Bank of Canada (#292), Alimentation Couche-Tard (#299), George Weston (#308), Toronto-Dominion Bank (#337), Enbridge (#345), Bank of Nova Scotia (#430), Onex (#447), and Suncor Energy (#476).

Web Integration

Want to learn more about the Fortune 500 Global rankings, which companies made the list, and who is #1? Log on to www.fortune.com and search the Global 500.

Whether it is through operational growth, strategic alliances, formal partnerships, mergers, or acquisitions, the global marketplace is becoming home to an increasing number of businesses seeking to operate via an international-based business model.

LO2   Why Go Global?

Companies look to move beyond their domestic markets for a combination of reasons. For simplicity purposes, these can be categorized around the following (see also Figure 3.2):

- New market opportunities
- Cost reduction opportunity
- Resource base control
- Closeness to markets
- Economies of scale

FIGURE 3.2   **Why Go Global?**

New Market Opportunities

As explained in Chapter 1, companies need to recognize that markets do mature and that new opportunities for untapped markets for current and future product/service offerings need to form a core part of the strategic planning process. As domestic markets become saturated, organizations will begin to look beyond their current countries and markets in an effort to discover and leverage new markets for the products and services they offer. For many Canadian companies, the natural tendency is to look first to the United States (given its close proximity) for potential growth opportunities and then turn their attention internationally, although this is not always the case. With the rapid growth of the emerging developing economies of the world, tremendous new market potential is being realized by a variety of Canadian and international-based organizations. As noted in Chapter 2, our Canadian banks continue to invest in new market opportunities in the United States, Central and South America, and Asia. Educational institutions—such as Queen's University, in Kingston, Ontario—are developing new markets for knowledge-based services in Saudi Arabia, the UAE, and other parts of the world. Magna International is active in Russia, CAE Inc. has flight simulator training facilities worldwide, Brookfield Asset Management has over 80 000 people in more than 30 countries managing its capital interests in real estate, renewable power, and infrastructure assets (utilities, energy, communications). Alimentation Couche-Tard (see the Business in Action feature) and Canadian Tire have both undertaken ventures into the United States. All of this is in search of new markets and organizational growth. It should be noted that the search for new markets is not a one-way focus, with fully developed economies, such as the United States and Canada, looking for new markets elsewhere around the world. Companies from emerging economies have taken the same approach. China's meteoric economic rise has been largely driven by an export strategy that has found opportunities for Chinese-manufactured products around the world. The same holds true for other Asian nations, South and Central American countries, and the developing economies of Eastern Europe. Although we have focused on organic growth in this discussion, companies can—and do—gain access to new markets via acquisitions as well. Alimentation Couche-Tard is an example of a company that has done just that (see Business in Action: Alimentation Couche-Tard). The ability to assess global market needs, manufacture products or develop services in response, and then engage in global trade to gain access to these markets has been fundamental to the development of today's global marketplace.

Business IN ACTION

Alimentation Couche-Tard—A Fortune 500 Company

Starting with a single store operation in 1980 in Laval, Quebec, Alimentation Couche-Tard has grown into one of the world's largest convenience store operators, and one of the world's 500 largest companies. This phenomenal achievement has been the result of a carefully orchestrated acquisition strategy matched by a well-managed operation that has consistently delivered double-digit returns on the capital it has employed. To say that acquisitions has been a critical part of the growth strategy is an understatement, as Alimentation Couche-Tard has successfully completed over 55 acquisitions between 1980 and 2018. Several recent acquisitions include Pantry Inc., a leading convenience store operation in the southeastern United States (2015), Topaz, the leading

© Graham Hughes/The Canadian Press

Its European operation consists of 2700+ store and retail-fuel locations, and Alimentation Couche-Tard has an estimated 2000+ stores under licensing agreements internationally. International locations include (but are not limited to) China, Vietnam, Indonesia, UAE, Saudi Arabia, Mexico, Costa Rica, and Honduras. The company reported net earnings of $1.6 billion (up from $1.2 billion in 2017) on revenues of $51.4 billion in 2018 (versus $38 billion in 2017). Revenue has grown an average of 5.1% annually over the past five years. Simply making an acquisition, however, does not guarantee success. Alimentation Couche-Tard's management team has been exceptionally adept in growing same-store merchandise sales year over year, consistently outperforming rivals, via a business model based on delivering value to the customer (time and convenience) and supported by effective merchandising strategies, food service and food product enhancements, prudent cost control, and key investments in distribution management and logistics. Alimentation Couche-Tard employs over 130 000 individuals worldwide, operating under local store banners such as Couche-Tard, Circle-K, Statoil, and Ingo.

convenience and fuel retailer in Ireland (2016), and CST Brands, the fourth largest convenience chain in North America (2017). Domestically, the company acquired 278 Esso-branded Canadian fuel and convenience stores in 2017. This history of a well-executed acquisition strategy, coupled with a disciplined approach to building additional stores within the existing network, has propelled the company's stellar growth record.

Alimentation Couche-Tard's operating footprint now includes location ownership or location licensing-management agreements worldwide. In total, Alimentation Couche-Tard's North American operation consists of over 9940 stores. Operations can be found in all of the Canadian provinces and in 48 of the 50 U.S. states.

Tracy Harris

Cost Reduction Opportunity

In terms of global competitiveness, organizations will locate in, and purchase inputs from, countries where the costs of productive resources enable them to generate a competitive advantage. They are attracted to countries where labour costs are relatively low and occupational skills are relatively high. This enables the organization to lower its overall cost base, thereby allowing the organization to maintain a competitive price in today's ever-demanding competitive markets. As an example, technology-based companies are attracted to India, given its well-educated and technology-focused labour pool. Numerous manufacturing processes have been globally shifted to China, given its lower labour costs and productive yields, while the garment industry has seen significant growth in Asia (Thailand, Vietnam, Bangladesh, Mongolia) and in Central America (Costa Rica, Guatemala, Honduras). North American manufacturers, such as the Hershey Company, have also shifted production to Mexico in an effort to take advantage of available lower-priced labour pools and lower their overall cost base. As competition intensifies, and the ability to truly differentiate products and services between one manufacturer and another is becoming more difficult, organizations are sensing an increasing pressure to use price as a weapon of competitive rivalry. In order to be effective with a price-focused strategy, organizations must, in turn, reduce their cost base in order to protect their operating margins and, ultimately, their profit. With labour representing one of the largest cost sectors for many manufacturers, the ability to significantly impact the cost base lies with the ability of firms to reduce such labour costs. This is what makes **offshoring** or **outsourcing** certain elements of the operation to regions where labour costs are lower so attractive.

Although labour is used as the primary example, decisions to invest abroad, or for foreign companies to invest in our domestic market, are not driven solely by labour costs. The same rationale of determining where and how to compete holds true for other cost sectors, whether they be raw materials, energy costs, technology-based costs, or politically imposed costs such as tariffs, duties, or other competition-based taxes. As an example, a number of Chinese companies are establishing manufacturing facilities in the United States and Canada. China's second largest dairy producer, Inner Mongolia Yili Industrial Group, has partnered with the Dairy Farmers of America to develop and manage a plant that produces powdered milk for the Chinese market.[5] In Kitchener, Ontario, the Suzhou Xingya Investment Company made a $20-million manufacturing investment for the development of a steel nail plant (United Enterprise), which produces steel nails targeted toward the U.S. market.[6] Kingston, Ontario is the recipient of a $225-million investment from Feihe International, a leading Chinese dairy processor, to build a plant with the ability to produce 60 000 tons of dry infant food annually.[7]

Faced with maturing markets in China, a reduced wage advantage due to higher labour costs in China, and an increasingly aggressive protectionist attitude in the United States, Chinese investments in new factory construction and acquisitions in the United States have grown substantially over the last two decades. As an example, from 2000 to 2017, Chinese companies invested an estimated $8.6 billion (USD) in new U.S-based production facilities.[8] Although labour costs are still higher in the U.S.A., the cost of land and utilities in some regional areas within the United States (e.g., South Carolina, Texas), when combined with strong state and municipal tax credits and incentives along with the avoidance of tariffs and duties on imported goods, has made such opportunities very cost-effective and appealing to Chinese companies. Add to this the reduced transportation costs associated with producing within the market being served, and the end result is that these cost savings have in many cases more than offset the higher labour costs.[9] The ratification of the Canada–China Foreign Investment Promotion and Protection Agreement (FIPA) in September 2014 is expected to generate similar results for Canada, as the act's intent is to provide a more streamlined approach to setting up business in each country and offers greater legal protection to companies doing business within each of the respective countries. Going back to our example of Suzhou Xingya Investment Company's decision to locate in Kitchener, the rationale for this move came down to two key components. First, Canada represents next-door-neighbour proximity to the U.S. market, and second, manufacturing in Canada eliminates the exposure of Suzhou to tariffs the U.S. would have imposed on the importing of steel-head nails had they been manufactured in China. The tariff avoidance, coupled with Canadian levels of productivity, are what made this investment such an attractive option to Suzhou Xingya Investment Company.

Offshoring is transferring a component (operations, service, support) of a firm's business system to another country for the purpose of reducing costs, improving efficiency or effectiveness, or developing a competitive advantage.

Outsourcing is contracting out a portion of, or a component of, a firm's business system for the purpose of reducing costs, improving efficiency or effectiveness, acquiring expertise, or developing a competitive advantage.

Organizations facing increasingly competitive markets will seek the most efficient and cost-effective product/service delivery systems as a methodology for maintaining cost competitiveness and earning higher margins and profits. An additional side benefit is that by investing in these markets, foreign firms can also diminish concerns relating to protectionism, duties, and other tax levies designed to protect domestic economies.

Resource Base Control

In some business sectors, organizations look globally in an effort to ensure their business portfolios continually add the required resource base necessary for an adequate future supply to support the products and services they offer in the marketplace. This is particularly true of the energy and commodity-based resource industries. Specific to Canada has been significant interest by foreign firms in acquiring ownership of our natural and energy resource bases. Oil-producing companies, mining companies, and other natural resource–intensive companies have all been active in making direct investments into Canada or obtaining ownership stake in our resource base via business acquisitions. For example, since 2000, over $160 billion has been invested in the Alberta oil sands project,[10] with a significant percentage of the investment coming from foreign companies. Although the recent drop in energy prices coupled with increasing operating costs, lower costs for renewable-energy alternatives, and regulatory and environmental delays in pipeline development (to flow the crude oil to refineries) has slowed current investment levels into this regional energy sector (down 45% between 2014 and 2017), it is hoped that a formal energy policy—and more supportive government action, as it is showing with regard to the $40 billion LNG pipeline project in British Columbia—will enable Canada to continue to benefit from this important sector of our economy, which generates $19 billion in government revenue and employs over 500 000 individuals. Partners in the LNG pipeline project include Royal Dutch Shell (Netherlands), Mitsubishi Corp. (Japan), Petronas (Malaysia), PetroChina Co., and Korean Gas Corp.[11]

As mentioned in Chapter 2, significant acquisitions by foreign firms into Canada did occur in the early 2000s, largely for the purpose of obtaining and controlling mineral rights. Xstrata's purchase of Falconbridge and Vale Limited's purchase of Inco are examples of the energy- and mining-related acquisitions that have taken place. More recently, the acquisition by IPC (a subsidiary of Norwegian-based Lundin Peetroleum AB) of Calgary's BlackPearl (oil and gas producer) in 2018 for $622.5 million (CAD) further reinforces this desire by firms and countries across the globe to develop an ownership stake in the finite natural resources possessed by our world. China, active internationally in this regard, has also been quite active over the past several years in Canada via its sovereign wealth fund, which is called the China Investment Corporation. Two deals this fund completed at the end of the last decade were (1) an $817-million investment for a 45% stake in Calgary's Penn West Energy Trust's Peace River oil sands project in Northern Alberta, as well as an additional $435-million investment for a 5% stake in Penn West Energy Trust overall (May 2010), and (2) a $1.74-billion investment for a 17% stake in Teck Resources Ltd. (July 2009). China Investment Corporation also has holdings in Kinross Gold Corp. and Potash Corp (now called Nutrien Ltd.). Sinopec, China's state-owned energy firm, also invested $4.65 billion for a 9% stake in Syncrude Canada, and in 2009 PetroChina Co. purchased a 60% stake in oil sands projects owned by Athabasca Oil Sands Corp.[12] As was discussed in Chapter 2, Australia's BHP Billiton's attempted takeover of Potash Corporation was largely driven by BHP Billiton's desire to broaden its resource base. This discussion is not meant to imply that Canada is at the mercy of foreign companies. We have also seen significant investment by Canadian firms into foreign markets for the same reasons. For example, Canadian companies have been some of the biggest players in the development of the African mining sector: at the end of 2012, Canadian companies—viewed as a "quiet powerhouse"—had mining assets valued at $90 billion in the Americas (excluding Canada), $22 billion in Africa, and $11 billion in Asia. In total, Canadian-owned mining assets globally (outside of Canada) totalled $148 billion. In addition, a number of Canadian-based pipeline development companies, frustrated by development delays at home, have embarked upon significant acquisitions to continue to grow their businesses. The period 2016–18 saw two significant deals involving Canadian companies in this regard. Enbridge Inc.'s acquisition of Spectra Energy Corp. (U.S.) for $42.8B (USD) was one of the largest energy-related deals in recent history. TransCanada Corp., another Canadian-based energy company, purchased Columbia Pipeline Group Inc. (U.S.) for $12 billion (USD).[13]

> The key fundamental in resource base acquisition strategies lies in seeking to control supply sources or influence the use of such sources, as well as being able to generate lower costs or better value by having more control over resource-based factors of production.

Closeness to Markets

Companies also look to expand their business operations across the globe for the purpose of being "close to markets." Emerging developing economies in Asia, Eastern Europe, the Middle East, and South America all represent new opportunities for growth for international players. The Brookings Institution, a private non-profit organization focused on independent research initiatives associated with globalization challenges and policy setting, monitors on an ongoing basis the global metro trends relating to employment and GDP growth. In its recent Global Metro Monitor 2018 release, Brookings has found that, during the period 2014–16, 300 of the largest metropolitan areas globally accounted for 36% of global employment growth and approximately 67% of global GDP growth. These large metropolitan areas generate approximately 50% of the world's global GDP, account for 23% of its employment, and are home to 24% of the world's population. Within these metropolitan areas the fastest growth occurred in metro areas within China, the Asian-Pacific region, and the Middle East and Africa. Metropolitan areas focused on technology, manufacturing specializations, utilities, tourism, and trade were identified as the growth leaders, outpacing metro areas with high concentrations of financial and professional services. Emerging economies were home to 80% of the 60 top-performing metropolitan areas. Although this would imply that the emerging economies are the focus going forward, advanced-economy metropolitan areas such as Dublin, Ireland, and the California cities of San Jose, San Francisco, and Los Angeles also saw significant economic growth. China as a country led the metropolitan growth focus overall, with 17 of the top 30 performing cities.[14]

Establishing facilities within developing economic regions enables companies to operate closer to these emerging markets and to react more quickly to market opportunities and trends. Metropolitan areas (as noted above) become particularly attractive as their large-population, high-density environments result in an easier ability to connect with customers at lower costs. These areas also generally offer a larger labour pool from which to build upon and a stronger supporting infrastructure grid (utilities, highways, terminals, etc.). Becoming a domestic producer in these areas often enables such companies to create a stronger affiliation for their products and services and overall brands, thereby reinforcing the value of their presence to the local market. For example, resulting from their substantial investments in manufacturing facilities in China—created in partnership with Chinese auto manufacturing companies—both Volkswagen AG and General Motors have generated significant local demand for their vehicles. Their investments have created jobs for local residents, enhanced the spending capabilities of the population via the wages they pay, and generated demand for their products and services as a result of their presence in these areas. Italian carmaker Fiat S.p.A.'s acquisition of a controlling interest in North America–based Chrysler in 2014 was directly related to Fiat's desire to gain immediate access to the North American market via dealer networks and manufacturing facilities. Apple, Facebook, Salesforce.com, Google, IBM, Oracle, PayPal, Dell, and Microsoft all have made substantial investments and created a significant presence in Dublin, Ireland.[15] Canada's CAE Inc., which designs, develops, and manufactures flight simulators and related equipment, has expanded its training sites globally in order to bring its product and training service offerings directly to its ever-expanding client base (see the Business in Action feature).[16] Engaging an organization into new markets often returns the added benefits of identifying new ideas as markets become better understood, developing new products/services in response to those needs, gaining greater market diversification as new markets grow and opportunities are capitalized on, and benefiting from learning new business methods.

Business IN ACTION

CAE—An Innovation and Technology Leader

Having developed a network of over 160 training centres across the globe, CAE Inc. is the recognized world leader in modelling, simulation development, and training for the civil aviation, healthcare, and defence industries. Possessing the most advanced flight simulation technology in the world, CAE annually trains over 220 000 civil and defence crew members, including more than 135 000 pilots. CAE's training programs cover the full spectrum of commercial aircraft, regional jets, and helicopters. Founded in 1947, this Canadian-based company employs over 9000 people worldwide, with 90% of its revenue being generated from international activities and worldwide exports. Core businesses include sales of simulation products and training services to both civil and military clients. Its close relationships with the military operations of both the United States and the United Kingdom, along with preferred supplier status to military manufacturers such as Lockheed Martin, has enabled CAE Inc. to become an integral part of the training and support of military jet, support craft, and helicopter crews. With annual revenues in excess of $2.8 billion (USD) as of March 2018 (up 5%

The Canadian Press/Andy Rain

over 2017), CAE Inc. has developed flight simulation technology for almost every modern airliner, and has sold its products and services to over 3000 airlines, aircraft operators, and manufacturers worldwide.

Key to growth looking forward is CAE's "emerging market" footprint. Solidly positioned as the "go to" simulation training company in North America and Europe (together they represent 65% of revenue), CAE is responding to emerging-country demand for pilot and crew member training. With annual passenger air travel growth rates near double-digit levels, these developing economies represent an important future opportunity to expand its business presence. CAE estimates (November 2017) that the training systems

integration market is valued at more than $15 billion (USD), and that more than 255 000 new airline first officers will require support training over the upcoming decade. The total number of active pilots globally could reach as many as 440 000 by 2027. Joint ventures and long-term training agreements have been arranged with a number of air travel providers in India, the Middle East, Latin America, Southeast Asia, and China. CAE is a publicly traded company on both the NYSE (New York Stock Exchange) and the TSX (Toronto Stock Exchange). CAE has consistently ranked as one of Canada's leading companies in research and development investments, investing an estimated 10% of annual revenues in pursuit of market-leading products and services.

Web Integration

Want to learn more about CAE Inc.? Visit their Web site at **www.cae.com**.

Economies of Scale

In terms of creating competitive advantages, organizations seek to develop, manage, and leverage global production and distribution networks. These **economies of scale** can be realized in the sourcing and production of products; the centralization of services such as marketing; and the sharing of manufacturing and infrastructure facilities to supply products and services to the global market. In industries such as automobiles, retail, or computers, for example, internationally focused companies are actively competing for the same customers in numerous global markets. In many cases, the products these companies create are purposely designed for global consumption in order to facilitate operational efficiency and to spread development and production costs across larger volumes. For example, the same car (with perhaps just a few modifications for local markets) can be produced and traded around the world. Toyota, with its TPS (Toyota Production System) process approach, has developed and perfected flexible assembly lines that enable Toyota to quickly change the model being produced in response to shifts in overall demand. Its Yaris and Prius models are examples of vehicles that have been designed for the global (versus a region-specific) marketplace. As a dominant competitor in the discount retail sector, Walmart's overall size and buying power enable it to spread the purchasing costs of goods and services across a large volume of stores, thereby reducing its overall cost on a per unit basis. Amazon.com's market reach, via its ecommerce-based business model, which enables Amazon not only to sell items to the marketplace, but also to act as a conduit for other companies to use its technology platforms for the same purpose, is able to spread the underlying cost of supporting its technology across a large volume of customers (business and individual). For both Walmart and Amazon, the sheer volume of goods and services sold has enabled each company to develop a cost advantage relative to rivals, which it can then leverage into lower prices while protecting its underlying profit margin.

Economies of Scale are reductions in the cost base of an organization as a result of greater size, process standardization, or enhanced operational efficiencies.

LO3 Global Market Stability: The Role of Government

The meltdown of the financial services sector in the fall of 2008 and the accompanying recession of 2009 have brought to the forefront the interdependency and connectivity that exists in the global marketplace. The free flow of debt services and credit facilities, along with an absence of a unified financial regulatory system for the global markets, resulted in a significant domino effect across the global financial services sector, with the end result being severe **liquidity** and **solvency** issues within numerous worldwide banking and financial institutions. In response to this crisis, the G7/8 and G20 organizations, via their respective forums, have agreed to implement financial protocols and regulatory policies focused on ensuring that the situation does not reoccur. Although this will take time, governments across the globe have jointly committed to developing such a regulatory environment with the purpose of managing financial and market risk in a steadily evolving global market. These financial and regulatory fundamentals are essential in ensuring that the global marketplace grows in a manner that minimizes economic disequilibrium from occurring within singular economies, avoids an overdependency toward protectionist-based marketing practices, and manages financial and market risk in a manner that minimizes the potential for unsustainable growth (i.e., economic bubbles) or counterproductive practices. They alone, however, do not fully define the role of government with respect to the management of risk and growth in today's global environment. In fully defining their role, governments, in union with each other, need to commit to six fundamentals (the first five of which have been emphasized by Jeffrey Immelt, former CEO of General Electric)[17] as committed participants in today's interconnected global market environment. These six key fundamental building blocks of global market development (see Figure 3.3) are as follows:

- Ongoing commitment to international trade system
- Market openness

Liquidity refers to the cash position of a company and its ability to meet its immediate debt and operational obligations. It also refers to the ability of the company to convert existing assets to cash in order to meet such obligations.

Solvency refers to the long-term stability of the company and its ability to meet its ongoing debt and operational obligations, and to fund future growth.

FIGURE 3.3   **Fundamentals of Global Economic Stability**

- Absence of protectionism
- Adherence to the fundamentals of fair trade
- Balanced economic development
- Responsible sovereign debt management

Ongoing Commitment to International Trade System

Ongoing commitment to an international trading system refers to the need for countries to commit (and adhere) to the trade policies and agreements overseen by the WTO (World Trade Organization). Created in 1995, the WTO's main role is to establish the parameters for multilateral trading now and for the future. Constantly evolving, the WTO provides regulatory and policy-based guidance on issues relating to the flow of goods and services, the protection of intellectual property, dispute resolution associated with trade quarrels between countries, and trade policy review associated with the policies individual countries are putting into place. A key purpose of the WTO is to ensure that transparency exists between countries and globally with respect to the manner in which trade is conducted. Its overriding objective is to ensure that trade flows smoothly, fairly, and predictably. This includes creating rules relating to the use and acceptance of tariffs and subsidies by governments as well as anti-dumping measures. According to the WTO, liberal trade policies that enable an easing of restrictions associated with the flow of goods and services sharpen competition, motivate innovation, and ultimately lead to economic success for the participating countries. Since its inception, data collected by the WTO have demonstrated a statistical link between freer trade and economic growth. Countries that have embraced the underlying concepts of free trade are able to leverage their comparative advantages as a mechanism to stimulate economic growth and then further evolve their economies in a way that broadens their economic base, thereby enabling them to compete more fully in the global market. Efficiencies are gained by having countries produce the products and/or offer services that they do best, and then rely on other countries to offer the products and services to them based on their underlying advantages. This enables all countries to benefit from a global marketplace, of which each trade member is offering to each other the best products and services at the best price. In addition to the work noted above, the WTO also provides a variety of support services to developing countries and emerging economies. As of June 2014 the WTO had more than 160 members, representing over 97% of world trade. Figure 3.4 provides an overview of the services offered by the WTO.[18]

Having commented above on the mission and intended value that the WTO brings to the global marketplace, its effectiveness and "reason for being" is being challenged today like never before. Since 2016, with the emergence of the Donald

FIGURE 3.4   **WTO: Key Services**

- Administers trade agreements
- Acts as a forum for trade negotiations
- Settles trade disputes
- Reviews national trade policies
- Assists developing countries in trade policy issues via technical assistance and training
- Links with other international organizations to ensure the smooth flow of trade

Trump presidency in the United States, the WTO has been facing a series of ongoing disputes as nationalistic and protectionist policies by the world's largest economy have resulted in aggressive tariff and restrictive trade policies being implemented by the United States, and retaliation by countries responding to such measures. The current dispute between the United States versus Mexico, Canada, and the European Union over steel and aluminum tariffs, and the heavy import duties and tariffs that the U.S. has levied against China (and on which China has responded with its own set of import duties), has challenged the free trade model around which the global economy has evolved. To date, it is too early to determine if the above-mentioned shift in trade dynamics is the new way of doing business, or if such aggressive measures will subside going forward and a return to the broader multilateral trade model will take place.

Credit Facilities is a general term that describes the variety of loans that could be offered to a business or a country.

Web Integration

Want to learn more about the WTO? Visit **www.wto.org**.

 ## Business IN ACTION

Global Spotlight—International Monetary Fund

In addition to the WTO, the IMF (International Monetary Fund) serves a vital role in managing and supporting the international trading system. Its primary purpose is to ensure the stability of the international monetary system. Focused on strengthening the global financial system, the IMF contributes to the international trade framework by (1) monitoring global economic and financial developments with an emphasis on crisis prevention (and global responses to crises that may occur), exchange rate stability, and balanced economic growth; (2) the issuance of temporary or short-term loans to countries that have balance of trade imbalances, thereby eliminating liquidity issues within these countries; and (3) the lending of **credit facilities** to low-income countries for the purpose of poverty reduction and economic development and providing technical support in the development of such poverty-reduction strategies. Following the financial crisis of 2008, the IMF expanded its role to include the lending of expertise and financial resources to countries pressured by sovereign debt issues. The IMF played a key role in the development of a solution to the sovereign debt issues challenging the governments of a number of

European Union members in 2010 and 2011. IMF loans during this period included $40 billion to Greece, $30 billion to Ireland, and $39 billion to Portugal. IMF loans to emerging markets during the 2008-09 financial crisis totalled an additional $60 billion. Going forward, in addition to the responsibilities noted above the IMF has now identified as a priority providing insight and expertise in making growth sustainable, given the unaddressed and growing concerns relating to climate change and its impact on the global ecosystem. It also continues to monitor the financial policies and actions of global markets to ensure that an efficient and effective global financial safety net remains in place to minimize the consequences of significant financial disruption, as occurred in 2008. Created in 1945, the IMF has grown from its original membership of 29 countries to 189 countries. Member countries can request IMF financial assistance if they are unable to meet required international debt payments and are unable to find sufficient funding elsewhere. The intent of such loans is to assist countries struggling with massive debt to correct such balance of payment challenges in order to restore overall economic stability. As an example, in 2018 the IMF issued its largest loan ever—$57 billion to Argentina in an effort to assist in stabilizing that country's economic system. Such loans are not provided without requirements for substantial economic policy change. The idea is to provide immediate financial relief while an underlying restructuring of a nation's financial structure and position takes place. In the Argentina example, the country was required to commit to a "Zero Deficit" action plan as part of the loan provisions.

Bloomberg via Getty Images

Web Integration

Want to learn more about the IMF? Visit **www.imf.org**.

Business IN ACTION

Global Spotlight—World Bank

Recognizing the relationship between economic growth and the elimination of poverty in the world's poorest countries, the World Bank provides low-interest loans, interest-free credits, and grants to developing countries for the purpose of funding development projects in areas such as education, health, public administration, infrastructure, financial and private-sector development, agriculture, and environmental and natural resource management. Providing both financial and technical assistance, the World Bank's mission is to work with developing countries to eliminate poverty, enhance growth via sustainable practices, and create individual opportunity and hope. In undertaking initiatives within countries in need, the World Bank seeks to (1) build capacity through the strengthening of governments via education of government officials, (2) assist in the creation of legal and judicial frameworks within these countries, (3) assist in the development of financial systems to support the development of an economic platform, and (4) combat corruption. Established in 1944, the World Bank has 189 country members and more than 10 000 employees worldwide. Its two core goals are to end extreme poverty by decreasing the percentage of people living on less than $1.90 a day and

to promote shared prosperity by fostering the income growth of the bottom 40% for every country. Since 1947, the World Bank has funded over 12 000 development projects globally. An outcome of its mission has been its ability to reduce the number of people worldwide who live on $1.90 per day from 1.9 billion (in 1990) to an estimated 736 million (as of 2015). A major emphasis of its work for the upcoming near term will be in the region of Sub-Saharan Africa, where the percentage of people living in extreme poverty continues to represent a significant percentage of the extreme poor.

AFP/Getty Images

Market Openness

Market openness refers to the need for developing economies to maintain a focus on the core elements of an open economy: the law of supply and demand, the encouragement of entrepreneurship and wealth creation, and the willingness to encourage and support private ownership. It also relates to the willingness of countries to open their borders to competitive goods and services in order to maximize benefits (import and export) to their citizens and residents. This translates into supporting the movement of goods and services, capital, foreign trade, and labour into and out of the country with few to no restrictions. The ongoing development of free-trade agreements; minimization of trade disputes; resistance to the concept of the nationalization of core economic sectors; abolition of the use of tariffs, taxes, and duties to artificially control prices; and elimination of unfair trading practices are all components of an open market system.

Absence of Protectionism

As defined in Chapter 2, protectionism is the intent of economic policies that are put in place to protect or improve the competitiveness of domestic industries via impeding or restricting the openness of a market or markets to foreign competitors through the use of tariffs, trade restrictions, quotas, market-sector subsidies (agriculture is an example), artificial control of currency values, or other related activities. The need to resist protectionist responses, associated with trade disputes or global market evolution, refers directly to the tendency for governments to initiate policies and practices whose intent is to protect domestic markets to the general detriment of the global marketplace. Such action generally arises when governments attempt to respond to competitive imports, which are appearing to cause a significant shift in a trade relationship between countries. The action is typically triggered by a perception that the impacted domestic market sector is unable to compete, generally due to higher costs, against the imports flowing into the country. The immediate response is therefore more likely to be based on political gain versus economic fundamentals. The danger, of course, is that such actions generally trigger similar responses or retaliatory actions on the part of the impacted trading partner, resulting in further economic stagnation and preserving underlying market inefficiencies. Although the perception by governments could be that such actions are necessary for the immediate good of the economy, protectionism largely has detrimental effects on the marketplace in the long run, and often results in economic inefficiencies and higher prices for consumers due to the absence of, or significant restrictions levied against, external competitors. As noted previously in this chapter, the actions of the administration of U.S. President Donald Trump are largely driven by the perception that the actions the U.S. has taken with respect to its trading partners will provide an immediate, positive return to the U.S. economy. President Trump's position is that the openness of the U.S. economy relative to the less-open economic market environment of its trading partners has had a long-term negative impact on the economic platform of the United States. Leveraging the current economic might of the United States with respect to the global economy, President Trump hopes to open the borders of trading partners in what is interpreted as a more level playing field for all. Countries that are not willing to do this run the risk of having duties and tariffs relating to products and services that they export to the United States levied against them, thereby making such products and services less price competitive with respect to domestic products and services manufactured or produced in the United States. The critical question going forward is the long-term impact that these trade wars will have on the broader global economy and on the trade relations between the countries involved.

Adherence to the Fundamentals of Fair Trade

Adherence to the fundamentals of fair trade relates directly to the commitment on the part of governments to support and enforce the intellectual and patent property rights of companies, adhere to generally accepted labour practices, and commit to environmental standards agreed upon by the global marketplace. The expectation associated with fair trade compliance is that governments will seek to eliminate **black market** activities, which violate the intellectual and property rights of developers and manufacturers of products or services. Examples of industries constantly under assault from black market knock-offs range from software and electronic handheld devices to luxury articles such as purses and watches. The motion picture and music industries have both suffered significant revenue and profit degradation due to black market unauthorized reproductions of copyrighted materials. Black market industries and intellectual property infringements are not restricted to developing countries. Although much has been written regarding significant black market activities for electronics, motion pictures, and software products in Asia and Mexico, fully developed economies face ongoing battles in this sector as well. For example, for decades Italy has been fighting a piracy culture in the manufacture of handbags.[19] Canada has felt considerable pressure from the motion picture industry to stem black market activities with regard to pirated "bootleg" copies of new film releases. Unauthorized downloading of copyrighted music and video content continues to make the news in the United States.[20] Global fair trade fundamentals also include adherence to anti-dumping regulations, the inappropriate use of subsidies to protect or provide competitive advantage to specific industries, and other difficulties that may arise within a country relating to the ability to adhere to WTO agreements and requirements.

Black Market is the illegal market that arises within economies where goods are scarce, taxation on such goods is high, or the prices of legitimate goods are beyond the capacity of significant segments of the population to buy.

Balanced Economic Development

A key fundamental that governments must work diligently toward is the development of well-balanced economic growth within their respective economies. Governments must look to ensure that the total focus of an economy is not export driven, with the intent of simply supplying products or services to other countries. The development of the domestic side of the economy must be pursued in order to minimize reliance on external buying sources. The development of internal markets for goods and services results in a stronger economic base and expanded economic activity, which is essential to ensuring that nations create stability and growth in the standard of living for their citizens and residents. A core area of the development of the domestic side of the economy lies with the fundamentals of economic market stability first identified in Chapter 2: established factors of production, a national monetary policy and banking system, manageable levels of national debt, low inflation, and a climate of political stability. For economies to experience long-term and sustainable growth, the purchasing power of its residents coupled with the domestic consumption of goods and services must occur in addition to export-driven manufacturing or production considerations. This internal exchange of goods and services drives economic vitality, which creates domestic-based wealth, enabling the emergence of buying power and the ongoing demand for additional goods and services. The current growth within the Chinese economy is a good example. Initially based on manufacturing platforms focused on supplying goods and services to external markets, China's accelerated GDP growth is the result of not only an increased export-based economy, but also one that is generating goods and services domestically for its emerging middle and upper class. The economy also has been the recipient of considerable foreign direct investment (FDI) in addition to domestic (Chinese government) investment that is geared toward developing the infrastructure and capacity to meet this growing domestic-based opportunity.

The development of internal markets for goods and services results in a stronger economic base and expanded economic activity, which is essential to ensuring that nations create stability and growth in the standard of living for their citizens and residents.

Responsible Sovereign Debt Management

Sovereign Debt is debt issued or guaranteed by a national government.

Responsible management of **sovereign debt** refers to the obligation that government leaders have to manage their economies in a fiscally prudent manner. In many cases countries will need to develop and carry deficits to effectively manage economic volatility and meet the diverse needs of their citizens. Emerging economies in particular often need significant financial support (World Bank, IMF) to initiate the fundamental changes needed to get economic activity off the ground. The use of debt, however, must be done in a manner that recognizes the obligations it will inflict on both current and future generations. Countries must seek to develop stable economic platforms that result in long-term balance of trade positions and that do not jeopardize economic growth due to overburdening deficit obligations. When sovereign debt gets out of hand, the end result can be significant negative pressures on the ability of the economy to grow, loss of control over inflation, political unrest due to the magnitude of taxation, or the reduction in services required to restore fiscal balance. The sovereign debt challenges facing the governments of Greece, Portugal, Italy, and Spain, their impact on the citizens of these countries, and their impact across the European Union and to the value of the euro are representative of the challenges countries will face when they take on too much debt. The growing debt situation globally, however, is becoming even more challenging, as 24 of the 59 countries that the IMF classifies as "low-income developing countries" are either in a debt crisis or are teetering on the brink of falling into one. These include (but are not limited to) countries such as the Republic of Congo, Mozambique, Chad, Sudan, Afghanistan, Haiti, and Yemen.[21] One only has to look at the current political stability challenges in Argentina and Venezuela to see the ramifications of burdening debt on a country's overall economic solvency. Concerns exist, as well, surrounding the amount of debt the United States government has issued since the financial crisis of 2008–09. The national debt of the United States climbed to an all-time high in February 2019 to $22+ trillion. The total debt of the U.S. now exceeds its GDP. In 1988 the U.S. debt was approximately 50% of GDP.[22] Canada itself experienced the harshness of burdening national debt back in the mid-1980s, when high levels of debt significantly impacted economic growth. It was only through prudent government action and restrained fiscal spending that our national debt was brought back under control. Today, thanks to the measures put into place in the 1990s, Canada's national debt position is one of the strongest of the developed economies, with our debt-to-GDP ratio well below that of most other nations. This strength enabled us to initiate the financial stimulus packages needed to prop up our economy as a result of the financial crisis of 2008–09, with fewer concerns than other nations experienced relating to the long-term negative consequences to our economy from taking on this additional debt.

Business IN ACTION

Global Spotlight—People's Republic of China

Over the past decade, the People's Republic of China has been one of the world's fastest growing economies. In fact, since 1978, China's economy has grown at a staggering 9.9% per year (Figure 3.5). During the period from 2000 to 2012, the economy of China went from being approximately one-ninth the size of the U.S. economy to a little over half its size. With a 2017 GDP of approximately US$12.2 trillion (GDP at current prices), China ranks as the second largest economy in the world and accounts for approximately 11% of gross world product.

In 2007, exports made up a significant percentage of GDP activity. Today, China's economy is driven by a much broader economic platform. Domestic consumption now drives approximately 50% of GDP growth, with investment and government services contributing an additional 40%. Net exports now represent just over 10% of overall economic activity. Given this rapid pace of growth, Chinese markets now represent a significant

market opportunity for countries around the world. Imports into China have risen significantly over the past decade, resulting in China being the world's second largest trading partner (behind the U.S.). The United States is currently China's largest trading partner, although trade with a number of Asian countries, in particular, is rapidly growing. Japan, South Korea, Hong Kong, and Australia, for example, all have developed significant trading relationships with China. In fact, China is the largest trading partner for over 32 countries globally.

Although China's economy has grown rapidly over the past 30 years, significant headwinds are causing its growth to slow. As its economy matures, its overall growth rate, although still robust, has declined in recent years. For example, 2018 had China's economic growth rate at 6.4% (the weakest since 1990), with this further declining to 6.2% in 2019. Pressure from the United States, its largest trading partner as noted above, to redesign its

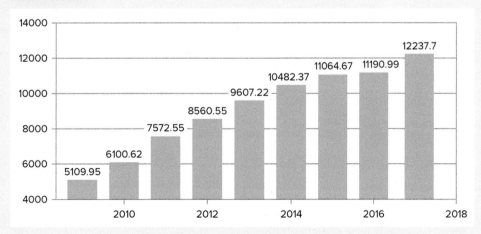

FIGURE 3.5   China—GDP Growth Annually, 2009-2017

Source: www.tradingeconomics.com, National Bureau of Statistics of China.

trading relationship, along with a general cooling of global growth, are both placing downward pressure on China's growth. In seeking to redesign its trade relationship, the United States has used its leverage as the largest purchaser of China's goods and services to aggressively encourage China to open its economy further to U.S. export providers. It has used tactics associated with tariffs and duties on Chinese imports to communicate its desire to re-frame the trade relationship between the two countries. It is anticipated that adjustments to the trade relationship between the two countries will continue to evolve going forward. The diplomacy and negotiations surrounding these trade discussions are expected to further impact China's economic growth in the near term. The maturing of the Chinese economy has also brought with it a desire for a higher standard of living among the Chinese population. This has resulted in upward pressure on wages and related social safety net costs. These activities have resulted in an evolving reduction in China's overall wage cost advantage relative to other fully developed economies.

A final concern relating to China's economy lies with the significant government spending that has taken place in support of China's growth. The country's total debt-to-GDP ratio is thought to be in the 300% range, placing the total value of the country's debt (from all sources) at over $35 trillion (USD). Its

massive infrastructure and factory-based investments have largely been driven by low-interest government-backed loans, resulting in what some perceive to be a potential overbuilding of capacity within the broader economic system. As growth slows, China will need to work toward a more balanced economic platform, driven by lower levels of government stimulus (infrastructure and service investments), credit tightening, and broader structural reforms to the economy. With China's economy slowing down, the level of imports has fallen while exports have remained stable, most notably due to an economic recovery in the U.S. The end result is that China's **balance of trade** surplus in January 2019 was estimated at US$391 billion, which although down from a high of $570 billion in November 2018 (one of the highest ever recorded; see Figure 3.6), demonstrates the perceived inequality of its trade relationship with a number of its trading partners, most notably the United States. Hence the reason for the aggressive actions on the part of the United States to re-balance the trade relationship between the two countries.

China's economic slowdown should not be inferred as being directly caused by U.S. trade negotiation tactics. As noted above, the historical growth, largely

Balance of Trade is the relationship between imports and exports over a defined period of time. A positive balance (where exports exceed imports) is known as a trade surplus. A negative balance (where imports exceed exports) is known as a trade deficit.

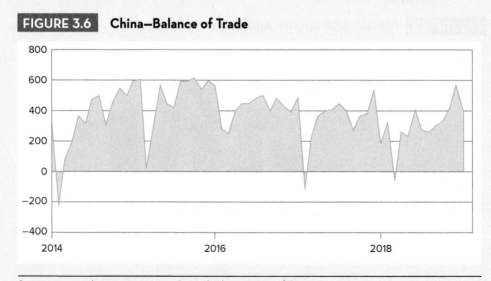

| FIGURE 3.6 | China—Balance of Trade |

Source: www.tradingeconomics.com, General Administration of Customs.

driven by low-value, labour-driven exports, is being replaced by a much more balanced economic approach and an overall improvement to the societal standard of living. Rising wages, stronger domestic consumption, rapid urbanization, welfare program and social safety net funding, and stronger financial discipline have all contributed to this evolutionary transformation. Despite this slower growth, China remains and will continue to be a dominant force in global trade and broader world economics. In his speech to the World Economic Forum in September 2018, Chinese Premier Li Keqiang indicated that, despite increasing trade tensions globally, China remains well positioned to respond to the challenges impacting its growth and remains committed to the principles of multilateralism and free trade.

Business IN ACTION

Global Spotlight—Emergence of the G20

In growing recognition of the influence that emerging economies have had on the global marketplace, in 1999 a broader economic forum was created beyond the original G7 forum and its representative countries. This broader forum is the G20, and its intent is to ensure a consultative process of all major global players relating to matters such as global economic governance, global financial stability, and transparency in fiscal policy. The G20 represents the 20 largest economies in the world. Consisting of both fully developed economies and emerging economies, the G20 represents more than 80% of the world's GDP. G20 countries also represent approximately two-thirds of the world's population. Attendees at the G20 forums include the finance ministers and central bank governors of 19 countries, as well as a financial representative from the European Union and a representative from the European Central Bank. In addition to the European Union, the 19 countries that make up the G20 are shown in Figure 3.7.

Typical G20 summit agenda items include tackling investment and infrastructure initiatives to stimulate and/or sustain global growth, responding to environmental sustainability challenges, creating and approving policies relating to trade management, and fiscal and financial regulation practices. In addition, the G20 summit will also look to generate responses to issues challenging the global economy and the members of the G20 at the time of each summit. Important topic items associated with the 2019 G20 summit included climate change, counterterrorism, and migration and refugees.

FIGURE 3.7   **G20 Members**

Argentina	Japan
Australia	Mexico
Brazil	Russia
Canada	Saudi Arabia
China	South Africa
France	South Korea
Germany	Turkey
India	United Kingdom
Indonesia	United States of America
Italy	European Union

Source: www.G20.org.

LO4 Global Market Trends

Recognizing that the global market is a complex entity with all sorts of economic triggers and events happening on an almost daily basis, the following points are offered as an assessment of the key trends and influencers that will most likely impact the global market over the upcoming near to mid-term. The overarching theme of these comments is summarized in Figure 3.8.

1 The global marketplace will continue to grow, although that growth is anticipated to be slower going forward versus what we have seen over the past decade. The International Monetary Fund anticipates that global growth will be in the 3.5% range annually through 2020. Although reduced energy prices have created a positive growth environment for most countries (Canada, Russia, and Venezuela are examples of exceptions), overall lower levels of investment globally brought on by uncertainty relating to trade relations will offset this growth incentive. For companies, weaker overall demand means weaker markets for products and services, which results in reduced incentives to invest. China will continue to lead the way in terms of growth influence; however, that growth will be significantly slower than the rapid growth experienced over the front end of this decade (10%+ annually). IMF growth forecasts for China are trending downward and lie in the 6% to 6.5% range through 2020. The U.S. will be another bright spot from a growth perspective, with annual growth anticipated in the 3% to 3.5% range. Other emerging-nation and developing-economy markets are anticipated to grow annually in the 4.5% to 5% range. Where concern lies is with Europe and petro-based economies (such as Canada). The euro area, according to the IMF, is expected to see growth of approximately 1% to 2%, with recessionary concerns still in the picture. **Deflation**, along with political fragmentation within the Euro Zone, could further complicate things. Ongoing austerity measures in Greece, Spain, and Italy, for example, add to political fracturing. Switzerland's recent uncoupling of the Swiss franc to the euro, along with Great Britain's decision to leave the EU (Brexit), will add additional pressure on the European Union

Deflation occurs when prices fall. The concern with deflation is that falling prices reduces revenue and income, which affects the ability to meet debt obligations as well as impacting government tax revenue.

FIGURE 3.8 **Forces Shaping the Global Economy**

Global Rebalancing

Emerging economies will continue to grow at a faster rate than fully developed economies and, as such, will increase their influence in the global marketplace.

Innovation and Reinvention

Companies based within fully developed economies will need to continually reinvent themselves and innovate to become more productive and leading-edge in the face of stronger global competition.

Acceleration of Technology and Interconnectivity

The global marketplace will continue to become increasingly connected, and technology will level the playing field between larger and smaller players.

Planet Sustainability

Climate change, environmental sustainability and resource conservation challenges will exert a greater influence on political, regulatory, and business decision making.

Protectionism and Nationalism

Countries will face increasing pressures relating to social stability, sovereign debt, immigration and cultural assimilation, and domestic market protectionism in response to accelerating global change.

The Rise of State Capitalism

Governments and businesses will continue to become more interconnected. The economic model is changing as governments are becoming more active partners in the pursuit of business opportunities.

Source: Adapted and updated from "Global Forces: An Introduction," Peter Bisson, Elizabeth Stephenson, S. Patrick Viguerie, *McKinsey Quarterly*, McKinsey & Company, June 2010.

governing body and the European Central Bank to maintain stability and stimulate growth. Eastern European nations are expected to outperform their western European counterparts. Germany, a general economic barometer of EU economic growth, experienced a slight economic contraction at the end of 2018, reinforcing this concern with respect to forward growth possibilities. Russia, given its heavy dependency on energy to drive economic growth, along with current economic sanctions levied against it due to the situation between Crimea and the Ukraine, as well as increased friction with the United States, has been challenged economically and is facing recessionary pressures at the time of this writing.

2 Economic specialization will continue to be the trend as the ongoing evolution toward the implementation of global free trade continues. The use of technology and supply chain logistics will continue to act as primary drivers of this market approach. Speaking of technology, it has and will continue to be the great equalizer in today's global environment. Technology advancements will continue to enhance productivity and drive economic growth. Emerging nations that possess the ability to leverage technology will be able to compete far more quickly in the global marketplace than ever before. Continued advances in communication technology will further increase the connectivity of markets. In response to this environment, companies will be pressured to heighten their need to view innovation and technology applications as fundamental to their competitive survival. Those that fail to adapt to the changes occurring in their market sectors will find the products and services they offer less competitive at faster rates than ever before.

3 The global financial meltdown of 2008, and the related long-term consequences of the sovereign debt incurred by many countries in response to it, will continue to impact the global marketplace in the near term. As new fiscal and financial regulation is implemented, this will most likely result in tighter credit markets, particularly in the small business sector, and will contribute to the overall slower pace of global economic growth being forecast. As noted above, the European Union, given the current sovereign debt issues challenging a number of its members, could be particularly vulnerable to such a drag on growth.

4 The United States and China's political and trade relations will remain critical to global health. As key economic drivers of the global market, the two largest economies of the world will continue to significantly influence the ongoing interaction of global trade. The significant trade imbalances that exist between these countries will need to be closed through a cooperative management process. Concerns relating to the undervaluation of the renminbi (Chinese currency, also referred to as the yuan) against the U.S. dollar will be a continued point of discussion in the near term. Access and openness to China, the world's fastest-growing major market, will remain a priority for many North American and European-based businesses. As indicated in other parts of this chapter, the recent aggressive implementation by the United States of tariffs and related duties on foreign imports, particularly from China, will continue to place "drag uncertainty" on the global economy in the near term. For China, in addition to maintaining these trade relations are rising concerns relating to a potential real estate bubble, as well as the significant debt being taken on by government as it looks to meet the infrastructure and investment requirements of its growing economy. The economic slowdown also adds new pressures relating to potential spikes in unemployment and overall economic excess capacity.

5 Demographics globally will continue to influence both trade and political decisions. Aging populations in North America, Europe, and some parts of Asia (China and Japan) will require broader immigration policies in order to meet the employment, productivity, and social service funding needs of these countries. At the same time, countries with significantly younger populations (Middle East, Turkey), where large percentages of citizens are under age 30, will be challenged to meet the employment needs of their youth.

6 Agricultural subsidy programs will remain a major focal point of global trade discussions. Emerging economies, a number of which rely on agriculture as a core component of their economic development, will continue to lobby for the elimination of agricultural subsidies in fully developed nations, particularly in Europe and North America. These subsidies, from the position of emerging economies, keep prices artificially low in fully developed economies (nations), making it more difficult for developing economies to penetrate these markets and thereby hampering their efforts to grow their economies. In turn, fully developed economies view such subsidies as being necessary to protect their agricultural industries and, thus, are reluctant to reduce or eliminate these programs.

7 Global warming, carbon cap and trade legislation, responsibilities pertaining to the Paris Agreement, other environmental agreements (Copenhagen and Kyoto accords), and other macro-level environmental issues and policies will become more and more integrated into the decision-making process of businesses and governments. Developed and emerging nations will need to work together on a global response to growing environmental and sustainable business practices in a way that meets societal concerns and maintains a level playing field for businesses within their respective borders. This subject matter is covered in more detail in Chapter 4, The Environment and Sustainable Business Practices.

The Paris Agreement's central aim is to create a unified global response to the threat of climate change. Its core objective is to keep the global temperature rise in the current century below 2 degrees Celsius, measured against a baseline temperature that the world experienced during pre-industrial times. Although 2 degrees is believed to be the least-acceptable position, the focus of activities associated with participating countries in the agreement is to pursue a temperature enhancement allowance of no more than 1.5 degrees Celsius above pre-industrial times.[23]

8 The global marketplace will become more and more a political economy. The interdependence between countries and companies will continue to grow. Technology, specialization, and the integration of the global financial marketplace will mean that actions and activities in one sector of the world will impact other sectors faster than ever before. Trade infrastructure, depending upon its level of development, will be both a facilitator and inhibitor of trade. As trade growth continues to exceed infrastructure growth, bottlenecks will occur and strain will be placed on the global trading system (ports, transportation, warehousing, etc.). This will require governments to continually spend investment dollars in an attempt to meet the growing trade demands within their country and region. Although protectionism and nationalistic tendencies will become a stronger influence in trade discussions and negotiations, **free trade agreements** should continue to act as the cornerstone of the evolution of country-to-country agreements toward broader free-trade zones. This would appear to be especially true in the Asian region, as ASEAN (Association of Southeast Asian Nations) will continue to broaden the number of countries included within this Asian free-trade zone.

9 Political unrest has to be viewed as a potential wild card going forward. Situations of political instability can wreak havoc on not only regional economies but the entire global economy, given its interconnectivity. Political ideology changes brought upon by the frustration with austerity measures, high levels of unemployment, or instability due to disagreements pertaining to geographic boundaries, tribal and/or religious differences, or ethnic backgrounds remain an ongoing concern in today's rapidly changing world. With economic growth in general comes an improvement in the underlying fabric of economies. Standards of living should rise, people should become better off, and poverty should be reduced or ideally eliminated. This, unfortunately, does not all occur in harmony across all class stratifications within society. In a number of the regions of the world income disparity is growing, not dissipating. Social and cultural clashes are increasing, and legal and political structural platforms are being challenged. Our ability to manage such crises and minimize global regional conflicts and/or outright war are fundamental to the economic stability of our global marketplace.

> **Free Trade Agreements** facilitate international trade between companies that is not constrained or regulated by governments, and that is not impacted via the use of tariffs, duties, or other monetary restrictions.

Technology, specialization, and the integration of the global financial marketplace will mean that actions and activities in one sector of the world will impact other sectors faster than ever before.

The Concept of International Trade   LO5

There is a common misnomer that trade occurs between countries. In actuality, trade occurs between organizations and individuals. Although countries report movements in GDP and their balance of trade (the relationship between imports and exports) as indicated, such movements are the result of the activities of organizations and individuals who seek to do business within their borders or from within their borders. Sovereign wealth funds, such as the China Investment Corporation, Kuwait Investment Authority, Abu Dhabi Investment Authority, and Singapore's Temasek Holdings, although financed by national account surpluses, are separate organizations that focus on developing investment interests in support of economic activities within their countries. These businesses and individuals could be either domestic residents of the country being assessed, doing business within the country as a result of direct investment or market opportunities that have been developed, or offering opportunities to be developed. As indicated earlier in this chapter, common reasons for seeking opportunities internationally include the appeal of new markets, diversification of operations, closer proximity to key markets, enhanced productivity and supply chain competitiveness, improvement of an organization's overall competitive position, and resource and technology acquisition.

What has allowed trade to flourish is a willingness on the part of the marketplace to engage in the concept of specialization. Specialization is the separation of tasks within a system. From our perspective, it reflects the identification and separation of tasks within a business whose purpose is the development and delivery of goods and services to the marketplace. Specialization recognizes that by having some entities (organizations and/or individuals) provide certain parts of the process, greater efficiencies and productivity will result. Whereas the development of domestic specialization recognizes that certain companies and individuals within a country will be the most efficient and effective at producing particular goods and services, international trade recognizes that the most efficient and effective mechanism for the production of goods and services lies in the development of clusters of specialization across countries. Rather than replicate the development of business systems for the manufacturing and delivery of all goods and services within each country, organizations and individuals have developed international trade, based on specialization, as the framework for meeting the needs of the global marketplace. Combining the concept of trade with capital investment and the desire to seek the most productive and cost-effective systems for the manufacturing and delivery of goods and services is the core component behind the rise of the developing economies of the world and the rapidity of technological advances globally, to the benefit of all. It has also resulted in an overall reduction in the prices of many goods and services, resulting in enhanced purchasing power for consumers.

> What has allowed trade to flourish is a willingness on the part of the marketplace to engage in the concept of specialization.

Business IN ACTION

Canada Goose

When the world thinks about extreme weather clothing, the world thinks about Canada Goose. For more than 55 years, this Canadian-owned apparel manufacturer has been creating high-quality jackets and parkas in Canada. Whether they are going to McMurdo Station in Antarctica, participating in a dogsled race in the Yukon or Alaska, or trekking to one of the most remote locations winter can offer, people who live, work, and play in the coldest places on Earth trust Canada Goose as the brand to keep them warm. What started as a small Toronto-based business in 1957 under the name Metro Sportswear Ltd. has become a global brand. Their heavy-duty parkas, a main focus of their operations in the 1970s and 1980s, became vital tools of the Canadian Rangers, various municipal police departments, and other industrial workers. David Reiss (son-in-law of founder Sam Tick), at the time an employee of Metro, purchased the company in the 1980s and, in addition to manufacturing white-label products, created a small collection of jackets as Snow Goose.

Jerome Cid/Dreamstime.com

In 2001, Dani Reiss (who joined Canada Goose in 1997) took over the company from his father, David. He decided that there was a future in stopping private-label manufacturing and marketing solely under the brand named Canada Goose, a brand he had taken to a trade show in Germany where he had received a very positive response. Dani recognized the value of Canadian outerwear being manufactured in Canada and what that could mean in the long term to consumers. He saw an immediate comparison to manufacturing the world's warmest parkas in Canada with making the world's best quality watches in Switzerland. It made sense that real brands be manufactured where they are born. Backed by a reported $250-million stake in the company by Bain Capital in 2013, Canada Goose continues to build its brand strength and reach internationally. A key understanding to this agreement with Bain Capital, which Dani Reiss felt was fundamental to the company's business model, was the commitment to keep manufacturing in Canada. In 2014, the company boasted worldwide sales of over $200 million, compared with sales of roughly $3 million when Dani Reiss took over the company from his father. The company has continued to grow, reaching a record sales level of $591 million in fiscal year 2018, a 46% increase over 2017 ($404 million). Net income over the past three years has grown from $30 million in 2016 to $94 million in 2018. Today Canada Goose is present in every major European market, with ecommerce adding additional growth strength across the globe. The company is also experiencing strong market penetration in Japan and Korea and a growing presence in China. The United States and Canada markets remain equally attractive, with double-digit growth expected to continue into the foreseeable future. The company continues to evolve its business model as markets and consumer connections change. Its current DTC (direct to customer) business model expansion, supported by ecommerce site and retail store expansion, has gained significant traction and is core to bringing Canada Goose to the world. Its focused strategy on being best-in-class has enabled it to effectively differentiate itself relative to rivals and drive significant customer loyalty for its brand.

For Dani Reiss and Canada Goose, the company is more than just a manufacturer of parkas—it is also

David L. Moore—US West/Alamy Stock Photo

about protecting the environment where Canada Goose products are worn. The company is a proud sponsor of Polar Bears International, where Dani also serves as chairman of the board, and a major supporter of the Conservation Alliance, an organization focused on protecting threatened wild places across North America.

Canada Goose has come to represent the true spirit of exploration, quality, authenticity, and great Canadian craftsmanship. The Canada Goose Arctic Disc logo is one of the most easily identifiable logos on parkas and jackets in the world.

Web Integration

For more information on Canada Goose products, its business, its partnerships, and plans for the future, visit www.canada-goose.com.

FIGURE 3.9   **XYZ Corporation: Domestic Operation**

Evolution of a Global Presence

Shifting to a global presence for an organization is a strategic decision that requires considerable thought as to where and how to compete. This strategic assessment would include decisions relating to not only the identification of potential foreign buyers, thereby opening up new markets, but also an assessment of the organization's business system to determine if there are parts of the business system that could be made more efficient and cost competitive if they were initiated elsewhere. Also critical to this assessment process is the magnitude of investment that would be required in order to gain access to such new markets or replicate portions of the supply, manufacturing, or distribution logistics processes offshore.

To illustrate some of the considerations required, let's use the XYZ Corporation, a Canadian manufacturer of electronic tracking systems, as an example. Figure 3.9 illustrates XYZ Corporation's current business system. XYZ is a domestically focused organization. Its suppliers (providers of components for its electronic sensors) are Canadian-based companies. Final assembly of its various sensor products (manufacturing) takes place at its main facility in Moncton, New Brunswick, and buyers of its products are Canadian-based organizations.

In assessing its position in the marketplace, the XYZ Corporation is realizing that its customers are pressuring XYZ to reduce its costs in order to be more competitive with other domestic and foreign competitors who are manufacturing similar products. Reviewing its business system, XYZ Corporation determines that it is able to acquire some of the components necessary for the manufacturing and assembly of its tracking systems from companies based in Asia. These components can be purchased at a lower cost (including shipping costs) than what is being charged by current domestic suppliers. As a result, XYZ Corporation's business system is modified as shown in Figure 3.10.

FIGURE 3.10   **XYZ Corporation: International Exposure**

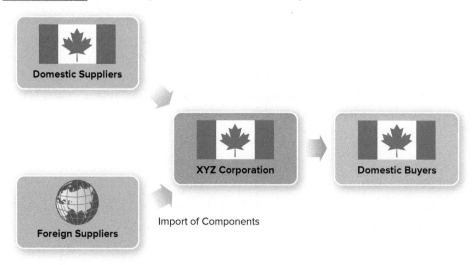

FIGURE 3.11   **XYZ Corporation: International Presence**

Searching for new opportunities to further grow, and recognizing a demand for its high-quality electronic tracking systems beyond Canada, the marketing and sales team of XYZ Corporation, via work with Export Development Canada, foreign agents, freight forwarding companies, and other industry trade organizations, begins to supply electronic tracking systems to foreign buyers in both the United States and abroad. To achieve initial closeness to its customers, sales offices and sales agent relationships are created in a number of countries when demand for the product warrants such investment. This initial move into the international marketplace shifts XYZ Corporation's business system to that shown in Figure 3.11.

As foreign markets develop and XYZ Corporation's penetration of these market opportunities improves, XYZ Corporation may make the strategic decision to not only have a sales presence in these markets, but also develop a full manufacturing presence. This, of course, would require a significant strategic assessment of current and future market opportunities, as well as an understanding of the capital investment requirements, the operations and logistics requirements of operating a full-fledged manufacturing facility in another country, and legal and risk considerations and concerns with transporting its intellectual and patent properties. In order to minimize some of these risks and to meet the development requirements of the foreign country, this may result in a partnership or strategic alliance with a domestic-based company. In making the decision to go forward, XYZ Corporation's business system is further transformed as shown in Figure 3.12.

FIGURE 3.12   **XYZ Corporation: International Operation I**

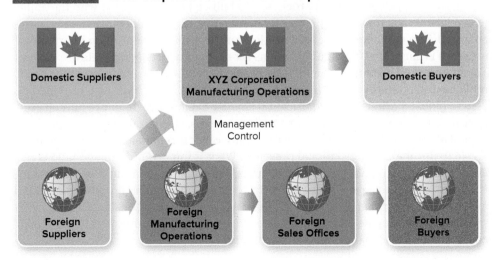

FIGURE 3.13   XYZ Corporation: International Operation II

Depending on market dynamics, competitive pressures, production efficiencies, and overall cost considerations, a final evolution could be that as shown in Figure 3.13. In this situation, manufacturing has been fully shifted to an offshore location, with support services, head office, and critical intellectual proprietary-based staff positions and responsibilities remaining in Canada.

Figure 3.13 does not conclude that all organizations will eventually evolve and choose to move their core manufacturing operations outside of Canada. It should also be understood that a number of entities may not evolve beyond those operating configurations illustrated in Figures 3.10 or 3.11. The overall evolution is dependent upon the opportunities presented, the competitive pressures the company is feeling, the capital available to the company, and the operational efficiencies the organization is aspiring toward in order to develop a sustainable competitive advantage. What is also not fully illustrated in Figures 3.10 to 3.13 is that the size of the organization is also growing, which will result in employment opportunities domestically and abroad. It should also be noted that, while organizations could outsource portions of the manufacturing process and other related operations, a majority may choose to keep their skilled employee requirements (product design and development, engineering, technology support) in house. Keep in mind as well that, as Canadian companies seek to gain an international presence, so too do other organizations worldwide. The figures illustrated above could easily be adjusted to illustrate the expansion of foreign firms into Canada. (For example, the decision of Feihe International, a leading Chinese dairy processor, to build a plant in Ontario with the ability to produce 60 000 tons of dry infant food annually, as mentioned previously in this chapter.) Also, although one configuration for the establishment of an international presence is illustrated, the configurations for entry into foreign markets are endless. The Internet and ecommerce models have, in many industries, eliminated the need to replicate full operating structures in foreign countries. They have also provided access to global markets with significantly smaller capital investment requirements—a particularly attractive feature for small businesses. Organizations with significant capital at their disposal may choose to acquire other foreign-based firms as a mechanism to develop an international presence. What is important to understand is that actions relating to developing a foreign presence and in creating a global trading business platform require significant strategic thought, planning, and learning. It also significantly changes the risk for the company, as trade considerations such as tariffs and duties come into play, as do currency exchange rates, political and legal considerations, and social and cultural differences.

Business IN ACTION

Export Development Canada (EDC)

Want to expand internationally, but don't know where or how to start? Export Development Canada is a great place to look for help. EDC provides Canadian companies that are looking to expand internationally with innovative financing, insurance, and risk management and technical and educational support. A self-financing Crown corporation, which operates at arm's length from the the Government of Canada, EDC's primary role is to assist Canadian companies in navigating what is, for many, the uncharted waters of international expansion. This includes providing educational programs to familiarize businesses with trade regulations and protocols; assessing the export readiness of an organization; providing assistance in securing the financial support needed for international expansion; providing guidance in business plan development; and linking businesses with foreign agents and freight-forwarding companies that facilitate trade in the global marketplace. In addition to these core services, EDC also provides internationally focused businesses with critical information relating to global economic trends and changes in international trading laws.

Founded in 1944, EDC has worked with Canadian companies seeking to do business internationally, with the end result being the support and facilitation of over $1.4 trillion in investments. 2017 was a particularly busy year, with EDC providing support to over 9400 Canadian companies, of which over 30% were looking to create and/or expand business opportunities in emerging markets. In all, over $104 billion in investments were made in 2017, resulting in the generation of $67 million in GDP growth and in support of an employment workforce of over 500 000 people. 2017 also saw EDC entrusted by the Government of Canada to create the Canadian Development Finance Institution, whose core mandate is to provide financial services and support to private-sector organizations focused on sustainable development and poverty reduction in developing nations. Figure 3.14 shows areas of EDC business facilitated by geographic market.

EDC's expertise has enabled it to develop a capital position exceeding $10 billion, thereby ensuring that the organization remains well-positioned to assist Canadian companies in developing international trade opportunities going forward. An accomplished leader in Canada's export trade development, EDC has been recognized as one of Canada's top 100 employers for eight consecutive years. With recently added branch offices in Singapore and Australia, EDC now has over 20 locations globally to assist Canadian companies in connecting with business opportunities around the world. Although the bulk of EDC's work is still in support of Canadian businesses looking to expand south of the border (58% to the U.S.A. and Caribbean), 17% of business facilitated now lies in the Asia/Pacific region, 13.6% in Europe, 7.5% in South and Central America, and 5% in Africa. Its newly opened Singapore office, as an example, supported investments of over $1.1 billion in its first year of operation.

FIGURE 3.14 EDC Business Facilitated by Geographic Market

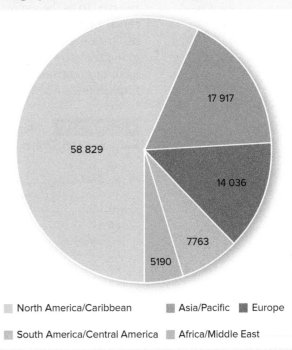

Legend:
- North America/Caribbean
- Asia/Pacific
- Europe
- South America/Central America
- Africa/Middle East

Values shown: 58 829 · 17 917 · 14 036 · 7763 · 5190

Source: EDC Annual Report 2017, "Trade Unlimited," p. 2, https://www.edc.ca/EN/About-Us/Corporate-Reports/Pages/default.aspx. Used with permission.

A Note on Currency Exchange Rates: How Are They Influenced?

As the marketplace continues its evolution toward a global playing field, organizations and individuals will become more and more focused on the changes to currency values and the corresponding impact such changes will have on sales and profitability. In Chapter 2, The Canadian Economic Environment, a brief discussion was provided as to how currency exchange rates, particularly when assessed against those of the United States (our largest trading partner), influence our overall competitiveness.

A currency exchange rate is the relationship between the value of one currency to another at a particular point in time. As an example, on February 24, 2019, the value of the Canadian dollar to the U.S. dollar was $0.76, meaning that it would cost us, as Canadians, $1.31 to purchase $1.00 USD. Using this same date, the euro on this day, as valued against the Canadian dollar, was $1.48, again meaning that you and I would have to pay $1.48 Canadian to purchase one euro. Conversely, a European visitor to Canada could purchase $1.00 Canadian with 0.71 euros.[24]

An easy way to think of currency exchange rates, which are set up to float relative to each other, is to think of it in terms of the concepts of demand and supply. A **floating exchange rate** is one whose value is allowed to move relative to other currencies; the value of the currency is set by foreign exchange market and is influenced by the demand for that currency via the "forex" market. As demand for a particular currency goes up so does its value. As demand drops, its value will as well. This is referred to as the appreciation and depreciation of currency value. In general, a currency that reflects an appreciating value against other currencies is a sign of a healthy or upward-trending economy. Conversely, when the value of a currency falls, it is often the reflection of a downward-trending economy. What influences movement of a currency is explained in more detail in the section below titled "Foreign Exchange Rate Influencers." Figure 3.15 shows the movement of the Canadian dollar

Floating Exchange Rate is one whose value is allowed to move relative to other currencies. The value of the currency is set by foreign exchange market and is influenced by the demand for that currency via the forex market.

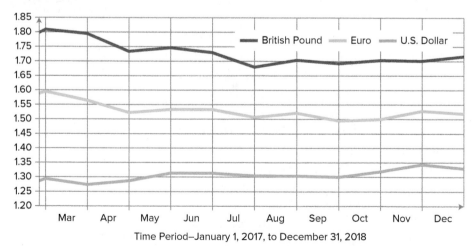

FIGURE 3.15   **Monthly Exchange Rates, Canadian Dollar vs. British Pound, Euro, and U.S. Dollar**

Source: Bank of Canada, https://www.bankofcanada.ca, February 24, 2019.

relative to the British pound, the euro, and the U.S. dollar for the period January 1, 2017 to December 31, 2018. As you can see, the Canadian dollar's overall value with respect to these currencies has been relatively flat, indicating that the underlying currency relationship is at what markets consider to be currency equilibrium.

As discussed in Chapter 2, changes in currency relationships with trading partners (i.e., Canada and the U.S.) impact that relationship. Countries with low currency valuation relative to their trading partner can benefit from lower costs as their products enter the importing trading partner. Countries with higher valuation will see the prices of their products rise as they are imported into their trading partner. Recognizing that a balanced relationship is best for all, governments attempt to manage their underlying economic fundamentals (interest rate management, etc.) as a way to minimize currency movement to a point where overall economic growth becomes impacted. In fact, some countries will fix the rate of the currency in relationship to a trading partner in order to maintain this control; this practice is called **pegging** a currency.[25] Although not always the case, countries with fixed rate or pegged currencies will generally fix such values against their major trading partner's currency. Bermuda, as an example, maintains a pegged rate of $1.00 Bermuda equalling $1.00 USD; this rate has been unchanged since 1972.[26]

> **Pegging** is when the value of one country's currency remains constant against another currency. It is also referred to as a fixed exchange rate.

Foreign exchange rate influencers In closing off this introductory discussion to currency exchange, when measured against other currencies (the global benchmark currency remains the U.S. dollar), the value of a nation's currency is influenced by six predominant factors (see Figure 3.16):

1 **GDP movement:** The movement (economic expansion or contraction) in the GDP of the country in question.

2 **Governmental budget deficits/surpluses:** The ability of the country's leaders to develop and adhere to realistic governmental budgets that present to the global community stable and realistic spending patterns and maintain sovereign debt exposure at acceptable levels.

FIGURE 3.16   Foreign Exchange Rate Influencers

3 **Trade balance:** The ability of the country to operate within an acceptable balance of trade range, avoiding huge balance of trade deficits that will necessitate ongoing borrowing to cover such deficits.

4 **Consumer price movements (PPP):** The ability of the country to maintain its rate of inflation within acceptable target ranges, thereby ensuring real growth versus purely inflationary growth within its economy, resulting in improvement in the purchasing power parity (PPP) of the currency.

5 **Capital mobility and supply:** The supply of capital and the ability to establish and utilize credit by a country and its businesses and individuals.

6 **Movement in domestic income level:** The movement (growth or decline) in the domestic level of income its citizens are earning. Increases in the domestic level of income have positive influences on the standard of living of a country's citizens, resulting in a positive influence on the value of the currency.

Strong economic growth, which is balanced domestically and internationally and improves the standard of living of the citizens of a country, and which is developed within a context of prudent government debt and fiscal management policies in an environment of controlled inflation, will result in an upward value of a nation's currency when measured against other countries' currencies. Conversely, nations that see reversals in the areas mentioned above will see an erosion of the value of their currency when measured against other countries' currencies.

The Canadian dollar spent a substantial part of the 1990s, and the first part of the current century (see Figure 3.17), devalued against the U.S. dollar, largely as a result of our sluggish economic growth and our high national debt (when measured against GDP) during that period. As emerging nations increased their demand for the products/services we exported (energy, natural resource commodities), our economy grew. Governmental policies designed to relax trade restrictions, reduce budget deficits, and pay down sovereign debt, coupled with attractive interest rates and low levels of inflation, all combined to move our Canadian dollar to parity (equal) with the U.S. dollar in the front end of this century, and continuing through the financial crisis of 2008 and the ensuing recovery through 2013. Now with growth

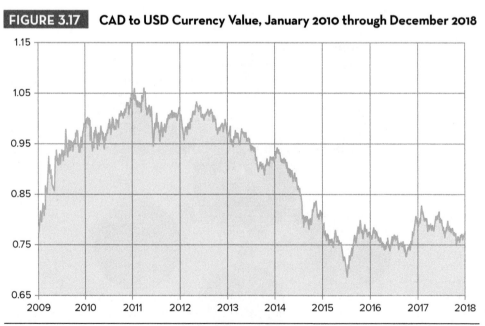

FIGURE 3.17   **CAD to USD Currency Value, January 2010 through December 2018**

Source: Adapted from XE Currency Charts, https://www.xe.com/currencycharts/?from=CAD&to=USD&view=10Y, February 24, 2019.

in emerging nations slowing and energy prices down, our dollar has returned to levels that many feel are more appropriate for our economic makeup and the overall size of our economy relative to the broader global market.

The United States dollar, as one will sense when they read more on this subject matter, remains the benchmark global currency, largely because of the size of the U.S. economy, its position as the predominant purchaser of goods and services globally, its historical strong economic growth, and its political flexibility. Although abetted by the relatively strong U.S. recovery underway, as well as the lagging economic stability in Europe, concerns relating to U.S. sovereign debt and the potential drag that may result on its economy have caused a number of nations to question whether the U.S. dollar should remain the benchmark going forward. An in-depth discussion of the interrelationship of currency exchange rates on the growth potential and profitability of organizations is beyond the scope of this textbook. Additional references to its influence will be discussed in later chapters relating to understanding business finances. For now, it is enough to recognize that in assessing global market opportunities, currency exchange rates are part of the discussion process.

> Strong economic growth, which is balanced domestically and internationally and improves the standard of living of the citizens of a country, and which is developed within a context of prudent government debt and fiscal management policies in an environment of controlled inflation, will result in an upward value of a nation's currency when measured against other countries' currencies.

Management Reflection—Challenges of Managing in Today's Global Environment

LO6

Competing in today's global economy requires a combination of efficient and effective production and manufacturing systems, well-organized and expertly supported trade facilitation processes and distribution logistics, and a solid network of financial intermediation and support. In other words, it's not just about selling products overseas, but it requires organizations and their management teams to view their business system as an integrated trading model. Shifting the organization's focus to that of an international player beyond Canada's boundaries requires a comprehensive review of the financial risks, political risks, legal risks, and reputation risks the organization will face. For managers, this means ensuring a comprehensive strategy is developed that fully outlines the level of capital investment required, the impact the expanded sales channel will have on cash flow and cash operating cycles, and the level of consulting, education, and trade services and expertise that will have to be developed or procured. The global market also challenges managers to look beyond their own local markets to determine where current and future competition will come from, what new products and services are being developed, and what potential disruptors on the horizon could render the organization's products and services less competitive or completely obsolete. In expanding internationally, managers will find that compliance management (trade, customs, security) and risk management (market, financial, intellectual property), along with global technology-based connectivity issues, will demand more and more of their time. Cultural and social issues relating to staffing, customer attitudes, and foreign market needs will present a whole new set of employment and organizational structure requirements and challenges. Add to this the complexity of the impact of currency exchange, protectionist attitudes within some governments, increasingly complex environmental rules within some geographic regions, and growing product liability concerns from globally integrated manufacturing and supply chains, and it is no wonder that a move to becoming a global player can—and will—keep many managers up at night. However, if the risks are managed, then the potential for organizations to successfully grow their companies globally is almost without limit.

Shifting the organization's focus to that of an international player beyond Canada's boundaries requires a comprehensive review of the financial risks, political risks, legal risks, and reputation risks the organization will face.

Chapter Summary

Developing economies possess one-third of the world's population. Specialization has enabled many small players to broaden their markets into the global arena by integrating their products and services into the business systems of larger organizations. The use of technology, a key market flattener (in levelling the playing field between large and small organizations), has resulted in much shorter developmental processes, quicker market access, and stronger, immediate competitive positions for organizations seeking to move onto the global stage. In reading this chapter, you have gained a greater understanding of the challenges the global market presents to managers and of the trends managers will have to continue to track going forward. The chapter focused on defining why organizations seek a global presence and the role government will play in developing the rules and facilitating the process of international trade. Highlighted within this chapter were political economy support organizations including the WTO, IMF, World Bank, EDC, and G20. Although "macro" in the breadth of information presented, the commentary applicable to each of these organizations attempted to define just how they fit into the evolving international trade framework. Also offered in this chapter was an overview of the concept of international trade and a brief glimpse of the process associated with the evolution to a global presence by a domestically focused business organization. The chapter closes with a discussion of the challenges of managing within the global marketplace and, in particular, the unique challenges that lie before Canada as our businesses and individuals seek to compete on an international basis.

Developing Business Knowledge and Skills

Key Terms

IPO (initial public offering) *pp. 88–89*

offshoring *p. 95*

outsourcing *p. 95*

economies of scale *p. 99*

liquidity *p. 100*

solvency *p. 100*

credit facilities *p. 102*

black market *p. 105*

sovereign debt *p. 106*

balance of trade *p. 108*

deflation *p. 110*

free trade agreements *p. 113*

floating exchange rate *p. 120*

pegging *p. 121*

Questions for Discussion

1. What are the five major reasons that companies often consider when looking to move beyond their current domestic position and into the global marketplace? (LO2)

2. What do you believe is the primary role of government with respect to the facilitation of international trade and the support of global trade growth? (LO3)

3. In your mind, which organizational entity is more important to the stability and growth of global trade, the G8 or the G20? Why? (LO4)

4. Recognizing that the information provided in this chapter is not all-inclusive, what globalization trends do you feel will most likely impact Canadian companies in the next five to ten years? (LO4)

5. What do you believe is the overarching challenge that managers of Canadian businesses face in competing in today's global marketplace? (LO6)

Question for Individual Action

Conduct a review of Canadian businesses that are actively competing on an international basis. For each of the five reasons why companies go global that are presented in this chapter, identify a Canadian-based company that has chosen to go global for that reason.

Team Exercise

With nearly US$100 billion to invest abroad, the China Investment Corporation (CIC) is considered by many to be well on its way to becoming one of the most influential investment funds in the world. With US$200 billion in managed assets, CIC, established in 2007, was created to act as a vehicle to diversify China's foreign exchange holdings and maximize returns (within defined risk tolerance levels) on its investments for its shareholders. CIC is currently divided into two subsidiaries, CIC International and Central Huijin (domestic investments). CIC International manages the overseas portion of the portfolio. Examples of CIC International's investments in the United States include a US$3-billion investment in the Blackstone Group, and a US$5.6-billion investment in Morgan Stanley. In July 2009 CIC made its first major investment into Canada, purchasing 17% of Teck Resources Ltd. for US$1.74 billion. It also has a 5% stake in Penn West Petroleum Ltd., as well as making a number of other energy-related investments in Canada.

As a team, research CIC and prepare a presentation on its organizational focus and intended strategy going forward. Include within this presentation your position concerning security concerns that have arisen due to China's increasing global acquisition attempts. Does CIC's current strategy of purchasing minority (non-controlling) stakes in companies abroad concern you?[27]

Case for Discussion

National Basketball Association (NBA)—Can Basketball become #1 Globally?

The National Basketball Association (NBA) has a plan. Their vision is to have basketball become the #1 sport globally. To do this means they need to accomplish two things. First, they need to put a basketball into the hands of more and more children and adults and inspire them to learn how to dribble. Second, they need to supplant soccer, known as football to the broader global marketplace, as the sport of choice.

Both, at this stage, seem to be daunting tasks, but the NBA thinks that though this will take time it is attainable. In fact, the NBA has already started to implement key aspects of this strategy. Take China as an example. The NBA has been aggressive in the development of basketball in the world's most populous country. Today, the NBA is China's most popular sports league, and over 300 million Chinese play basketball. In addition, almost 190 million Chinese streamed the 2017 NBA Finals on their mobile devices.[28]

The NBA has also developed licensing arrangements for team logos to apparel manufacturer MK Trend of South Korea, as well as video game development rights to Marvelous Entertainment of Japan. Exhibition matches are now taking place in Africa and continue to be played in China and Europe as well. An NBA merchandise store has also been opened in Manila. All of this, of course, is designed to generate greater awareness and enthusiasm for the game, as well as generate new sources of revenue for the NBA. Going back to the growth of basketball, and particularly the NBA in China, in 2015 the league completed a digital video rights deal with Tencent Holdings (China) worth an estimated $500 million (USD). The NBA followed this with a deal with Weibo, a popular microblogging platform with more than 400 million monthly active users, which allows the league to post game highlights and related stories and communicate event information to its audience.

The above-mentioned licensing arrangements are expected to further add to this new revenue opportunity as well. The NBA has also been aggressively targeting the international media as a way to "sell" the game. With 108 players from 42 countries on its team rosters, events like the "Rising Stars Challenge" (part of the all-star game package), which pits the best young international players against the best young U.S. players, and NBA Global, which has regional NBA stars (such as those who come from Africa) competing against international players, offers an excellent showcase for international media reporters to view and comment on. In addition, ongoing visits by international media representatives and potential commercial partners to the NBA's head office are both encouraged and actively sought. All in the name of promoting the game, its stars, its growing international composition, and of course its revenue base.

While Asia and Africa look promising, the NBA still recognizes Europe as a key linchpin to its global strategy. There is growing interest in the NBA in Europe, largely the result of the increasing number or European players now playing in the NBA, as well as the league's decision to shift its Sunday afternoon television schedule, time wise, to deliver a game to Europe each Sunday in prime time. Still, soccer is king in Europe, and across the globe, with over 50% of the world's population actively engaged in the FIFA World Cup (held every four years). European football is not only a well-established sport, but it is, in many countries, an enshrined institution, with almost fanatical allegiance for soccer clubs

CHAPTER 3 The Global Marketplace

and countries alike. The trick to becoming #1 is to elevate basketball to the point where children in Europe are willing to trade kicking the ball for dribbling it.

With the North American market felt to be largely saturated, seeking revenue opportunities elsewhere only makes sense. Still, the road to becoming #1 globally, although ambitious, does present some significant challenges. Current travel technology, as an example, simply does not allow for a full-season of global-based teams (Europe or China) to compete against one another. If executed properly, however, the NBA does see a time, in the near future, where its efforts to globalize the league will result in revenues outside the U.S. exceeding its revenue from U.S. sources. If #1 globally is not attainable, being #2 directly behind soccer does carry with it considerable financial benefits.[29]

Questions

1. Do you think that the NBA can supplant soccer with basketball as the #1 sport globally?

2. Is the idea of becoming #1 globally too broad a strategic objective?

3. If you were the NBA, where would you focus your resources? In your opinion, would you focus on China and Asia? Would Africa, where there is a lower profile but significant potential opportunity, represent a better use of resources than further penetrating Europe? Then there is South and Central America, which were not mentioned in the case—would you deploy resources there?

4. What would be your high-level expansion plan for the NBA?

5. For the NBA, are licensing arrangements the best way to inspire the development of basketball, or is it really more about generating new revenue sources for the NBA?

CHAPTER 4

The Environment and Sustainable Business Practices

LEARNING OBJECTIVES

This chapter is designed to provide students with:

LO1	An overview of the business practices that created the environmental sustainability issues challenging us today
LO2	An understanding of the major environmental sustainability challenges the global marketplace must respond to
LO3	An appreciation for the complex factors that affect the ability of governments, organizations, businesses, and individuals to respond to the current environmental sustainability challenge
LO4	An understanding of the need for organizations to successfully integrate environmental sustainability stewardship into their strategies, operations, and processes

Snapshot

What to Expect in This Chapter

This chapter focuses on the environment and sustainable business practices. The content emphasized in this chapter includes the following:

- The Consumption Journey
- The Sustainability Challenge
  - Climate Change
  - Pollution and Health
  - The Energy Crunch
  - Resource Depletion
  - The Capital Squeeze
- Business's Response to the Sustainability Challenge
  - Trade Management
  - Eco-Efficiency Management
  - Strategic Integration
- Management Reflection—Sustainability Balancing Act

Business IN ACTION

Cascades—Green by Nature

For the eighth consecutive year, 2018 had Cascades being recognized as one of Quebec's most responsible organizations and brands, as well as being included in Canada's Top 50 Corporate Citizens. But the accolades don't stop there. Mario Plourde, the President and CEO of Cascades, was the 2019 recipient of the Clean 50 and Clean 16 awards. These annual awards presented by the Delta Management Group recognize individuals for their outstanding contributions to sustainable development and clean capitalism in Canada. 2018 also saw Cascades recognized with the Platinum Supplier of the Year award by the Hygiene and Maintenance category at the Balpex Supplier Summit, and it received the Leadership Award from the Canadian Industry Partnership for Energy Conservation (CIPEC) for its commitment to energy efficiency.

© Roman Milert/Alamy

Employing just under 11 000 people, with operations in North America and Europe, this $4.4-billion Quebec-based company celebrated 50 years of service in March 2014—50+ years of service underlined by a commitment to the concepts of reusing, recovering, and recycling. Its continuous efforts and underlying management philosophy have resulted in an innovation-based approach to business predicated on sustainable business practices, resulting in the development of a portfolio of environmentally friendly products. The company is currently the #1 paper collector in Canada, the #5 tissue producer in North America, the #6 containerboard producer in North America, and the #2 coated recycled boxboard producer in Europe. 100% of the fibre used in its products is sourced responsibly and is FSC verified as 82% recycled. With a focus on customers and innovation, the company's product lines and new product launches consistently focus on sustainability-framed packaging and logistics solutions. As an example, its Evok polystyrene foam packaging product contains 50% recycled material, its Ultratill low-density PETE packaging contains 80% reusable materials, and its Northbox insulated containers are made with FSC certified recycled materials.

What clearly makes Cascades unique is the organization's culture, one that is focused on driving sustainability across all areas of business. Initiated in 2010 and followed up with updates to the plan on a three-year cycle, Cascades incorporates its sustainable development plan as an integral part of its overall strategic planning process. The current 2016–2020 sustainable development plan contains three priorities (planet, partners, and prosperity) supported by ten measurable objectives considered to be key performance indicators of the company's ability to further enhance its sustainable development practices. These ten objectives are as follows:

Area	Goal	Target
Greenhouse gas emissions	Conversion of operations steam boilers to natural gas	Greenhouse gas emissions reduced by 51% between 1990 and 2015. A reduction of 11% occurred between 2013 and 2017, with the 2020 target being a further reduction of 12% by 2020.
Residual materials (waste)	Increase amount of waste materials recovered or reduced	71% of waste is recovered with a 2020 target of 80% recovery.
Water	Reduce the amount of waste water to 8.9 cubic metres per metric tonne of saleable products by 2020	Cascades plants' average water consumption is 9.9 cubic metres per metric tonne of saleable products versus an industry average of 65 cubic metres per metric tonne.
Sustainable procurement	Source materials from responsible suppliers	Over 40% of all purchases are sourced from responsible suppliers with a 2020 goal of raising this to 60%.
Innovation	Develop and market new products	Sales of innovative and eco-responsible products were up by more than 30% in 2017 (versus 2016), with sales from new products exceeding the 2020 goal of 20%.
Financial performance	Optimize the return on capital employed (ROCE)	Although ROCE was down in 2017 (3.7% vs. 5.2% in 2016), the company has made considerable investments in plant and operations modernization with an ROCE goal of 8% by 2020.
Health and safety	Reduce occupational injuries and illnesses	Reduce to 2.2 days per 200 000 hours worked, with a 2020 objective of 1.6 days.
Employee engagement	Increase the level of employee commitment	56% based on results from AON Hewitt employee opinion survey, with a target of 65% by 2020.
Community involvement	Increase financial contributions to communities where we operate	83.5% participation of units for at least three community-based initiatives.
Energy	Quantity of energy purchased to make our products	Cascades plant average is 9.9 gigajoules per metric tonne of saleable products vs. an industry average of 25.76 gigajoules per metric tonne of saleable products.

The Cascades management team is committed to ensuring the company operates with a belief that nature does not belong to us, but that we are simply borrowing it. The company's philosophy is to manage resources naturally, and that financial results can be the outcome of a proactive resource management approach. The vision of the company's ownership and management team is to ensure that sustainable development and its underlying business practices are part of the organization's core DNA. To do that means Cascades needs to continually work to improve its practices and the sustainable composition of its products—something the company fully intends to keep doing.

Web Integration

Want to learn more about Cascades and its 2016–2020 sustainable development plan? Visit **www.cascades.com/en/sustainable -development/overview/**.

Business IN ACTION

Canada and Water Consumption

According to the latest statistical information, our country ranks fourth in terms of water utilization per capita (per cubic metres) despite having only 3% of the world's population. Only New Zealand, the United States, and Estonia use more water per capita than Canada with respect to water consumption. Graded on the basis of A, B, C, and D, Canada received a "C" for its water conservation practices by the Conference Board of Canada in 2016. The Conference Board of Canada study reinforced a prior study conducted by the OECD (Organisation for Economic Co-operation and Development). The OECD, which studied water use in 29 different countries from 1980 to 2000, ranked Canada 28th out of 29 countries at that time. The Conference Board of Canada's 2016 report also ranked Canada second in the world in terms of water consumption. Again, only the residents of the United States, on a per capita basis, used more water than Canadians. At that time, according to the Conference Board of Canada, Canadians used an estimated 1500 cubic metres of water per person per year. This was double the 16-country average identified in the Conference Board study, and more than nine times greater than the number-one ranked country, the United Kingdom (est. 155 cubic metres per person per year).

Recent data show that conservation efforts in Canada are having positive results (down 30%). Our current utilization is just over 1000 cubic metres. Still, of the 20 countries that made up the

© Kelly Ann Tierney/Getty Images

comparison, 14 countries had water consumption, on a per capita basis, of under 700 cubic metres—less than 70% of Canada's consumption level. Although Canada's largest water consumer is industry (68%), Canadian households use more than 300 litres of water per day.

Water Consumption in Canada: Quick Facts (McGill Study 2016)

Number of litres of water used by Canadians per day	329 litres
Percentage of water used in the bathroom	65%
Amount of water used in an 8-minute shower	76 litres
Amount of water a dripping tap will lose annually (6 drops/min)	1200 litres

So, why is it that Canadians use so much water? The Conference Board of Canada study pointed to two key factors. First, Canada as a whole suffers from a lack of widespread water conservation practices. As an example, agriculture, the largest industrial user of water in Canada (80%), is particularly inefficient, recycling less than 30% of the water it uses. While many countries worked toward reducing water consumption over the 20-year period between 1990 and 2010, Canadian water consumption actually increased by 26% during this same period (although, as noted above, this is trending down). The second reason given for our high water utilization has to do with the price of water in Canada. In many areas in Canada the price of water is significantly less than it should be, with overall revenues falling short of the levels needed to cover operational, repair, upgrading, and water delivery expansion costs. A number of municipalities have not initiated water metering technologies, with many municipalities simply charging a flat rate regardless of the amount used. Data point to the fact that if Canadians are charged for water on the basis of use, where rates increase in proportion to the amount used, then the volume of water consumption does drop. Canadians being charged for water via a metering process have consumption levels approximately 20% lower than those paying for water on a fixed-rate basis. Having said this, only an estimated 56% of Canadians are subject to water metering. A number of municipalities have actually reduced rather than increased the price of water, with the end result being that high users of water receive discounts, not surcharges, for their heavy consumption. This lack of proper pricing has resulted in an aging and seriously deficient water infrastructure system. Experts estimate that Canada will need to spend billions of dollars in order to meet the future needs of our country. In addition to responding to these aging infrastructure concerns, pricing also aids in the creation and buy-in for conservation practices. As demonstrated by initiatives undertaken by other countries, increasing the cost of water is one of the best incentives for reducing water consumption.

As Canadians, we need to contemplate the inefficiencies that lie within our water consumption practices and build the methodologies and infrastructure that will transition us from a water waster to a water conservationist. Water, much like oil, is a finite resource. The amount of water that exists globally is shrinking. Global warming, population growth, and industry expansion are all working toward depleting this precious resource. In 2001, the federal Commissioner of the Environment and Sustainable Development declared fresh water in southern Canada to be heavily used and overly stressed. As Canadians, our task is to protect and respect this finite resource, through stronger conservation practices and through pricing strategies that ensure our water resource is managed to the benefit of not just current but also future generations.

Web Integration

Want to learn more about Canada's water conservation and water management initiatives? Visit the Conference Board of Canada Web site at **www.conferenceboard.ca**, or Google "Canada's water consumption practices."

LO1   The Consumption Journey

During the mid-to-late 1700s, the world embarked upon a significant change when the marketplace of Great Britain/Europe began the shift from being a largely agricultural-based society to being one transitioning toward a production-based model. Supported by population growth, an increase in trade and inventiveness, and a growing emphasis on wealth creation, the concept of mercantilism backed by the rise of business systems fundamentally changed the course of economic development and direction forever. This transitioning period, which historically has been referred to as the Industrial Revolution, marked the beginning of a societal shift toward technology and scientific methodologies as mechanisms for economic development. It also marked the change in societal behaviour from self-sustenance to a consumption-inspired marketplace. Driven to meet the needs of this newly emerging society, entrepreneurs and merchants identified and responded to the needs of society in an unprecedented way. This increase in the demand for products and services resulted in the need for greater production, more efficient operations, and a growth in specialization. Technological innovations such as the assembly line, replaceable parts, and factory-based, labour-driven business systems all evolved in response to the growing demand being experienced. The concepts of specialization and outsourcing were both born during this period as organizations sought to create greater efficiency and scale to meet this new demand, as well as capitalizing on the opportunity for wealth and success this "new age" offered.

This societal shift, however, also marked the advent of another defining moment for the global marketplace. This new shift was the dramatic intensification of destructive pressures on our environment. With the Industrial Revolution, and the centuries that followed, businesses and organizations—while focusing on responding to meeting the insatiable appetites of society—pumped billions of kilograms of toxic materials into our air, water, and land. Absent of regulations for governing business behaviour, prosperity was measured by activity and monetary gain, not by long-term legacy and **environmental stewardship**. In many cases, the huge amount of waste that was generated was simply buried, with little concern over its long-term impact on future generations and on the biological species with which we share our planet. Fast-forward to the 20th century, when as humans we began to sense the environmental degradation that is occurring as developed-nation economies, whose cultures have been largely built around economic performance, become enlightened to the consequences of poor resource management and the toxicity that practices up to this time have allowed to seep into our global environment. In response both to growing scientific evidence and to the occurrence of environmental disasters, governments began to create minimum levels of regulatory environmental compliance for a growing number of business sectors (see Figure 4.1). These regulations, for example those associated with pollution and waste, were designed to provide some element of accountability and control with respect to environmental management within the business and public sectors.

Forced to absorb unexpected costs and their corresponding impact to profitability as a result of the legal liability that regulatory compliance mandated (fines, cleanup expenses, injury claims, etc.), a number of organizations began to see the true value in implementing eco-management initiatives and in incorporating

> **Environmental Stewardship** is the integration of sustainability values into the managing of environmental resources.

FIGURE 4.1   **Societal Response to Environmental Degradation**

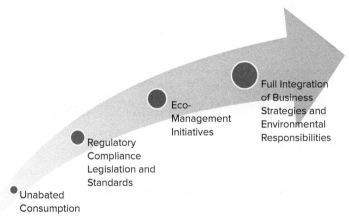

- Full Integration of Business Strategies and Environmental Responsibilities
- Eco-Management Initiatives
- Regulatory Compliance Legislation and Standards
- Unabated Consumption

environmental policies into their business operations. This need to mitigate risk and organizational exposure to significant economic consequences led organizations to begin to develop environmental policies and environmental management systems in order to reduce, measure, and monitor their risk exposure to enacted legislation directly impacting their industry sector and business operations. These policy initiatives resulted in the base-level development of operational protocols and practices relating to pollution prevention, recycling, and environmental health and safety assessment. The benefit of this risk exposure recognition is that the marketplace began to come to terms with the impact of the unabated consumption practices to date, and the consequences of such activities to our environment.

So, where do we go from here? With the global emergence of economies from developing nations around the world, the acceleration of our consumption of the world's resources continues to increase. The true finite nature of these various resources is truly beginning to be more fully understood in a manner never seen before. Continued unabated **degradation** of our air, land, and water as the accelerated rate of global economic growth continues has the makings of a massive environmental and planetary disaster. For businesses and the planet to survive, organizations must make the transition from simply a compliance/eco-management approach to a sustainable business strategy approach. This means we must become fully successful at integrating environmental responsibilities into our business strategies.

The goal is to design and redesign business processes in a way that, while allowing for increased wealth and enhanced competitive advantage, incorporates the principles of humankind and resource protection and sustainability for the future. This requires organizations to integrate sustainable development and resource management into their core mission, vision, values, codes of conduct, and business systems. This process is much more than just compliance or prevention. Its core fundamental is the integration of the relationship of society, the environment, and economic benefit into every facet of the organization's decision-making process. The successful development of economies and nations can no longer simply be measured in terms of domestic consumption growth, production-based productivity indexes, and GDP growth. To do so simply means the potential disregard for the value of our natural resources, the nature of our planet, and the true well-being of our society. Successful economic development ratings need to go beyond production and consumption indices and include additional measures such as the protection of our biosphere, sustainable use of global resources, energy conservation, environmental restoration, waste reduction, safe waste disposal practices, and public education toward planetary stewardship.[1]

Degradation is the deterioration of the environment through the depletion of resources and the destruction of ecosystems.

> The goal is to design and redesign business processes in a way that, while allowing for increased wealth and enhanced competitive advantage, incorporates the principles of humankind and resource protection and sustainability for the future.

Business IN ACTION

Canada and the Environment—Sounding the Alarm

Climate change is without a doubt one of the most serious threats globally. The impact of the industrial and manufacturing bases created within fully developed countries is now being further expanded as developing nations accelerate their economic platforms and the required accompanying infrastructure. Scientific data continue to substantiate the direct correlation between our actions relating to economic development and the consequential outcomes relating to global warming, sea level rise, extreme weather events, and the overall sustainability of our planet. In order to stem the further degradation of our environment going forward, governments, businesses, and individuals need to effectively work together to create solutions that minimize (and, ideally, halt) the contributions to environment degradation. In this regard, it is imperative for each country to look at its track record relating to its environmental conduct and demonstrate to the global community at large our contributions in response to this monumental environmental challenge.

In her role as the Environmental Commissioner of Ontario, Dianne Saxe sounded the alarm relating to climate change at the Kingston Climate Change Symposium held on January 17, 2019. In her comments relating to the critical pivot point we are facing, Saxe's comments centred around the fact that climate is now changing everything. In this regard, her comments were intended to drive home the point that climate change is here, it is affecting us now, and its impact lies much worse in the years ahead. For us as Canadians, and for the global marketplace at large, we are determining our future now by the decisions we are making today.

To put it bluntly, today's planetary environment finds itself experiencing

- The highest CO_2 levels in the history of civilization (see Figure 4.2). It is of critical concern that this has occurred at exponentially increasing growth rates, from 278 parts per million in 1750 to 410 parts per million in 2018. The last 30 years alone have seen CO_2 parts per million jump from 350 to 410.

- The highest temperatures in human civilization, coupled with the greatest variations in temperature anomaly (see Figure 4.3). It is estimated that as much as 90%+ of this extra heat is captured in the oceans, thereby contributing to the extreme weather activities we have all seen, felt, or heard of as we go about our daily lives.

So, just how far-reaching are the effects of climate change? Climate change will impact us as Canadians, as well as across the globe, in a number of critical ways. Some, but not all, of these impact factors are as follows:

- Climate extremes will become more common as temperatures rise and temperature variation volatility increases, with the results becoming more damaging. Higher average temperatures will become more unevenly distributed, resulting in heightened probability of floods, fires, drought, wind, and heat in areas that historically have seen little impact from such events.

FIGURE 4.2 CO_2 Emission Growth, Parts per Million (PPM)

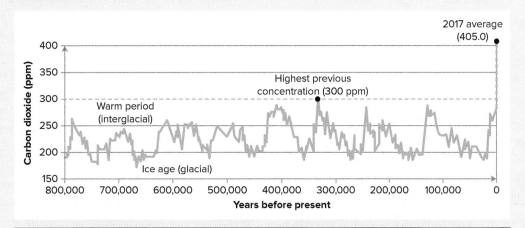

Source: Lüthi, D., M. Le Floch, B. Bereiter, T. Blunier, J.-M. Barnola, U. Siegenthaler, D. Raynaud, J. Jouzel, H. Fischer, K. Kawamura, and T.F. Stocker. (2008). "High-Resolution Carbon Dioxide Concentration Record 650,000–800,000 Years Before Present. *Nature*, Vol. 453, pp. 379–382. doi:10.1038/nature06949.

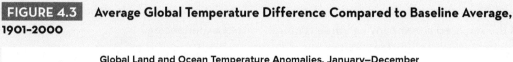

FIGURE 4.3   Average Global Temperature Difference Compared to Baseline Average, 1901-2000

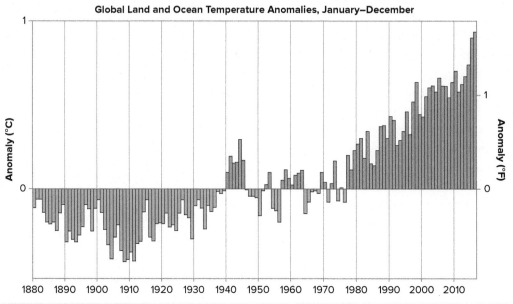

Source: U.S. National Oceanic and Atmospheric Administration (NOAA), *Climate Change—Global Temperature*; Climate Action in Ontario, *2018 Greenhouse Progress Report*, p. 22.

- Property, particularly along coastal areas, will become exposed not only to flooding, but also to full and permanent submersion as a result of rising sea levels. As an example, studies have indicated that as many as 10% of Canadian properties reside in these high-risk areas.

- Insured losses relating to catastrophic events are growing rapidly and are expected to continue to climb, resulting in significant costs to the insurance industry and society at large.

- Heat impact associated with climate change will make forests more prone to diseases, pests, and risks such as forest fires, forest die-back, and loss of winter cover. In Canada, the Ministry of Natural Resources and Forestry recorded 1325 forest fires in 2018.

- Food and farming will be impacted as well. Climate change may result in longer growing seasons in some areas, but the season length will be less predictable and subject to higher probability of droughts, floods, pests, and weather instability.

- As noted above, oceans have been the primary storage facility for the increased heat being generated by global warming. Ocean temperature rise will continue to trigger the loss of sea ice and will cause changes in ocean currents and balance.

Given the damage done, the critical question now has become "Is it too late?" It is true that our prior actions do mean we are in for big changes regardless of how quickly we act to change our current way of life. There is a belief, however, that we still have time to manage the severity of the impact going forward—therefore, the choices we make today do matter. Action is required on the part of Canadians and our governments, as well as other governments worldwide. The good news is that we do, in many cases, know what works. It is fundamentally imperative that we invest in solutions that significantly reduce and move us away from our reliance on fossil fuels. In addition, key to this process is to put into place regulations and programs that require polluters to pay for their actions and that regulate such activities going forward. Solutions such as cap and trade programs, carbon tax programs, grant programs focused on energy retrofits to existing buildings, housing, and institutions, and electric vehicle sales all are first steps in minimizing the exponential growth in carbon emissions. We as individuals can—and also must—contribute to re-inventing how we behave on a day-to-day basis by reducing our own carbon footprint and by actively speaking up and using our purchasing power as mechanisms to influence business and government behaviour.

As Canadians, it is imperative we recognize that growing GDP and the expansion of our economic platform cannot be accomplished at the expense of the environment. We must realize that demonstrated improvement in our quality of life must also demonstrate the sustainability of such growth and quality improvements. Our physical resources are finite and become scarcer with each passing decade. To improve our overall performance we need to seek greater levels of commitment at all levels of government, and across all sectors of society, in a way that

promotes economic growth without further degrading our environment. Without a significant increase in our attention to environmental sustainability as fundamental to our economic decision-making process, we expose our quality of life to significant long-term risk. Other countries in our world have demonstrated that significant improvements can be realized with little risk to the economic vitality of their societies. We need to realize that we too can be both economically focused while being "stewards of the planet." The two go hand-in-hand. This means that we must lower greenhouse emissions, be wiser in our consumption of finite and scarce resources, and reduce the amount of waste we are generating. Businesses, given their unique position in the economic fabric of our society, are well-positioned to take the lead in this regard.

The Sustainability Challenge

LO2

The United Nations (UN) estimates the 2017 population of our planet as being approximately 7.55 billion people. The UN estimates that in 2030, assuming no significant changes in fertility rates, the global population will exceed 8.5 billion (see Figure 4.4), with this further growing to as much as 11 billion by the year 2100.[2] This represents an estimated 48% increase in residents of Earth over this period. What was initially a trend of declining birth rates in more developed economic regions of the world at the start of this century no longer became the case, as birth rates in many countries in the developed world (Canada included) actually increased over the 10-year period 2002 to 2012. Today, the world's population continues to grow, although the growth rate has slowed in recent years. During the 10-year period

FIGURE 4.4   **UN World Population Projection, 2015–2100**

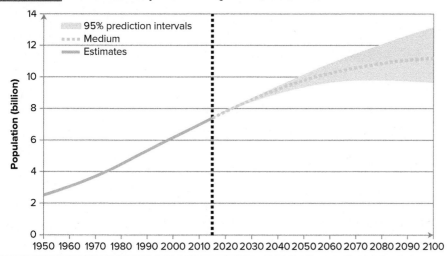

Source: United Nations Department of Economic and Social Affairs Population Division, "World Population Prospects, The 2017 Revision, Key Findings, Advance Tables," p. 2. Reprinted with the permission of the United Nations.

mentioned above the growth rate was approximately 1.24% per year. This global growth rate today has decreased to approximately 1.1%. Still, at this lower growth rate we are adding an estimated 83 people annually to the world's population. Although developed countries will not significantly impact the overall population going forward, it is important to note that given the anticipated population increases in emerging and developing regions of the world such as Africa (see Figure 4.5), the UN's date for world population stabilization will most likely not occur until around the year 2100. Although one could argue the exact numbers associated with this anticipated population increase (as statistics from less developed areas of the world may not be fully reliable), one thing is certain: population growth over this century is inevitable, and given the growth anticipated significant stress is going to be placed on our planet with respect to resource depletion, climate management, and the health and safety of our global residents.[3]

In assessing the challenges going forward (see Figure 4.6), governments, businesses, and we as citizens must respond in ways never thought of before to five critical sustainability challenges: climate change, pollution and health, the energy crunch, resource depletion, and the capital squeeze.

Climate Change

Did you know that a 1°C rise in average temperature can have devastating effects on crop yields? Recent research by David Lobell of Stanford University (published in the periodical *National Climate Change*) has concluded that the rise in global temperatures will reduce corn crop yields across our planet.[4] This is particularly true when the temperature moves above 30°C. Increasing the average temperature a little impacts the number of hot days and, as noted, days above 30°C are particularly damaging. According to Lobell's work, every day the temperature is above 30°C,

FIGURE 4.5   **World Population Forecast with Africa's Percentage Share**

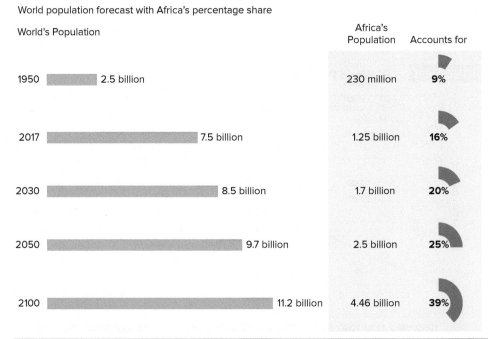

By the End of the Century, 40% of People will be African

World population forecast with Africa's percentage share

World's Population		Africa's Population	Accounts for
1950	2.5 billion	230 million	9%
2017	7.5 billion	1.25 billion	16%
2030	8.5 billion	1.7 billion	20%
2050	9.7 billion	2.5 billion	25%
2100	11.2 billion	4.46 billion	39%

Source: Adapted and based on United Nations Department of Economic and Social Affairs, Population Division (2017), "World Population Prospects: The 2017 Revision," New York: United Nations.

FIGURE 4.6   The Challenges Going Forward

crop yields can diminish by up to 1%. Move up 2°C to 32°C, and the impact is twice that found at 31°C. Given anticipated global temperatures going forward, this could impact corn growing areas, such as Africa, by as much as 20% of their yields by the middle of this century (assuming Lobell's data are accurate).

Although the debate on climate degradation is ongoing, for the most part scientists appear to be in agreement that time is running out on our ability to respond to the climate change trends underway and that if we don't act quickly we will be placing our planet at significant risk. Just how much time do we have? The general estimate is probably less than 40 years. Just what do we need to do within this 40-year period? To significantly reverse the downward spiral associated with climate change, we need to cut carbon-based emissions during this period by at least 50% from their current levels. Recognizing that the consumption society we have created was built over approximately 200 years, our climate change revolution will need to reverse these trends in 20% of the time—a time when our global population, as noted above, is expected to increase by more than 48%. Can this result be realized over this period of time? According to a McKinsey Climate Change Special Initiative the answer is yes—*if* we are successful in five key areas (see Figure 4.7).[5]

Although building a reduced-carbon economy will require new capital investments, a number of initiatives can be put into place using existing technologies and little to no new capital. As an example, shifting to low-energy lighting, switching to electric or at least more fuel-efficient vehicles, and continuing industrial process zero-emission initiatives can significantly reduce the negative impact. Decarbonizing the energy supply by continuing to apply alternate solutions—such as wind, solar, geothermal, biomass, hydro, and even nuclear, where applicable—will further reduce the carbon footprint. If we can successfully employ carbon-capture technologies around carbon-based fuels such as coal, we further reduce the carbon-based emissions flow. This is particularly true in China and the United States, where coal continues to be a major energy source.

Transportation is another key area where a significant improvement can be achieved. The Global Fuel Economy Initiative expects the number of cars worldwide to triple between now and 2050. Unchecked, this rapid growth in vehicles and their

FIGURE 4.7   Building a Reduced-Carbon Economy

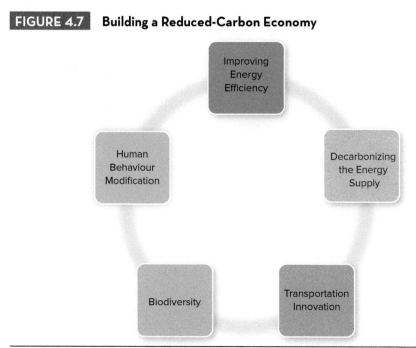

Source: Beinhocker and Oppenheim, "Building a Post-Carbon Economy," McKinsey & Company, February 2009, http://whatmatters.mckinseydigital.com/climate_change/building-a-postcarbon-economy, accessed March 2011.

carbon-based emissions can have serious climate degradation implications. Having said this, a report titled "50by50: Prospects and Progress," by George C. Eads, Charles River Associates, indicates that with proper action this growth can be managed. Critical to this action is ensuring that governments and manufacturers set fuel economy as a top priority, and that worldwide binding fuel economy targets are set. Creating a regulatory and financial environment that moves manufacturers to stress fuel economy instead of performance could enable us to cut fuel emissions by 50% between now and 2030. According to Eads, fuel economy averages in new cars should be able to reach 2.27 litres per 100 kilometres during this period. All of this could be built around technologies relating to advancement in internal combustion engine design, hybrids, electric vehicles, and next-generation biofuels.

Protecting our green carpet also needs to remain a top priority. "Green carpet" refers to our forests, trees, and plant life. Farming, logging, and energy consumption have resulted in a serious erosion of our green carpet.[6] Deforestation, which is the massive clearing of Earth's forest, continues to be a major issue in many developing countries. Honduras, Nigeria, Benin, Ghana, Indonesia, and Nepal have all experienced a huge reduction in their forest areas due to massive clearing of their green carpets. Deforestation largely occurs due to agriculture and logging initiatives as countries seek to create an economic base in order to increase the standard of living of their citizens. In addition to the loss of plant and animal species resulting from deforestation, this process also robs Earth of its ability to deal with natural carbon dioxide emission absorption. Although the largest contributor to carbon dioxide emissions is the burning of fossil fuels (approximately 77%), deforestation accounts for an estimated 22% of this problem.[7] In addition to the loss of our ability to offset carbon dioxide emissions with our green carpet, deforestation also contributes to the water cycle and to overall management of Earth's average temperature. Keeping our green carpet is one of the easiest and least expensive ways to combat global warming. Forestry management guidelines—and adherence by all countries—is a needed first step in our fight against global warming. Reforestation education initiatives, particularly in developing nations, are key to successfully maintain and effectively improve our balance between nature and economic growth.

FIGURE 4.8   **Quick Facts Relating to Climate Change**

Sea Ice	Sea Level	Carbon Dioxide	Global Temperature
Is diminishing 413 giga-tonnes per year. We are losing an estimated 12% of Arctic ice per decade. 2012 recorded the lowest extent of sea ice on record.	Is rising 3.2 millimetres per year. Sea levels have risen an estimated 178 mm (7") over the past 100 years. The rate of rise continues to accelerate.	Has risen to 411 parts per million, and is at highest levels in the last 650 000 years.	Has risen just over 1°C (1.9°F) since 1880. 18 of the 19 warmest years on record have occurred since 2001. 2016 was ranked as the warmest year on record.

Source: NASA Global Climate Change, *Vital Signs of the Planet,* https://climate.nasa.gov/, referenced February 27, 2019.

As demonstrated above, our ability to respond to the climate change challenge lies, in large part, in changing current practices and making stronger use of existing technologies. Success lies in our ability to change human behaviour (which scientists believe, with a 95% probability, is responsible for the climate change challenges we face)[8] as much as it lies in the development and application of new technologies. (See Figure 4.8 for a series of quick facts related to climate change.) This will require a shift in values and lifestyles. Yes, governments and regulatory agencies must enact new policies and create additional incentives (or penalties) in order to kickstart this transition. This can be via stronger use of incentives such as a carbon tax or cap and trade systems; stronger adoption of compliance methodologies such as those proposed in the Kyoto Protocol (1997), the Copenhagen Accord (2009), and most recently the **Paris Agreement** of 2016, revisited in 2018 (see Business in Action), or similar forthcoming global initiatives; and stronger use of tax or investment incentives for transitioning businesses to renewable strategies and making the investments in research and development to spur new technologies.

Paris Agreement has an overall objective to bind all nations to a "common cause" response to the emerging crisis associated with climate change.

Although such governmental and regulatory policies and initiatives will up the compliance scale, it is we as managers and individuals who need to take climate change responsibility into the boardroom and into the business operation to ensure the behaviours exhibited reflect a true integration of environmental sustainability practices into our organizational and corporate strategies.

Business IN ACTION

The Paris Agreement—Canada

Drafted in December 2015, the Paris Agreement's overall objective is to bind all nations to a "common cause" response to the emerging crisis associated with climate change. The central aim of the agreement is to develop mechanisms and methodologies to ensure that the global temperature, currently at historical highs, does not exceed 1.5°C above pre-industrial levels. Critical to this agreement is the willingness of nations to put forward their best efforts to meet specific individual targets for each

© Bernie Epstein/Alamy

country and to appropriately mobilize the allocation of financial resources, technology, and regulatory policies with respect to greenhouse emissions and related climate change challenges. As of this writing over 195 countries, representing 97% of global GHG emissions, agreed to commit to more aggressive response targets, including the pledge to hold global temperature increases to below 2°C, with a further defined target of 1.5°C above pre-industrial levels.

The agreement, which was officially signed on April 22, 2016 (Earth Day), requires countries to regularly report their individual and collective progress toward the achievement of their agreed-upon targets. Recognizing that each country is at a different stage of economic evolution and has different resource capabilities toward responding to climate change, the agreement looks for each country to specify the targets and overall long-term strategy it intends to initiate and execute on in order to meet its contribution requirements to the overall global goal of greenhouse gas emission reduction. As a participating member, Canada has outlined its commitment to creating a cleaner, more innovative economy that will balance the need for environmental protection and reduced greenhouse emissions while pursuing future economic growth. Specific to this, Canada is looking, as its mid-century strategy, to reduce emissions by 80% by 2050 (benchmarked against 2005 levels).

For Canada to be successful in executing on its pledges significant behavioural change will be required by the industries, companies, and people that make up our economy. Cost-effective emission abatement methodologies will need to be both created and effectively executed on. This will require significant capital investment and innovative solutions fundamental to building a clean technology sector and revamping how our underlying production and product transformation processes operate. Private-sector R&D investments combined with funding support from all levels of government will be needed to drive this innovation process. In addition, government will be challenged to create and implement even stronger regulatory policies relating to carbon pricing and penalties for violation and/or inaction. Although the task may seem daunting, Canadians can and should view this challenge as an opportunity. Taking a leadership role in the active development of clean air and emission reduction technologies that can then be shared with the rest of the world represents a significant economic opportunity. Most Canadians recognize the need to mitigate climate change and limit the increase in global average temperature. To be successful in our response, however, requires a true collaborative effort on the part of our provinces, territories, municipalities, businesses, and the broader community of global stakeholders core to Canada's success. Having said this, the magnitude of change is significant, and the need for quick and decisive action understated. The clock is ticking. The Paris Agreement needs now, more than ever, to produce the results fundamental to our planet's sustainable survival.

Pollution and Health

When we look at global mortality rates, we often are reminded of the horrid diseases that take so many lives prematurely. Heart disease, cancer, HIV/AIDS, Ebola, and malaria may immediately come to mind as possible reasons for premature death. But how many of us think of pollution as a major killer of humans? Recent research by David Pimentel of Cornell University estimates that as many as 62 million deaths per year—representing an estimated 40% of deaths globally—may be attributed to environmental factors such as organic and chemical pollutants. Essentially, the cause of death is the air we breathe and the water we drink. According to the World Health Organization (WHO), as many as 1.1 billion people live in areas that do not have access to clean and safe drinking water. Lack of water sanitation alone is a major cause of death worldwide. Unsafe drinking water can be the result of untreated sewage and contaminated surface water. In a number of developing countries, many people simply dump their garbage and waste into the same water they use for drinking and bathing.[9] See Figure 4.9 for a visual representation of the worst pollution sites in the world.

FIGURE 4.9 **Contaminated Sites Assessed by the American NGO Pure Earth**

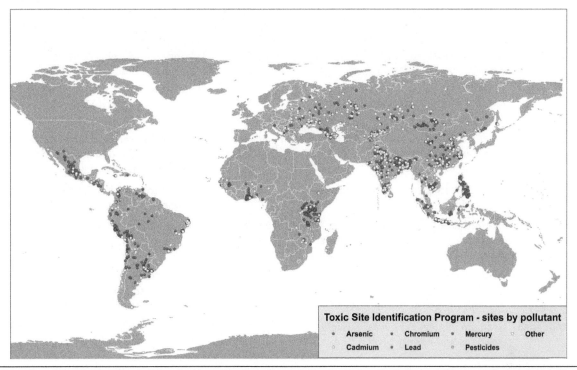

FIGURE 4.9 **Contaminated Sites Assessed by the American NGO Pure Earth**

Source: Taken from "The World's Worst Pollution Problems: The Toxics Beneath Our Feet," Pure Earth (formerly Blacksmith Institute), New York, USA, p. 14. Used with permission of Pure Earth.

Air pollution is another major killer. The WHO estimates that more than 3 million humans die each year from pollution-triggered diseases such as pneumonia, bronchitis, and lung cancer. It comes as a surprise to many of us in fully developed countries such as Canada that indoor pollution from smoke and ash from open indoor stoves is more of a deadly killer than outdoor air pollution.[10]

Our health is also affected by the thousands of toxins released into the air and the environment by businesses and organizations that have operated—or that currently are operating—across the globe. The highly respected Pure Earth Blacksmith Institute, in partnership with Green Cross Switzerland, listed the top six toxic threats to mankind in its 2015 update of its 2012 report on the world's worst pollution problems; these threats are summarized in Figure 4.10.

The Pure Earth Blacksmith Institute has identified more than 2300 sites that contain these leading toxins (lead, mercury, chromium, cadmium, pesticides, and radionuclides), affecting an estimated 95 million people and accounting for 14.7 million disability-adjusted years of life lost (with particular impact on children).[11] According to the Pure Earth Blacksmith Institute, 1000 of these sites are considered toxic hot spots. Argentina, Indonesia, and Nigeria are among the world's top 10 most polluted places, and in Dzerzhinsk, Russia, for example, the ongoing dumping of chemical waste has contaminated the groundwater to such an extent that the life expectancy for residents has fallen to age 42 for men and age 47 for women. This identification work, however, is far from complete. Initial estimates, based on work in progress, indicate that the number of sites globally impacted by toxic pollutants could be double the current 2300 sites identified, and the number of people impacted could be more than 100 million, most of whom live in low-and middle-income countries. The Pure Earth Blacksmith Institute, Green Cross Switzerland, and the World Bank (with $500 million in funding) are leading the international effort to clean up global toxic waste. Preliminary funding estimates for such initiatives, aimed at tackling the worst of these sites, could run as much as $1 billion or more. The positive news is that,

FIGURE 4.10   **Pure Earth Blacksmith Institute: Top Six Toxic Threats**

Toxic Threat	Pollution Location	Estimated Global Impact (millions of people)	Major Health Risks
1. Lead	Air, water, soil, food, dermal contact... metal smelting and mining	26	The #1 current concern. Neurological damage, reduced IQ, anemia, nerve disorders, lead poisoning
2. Mercury	Air, water, food, dermal contact... chlorine gas, batteries, electrical switches	15–19	Damage to brain, kidney, stomach, intestines, lungs. Used in mining and other industrial activities.
3. Chromium	Air, water, soil, food...metal and steel processing, welding, tanning	13–17	Damage to gastrointestinal, respiratory, immunological systems, reproductive systems.
4. Cadmium	By-product of nickel-cadmium batteries, fertilizers, coatings, and plastic stabilizers; by-product of zinc mining	5–9	Renal and bone disease and other related conditions.
5. Pesticides	Groundwater and water sources	5–8	Damage to neurological, reproductive, and dermatological systems. Three million acute illnesses annually.
6. Radionuclides	Uranium mining, mine waste, nuclear weapons and energy production	22	Damage to cells, cancer, and death (high doses).

Source: McCartor & Becker, "World's Worst Pollution Problems 2010: Top 6 Toxic Threats," Blacksmith Institute, New York, NY, USA, and the Weather Channel, 6 Top Toxic Threats, https://weather.com/health/news/top-toxic-threats-of-2015, October 21, 2015.

unlike other types of pollution or communicable diseases, in many cases cleaning up these toxic sites is a one-time expense. Once cleaned up, and assuming additional dumping does not take place, the remediation effort involved would most likely be a one-time intervention. To date, involvement in this cleanup process by companies within the industries that have caused the issues has been on an ad hoc basis. Our role, as managers and as planetary citizens, is to move decisively in this area to fund the types of initiatives the Pure Earth Blacksmith Institute is spearheading. This means fully integrating our present and future environmental responsibilities into our business strategies.

Business IN ACTION

Alberta's Oil Sands

Alberta's oil sands represent approximately 142 000 square kilometres of land, clustered in the northeastern section of the province. Largely concentrated in three regions (Peace River, Athabasca, and Cold Lake), and representing an area approximately the size of the state of Florida, its bitumen-based deposits represent vast energy resources (oil) which, if fully developed, would propel Canada, within the next 25 years, to become the fourth largest oil producer behind Saudi Arabia, the United States, and Russia.

In fact, the area represents the third largest known oil reserve in the world, trailing only Saudi Arabia and Venezuela. Since 2000, foreign and domestic companies and country-based sovereign wealth funds have invested over $100 billion in developing the required infrastructure to harvest the economic benefits of the oil sands' underlying reserves. Capital investment in Alberta's upstream energy sector (of which the oil sands project is one component) was an estimated $28 billion in 2016, $26 billion in 2017, and $23 billion in 2018. Although investments in the oil sands project itself have diminished in recent years, due to the lower price of crude oil and delays in the development of further transportation pipeline capacity, future investment is still anticipated going forward. As an example, Imperial Oil announced in November 2018 that it would go ahead with an additional $2.6-billion investment in its Aspen project in Northern Alberta.

At its height, proponents of the oil sands initiative projected that the development of the oil sands to its full economic potential could generate as much as $2.4 trillion in gross revenues, creating over 800 000 jobs and over 3.2 million person-years of employment; generate more than $172 billion in wages and salaries; and add more than $570 billion to federal and provincial government tax coffers (personal and corporate income tax, sales tax, etc.). For the Alberta government and its residents, the additional benefits from this project come in the form of not only the positive impact relating to the economic growth, but also the receipt of Bitumen Royalties from oil sands development participants, estimated at $1.48 billion in 2017 (down from $4.4 billion in 2013), which provides the government with a significant revenue source for which to fund province-wide services. So why all the fuss? What could possibly be so concerning about this project, given the tremendous economic benefits noted above? These same economic benefits driven from the oil sands development are offset by more than significant environmental concerns—greenhouse gas emissions and related air pollution, water consumption, groundwater contamination, and the absence of land reclamation abilities and initiatives, to mention a few.

Extracting oil from the bitumen-rich sands requires extensive processing, which produces between 3.2 and 4.5 times the greenhouse emissions per barrel compared to extracting oil from a conventional crude oil deposit. Already representing approximately 7% of Canada's total greenhouse emissions, the oil sands, given its current and anticipated development activity, is the fastest growing source of greenhouse emissions in Canada. To put this into perspective, if Alberta were a country it would have the highest per capita greenhouse emissions in the world. Sulphur dioxide and nitrogen dioxide, two major extraction by-products, are major contributors to acid rain formation. Producing a barrel of oil from bitumen creates

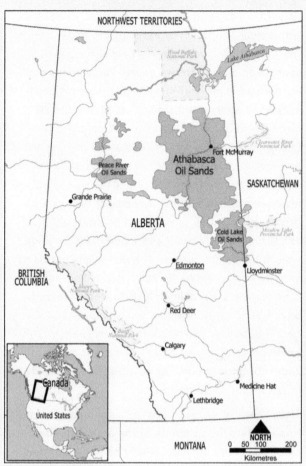

© Norman Einstein

more than twice the sulphur dioxide and nitrogen dioxide emissions than are typically generated through conventional oil extraction processes. According to the Pembina Institute, in 2006, extraction operations in the oil sands released an estimated 45 000 tonnes of nitrogen oxide and 115 000 tonnes of sulphur dioxide into the atmosphere. Proponents of the development of the oil sands do point toward the fact that Alberta, in response to these air pollution concerns, has established the Alberta Air Quality Objectives (AAQO), which are intended to provide protection of the environment. Again according to Pembina, however, AAQO guidelines are judged to be more lenient than those issued by the World Health Organization, and these less stringent guidelines have frequently been exceeded by oil sands operators.

The intensive extraction process of the bitumen in the oil sands also uses a great deal of water. In 2011, oil sands operators used the equivalent of the residential water use of 1.7 million Canadians, almost none of which is returned to the natural cycle. This withdrawal of water is threatening the ecosystem of the Athabasca River, as well as other natural-based sources across the three-reserve region. The waste water used in bitumen-based mining operations is subject to a zero-discharge policy due to the significant number and level of toxins (referred to as tailings) found within it. This water, since it cannot be recycled, is being stored in tailings ponds or re-injected deep underground. At 2014–15 production levels, more than 200 million litres of tailings are produced each day. Given the amount of bitumen extracting already taking place at oil sands mining sites, a significant number of these tailing ponds have already been created. In fact, these tailings lakes now cover an area approximately 50% greater than the city of Vancouver. Add to this a recognized concern that tailings lakes could possibly seep, and the environmental impact of this seepage is not yet fully known or understood. Figure 4.11 shows a satellite image of the oil sands area.

Then there is the additional issue of land reclamation. To date, less than 1% of the area disturbed by oil sands mining has actually been certified as "reclaimed" by the government of Alberta. A big reason for this is that the bitumen extraction projects currently in operation are at the front end of their life expectancy curve. Many projects have a lifespan of 20 years or more, so reclamation remains in its very early stages. Although the Alberta Environmental Protection and Enhancement Act is intended to oversee and safeguard the reclamation of oil sands mining lands, critics of the project contend that this oversight is inadequate and is putting Albertans and Canadians at financial risk—a risk that will not be fully understood until many years from

FIGURE 4.11   Athabasca Oil Sands—NASA Photo

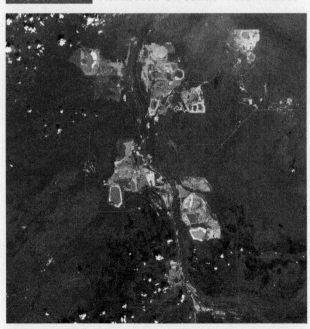

Source: NASA Earth Observatory, "World of Change: Athabasca Oil Sands," https://earthobservatory.nasa.gov/world-of-change/Athabasca.

now. The major issues lie in the inability to return the boreal forests being destroyed by mining to their natural state and the still emerging technology of reclamation of tailing waste currently being stored in the human-made tailing ponds. Lands associated with decommissioned wells also represent challenges, with the average reclamation period in the six-year range.

There can be little doubt the economic benefits of developing the oil sands are numerous. Equally evident are the environmental risks posed by this development. Can these risks be mitigated or avoided to develop the oil sands in an environmentally sustainable manner? This is a question that remains to be answered.

The Energy Crunch

At this time, our entire global economy remains significantly dependent on fossil fuels (Figure 4.12). As an example, before commercial production of oil began in the mid-1800s, it was estimated that the global supply of oil was approximately 2 trillion barrels. Since commercial production began, our consumption pattern has continued to grow to the point where we have consumed approximately one-half of this amount (1 trillion barrels) and have reached annual demand levels of 30+ billion barrels per year. Although the global recession of 2009 and 2010, combined with energy conservation and efficiency efforts, has slowed the appetite for oil and fossil fuel-based energy sources in general (oil, gas, coal), energy consumption has continued to increase each year, reaching a new all-time high in 2017.[12]

FIGURE 4.12   **World Energy Consumption**

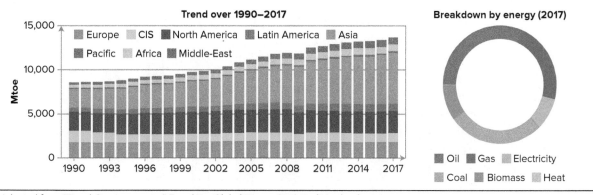

Source: Adapted from "Trend Over 1990–2017," Enerdata, *Global Energy Statistical Yearbook 2018.*

Recognizing the slower growth rates anticipated globally for the near term, the long-term outlook for energy consumption is still considered to be moving upward. According to Enerdata, global energy consumption in 2017 grew at a rate of 2.3% (vs. 1.1% in 2016), with China, now the world's largest energy consumer, doubling its energy growth during this period. China's overall energy consumption was up 2.9% in 2017 versus 2016. China is not alone in its growing appetite for energy. India, Indonesia, Malaysia, and South Korea all continue to see upward growth in their energy needs, as did many European countries and Canada. This increase in energy consumption occurred across all energy sectors including coal, considered to be one of the most environmentally harmful energy sources. This increase in the demand for coal was largely driven by increased consumption in India and Turkey. As previously indicated, demand for gas, oil, and electricity are also trending upward. With this upward demand in consumption, the global marketplace, despite its sustainability efforts, has also seen a rise in CO_2 emissions during this period (Figure 4.13); CO_2 emissions globally rose 2% in 2017, following three years of stagnation. In general, much of this increase was driven by consumption in non–OECD (Organisation for Economic Co-operation and Development) countries (+2.6%), with Russia (+5.8%) and India (+4%) seeing the highest spike in CO_2 emissions, but OECD countries also saw an upward tick in their emission levels (+1.3%).[13]

Looking forward, global energy consumption is estimated to increase by as much as 30% or more by 2040, with global electricity demand doubling during this period. Africa alone will require almost three times more energy in 2040 than it is consuming today (see Figure 4.14).

FIGURE 4.13   **Growth of CO_2 Emissions in 2017**

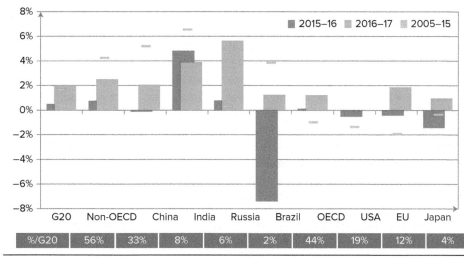

Source: Adapted from Enerdata, *Global Energy Statistical Yearbook 2018.*

FIGURE 4.14 **Energy Consumption Estimates to 2040**

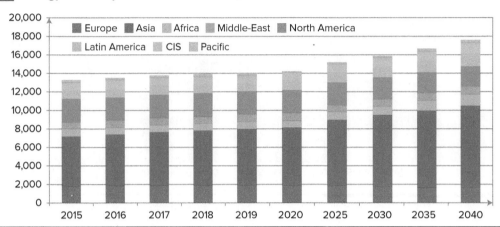

Source: Adapted from *Global Energy Statistical Yearbook 2018.*

For many developing countries, it is all about building the domestic capacity needed to respond to the economic development occurring within their borders and around their regions. Capacity investments are needed in a number of energy-consumption-intensive sectors to enable this economic development to take place. This will require an ongoing dependency in the near term (estimated to 2030–35) on fossil fuel–based energy, although the shift toward electricity and renewables will continue to accelerate. It is anticipated that the consumption of electricity will double between now and 2050, and that renewables will finally overtake oil as a percentage of the overall energy mix (2050). Having said this, the dependency on fossil fuels will still exist, with 65% of energy still being driven from oil, gas, and coal14 (see Figure 4.15). The critical component of the energy shift will be the ability of new-build renewable energy substitutes to be developed and implemented at lower cost points than traditional fossil fuels. This is happening across the globe, with a number of countries seeing the scale tipping in the favour of renewables around 2025. The utilization of governmental grants and regulatory processes could accelerate this transformation, particularly in the OECD countries.

Recognizing that the global marketplace is going to require significantly more energy over the next decade, and that it will need to come from largely existing energy sources, the question becomes whether we have enough supply to deliver on this mandate, let alone the potentially hazardous consequences that this reliance will place on our planet and the air that we breathe. The response to the question relating to supply is that it depends on two core ingredients: (1) resource availability, and (2) improvements in energy productivity from the sources we have available.

Resource availability Although the marketplace has been experiencing a temporary glut in energy production (resulting in the sharp downward pressure on price from mid-2014 and through 2018), the long-term assessment is that rising energy consumption will negate this current surplus, and that the tight relationship between supply and demand will resume. This conclusion is not based primarily on the **peak model theories**, which suggest that the finite supply of these non-renewable sources is coming to an end, but more on the key factors that determine our ability to draw on existing resource availability at this time (see Figure 4.16).

As Figure 4.16 illustrates, the supply side of the demand/supply relationship is influenced by seven key factors. These factors are as follows:

- **Current supply development constraints:** refers to how quickly we can develop the production of existing known resource supplies. This relates to how

Peak Model Theories are based on the belief that resources are finite and that, at some point in time, the availability of such resources will pass their maximum production point and begin to decline.

FIGURE 4.15   **Long-Term Energy Demand per Fuel Source**

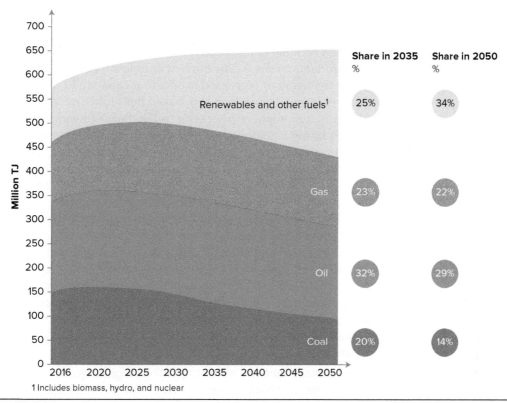

1 Includes biomass, hydro, and nuclear

FIGURE 4.16   **Key Factors Impacting Energy Supplies**

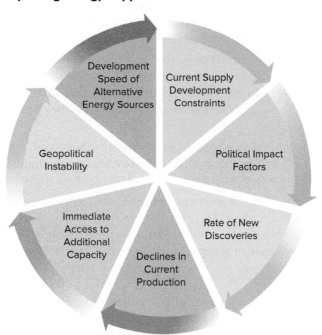

quickly capital investment in existing and new sources of energy can result in such energy sources being moved from a state of known, but not developed, to "into the pipeline." This would include the cost/benefit trade-off of developing such opportunities. It would also include transportation capacity constraints and refining constraints that could bottleneck or impact the delivery of final products to users. The current energy supply glut being experienced is largely the result of increased production capacity in North America. Both the Alberta oil sands area and U.S.-based hydraulic fracking have resulted in significantly new supplies of energy (oil and gas) flowing into the marketplace. U.S.-based fracking alone has generated an additional 11.5 million barrels of oil per day (November 2018), and is expected to top 12 million barrels of oil per day in 2019.[15] Canada added an additional 2.8 million barrels per day in 2017.[16] Although this supply injection has eased oil and natural gas supplies in the near term, it is anticipated that production volumes in the U.S. and Canada will begin to decrease around 2025, despite anticipated demand from developing economies. A key factor to watch, however, is the impact that low prices have on overall market economics. While low prices benefit consumers, low prices for oil, gas, and coal impact the broader marketplace in two ways. First, low prices will reduce the desire of oil-producing companies and nations from investing in new capacity, thereby tightening the relationship between demand and supply. Second, low prices for oil will impact the tipping point for transitioning to renewables, as the cost savings of shifting to renewables may be negated.

- **Political impact factors:** refers to political, legislative, or environmental action that constrains the ability of companies and organizations to proceed with supply development. An example is the current disagreement among nations relating to ownership rights for arctic lands that have been found to possess energy reserves. It would also refer to the environmental impact requirements, existing and new-to-come, that will impact costs and time associated with the pre-infrastructure development process. The ongoing and costly discussions between Canadian-based companies and the individual states within the U.S., and provinces within Canada, with respect to pipeline development (i.e., Keystone XL pipeline, Trans Mountain Expansion, Energy East, Northern Gateway Pipeline) are good examples, along with the decision of New York State in January 2015 to ban hydraulic fracking within the state.

Feed-in Tariff refers to government payment subsidy arrangements whereby participants are paid a guaranteed premium for energy developed through the adoption of alternate energy sources.

- **Feed-in tariff** subsidies and other grant/investment programs developed by governments to support the development of energy alternatives or improvements in energy productivity would also fall under this impact factor. Political impact factors can be viewed as either positive or negative influences on supply.

- **Rate of new discoveries:** refers to the identification of new sources of fossil fuels. New exploration technologies have resulted in the identification of fossil fuel reserves in areas where such reserves were not known to exist.

- **Declines in current production:** refers to the reduction in current supply volume due to energy sources drying up or being taken offline. The closing of a well due to the exhaustion of the oil supply associated with that well is an example of a supply contraction contributor. An additional example is the significant price instability that occurred during the latter half of 2014 and into 2015. This rapid drop in oil prices due to a heightened supply situation resulted in a number of companies cancelling capital investment plans intended to increase production capabilities. As an example, one of Canada's leading energy companies, Suncor, cut capital spending by $1 billion and initiated significant layoffs in January 2015 in response to falling oil prices.[17]

- **Immediate access to additional capacity:** refers to the ability of current suppliers to tap into excess capacity to meet the demand needs of the marketplace. The ability of OPEC to increase supply capacity from existing sources is an example. Enhanced production capability in Alberta, resulting in greater resource extraction from existing oil sands sites, is another example of our ability to add capacity to the supply side.

- **Geopolitical instability:** refers to instability in the countries or regions that supply our global energy needs. The instability in the Middle East, Venezuela, and in North Africa (Libya, Nigeria) over the past few years is reflective of how supplies can be disrupted due to geopolitical instability. The current instability between Russia and the Ukraine has also generated concern relating to future potential supply disruptions for natural gas flowing into Europe.

- **Development speed of alternative energy sources:** refers to the speed at which alternate energy sources can be brought online and achieve the necessary scale and cost structure to be viewed as viable options for energy consumers to consider when looking to meet their current and future energy needs. Political action may or may not be a primary driver of this scale and cost structure development process.

Improvements in energy productivity   Energy productivity is all about improving the efficiency of energy production currently taking place, as well as reducing the overall demand for such energy in a manner that does not compromise economic growth. This is where behavioural change and investment in technology come into play. Energy productivity is a measurement of the productivity achieved from each input of energy consumed. Based on the McKinsey Global Institute's research, we, as a global economy, currently consume 12 600 BTUs of energy for each dollar of global GDP output.[18] Although some improvement in energy productivity has been achieved, averting an energy crunch's negative impact to global growth means that we will need to either reduce the amount of energy input per dollar of GDP output, or create more GDP output from the same level of energy input. The approach will, most likely, be a combination of both. Capital investment in new technologies will, hopefully, generate greater output per energy input requirement, and lead to energy savings through reduced consumption. An example of this latter point would be the Energy Star ratings for appliances that require less energy to operate. Behavioural changes will highlight energy conservation in order to reduce the energy input required for each dollar of GDP output. Getting consumers to switch from incandescent lights to fluorescent lights in their homes is an example of a behavioural change. Success in improving energy productivity will need to underscore any global energy policy going forward. Without improvements to energy productivity initiatives, our energy dependency and the tightness of supply that is occurring will continue to magnify.

Resource Depletion

Resource management refers to our ability to actively manage existing supplies of materials and regenerate new supplies in a way that minimizes resource depletion. As we have discussed throughout this chapter, our industrial and technology-based society is based on the acquisition and consumption of materials found in, and on, our planet. These materials form the basis for the creation of goods and services designed, in large part, to improve our standard of living. Some of these resources are more renewable than others. What has grown significantly, however, is an overall concern that the replacement rates on renewable resources lag far behind their consumption. This

Resource Management is the ability to actively manage existing supplies and regenerate new supplies of materials in such a way that we minimize resource depletion.

concern is further compounded by the acceleration of non-renewable resource consumption, which in some areas has grown to the point where resources are well past their peak supply points. With the projected population growth for our planet noted above, combined with the tremendous economic growth in emerging economies across the globe, this resource depletion curve continues to accelerate. As indicated in the previous section, much of the discussion around resource depletion has focused on the energy sector. This concern, however, goes well beyond oil and other fossil fuels. Resource depletion is being felt across such areas as mining, fishing, agriculture, and water. The depletion of these supplies is more time-sensitive in some areas than in others. Whereas abundant supplies of some ores may take us well into the centuries to come, total supply levels in other resource areas do not present such leeway. Lithium, for example, may not exist as abundantly as zinc or copper. Mineral depletion could potentially be offset by our capability to make greater use of technology to mine hard-to-reach supplies, or to create synthetic or mineral substitutes. For other categories of resources, however, this is not always the case. Fishing, for example, is an area where very real concern exists relating to the depletion of our global fixed stock supply. Ten to 12% of the world's population depends on fisheries and aquaculture for their livelihoods. Fish account for 17% of all animal protein in the world, and 26% of fish are consumed in the poorest, least-developed nations. The World Economic Forum, in its July 2018 report on Environmental and Natural Resource Security, reported that 29% of commercially important fish stock is overfished, and an additional 61% is being fully fished (see Figure 4.17). The overarching concern lies in the fact that nations continue to heavily subsidize fishing in a way that has encouraged this significant trend toward overexploitation of fishing stock. The World Economic Forum is recommending the removal of these government subsidies, which encourage overfishing and overall excess capacity in this industry as soon as is possible (with an initial target of 2020).[19]

Equally concerning is the impact that overuse is having on water supplies globally (Figure 4.18). The replacement rate of fresh water is declining across our planet. According to a UN environmental outlook, it is estimated that by 2025 as many as 1.8 billion people will be living in areas with absolute water scarcity, and two-thirds of the world's population will be living under water-stress situations where the availability of water to meet domestic, agriculture, industry, energy, and environmental needs will be compromised.[20]

A key problem in this regard is groundwater depletion. Water tables are falling across the globe. An Earth Policy Institute estimate indicates that water tables are down in countries containing more than half the world's population. Groundwater is essential to agriculture (irrigation), industry (hydroelectricity), and domestic use (residential needs). Excessive pumping of groundwater results in the drying up of wells, the lowering of water in lakes, rivers, and streams, the deterioration of water quality, and increased costs as governments, organizations, and businesses strive to gain greater access to this valuable resource. Las Vegas, for example, is being

FIGURE 4.17   **Commercial Fish Stock Concerns**

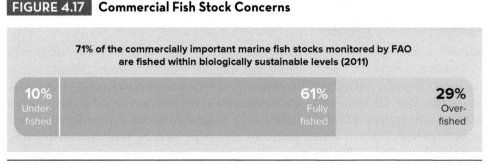

Source: Food and Agriculture Organization of the United Nations, World Economic Forum, July 13, 2018.

FIGURE 4.18   **Global Physical and Economic Water Scarcity**

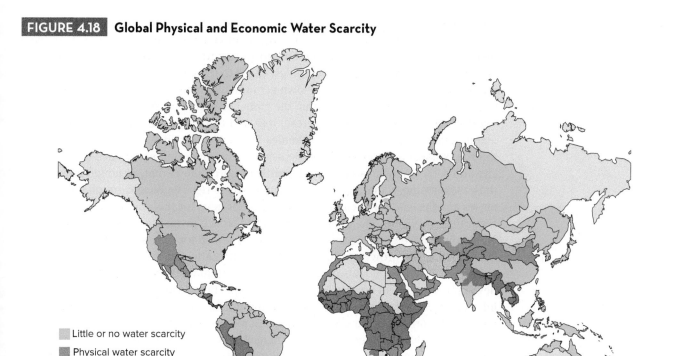

Little or no water scarcity

Physical water scarcity

Approaching physical
water scarcity

Economic water scarcity

Not estimated

Source: United Nations Department of Economics and Social Affairs. "Managing Water Report Under Uncertainty and Risk," The United Nations World Water Development Report, Vol. 1, p. 125.

challenged by a long-term water crunch. The city, whose population has doubled over the past two decades and is projected to continue to grow, is in danger of running out of water. The Lake Mead Reservoir, a major source of water for Las Vegas, Los Angeles, and Phoenix, has recently experienced some of the lowest water levels since it was built. Plagued by recent droughts and an ongoing drain on the existing water supply, the Southern Nevada Water Authority (SNWA) has been seeking to build a 450-km pipeline, as well as supporting infrastructure (pumping stations, power facilities, regulating tanks, etc.), to bring groundwater from areas in eastern Nevada to Las Vegas and vicinity. The cost of this project—which initially planned to sink 195 wells as deep as 500 metres to tap deep-water sources—is estimated at more than $2 billion.[21] Currently tied up in court, given the potential impact this initiative would have on water tables across the state, Las Vegas to date has relied on significant water conservation initiatives to keep its taps running. The SNWA also continues to look at the idea of investing in water desalination plants along the coast of the Pacific Ocean and piping it the approximately 300 miles to Las Vegas to meet the city's increased water demands over the upcoming 50 years.[22]

The Capital Squeeze

Over the past two decades, the global marketplace has benefited from an excess supply of capital at very attractive rates. Developing economies driven largely by export-centric practices supplied the fully developed economies of the world with a vast array of goods and services. With most of their trade focused externally, these economies developed considerable capital reserves. As noted in Chapter 3, the People's Republic of China's currency and gold reserves topped US$3.9 trillion at the close of 2014. These

Sovereign Wealth Funds are country- or state-owned investment funds.

reserves, coupled with the rise of **sovereign wealth funds** within many of these economies and supported by a propensity toward individual savings by their citizens, have resulted in the global marketplace having access to cheap money in volumes never before seen. Fully developed economies, eager to stimulate their own growth, tapped into these dollars to finance their own economic expansion. The end result is that a significant number of nations within the global economy have leveraged their growth via these developing economies' reserves. Add to this the very low rate of savings many of these fully developed economies have experienced among their citizens, and the end result is an overwhelming dependency on emerging economies to meet their capital needs. So, why is this a problem? It is a problem in that, although historically these developing economies have expanded their reserve base through export surpluses and the lending of capital externally, their need for this capital internally is dramatically increasing. The capital needs of the world, given the growth we have seen within these developing economies, will create a need for capital never seen before. A quick look at the growth within Asia, Africa, and Latin America demonstrates the requirement for huge amounts of capital investment that will be needed for infrastructure development such as homes, intermodal transportation systems (ports and highway infrastructure), water systems, hospitals, and public service buildings. Added to this is the need by private domestic and international companies to build factories, plants, and office buildings. According to an analysis compiled by McKinsey & Company via research undertaken by the Economic Intelligence Unit, the global demand for capital, for investment purposes, is expected to top $24 trillion in 2030, assuming that anticipated GDP growth targets are realized. Based on forecasts of GDP growth and anticipated savings rates, this could mean a shortfall of close to $2.5 trillion between what the global marketplace needs and what it can provide.[23] The consequence of this massive capital infusion requirement and the projected capital shortfall will be as follows:

1. Access to capital, particularly by fully developed economies, will become more difficult. This will be due to (a) the low savings rates of their citizens, resulting in little investment capital being generated internally, and (b) the increasing need of developing economies to use their capital reserves for internal, domestic investment, thereby reducing the supply they are able to lend elsewhere.

2. A reduction in savings will most likely occur among citizens in developing economies as their domestic economies grow and as consumption-based practices permeate the lives of their citizens. Simply put, in order to enhance their quality of life, these citizens will save less and spend more obtaining the goods and services that will make their lives easier and more fulfilling. Historically, as economies grow and citizens become wealthier, savings rates decline.

Cost of Capital is the cost of company funds (both debt and equity).

3. The **cost of capital** (interest rates) will increase as the demand for capital for investment purposes exceeds the supply. For governments that financed their current deficits with the low interest rates, their cost of debt will rise as their credit facilities mature and require renewal underwriting.

Financial Protectionism refers to government actions or policies that restrict or restrain the outflow of funds from one economy to another.

4. A form of **financial protectionism** could creep into the global capital marketplace as countries with surpluses seek to keep their capital for internal and external investment in a manner that provides them with a global competitive advantage, offering lower cost of capital to domestic players and higher, risk-laden cost of capital to external borrowers.

The end result of this impending "capital crunch" will be that access to cheap capital will no longer be the large contributor to global growth it has in the past. In fact, the reverse may be true. The inability to gain access to needed funds may result in growth slowing. The scarcity of capital may also increase the gap between countries that have access to capital and those that do not. It also will most likely result in higher taxes and fewer services in those countries forced to pay significantly higher interest rates on existing deficits.[24]

Business IN ACTION

ExxonMobil and Algae Biofuels—Will the Research Effort Yield a Transportation Fuel Option?

In June 2009, ExxonMobil, currently the world's largest publicly traded energy company, announced a $600-million investment in a research and development alliance with Synthetic Genomics Inc. (SGI) for the purpose of developing advanced biofuels from photosynthetic algae. The intent of this investment is to produce a low-net-carbon transportation fuel. With renewable energy alternatives becoming increasingly important, and with the competing demand for agricultural products, such as corn, between the food chain and the production of biofuels, the marketplace is actively seeking viable alternate fuel options.

The Canadian Press/Gene J. Puskar

Although some countries, such as Brazil, have been successful in developing significant scale for agriculture-based ethanol production, most experts now agree that the conversion of corn, sugar cane, and other agricultural-based products to alternate fuels results in three significant benefit offsets: (1) increasing prices to the food products based on the same agricultural source, (2) increasing amounts of land relegated to biofuel-based production, which removes it from producing food to meet global needs (and the corresponding deforestation that may be required to make such land available), and (3) increasing energy required and pollution realized from the ethanol production cycle.

In initiating this research, algae-based fuels, it is hoped, will deliver on the benefits of biofuel while eliminating the offsets noted above. The production of algae-based fuels, for example, does not rely on fresh water or need arable land. The algae-based source for this fuel can be produced using sea water or waste water. Algae are also biodegradable and can be produced with minimal environmental impact. It is hoped that the oils produced by the algae can be processed using existing technologies and refineries and would yield a product that can be used as fuel by our current transportation-sector technologies and infrastructure. Algaculture, as the process of farming algae is called,

is also being assessed with respect to its ability to produce vegetable oil (among other things), in addition to bioethanol, biogasoline, and biodiesel products. Algaculture is also believed to have a positive impact on global warming, as the photosynthetic process used to grow algae (sunlight and carbon dioxide) offers positive green carpet–based greenhouse gas mitigation benefits. Equally important is the output efficiency that algaculture offers. According to ExxonMobil researchers, algae potentially had the promise of yielding 2000 gallons of fuel for each acre of algae production per year. Current biofuel sources, such as corn (250 gallons per acre per year) and sugar cane (450 gallons per acre per year), produce significantly less biofuel annually. It was also believed that algae could be grown more quickly than their land-based alternatives and thereby yield potentially greater efficiencies in the production process.

Now ten years into this project, SGI and ExxonMobil have indicated that they believe they have solved a critical challenge in making biofuel from algae. "By tweaking a particular gene in a certain species of algae, they were able to make the algae produce twice as much fat, but still enable the algae to grow as quickly as usual." Assuming that they can execute on this knowledge, Exxon and its partners believe that they could produce as much as 10 000 barrels of algae biofuel per day.

ExxonMobil is not alone in its research into the viability of algaculture-based techniques for the development of algae-based biofuels. A number

Kyodo/Newscom

of competitors have also been assessing the potential of this market sector. Chevron Corporation, a major competitor to ExxonMobil, for example, has partnered with the U.S. Department of Energy's National Renewable Energy Lab to facilitate the commercialization of algae-based fuels. The actual widespread commercialization of this potentially viable alternate fuel source is still a ways off. If successful, however, it could play a vital role in reducing carbon emissions and in reducing our dependency on fossil fuels for our business and transportation needs.

Web Integration

Want to learn more about algae-based fuels? Visit the National Algae Association's Web site at **www.nationalalgaeassociation.com** or the California Center for Algae Biotechnology at **algae.ucsd.edu**.

LO3, LO4   Business's Response to the Sustainability Challenge

Businesses alone cannot solve the environmental sustainability challenge that currently confronts us. It will take the combined efforts of governments, organizations, businesses, and individuals to define how we can achieve the level of economic development that will result in an improved standard of living for all global citizens while at the same time protecting this planet we call home. What is important, however, is that businesses, and the people who manage them, take a leadership role in tackling this challenge. The approach to this challenge is not an easy one. It will take an integrated process spanning key tactical decision-making areas, framed by strategic inclusion and broad market support. This process will need to be driven by a top-level management approach that analyzes an organization's current practices, sets sustainable development policies and objectives, and designs and executes an implementation plan that is integrated within an organization's overall strategic plan and supported by key metrics capable of measuring and monitoring success. This commitment will be firmly rooted in the organizational culture and endorsed by members of the stakeholder community who recognize the critical need for environmental sustainability as a core component of the organization's DNA (see Figure 4.19). The more we learn about how our practices impact our environment, the more we need to manage it in order to minimize its degradation. The approach being offered, therefore, is not static but dynamic in that adjustments to it can, and should, take place in order to maximize the effectiveness of the organization's response to the challenges previously noted.

Responding to these challenges will require a definitive and dramatic shift in the way we think about business. Success will require us to rethink our attitude toward trade and the cost/price relationships associated with it. It will also require us to rethink our approach to how we utilize our resources (eco-efficiency management) to develop the products and services we offer to the global marketplace. The process cannot, however, simply stop at the development of tactical initiatives. Management, supported by its stakeholder base and the community at large, must redefine the culture and the thought process of the entire business system. This can be

FIGURE 4.19   **Responding to the Sustainability Challenge**

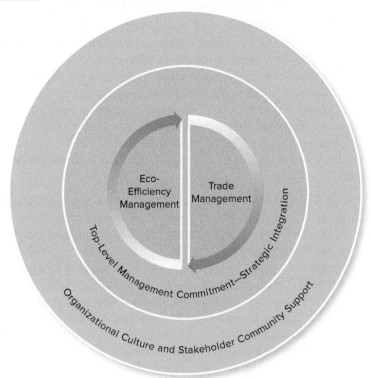

Source: BSD, "Business and Sustainability Development: A Global Guide," 2010 International Institute for Sustainable Development, www.isd.org, April 2011.

accomplished by creating an approach that contributes positively to the global response to the challenges present today, and to the ones that lie ahead in the years to come. With this in mind, the following discussion is a cursory overview of what is required by businesses in order to effectively respond to the sustainability challenge now upon us.

Trade Management

Trade management involves shifting the impact of trade and economic development away from being the primary driver of environmental harm and planet degradation toward being a process that exists in an arena of environmental sustainability. To achieve success, global market participants must be unanimous in their agreement for the transitioning to, and maintenance of, three critical trading practices:

1 Participants in trade and economic development must agree to pay for the social costs of environmental degradation. It cannot be an option or choice, on an ad hoc basis, as to whether one should participate. Loopholes or lax industry standards that permit inefficient outcomes relating to environmental protection need to be identified and corrected. Retailers and manufacturers must demand that supply chain partners adhere to such practices as well.

2 Participants across markets need to support and accept pricing policies that reflect the full cost of expenses incurred in order to achieve environmental sustainability. This would include charges associated with taxes imposed, emissions fees required, and cap and trade mechanisms initiated by various economic sectors. It also recognizes the reality that costs associated with the development and application of new technologies and sustainability processes need to be recovered as part of an organization's pricing strategy.

3 Participants must block the ability of market players to obtain and leverage a competitive advantage as a result of efforts to avoid environmental costs. Global trade participants must develop and adhere to an equal playing field that eliminates practices of non-enforcement or loosening of existing regulations, blockage of the implementation of new, required regulations, and the creation of safe havens for environmental abusers. Recognizing that adherence to environmental sustainability standards and policies currently varies across the globe, the World Trade Organization (WTO) and other such global entities will need to create and manage definitive timetables for compliance.

The movement to a global sustainability model will take time and will be a challenge. This is particularly true when the impact of the costs associated with the transition period needs to be factored in to the prices you and I pay for the products and services we use. The fragility of the global economic recovery, coupled with the significant sovereign debt loads many countries are facing, will add additional hurdles to this initiative. The ability to redefine our trade culture is, however, imperative to the implementation of a successful global sustainability model. Redesigning our trade mentality from that of a consumption model to one that is built around responding to the environmental challenges identified earlier in this chapter is predicated on the ability of businesses to make such investments knowing that costs can be recovered and that, in doing so, such investments do not result in competitive disadvantage.

> Trade management is shifting the impact of trade and economic development away from being the primary driver of environmental harm and planet degradation, to that of a process that exists in an arena of environmental sustainability.

Eco-Efficiency Management

Eco-efficiency Management is the tactical shift required within our business operations to maximize the efficiency of our resource utilization and minimize or eliminate the resulting current degradation to the planet.

Eco-efficiency management refers to the tactical shifts required within business operations to maximize the efficiency of resource utilization and minimize or eliminate the resulting current degradation of the planet that such operations bring. Eco-efficiency management can be thought of as consisting of two broad categories of operational reassessment: resource management and emissions management.

Resource management   For market participants, resource management focuses on shifting away from the old consumption model whereby resources acquired entered into the transformation process with the end result of producing a product and disposing of waste. What was not sold to the market was simply tossed out. Waste disposal was treated as a "bad and unavoidable cost," so efforts to minimize this expenditure led to minimal efforts to protect the environment (see Figure 4.20).

Although a number of organizations globally still view their existence framed around this consumption model, we are seeing significant strides toward replacing this model with what is called the resource management model (see Figure 4.21).

FIGURE 4.20   Consumption Model

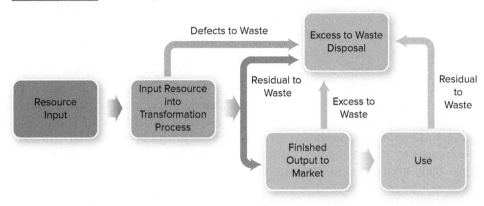

The resource management model has evolved as a result of three fundamental shifts in the thought process associated with waste:

1. The recognition that resources are finite for many market sectors. With increasing global demand, procurement of these resources is resulting in additional "bring to market" costs that are resulting in an upward trend, price-wise, on such commodities and materials.

2. The recognition that resource efficiency, while possibly leading to slightly higher costs in the short run, can lead to lower overall costs in the long run. Investments in 4R initiatives (to reduce, reuse, recycle, and recover) are yielding long-term cost savings to those organizations that effectively undertake 4R programs.

3. Societal pressure. Perhaps one of the most noticeable areas of environmental degradation, the relative strength of a company's waste reduction and waste prevention strategies, is becoming closely linked to company image and brand reputation.

The end result of these three shifts is that more companies are taking a 4R approach to resource management, which has resulted in a more circular approach to the consumption model whereby the emphasis has moved from waste disposal and treatment to that of waste reduction, prevention, and, ideally, total elimination, as shown in Figure 4.21.

FIGURE 4.21   Resource Management Model

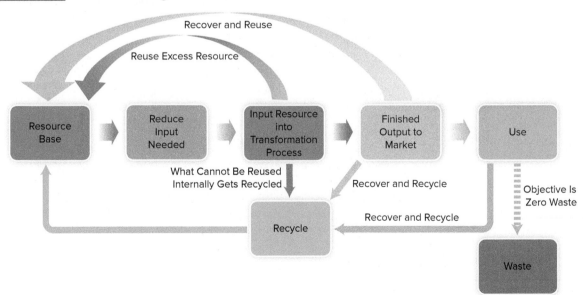

The desired outcome of the resource management model is twofold. The first outcome is to achieve the goal of zero waste, which eliminates further degradation of the environment due to the cessation of landfill-based pollution-creating activities. The reduction of waste not only assists in reducing the direct operational costs of the business involved (waste packaging and removal, etc.), but also generates considerable secondary societal benefits and cost savings in terms of lower waste treatment costs, disposal costs, storage costs, energy costs, and cleanup costs (e.g., brownfields remediation). Where we ultimately want companies to transition toward is what is called Cradle-to-Cradle sustainability management (see Figure 4.22). **Cradle-to-Cradle sustainability management** is the process whereby organizations create production and distribution techniques that are not just more efficient but are truly waste free. In Cradle-to-Cradle processes, all inputs and outputs are viewed as being underlying nutrients, either technical or biological. Technical inputs and outputs (nutrients) need to be created with the full intent of recycle, redesign, or reuse outcomes. Biological inputs and/or outputs (nutrients) need to be created realizing that any component not consumed must be compostable. Cradle-to-Cradle sustainability management means that organizations go beyond taking responsibility for the disposal of goods and services, to that where there are, ultimately, no unused goods or services to dispose of or recycle back into service. Biological nutrients are naturally dissolved and technical nutrients disassembled and redesigned in a manner that results in zero waste.[25] Cradle-to-Cradle processes require organizations to achieve a heightened understanding of the relationship among chemicals, environmental properties, component development, material flows, etc., in a way that optimizes an organization's products and services around not just economic value, but also environmental and societal value.

The second outcome is preservation of resources, which prolongs our ability to tap such resources into the future. This preservation is accomplished through modifications to internal resource and product/service transformation systems via (1) technologies and the use of renewable resource substitutes that reduce the quantity of a finite resource required within the transformation process, and (2) where finite

> **Cradle-to-Cradle Sustainability Management** is the process whereby organizations create production and distribution techniques that are not just more efficient but are truly waste free.

FIGURE 4.22   **Cradle-to-Cradle Sustainability Management**

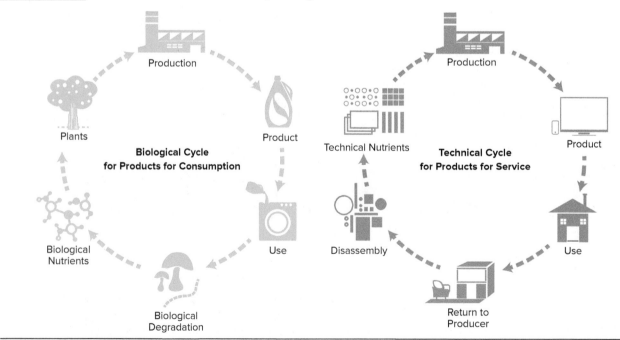

Plants

Production

Product

Biological Cycle for Products for Consumption

Biological Nutrients

Use

Biological Degradation

Technical Nutrients

Production

Product

Technical Cycle for Products for Service

Disassembly

Use

Return to Producer

Sources: wakeup-world.com; Katrin Geist; Cradle 2 Cradle.

resources are required, the development of a strong "reusing" of the excess not fully consumed within the initial transformation process. This is further supported by a strong recycling process that maximizes alternate uses of excess resources and resource by-products that cannot be looped back into the internal resource reuse system. Finished output to the marketplace is also accompanied by strong recovery and recycling systems to maximize the reuse potential of product/service by-products, including the final recovery of such products once their use in the marketplace has ended due to consumption practices or obsolescence.

Resource management also includes improving the durability of products to increase their lifespan, rebuilding or replenishing resources used (e.g., reforestation), reducing the energy consumption used in the associated transformation processes, and reducing or eliminating the use of toxic materials and chemicals within such processes.

> The goal is to create a sustainable resource management model geared toward reducing the material and energy intensity of creating products or services while still being able to produce economically viable products that enhance the lives of global residents.

Business IN ACTION

Canon—Managing Materiality and the Environment

Stakeholder surveys are pointing out more and more the need for organizations to organize their business activities around the global environmental issues challenging us. The reuse and recycling of materials, the reduction of waste, the prevention of water and soil pollution, and the reduction of energy consumption are all impacting the decision-making process within businesses more so than ever before. So too is the increasing regulatory environment within which companies need to operate. Regulatory risk, risks relating to market/technological change, and physical risks associated with extreme weather events (hurricanes, floods, tornadoes, etc.) are all having an impact on the competitiveness and underlying cost structure of organizations operating in today's global environment. So just how should companies respond to such challenges?

Our hope is that many will respond the way that Canon has. Central to Canon's business strategy and core to

© Tracy Leonard

its operational decision making is the belief (kyosei) that it has a responsibility to work in harmony with our environment, and that it has a fundamental obligation to leave a prosperous planet for future generations. Critical to this assessment is a need to understand the characteristics of its own operations and how they impact the environment. In drawing conclusions relating to this, Canon looks to identify concerns and outcomes relating to its use of materials in its products from four

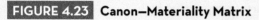

FIGURE 4.23   **Canon—Materiality Matrix**

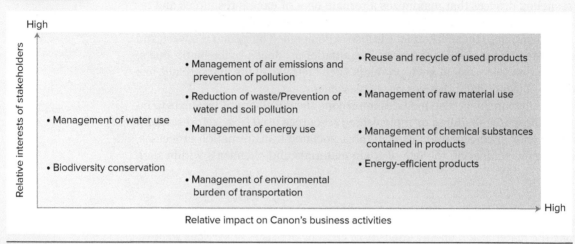

Source: Adapted from Canon Global.

particular views: (1) is Canon contributing to a low-carbon society, (2) is it contributing to a circular society (zero waste), (3) is it eliminating its use of hazardous substances and preventing pollution, and (4) is it contributing to a society in harmony with nature. In drawing conclusions relating to these outcomes, Canon actively assesses its use of materials on the basis of its "Materiality Matrix" (see Figure 4.23). In doing so, Canon poses questions such as: Are we designing products and developing recycling technologies that reduce our dependency on natural resources? Are we assessing our shipping protocols to ensure compliance and minimize the risk of environmental contamination? Are we analyzing new business opportunities against biodiversity conservation benchmarks, and are our operations contributing to the reduction and cessation of pollution and other climate change causative factors?

Canon, as a global entity, has pledged to initiate and participate in the urgent call to combat climate change and its impact. It has also committed its organization and the people who work for it, on behalf of all of its stakeholders, to meet the required actions outlined in the Paris Agreement and the SDGs (sustainable development goals) adopted by the United Nations in 2015. Canon is proud of its long and steadfast focus on protecting and preserving what it believes is our most precious resource: the world we share. As citizens of this planet, we would truly benefit from more organizations embedding in their strategies the values that form the basis of decision making at Canon.

Web Integration

To learn more about green initiatives at Canon Canada, see **www.canon.ca**.

Emissions management   Emissions management is focused on achieving a position of "zero global emissions." The long-term focus should be a global market that produces zero pollution/waste in the air. To accomplish this objective, market participants must do the following:

1. Commit to attacking pollution at the source rather than after it is created. This means looking at the current inputs in an operational process and seeking to develop substitutes for such inputs, or investing in or creating technologies that eliminate such waste prior to it moving into the air. Of critical importance to the achievement of this environmental need is that a timetable for compliance for phasing out hazardous inputs in output processes (i.e., production and manufacturing) is established and adhered to. Where required, education and

training, along with financial support in the form of credits or other economic incentives, grants, and/or loans, should be provided to ensure compliance.

2 Prove, prior to implementation, that the processes being employed in new operations will do no harm to the air.

For such an approach to be effective, market participants must be transparent in their operational approaches, and must fully communicate to workers, consumers, and the global community at large the information relating to their environmental performance. As with our discussion surrounding trade management and resource management, the ability for the global marketplace to transition to a "zero emissions" policy will be a challenge to say the least. For many developing economies, it requires not only access to the latest technologies, but also a considerable educational effort. It also means acceptance of the trade-offs required with respect to rapid economic development versus environmental sustainability.

Strategic Integration

Our opening discussion in this chapter focused on the consumption society that has evolved around our current and historical trade practices. We then discussed the impact that such an approach has created with respect to our environment. Although we have transitioned from unabated consumption to a marketplace partially governed by environmental regulatory and legislative compliance, our global society needs to further evolve well beyond our current position. A number of companies have initiated eco-management tactics for resource management and emissions control. In some cases this has been driven by compliance requirements, whereas in others it has evolved as a result of an understanding of the benefits it brings along with a desire to participate in environmental stewardship activities. Societal pressure, often driven by external groups and concerned citizens, has also resulted in a greater awareness and understanding of the environmental challenge we are now facing. For the global marketplace to be truly successful in responding to this challenge, businesses need to completely integrate environmental responsibility into their business strategies. This means balancing what it takes to be a successful business with doing the right thing for society (see Figure 4.24).

Strategic integration means that businesses need to see environmental sustainability as an integral part of value creation and that this creation includes sustaining and enhancing the resources we depend on well into the future. The problem is not that we are unaware of what needs to be done, but rather lies in how to do it. Environmental sustainability is a highly complex challenge that reaches to an organization's core. Integrating it into the organization's long-term strategic plan requires, in many cases, redesigning the business model. Successful execution in this regard requires experience and expertise in an area where many businesses simply do not possess such skills beyond their compliance requirements. It is this gap between intent and action that is preventing organizations from moving beyond compliance and eco-management tactics to a position of true strategic integration. So, how do we get businesses to strive for full environmental sustainability integration into their business strategies? First, managers need to recognize the long-term benefits such integration can bring; second, they need to develop the capabilities to successfully conduct a critical self-assessment of how such benefits can be realized within their organization.

Strategic integration means that businesses need to see environmental sustainability as an integral part of value creation and that this creation includes sustaining and enhancing the resources we depend on well into the future.

FIGURE 4.24 The Sustainability Balancing Act

Long-term benefits of environmental sustainability strategic integration For many businesses, environmental sustainability is focused on two short-term outcomes:

- Improved corporate image
- Regulatory compliance

Although these are valid outcomes, integration of environmental sustainability practices into an organization's strategy can yield significantly greater long-term benefits that often are overlooked by organizations and their management teams. Some of these include:

1. **Pricing power:** a stronger brand increases an organization's pricing power.

2. **Enhanced efficiencies:** resource intensity reduction techniques lead to greater long-term operating efficiencies and stronger supply chain management. This can lead to higher margins and an overall lower cost base, which can be leveraged into a competitive advantage.

3. **Customer retention:** improved customer loyalty leads to lower customer desertion rates, resulting in greater opportunity to leverage additional revenue from these customers and lower customer transaction costs.

4. **Stronger employee base:** employee engagement via sustainability initiatives can result in greater employee retention, stronger recruitment positioning, and higher levels of employee motivation and productivity.

5. **Strong environmental management:** leads to lower risk exposure, which can result in lower insurance premiums, lower capital costs, and greater access to capital.

6. **New business options:** can lead to new skill development within the organization, which can lead to the creation of new business opportunities and an enhanced ability to enter into new markets.

Capabilities: Critical self-assessment The full immersion of environmental sustainability into the strategic planning process means integrating it throughout our culture, operations, and processes. It also means ensuring the skills necessary for assessing environmental sustainability are embedded within our organization's business acumen. To be successful in such an integrative approach, organizations and their management teams need to recognize where and how their current practices are impacting the environment. Once identified, they need to create a well-organized approach to responding to these issues. Figure 4.25 offers a decision guide to assessing and integrating environmental sustainability into an organization.

Organizations must first understand how environmental sustainability is affecting, or will affect, their businesses. This means developing a clear and succinct understanding of what sustainability is and communicating it across the organization. This initial impact assessment is followed by a comprehensive analysis of the key drivers of environmental impact and degradation and how each of these identified areas will impact the business system and market positioning. A key outcome of this analysis is the identification of the opportunities such drivers offer, the threats that are present, and a conclusion as to the gaps that exist as well as the risks associated with such gaps. A key aspect of this identification process is also the identifying of channel partners, stakeholders, and external agency partnerships that are considered critical to overall success, as well as the identification of key capabilities that are required but currently do not exist within the organization. Once the gap and risk analyses are completed, the organization will then need to build a thorough business plan that defines how a commitment to environmental sustainability can be integrated into its culture, operations, and processes. This will include both near-term and long-term requirements, impact factors, and a thorough understanding of the cost/benefit trade-off such commitments will mean. Evolving out of this business plan will be the development of a timetable and the establishment of targets and performance metrics to guide the plan's execution. Also key to this stage of the process is the identification of internal champions designated to ensure committed resources are effectively allocated in pursuit of the organization's sustainability objectives. Resource commitment means ensuring full integration takes place across both the primary activity areas and the supporting activity areas of the value chain.

FIGURE 4.25   Integrating Environmental Sustainability

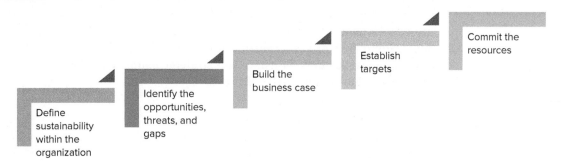

Define sustainability within the organization

Identify the opportunities, threats, and gaps

Build the business case

Establish targets

Commit the resources

Strategic integration of environmental sustainability initiatives, for many companies, means rewiring the organization. In many cases, this will require the organization to seek help and support from external parties. It means working both forward and backward with, and through, channel partners. It means reframing the financial models around which a business has been fundamentally built. It also means committing to a long-term plan that, once started, requires revisiting every organizational process.

What generally is not understood is that, for many companies, significant financial investment often is not required to transition to a more environmentally sustainable organization. For example, in examining its footwear design and manufacturing processes Nike realized in hindsight that for every two pairs of shoes it produced it discarded enough waste to have produced a third pair of shoes.[26] Simply by shifting to a more efficient resource management model, Nike is now looping what used to be waste back into its **productivity cycle**. The creation of this closed-loop system, with the goal of zero waste, has saved the company millions of dollars per year. The positive impact of this change benefits both the environment and the organization's bottom line. As has been demonstrated by Nike, in many cases significant progress can be realized through policy changes alone. The key is to build awareness as to how the current practices and processes an organization undertakes impact environmental degradation. Once this awareness and sensitivity is understood the platform for change materializes, and initiatives responding to such degradation are brought into place.

Productivity Cycle includes the processes involved in transforming materials into a product or service available for sale in the marketplace.

Management Reflection—Sustainability Balancing Act

In the U.S. state of Wyoming, there is a natural hot spring pool called the Morning Glory Pool. For decades, this pool—with its distinctive blue colour—attracted visitors from around the world. Over time, visitors began to view the hot spring pool as a giant, natural wishing well, and tossed in coins as they made their wishes. So, what does this have to do with environmental sustainability? Well, what was once a pool of distinctive blue water is now yellow and green. The coins tossed into the pool have blocked its natural heat vents, thereby reducing its temperature. Also, the chemicals in the coins have reacted with the hot spring water, causing bacteria to grow and creating the yellow ring that dominates the outside perimeter of the pool today. What has happened to the Morning Glory Pool reflects the way we have approached our environment. For a number of centuries, actions taking place "one coin toss at a time" have resulted in the planetary conditions that now challenge us. Environmental degradation is real and material. To think that we, as business managers, do not have a role in addressing such issues can no longer be a position by which we operate our companies. The belief that the primary business objective is to maximize return on equity regardless of environmental consequences needs to be shifted to one that is built around the sustainability balancing act illustrated in Figure 4.24. Managers cannot rationalize that sustainability has no impact on their business. Going forward, successful companies will be those that fully integrate environmental sustainability into their strategic planning process and recognize the long-term value creation that will result.[27]

Chapter Summary

The purpose of this chapter is to expose students to the environmental sustainability challenge that is now impacting governments, organizations, businesses, and individuals as we seek to continue to grow and expand the global marketplace. The chapter opens by framing what is termed the "consumption journey," or how our economic evolution has driven the environment degradation to the level that we now face. This is followed by a discussion of the major environmental sustainability issues that lie before us: climate change, pollution and health, the energy crunch, resource depletion, and the capital squeeze. Commentary is offered as to the current and future challenges the global marketplace will need to respond to in each area as we continue to attempt to create and supply the increasing level of products and services desired worldwide. Recognizing that business, on its own, cannot provide solutions to all of these impact factors, the chapter then transitions into discussing the key requirements businesses need to incorporate into their planning processes if we are to reverse the escalating environmental degradation we now face. These include fundamental changes to the way we perceive trade, the need to initiate effective eco-management initiatives, and the need to ensure that environmental sustainability best practices are fully integrated into our strategic planning process. To be successful, managers must identify and understand how the implementation of environmental sustainability practices can benefit their organizations in the long run, and how to identify the gaps that exist within their organizational culture, operations, and processes. This identification and self-assessment process is highlighted as the chapter closes, thereby providing managers with an understanding of the steps organizations need to transition through in order to succeed in integrating environmental sustainability practices into their strategy.

Developing Business Knowledge and Skills

Key Terms

environmental stewardship *p. 133*

degradation *p. 134*

Paris Agreement *p. 141*

peak model theories *p. 148*

feed-in tariff *p. 150*

resource management *p. 151*

sovereign wealth funds *p. 154*

cost of capital *p. 154*

financial protectionism *p. 154*

eco-efficiency management *p. 158*

Cradle-to-Cradle sustainability
management *p. 160*

productivity cycle *p. 166*

Questions for Discussion

1. Identify the five major environmental sustainability challenges going forward. Which one concerns you the most? Why? Is something missing from this list? If so, what is it? (LO2)

2. What are the key success factors associated with building a reduced carbon-based economy? (LO2)

3. What are the key factors that will influence the availability of energy supplies over the short term? (LO2)

4. Which do you feel is the easier response for businesses to enact with respect to environmental sustainability challenges, trade management adjustments or eco-efficiency adjustments? Why? (LO3)

5. What is the primary difference between the consumption model and the resource management model? (LO4)

6. Identify what you believe are the primary benefits companies can expect as a result of integrating environmental sustainability practices into their overall strategy. (LO4)

7. What do you believe is the greatest barrier to organizations fully integrating environmental sustainability initiatives into their business strategies? (LO4)

Questions for Individual Action

Research the concept of Cradle-to-Cradle sustainability management. What are the core components fundamental to this sustainability approach? Why is it that all companies have not committed to operations built around Cradle-to-Cradle sustainability methodologies? Where does the fault lie? What can we do as consumers and commercial buyers to accelerate the trend toward Cradle-to-Cradle sustainability management methodology adoption? Prepare a presentation outlining your position. Be prepared to present this to your fellow classmates.

Team Exercise

Adopted on Earth Day in 2016 and reaffirmed in 2018, the Paris Agreement is an international agreement linked to the United Nations' sustainability development goals. The agreement looks to get participating countries to commit to binding targets relating to CO_2 emissions and related climate change causation factors in order to ensure that the temperature of our planet does not increase by 2°C when measured against pre–Industrial Revolution temperatures. Ideally, the ceiling, although set at 2°C, carries with it an underlying objective of minimizing such an increase in temperature to no more than 1.5°C. As a team, research the current status of this agreement. Which countries are participating? Which are not? What primary concerns surrounding this agreement have resulted in some countries choosing not to participate or allowing their binding target commitments to fall short of the commitments needed to stem global warming and meet the temperature warming ceiling? Do you believe this agreement will be successful in the long run? What about Canada? Just where do we stand with respect to what needs to be done and what we are doing? Prepare a presentation on this subject and be prepared to present your findings to your fellow classmates.

Case for Discussion

Canada has a problem. So, too, do a number of other countries globally. The problem is what to do with nuclear waste. Although nuclear power facilities have been around for decades, and research on radioactive waste has been assessing the situation for more than 30 years, no one has yet figured out what to do with it. In fact, no country in the world as of this writing has a permanent radioactive waste storage facility (although Sweden and Finland are in the process of creating permanent underground storage repositories). In Canada, for example, radioactive waste up to this point is being stored temporarily at plants and research facilities. The Nuclear Waste Management Organization (NWMO), created by the federal government in 2002, has been tasked to solve this problem. Their solution is to bury what will be an estimated 3.6 to 5.5 million used fuel bundles (depends on number of reactors operating), created by our nuclear reactors, a half-kilometre below the ground in a deep geological repository.[28] The waste will be secured in corrosion-resistant containers, shielded by human-made barriers of clay, and isolated from the environment and groundwater.

This solution is what is believed to be required, as nuclear waste will continue to emit radiation at hazardous levels long after it is buried (estimates peg this at more than one million years). So, who wants this in their backyard? Well, to date, 22 communities in Canada have shown an interest. These communities, interested in the promise of significant permanent employment and construction job-related opportunities, can be found mainly in Ontario and Saskatchewan. A key component of the selection process lies in the geological match between what the NWMO needs to build the required repository and the town's location. Potential matches at the preliminary assessment stage included the towns of Ignace, Ear Falls, and Schreiber, Ontario, and English River, Pinehouse, and Creighton, Saskatchewan. Why this level of interest? Many of these communities are located in isolated areas, and are currently economically depressed and struggling to survive. The lure—jobs and economic revitalization! As noted above, the facility, once built, could provide hundreds of jobs. In addition to the waste management facility, NWMO also intends to build a "Centre of Expertise" on the site for research purposes, and expects to attract

FIGURE 4.26   **NWMO—Nuclear Waste Deep Geological Repository Plan**

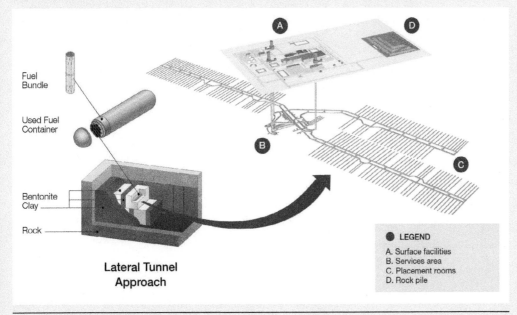

Fuel Bundle

Used Fuel Container

Bentonite Clay

Rock

Lateral Tunnel Approach

LEGEND

A. Surface facilities
B. Services area
C. Placement rooms
D. Rock pile

Source: © NWMO. Used with permission.

experts in the field from all over the world. Leading up to the opening of the facility and the centre is the estimated $24 billion in construction projects needed to support it. Once started (still a few years away), the construction alone is expected to take until 2035. For Ignace, Ontario, the potential economic spinoff was such that the town council at the time (2009) was the first community to communicate its interest to NWMO. That does not mean that everyone in Ignace is on board. People there agree that something needs to be done to save their town, but not everyone is sure this is the right solution.[29]

The views and opinions expressed in this case study do not necessarily reflect the official policy or position of the NWMO. For more information about the NWMO and its project, please visit www.nwmo.ca.

Questions

What do you think? How do you feel about NWMO's solution regarding radioactive waste storage? Is this the right approach to this problem? Anti-nuclear groups believe we should cease considering nuclear energy as a solution to our future energy needs until we have a solution for the waste it generates. What is your position? What about the transportation risk? NWMO estimates that transporting 3.6 million bundles to a permanent underground repository location would require 53 shipments per month, by road, for 30 years. If you were a resident of Ignace, Ontario (or one of the other towns that has indicated interest), how would you feel?

PART 2

CHAPTER 5

Ethics and Corporate Social Responsibility

LEARNING OBJECTIVES

This chapter is designed to provide students with:

LO1	An understanding of the key challenges managers and members of an organization's board of directors face when wrestling with the concept of ethics
LO2	An overview of techniques managers can use when making decisions involving ethical issues
LO3	An understanding of the role of the board of directors in developing the culture of the organization with respect to ethical codes of conduct and behaviour
LO4	An introduction to the growing importance of corporate social responsibility (CSR) in the marketplace and the various levels of CSR involvement
LO5	An understanding of the complexity and challenges associated with integrating CSR and corporate strategy

Snapshot

What to Expect in This Chapter

This chapter focuses on the role of ethics and social responsibility within the managerial decision-making process. The content emphasized in this chapter includes the following:

- Ethics in Management
- What Is Ethics?
  - Ethics and the Individual
  - Ethics and Culture
  - Ethics and Small Business
  - Regulating Ethics
- What Is CSR (Corporate Social Responsibility)?
  - Why Is CSR Becoming So Important?
  - The Interdependency of CSR and Corporate Strategy
  - The Challenge Behind CSR Implementation
- A Note Pertaining to Not-for-Profits
- Management Reflection—It Is All About Trust

 Business IN ACTION

Josephson Institute's 12 Ethical Principles for Business Ethics

Michael Josephson, an influential and internationally recognized leader in the development of character education relating to youth and business ethics, is the driving force behind the creation of the Joseph and Edna Josephson Institute of Ethics. The focus of the institute is to promote and support the education of youth in understanding the importance of professional ethical behaviour and in guiding the creation of sustainable ethical cultures within businesses and organizations. An author of more than a dozen books on this important topic, Michael has assisted corporations, state legislatures, government agencies, and professionals in strengthening their understanding and commitment to ethical decision making.

A firm believer that we, as managers, should conduct business on the basis of what is right or

3D_Creation/Shutterstock.com

wrong, not what is legal or not legal, Michael offers to all of us, in his 12 Ethical Principles for Business Executives, a standard by which to govern our professional careers. These 12 ethical principles are as follows:

1. **Honesty**—Be honest and truthful in all your business dealings. Do not deliberately mislead or deceive others via misrepresentations, omissions, partial truths, or any other means.

2. **Integrity**—Always do what is right, even when pressured to do otherwise.

3. **Promise-Keeping and Trustworthiness**—Be forthcoming in supplying relevant information and expedient in correcting the misinterpretation of facts. Make every effort to fulfill promises and commitments made. Do not interpret agreements strictly from legalistic perspectives simply to avoid compliance or create justifications for one's actions.

4. **Loyalty**—Always behave in a manner that is worthy of trust, and demonstrates fidelity and loyalty. Avoid unscrupulous actions and influences or conflicts of interest. Refrain from discussing or using information learned in confidence and friendship for one's personal advantage.

5. **Fairness**—Be fair and just in all dealings. Do not exercise power arbitrarily. Fairness requires a commitment to justice, the equal treatment of individuals, tolerance for and acceptance of diversity, open-mindedness, and a willingness to admit when one is wrong.

6. **Concern for Others**—Successful managers and executives are caring, compassionate, benevolent, and kind in their interactions with others.

7. **Respect for Others**—Successful professionals demonstrate a consistent respect for human dignity, autonomy, privacy, and the rights of others, regardless of race, creed, national origin, gender, or economic or societal circumstance.

8. **Law Abiding**—Ethical executives abide by the laws, rules, policies, and regulations that govern and relate to their business activities.

9. **Commitment to Excellence**—Successful managers and executives commit to excellence in all duties and interactions.

10. **Leadership**—Ethical managers understand the responsibilities and obligations of their positions, and commit to being positive ethical role models in the pursuit of their objectives. Their conduct reflects these principles.

11. **Reputation and Morale**—Managers and executives understand their obligation and responsibility to protect and enhance the reputation of the companies they work for, and they recognize how this reputation can and does impact the morale of their employees.

12. **Accountability**—Ethical managers take and accept the personal accountability for the decisions they make.

As you complete your education and begin your journey in pursuit of both your business and personal goals, keep in mind that "Character Is What Counts," and be conscious of your actions and committed to behaving in a manner that follows the 12 important points identified above.

Ethics in Management LO1

The positive impact of ethical influences in managerial decision making is only as good as the moral, ethical, and behavioural frameworks that surround it. At its fundamental base, it is knowing right from wrong in the workplace setting and having the appropriate safeguards and ethical guidance mechanisms in place to guide the decision-making process. As the next section of this chapter (What Is Ethics?) focuses on, the determination of just what is right or wrong is not that simple to understand, especially when in some instances it is more lucrative to act unethically versus ethically. What is also typically underestimated, however, in drawing such conclusions about how to act is the impact and effect that unethical decisions make on the broader stakeholder community who interact with us and our company on a day-to-day basis.

As an example, we would all agree that the events of the Enron scandal of 2001—in which three senior-level managers were charged with defrauding their employer (Enron) of over $60 million, along with a variety of associated crimes including securities fraud, wire fraud, and making false and misleading statements—were wrong. The hidden tragedy associated with the Enron scandal is that it is estimated more than 21 000 individuals were harmed as a result of the loss of jobs and the loss of pension savings stemming from the bankruptcy of Enron, and the loss of Arthur Andersen LLP's licence to practise in the United States due to its failure to effectively audit Enron's books.

Ponzi Scheme is a type of investment fraud that involves the payment of purported returns to existing investors from funds contributed by new investors.

In March 2009, Bernie Madoff pleaded guilty to 11 federal felonies including securities fraud, investment adviser fraud, money laundering, theft from an employee benefit plan, falsifying SEC filings, and perjury associated with the **Ponzi scheme** he created while overseeing his investment company, Bernie L. Madoff Investment Securities LLC. Madoff, one of the most active traders in the marketplace, achieved what many described as legendary fame for the double-digit returns his company was able to return to investors. What was hidden for so long was that Madoff was using money from new investors to reward older investors, while at the same time siphoning off significant amounts of money for himself. Equally concerning was the fact that reputable financial institutions, credible hedge funds, and prominent investors were included among the ranks of those swindled by Madoff. Fairfield Greenwich Advisors, an investment management fund, was reported to have had more than 50% of its investment portfolio (an estimated $7.5 billion) with Madoff. Australian bank Bank Medici and Spanish bank Banco Santander both had exposure with Madoff in excess of $2 billion. The Dutch bank Fortis, the Swiss bank Union Bancaire Privée, the British bank HSBC, and the French bank Natixis SA, to name a few, were all investors with Madoff. In total, the reach of Madoff's Ponzi scheme is estimated to include thousands of investors, including not-for-profit organizations and charities, universities, pension plans, prominent Hollywood personalities, and professional sports stars. Some individual investor losses were in the tens to hundreds of millions of dollars. In all, prosecutors estimated that Madoff's fraudulent activities resulted in him scamming investors out of an estimated US$13 billion, making it one of the largest Ponzi schemes ever. On June 29, 2009, Madoff was sentenced to 150 years in prison, the maximum allowed under the law.[1]

On May 30, 2014, Robert Fast, founder of Marathon Leasing Corporation, and his daughter, Danielle Fast-Carlson, were sentenced to prison and ordered to pay restitution exceeding $17 million to investors (more than 200 persons) whom they defrauded in the course of conducting business on behalf of Marathon. In finding the two guilty of the charges brought against them, the Saskatchewan court concluded that both Robert Fast and his daughter misled investors via intentional acts or omissions, offered false statements relating to the financial stability and solvency of Marathon, and intentionally used money from new investors to pay interest payments to other investors. The judge also concluded that although the two were aware that the cash flow of the business was insufficient to keep it afloat while making interest payments to investors, they continued to make such payments, and intentionally embellished the track record of the business to create the perception that it was financially solid and growing. They also continued to accept investment money despite being restricted from doing so by the Saskatchewan Financial Services Commission.

Although these three examples illustrate what many of us conclude is straight-forward unethical behaviour, not all such decisions are that clear-cut. Consider the following examples in illustration of this conclusion.

- Accusations in 2017 that Apple Inc. and Samsung purposely slowed down older phones (which the company claims was in response to decaying battery life) without first warning customers. Lawsuits are now pending that charge the two companies knowingly did this, via software updates, in a bid to encourage consumers to upgrade to newer models. At the time of this writing both Apple and Samsung have been fined by Italy, as an example, for this intended "planned obsolescence."[2]

- CEO of Turing Pharmaceuticals Martin Shkreli's decision to dramatically increase the price of the life-saving pharmaceutical Daraprim from $13.50 per pill to $750 per pill to drive stronger profits immediately after acquiring Daraprim in 2015.

- Bloomingdale's Christmas 2015 holiday ad, which was quickly removed from the media—with an apology from Bloomingdale's—after accusations that it was inappropriate and in poor taste. Search the Web for "Bloomingdale's Christmas Ad 2015" to find more information on this incident.

- Amsterdam-based clothing and fashion company Mexx's 2011 international marketing campaign, which caused a stir with respect to the presentation of the children in one of its advertisements. For some critical perspectives on the controversy, search the Web for Mexx 2011 international children's marketing ad controversy.

Whether it be the faking of quality reports, as has been alleged against Volkswagen and Japanese manufacturers Kobe Steel and Toray, or questionable actions by automobile manufacturers Nissan and Subaru, which allowed unqualified inspectors to assess cars at their final quality assurance checkpoints, to Wells Fargo's admission that it charged as many as 570 000 customers for auto insurance they did not need,[3] managers and executives are constantly being evaluated against their ability to make good ethical business decisions.

Not only are the decisions themselves being evaluated, but the communications and responses to the decisions made are making interaction with the broader stakeholder community even that much more important given the speed and reach of social media. Just ask United Airlines President Oscar Munoz, criticized initially for his company's treatment of passenger David Dao, who was dragged off of a United Airlines plane by two security officers in 2017; Munoz was then further attacked via social media for his communication and handling of the incident internally and externally.[4] As we can see, not all decisions, many of which carry potential ethical implications, are clear-cut. Many fall into what is called the "grey area" of decision making (discussed later in this chapter). What is clear, however, is that how we respond to the challenges of grey area decisions will carry with it a legacy of impact on us, both personally and for the organizations we represent.

What Is Ethics?

LO2, LO3

What causes people to behave like Bernie Madoff and Robert Fast did? What drives a major component of an organization's senior management team to become involved in records falsification and the misrepresentation of results, bribery, and/or corruption-based activities? After all, the cases mentioned above are hardly the only ones we have become witness to over the past few years. In 2009, Canadians

FIGURE 5.1   **Prime Minister Justin Trudeau with Jody Wilson-Raybould**

THE CANADIAN PRESS/Sean Kilpatrick

in Quebec learned how investment money manager Earl Jones misused an estimated $12 million of the funds entrusted to him to pay for his life of luxury, which included the purchase of cars, condos, and private schooling for his children. Those impacted included Jones's own brother and sister-in-law.[5] Canadian Conrad Black, who once headed Hollinger International Inc., was convicted of obstruction of justice in 2007 and, along with three former executives of Hollinger, was convicted of siphoning more than $6 million out of the company. Think of the company names Enron, WorldCom, and Tyco, and some of North America's greatest corporate fraud cases come to mind. These types of situations are not limited to the private sector; both government and the not-for-profit sector have had their challenges. Canada's federal government (e.g., the 2004 sponsorship scandal) and a number of provincial governments (e.g., Quebec's construction industry/labour unions/politics, Nova Scotia's legislature expenses scandal, Ontario's Lottery Corporation expenses scandal, British Columbia's BC Rail sale controversy) have faced questions surrounding their ethical behaviour.[6] Fast forward to 2019, when Prime Minister Justin Trudeau and his Liberal party found themselves facing ethical behaviour charges from opposition parties and the Canadian public at large for their alleged involvement in the SNC-Lavalin Group Inc. affair. The focus of the allegations, around which two members of cabinet resigned, was the implication that government officials were alleged to have pressured then Attorney General Jody Wilson-Raybould to resolve the corruption and fraud case against SNC-Lavalin Group in a manner that spared the company from criminal prosecution. SNC-Lavalin Group was under investigation and facing fraud and corruption charges relating to an estimated $48 million in payments to Libyan government officials between 2001 and 2011.[7]

The breach of ethical obligations is not strictly limited to government and the for-profit sector. The Orion Foundation (closed in May 2010), a charity supposedly in support of fighting AIDS in Africa, is alleged to actually have been operated for the private gain of its founder, who is alleged to have benefited from hundreds of thousands in management fees, trips to Las Vegas and Cuba, and home renovations, with auditors finding little money actually flowing to the intended cause.[8]

So, why are we seeing and hearing about such brash dismissals of what we, in general, define as unethical behaviour? To answer this question we need to assess ethics within an organization at two levels. The first level has to do with the individuals themselves. The second level is the culture of the organization within which individuals work.

Ethics and the Individual

Ethics is a reflection of the moral principles or beliefs about what an individual views as being right or wrong.

In its purest sense, the term **ethics** reflects the moral principles or beliefs about what an individual views as being right or wrong. These beliefs are built in part around the norms or standards of conduct society views as acceptable behavioural practices. In many ways, ethics can be thought of as an invisible hand that guides each of us as we make decisions.[9] Because ethics is so personal, herein lies the problem, or challenge, with respect to assessing the ethical boundaries within which an individual will operate. Individual motivations, cultural and environmental upbringing, personal pressures, and lack of information or ignorance will all influence—positively or negatively—an individual's ethical behaviour. For some, ethics is based solely on legality: if it is legal, it is therefore ethical. For others, it is about fairness: if the situation I find myself in is perceived to be unfair, then I am entitled to any course of action to right the wrong. Misinterpretation of what society values also plays into questions relating to ethics. If society has demonstrated both reward and a blind eye to particular actions, then such actions will become, in the minds of some individuals, acceptable practices. If self-worth is communicated on the basis of what you have, the size of your house, and the type of car you drive, then individuals will become driven to achieve this level of societal acceptance to the point that it changes the type of person we should aspire to be. Rather than being viewed as a values-based decision model, the desired outcome is viewed as an economics-based decision model.

> In many ways, ethics can be thought of as an invisible hand that guides us as we make decisions.

As managers, we are challenged daily with a multitude of decisions, many of which may carry ethical overtones to some degree. Although decisions associated with financial integrity seem to dominate the spotlight, ethical decision challenges can occur across a wide operational spectrum. Is the discovery of mould or exposed asbestos in the workplace followed by the choice to cover it up rather than remove it unethical behaviour? What about biases associated with employees because of gender or ethnic background? How about not hiring a candidate for a position that requires extensive training because she mentioned she is pregnant, thereby resulting in your belief that she will take a full year of maternity leave when her child is born?

The same holds true for our employees. They, too, are challenged daily with decisions relating to ethics. Is an employee who routinely comes in late, takes extended lunch breaks, and then leaves early from work guilty of unethical behaviour? Is calling in sick when you are not ill in order to have an extended weekend unethical behaviour, even though the company provides you with 12 sick days per year? What about asking the gym where you work out to give you a letter that states you have attended at least three times per week for the past year, as this is what is required for your employer to reimburse you for your membership, when in actuality you have been going to the gym this often for only the past month? How about a bartender who gives a "friend" a couple of free drinks one night because they want to impress them, even though the company policy forbids employees to give away drinks?

Taking a poll of your fellow students regarding their responses to the questions asked above might yield some surprising results. Some individuals may view all of the examples provided as unethical behaviour. Others may see unethical actions in only some of the examples. Again, this points to the dilemma of ethics. Each of us has a different interpretation of what is acceptable or non-acceptable behaviour. This interpretation is influenced by our own personal upbringing as well as societal and other external influences. With respect to business decision making in general, the formation of our ethical interpretation—and, therefore, the invisible hand that guides us—comes from four fundamental sources (see Figure 5.2).

These sources are individual, societal, professional, and business culture influences. In making decisions, we need to think in terms not of what is in our personal best interests, but of what is in the best interests of the stakeholders and the public

FIGURE 5.2   **Ethics Wheel**

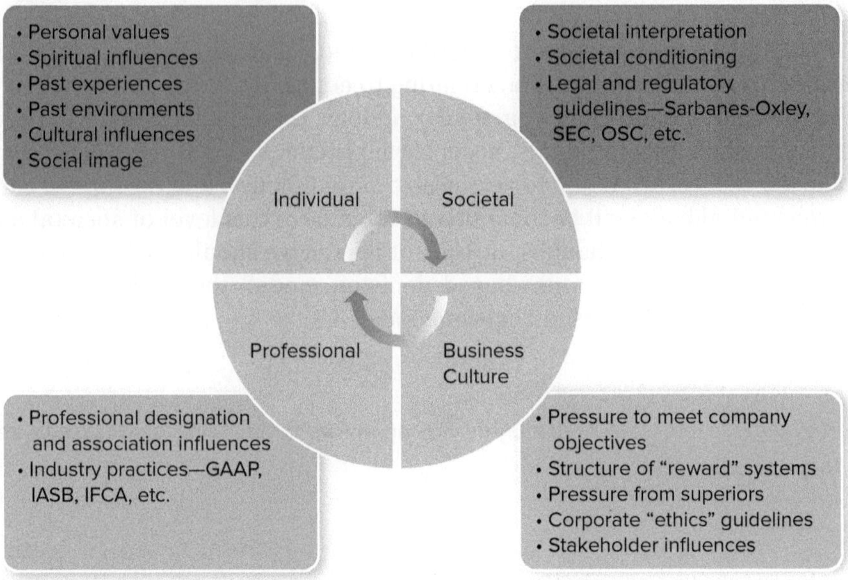

- Personal values
- Spiritual influences
- Past experiences
- Past environments
- Cultural influences
- Social image

- Societal interpretation
- Societal conditioning
- Legal and regulatory guidelines—Sarbanes-Oxley, SEC, OSC, etc.

Individual   Societal

Professional   Business Culture

- Professional designation and association influences
- Industry practices—GAAP, IASB, IFCA, etc.

- Pressure to meet company objectives
- Structure of "reward" systems
- Pressure from superiors
- Corporate "ethics" guidelines
- Stakeholder influences

at large. A key aspect of this process is to recognize where the boundaries lie, which should aid us in framing our decisions. As a CEO, I, like many other managers, was challenged a number of times by decisions that carried with them ethical issues. In weighing the ethical considerations associated with these decisions, I utilized what I term the "triple-yes" rule (see Figure 5.3) to determine whether the ethical issues from the decision were effectively dealt with.

> The triple-yes rule is as follows: In making decisions, we need to think in terms not of what is in our personal best interests, but what is in the best interests of the stakeholders and the public at large.

A key aspect of decision-making is being able to live with your decisions. I have found that using the triple-yes approach causes one to fully assess the ethical ramifications of the decisions made and the preservation of personal integrity, which is so fundamental to the role of a manager, employer, and individual in today's society. A second methodology that I have found of value, and use in conjunction with the

FIGURE 5.3   **The "Triple-Yes" Rule**

- Yes #1—Does the decision that I am making fall within the accepted values or standards that typically apply to all organizational environments?

- Yes #2—Would I be willing to have this decision communicated to all of my organization's stakeholders, and have it reported on the front page of the newspaper or serve as the lead story on a news channel?

- Yes #3—Would the people in my life with whom I have a significant personal relationship (family, spouse, etc.), as well as managers of other organizations, approve of and support my decision?

FIGURE 5.4   **The Ethical Decision-Making Process**

Identify whether an ethical dilemma exists.	In recognizing the dilemma, gather as many facts about the situation as possible.	Evaluate the alternatives available from the perspective of the various ethical positions.	Choose what you believe to be the best alternative, and then "test" it, with a valued adviser, to ensure your correct interpretation.	Initiate your decision and closely monitor the results.

triple-yes rule, is what I refer to as the ethical decision-making process (see Figure 5.4).

This ethical decision-making process is designed to get a manager to slow down and think through all the consequences of a decision they are about to make. With respect to this process, the two key elements are (1) ensuring you have initiated the proper depth of assessment to fully understand the ethical dilemmas and/or consequences that may permeate the decision or exist below its surface, and (2) testing your interpretation of your intended decision with a mentor or key adviser to ensure you are correctly interpreting the situation and that your decision-making frame of reference is complete. This check with a sounding board can—and, in many situations, will—bring forward potential issues you may not have thought of.

The most important skill you can bring to the workplace is your **integrity**. You can be the brightest individual, possessing the best skills and backed by the best training, but if people cannot trust you they will not want to work with you. Business is about team work and being able to execute strategy and make decisions in a team-based environment. This means you have to be reliable, trustworthy, and honest. It also means being willing to take responsibility for mistakes you have made. Ethical behaviour, and the decisions associated with it, means being able to look in the mirror each day and know that you are defined by your actions and have the courage to do what is right for the people who work with you and support you.

Integrity is honesty, reliability, ethics, moral judgment.

The most important skill you can bring to the workplace is your integrity.

 Business IN ACTION

Working Canadians and the Pressure of Ethical Standards

In 2013, a survey conducted by Ipsos-Reid offered an interesting insight into the relationship between workplace pressures and the adherence to ethical standards. The survey polled over 1000 individuals in both private- and public-sector Canadian organizations. According to this survey, more than four out of ten Canadians had witnessed ethical compromises or wrongdoing at work. This included clear examples of breaches of ethical conduct, such as bribery, fraud, and tampering with financial results, as well as "conflict of interest" ethical compromises such as insider trading and misrepresentation of financial statements. Also cited in the survey were ethical violations relating to stealing, falsifying of time sheets and/or expense reimbursement reports, fraudulent employee benefit reimbursement submissions, and misuse of company property for personal gain and/or benefit. Of equal concern was that in witnessing the above-mentioned actions by other employees, almost 50% of these actions were not reported to the companies that these witnesses worked for.

Canadians are not alone in their observance of and feelings of pressure relating to ethical standards in the workplace. According to the Ethics and Compliance Initiative (ECI) 2018 report, employees in more than 16 countries felt pressured to bend the rules or compromise their ethical standards in order to safeguard their jobs. Equally concerning, most workers indicated that in many cases they would not report ethical violations observed. This was in large part due to the belief that most felt such reporting would not remain confidential (74%), or the reporting would not do any good (69%), and many felt they would be branded a "snitch" if they reported such activities (63%).

As managers, these results have to be alarming. More importantly, they are a signal to us that something is missing in the underlying fabric of the organization's culture with respect to ethical guidance. A key conclusion was that many employees felt reluctant to come forward with accusations of wrongdoing due to their lack of faith the claims would be properly investigated and with adequate "whistleblower" protection for them. The Canadian survey found, as an example, that only a little over 30% of employees felt these accusations would be properly investigated and that disciplinary action would be applied. Another issue was the perception that in applying disciplinary action sanctions may not be applied consistently, and policies may not exist to protect informers from retaliation from impacted employees.

The failure to offer guidance, support, and protection is not the only concerning result stemming from the surveys. The Canadian survey (again, as an example) also found that one in three individuals surveyed felt that delivering results was more important than doing the right thing, and roughly 25% of those surveyed were willing to compromise their personal ethics if it was required to keep their job. Such results clearly point to the need for managers, boards of directors, and society as a whole to create a culture of support for their employees, and to communicate clearly the long-term impact that ethical compromise can have on the organization's reputation, its financial results, and the personal reputation of those involved. Strong corporate cultures, focused on risk management and clearly communicated ethical guidelines and expectations, are required to ensure the actions and consequences reflected in the survey and attitudes illustrated above do not occur within the organizations we manage.

Ethics and Culture

Much of this textbook has focused on the need for businesses to build efficient structures and processes in order to succeed. Chapter 8 comments on the need to create a positive work culture where employees are motivated and create high-performance teams to define and execute strategy and tactics in a way that results in a sustainable competitive advantage over their competitors. The responsibility for cultural development does not end, however, with motivation and employee performance. An additional critical component of an organization's culture is the defining of the boundaries of acceptable behaviour for its management team and employees. Just as companies are vulnerable to shifts in market conditions, changes in the intensity of competitive rivalry, disruptive technologies, and changing customer behaviour, so too are they vulnerable to the serious consequences and brand equity erosion that accompanies unethical behaviour within their management and employee ranks. For many organizations, the responsibility for developing policies relating to values, ethics, and financial integrity lies with the organization's **board of directors**. Yes, management needs to execute the policy, but first the board of directors needs to define the parameters of what is meant by ethics and integrity and develop the necessary structure and processes that will enable it to gauge the conscience of the organization. Where a board of directors does not formally exist, advisory boards, equity partners, and individual owners need to ensure the parameters that define ethical behaviour and business integrity are in place and are fully communicated to all employees.

> Just as companies are vulnerable to shifts in market conditions, changes in the intensity of competitive rivalry, disruptive technologies, and changing customers, so, too, are they vulnerable to the serious consequences and brand equity erosion that accompanies unethical behaviour within their management and employee ranks.

Board of Directors is the term for the governing body of a corporation, comprising individuals chosen or elected to oversee the management of the organization; an appointed or elected body of a for-profit or not-for-profit corporation that oversees and advises management on issues challenging the organization on behalf of its stakeholders and shareholders.

In forming a culture of ethical behaviour and financial integrity, boards of directors are, in essence, trying to establish the accepted zone of business actions and activities for an organization. The establishment of this structure within the culture keeps an organization's decision-making process and its activities within what is considered to be the "green zone" of accepted business principles around which a company is to operate. The green zone acts as a barrier to keep managers and individuals from straying into the zone of ethical and decision-making uncertainty (the grey zone), or the zone of clearly defined unethical behaviour (the red zone) (see Figure 5.5).

Building this behaviour-containment process begins with the establishment of the mission and core values of the organization and flows through its goals and objectives and right into its business decision-making framework design process. The process, however, does not end here. To truly create a culture of ethical behaviour and financial decision integrity, the board of directors (or owner-representative body) must be active in the ongoing monitoring of the organization and take a leadership role in the tightening of such processes when and where it is required. For example, if a board of directors is expecting its CEO regularly to justify his/her actions and the organization's performance, then this periodic assessment needs to include not only financial and business result benchmarking but also financial integrity and ethical behaviour

FIGURE 5.5   **Zones of Decision Making**

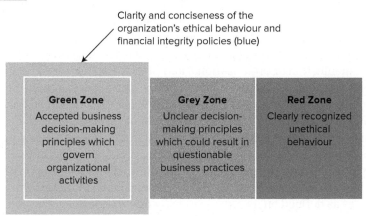

Clarity and conciseness of the organization's ethical behaviour and financial integrity policies (blue)

Green Zone	Grey Zone	Red Zone
Accepted business decision-making principles which govern organizational activities	Unclear decision-making principles which could result in questionable business practices	Clearly recognized unethical behaviour

benchmarking. For boards to effectively create a culture of ethical behaviour and financial integrity, they must commit to the following specific actions:

1 The board must clearly define and establish boundaries of acceptable behaviour and financial integrity, and create performance standards to evaluate adherence to these parameters.

2 These boundaries must be clearly understood and communicated to all employees in the form of a policy or code of conduct. This code of conduct is not limited to financial integrity, but should clearly identify boundaries associated with ethical behaviour, both internal and external, and the consequences for failure to adhere to such a policy or code of conduct. A key requirement at this level is that senior management fully buy into the development process and the integration of the code of conduct into the organization's policies, protocols, and overall culture.

3 The board of directors must appoint a representative (individual or committee), at the board level, whose responsibility is to audit managerial and employee performance and action in critical areas of this policy or code of conduct. This representative or committee would also be a key participant in reviewing compensation packages and other personnel-related policies to ensure these are not designed in a way that would encourage unethical behaviour.

4 The board of directors must create and support a mechanism for the reporting of ethical concerns within the organization (called **whistleblowing**), with such a process designed in a way that ensures employees who utilize such a process are not penalized or ostracized.

5 The board of directors or its representative must interact with senior management and external agencies monitoring the organization's activities in order to discuss issues that could arise with respect to management or employees, and represent the best interests of the organization and its shareholders with respect to questions of ethical behaviour or financial integrity.[10]

> To truly create a culture of ethical behaviour and financial decision integrity, the board of directors (or owner-representative body) must be active in the ongoing monitoring of the organization and take a leadership role in the tightening of such processes when and where it is required.

The key takeaway from the list above is that the board of directors, as representatives of the stakeholders of an organization, must see itself as the creator and sentinel of the organization's conscience. To ensure this occurs, boards must take a lead role in the development of management compensation policies, the shaping of an organization's personnel policy, the review of senior management's performance, and the communication of organizational activities to stakeholders. Board members should never be caught blindsided by events such as what occurred at Enron, or are currently challenging SNC-Lavalin. By actively developing an ethical behaviour and financial integrity policy and process, the board of directors and its members can define what is acceptable behaviour for the organization's employees and develop the parameters necessary to keep behaviour clearly in the green zone. Should such behaviour move beyond the green zone, the board, via its auditing process, should be able to react to such unethical practices quickly and in accordance to established consequences as defined by its organizational **code of conduct**. The board of directors and the organization's senior management team should also set the expectation

Whistleblowing is the process through which an individual informs someone in authority of a dishonest act or the dishonest behaviour of another person.

Code of Conduct is the name for a statement that describes the required responsibilities, actions, and rules of behaviour of an organization's employees.

and look for full compliance to the organization's code of conduct by supply chain and channel distribution partners. The shared risk and liability exposure that supply chain and distribution partners (as well as all related or interdependent business organizations) have with an organization cannot be overemphasized given the vast global reach of outsourcing and offshoring, which are now embedded into many organizations and their operations.

> The board of directors, as representatives of the stakeholders of an organization, must see itself as the creator and sentinel of the organization's conscience.

The Bombardier Code of Ethics and Business Conduct, a comprehensive guide to addressing ethical behaviour and financial integrity requirements at Bombardier, is an excellent example. It explains employee obligations with respect to the working environment, business practices and relationships, and interaction with external stakeholders. Bombardier provides this Code of Ethics and Business Conduct in 14 different languages. Information on how to access the code is provided at the end of this chapter.

Ethics and Small Business

Up to this point, our discussion has largely focused on how larger organizations can respond to the ethical challenges faced by managers and members of boards of directors. Like these larger organizations, small businesses are challenged daily by ethical dilemmas relating to both individual employee behaviour as well as company-wide interactions with the broader stakeholder community. Unlike larger organizations, which have full-time HR departments and, in many cases, full-time employees dedicated to ethics monitoring and training, small businesses generally do not have the financial resources, knowledge and competencies, and supervisory depth to effectively manage the variety of ethical dilemmas that could challenge both the organization and its employees. At the same time, the same risk and repercussions can impact the small business that impacts larger organizations. Customer loyalty, company reputation, financial relationships (debt and equity-based), credibility with channel partners, and financial loss due to theft and pilferage are all impacted by the unethical actions of small business owners and their employees. So, how can small businesses create and sustain an underlying business model that is built around a strong ethical foundation? The following recommendations, outlined by Donovan A. McFarlane in "The Importance of Business Ethics to Small Ventures," are offered to assist small business owners with developing or improving ethical practices within their business, and establishing guidelines/policies for creating an ethical decision-making culture.[11]

- Always conduct business in good faith and make the development of long-term goodwill between you and your stakeholders fundamental to your philosophy of doing business.
- Create a professional code of ethics for your business and actively communicate this to your employees.
- Emphasize to employees the importance of ethical values as core to the actions that are undertaken in pursuit of customer growth and retention, and overall business profitability.
- Encourage and reward moral courage on the part of owners and employees, even in situations where such actions cost the organization business and/or profitability.

- Develop a mission statement and strong strategic vision for the organization (discussed more fully in Chapter 6) that is built on a foundation of business ethics and moral conduct.

- When developing, reengineering, or innovating new products, ensure that ethics and social responsibility are part of the decision-making process in order to guarantee that society's best interests and safety are placed first.

- Realize that social and ethical responsibility, in the long run, define who you are and what your business is truly all about.

Business IN ACTION

The Concept of Fraud

Fraud, by its definition, is a deliberate, dishonest action, on the part of any individual, in order to drive gain or advantage. To be considered fraudulent, an action must generally demonstrate five key characteristics. These characteristics are as follows:

- A false statement of material fact must be given.

- The deliverer must possess the knowledge that the statement is untrue.

- The deliverer must communicate the knowledge with the intent to deceive the recipient (victim).

- The recipient (victim) must rely on the information communicated to engage in an action.

- The recipient (victim) incurs definable damages as a result of the action.

In business, fraud is one of the most serious breaches of ethical standards that can be committed by employees within an organization. As managers, it is important to recognize that the ability to commit fraud can, in many cases, be traced back to the underlying fabric of the culture we have allowed to evolve within our organization. In order for a fraudulent environment or culture to grow and exist within an organization, three underlying features must exist. These are opportunity, motive, and attitude/rationalization (see Figure 5.6).

Opportunity refers to the belief, by an employee, that they can initiate and/or perpetuate a fraudulent act and get away with it. Motive is a reason, incentive, or pressure for a person to commit fraud. Attitude/rationalization refers to the fact that some individuals may be predisposed to committing fraud and/or find it easier to rationalize the reasoning behind such conduct. For

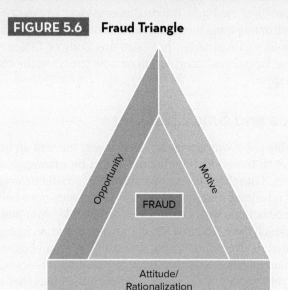

FIGURE 5.6   **Fraud Triangle**

many of us, the conclusion we often reach is that fraud is largely the result of an underlying greed or desire for financial gain. While this is true in a number of situations, the underlying reasons for fraud are more complex. Fraud can also be driven by social incentives and pressure, as well as by a malevolent work environment. Referring back to a previous Business in Action, "Working Canadians and the Pressure of Ethical Standards," we see that the need to meet company results and/or objectives can, in some cases, inspire or trigger fraudulent activity on the part of individual employees. So, too, can the quest for status, recognition, or promotion. Malevolent work environments where checks and balances are absent; disenchantment for an organization; and/or heightened levels of disgruntled employees also trigger fraudulent action. In the fraud triangle, opportunity—the belief that an individual can get away with fraud—is fundamental to the decision to commit a fraudulent act.

With respect to the characteristic of attitude/rationalization, those who commit fraud often possess or create an underlying rationale for their actions. In some situations, individuals who have committed fraudulent acts will actually transfer the blame of their actions onto others, including the organization. For others, a common rationalization lies in a perceived belief of ignorance. They will often state that they did not realize the actions committed constituted fraud, or that they were actually hurting others as a result of their actions. Still others will focus on moral justification, a perception of entitlement, or a temporary lapse of judgment.

So, what heightens the probability that fraud could occur within an organization (or a department or division within an organization)? Pamela Murphy, Associate Professor and E. Marie Shantz Fellow in Accounting within the Queen's University School of Business, along with her colleagues, has conducted significant research in the area of understanding fraud. Based on her research, Murphy has concluded that the following characteristics are inherent contributors toward creating an environment of fraud:

- An environment where people protect their own interest above all other considerations. In other words, people are out for themselves.

- An environment where people are expected to do whatever it takes to further the organization's interests, and these interests are to the exclusion of all other interests.

- An environment which communicates to its people that there is no room for their own personal morals or ethics, and work is only considered to be substandard when it hurts the organization's interests.

So, how do we prevent fraud from occurring? A key component of fraud management is the development of internal reporting and assessment controls. These by themselves are not the total solution, however, as cases have shown that individuals, particularly in collusion with others, can override such controls, or simply choose to ignore them. Above and beyond this, organizations need to heighten the discussion, via fraud training, to enable managers to better understand the underlying factors impacting the fraud triangle (Figure 5.6), particularly in the areas of social motive and rationalization. Managers also need to think through the underlying message the organization is sending to its employees with respect to achieving company objectives and related financial performance. In addition, managers need to ensure that adequate cross-functional interaction is occurring across organizations in order to minimize the underlying potential for collusion to permeate within the organization. Finally, managers need to recognize the importance of ensuring that when such breaches occur, guilty employees are properly disciplined and that employees involved in the investigation are fully protected from retaliation.

Regulating Ethics

Recognizing the concerns associated with defining ethics and the challenges organizations face in regulating the behaviour of their employees and management teams, governments and agencies worldwide have created regulations that define how organizations should comply with financial integrity obligations and ethical decision making and behaviour. The criminal acts associated with organizations such as Enron, Tyco, and WorldCom in the United States led to the passing of the Sarbanes-Oxley Act of 2002 (SOX). In Canada, the equivalent to SOX grew, initially, out of a provincial government of Ontario budget measures act titled Bill 198 (in Canada, securities regulation is handled at the provincial level versus the national level, as is the case in the United States). This was further supplemented by multilateral instruments (regulations) titled 52-108, 52-109, and 52-100, all of which now form the basis of our various provincial securities commission responses to questions of financial integrity and ethical behaviour. These acts, and the accompanying multilateral instruments, focus on protecting the interests of investors and all stakeholders by heightening the financial operational requirements of organizations around such areas as auditor independence, audit committee responsibilities, CEO and CFO accountability for financial reporting and internal controls, faster public disclosure, and stiffer penalties for illegal activities. Similar acts, many that are referred to as Sarbanes-Oxley equivalents, have been adopted in countries globally. Japan's Sarbanes-Oxley Act equivalent is referred to as J-SOX; in Australia, the Sarbanes-Oxley equivalent is referred to as CLERP 9 (Corporate Law Economic Reform Program Act).[12]

The financial crisis of 2008 carried with it a whole new need for financial integrity reform. Whereas the response by governments to business misrepresentation and fraud rests fundamentally in Sarbanes-Oxley (and equivalents), the financial crisis demonstrated heightened concern about the relationship between ethics and risk management. Concerns over the degree of financial leverage that had permeated the marketplace, along with an absence of necessary levels of liquid asset management required to protect against such exposure, is one of many of the market challenges this crisis brought, and around which governments are now seeking to place boundaries. Both international and national organizations—such as the International Accounting Standards Board and the Financial Accounting Standards Board—have called for heightened reporting standardization and regulation to ensure such a situation does not repeat itself. The G20 has agreed, in principle, to the development of high-quality global accounting standards, and initiatives are now underway to make this a reality. A key outcome of all these initiatives will be the development of a single set of global reporting standards that utilize consistent reporting methodologies, provide accurate, unbiased information, and offer full risk disclosure, regardless of the location of the business, organization, or financial institution.[13]

Forensic Accounting is the integration of accounting, auditing, and investigative skills.

Forensic accounting In addition to the heightened regulatory responses to issues pertaining to ethical behaviour and financial integrity, the field of **forensic accounting** has grown significantly over the last decade. Forensic accounting is the integration of accounting, auditing, and investigative skills. Forensic accountants are specialists in looking beyond the numbers in order to interpret what exactly is transpiring within an organization. Forensic accounting audits and investigations are critical to determining the potential extent of damage an organization may have incurred due to unethical employee behaviour or financial integrity issues. They are also key to providing assistance at trial, and during pretrial discovery periods, in order to provide a professional and credible opinion on the cause and effect of actions taken by individuals, or to settle disputes relating to valuation, economic damage, breach of contract, fraud, and personal injury, to name a few.

 Business IN ACTION

The Ethisphere® Institute World's Most Ethical Companies®

Since 2007, Ethisphere Institute, a global leader in the identification and advancement of ethical business standards, has identified what it believes are the world's most ethical companies. For Ethisphere, the companies recognized truly go beyond making statements about doing business ethically, exhibiting business ethics daily in their actions. The companies that make the list not only have implemented and adhered to ethical business standards as a part of doing business, but also are recognized as having exceeded legal compliance minimums and have assisted in developing their respective sectors' best practices. As identified by Ethisphere, these are companies that force other companies to follow their leadership or fall behind. They also are companies that recognize the importance of ethical leadership as a silent but critical component of their overall business model and its underlying profit drivers. In 2019, after a rigorous assessment process, 128 companies made the list, representing 50 industries and 21 countries. Among these 128 companies three Canadian companies were recognized for their outstanding ethical conduct: Bank of Montreal (BMO) (banking); Capital Power (energy and utilities); and Covenant Health (non-profit health care provider). Both BMO and Covenant Health are past recipients of the honour, while Capital Power is a new addition to the list.

So, what does it take to become one of the world's most ethical companies? Ethisphere Institute assesses each nominated company against what it has coined an Ethics Quotient®. The framework behind the quotient consists of five categories. These five categories, and the overall weighting assigned to each, are shown in Figure 5.7.

The review process undertaken by Ethisphere is a thorough one. In addition to a complex set of formulas for arriving at its conclusions, the review process

ETHISPHERE®
GOOD. SMART. BUSINESS. PROFIT.®
Used by permission of The Ethisphere Institute

also includes a number of verification steps, and can be followed with requests for additional documentation, independent research, and/or interviews with company leadership. Covenant Health, as an example, has been recognized for the fourth consecutive year, excelling across the board in its commitment to ethical governance, corporate social responsibility, stewardship of human and financial resources, legal and risk management, and cultural diversity. BMO, a recipient for the third year in a row, looks to deliver more than just financial returns to its investors. The company looks to demonstrate a rigorous commitment to delivering a positive collective impact to all stakeholders, and seeks to demonstrate principled behaviour guided by a strong set of ethical values and conduct.

For BMO, Covenant Health, and Capital Power, placement on the list signals to their stakeholders—and particularly their customers—that these organizations conduct themselves at the highest level of ethical standards, and that their day-to-day actions are reflective of a culture predicated on trust and developing best practice approaches in all their interactions.

FIGURE 5.7   Ethisphere Decision Criteria

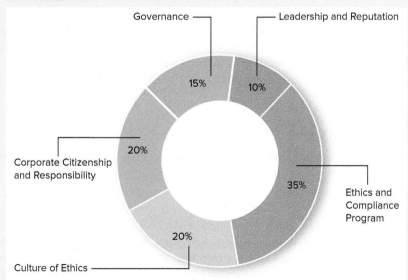

Source: Used by permission of The Ethisphere Institute.

LO4, LO5

What Is CSR (Corporate Social Responsibility)?

So, just what is the moral purpose of business? Is it simply to earn profits? Is it limited to providing jobs, buying and selling products and services, and making capital investments that will return a positive ROI (return on investment) to its investors and shareholders? One would like to believe that the responsibilities of business extend beyond this limited moral purpose and strive to create a broader and healthier relationship with society. One reason why corporate social responsibility, as a buzzword, generates such debate in companies, boardrooms, and across society is that, like the definition of ethics, its meaning, and the interpretation of that meaning, is different for almost everyone. For some, it is about not doing anything illegal or dishonourable, or simply supporting a personal or "pet" public project with which a business owner or management team has some connection. For others, it is interpreted as being "philanthropic," in the form of donations to causes that are viewed to be of value to society. A third interpretation might simply be the restoration of environmental degradation that is determined to be a consequence of the operations and actions of an organization, thereby protecting the brand and the image of the organization. One thing is certain, however. The old belief that if an action is profitable then it automatically serves the public's best interest no longer applies. To understand the concept of corporate social responsibility, businesses and organizations must first recognize that business and society are interconnected and interdependent. The relationship between the two is not "win or lose," but rather needs to be based upon the fundamental realization that decisions being made within the business organization need to result in profitability, but also need to be in the best interests of society. This is, in essence, what **corporate social responsibility (CSR)** is all about. It is the understanding that the purpose of an organization is to create shared value (business and society) by strategically integrating into its actions a partnership mentality with society where the objectives of both parties are met. It means treating the public interest as a key stakeholder in an organization's operational success, thereby resulting in an attitude shift from "winning for me," or "looking out only for me," to one of participating in activities that enable the organization to win while serving the public good. Making decisions in this broader context is the key to moving the organization beyond the development of a strong corporate reputation and image, which may or may not add value to society, to that of an organization whose core premise is built on creating shareholder value by actively partnering in environmental, social, and public policy programs and initiatives that contribute to the long-term health of society.

Corporate Social Responsibility (CSR) is the understanding that the purpose of an organization is to create shared value (business and society) by strategically integrating into its actions a partnership mentality with society where the objectives of both parties are met.

Why Is CSR Becoming So Important?

Recognizing this underlying uncertainty by many with respect to what CSR is all about, why is it then becoming so fundamentally important in the minds of so many executives and members of their boards of directors? The answer lies in the recognition that consumers, in general, are going beyond asking what companies stand for. They are looking for companies to become a force for change across society through their actions and business activities. What has historically been a relatively slow but definitive evolutionary trend on the part of consumers worldwide to demand that companies stand for more than just profits to benefit their shareholders is now an accelerating expectation for companies and their decision makers to advance the progress of the world, particularly in terms of social justice and climate care.

Demonstrating an example of this, a 2017 survey by Cone Communications pointed toward the following trends in the United States business arena:[14]

1. Consumers are increasingly becoming concerned about important social and environmental issues and are looking for companies to become leading advocates in ethical and value-based responses to them. 79% of those surveyed expect businesses to improve their CSR efforts, and 63% are looking for business to drive social and environmental change going forward.

2. CSR continues to be a decision differentiator on the part of many consumers. Data collected over the last 25 years conclude that consumers want to support companies whose values align with theirs and are increasingly willing to purchase products tied to social causes and benefits. In fact, 76% of those surveyed indicated that they would refuse to purchase a product if they found that the company supported beliefs contrary to theirs.

3. Being a good employer is one of the most important characteristics of a responsible company. This means employers are expected to take care of the people who work for them, but also operate in a way that protects the environment and benefits society.

4. Consumers also want companies to take a stand and address issues that are active in today's society. These include issues such as domestic job growth, racial equality, women's rights, cost of education, immigration, climate change, gun control, and LGBTQ rights.

5. Millennials are the demographic placing the greatest emphasis on CSR, seeking out responsible products where possible, holding companies accountable for their actions, and researching company business practices as part of the purchase decision process. 80% of respondents indicated that they believe businesses have an obligation to help people and to take action to improve societies performance on the issues identified in #4 above.

As the Cone Communication study demonstrates, giving back to society; helping others; operating ethically, honestly, and lawfully; being environmentally responsible; offering quality products and services at fair prices; and caring about the impact of their products both globally and the way they are used by their customers are considered to be fundamental to the CSR definition. Being environmentally responsible and treating employees fairly were identified as well as key performance measures in terms of what companies need to do to be viewed as more socially responsible. Creating energy-efficient and environmentally sensitive products, providing appropriate levels of pay and benefits for employees, demonstrating equality and equity in hiring practices, caring about the public's well-being, and helping people in need ranked high on the consumer importance list.

The results depicted in the Cone Communications survey appear to reaffirm similar research conducted by Bonini, McKillop, and Mendonca and published in *The McKinsey Quarterly* in 2007.[15] In a research brief titled "What Consumers Expect from Companies," Bonini, McKillop, and Mendonca identified a number of important areas where consumers felt that companies were doing an unsatisfactory job. The identified areas included transparency about business practices, transparency relating to product and service risks, the development of socially and environmentally responsible products and services, and fair pricing and appropriate accessibility levels of products and services. Consumers also felt that companies performed inadequately with respect to issues associated with political influence, acceptable profit levels, and compensation plans relating to senior management. It should be noted that not all industries or market sectors studied exhibited the same level of concern relating to the perceptions associated with areas of performance identified above. Some market sectors, such as the petroleum industry, exhibited heightened concern in the areas of pricing and environmental impact, while other areas, such as retail, focused their concerns more toward energy consumption, packaging, employee pay and benefits, and the impact of large retailers on local competitors within their communities. For pharmaceutical companies, consumers identified the need for greater equality of health care between fully developed and developing countries as a key concern.

Although the field of CSR is still evolving, the implications of the work done to date are leading managers and boards of directors to three key conclusions relating to the development and execution of business strategy:

1 Consumers are paying attention to companies and their positioning with respect to CSR. Companies perceived as being CSR conscious are finding true opportunities for differentiation, while companies that are lagging in the development and execution of CSR initiatives are being increasingly challenged by individual consumers and activist groups.

2 A true key to creating a positive CSR bond with consumers is by demonstrating, through the products and services being offered, the social benefit of the organization's offerings. This can and increasingly will make the difference in the minds of consumers at the time of the purchase decision.

3 Communication strategies are the critical link between consumers and organizations. To be effective in leveraging the CSR initiatives undertaken, organizations need to communicate to their stakeholders how they respect and give back to the communities within which they operate, and how they holistically manage the environment and resource base that they use in the design, development, and delivery of products and services.[16]

The result of the two works identified above, as well as others in this field, point toward the same conclusion: companies that do a better job of understanding consumer perceptions and expectations relating to CSR, and that utilize this knowledge in the delivery and support of their product/service value propositions, ultimately will be more successful in winning the public's trust.

Business IN ACTION

Canada's Best Corporate Citizens, 2017

On June 6, 2017, Corporate Knights and its sponsoring partner, CIPEC (Canadian Industry Partnership for Energy Conservation), released their annual rankings (now in its 16th year) of Canada's 50 Best Corporate Citizens. For the second year in a row, the title of Canada's best corporate citizen went to Vancouver City Savings Credit Union. Vancity, as it is known, was awarded this title based on an assessment of 14 key performance criteria focused on transparency of business practices, CEO-to-average worker pay ratio, executive diversity, waste productivity, supply chain and clean-air productivity, and employee turnover. Companies considered in the selection process included those with revenue of at least $2 billion, employing 2000+ employees, the 10 largest cooperatives in Canada, and the members of the TSX 60.

In addition to Vancity, Desjardins Group, HSBC Bank Canada, Hydro-Quebec, and Cameco Corporation rounded out the top 5. HSBC Bank Canada (ranked #3) was singled out by Corporate Knights for having the highest percentage of women in executive positions. Overall, the financial sector led the way with seven companies from this business sector positioned in the top 10 of Canada's best corporate citizens. Utilities and energy companies took up the other three spots in the top 10. Mountain

Equipment Co-op (#15) was the top finishing consumer products provider.

The 50 Best Corporate Citizens—which, according to Corporate Knights, are doing the most to advance a more fair and sustainable world—are shown in Figure 5.8.

FIGURE 5.8   **Best 50 Corporate Citizens in Canada**

- Vancity
- Desjardins Group
- HSBC Bank Canada
- Hydro-Quebec
- Cameco Corp.
- Enbridge Inc.
- Royal Bank of Canada
- IGM Financial
- The Co-operators
- Sun Life Financial
- Hydro One Limited
- Bank of Montreal
- Manitoba Hydro-Electric Board
- Enmax Corp.
- Mountain Equipment Co-op
- Transat AT Inc.
- Ontario Power Generation

- Toronto-Dominion Bank
- Teck Resources
- Kinross Gold
- Suncor Energy
- Cenovus Energy
- TC Transcontinental
- Agrium Inc.
- Celestica Inc.
- Telus Corp.
- Rogers Communications
- Intact Financial
- CIBC
- Transcanada Corp.
- Domtar Corp.
- BCE Inc.
- Agnico Eagle Mines
- Bank of Nova Scotia

- Husky Energy Inc.
- Cascades Inc.
- Aimia Inc.
- Canadian Tire Corporation
- Catalyst Paper Corp.
- Capital Power Corp.
- Bombardier Inc.
- Pacific Exploration and Production
- Potash Corp.
- National Bank of Canada
- WSP Global Inc.
- Yamana Gold Inc.
- Maple Leaf Foods
- Canadian National Railway Co.
- Loblaw Cos. Ltd.
- Federated Co-operatives Ltd.

Source: "Top 50 Best Corporate Citizens 2017," Sustainalytics.com.

The Interdependency of CSR and Corporate Strategy

With a broad-level understanding of CSR in place, let's now take a closer look at how we can achieve the establishment of a CSR culture into our business organization and systems. Prior to commencing with this discussion, however, it is important to recognize that businesses alone cannot solve all of the world's problems, nor do they have the resources to do so. What businesses can do, however, is identify where they can have a positive effect on society (people, communities, environment) and actively incorporate these initiatives into their overall strategy.

As mentioned in the opening discussion on corporate social responsibility, interpretation as to what this responsibility constitutes does vary by individual and organization. One way to visualize the current variety of approaches associated with corporate social responsibility is to view it via the CSR pyramid (see Figure 5.9).

The CSR pyramid illustrates the four primary views associated with the integration of CSR into an organization. At the bottom of the pyramid are the two

FIGURE 5.9   **CSR Pyramid**

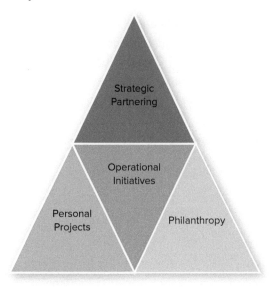

methodologies that represent arm's-length organizational CSR involvement. At this lower level of the pyramid, participation in CSR initiatives is predominantly focused on personal projects by a business leader(s) or by philanthropic involvement through cash or in-kind donations. Although both of these methodologies do provide a positive contribution to society, in many cases they are the result of decisions that do not significantly influence forward-looking corporate strategy but rather seek to enhance or reinforce the company's image or brand in the marketplace. Their role, in terms of organizational benefits, is largely focused on generic social issues (in many cases, personally driven) external to the organization's operations and long-term competitiveness. An example of "philanthropy," from the base level of the CSR pyramid, is Walmart's decision to provide (through *The Oprah Winfrey Show*) the McGhee sextuplets of Columbus, Ohio, with a generous gift of $250 000 in products and services to help the family transition the six children from infancy to adulthood.[17] An example from the "personal projects" area of the pyramid is the M&M Food Market's annual BBQ day in support of the Crohn's and Colitis Foundation of Canada (CCFC). Again, the initiative is noteworthy in that it is in support of a social issue. Mac Voisin, founder and chair of M&M, and M&M franchisees have raised more than $26 million for CCFC.[18] Although these examples are monetary-based, it should be noted that many companies are actively involved, at these levels, within their communities not only in terms of money, but also in terms of time and talent, referred to as "in-kind services." When the YMCA of Kingston, Ontario, made the decision to build a new aquatics centre, the Kingston organization Homestead Landholdings Inc. donated land adjacent to the YMCA and provided engineering design and development support and project management expertise toward the new centre. Without the expertise provided by this commercial development organization, the Kingston YMCA would not have been able to undertake the project without considerable additional expense.

The true integration of CSR initiatives into corporate strategy does, however, require movement beyond the base level. A key transition component to this evolution is for a company to start to view operational systems and tactics with social responsibility outcomes in mind; this forms the middle area of the pyramid, called "operational initiatives." This area is separated from the two base-level

FIGURE 5.10 Integration of CSR into Strategy I

Create CSR awareness through personal projects, policy development, and "good citizenship" initiatives.

Initiate business system benefits that enhance efficiencies while minimizing environmental harm.

View business system operational benefits and societal benefits jointly.

Fully integrate CSR initiatives into company planning and strategy... partnering with society.

areas by the transition from arm's-length social issues to that of social issues impacted as a result of the organization's day-to-day operations. The emphasis here is an awakening, within the organization, of a desire to mitigate social harm as a result of its business system activities (see Figure 5.10). The decision-making focus lies in seeking to enhance efficiencies while, for example, minimizing environmental harm.

An example is the use of water in the extraction of bitumen by energy-based companies associated with the Alberta oil sands project (and commented on in Chapter 4). Over the past few years, the industry has developed water recycling technology that enables an industry average recycling of 80% of the water used (with a number of more efficient companies, the steam injected into the extraction process has reached 90% to almost 100% recyclable levels). In addition, the current steam to oil bitumen ratio is approximately 3 to 1. With an industry average recycle recovery rate of 80%, this results in an estimated 0.6 barrel of (brackish) water per barrel (bbl) of oil produced. Again, new technologies being employed anticipate the ratio of water to bitumen to be reduced to 2 to 1, and industry recycling averages to move up to 90%. This will result in a reduction in water use to 0.2 bbl of (brackish) water per bbl of oil.[19] As this is non-potable water taken from deep-well sources, the efficiency gains via recycling and use reduction will reduce the cost base associated with the deep-well water source tapping process and the bitumen extraction process, as well as generate the secondary benefit of enhanced water conservation.

As with the discussion associated with personal projects and philanthropy, this movement toward efficiency enhancements yields positive, although in many cases secondary, benefits to the social agenda. It does not, however, result in the true integration of social responsibility into the strategy development and execution process of an organization. Achieving this level of corporate social responsibility requires a cultural shift within the organization to the top of the pyramid, which is an area titled "strategic partnering." This transition to true corporate social responsibility is identified by two fundamental shifts in the integration of strategy and the social agenda. These two shifts are:

1. The organization's decision-making process evolves from one that responds to social issues identified (in many cases, from external sources) as being pertinent to the organization, to a process that treats corporate social responsibility as a core root of the organization's strategic planning process.

2. The organization recognizes that certain social issues impact the key drivers of its competitiveness and, therefore, seeks to actively develop the necessary social partnerships in order to leverage such competitiveness in a way that positively impacts the people, communities, and environment around which it conducts its business.

FIGURE 5.11   **Integration of CSR into Strategy II**

Create CSR awareness through pet projects, policy development, and "good citizenship" initiatives.

Initiate business system benefits that enhance efficiencies while minimizing environmental harm.

View business system operational benefits and societal benefits jointly.

Fully integrate CSR initiatives into company planning and strategy... partnering with society.

Although not always the case, for many companies this is a two-step process (see Figure 5.11). The first phase is shifting the analysis of its business system beyond simply enhancing efficiencies and effectiveness, with secondary benefits derived to society, to that of fully viewing the benefits to society and the organization's operations jointly. This means providing full transparency of its business practices and the risks associated with the products/services it offers, as well as creating socially and environmentally responsible products.

The difference between this stage of CSR evolutionary development and the prior one is based on the organization's acknowledgment of its interdependence with society and that the benefits derived from the desire to maximize social benefits across its operations and overall value chain will also assist in maximizing business gains. This means auditing each area within the business system, identifying the positive and negative social benefits that result from the organization's activities within each one, and then seeking to change the organization's activities within each business system area in a way that provides the greatest operational value while achieving the greatest social benefit. This business system evaluation process should enable the organization to identify the negative contributors to the social partnership, thereby providing an opportunity to remedy such practices and transition this work into competitive advantages and new strategic value.

This type of decision making and cultural transition requires leadership from the top. It means conducting a complete risk/reward audit of the full business system and strategic approach to the social partnership. For managers, this approach needs to be conducted on two levels. The first is to identify key social interactions that will occur on a day-to-day basis throughout the organization's business system. By assessing each of these areas of responsibility, managers can then move to step #2, which is to identify those social impacts that are critical to the organization's success and then create definitive and sustainable solutions to such issues. Figure 5.12 provides an example of some of the key factors that could form part of this business system CSR audit process.

A fairly recent situation in the rental car industry illustrates this interdependency between the organization and social responsibility. In February 2011, the National Highway Traffic Safety Administration (NHTSA) in the United States released the results of a recently completed study of major car rental companies. The study looked at the percentage of vehicles subject to recall that were being rented out to customers prior to the recall defects being repaired. This study was initiated because of growing concerns relating to incidents with rental vehicles and allegations of personal injury and death due to rental car company practices pertaining to recalls. Most notable was an incident involving two California women who were killed in an accident involving an Enterprise Rent-A-Car vehicle. In this particular situation, the car they were driving, a Chrysler PT Cruiser, had an outstanding recall on it. The recall was for a possible leak in the power-steering fluid reservoir, which could result in the engine catching fire. The two women were killed when, while

FIGURE 5.12   **CSR and the Four Quadrants of Managerial Responsibility**

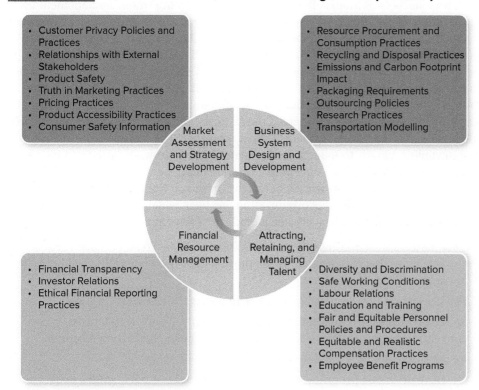

driving, their engine caught fire, resulting in them hitting an oncoming semi-tractor trailer. The investigation that followed showed this same vehicle had been rented out to others prior to the two women, with the recall repairs never made. The follow-up study by the NHTSA continued to raise concerns about the practice of renting out vehicles prior to ensuring that those subject to recalls are repaired. The study confirmed that the big three industry players—Enterprise, Avis/Budget, and Hertz—were, at the time, continuing to rent vehicles with outstanding recalls on them during the 90 days following the recall notice in more than 50% of the recall situations analyzed. In fairness to the industry, change did occur. Hertz's revised policy is that it will not rent or sell to consumers vehicles that have received a recall and will ground these vehicles within 24 hours of receiving notice. Hertz cited safety advocates and public attention to the situation as primary reasons for the policy change.[20] The AvisBudget Group (Avis, Budget, Payless), and Enterprise Holding (Alamo, Enterprise, National) have also implemented similar policies. "Product safety" is a key CSR impact factor in the "Market Assessment and Strategy Development" zone of the four quadrants of managerial responsibility. For the rental car industry, a true corporate social responsibility approach—which envisions a partnership with society—would, at the forefront of decision making, recognize the need to balance the safety of its customers with its desire to drive volume and profitability from its car rentals. Such an approach would shift away from making decisions on a reactive basis, interpreting what is a sufficient reason to ground a fleet of vehicles (i.e., making internal judgments as to what may or may not constitute risk to customers), to an operational position where any recall or potential threat to customer safety results in the grounding of the vehicles involved until such repairs are made (i.e., what Hertz is now doing). The pending movement to autonomous driving vehicles, coupled with the increase in the variety of technology-based devices now present in today's vehicles, will continue to challenge the rental industry, and the automotive industry at large, as to how to proactively make such decisions going forward.

Steam Whistle Brewing, a micro brewer serving the Ontario, Alberta, and British Columbia markets, is an excellent example of a company whose management team has worked diligently to incorporate green and sustainability-based initiatives across the four quadrants of managerial responsibility and to embed such initiatives into its business practices. The company has been recognized in the past by MediCorp Editors (*The Globe and Mail*) as one of the Top 50 Greenest Companies and is a recent recipient of the CIPH National Water Wise Award, as a result of its commitment to water conservation and purification within its core operations. The company in the past has also received the Ontario Minister's Award for Environmental Excellence, the Toronto Green Award, and the ECR Excellence in Corporate Responsibility Award (to name a few). Steam Whistle Brewing reflects in its operational decision making the concept of environmental stewardship, resulting in one of the most sustainable breweries in North America.[21] Socially responsible impact factors that illustrate why this organization has been widely recognized for its commitment to environmental excellence include the following:

- Its signature green bottles are made of 30% more glass, resulting in a recycling and refill rate that is more than twice the standard brown-bottle-based industry average.
- The brewery is powered using 100% green energy from Bullfrog Power.
- Its refrigeration system is chilled using deep water from Lake Ontario (versus conventional refrigeration systems), thereby reducing its carbon footprint.
- Its delivery trucks are fuelled with biodiesel.
- Its waste diversion program sends leftover food items from brewery events to a local street mission. Organic waste is sent to commercial composting. Cardboard, shrink wrap, broken glass, and sheet metal are all recycled, as well.
- It provides employees with showers and towel service and a secure and sheltered bike storage program, which encourages them to come to work via a "clean air commute."
- Its energy systems and its water savings systems have resulted in significant reductions to water (two-thirds reduction) and energy use (25% reduction).

Organizations that are able to climb to the top of the pyramid and develop the necessary social partnerships in a way that positively impacts the people, communities, and environments around which they conduct their business are those that are able to fuse and synthesize their organization's values and financial aspirations into such a partnership (see Figure 5.13). These organizations have learned how to leverage their business competencies and capabilities to utilize their resource base and their expertise to drive maximum benefit for society and, as a consequence, themselves as well.

FIGURE 5.13   **Integration of CSR into Strategy III**

Organizations that are able to climb to the top of the pyramid and develop the necessary social partnerships in a way that positively impacts the people, communities, and environment around which they conduct their business are those that are able to fuse and synthesize their organization's values and financial aspirations into such a partnership.

In reaching these levels, organizations and their management teams recognize that the long-term health of society is fundamental to the long-term health of the organization; the two are interconnected versus being separate and distinct. As was indicated earlier, the achievement of this level of fusion between society and the organization needs to be the result of a focused execution strategy across critical business system components and long-term strategic planning and positioning. An example of the fusing of positive societal impact with corporate strategy and business system needs is Gap Inc. Women make up 70% of Gap's workforce, with many of these employees residing in developing nations. Recognizing that the long-term health of Gap Inc. is based on the ability of these workers to excel in the workplace, in 2007 Gap Inc. initiated the P.A.C.E. program (Personal Advancement and Career Enhancement). This program focuses on training female garment factory workers to have both workplace and social skills, so that they can develop the efficiency skills needed to handle their existing jobs as well as the professional and personal skills needed to advance. The company realizes that by moving these workers beyond their entry-level jobs, they personally advance and thrive and so too do the communities in which they live. According to Gap Inc. and its partners, the International Center for Research and Women and the Swasti Health Resource Center, more than 200 000 women have participated in the program, and women who completed the program were promoted 4.7 times faster. Initially implemented in India, the program has now been expanded to countries such as Bangladesh, Cambodia, China, and Vietnam (16 countries in all), with a commitment to educate and empower more than 1 million women by 2022.[22]

Chip market leader Intel Corporation also has reformulated its philanthropic approach over the past few years. Again, it is a situation where Intel has redirected its efforts in a way that works with its business strategy—the end result is the creation of a strong society/business partnership. For example, one sector where Intel focuses its monetary and organizational support lies in the area of engineering and math education. Intel has invested in teacher training programs in partnership with ministries of education, with the end result of providing support to more than 8 million teachers in 70 countries. The company also provides resources to support the Intel Science Talent Search, one of the oldest student science competitions in the United States. The Intel International Science and Engineering Competition attracts more than 6 million participants worldwide for awards and scholarships exceeding $5 million, across a variety of research categories.

For companies like Gap Inc. and Intel Corporation, the anticipated benefits of investments in social partnership go beyond simply enhancing the corporate reputation. For these companies, the social strategic partnerships they become engaged in are all integrated with the corporate strategy with the intent of producing long-term value creation and competitive advantage. The investments in social initiatives are complementary to the organization's business goals and objectives. Although the benefits derived may be longer-term, if properly executed the intended outcomes of reduced business risk, increased revenue, or operational cost reductions can be realized as a result of such social integration strategies.[23]

Business IN ACTION

McDonald's Corporation

What does a comprehensive ethics and corporate social responsibility program look like? One would be hard-pressed to find a more comprehensive example than that of the McDonald's Corporation. In its annual "Values in Action" commitment McDonald's breaks its efforts down into several categories: sustainability priorities, good food, good sourcing, good planet, good people, good community.

McDonald's ensures strong corporate governance via a variety of means. First, its corporate governance principles require that all of the members of its board (save for its CEO and president) be independent of management. All directors of its board must also abide by a code of conduct, and six standing committees are charged with key roles in contributing to the oversight of management and the decisions management makes. McDonald's regularly updates its Standards of Business Conduct to reflect its ethical ambitions.

McDonald's ensures the sustainability of its supply chain by sourcing fish from fisheries with favourable sustainability ratings and beef from abattoirs with certified animal welfare policies, and has begun to maintain an environmental scorecard for suppliers of its other agricultural products. McDonald's has also conducted a number of initiatives to reduce waste in its packaging (the #1 concern of customers); in 2008, 82% of its consumer packaging came from

renewable materials and 30% came from recycled fibre. McDonald's has pledged that by 2025 it will seek to have 100% of its packaging recyclable, and that 100% of its packaging will come from renewable, recycled, or certified sources. McDonald's participates in a number of environmental initiatives, such as the LEED Retail Pilot Program, and has created a Global Energy Council to compile best-energy practices from its worldwide operations. To this aim, McDonald's has partnered with its franchisees to reduce greenhouse gas emissions by 36% by the year 2030, and has set a goal of a 31% reduction across its supply chain.

While maintaining a perceived historically unhealthy menu (it is fast food, after all!), McDonald's has made a concerted effort to improve the healthiness of its offerings by eliminating trans fats from its U.S. restaurants and by introducing healthier options, such as salads and wraps, in recent years. McDonald's also provides nutritional information for all of its products, and has initiated a global approach for food safety management.

McDonald's seeks to augment its employee experience by providing retirement plans, profit-sharing, and other benefits. McDonald's also operates seven Hamburger Universities, which serve as training centres for restaurant employees and corporate staff. McDonald's strives to create a comfortable environment for people of all cultures and backgrounds to work in, and has received several diversity awards.

McDonald's community involvement includes a long history of Olympic sponsorship and various philanthropic initiatives (on local, regional, national, and international scales). Undoubtedly, however, McDonald's Corporation's best-known charitable initiative is the Ronald McDonald House Charities.

McDonald's Corporation's wide-ranging efforts in CSR and ethics have certainly done well for its business. *Forbes* magazine has named it one of America's most inspiring companies as determined by consumers.

© Tracy Harris

The Challenge Behind CSR Implementation

Given what we have discussed about CSR up to this point, we legitimately should wonder why all organizations have not raced swiftly to the top of the CSR pyramid. For many companies, transitioning to the top of the CSR pyramid would require a significant change not only in operating procedures and processes, but also in the entire culture of the organization. In many industries, such a change will require significant investment up front and potentially an additional cost layer to the operating budget. CSR research does indicate that a majority of customers have indicated a willingness to pay more for products/services, but the unanswered question is just how much more. The risk for companies willing to consider a CSR transformation is, of course, "If we do it and our competitors do not, how will that impact our competitiveness?" A second and equally pressing problem lies in quantifying the benefits of CSR initiatives. In other words, how do we assign a financial value to enhanced corporate reputation, improved employee recruitment and retention, or the attractiveness of long-term, value-based social initiatives? In addition to the initial potential outcome value of CSR initiatives, considerable uncertainty exists in how to realistically create and measure the metrics needed to evaluate these very subjective areas. Finally, although CSR ideas may appear to be logical, under normal economic conditions what will be the impact toward sustaining these initiatives in periods of global market or company distress? Will shareholders be willing to sacrifice returns during such periods to maintain a longer-term social contract in areas that benefit non–financially committed stakeholders?

The answers to the questions posed above lie in the ability of management and the board of directors to create the necessary data that demonstrate how CSR initiatives are—and why they need to be—fully integrated into an organization's strategy and operations. This means developing the very metrics identified above, which will enable investors to understand their value and to see how a conscious effort toward the "triple bottom line" of people, planet, and profits really does enhance the final P—profits. Such an outcome can be achieved only by a disciplined approach to business planning that identifies CSR as a core pillar within the strategic planning process. Equally challenging for management and the board of directors will be the task of communicating the societal partnership benefits to the external stakeholders and communities while communicating, internally, the win/win nature of the arrangement.

A Note Pertaining to Not-for-Profits

The March 8, 2011, front-page headline on the *Toronto Star* was "Game Over for Shady Charity"; the accompanying subheading indicated that an organ donation association's licence had been yanked after an audit confirmed the charity misspent cash it raised. The article went on to detail how the Organ Donation and Transplant Association of Canada, which made emotional pleas to Canadians to help save lives, had in actuality spent most of the money it raised on fundraising fees and administrative expenses. In fact, it was reported to be one of six health-based charities where more than 70% of the amount raised was spent for reimbursing telemarketers and covering other administrative expenses (the CRA, in 2009, communicated a directorate that indicated 35% was the maximum safe level for fundraising costs). The audit also found that the charity had initiated practices designed to hide its high costs. This resulted in the charity reporting that only 20% of revenues raised went to fundraising and administrative expenses, when the audit concluded that 71% of the dollars raised were used to cover such expenses.[24] As is typical with most fraudulent schemes, it is not just the fact that generous donors do not see their money going to its intended use. Canada Revenue Agency (CRA) also continually warns Canadians that contributions to charity schemes can very well lead to a reassessment of one's income tax submissions. An April 2018 report by Global News reported that the CRA has denied over $7 billion in tax claims due to charity-based scams, reviewing over 200 000 tax returns in the process, for submissions relating to charity-tax-shelter contributions and deductions. Individuals impacted not only lose the charitable deduction upon which the tax return was based, but also may face penalties and interest charges for the loss of the tax break provided (when intentionally involved) due to the charitable donation.[25]

For not-for-profits and charities, the goodwill associated with the work they do and the integrity with which they conduct themselves is fundamental to their existence. Unlike for-profit entities, which can use private equity as a basis for acquiring the capital needed to sustain themselves, not-for-profits are heavily dependent upon monetary gifts (donations) from others to keep their operations rolling. For each Organ Donation and Transplant Association, there are hundreds of charities that conduct their business operations in a fully transparent and ethical manner. The challenge for these not-for-profits is how to communicate to potential donors the legitimacy of their work in a donation environment that is becoming increasingly concerned about fraud. Canadians are generous supporters of the not-for-profit sector, but recent survey results reflect a growing uneasiness with the industry as a whole. With over 86 000 charitable organizations in Canada, most of which collect less than $500 000 each year, it is often difficult for individuals to draw conclusions as to which charities to support. Canada Helps and Capital One Canada in completing their annual charity fraud awareness quiz have reported that more than 65% of Canadians were worried about fraudulent charities, and more than 50% indicated they were less likely to give to charities because of fraud concerns.[26] For managers of charities and not-for-profits, these numbers are nothing but alarming. Not-for-profits and charities must earn and maintain the trust of Canadians in order to be the recipients of their generosity. This means that these same managers must be able to communicate to Canadians the legitimacy of their organizations, be able to provide clear outcomes for the programs and services that they are providing, and be fully able (and credible) to provide prospective donors with an accounting for how their organization spends their money.

In an effort to assist Canadians in determining the efficiency of Canada's major charities (raising over $1 million annually), *MoneySense*[27] has created an evaluation-based methodology and publishes the results in its publication titled the Annual Charity 100. The evaluation behind this ranking of Canada's top charities takes into consideration a charity's fundraising efficiency and its governance model, financial reserve position, and overall efficiency in the way it spends the dollars it receives. Based on this assessment process, the charity is then provided a "charity efficiency grade" (a letter grade of A, B, C, etc.). As an example, in 2018, the Canadian Red Cross Society received a letter grade of A– for its overall efficiency, a B+ for its fundraising effort, an A– for its governance practices, and an A for its financial reserve position. Its final grade was a B+. Conversely, Cystic Fibrosis Canada did not score as well across these performance criteria, receiving an overall grade of C+ for its charity-operations efficiency (this is not to imply that one should not contribute to this cause). A lower grade relative to rivals does not mean that a charity is dishonest, it just means that its overall operational efficiency is not at quite the same levels as its peers. In this regard, the Charity 100 provides a valuable tool for charity managers and decision makers as well, as they can seek to use this tool as a benchmark for improving their overall mission and service delivery protocols. For us as Canadians, as generous as we are, we all want to believe that our donations are being put to good use. In this regard, buyer beware—or, in this case, "donor beware" does apply. Take the time to research the charities you are asked to contribute to, and be sure that they are using your gifts in the way in which you intend them to be used.

Management Reflection—It Is All About Trust

Business courses worldwide continually reinforce the need for organizations to encourage entrepreneurship, innovation, and risk taking. Managers and executives have hundreds of articles and books at their disposal on how to manage and motivate their employees. Organizations continuously look for ways to empower people to develop new processes and operating efficiencies. So, just what is the common thread that allows for all these things to occur within successful organizations? The common thread is trust. Trust is fundamental to all that we do and to everyone that we interact with. As indicated in this chapter, the best asset you can bring to work, on a day-to-day basis, is your integrity. This means being honest, respecting the dignity of others, listening before you speak, being accountable for your mistakes, doing what you say you are going to do, demonstrating transparency in the decisions you make, not presuming you have all the answers, and thanking people for their feedback. Successful managers are open and authentic. They encourage open discussion, communicate their concerns, actively discuss risk, and don't manipulate people or distort facts.

The same holds true for organizations. Trust is a two-way street. To effectively create a societal partnership, organizations need to gain the trust of the external stakeholders who will be impacted by the decisions being made. Corporate social responsibility is just that. It is all about trust. It is making sure that other parties do not perceive the existence of a hidden agenda. It is ensuring that the organization is not distorting or hiding the facts in order to create private gain. It is not trying to spin our public relations in a way that sugarcoats a broken commitment. It is a willingness to address the tough actions quickly and not break the confidence of others when doing so.

As managers, we have an obligation to our employees, our organization, our society, and our planet to make decisions that benefit all, and to do the right thing. Remember, our value and our rewards come from what we do.

Chapter Summary

The purpose of this chapter is to provide students with an understanding of the importance of ethics in the decision-making process, for both individuals and managers. In this regard, the chapter focuses on identifying the critical elements that make up the interpretation of ethical behaviour and financial integrity. It also discusses the challenges that managers, employees, and organizations and their boards of directors face in attempting to build and maintain an ethical environment. The chapter also discusses the concept of corporate social responsibility (CSR) and the development of societal partnerships as a core component of strategic planning. The chapter comments on the growing importance of CSR, the various levels of CSR that exist in today's market environment, and the transition process that occurs as organizations become more connected to the societal partners they influence and, ultimately, can work with for the betterment of all. The chapter also provides a summary overview of the challenges organizations face in implementing CSR into their business strategy. The chapter closes with a discussion of the importance of integrity in the not-for-profit field and the need to demonstrate full operational transparency as a key success factor within this process. The management reflection offers some final comments on the importance of trust as the basis of all decision making and human interaction within the workplace.

Developing Business Knowledge and Skills

Key Terms

Ponzi scheme *p. 174*

ethics *p. 176*

integrity *p. 179*

board of directors *p. 181*

whistleblowing *p. 182*

code of conduct *p. 182*

forensic accounting *p. 186*

corporate social responsibility (CSR) *p. 188*

Questions for Discussion

1. What do you feel is the main challenge for managers and boards of directors with respect to ingraining ethics into an organization's culture and decision-making environment? (LO1)

2. What is the difference between ethics and financial integrity? How are they interconnected? (LO1)

3. With initiatives such as Bill 198 and Sarbanes-Oxley (SOX) put into place, and new global reporting standards coming on-stream in this decade, do you feel that government and regulatory bodies on their own can fully define and manage business ethics and ensure financial integrity? Why, or why not? (LO2)

4. What does a board of directors and an organization's senior management team need to do in order to ensure that decision making stays in the "green zone" of accepted business principles that govern organizational activity? (LO3)

5. What do you feel is the major barrier preventing organizations from reaching the top of the CSR pyramid? (LO4)

6. Do you feel that consumer concerns relating to CSR will accelerate in the years to come? Will this be enough to fundamentally change the current view of CSR around the board of directors' table? (LO5)

Question for Individual Action

Arrange an interview with an owner of a small or medium-sized business, or the executive director or CEO of a not-for-profit in your community. Ask this individual if they have created a Code of Conduct for employees. Ask this person, as well, if any formal ethics-based training has been initiated within the organization. Be prepared to share the results of your interview with your class.

Team Exercise

Using Bombardier Inc.'s Code of Ethics and Business Conduct[28] and your university/college's academic integrity policy as templates, create a Code of Conduct for this business course. Be sure to make your code all-inclusive, commenting on areas beyond simply academic honesty. Look to broaden your policy to include commentary pertaining to work environment, peer and external stakeholder relationships, team-based exercise support, and classroom practices. Present your Code of Conduct to your peers for review and discussion.

Case for Discussion

Payday Loans

Your car, which you need for work purposes, has just broken down. It's going to cost $300 to repair it. Money that, unfortunately, you don't have. What are your options? Many Canadians would turn to friends or family to borrow the needed $300 with a promise to pay them back on their next payday. Others might use a credit card, be willing to access their account overdraft allowance, or dip into a line of credit. But what if you didn't have access to any of the above options? Where would you get the needed $300? If you have a job or any other reliable source of income you could get an advance, until your next paycheque, from a payday loan provider.

About 7% of Canadians have used the services of the approximately 1360 payday loan outlets (down from 1440 in 2015) across the country.[29] Payday loans are described as convenient, economical, unsecured short-term loans designed to meet unexpected cash needs. In general, payday loan providers offer these loans for an average of two weeks, although loan terms can typically range between 7 and 42 days and vary by province and provider. Payday loan providers also provide loans on an installment basis, with APRs as much as 40%+. The Canadian Payday Loan Association, which represents 815 retail financial service outlets providing payday loans and serves nearly 2 million Canadians annually, stresses that such loans should be for occasional use only and are not a solution to covering ongoing budgetary shortfalls due to living beyond your means or poor financial/budgetary management.[30]

Quick Facts—Payday Loans, Province of Ontario, 2014[31]

Estimated number of Ontario residents who take out a payday loan	400 000
Number of payday loan locations in Ontario	796
Approximate value of payday loans issued in Ontario	$1.1 to $1.5 billion
Average payday loan amount and term for the province of Ontario	$460 for a two-week term

This service is regulated by the provincial governments; each province has set a maximum that can be charged in fees and interest. Although convenient, these short-term loans are perceived by many to be a very expensive way to borrow money compared to other loan or credit facility options. According to the Financial Consumer Agency of Canada, a payday loan can cost up to 10 times more than borrowing from other sources. The table below illustrates the cost of borrowing $300 for 14 days from the short-term credit options typically available to individuals.

Source of Loan	Cost
Payday loan	$45.00*
Line of credit	$ 5.81
Credit card cash advance	$ 7.42
Overdraft	$ 7.19

*Adjusted for 2018 Ontario legislation rate cap

Source: Example adapted from Financial Consumer Agency of Canada: http://www.fcac-acfc.gc.ca/Eng/resources/publications/creditLoans/Pages/Payday-Precir-D1.aspx.

Remember, the example above is only for a two-week period. If a borrower does roll over a loan repeatedly, additional fees are incurred each time. Such a practice would result in that $300 loan incurring a cost of borrowing of 390% on an annual basis. In addition to the borrowing costs incurred, in the event of default payday loan borrowers are also typically charged a returned item fee plus interest. Money Mart, one of Canada's largest payday loan providers, as an example, charges borrowers $40 (at the time of this writing), plus interest, for defaulting on a loan (labelled a returned item fee).[32] Online payday loan providers such as GoDay.ca or Payday247.ca offer borrowing packages similar to those being sold by traditional storefront operators. Applications are accepted and approved 24/7 and individuals can receive their money in as little as one hour.

So why do people use payday loans? One factor is that you don't need a good credit rating to get a payday loan. For all of the other sources above, a customer would need to have an acceptable credit rating in order to have access to these bank products. Payday loans are the only source of borrowing available for Canadians with a poor credit rating or no credit rating at all. As Stan Keyes, head of the Canadian Payday Loan Association, points out, "what alternative do borrowers have?" It is precisely the fact that payday loan outlets charge very high fees to people who need cash quickly, but have no other options, that has led to accusations of exploitation for the industry. But concerns don't stop there. In addition to charging high fees, the payday loan industry has also been criticized for targeting low-income neighbourhoods and areas with a high number of people receiving social assistance. Keyes argues that the outlets are "simply located where the commerce is." However, opponents of the industry claim this enables the payday lenders to take advantage of society's most vulnerable members. Jerry Buckland, author of *Hard Choices: Financial Exclusion, Fringe Banks and Poverty in Urban Canada*, argues that Canada has a two-tier system of banking that contributes to income inequality.[33]

The Government of Canada, in looking at payday loans (2016), has concluded that fewer than half of those utilizing the payday loan system realized that other lending alternatives were available to them. More than 60% indicated they did not have access to a credit card, and just under 90% indicated that they did not have access to a line of credit. In borrowing the money, almost half of those responding to the Government of Canada study indicated that they were borrowing money to cover unexpected expenses, such as the car repair used in this case example. Another 40%+ indicated that they needed the money for expected expenses, such as utilities, which they needed to pay within a certain time frame. 53% of borrowers reported incomes of less than $55 000 per year, with just under 30% reporting incomes of less than $32 000 per year.[34]

An analysis of the industry by the Province of Ontario (May 2014), conducted by Deloitte, not only expressed concerns relating to the potential vulnerability of low-income earners who depend on payday loan providers, but also pointed toward the anticipated growth of this industry as online and mobile technology-based lending approaches continue to evolve. The ability to get "fast money" online, 24/7, poses the high cost of borrowing concerns and also increases the challenges by the province to regulate such activities and fully ensure consumers are protected from unlicensed vendors and "lead generator" software used to seek out potential borrowers in order to generate additional lending activity.[35]

Many activists are just as critical of the provincial governments as they are of payday loan providers. Yes, provinces have established payday loan legislation and regulations to govern this market sector. Concern, however, does exist that the consumer protection provisions within these regulations could do significantly more at minimizing the costs associated with payday loan borrowing. In response to this pressure a number of provinces over the past few years have introduced and implemented legislation tightening lending regulations within this financial services sector. As an example, the provinces of Ontario and Alberta have both enacted legislation which limits the cost of borrowing to $15 per $100 advanced for loans of fewer than 62 days in duration. For loans exceeding 62 days in duration, or advancing more than $1500, the annual interest rate is capped at 60%.

Research in this area is indicating that the typical payday loan borrower takes out multiple loans over a one-year period. Assuming this is the case, concerns are being raised that such activity could mean customers are using loans to pay for reoccurring expenses and/or repaying prior loans and associated fees. This exposes such borrowers to the risk of a "debt cycle" of continuous payday loan borrowing.

So what is the solution? One Canadian financial institution has recognized the void in the short-term, small-loan market and has begun to offer an alternative. Vancity, British Columbia's largest credit union, has started a program offering same-day, short-term loans to its members. The program aims at "bridging the gap between a payday loan and a traditional loan." While significantly cheaper than a payday loan, the interest rate charged by Vancity is comparable to that charged for a credit card cash advance. For example, if you were a member of Vancity and needed that $300 loan in order to pay for your car repairs, you could borrow the $300 for two months with the amount required to be repaid at the end of the two-month period being $307.50 (reflecting an interest rate of 19%).[36]

Questions

1. Are payday loan companies simply filling a need that other financial institutions have ignored, as proponents say, or do they prey on the vulnerable and promote income inequality, as detractors say?

2. Should governments take a more aggressive approach with respect to regulations and legislation governing interest rate maximums?

3. Payday loan providers indicate that higher interest rates are required in order to offset their operating costs and higher risk of default. If governments enact rate caps below their required rate spreads, resulting in the disappearance of these providers, who will service this market sector, which often does not have access to traditional banking credit facilities?

4. Does the anticipated easy access to "fast money" 24/7 concern you? Should this be a consumer decision, or should governments more aggressively regulate or prohibit growth in this sector?

5. What about technology? Instant Financial Inc., a Vancouver-based start-up, released an app that allows employees who are paid by the hour to get their day's earnings after each shift. Employers pay for use of the app, thereby providing this service "free of charge" to their employees. Walmart is working with a similar arrangement as well. Will technology such as this eliminate the challenges described in the case?[37]

CHAPTER 6

Developing a Business Strategy

LEARNING OBJECTIVES

This chapter is designed to provide students with:

LO1	An understanding of the concept of business strategy
LO2	An appreciation of the importance of developing a strategy within a business operation
LO3	An overview of the key areas around which business strategy is developed
LO4	Exposure to the fundamentals of the strategy planning and implementation process
LO5	An understanding of the unique strategy planning requirements of the not-for-profit sector

Snapshot

What to Expect in This Chapter

This chapter provides students with an introductory overview of business strategy and the strategic planning process that management teams undertake in order to determine the market position they visualize their companies owning, and the actions they intend to pursue, within the market segments in which they choose to compete. The content emphasized in this chapter includes the following:

- The Concept of Business Strategy
  - Strategy Made Simple
- Core Elements for Assessing Business Strategy
  - Purpose
  - Markets
  - Products and Services
  - Resources
  - Business System Configuration
  - Responsibility and Accountability
- The Strategic Planning Process
  - I/E (Internal/External) Analysis
  - Competitive Advantage(s) Identification
  - Strategy Development
  - Strategy Execution
- Strategy Challenges in the SME (Small and Medium-Size Enterprises) Sector
- Strategic Planning in the NFP (Not-for-Profit) Sector (Social Economy)
- Management Reflection—The Need to Plan

 Business IN ACTION

Scotiabank—Executing Strategy Globally

Scotiabank is a multinational financial services provider and one of Canada's most international banks. Established in 1832 in Halifax, Scotiabank offers a broad range of financial services including personal and commercial banking, wealth management, and corporate and investment banking to more than 25 million customers globally.

For Scotiabank, its historical and future success is predicated around three key fundamentals. A committed team of more than 97 000 employees who work together to offer customers expert advice, guidance, and solutions relating to financial services and wealth management. A well-diversified and balanced portfolio of products and services customized to customer needs globally. A clearly focused strategy that revolves around the pillars of customer service, leadership depth, effective resource deployment, digital transformation, diversified business mix, and efficient and effective organizational processes and cost management.

For Scotiabank, strategic success lies in its growing global diversification, which is designed to minimize potential revenue and earnings volatility associated with any one specific region of the world. Recognizing that economies will, most likely, experience uneven growth in the mid-to-longer term, Scotiabank will continue to look internationally for growth, particularly in

© Ivansabo/Dreamstime.com/GetStock.com

those markets that possess young, under-banked and growing populations supported by a well-educated workforce and a growing middle class. One such attractive area that has been on Scotiabank's radar is the Pacific Alliance countries of Mexico, Peru, Colombia, and Chile, coupled with a secondary emphasis on the Caribbean and Central America. This regional area (Pacific Alliance) possesses more than 224 million people, has a combined GDP of approximately $2 trillion, and represents the eighth largest economy in the world. The recent acquisitions

of Cencosud S.A.'s financial services in Chile, and a majority stake in Banco Bilbao Vizcaya Argentaria S.A.'s retail business in Chile, are good examples of Scotiabank's selective acquisition strategy to further grow its international presence in this region. The Pacific Alliance, where Scotiabank is the fourth largest banking operation, now makes up 70% of the bank's international profile, which accounts for 31% of its total business lines earnings and is supported by a customer base of more than 15 million customers. LatinFinance recognized Scotiabank as the 2018 bank of the year in Latin America and the Caribbean.

Although focused internationally, this does not mean that Scotiabank intends to decrease its focus on Canada, which continues to represent approximately 50% of the bank's earnings (and 59% of its asset base). Now the third largest bank in Canada, and one of the 25 largest in the world (10th largest in the Americas), Scotiabank intends to continue to build on its solid footing in Canada. In fact, two recent key moves in Canada, the $2.6-billion (CAD) acquisition of MD Financial Management, a wealth-management company headquartered in Toronto, and the $950-million (CAD) acquisition of Jarislowsky Fraser Ltd., Canada's third-largest active money manager (located in Montreal), point to exactly that (both acquired in 2018). This follows earlier moves to further ingrain itself in the Canadian marketplace,

FIGURE 6.1   **Scotiabank—Business Lines Global Presence**

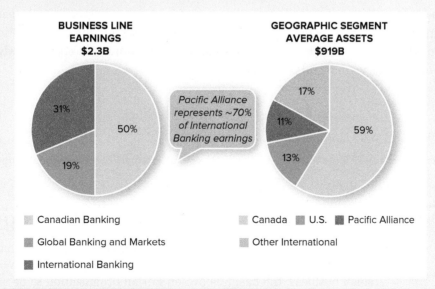

Source: Data and adaptation taken from Scotiabank Investor Presentation, Q3, 2018.

such as the rebranding and launch of Tangerine (formerly ING Direct Canada, acquired in 2012), and a partnership with Canadian Tire Corporation to develop a cross-promotions program that will enable Scotiabank to offer new and expanded financial services to Canadian Tire customers. Underpinning this relationship was Scotiabank's acquisition of a 20% stake in Canadian Tire's financial services business (2014), as well as an additional $2.25 billion in credit card receivable financing. For Scotiabank, these types of deals offer an opportunity to attract new customers and to tap into the lucrative credit-card business. Canadian Tire's financial services division manages an estimated $4.4 billion in receivables and has 1.8 million active customers. For example, in 2014 Scotiabank estimated that more than half of its new customers in Canada have come as the result of its active partnership expansion and indirect marketing channels strategies—which, in addition to Canadian Tire, include such successes as the SCENE program with Cineplex, sports partnerships (Tangerine is now the exclusive bank of the Toronto Raptors), and expanded brokerage and auto-lending channel intermediaries.

Going forward, Scotiabank's strategic focus remains unchanged. At its core, it intends to maintain and grow its presence in Canada while selectively looking to expand its presence in high-growth markets, particularly within the Pacific Alliance. The key pillars behind its growth ambitions lie in increasing its customer service focus, further enhancing the depth and diversity of its leadership, and continuing to reinvent the way it does business in order to better serve customers while reducing structural costs. The key

to this strategic focus lies in what it perceives to be opportunities in the areas of wealth management and insurance business growth internationally, increasing emphasis on automated transaction services and indirect banking (Tangerine), and accelerated emphasis on leveraging the organization's expertise in electronic transaction and credit card management.

Having said this, Scotiabank does not intend to pursue growth just for the sake of growth. Part of the strategic decision-making process within any business is to assess the success of a company's current portfolio in addition to looking for new growth opportunities. At Scotiabank, CEO Brian Porter and his team are doing just that. In overseeing Scotiabank since 2014, Porter and his management team continue to refine Scotiabank's global reach and mix. This has resulted in the divestment or pending divestment of a number of businesses within its portfolio in approximately 22 geographic markets. Included in this "pruning exercise" based on growth and profitability potential are banking operations in nine Caribbean countries, as well as a life insurance business presence in both Jamaica and Trinidad. Going forward, the bank's emphasis will shy away a bit from further large acquisitions—at least in the near to mid-term. Acquisitions require time to digest the new companies into the bank's operation. The value of these acquisitions lies in the ability to grow the organizations once the purchase is completed. For Scotiabank, this means a stronger emphasis on "organic" growth in order to leverage the opportunities perceived to exist within the markets the newly acquired companies serve.

Web Integration

Want to learn more about Scotiabank? Go to **https://www.scotiabank.com/ca/en/about/inside-scotiabank/corporate-profile.html**.

LO1, LO2 The Concept of Business Strategy

The development of an organization's business strategy is fundamentally one of the most important responsibilities of a senior management team or, in the case of a small business, the business owner. For an organization to be successful over the long term, managers need to have a game plan as to where and how to compete in the markets in which they intend to serve. As was pointed out in Chapter 1, the

FIGURE 6.2   **Interdependency of Strategy and Tactics**

long-term success of an organization, and its ability to evolve and grow, is predicated on two fundamental principles (see Figure 6.2):

1. the ability to define and create a strategic direction and market position for the organization (strategic plan); and

2. the ability to execute the core tactical initiatives within the plan in a manner that ensures the organization's success.

This chapter deals in detail with the first part of this equation, the development of a business strategy. It also provides an overview of the execution of this strategy to achieve the organization's objectives (covered more extensively in the remaining chapters of this textbook).

> The long-term success of an organization and its ability to evolve and grow is predicated on two fundamental principles: the ability to define and create a strategic direction and market position for the organization (strategic plan), and the ability to execute the core tactical initiatives within the plan in a manner that ensures the organization's success.

Strategy Made Simple

For many students, the concept of business strategy is one of the most difficult to understand and apply. This is largely due to the fact that strategies are generally customized for each business, given the market conditions that they face and the desired business goals they aspire to reach. In its most basic form, business strategy is all about understanding what opportunities exist in the marketplace and which ones should be pursued. Based on these conclusions, managers then have to decide upon their path of action in pursuit of capitalizing on the opportunities chosen (see Figure 6.3). Think of strategy simply as being summarized by the answers to three questions: "Where do we want to play," "Why is this the best use of our resources," and "How do we plan to win." By answering these three questions, we develop the seeds for what is called our intended or deliberate strategy; that is, the specific direction and actions we plan to take in order to guide our organization's decisions going forward. Whether we can hold our course or are forced to change our direction is based on our abilities to execute our strategy, given competitive actions and external market influences.[1]

FIGURE 6.3   **Business Strategy in Simple Terms**

LO3   Core Elements for Assessing Business Strategy

For business managers, the development of a business strategy means making decisions and determining direction in six key areas (see Figure 6.4):

1. Purpose
2. Markets
3. Products and services
4. Resources
5. Business system configuration
6. Responsibility and accountability

Purpose

Mission defines an organization's purpose or reason for existence.

Purpose refers to the mission of the organization and the vision its managers or owner(s) have for the business. **Mission** refers to the fundamental purpose the business has identified as being its predominant reason for existence. Mission statements usually identify the broad goals around which a company was formed. They also can reflect on how an organization will get to where it wants to go. For example, RBC's (Royal Bank of Canada) mission or purpose is "helping clients thrive and communities prosper."[2] One of Canada's best known integrated energy companies, Suncor's mission is to "create energy for a better world."[3] Blackberry's mission, or statement of purpose, is "to be the world's leading provider of end-to-end mobility solutions that are the most secure and trusted."[4]

Mission statements, when combined with ethics policies, codes of conduct, and statements of behaviour or values, guide the overall direction and activities of a business. Decisions made by managers within an organization should reinforce the mission the company is aspiring toward.

Vision is a forward-thinking statement that defines what a company wants to become and where it is going.

A **vision** statement is a forward-thinking statement that defines what a company wants to become and where it is going. It is often referred to as the "big hairy

---

FIGURE 6.4   **Core Elements of a Strategy**

audacious goal" (BHAG) of an organization, or its strategic business statement. As an example, RBC's vision is "To be among the world's most trusted and successful financial institutions."[5] Suncor's vision is "To be the trusted stewards of valuable natural resources. Guided by our values, we will lead the way to deliver economic prosperity, improve social well-being and a healthy environment for today and tomorrow."[6] Jim Treliving (of *Dragons' Den* fame) and his partner George Melville's initial vision for Boston Pizza was to have it become Canada's #1 casual dining chain.[7] This has now evolved into positioning itself to be the gathering place in every community in Canada to share great food and even better occasions.

An example of the integration of mission, vision, and strategic intent, which outlines what an organization aspires to become and how it plans to achieve it, is shown in the accompanying Business in Action, which revisits the Canadian company CAE, initially referred to in Chapter 3.

Business IN ACTION

CAE—Revisited

Our vision is to be the recognized global training partner of choice to enhance safety, efficiency and readiness.

Our mission...Through the training we provide, our mission is to make air travel safer, defense forces mission ready and medical personnel better able to save lives.

Our strategy...We address safety, efficiency and readiness for customers in three core markets: civil aviation, defense and security, and healthcare. We are a unique, pure-play training company with a proven record, of more than 70 years, of commitment to our customers' long-term training needs. We offer the most innovative and broadest range of comprehensive training solutions across a global network by incorporating a combination of live training on actual platforms, virtual

training in simulators and extended reality applications, and constructive training using computer-generated simulations. Our strategic imperatives focus on the protection of our leadership position and growing at a superior rate than the underlying markets.

Our six pillars of strength...We believe there are six fundamental strengths that underpin our strategy and position us well for sustainable long-term growth:

- High degree of recurring business;
- Strong competitive moat;
- Headroom in large markets;
- Underlying secular tailwinds;
- Potential for superior returns;
- Culture of innovation.

Source: Used by permission of CAE.

As part of developing and reviewing a business strategy, managers or business owners will revisit their mission and vision statements to ensure they are still applicable and represent desired outcomes for the firm's direction and decision-making process. Required changes will be made at the front end of the strategic planning process. A review of these two "purpose" fundamentals is a necessary first step in deciding where and how to compete.

Markets

Markets refers to the specific markets or market segments the business sees itself competing in. As part of the strategy development process, managers and owners need to assess their success in existing markets and evaluate the potential of new markets. Markets should be assessed in terms of their current and future profitability and growth potential. Markets that represent opportunities for future growth and enhanced profitability will receive greater managerial attention and resource support. Markets that have become unprofitable or marginally profitable and lack significant future growth will be evaluated in terms of market exit strategies or **harvesting** strategies.

Harvesting is a strategy that reflects a reduced commitment to a particular market given its perceived weak future growth or profitability potential.

Products and Services

Products and services refers to a review of the current products and services offered by a business, as well as potential new products/services that are to be added to the products portfolio (see Figure 6.5). This review is triggered by an assessment of the opportunities that the organization has decided to explore as a result of its market assessment (previously mentioned). Over time, products and their related services can become obsolete or no longer desired by the organization's customers. This can be the result of technological innovation, changes in consumer needs and tastes, or new direct substitutes for existing products and services being offered by competitors. A critical part of the strategy development process is to determine which products and related services are to remain part of a business's portfolio, as well as which are to receive additional R&D (research and development) support, and which new ones are to be added.

Examples of strategic business decisions regarding services could relate to whether customers should be offered payment terms for buying products, whether financing options should be offered by the company itself or sourced to an external financing supplier, and so on. An example of a company constantly evolving its portfolio is Apple Inc. Originally a personal computer manufacturer, the company's product portfolio has evolved to include tangible products such as the iPod, iPhone, iPad, Mac computers, and Apple TV, along with support services such as proprietary operating systems, iTunes, and the App Store, as well as Apple's many patents used to support its underlying technologies. Highly publicized new additions to the portfolio include Apple Pay (2014) and Apple Watch (2015); 2015 also brought forward speculation that Apple was actively involved in undertaking the development of an electric automobile and/or autonomous-driving vehicle software (called Project Titan), with

FIGURE 6.5   Portfolio Analysis

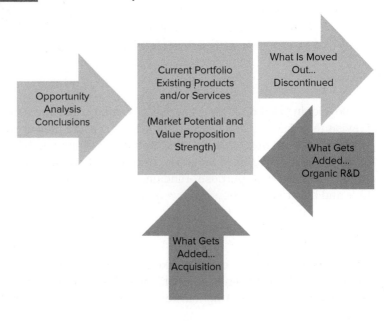

TABLE 6.1	Recent Apple Acquisitions
Acquired Company	**Focus**
Texture (2018)	Digital magazine distributor
Shazam (2018)	Music identifying app
Spektral (2018)	Digital camera technology enhancement
Beats (2014)	Headphones, music services, etc.
Laserlike, Pullstring, and SilkLabs (2019)	Artificial intelligence (AI)
Platoon, DataTiger (2018)	Analytics
Dialog (2019)	Semi-conductor chip maker and supply chain partner
Akonia Holigraphics (2018)	Augmented reality (AR)
Buddybuild (Vancouver-based) (2019)	iOS development and support

Source: Based on data taken from "Top 7 Companies Owned by Apple," Investopedia.com.

production as early as 2021.[8] In all, Apple spends billions annually (approximately $14 billion in 2018) on research and development (R&D) in support of new product development and existing product iterations.

In addition to its organic (internal) product development Apple has been aggressive in acquiring companies, which enables it to both access emerging technological innovation and add specific products to its portfolio. Table 6.1 provides a partial list of recent acquisitions undertaken by Apple to continually grow and/or enhance existing products within its product portfolio, or to shape and support anticipated market opportunities going forward. Apple has made over 100 acquisitions since the late 1980s.[9]

As mentioned in previous discussions within this textbook, strategic decisions are not just about adding products or services. Strategy also focuses on reducing support and/or eliminating products or services whose growth and profitability potential no longer meet a company's expectations. Examples of products discontinued by Apple over the company's evolution include a variety of personal computer and Mac models, iPod models, printers, servers, external drives, as well as early versions of iPhone, iPad, Apple TV, and operating systems and other support software.

Resources

Resources refers to the allocation of a business's resources in support of its strategic decisions. Businesses, like all of us, have only so many resources. Capacity limitations exist as to the amount of products businesses can produce, the amount of money they can commit to projects, and the variety of tasks their workforce can handle at any given time. In recognizing this, as part of the strategy development process businesses must make decisions on where to allocate these limited resources. Similarly, businesses may not have the expertise in-house to effectively execute strategies. In this situation, managers will have to decide if they need to go out and acquire required expertise, or if their plans need to be modified or redirected due to the lack of competencies or technology within a business in order to succeed with a desired strategic direction. The decision by Target Corporation in January 2015 to cease doing business in Canada and wind down its Target Canada subsidiary is a good example of a company resource allocation decision. Having already invested nearly $7 billion in its Canadian retail operation, representing roughly 4% of Target's North American sales revenue, Target Corporation felt that perceived required investments of an additional $2 to $3 billion did not warrant the expected return that such an additional investment would generate. Target's estimates of potential profitability in Canada (or lack thereof), now pushed out to beyond 2021, versus the required expenditures to keep the Canadian operation solvent simply did not support staying in Canada. The resources could be better used elsewhere in areas where acceptable returns on such investments made better sense for the organization overall.[10]

Business System Configuration

Business system configuration refers to modifying the organization's infrastructure and the way it does business to ensure the success of the plan. This could mean making changes to the organization's distribution outlets, warehousing or product delivery, plants and facilities, manufacturing or assembly processes, marketing campaign, and so on. (The development and management of business systems is covered in more detail in Chapter 8.)

A good example of a business configuration strategy shift is one that is occurring within fast-food giant McDonald's. As part of its overall evolution, McDonald's has utilized a combined franchise and company-owned store model. An outcome of its strategic planning process in 2015 (further reinforced in the Growth Velocity Plan of 2017), McDonald's has made a decision to definitively change its business delivery model to that of purely franchise-owned storefront operation. In this regard the company began to sell its company-owned stores, which in 2015 represented 20% of its total number of storefront operations, to individual franchisees and franchise and licensing syndicates. The goal is to reduce the total amount of company-owned stores to 5% of the overall store total. This shift in the business delivery system, as shown in Figure 6.6, illustrates a downward trend in the number of company-owned store operations (10% of total at the end of 2017) and the subsequent reduction in the number of employees directly employed by McDonald's. Further reductions were seen in 2018 as the number of people working directly for McDonald's dropped to 210 000, and the number of company-owned stores now represents only 7% of the total.[11] Reducing the number of stores it is actually operating has allowed the McDonald's Corporation to move its operational focus and expenditures and capital investment and marketing support away from day-to-day storefront challenges (now handled by franchisees) toward customer service and support training, social and environmental issues, technology modernization (kiosks, ordering and delivery support apps, etc.), along with quicker-to-market menu additions, changes, and promotions.[12]

FIGURE 6.6   **McDonald's Shifting More Restaurants toward Franchising**

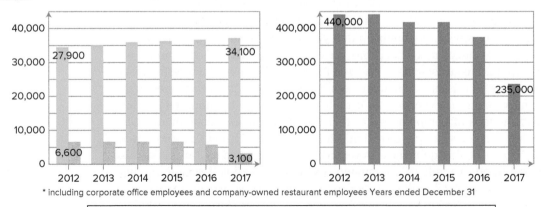

* including corporate office employees and company-owned restaurant employees Years ended December 31

■ Franchise restaurants   ■ Company owned restaurants   ■ Directly employed people*

Responsibility and Accountability

Responsibility and accountability refers to identifying who within the business will be responsible for each aspect of the strategic plan. A fundamental underlying element to the success of a business strategy is to identify the key objectives to be achieved and who will be responsible for their attainment. To assist managers in meeting such objectives, initiatives within a strategic plan are built around what are termed SMAC principles: specific, measurable, actionable, and controllable. (Another popular acronym in this regard is SMART: specific, measurable, actionable, realistic, and time sensitive.) For example, a manager who is given an objective to "increase sales" has little to base his overall effort on or success against, and accountability measures for evaluation purposes are not really identified or communicated. Modify this directive based on SMAC (or SMART) principles, and it becomes "increase the sales revenue of products A, B, and C by 10% over the upcoming three-month period, with 50% of the sales growth coming from new customer accounts and 50% coming from higher sales to existing customers." The manager in charge of products A, B, and C now has a much clearer idea of the objective he/she has been given, and understands the accountability measures against which he/she will be evaluated. These SMAC (or SMART) principles could be further expanded to define which customer segments will be attacked, how much money will be provided for promotional purposes (budget), and how staff involved will be rewarded for the success of this initiative. Strategic plans must identify who is responsible for each element within the plan and also identify how accountability for the success of the plan will be measured.

As you have probably sensed, considerable crossover and interaction exists among the six areas noted in this section. Developing a business strategy looks at each of these areas individually, but also holistically in determining the road an organization should take. Decisions and adjustments relating to products and markets impact the business configuration. Likewise, a revision to the organization's mission or a shift in its vision can result in its strategy taking a whole new course. Competitor actions and the resources that an organization has at its disposal will influence decisions on where and how to compete. Developing a business strategy is a lot like planning a trip. You need to determine where you are, where you want to go, and what the best route to take is given the amount of money you have to spend, your means of getting there, and what you hope to accomplish on the trip. For businesses, a strategic plan is its road map to success. It defines a specific route the business intends to undertake, provides benchmarks to measure its success along the way, and identifies where and how the organization will interact with its customers as it seeks to meet its overall mission and vision.

> For businesses, a strategic plan is the road map to success. It defines a specific route the business intends to undertake, provides benchmarks to measure its success along the way, and identifies where and how the organization will interact with its customers as it seeks to meet its overall mission and vision.

The Strategic Planning Process   LO4

With a base-level understanding of strategy and the core elements that are assessed as part of its development, let's now turn our attention to how managers and organizations actually take this knowledge and information and turn it into the stated "road map" (organizing framework) for success. The building of this road map is called the strategic planning process. This process is all about observations, analyses, choices,

FIGURE 6.7   **Strategic Planning Process**

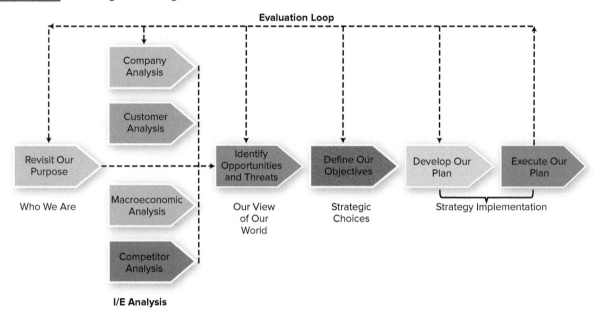

and actions. Again, recognizing that strategy is specific to each company and therefore may require some tailoring of the approach, the following represents a general overview of the steps associated with the development of a strategic plan (see Figure 6.7):

- **Revisit our purpose:** Who are we and where do we want to go?
- **Undertake an I/E (internal/external) analysis to understand our environment:** What changes or shifts are occurring that threaten us or that provide us with opportunities? This analysis can be broken down into two components:
  - *Framing*—determining what is going on in the external environment.
  - *Baselining*—given what has changed or is changing externally, what are our underlying competencies, capabilities, and overall capacity as a company, assessed against what we feel we need to do and rival company capabilities and competencies.
- **Assess our view of our world:** Based on what we know, what are our choices?
- **Choose a direction:** Given our capabilities, competencies, competitive advantages, and resources, which strategic choices should we pursue (where will we play)? What threats must we respond to?
- **Implement our strategy:** How do we develop the strategic thrusts and tactics to achieve our objectives and successfully execute the plan (how we will win)? What key resources or skills can we leverage, or must be acquired in order to succeed?

The strategic planning process is really an organizing framework around which the company can first assess what is changing in its macroeconomic environment, what strategies its competitors are pursuing, who its customers are and how they are changing, and what its capabilities, competencies, and advantages are. Given this analysis, its focus then shifts toward identifying the opportunities that exist in the marketplace, choosing which opportunities to pursue, and then developing an implementation plan to successfully achieve the identified objectives. With this in mind, let's take a quick look at each of the phases within the strategic planning process in order to better understand a management team's focus (see Figure 6.8). Note that the need to revisit an organization's purpose (mission and vision) was discussed earlier and will not be repeated here.[13]

FIGURE 6.8   **Where Is Our Focus?**

Stage of Strategic Planning Process	Focus
Revisiting Our Purpose	Assessing the fit of the current mission and vision of the organization
I/E Analysis	Understanding the external and internal environment External—PESTEL, Porter's Five Forces, competitor SWOT Internal—company SWOT, 3C analysis—competencies, capabilities, capacity Customer—changes in attitudes, behaviour, needs
Our View of Our World	Given what we know about ourselves, our customers, our competitors, and the overall environment, what are our options? What is/are our competitive advantage(s)?
Strategic Choices	Which opportunities make the most sense, given our market position, resources, and environmental dynamics? What threats must we respond to?
Strategy Implementation	Develop the plan. Define the key performance indicators for monitoring it. Execute it.

I/E (Internal/External) Analysis

The I/E (internal/external) analysis is all about assessing business risk and change in four key areas. These areas are identified as macroeconomic, industry, competitor, and company. The external portion of the I/E analysis focuses on understanding what is influencing markets today and what will influence them going forward. In many cases, it is an assessment by management of the magnitude of change that is occurring within a given market arena and what shift in business risk has occurred, or will occur, as a result of such changes. The business models that we discussed in Chapters 1 and 2 (PESTEL, Porter's Five Forces, competitive markets, 3C analysis) are all critical in assisting us with the development of this analysis, as is the inclusion of **SWOT** (strengths, weaknesses, opportunities, threats) analysis (see Figure 6.9).

SWOT stands for strengths, weaknesses, opportunities, and threats.

FIGURE 6.9   **I/E Analysis: What the Models Tell Us**

Business Model	Focus of Analysis
PESTEL	Guides us in developing an understanding of the macro-economic environment—Political, Economic, Societal, Technological, Environmental, Legal
Porter's Five Forces	Guides us in understanding the dynamics of the industry within which we compete—Porter's Five Forces are: • Intensity of rivalry within the industry • Threat of new entrants into the industry • Threat of new product/service substitutes within the industry • Power or control of suppliers within the industry • Power or control of buyers within the industry
Types of Competition	Guides us in understanding the nature of the industry's competitive landscape: • Perfect Competition • Monopolistic Competition • Oligopoly • Monopoly
SWOT Analysis	Strengths, Weaknesses, Opportunities, Threats S & W = Strengths and Weaknesses focus internally O & T = Threats and Opportunities focus externally (macro-environment) Emphasis is to leverage strengths, mitigate weaknesses, pursue opportunities, and manage threats
3C Analysis	An assessment of our competencies, capabilities, and capacity with respect to the resources we possess

As was discussed in earlier chapters, conducting a PESTEL analysis enables us to get a sense of the broad market environment and external influences that could impact demand for our products and services, and change the nature of the way in which we do business. This would include assessing the potential impact of factors such as geopolitical events, new regulations, economic growth potential, foreign exchange rate influences, inflation, demographics, societal changes, accessibility to credit, technology disruptions, environmental impact factors, and legal exposures in the areas of product liability and environmental risk management.

At the industry level, our main focus would be on Porter's Five Forces. The value of Porter's Five Forces lies in its ability to assist us in identifying fundamental changes or disruptions to the industry within which we compete with respect to five key areas (as previously noted in Chapter 2):

1. Rivalry among existing competitors

2. Threat of new entrants

3. Threat of substitute products or services

4. Bargaining power of suppliers

5. Bargaining power of buyers

The following examples illustrate how, having conducted a Porter's Five Forces analysis, we are able to recognize changes or disruptions that are occurring in key market areas. The growth of PayPal and the arrival of Apple Pay and Google Wallet (as a result of the technological innovations behind the smartphone and smartwatch) possess the potential to fully disrupt the existing credit card and debit card marketplace. Apple Pay and Google Wallet seek to render the physical plastic credit card obsolete, thereby impacting existing card manufacturers, while PayPal's focus, along with other similar providers such as Alipay in China, is to offer an alternate payment system that replaces credit cards at large. Chase Bank, one of the largest banks in the United States, announced in 2018 that customers can use Apple Pay and other mobile wallet services for card-free access at over 16 000 ATMs across the U.S.[14] Wireless phones (cell phones) have become a direct substitute for land-line phones as well as for physical plastic cards (credit, debit, loyalty, etc.) for a significant percentage of the population. Online shopping is reducing the traffic at malls and bricks and mortar retail outlets, thereby impacting the revenue potential of mall and shopping centre–based tenants. Companies such as Serta, Simmons, and Sealy, involved in traditional business models relating to the manufacturing and selling of mattresses, are seeing their market sector disrupted by new ecommerce-based entrants such as Casper, BedInABox, and Canadian-based Endy Sleep. Traditional automobile manufacturers such as Toyota, Ford, GM, and Volkswagen are seeing well-capitalized new entrants, such as Tesla, Google, and Apple, move into their industry sector as enhanced technologies associated with automobile development, coupled with improvements in alternate fuel technologies (electric, hydrogen fuel cell), shift the underlying competencies required for success. Canada Post and the United States Postal Service are facing reduced revenues due to substitute products such as text messaging and email impacting overall mail volume. Using Canada Post an an example, the first three quarters of 2018 showed that although parcel delivery revenue was up by $92 million (due to online shopping deliveries), transaction mail (letters, etc.) revenue decreased by $103 million and direct marketing revenue fell by $5 million.[15]

Shifting the emphasis to competitive rivalry analysis, we see that Walmart, given its economies of scale and buying power, is able to exercise considerable price control over its suppliers and then leverage such cost advantages against its direct and indirect competitors. Competitive rivalry intensity continues to rise within the retail and grocery sector in Canada. Over the past decade, the grocery sector in Canada has been adding square footage at a rate faster than the Canadian market is growing. U.S.-based players, such as Walmart and Costco, account for a major part of this growth, but Canadian-based grocers, such as Loblaw Companies, Metro Inc., and Sobeys Inc., are also adding square footage and spending millions of dollars in existing store expansion and upgrades to further strengthen their market positions. Add to this the arrival and development of specialty and ethnic-based grocers such as Whole Foods Canada, T&T Supermarkets, and Groupe Epicia, along with Sobeys' intended expansion of Ontario-based Farm Boy (acquired for $800 million in 2018), and we end up with the percentage increase in square footage exceeding the percentage growth in population by almost three to one.[16] The end result of this increase in competitive rivalry, coupled with the absence of inflation and a weakened Canadian dollar impacting costs, is the potential downward pressure on margins as the cost of gaining or maintaining a share of the customer's wallet increases.

Business IN ACTION

HBC—Reinventing Itself in the Age of Digital Transformation

Established in 1670, the Hudson's Bay Company (HBC) has been one of Canada's most iconic and well-recognized retail operations. Originally a fur-trading company with trading posts across the early Dominion of Canada, HBC today is an international retailer owning such prominent banners as HBC, Saks Fifth Avenue, Lord & Taylor, and Home Outfitters, possessing over 480 stores, employing an estimated 66 000 people, and with a market capitalization value of approximately $2 billion (as of March 2019). With retail, however, as with many other market segments these days, historical success is no longer a predictor of future performance. Like many other retail players (Macy's, Bloomingdale's, Kohls, Sears, etc.), HBC is being challenged like never before by the digital transformation taking place in today's retail arena. The emergence of Amazon.com, along with a host of ecommerce-savvy specialty players, has resulted in a significant change in the way customers approach and ultimately make purchase decisions. As mainly a bricks and mortar business model operator, the Hudson's Bay Company found itself poorly positioned and slow to react to these changes. Recognizing the need to change, in 2017 HBC embarked upon a strategic reassessment of how it conducts its business. Undertaking a formal strategic planning process similar to that outlined in this chapter, HBC identified critical areas

Rick Madonik/ZUMA/Newscom

where change needed to occur. This resulted in a significant resource allocation shift and overall decision-making focus to transform HBC into a fully integrated and digital-savvy omnichannel player.

Becoming a digital player is no easy task, particularly when one needs to play catch-up against "best of breed" players who have already made significant investments, have created lean operations, and have fully leveraged the capabilities of social media and other digital marketing components. For HBC, becoming an omnichannel player meant literally redefining its marketing approach, redirecting its resources, and reformulating its operating processes, all the while looking to enhance its ability to respond to and satisfy customers both in terms of their specific needs as well as how they now shop. A key objective of its

Jeff Whyte/Shutterstock.com

transformation was (and remains) the need to shift its culture and formal decision-making structure to view its interactions with customers not from a bricks and mortar mentality but rather from that of a seamless in-store and online shopping experience, where there is complete integration between the salesperson on the floor and the online operation. Keep in mind that all of this needed to be accomplished in an environment of rapid change and significant disruption.

So how is HBC doing? Although the initial execution was not as effective as hoped, the organization is well into its turnaround and overall transformation. Under newly appointed CEO Helena Foulkes (February 2018), the organization is moving fast and furious to adjust to the new market environment and to reposition HBC as a relevant player in today's retail arena. Recent actions by Foulkes and her management team include:

- Enhancing HBC's online direct-to-consumer presence in North America.

- Restructuring Marketing and IT and integrating digital functions throughout the company.

- Divesting of real estate to raise the required capital to fund the transformation initiatives.

- Creating and executing on a seamless purchase and interactive experience for its customers.

- Closing its underperforming Saks Fifth Avenue stores (approx. 15% of stores).

- Shutting down its 37 Canadian-based Home Outfitters stores and integrating its product lines into the HBC stores.

- Divesting itself of its Lord & Taylor division (sold to Le Tote for just an estimated $100 million USD).

- Merging its European operations, Kaufhof, with top rival Signa Karstadt in order to consolidate its European localization approach.

- Streamlining its operations and reducing the overall debt load the company is carrying due to prior acquisitions and expansion.

Although on the right track and seeing some positive results from its efforts, HBC's challenges going forward remain formidable. TJX, owner of Marshalls, TJ Maxx, Winners, and HomeSense, continues to expand and represents a significant threat to Saks and The Bay's customer base, as does a repositioned Macy's. Bed Bath & Beyond is also further entrenching itself into Canada and will represent a challenge to HBC as it shutters its Home Outfitters and Lord & Taylor stores and reduces the amount of this product line in its The Bay stores. Walmart Canada and Canadian Tire also carry similar merchandise, and the "Amazon effect" continues to siphon away customers. For HBC the key hurdle at this critical moment of change in the retail sector will be its ability to adapt to the evolving needs of customers in a way that maintains their loyalty and commitment to this iconic brand and that delivers to the marketplace a seamless, best-of-breed shopping experience, thereby enabling it to outperform its direct and indirect rivals. In looking to achieve this, strategic discussions going forward will ultimately define where and how resources are to be allocated. For HBC this means it is as important to understand what not to do as it is to know what to do.

Identifying anticipated moves by major and up-and-coming competitors is also a key component of the external analysis. Businesses need to anticipate and react to new initiatives and changes in strategies and market positioning by their competitors. Walmart and Costco's expanded presence in Canada has required organizations such as Loblaw Companies, Metro, and Sobeys to develop strategies in response to this heightened competition in the grocery sector. All are further refining their business models, testing express store options in urban areas, offering online "click and pick up" services, and rebranding stores in order to create closer regional connections with customers. HBC, as mentioned in the Business in Action, is redefining its business approach and overall customer interaction model in response to the digital transformation taking place in today's retail sector. Canadian Tire has modified its store design in an effort to increase its product/service offerings (kitchen and bath, house and home) and drive additional dollars from its customer base in response to changes in the competitive landscape. It has also shifted its product selection toward sports-related products and services (fishing, hockey, etc.) in order to minimize its exposure to Walmart, Home Depot, and Lowe's across more general product categories relating to home maintenance, etc. Tim Hortons and Starbucks both will need to continue to respond to McDonald's growing presence in the coffee market. Assessing competitors means looking at their operations, understanding how they intend to attack the marketplace, determining what message they will send to consumers as part of their positioning/differentiation strategies, and identifying what their perceived competitive advantages are (price, brand awareness, product quality). It also means assessing their management team and getting a feel for how managers make decisions, what their vision for the organization is, and how quickly they will react to shifts or changes in your organization's strategy. A popular way to assess a competitor is through the use of a SWOT analysis. A SWOT analysis asks managers to analyze a competitor on the basis of four elements: what are the competitor's strengths, what are its weaknesses, what market opportunities will it seek to attack, and what threats does it pose to your organization if it is successful in its operating initiatives, new market thrusts, and overall strategies to grow the company. Reviewing the annual reports of competitors, reading their quarterly earnings reports and forward-looking assessments of the future, and listening to their C-level management team's comments relating to market conditions and opportunities are also excellent sources of information relating to intended competitor strategies and actions.

Businesses need to anticipate and react to new initiatives and changes in strategy and market positioning by their competitors.

A customer analysis focuses on trying to identify what shifts have taken place in our customer base in terms of attitudes, behaviours, and needs. The analysis will take into consideration demographic changes to our customer base, shifts in the desires of customers for the types of products and services they are looking to buy, and the impact of the economic climate on both current and future demand for our goods and services. A key outcome of this analysis is the identification of any significant shifts in customer expectations and requirements for our products and services in the markets we serve. The customer analysis will also look to assess our existing customer base for new sales and revenue-generation opportunities, as well as to identify opportunities to reach new customers through new market development (finding new market segments to serve), new product/service offerings, or potentially as a result of acquiring a company and its customer base. As noted previously, Chase Bank was one of the first banks to align itself with Apple Pay for its credit card and debit card business. Chase, in analyzing the opportunity associated with Apple Pay, has found that users of Apple Pay tend to be younger (on average, 9+ years younger than their traditional customer), higher earners (earning roughly 21% more than the average customer). They also tend to be more frequent users of credit cards (an average of 18% greater frequency). For Chase, adding this payment option to its credit card portfolio has enabled it to tap into a financially attractive and engaged customer, just the type of customers banks like. The more transaction-active customers are, the more underlying revenue the bank can generate by offering such "ease of use" services. In February 2015, Chase had more than a million customers using Apple Pay. Today, Apple Pay has over 250 million users globally, with over 4900 banks supporting this product (including Canada's major banks) and over a billion transactions being reported quarterly.[17] As the evolution of digital payment options grows, Chase, as an early adopter of technology, views itself as being well-positioned to attract additional customers within this demographic, and therefore able to fully leverage its portfolio of products and services, increasing both its customer count as well as the revenue generated from the services it offers.[18] Mars, traditionally thought of as a confections and food company (M&Ms, Milky Way, Snickers, Uncle Ben's, Masterfoods), has via a series of recent acquisitions transitioned itself into one of the largest manufacturers of pet food. Mars pet care brands include Nutro, Iams, Royal Canin, Whiskas, Greenies, and Pedigree, to name a few.[19]

> A customer analysis focuses on trying to identify what shifts have taken place in our customer base in terms of attitudes, behaviours, and needs.

As part of the organizational evaluation process, managers (and business owners) need to assess the competencies of their own organization and the level of resources (financial, operational, etc.) they have access to in order to determine what their capacity and overall capabilities are as a company. This is the internal portion of the I/E analysis. Just as managers are encouraged to assess competitors via a SWOT analysis approach, managers also are encouraged to conduct a SWOT analysis on their own organization. For organizations to properly assess their position in the marketplace and the probability of success of the various business opportunities they are considering, a full internal audit (strengths and weaknesses) of the firm's financial resources, organizational competencies, operational capacities, human resource skills, and overall capacity should be conducted and then measured against key competitors. By conducting such an internal analysis, managers can determine which markets the organization can successfully compete in and which initiatives should be avoided due to the resource, competency, and capacity limitations of the organization. For managers, the internal analysis represents a form of enterprise risk management. It seeks to identify the financial, operational, technological, and market risks that would need to be assumed if a certain opportunity were pursued, and measures the ability of the organization to be able to respond to—and manage—such risks prior to the implementation of these initiatives.

From this I/E analysis phase, the organization hopes to be in a position to determine where, and how, it wants to compete. A critical part of this I/E analysis process is to identify opportunities that exist for the organization, as well as any threats that may be present and that must be appropriately assessed from a risk perspective. Another key outcome should be the ability of the organization to define any temporary or sustainable competitive advantages it has over its competition.

Competitive Advantage(s) Identification

Competitive Advantage occurs when a company possesses capabilities that enable it to perform critical activities better than its rivals; this advantage enables it to generate greater sales and/or margins and creates preference for its products and services in the minds of its customers.

A **competitive advantage** is an advantage an organization has over its rivals that enables it to generate greater sales or margins, and creates preference for its products and services in the minds of its customers. Whether this advantage is temporary or sustainable for a longer period of time is determined by the strength of the competitive advantage equation as it relates to the advantage being assessed Figure 6.10).

FIGURE 6.10   **Competitive Advantage (VRIN) Equation**

For managers, a key outcome of the I/E analysis is identifying the competitive advantages an organization believes it possesses when compared to its competitors, as well as the advantages it attributes to its rivals. As noted above, a company enjoys a competitive advantage when it can provide customers with a product/service that offers more value than alternate products/services offered by its competitors. The key words in the definition of competitive advantage are *more value*. The ability to enhance the value of a product or service when measured against competitive offerings is what fundamentally entices customers to select your product as the best solution to their needs. Another way of stating this is that the real measure of a competitive advantage is the reason why a customer chooses to purchase your product over those of your competitors. Competitive advantages are either strategic or operational. Strategic competitive advantages can be thought of as "first mover" actions in a marketplace; that is, the ability to see how your organization can change the rules of the game in the markets the company chooses to compete in. Apple Inc.'s innovative approach to the integration of entertainment and technology, and the new customer demands being driven from it, is an example of a strategic competitive advantage. From this strategic sense of market direction and needs Apple has been able to create innovative products such as the iPhone, iPad, Apple Pay, and iPod. Operational competitive advantages are the result of being able to execute the day-to-day activities required of the transformation and marketing support processes within the organization in a manner that is superior to the same execution requirements of competitors. This means being more efficient and effective than competitors in the processes the organization undertakes to deliver products and services to the market, being more responsive to customer needs, offering superior quality, being able to offer new product enhancements faster, and being more flexible toward change as markets evolve. Figure 6.11 provides an overview of the four major areas where companies can seek to establish competitive advantage opportunities.[20]

FIGURE 6.11   **Areas for Establishing Competitive Advantage Opportunities**

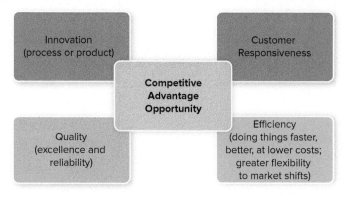

Strategy Development

For managers, the next step after completing the I/E analysis and identifying the organization's competitive advantages is to make decisions as to which opportunities to pursue and how resources will be allocated in support of these market opportunities. These decisions are then formulated into the organization's strategic plan, which can be thought of as possessing three parts: the corporate-level strategy, the business-level strategy, and the operating plan. The **corporate-level strategy** defines *what* the organization intends to accomplish and *where* it plans to compete (the markets to be focused on). It identifies which businesses to compete in, which new businesses to add, which business areas to exit, and where the business emphasis should be placed. In general, it is considered the high-level strategy that guides the organization's overall activities; think of it as outlining the "big picture." Once this direction has been determined, the organization then develops its **business-level strategy**. This defines *how* the organization intends to accomplish the corporate-level strategy. Business-level strategies respond to questions of how to compete in the market sectors where the organization has chosen to do business. This level of planning would be determining specific objectives it hopes to achieve for each of its identified business initiatives or business units. Finally, with these objectives identified and understood, the organization would develop the specific tactics or what is called its **operating plan**, which it will need to execute in order to ensure the business strategy—and, therefore, the corporate strategy—is met. Figure 6.12 provides an overview of what this process and its sequencing looks like.

Corporate-Level Strategy defines what the organization intends to accomplish and where it plans to compete.

Business-Level Strategy outlines specific objectives the organization hopes to achieve for each of its identified business initiatives and/or business units.

Operating Plan is a detailed, immediate-term set of objectives and corresponding tactics designed to achieve a specific business initiative.

FIGURE 6.12 **Strategy Alignment**

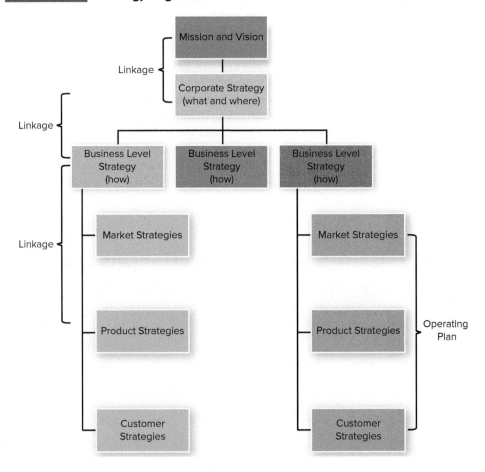

Let's use Shaw Communications Inc., one of Canada's largest residential entertainment and communications companies, as an illustration to highlight the relationship between corporate-level and business-level strategies. Headquartered in Calgary, Shaw Communications currently serves an estimated 3 million Canadians with wireless network services. As part of its ongoing commitment to its investment community, Shaw Communications continually seeks to refine its corporate focus for the organization. Pursuant to this, Shaw announced a total business transformation in fiscal year 2018. This transformation, a multi-year initiative, was designed to reinvent the company's business model and enhance the organization's ability to meet the needs of its customers. Core to this transformation was an objective of long-term growth built around a product portfolio consisting of broadcast services, residential and business data networking, video, voice, and Internet services, digital direct-to-home satellite TV services, and wireless communication (smartphone) services.

Shaw's vision is to be the leading entertainment and communications company, delivering exceptional customer experience through outstanding people who exhibit accountability for their actions, passion for their customers, integrity in their business dealings, and balance in their lives, and who work in a collaborative and cooperative team-based environment underscored by a positive, "can do" attitude. Its mission is to provide its customers with high-quality entertainment, information, and communication services, utilizing a variety of distribution technologies.

To achieve this vision and mission, Shaw Communications has established critical themes at the corporate level to guide the organization's decision-making and operation execution. These corporate strategy objectives can be summarized as follows:

1 To continue to build awareness for the brand through exceptional customer experience

2 To invest in and leverage leading technology in order to maintain and build our network advantage and to support emerging technology trends

3 To deliver a disciplined pricing and promotional strategy that enables us to maintain and grow our customer base

4 To improve upon our operational efficiencies in order to enhance productivity and improve customer service capabilities [21]

To ensure the achievement of these corporate objectives, Shaw Communications has developed an underlying business-level strategy for each of the corporate strategy objectives identified. These business-level strategies offer managers guidance on how the specific corporate objectives are going to be measured and realized. As an example, with respect to the corporate-level strategic objective of improving upon operational efficiencies and customer service capabilities (summarized for brevity), Shaw Communications is seeking its operational units to:

• Shift customer interactions to digital platforms

• Drive more self-install, self-help, and self-serve customer needs options

• Streamline the process of building and servicing its networks

With respect to the corporate-level objective of investing in and leveraging leading technology in order to maintain and build Shaw's network advantage and to support emerging technology trends, particularly in the wireless sector, Shaw identified the acquisition of Freedom Mobile in 2016 for $1.6 billion as an opportunity to build scale, adding 940 000 customers and 300+ points of distribution, and more importantly creating immediate access to the Ontario marketplace (Toronto and Ottawa), thereby expanding its service capabilities to over 16 million Canadians. This acquisition, coupled with the addition of the iPhone to its product portfolio of phone offerings, has enabled Shaw communications to grow its customer footprint significantly over the 2+ years following this acquisition. In addition, Shaw Communications continues to make significant investments in its hybrid fibre coaxial networks, WiFi networks, and wireless networks, as well as working with its strategic partners (Comcast, Nokia, and Broadsoft) to develop and deliver core network and infrastructure solutions that are considered to be best-in-class and enhance the overall experience of its customer base.[22]

Once corporate-level and business-level strategies and objectives have been identified, operating plans are developed that will ensure their successful execution. Key components of the operating plan development process include:

a. Specifics as to how to compete (for each business initiative or business unit)

b. Identification of the key revenue drivers and performance metrics (called KPMs) and an assessment of the total potential financial results the business can expect from a particular initiative

c. Identification of the upfront and ongoing cost commitments necessary to develop the market opportunity that the business has decided to focus on

d. Identification of the required market position and marketing communication initiatives required to support the business initiative or unit in question

e. Identification of staffing, infrastructure, and process realignment required in support of the initiatives undertaken

Figure 6.13 provides a summary of the key fundamentals that managers need to fully develop when formulating operating plans.

Again using our Shaw Communications example, operational objectives and key performance metrics (KPMs) that the company has identified to assess its performance in 2019 include:[23]

• Successful launch of its Big Binge promotion

• Deployment of Freedom Mobile operations in 140 Walmart locations

FIGURE 6.13   **Fundamentals to Operating Plan Formulation**

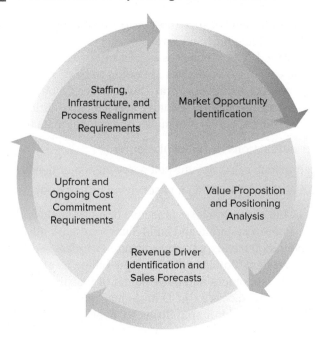

- Successful deployment of its 700 MHz network
- Further reduction in customer "churn" defection (customers leaving Shaw) below the current 1.28% desertion rate
- An EBITDA (earnings before interest expense and taxes, less depreciation and amortization) target of $2.2 billion
- A free cash flow (FCF) generation target of $500 million
- Capital expenditures not to exceed $1.2 billion

At the end of the day, the organization's strategic plan should identify where and how it intends to compete in the marketplace, identify which weapons of competitive rivalry it will leverage as its products/services battle for market share, and define the marketing and operational plans required to effectively and efficiently execute the plan. A good way to assess the "fit" of the strategy being recommended is to assess it against the five questions provided in Figure 6.14.

Prior to the implementation (execution) of the strategic plan, managers should review the plan with the intent of confirming the following:

1 The operational activities within the plan are properly aligned to achieve the plan's objectives.

2 The budgets established, and the money to be generated, are realistic when compared to sales forecasts.

3 The resources needed to successfully execute the plan are available or can be acquired.

4 A series of benchmarks or performance indicators have been established that will enable the management team to effectively monitor the plan's progress.

FIGURE 6.14 Five Critical Questions to Review When Developing Strategy

1. Does your proposed strategy leverage your organization's resources and capabilities?
2. Does your strategy fit with current and anticipated industry/market conditions?
3. Are the competencies that you plan to leverage considered to be sustainable for the required period?
4. Are the key drivers of your strategy consistent with the organization's strategic objective and position?
5. Do you have the ability and wherewithal to successfully implement the chosen strategy?

Source: Ken Wong, Queen's University.

At the end of the day, the strategy being recommended should define, for the organization, where and how it intends to compete in the marketplace, which weapons of competitive rivalry it will leverage as its products and services battle for market share, and the marketing and operating plans that will be required to effectively and efficiently execute the plan.

Strategy Execution

The final phase of the strategic planning process is the strategy execution phase. It is this portion of the process where management shifts its emphasis from what it wants to do, and hopes to achieve, to actively engaging the business into executing the desired strategic thrusts and tactics. It is in this stage where the organization

Directional Lock-In is the level of financial and operational commitment an organization incurs as a result of implementing the organization's strategies.

becomes fully committed to the plan, resulting in a degree of "directional lock-in" taking place. The level of **directional lock-in** directly equates to the level of riskiness of the plan, as the higher the capital amount and resource base being committed, the greater the impact on the organization should the plan not be executed properly and fail to meet its required objectives.

In the execution phase, organizations commit their capital resources for needs such as building plants, retooling existing plants, building new equipment, funding research and development for new products and services, undertaking marketing and advertising campaigns, funding warehouse and distribution logistics support, and hiring staff. The amount of investment into these items that is required by an organization at the front end of the execution of a strategy results in the degree of directional lock-in that a company experiences. The more money invested up front the greater the risk to the company, as the return of this investment is determined by the success of the strategy in the marketplace. For example, a small-business owner may decide to open up a second store for their retail business in a neighbouring town as part of a new business strategy. This decision requires the owner to make a considerable locked-in investment prior to the receipt of any revenue (sales) from this new location. The owner will have to build a building or commit to a lease for retail space. Inventory and equipment will need to be purchased. Staff will need to be hired. Such a decision could result in a capital investment running into the hundreds of thousands of dollars. Going back to our example of Shaw Communications Inc., one of the business initiatives commented on above was the acquisition of Freedom Mobile Inc. for US$1.9 billion. The decision to acquire Freedom Mobile represented a significant investment on the part of Shaw Communications. Once the acquisition takes place, Shaw Communications is "locked in" to this significant monetary commitment, and the supporting resources required to execute its intended operational strategy for Freedom Mobile in a manner that enables Shaw to grow its market reach and depth and contribute positively to its revenue model and underlying profitability, thereby enabling Shaw Communications Inc. to meets its vision of becoming the leading entertainment and communications company.

For any business to be successful in recovering its capital investment and covering the operating costs associated with delivering products and services to customers, the execution plans need to be effectively implemented. This means that their operations must be efficient, their marketing plans must be effective, their staff must deliver on meeting customer needs, and their management teams must make good decisions on how to respond to issues and challenges that occur as the strategy is executed. The end result is that the company has to generate enough revenue from the sale of its products and services to cover its operating costs, meet its financial obligations relating to debt it has taken on (if applicable), and return the investment back to the company. Only if this performance level occurs will the organization actually experience true growth.

A key requirement of the strategy execution phase is for managers to continuously monitor the success of the implementation of the strategy and to take corrective action quickly in the event that things are not going well. Managers keep their finger on the pulse of the execution of the strategy by measuring success against predefined benchmarks or objectives. Sales forecasts become sales targets for sales managers. Operations managers monitor and manage processes and materials purchases, as well as labour levels, to ensure that costs stay in line. Finance managers monitor the cash flowing into and out of the business to ensure the company can continue to pay its bills and that the revenue coming in from business operations is sufficient to meet current and future cash requirements. Periodic senior-level management meetings take place in order to fully evaluate the company's progress with the strategy and determine whether adjustments to the plan need to be made. They also focus on assessing the impact of competitor actions and responses to the plan.

FIGURE 6.15 **Monitoring Plan Success**

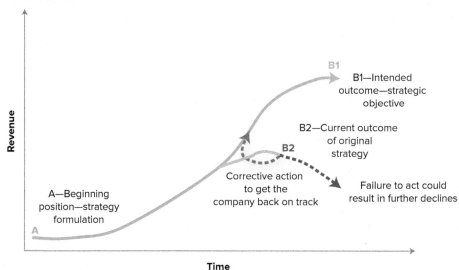

This ongoing evaluation process is designed to ensure that managers look to see if the organization, at the end of the business cycle period, will meet the objectives being strived for. If they sense that such objectives are not currently on track, then alternate corrective tactics or revised objectives will be developed and put into place to get the organization back on track or to minimize the negative consequences of a company's weak performance (see Figure 6.15).[24]

A key requirement of the execution phase is for managers to continuously monitor the success of the implementation of the strategy and to take corrective action quickly in the event that things are not going well.

Business IN ACTION

What Makes for a Bad Strategy?

This chapter has been focused on the fundamentals of strategic planning and how organizations can develop good business strategies. Did you ever think, however, about what makes for a bad strategy? Richard P. Rumelt has. In his book *Good Strategy/ Bad Strategy: The Difference and Why It Matters*, Rumelt, a management professor at UCLA, not only outlines the core fundamentals of what makes for a good strategy, but also offers insight to the strategy development traps that managers can fall into and that ultimately result in poorly planned or executed strategies. According to Rumelt, bad strategies can often be traced back to one or more of the following:

1) failure to face the challenge, 2) mistaking goals for strategy, 3) developing poor strategic objectives, or 4) building strategy around fluff.

In terms of failing to face the challenge, managers and strategists often fail to fully define the key issues that are impacting the company's overall performance and market position. An example of this could be an organization whose strategic objective is to increase its market share, yet fails to understand that its underlying business processes are inefficient, or its administrative bureaucracy overly cumbersome, thereby placing it at a competitive disadvantage relative to rivals in terms of costs and/or service effectiveness. Another example could be a shift in customer focus that results in a deterioration of market position. IBM specializes in providing high-value, high-margin consulting services. A key service delivered by IBM is assisting companies with the development and management of their in-house data storage and development needs. The marketplace, however, is trending toward an outsourcing of these centres to companies such as Google and Amazon. The impact to IBM is a reduction in the need for the data management consulting services they offer. A key part of strategic planning is not just to identify the objectives you want to achieve, but also to recognize the key obstacles that must be overcome in order to be successful in achieving those objectives.

With respect to mistaking goals for strategy, companies often create specific objectives and then interpret them as strategy. As an example, the XYZ Company's objective is to increase revenues by 20% and profit margins by 10%. Objectives on their own, however, do not constitute strategy. Strategy implies a specific set of actions designed to achieve a particular objective or outcome. It also implies knowing what should *not* be done, as much as it means knowing what needs to be accomplished. In order for organizations to be successful at executing strategy, organizations must understand the specific actions required and develop a measurable road map for success. Successful strategy execution is predicated on identifying what you want to do, and then creating, reinventing, modifying, or adjusting the business model in a way that enables you to achieve the strategic objectives identified.

Equally destructive as mistaking goals for strategy is the development of vague or bad objectives. In order to develop strategic initiatives, managers and decision makers need clarity with respect to where to allocate the organization's resources. Weak strategies often reflect "pie in the sky" desires versus offering specific and measurable direction for the organization to work toward. Additionally, Rumelt has found that many companies try to do too much at the same time. Instead of focusing on a limited number of priorities, thereby enabling the organization to concentrate its resources and efforts on specific initiatives, the organization attempts to support a laundry list of objectives. This results in the inability of the organization to truly accomplish any of the objectives in a way that creates competitive advantage and long-term strategic success.

Finally, organizations can fall into the "fluff" trap. Fluff refers to the organization's inability to truly define what it is that it wants to do. It also refers to an organization's inability to communicate the strategy in language that its employees will understand. As an example, our strategy is to position our company as the preferred customer-centric intermediary in the banking sector. What does this mean? How does this statement enable you and me, as the organization's managers and decision makers, to create specific underlying initiatives in pursuit of this strategic market position?

To be successful at strategy execution, strategists within the organization need to be able to accurately identify and assess the magnitude of the underlying challenges facing the organization, establish a focused approach on which challenges to respond to and how, and then develop and effectively communicate the coordinated actions that will enable the organization to effectively execute on the identified priorities. Rajeev Suri, the new CEO of Nokia, is doing just this. He has consolidated Nokia and spun off unprofitable businesses in order to stabilize the company. He and his team have identified the company's end-to-end networks, and supporting stand-alone enterprise software, as the current core revenue drivers, and as a result are focusing the company's resources on expanding Nokia's presence in this market. The company also continues to pursue 5G development as a core future earnings stream, particularly with respect to mobile radio products. In support of this, Suri and his team orchestrated the successful acquisition of Alcatel-Lucent (2016), thereby enabling the two companies to consolidate their resources to better compete with Huawei and Ericsson, two key rivals in the business sectors noted above. In addition, recognizing the brand strength of Nokia, Suri remains focused on returning the company to the smartphone sector. This, however, is being approached differently. Rather than looking to compete head-to-head with Apple, Samsung, and other well-entrenched rivals, Suri is focusing the company's efforts on making Nokia a technology developer that will create innovative products in this sector and then license them to others for their use. The catch is that in order to use the Nokia brand, smartphone players will need to have Nokia handle the product and related technology development.[25]

Web Integration

Want to track Nokia's progress? Go to www.nokia.com.

Strategy Challenges in the SME (Small and Medium-Size Enterprises) Sector

For owners of small and medium-size enterprises (SMEs), taking the time to plan strategically is often one of the most difficult things on the "to do" list to accomplish. Unlike large organizations, which possess significant managerial resources with specific specializations, and which generally have a board of directors and a given level of emphasis on assessing strategic direction at defined periods of time, SME managers and owners often find themselves acting as the marketing, human resource, operations, and financial managers all rolled into one. Their daily, weekly, and monthly efforts seem to be focused on fighting fires or fixing problems. When they do get a chance to plan, it is often focused on short-term planning efforts, generally geared toward current-year initiatives. In addition to having little time to plan, small and medium-size business owners often lack access to the expertise and resources needed to undertake a strategy review. Having said this, the need to plan strategically is just as important for a small business as it is for a major multinational organization. Small and medium-size business owners must assess and anticipate the changes that are occurring within their markets, the need for their products, and new opportunities that could exist. Strategic planning also enables these managers and business owners to make more efficient use of their resources and to minimize impulse spending or copycat initiatives that may result in little to no revenue or profitability gains for the organization. A good example is the temptation to spend large amounts of money on a radio or television advertising campaign. To maximize the return on such an expenditure (or to make such an expenditure at all), business managers and owners should first determine whether this is the correct approach to reaching their primary target market, whether it is the best route to take in delivering such a message, whether it is the right time of the year for the message to be delivered, whether the anticipated return on the advertising investment warrants its costs, and whether this expenditure makes sense given the objectives the business hopes to achieve going forward. Creating a strategy for the business, determining where and how to compete, and laying out a plan for an upcoming specified period will enable SME owners to make better decisions as to how to allocate their monetary, staffing, and operational resources. Taking a planning cycle approach, as discussed in Chapter 1, will provide clarity and direction to the business and enable it to better define benchmarks against which operational performance can be measured.

The need to plan strategically is just as important for a small business as it is for a major multinational organization.

Business IN ACTION

Planning a Small Business Strategy

For Elwin Derbyshire, risk taking is nothing new. A veteran Canadian Tire Corporation dealer, Elwin has seen the competitive landscape change significantly over his illustrious career. He is a recipient of numerous community and Canadian Tire corporate awards and is the owner of Canada's largest-volume (sales) Canadian Tire store. Elwin credits much of his success to the belief that it is critical to understand market trends, both in terms of the consumers' wants and in-store technology. Understanding trends is only the start—you must then deliver products that meet the customers' needs. A key component of this process is competitive intelligence. Elwin diligently reads trade periodicals and monitors key market indexes to keep abreast of shifts in market dynamics and trends. Visiting both direct and indirect competitor retail operations also provides him with a sense of where the competition is going and what new trends are taking hold in the marketplace. Elwin is also a firm believer in the need to maximize the use of technology to drive operating efficiencies and effectiveness. Entrepreneurship is about risk taking. To quote a baseball analogy (a favourite of Elwin's), if you never take a step off first base, you will never steal (or reach) second base. Risk taking, however, can be managed. With Elwin, it means continuous interaction with suppliers at trade shows and Canadian Tire Corporation buyers, and seeking the involvement of his managerial people and other team members in the long-range planning and the day-to-day buying and service-related decisions in the store. Where is this decision-making effort focused? Right at the end user—the customer! In Elwin's mind, the emphasis is on the shopper and the delivery of a positive and unique shopping experience. The most important part in the customer's shopping experience in a "needs-driven" store like Canadian Tire is having the product that the customer came looking for. A lot of time is devoted to ensuring the store is stocked and products are on the floor, particularly with the flyer-advertised items—it is critical to deliver on what you promise. A key ingredient in the store's success is recruiting and training skilled staff and then following up and assessing staff competencies and empowering people with responsibility and accountability for getting the job done. Yes, there are some risks to being the first to introduce new products and enter new markets. In today's competitive retail environment, with increasing sales volumes, the inventory risks become larger (over $10 million in inventory in this one store), but the benefits can be huge. Possessing many years of business experience, natural leadership qualities, and an uncanny aptitude for instinctively sensing new opportunities, Elwin knows strategically where he envisions his operation going. As he states, "If you always do what you have always done, you will always get what you have always got." Reaching out to tap new customer needs and desires, involving his team in the community, and not waiting for customers to simply show up at the store are the key drivers in his strategy-planning philosophy.

Courtesy of Elwin Derbyshire

Vale Stock/Shutterstock.com

Strategic Planning in the NFP (Not-for-Profit) Sector (Social Economy)

LO5

Strategic planning in the not-for-profit sector poses some unique challenges over and above those mentioned up to this point in our discussion. Like for-profit entities, not-for-profits, in many instances, must develop strategies and tactics that produce positive financial results for the organization. If they don't, then they run the risk of becoming unable to sustain their operations. Where the difference lies, however, is in what drives the overall mission of the organization and to whom, collectively, the management team needs to respond. In the for-profit sector, the overarching objective of a business's strategy is ultimately focused on driving profitability and maximizing gains on behalf of business owners or shareholders. This is accomplished via the sale of goods and services, and funding is provided through operations, debt financing, or equity financing. In the social economy, not-for-profit leaders have a different mandate in that they are challenged to succeed while balancing the effectiveness of their economic activities (if they provide goods or services for a fee) with the social goal or purpose of the organization (see Figure 6.16). Their strategies involve a stronger inclusion of needs delivery based on the collective interest and social goals of a segment of society. Rather than having shareholders or direct business owners, their actions are assessed by some organized collective (membership base, government entity, or community board). Financing is, in many cases, the result of philanthropic donations, government allowances or grants, and private grants, in addition to dollars generated through the sale of goods and services, and/or dollars borrowed (debt financing). In a number of cases, there may actually be no revenue generated by the not-for-profit, making it totally reliant on external funding mechanisms, such as government.

In formulating and implementing strategy in the social economy, managers must ensure that their actions, in addition to guiding the economic activity of the not-for-profit (NFP), effectively respond to the following (see Figure 6.17):[26]

1 Mission balance: Maintain the balance between the need to create an effective economic base for the NFP while ensuring that the social mission and goals of the NFP are met.

2 Vitality: Enhance the **vitality** of the organization through maintenance and growth of its membership or community support base.

Vitality refers to the ability of the NFP to grow and sustain its membership base and donor base.

FIGURE 6.16 **Social Economy: Strategic Conclusions**

Private Sector		Social Economy
Profitability Maximizing Gains	Overarching Objective	Needs Delivery via Collective Interest and Social Goals
Management Shareholders	Influences	Democratic Foundation Organized Collective
Debt/Equity Financing Internal Reserves	Financing	Diversified Base—Members, Government, Community
Sales of Goods and Services	Predominant Revenue	Sponsorship—Government, Model Foundations, etc. Sales of Goods and Services

Source: Adapted from Réseau d'investissement social du Québec: *Guide for Analysis of Social Economy Enterprises.*

FIGURE 6.17 **Social Economy: Strategy Considerations**

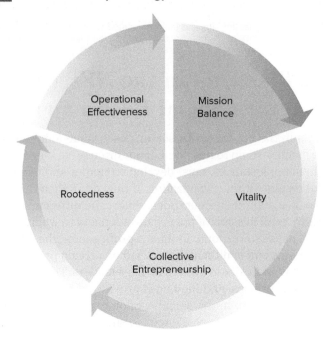

Source: Adapted from Réseau d'investissement social du Québec: *Guide for Analysis of Social Economy Enterprises.*

Collective Entrepreneurship ensures that the involvement of the community where an organization is located and the population that it serves are reflected in the formulation and implementation of the strategy.

Rootedness refers to the extent to which the NFP is interwoven into the fabric of the community that it serves and is supported by a broad representation of its organizations, businesses, and citizens.

3 **Collective entrepreneurship:** Maintain an atmosphere of **collective entrepreneurship**, which means ensuring that the involvement of the community where it is located and the population it serves are reflected in the formulation and implementation of the strategy.

4 **Rootedness:** Enhance the **rootedness** of the organization by strengthening partnerships and not-for-profit networks that are supportive of the mission and work of the NFP.

5 **Operational effectiveness:** Operate in a manner that demonstrates the products and services offered by the NFP are priced at levels that ensure their accessibility by the targeted social audience, and provide mechanisms for support for those who are in need yet truly unable to pay.[27]

Management Reflection—The Need to Plan

Sun Tzu, in *The Art of War*, comments that "strategy without tactics is the long road to victory; tactics without strategy is the noise before defeat." For managers, regardless of the size of their business, defining the direction of the company and determining where and how the business is going to compete is essential. Successful businesses have one very common denominator: they take the time to plan how the business will be positioned in the marketplace, and what markets it will serve, and then they execute the critical components of their strategy better than their competitors. A successful business person will be able to tell you why their business is different from its competitors and unique to its customers. In essence, they know what their competitive advantages are, and they know how to leverage them to ensure their business is "best of breed."

In summary, then, what constitutes a successful strategy? A successful strategy is one that properly assesses the external environment, defines the changes and opportunities within market segments the organization intends to serve, and effectively allocates resources and maximizes capabilities in a manner that is supportive of the products and services it delivers to the marketplace. A key outcome of the strategy formulation process should be the identification of the key competitive advantages the organization possesses and the successful leveraging of these advantages within its marketing communication and operational delivery processes. To be successful, the organization must be able to transfer the knowledge gained during the assessment process into a well-formulated strategy, which it then executes successfully to a defined target market in need of the goods and services being offered. To be successful in this regard, the organization needs to visualize this process from the customers' perspective. This means that as managers we need to fully understand the key buying criteria that customers are using in making purchase decisions, and then determine how our organization can best align our products and services to meet customer expectations identified via these criteria. This process is what will enable us to develop and sustain competitive advantages, and will help us determine how to most effectively allocate resources in order to drive innovation, efficiency, quality, and customer responsiveness initiatives. Only when we have fully understood what the customer wants, and how we can most effectively respond to this, will we be able to embark on a well-thought-out path toward profitability and organizational wealth creation.

Chapter Summary

This chapter provides students with an introductory overview of the concept of business strategy and of the fundamentals of the strategic planning process. A key emphasis within the chapter is the identification of the key elements that managers need to assess as they develop a strategy for their business or organization. These include the creation of vision and mission statements, defining the products/services to be offered, assessing the resources the organization has or has the capacity to acquire, configuring the business system to ensure the execution of the intended set of actions, and defining managerial responsibility and accountability to ensure its success. Also discussed, in detail, is the strategic planning process itself and the key stages within it (revisiting the organization's purpose, I/E analysis, the identification of strategic choices, strategy formulation, and strategy implementation). Included within this discussion is an understanding of the difference between corporate-level strategies, business-level strategies, and operating plans, and the linkages among the three. The chapter closes with some thoughts relating to the challenges that strategy development poses for small and medium-size businesses, as well as the unique influences that not-for-profits need to consider when assessing and developing their organizational strategies. For not-for-profits, strategic plan development is uniquely challenged by the balancing requirements between financial stability and meeting the needs of a collective interest, defined by its social mandate and, in many cases, the altruistic goals of an organized collective.

Developing Business Knowledge and Skills

Key Terms

mission *p. 212*

vision *p. 212*

harvesting *p. 214*

SWOT *p. 219*

competitive advantage *p. 224*

corporate-level strategy *p. 226*

business-level strategy *p. 226*   vitality *p. 235*

operating plan *p. 226*   collective entrepreneurship *p. 236*

directional lock-in *p. 230*   rootedness *p. 236*

Questions for Discussion

1. What are the six key areas that managers need to assess when developing a business strategy? How does managerial responsibility and accountability factor into this process? (LO3)

2. What are the major stages of the strategic planning process? Why is revisiting an organization's mission and vision such a critical beginning point of the strategic planning process? (LO4)

3. Why do managers need to assess the internal and external environment as part of the strategy development process? What key takeaways do you believe should be the result of this analysis? (LO3)

4. What is the difference among corporate-level strategies, business-level strategies, and operating plans? How are they interconnected? (LO4)

5. How is strategy formulation different in the not-for-profit sector when compared to the for-profit sector? In your mind, does this make the development of strategy in the NFP sector more challenging? Why, or why not? (LO5)

Question for Individual Action

Assume that *Canadian Business* magazine has asked you to write a short reflective commentary on the role of strategy and/or the strategic planning process as it relates to organizational growth and market position. You are to craft a creative essay that will communicate to readers your unique perspective on the role of strategy and the importance of strategic planning in the life cycle of an organization. The approach you take in responding to this question is open to you. You may choose to focus on a specific aspect of strategy or strategic planning, or tackle it at a more "macro" level. The intent is not simply to re-state information from the chapter, or to re-word basic definitions, but rather to develop a truly reflective discussion on the subject matter you choose to explore. You may quote other sources in your commentary, but remember that it is meant to be your personal interpretation. It should not be thought of as a research paper, but as a learning tool written from the position of a knowledgeable student within this field.

Team Exercise

Conduct interviews with two or three small-business owners in your local area. Ask them to describe their strategy development or business planning process. Discuss with them the strategy development approach presented in this chapter, and ask them to comment on some of the barriers they envision in utilizing this methodology as part of their business planning approach. Prepare a presentation that summarizes your discussions and provides recommendations for best practices for small businesses looking to assess their current market position and future strategy.

Case for Discussion 1

Agropur: Managing through Change in the Canadian Dairy Industry

The Agropur Dairy Cooperative (Agropur) was founded in 1938 as the Société coopérative agricole du canton de Granby. As a cooperative, its initial focus was to provide purchasing power on the supply side for its members. It quickly expanded to further its role and overall focus to include the processing of the milk produced by its members into products including butter, cheese, and most recently yogurt. Agropur's operations continue to grow, expanding its reach nationwide both through organic initiatives and by acquisition, culminating with its 2008 expansion into the United States. Today, operating from Longueil, Quebec, Agropur is the largest dairy-processing cooperative in North America. Its brands include such well-known names as Natrel, OKA, iOGO, Island Farms, Northumberland, and Sealtest. For 2018, the organization produced revenue of $6.7 billion and net earnings after patronage dividends and tax of $67.7 million.[28]

Agropur's primary competitors in the Canadian dairy processing industry include Toronto-based Parmalat Canada, a subsidiary of France's Lactalis, and Montreal-based Saputo. Privately held Le Group Lactalis is the largest dairy group in the world. Through Parmalat it manages a stable of well-known brands including Lactantia, Beatrice, Black Diamond, Astro, Balderson, and Galbani. Saputo (see the Business in Action in Chapter 7) is among the top 10 dairy processors in the world; it posted 2018 revenue of $11.54 billion and earnings of $853 million. Approximately 35% of the business is derived from the organization's Canadian operations. Some of Saputo's more well-known brands include Dairyland, Neilson, and Stella.[29]

As with any industry, market sectors are constantly in motion and change is occurring on a regular, if not accelerated, basis. In this regard, Agropur and its rivals mentioned above are continuously attempting to adjust to changing consumer preferences in the category. As an example, according to Statistics Canada milk consumption has been experiencing a downward trend in Canada, peaking at 98 L per capita in 1980 and now hovering around 65 L. Partly skimmed (2% milk fat) milk passed standard milk (3.25%) as Canadians' preferred type in 1976. In turn, demand for partly skimmed milk peaked in 1988 and has declined gradually since that time. Skim milk (usually defined as 0.5% milk fat or under) enjoyed some popularity in the 1990s and early 2000s, but never really caught on with Canadians in the way partly skimmed did. Substitutes such as soymilk and almond milk have emerged more recently and are attractive to a small group of consumers. In general, Canadians are drinking significantly less milk than they once did, and the milk they do drink is lower in fat.[30]

The story for ice cream is similar. Canadians' consumption of ice cream peaked at 13 L per capita in 1979, and now sits at around 4 L per person. However, over the same period yogurt has become one of the stars of the dairy industry. Consumption has grown from less than 2 L per person to 11 L per person. Functional and fortified yogurts are particularly attractive.[31]

The market categories of cheese and butter have also experienced an upward trend. Per capita cheese consumption by Canadians has grown from 12.4 kg to 13.38 kg over the past 10 years. While cheddar cheese has led the way, variety (fine) cheeses have also shown consistent growth over the period. Demand for cottage cheese and processed cheese has declined.[32] The Canadian Dairy Commission reports that per capita butter consumption has grown from 2.72 kg to 3.21 kg over the past 10 years.[33]

Understanding market trends is not the only challenge the management team faces in directing Agropur. In Canada, as an example, producers must also manage their way through the country's supply management system. The system limits supply in commodity sectors such as dairy in order to provide stable prices. This supply management system, put in place by federal and provincial government bodies interacting with producers, rests on three pillars. First, the system uses a national marketing agency to set production quotas. Second, provincial marketing boards set minimum prices producers receive for their products. Third, the system is supported by generally high tariffs on foreign inputs in the sector,[34] thereby managing and controlling the overall capacity in this market sector from broader global sources.

This supply management system is the envy of some and the bane of others, and the Canadian tariffs associated with agriculture, such as the supply management system noted above, were a central sticking point in the renegotiation of the North American Free Trade Agreement (NAFTA). The new agreement, the United States–Mexico–Canada Agreement (USMCA), provides the U.S. with expanded access (an estimated 3.6% of market accessibility) to the dairy sector. Together with the Comprehensive Economic and Trade Agreement (CETA) with the European Union and the Comprehensive and Progressive Trans-Pacific Partnership (CPTPP), global free-trade agreements open approximately 10% of the Canadian dairy sector to imports.[35]

Recognizing the change in market dynamics occurring within Canada's dairy sector, Agropur is looking to revisit its overall business strategy and draw conclusions relating to how it should compete going forward. In this context, Agropur's strategic execution up to this point has been focused around the following strategy pillars:

- **Brand strategy:** Agropur has focused its marketing efforts on building preference for its brands in Canada and strengthening them internationally. The cooperative's mission is to make Agropur Canada's most trusted dairy brand, and to continue to expand preference for the brand internationally. In support of this, for example, the Agropur logo has now been added to all international packaging.

- **Innovation:** The cooperative has looked to increase its emphasis on innovation as a way to maintain its competitive presence and edge. With respect to this, in 2016 the cooperative launched a series of innovation-based competitions under the umbrella Inno Agropur as a methodology for creating industry-shaping opportunities within the dairy sector. Inno Agropur is made up of three specific innovation thrusts. Inno Challenge is an open challenge focused on improving dairy processing techniques and driving higher levels of consumption. Winners in this challenge receive financial support and have access to the cooperative's R&D expertise to further evolve their ideas and concepts. Inno Accel is a business accelerator program that provides dairy sector start-ups with an opportunity to showcase their innovations and receive funding for moving their ideas from concept to reality. Inno Capital is a co-investment fund, providing seed capital in an open invitation format to businesses within the dairy sector (cheese, desserts/ice cream, yogurt, etc.). Inno Agropur is the largest open innovation initiative in the dairy sector in North America. Agropur is also a founding member of Scale AI, the Montreal-based supercluster focused on applying AI (artificial intelligence) methodologies within supply chains, thereby improving overall productivity and enhancing operational performance and maximizing the return on invested capital.

- **Reducing costs:** Agropur recently implemented what it calls the Agropur Operating System, intended to complement a focus on cost containment and operational efficiency with a focus on agility and employee empowerment. The company is committed to reducing its overall costs by $100 million by year-end 2019. As of this writing, the company had, via its efficiency and effectiveness efforts, successfully reduced costs by more than $41 million.

- **Human capital:** The company is committed to increasing customer focus, building stronger teams at all levels of the organization, harmonizing the corporate culture around the cooperative's core values and code of conduct, and creating methodologies for successful management succession into the future. Among many of the programs relating to these objectives are the organization's VisionR and LeadR programs, both designed to motivate and develop the next generation of managers at Agropur (succession management).

- **National and international development:** According to Agropur's annual report, the cooperative knows no borders and continues to grow by acquisition, in 2016 becoming one of the 20 largest dairy companies in the world. Agropur invested an estimated $1.6 billion on acquisitions in the four-year period between 2012 and 2016, resulting in a 63% increase in sales during this period.[36]

- **Corporate social responsibility (CSR):** A goal is making social responsibility core to Agropur's business, particularly with respect to milk and related product quality, animal welfare, employee health, safety, and well being, and community and societal commitments relating to ethics and environmental management.

Questions

In reviewing its strategic focus, Agropur has asked you to frame the current market situation challenging the organization. As a first step in this process, the company is looking for a briefing from you and your team regarding the following:

1. Using the information presented in this case, along with additional research on your part, offer an assessment as to the changes occurring within this market sector. At a macro level, what are the predominant disruptive forces impacting the dairy sector? In your opinion, are these forces changing the relationship between demand and supply?

2. Do you think that the current strategic focus of Agropur will remain valid going forward? Are there areas relating to these strategic thrusts where you would assign greater priority and stronger resource allocation? Are there critical areas of exposure that you feel are not adequately assessed within the action categories noted above?

3. Do you believe that Agropur's status as a cooperative is beneficial and adds to its value proposition? If so, what benefits does this possess that it can leverage in its communication message to current and prospective customers?

4. Given your analysis, what three specific recommendations would you make to Agropur's management team and board of directors that will enable Agropur to maintain or further create competitive advantage in the marketplace?

Case for Discussion 2

Target Canada—Lessons Learned

In 2011–12, Target Corporation set its sights on Canada as a result of purchasing the majority of leases for locations associated with The Hudson's Bay Company's now defunct Zellers brand. Not since the arrival of Walmart in 1994–95 has the entry of a company into the Canadian retail landscape been the subject of such discussion and overall anticipation. Committed to opening 124 locations within its first 12-month period, Target's initial investment of an estimated $3.1 billion (USD) was anticipated to start showing a profit at the end of its first year of operation (April 2013 to April 2014), with sights set on an early payback on the investment of fewer than five years. Instead of an operating profit, Target Canada reported a first-year operating loss of more than $1 billion (USD), cutting EPS (earnings per share) for the Target Corporation as a whole by $0.29 per share. Then 2014 added an additional $1 billion (USD) loss to the Canadian operation, bringing cumulative losses to year-end 2014 to $2+ billion (USD). Oh, and that initial investment payback of five years? Target, at the end of 2014, anticipated it would take approximately six years just to get to breakeven (assuming it could put its Canadian house in order), with no real determination of just how long it would take to be paid back for what had amounted to a roughly $7-billion investment into Canada. Reviewing all of its options, Target announced on January 15, 2015, that it would cease operations in Canada, close its 133 Canadian stores, and permanently lay off 17 600 employees. The decision was a simple one: shutting down its Canadian operation would lead to higher profits for Target Corporation overall. Additional investment into Target Canada, given its overall revenue potential, just was not a good strategic decision for Target to pursue. The better decision, according to Brian Cornell, CEO, Target Corporation, was for Target to cut its losses, leave Canada, and reallocate its financial resources elsewhere. (For Target Canada's average sales per day and operating losses, see Figures 6.18 and 6.19.)

FIGURE 6.18   **Target Canada—Average Sales per Day**

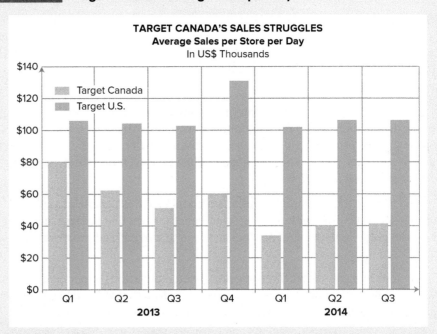

Source: Interstratics; Jonathon Rivait; *National Post.*

FIGURE 6.19 **Target Canada—Operating Losses**

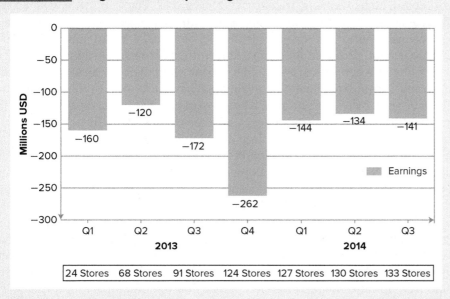

Source: Adapted from "Target's Failure Sends a Message to International Retailers," *The Toronto Star*, January 16, 2015.

Analysts can point to a number of quantitative factors that led to this decision. Average sales per day for Target stores in Canada were less than 50% of what Target realized in its U.S. stores ($40 per sq. ft. in Canada per day vs. $105 per sq. ft. per day in the U.S.). Operating margins demonstrated the same results, with Target Canada gross margins at 18%, well below Target Corporation's U.S. store performance of +30%. Estimated sales growth to move Target Canada to the level of performance of its U.S. operation was identified as being in excess of 20% annually, something Target Corporation just did not see materializing. EBIT (earnings before interest and taxes) was not expected to improve, and continued to be estimated in the –25% range—meaning quarterly losses for the foreseeable future would continue in the $100+ million range. Add to this a weakening Canadian dollar (relative to the U.S.), and the cost of doing business in Canada was expected to increase, not decrease, resulting in a further squeeze on margins, and possibly further depressing losses. On the bright side, exiting in 2015, while the dollar was weak, would mean that the cost of exiting for the U.S.-based Target Corporation would be cheaper, as lease buyouts and employee severance packages would be paid for by a stronger U.S. dollar. Added to this were tax benefits due to the write-off associated with the exit, which would free an estimated $1 billion in cash benefits to Target Corporation.

The bigger question to be asked, however, is why Canadians did not react to Target's value proposition in a way that would allow the company to be successful. Although Target's rationale for its poor performance initially centred on a disconnect between its supply chain management systems and actual store merchandise in stock, it can be readily concluded that while inventory management issues contributed to a poor customer experience, the issues underlying Target Corporation's failure in Canada run deeper. First, there was the already-crowded Canadian retail landscape

that existed prior to Target's arrival. Established competitors such as Canadian Tire, Loblaw, Metro, Sobeys, Walmart, Old Navy, TJX, The Gap, H&M, Giant Tiger, Dollarama, and Dollar Tree, to name a few, already possessed well-established and seasoned operations. The fact is that Target, via its initial announcement to come to Canada, provided its competition with approximately 24 months to prepare for Target's entry and to establish market share defence strategies, thereby preventing Target from easily acquiring market share. Add to this the fact that growth in retail sales in Canada has been relatively flat in recent years, and Target had little ability to attract new customers to its stores. Target also entered Canada absent an online, ecommerce distribution option. Ecommerce sales are the fastest growing section of Canada's retail sector, growing 12% to 15% annually. Lack of an omnichannel development strategy further limited Target's ability to drive traffic and create revenue streams. Recognizing that they would be a late entrant into the retail landscape in Canada, Target more than ever needed to demonstrate a strong, well-differentiated strategy and fully adapt to the purchase behaviour exhibited by shoppers in Canada. Unlike the psychological appeal of cross-border shopping, Target would now have to win Canadians on a day-to-day, head-to-head battle with its competitors. Doing so meant that Target would have to move beyond the perception that the Canadian marketplace was just an extension of the U.S. market, and that Canadians would immediately buy in to the "cheap chic" middle-class retailer position Target was able to carve out in the U.S. This upscale image just did not resonate with Canadians, who viewed Target as just another large American discount retailer. This, in particular, was all the more noticeable when Target's product mix failed to include many of the unique Target brands Canadians were aware of through their cross-border shopping experience. It was also perceived that those products that were brought north of the border were priced at higher price points than Canadians were used to paying at Target's U.S. stores. To be successful in Canada, Target stores also needed, to some degree, to reshape the shopping behaviour of Canadians. In the U.S., buyer behaviour has been effectively built around the one-stop-shopping concept. Although Canadians do accept this model at a base level, shopping behaviour in Canada does not embrace this the way that American shopping behaviour does. As an example, in the U.S. 21% of Target store revenue comes from food and pet supplies. In Canada, during its first two years of operation, Target Canada stores were generating only 14% of their overall revenue from these product categories.

Target's challenges in Canada did not end there. Canada, as a country, possesses a significantly more ethnically diverse population than the United States. Also, our regionalized geographic clustering, coupled with this ethnically diverse population, makes the application of a standardized business model across Canada significantly more challenging than what one experiences in expanding across the U.S. Add to this the operational challenges of trying to open 124 locations literally all at once, and the underlying supply chain issues, inventory problems, and product mix and pricing obstacles that Target incurred, and one can easily see why the venture ran into trouble right from the start. As Brian Cornell also commented, Target missed the mark from the beginning by trying to do too much too fast. Although Target was able to correct some of its underlying operational issues, the changes it made were not enough to inspire Canadians to shift their purchase behaviour and shop at Target. The losses were simply too great and the amount of time required to correct the situation was just too far out in the future for Target to maintain the course and remain in Canada.[37,38,39,40]

Questions

1. In reviewing the strategic planning process, what did Target Corporation fail to do prior to its entry into Canada that may have resulted in its biased perception of the extent of opportunity in Canada?

2. Looking back on the situation, and given what we know today, if you were managing Target Corporation, what approach to entering Canada would you have taken in order to mitigate the risk of failure?

3. If you were a member of the board of directors for Target Corporation at the time of the proposal to expand into Canada, what would be the three most important questions you would ask the management team about this opportunity?

4. Why have retailers like Walmart, Loblaw Companies, Canadian Tire, and TJX (Winners and HomeSense) been successful in Canada? What is it that they have done that Target did not do?

CHAPTER 7

Entrepreneurship and Forms of Business Ownership

LEARNING OBJECTIVES

This chapter is designed to provide students with:

LO1	An understanding of the concept of entrepreneurship and the key characteristics that successful entrepreneurs have in common
LO2	An appreciation of the core fundamentals that entrepreneurs need to demonstrate to potential investors and/or creditors that their business start-up possesses
LO3	A recognition of the risk exposure business ventures face and the importance of planning as fundamental to mitigating and managing such risk
LO4	An understanding of the different business ownership options available to entrepreneurs and the advantages and disadvantages of each
LO5	An overview of the evolutionary process that firms transition through over the course of their life cycle

Snapshot

What to Expect in This Chapter

As identified by the learning objectives, this chapter focuses on exposing students to the basics associated with entrepreneurship and the launching of new business opportunities. The content emphasized in this chapter includes the following:

- Entrepreneurship
- The Business of Entrepreneurship
  - Core Fundamentals
  - The Concept of Risk: Life in the "Uncertainty Lane"
  - Offsetting Risk Uncertainty: The Business Plan
  - Franchising: One Way to Mitigate Risk
  - Financing Your Business Start-up
- Business Ownership Options
  - Sole Proprietorships
  - Partnerships
  - Corporations
- Legal Ownership Evolution
- A Note Pertaining to Not-for-Profits
- Management Reflection—The Launch Decision

 Business IN ACTION

Saputo Inc.—A Case of Classic Entrepreneurship

With $500 that he had saved while working as a labourer, in 1954 a Sicilian immigrant and master cheese maker, Giuseppe Saputo, along with his wife, Maria, began making cheese in the corner of a cheese factory in Montreal. Their 17-year-old son, Lino, in the true spirit of a family operation, handled delivery of the cheese using his bicycle. Thus were the humble beginnings of one of Canada's many classic entrepreneurial success stories. Fast forward to March 31, 2018, and Saputo Inc., now publicly traded on the TSX (SAP), has market capitalization value of $17 billion (March 2019), 2018 revenue of $11.5 billion, and net earnings of $852 million. The operation, which spent the first two years of its existence focused on generating enough volume to be able to build its own factory, is now of international scale, employing approximately 15 000 people with operations in Canada, the United States, Argentina, and China. The company has made 30 acquisitions since 1997 and has spent over $6.9 billion during this

The Canadian Press/Ian Barrett

time period, with a major focus on expanding its USA, Argentinian, and Australian operations. The two most recent additions to Saputo's international presence in Australia, as an example, were its 2014 acquisition of Warrnambool Cheese & Butter Factory Company Holdings Limited for $450 million and the 2018 acquisition of Murray Goulburn for $1 billion.

Known in the industry as the "Mozzarella King" due to its commanding market leader position of 40% in the Canadian market, today Saputo Inc. is much more than just a cheese manufacturer. Through a series of well-planned organic growth initiatives coupled with timely acquisitions, Saputo's products stretch across a number of industry sectors such as powdered and condensed milk, cheese and butter, dairy products, and ice cream. The organization is structured around three sectors (Canada, USA, and International) and five operating divisions: Dairy Division (Canada), Dairy Foods Division (USA), Cheese Division (USA), Dairy Division (Argentina), and Dairy Division (Australia). Its stable of banners includes such well-known Canadian brands as Saputo, Neilson, and Stella. Continued acquisitions, both domestically and abroad, have resulted in Saputo Inc. becoming Canada and Australia's number-one dairy producer and one of North America's top three cheese producers. When the company started producing cheese in 1954, its initial production run was 10 kilos. Today, the company transforms over 10 billion litres of milk per year into various dairy products. Cheese production now extends well beyond mozzarella, including specialty cheeses such as havarti, brie, feta, and goat cheeses; manufacturing stretches across three continents, with 62 production facilities. Giuseppe Saputo stepped down as CEO in 1969, with Lino taking the helm and transitioning Saputo Inc. into the international player it is today. Lino (Emanuele) himself stepped away from the CEO position in 2004, and a third-generation Saputo, Lino A. Saputo Jr., serves as chief executive officer and chairman of the board as of this writing. Since the movement to a publicly traded company in 1996, the Saputo family's ownership in the company has been reduced to 33%. This percentage of ownership, however, makes this family one of the wealthiest in Canada (estimated net worth $10.4 billion). For the Saputo family and Saputo Inc., business is not just about money. The organization is an active supporter of athletic-based initiatives in Quebec and across Canada, including a strong sponsorship position in the 2010 Vancouver Winter Olympic and Paralympic Games. The company also actively invests in the communities where its employees live, and in environmentally responsible business practices. In Montreal, the company is a driving force in the establishment of a professional soccer team (Montreal Impact), and in the construction of the $17-million Saputo Soccer Stadium, of which $7.5 million of the construction costs were covered by a donation from the Saputo family. The stadium was further expanded in 2012 as a result of a $23-million investment by the Quebec government.

Web Integration

Interested in learning more about Saputo Inc.? Visit **www.saputo.ca**.

LO1 Entrepreneurship

At one time or another most of us have thought about the challenges and joys of running our own business. Media articles, documentaries, interviews, and commentaries reflecting on the lives and successes of stellar entrepreneurs—such as Mark Zuckerberg, Elon Musk, Lori Greiner, Gina Rinehart, Oprah Winfrey, Barbara Corcoran, Sara Blakely, Sergey Brin, and Larry Page, to name a few—stimulate the imagination of the lifestyle and benefits of successful entrepreneurship. This same media buzz often focuses as well on what it takes to be a successful **entrepreneur**, and what seems to be the age-old question: Are entrepreneurs born or can they be made?

Entrepreneur refers to a person who starts a business and is willing to accept the risk associated with investing money in order to make money.

FIGURE 7.1 MERFS

> **MERFS**
>
> M = Motivation
> E = Expertise
> R = Risk Management
> F = Focus
> S = Self-Belief

The idea that entrepreneurs are born and that they come into this world with DNA programmed toward entrepreneurship is an interesting one. It can, however, seemingly be easily disputed simply on the basis of observing the wide variety of personalities, backgrounds, and experiences possessed by individuals blessed with entrepreneurial success. If entrepreneurial tendencies and propensity for success are not relegated to a chosen genetically preselected few, then the conclusion results in a belief that entrepreneurs can be made. In reaching this conclusion, the critical question now becomes one of what behavioural patterns and thought processes do entrepreneurs possess that result in a different way of thinking about the art of creating and managing a business.

Significant research and analysis has focused on defining just that—the unique behaviours and traits that successful entrepreneurs seem to possess. Articles and commentaries relating to these behaviours and traits result in the generation of lists of attributes, in some cases identifying as many as 25 to 40 different characteristics. For simplicity, and in recognition of what appears to be the common conclusions reached across a broad assessment of these articles and commentaries, successful entrepreneurs seem to possess a set of common characteristics that can be easily remembered using the acronym MERFS (see Figure 7.1):

① Successful entrepreneurs are highly ***motivated*** individuals. They have an underlying desire or passion to excel, and a bulldog mentality and tenacity when it comes to striving for success. Failure is viewed as something that happens numerous times per day, and adaptability, determination, and perseverance are what enable such individuals to push through the obstacles that challenge them.

② Successful entrepreneurs have a demonstrated ***expertise*** in the arena encompassing the business opportunity they are pursuing. For entrepreneurs, the "devil *is* in the details." They are precise and methodical in the way the business is to be approached and how resources are to be allocated. They possess the customer contacts and supplier and channel partner networks needed to assist in getting the new business off the ground, and also understand, possess, or know where to acquire the specialized skills essential for success. Many successful entrepreneurs honed their skills as employees in the business sectors within which they ultimately will disrupt and/or compete.

③ Successful entrepreneurs view ***risk*** differently. It is not, in many cases, that they are willing to take on greater risk, it is that they are able to better manage the uncertainty and potential failure that risk implies. It is more about the perception that risk can be controlled and that the underlying stress associated with risk can be managed and counterbalanced. As an example, for many of us the idea of mortgaging our homes, borrowing seed money from family members, personally guaranteeing a business loan with our savings and/or other assets, and burning through cash infused into our business by investors represents a significant risk to our livelihood and a source of significant stress in our lives. For entrepreneurs, this exposure is counterbalanced by the passion of pursuing a dream and departmentalizing the risk exposure in such a way that enables them to keep such stress in check.

4 Successful entrepreneurs possess and can successfully communicate the vision they have for their business. This *focus* enables them to uniquely sense the opportunity that exists, be it in niches that existing businesses have yet to identify, innovation via the use of emerging technologies, or transforming current points of customer pain into viable product/service solutions. It also often means facing the "naysayers" who don't possess the same innovative curiosity and demonstrating the unique need that can be solved by the entrepreneur's proposed business model. It should be noted, however, that this focus is balanced by flexibility. Successful entrepreneurs possess an uncanny sense to recognize when it is time to shift gears or redirect the process, based on shifts occurring within the market and/or fine-tuning requirements associated with the initial business model.

5 Successful entrepreneurs truly believe in themselves. For many, they perceive that they have fully thought through the business opportunity, conducted the appropriate levels of research, understand the specific tasks that need to be executed to achieve success, and possess the knowledge and know-how to get the job done. This level of *self-belief* is what drives the confidence so often recognized within successful entrepreneurs. Self-belief is further illustrated by a willingness to break the rules; that is, to defy conventional wisdom, and to reinvent the way business takes place within the sectors where they choose to compete.[1] It is also reinforced by the entrepreneur's willingness to commit fully to the business idea in terms of time, talent, and treasure. This is what is referred to as "skin in the game" and, for many entrepreneurs, is underscored by a willingness to put it all on the line in pursuit of their dream.

So, is entrepreneurship right for you? Keeping MERFS in mind, think through the following quotes:

- I have not failed. I've just found 10 000 ways that won't work.—Thomas Edison
- Entrepreneurship is living a few years of your life like most people won't, so that you can spend the rest of your life like most people can't.—Anonymous
- What would you attempt to do if you knew you would not fail?—Robert Schuller
- Motivation is what gets you started. Habit is what keeps you going.—Jim Rohn
- Every worthwhile accomplishment, big or little, has its stages of drudgery and triumph: a beginning, a struggle and a victory.—Mahatma Gandhi
- Some people dream of great accomplishments, while others stay awake and do them.—Anonymous
- The most valuable thing you can do is make a mistake—you can't learn anything from being perfect.—Adam Osborne
- Success is walking from failure to failure with no loss of enthusiasm.—Winston Churchill
- Genius is 1% inspiration, and 99% perspiration.—Thomas Edison[2]

Business IN ACTION

Success Is in the Details

What makes the difference between a merely satisfactory delivery and a great delivery of a new and innovative idea to the marketplace? Well, if you ask Richard Branson, philanthropist, entrepreneur, and founder of the Virgin Group, his response would most likely focus on ensuring that you have a structure in place that ensures definitive attention to detail. In an article in *Canadian Business*, Branson discussed why attention to detail is so important and offered some tips that enable him to stay on top of the delivery of services across the many organizations that exist within the Virgin Group's portfolio. A key component of this process is to think of service delivery in conjunction with what you have identified as your company's core values, key mid-term strategic considerations, and the overall long-term vision. A second critical requirement is to continuously sample the products and/or services that your company offers, making notes on where deficiencies and improvements need to be made and then ensuring that such product and/or service delivery refinements are put into action. A core aspect of this sampling process is to take the time to speak with staff to ensure that you understand the organization's delivery model from their perspective. They are also great identifiers as to where bottlenecks are occurring and inefficiencies are creeping in. An open-door communication policy that encourages staff and customer suggestions for product and/or service improvements is fundamental to this detail-focused approach as well. In business, profitable market share is generated one customer at a time. Don't be afraid to take the time to ensure that each customer contact receives the level of attention necessary to create a loyalty bond between you and them. Remember that value proposition development and creating customer commitment is not so much about the

The Canadian Press/Reed Saxon

products and services offered, but the relationship experience that customers have with your business and you. Competitors should also be thought of as potential opportunities versus enemies. Interacting with key individuals in direct and indirect business competitors offers the opportunity to gain market knowledge and to uncover collaborative opportunities that may assist in further growing the scale and profitability of all involved.

The Business of Entrepreneurship   LO2, LO3

Core Fundamentals

In the opening section of this chapter our discussion focused on the underlying traits that are found in successful entrepreneurs. Let's shift our focus now to the business of entrepreneurship. By this, I mean let's focus on what it takes to develop a successful business. In a recent commentary on BNN relating to business ventures, two successful venture capitalists, Timothy Draper, founder of Draper Fisher Jurvetson (DFJ) of Silicon Valley fame, and Richard Nathan, managing director of Kensington Capital, one of Canada's leading venture capital firms, commented on the core fundamentals they look for in assessing a potential investment into a business start-up.[3] Their comments—remarkably similar, and further reinforced by the broader **venture capitalist** community—can be summarized around the following key points (see Figure 7.2).

Venture Capitalist refers to an individual who provides capital to a business venture for start-up or expansion purposes.

FIGURE 7.2   **The Business of Entrepreneurship**

1 **Quality of the Management Team**   Venture capitalists, angel investors, and financing organizations (banks, private equity companies, hedge funds, etc.) all have the same fundamental question when assessing the potential financing of a business opportunity: Who are the individuals behind the business idea? Looking at the management team and its underlying competencies and experience is a core first step in assessing the viability of a business opportunity. For many investors, knowing that the management team has had experience in the start-up of a new business venture makes a big difference in whether to lend or support the venture through an equity position. So what about new start-ups where this experience does not exist? Having access to individuals who possess this experience and expertise, via a mentorship or advisory role, is often required. In assessing the résumés of the business principals, investors are looking to determine if the management team is complete in terms of the skills required for success, if they are committed to the venture via "skin in the game," if they are enthusiastic and passionate about the venture to be undertaken, and if they are realistic about the obstacles and challenges they will face as they look to drive the venture to the point of sustainability. Many investors also want to feel confident that the CEO of the new venture can demonstrate that they can lead the organization right through the development and ramp-up phase and, ideally, to the point of an IPO (initial public offering).[4] A key additional point is flexibility and adaptability to make the changes and hard decisions required as the venture moves from an idea to full commercialization. Investors know that business plans, although a good starting point, often change as the business evolves. The key determinant becomes the perception of management's ability to recognize when such changes need to be made and then execute on this knowledge.

2 **Uniqueness of the Product/Service Offering**   In addition to assessing the marketing team, potential investors and creditors also look closely at the uniqueness of the product/service offering behind the venture. A key determinant is whether the new business venture offers a truly unique and different way of doing business. They will also assess whether the product/service to be launched is a replacement product for existing market offerings or something new that the market has not seen. Seasoned venture capitalists know that established firms in existing markets possess advantages over new business start-ups. These advantages can lie with brand reputation, economies of scale due to volume, financial capital capabilities, established marketing and distribution channels, and existing R&D departments, often capable of immediately responding to technological leap-frogging. As an example, let's take a quick look at Fitbit, to date one of the most successful wearable technology success stories. Founded in 2007 by James Park and Eric Friedman, Fitbit has leveraged an initial $400 000 investment of venture capital seed money into a viable player in the wearable device market sector, with sales of $1.5 billion USD (2018) and a market capitalization value of $1.5 billion USD.[5] In launching Fitbit, Park and Friedman initially created and successfully marketed a line of fitness and activity trackers, becoming one of the first movers within this market segment and generating significant interest in the products and services they offered. This initial success has been followed by an ongoing expansion and evolution of the product line to include not only trackers, but also watch-based wearable devices. Today, Fitbit holds a prominent position in the wearable device sector with products such as Versa, Charge, Inspire, Ionic, Ace, and Aria. Keep in mind, however that initial success does not mean long-term success is automatic. Success breeds interest and imitation, often by successful, well-financed companies seeking to grow. Apple, Garmin, and Samsung have all targeted the wearable device sector as profitable growth opportunities. Apple, as an example, carries into this market its brand reputation, a well-oiled marketing machine, a large contingent of app developers who can create new and innovative uses for the watch, and cash reserves at this time (2019) in excess of $240 billion USD.[6] For Fitbit to remain successful against Apple and other smartwatch/wearable-device competitors, Fitbit will need to continuously demonstrate real and/or perceived credible differences between its watch and those of its rivals. In assessing new business start-ups, investors focus on whether the start-up possesses some type of advantage-destroying innovation that reduces or eliminates the competitive advantages of existing rivals, a unique need that is not currently being satisfied by existing industry players, a unique intellectual capital (patents, etc.) that gives the start-up an advantage, or a business model innovation that enables the new entrant to compete without having to fully replicate the business model of existing competitors. Fitbit delivered on this in the early days of the wearable device market. Does Fitbit possess such advantages today, in a way that it will be able to maintain its momentum and growth in this segment against much larger rivals? Time will tell. To be successful, Fitbit will need to demonstrate that its value proposition and overall product/service uniqueness signals to its existing and prospective customers that it remains the preferred choice in this segment.

③ Market Size and Opportunity Alignment A third key evaluation attribute for potential investors and creditors is an understanding of the potential size of the market and the estimated time it will take for the organization to gain enough traction to reach a point of **cash flow positive**, **breakeven point**, and, ultimately, the targeted level of profitability. For investors, although the size of the market can be related to the potential of the opportunity, it is more about the amount of time it will take for the business to no longer rely on external capital to fund its operations. Operating below cash flow positive means the organization is burning cash and, therefore, may require future cash infusions. Operating below breakeven point means the organization is unable to generate profits in a way that ensures the longer-term stability of the organization. Both of these concepts will be covered in more detail in Chapters 13 and 14. For now, it is

Cash Flow Positive refers to that point in time when an organization is able to cover the actual cash expenses of an operation from the revenue it generates.

Breakeven Point (BEP) refers to the point where total expenses = total revenue. The income statement, which takes into consideration actual cash expenses as well as non-cash expenses, results in profit = $0.

important to recognize that market size and market penetration are essential to generating enough volume to enable the company to meet its profit objectives. For potential investors and creditors, this means understanding the business scale required to sustain the business, and the amount of time it will take for the organization to get to this point. This is then measured against the amount of capital needed to support the operation during the ramp-up period.

4 **Current Conditions within the Market**   A fourth component of the new business start-up process for potential investors and creditors has to do with understanding the current conditions within the market sector where the new business start-up is positioning itself. As indicated above in point #2, established firms are generally thought to have definitive advantages over new entrants into a market. What improves the chances of the upstart lies in the underlying disruptive nature of the market sector being targeted. Markets that are experiencing significant convergence often offer opportunity for start-ups. Smartphone manufacturers, exploiting the "supercomputer in your pocket" trend, stand ready to go head-to-head with established laptop and tablet manufacturers and marketers. The advent of digital-based technology has enabled Netflix to gain tremendous market traction against established network producers and DVD vendors. The greater the potential for market convergence, coupled with the fast cycling of technology through a given market sector, the riper the opportunities for entrepreneurial start-ups. A second condition that investors look to assess is the extent to which existing competitors are entrenched within a given business model, and the opportunity that exists to disrupt such models. Oligopoly-based markets, where there is limited competition and where established firms have become remarkably similar and, to some extent, lazy in their focus on innovation, offer true potential for new start-up disruption. Amazon caught the publishing sector sleeping when it launched in 1994, and continues to surprise existing competitors firmly entrenched in their old ways as it expands beyond its original business model format.

5 **Investment Hypothesis (Business Plan)**   Starting a business is much more than having a great idea for a unique or disruptive product/service offering or business model; it is really about management, and management requires planning. It is important for entrepreneurs to understand that start-ups are as much about how to create a sustainable business as they are about creating products. Potential investors and creditors want to see the underlying plan behind the start-up (business plan components are covered in more detail in the following section). Equally important, however, is that potential investors and creditors want to understand the critical pivot or **inflection points** the management team feels it will face, and the timing of such key events. Savvy venture capitalists, as an example, know that business plans are just guesstimates as to the road map that a business intends to follow as it seeks to gain traction in the marketplace. These investors are looking to key points within the plan that can demonstrate validated learning that things are progressing as intended and, if not, that the entrepreneur will be able to recognize this and adjust accordingly. In scientific terms, a business plan can be thought of as a hypothesis, and the traditional build, measure, and learn feedback loop, built around measurable metrics and followed by cause-and-effect decision making, should be the underlying fundamental of its execution. It is this ability to communicate measured progress along the way that demonstrates the concept of planning within a business plan, and the ability of the management team to manage the underlying uncertainty inherent within all business start-ups.

Inflection Points are decision points where the current path a business is taking is assessed relative to where the company is and where it should be.

Business IN ACTION

Payfirma (Merrco)—Making Payments Delightful, One Business at a Time

Established in November 2010, Vancouver-based Payfirma processes payments for thousands of businesses across North America. The services provided by Payfirma enable trade companies, professional service firms, publishers, and global online retailers, as well as not-for-profit organizations, to transact credit card and debit card payments across a variety of electronic platforms. Whether it be assisting a waste management and junk removal service company with implementing a mobile, point-of-sale payment system to complement their "weigh and pay" business model, or assisting an integrated digital marketing solutions company to process customer credit card purchases via a Web portal, Payfirma does it all.

Success to date for Payfirma has been due to a variety of key factors. First, the company was one of the first in Canada to offer a mobile payment app for the Apple iPhone. Second, the company continues to focus on innovation, developing multi-channel payment opportunities (smartphones, Web terminals, secure ecommerce payment services for selling online, recurrent billing payment services for fee collections, donations, etc.) in order to enhance its business reach. Third, the company offers interactive technologies that integrate mobile payments to traditional cash drawers, terminal payment systems, and printers in order to further meet business needs. Fourth, the company has successfully leveraged partnerships with other organizations to further grow its business reach. Two key partnerships that have assisted the company in reinforcing its credibility as a leading payment solutions provider are with CIBC and BluePay, a leading payment processor in the United States. Recognizing the fast-moving nature of technology and the continued expansion of service opportunities, in March 2014 Payfirma launched an open payment API for ecommerce along with a new resource service that will enable developers to build additional versatility into the online and mobile device market sectors and also strengthen underlying data collection capabilities, as customers seek to maximize the benefits of heightened reporting and expanded analytics.

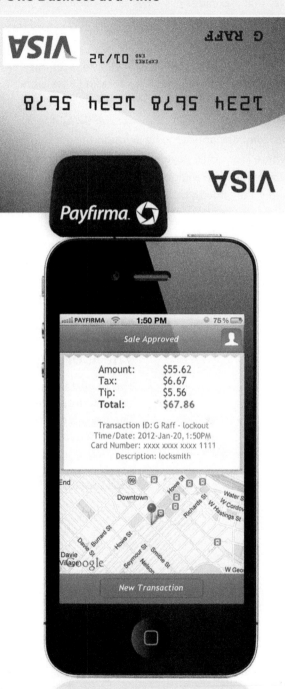

© 2015 Payfirma Corporation

For businesses doing business with Payfirma, the benefits lie in the simplicity of its use, as well as the improved customer experience the company adds to the business/customer interaction. The payment solution frees companies from bricks and mortar restrictions and enables them to complete the customer experience in a way that maximizes customer satisfaction.

So how did Payfirma founder Michael Gokturk do it? The company has benefited from angel investor seed money totalling $26 million. The company has also issued convertible notes totalling $3 million. This was followed by an additional $13 million round of financing in 2015. More importantly, Gokturk and his company appear to have found the gap between where electronic payment technology is today and where it will be tomorrow. The idea that payments should be able to take place in any space via any platform is not new. It is attention to detail, however,

and a focused emphasis on simplicity and meeting customer needs that have enabled Payfirma to carve a formidable niche in this market sector. Yes, there are larger U.S.-based rivals to contend with—such as PayPal's Braintree, Square Inc., and even possibly Apple Pay—but Payfirma's collaborative relationships have enabled its customers to transition quickly from a world of traditional legacy payment systems to one of cutting-edge payment technology. It is this collaborative support that has allowed Payfirma to create and solidify customer relationships in this increasingly competitive space.

Payfirma achieved breakeven cash flow in 2017, a major milestone for any start-up company. On October 22, 2018, Payfirma was acquired by Merrco, a private Toronto-based corporation, for an undisclosed amount.

Web Integration

Want to learn more about Payfirma? Visit the company's Web site at **payfirma.com**.

The Concept of Risk: Life in the "Uncertainty Lane"

The uncertainty associated with the commencement of a business venture is to some degree unavoidable. Despite our best efforts, success is never a certainty. The less an existing business and its structure can be leveraged in support of the new opportunity, the higher that uncertainty becomes (see Figure 7.3) and,

FIGURE 7.3   **Risk and Business Ventures**

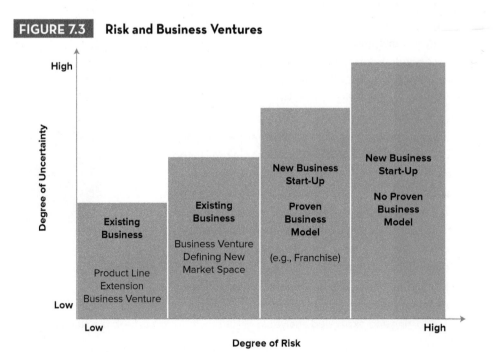

therefore, the greater the challenge to managers and entrepreneurs to fully recognize and define the magnitude of risk presented.[7] Companies initiating business ventures built around existing product lines, or capable of leveraging an existing business's competencies and experience, have some knowledge of competitors, market dynamics (PESTEL), technology application, cost structure, and revenue potential. Despite this knowledge going in, thereby reducing the risk/certainty profile of the venture, many still do not succeed. With new businesses where these competencies and experience are lacking, the risk/certainty profile is even more forbidding. The utilization of a proven business model or turnkey operation, such as a franchise (see below), can assist to some extent in mitigating this risk, but considerable uncertainty with respect to the probability of success remains. Entrepreneurs heading out into market space where no one has treaded before, and absent of any proven business model, expose themselves to the greatest risk and uncertainty. It is true that, in these types of ventures, with success can come considerable reward—just look at the current valuations of Facebook and Google as examples. Yet, for every couple of big winners, many more businesses simply cannot create the demand and scale to survive and, therefore, exit or cease to exist soon after they enter a given market.

Offsetting Risk Uncertainty: The Business Plan

As noted in the prior discussion relating to the investment hypothesis, mitigating uncertainty and risk is all about planning. By planning, organizations create a definitive path to navigate through the turbulent waters of risk and uncertainty and define, in advance, how to respond to the critical make-or-break issues that will challenge them. New venture assessment focuses first on the development of a business plan, and then on assessing the viability of the plan to work and to meet its identified objectives. The business plan describes the business, assesses the opportunity given market and competitive conditions, defines the strategy, details the management expertise and operation-based and marketing-based tactics, provides financial validation, and explains why you will succeed (see Figure 7.4).

In reviewing the business plan, we look to assess the viability of the economic base, validate the size of the target market, assess the competitive landscape, draw conclusions on the level of saturation that already exists in the market, determine the validity of the cost estimates and capitalization requirements offered, and ensure that we understand how the business will connect with, and acquire, the necessary customers to ensure success. An easy way to think about what a business plan needs to deliver is shown in Figure 7.5, the five "rules of the road" for business plan development.

Upon reading a business plan, you should be able to determine who the customer is, why the business will be successful in reaching these customers, how the business

FIGURE 7.4 **The Business Plan**

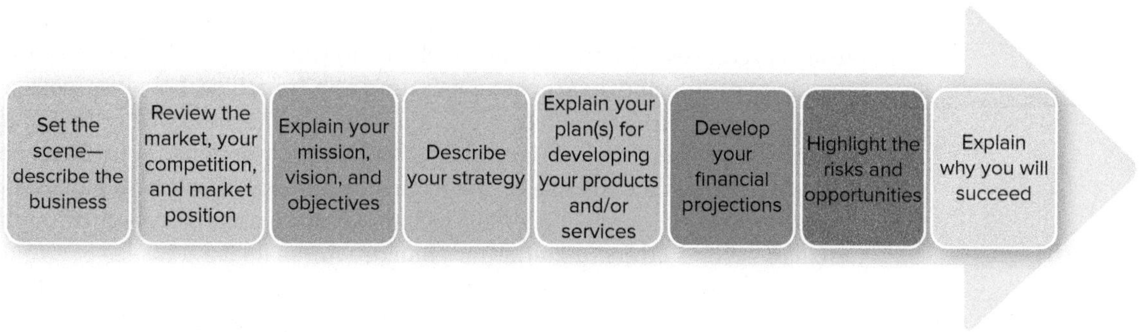

FIGURE 7.5   **Business Plan: Rules of the Road**

- Rule #1—Know Your Customer
- Rule #2—Know Why You Will Win
- Rule #3—Know How You Will Win
- Rule #4—Know What It Will Take to Win
- Rule #5—Demonstrate Why Others Should Believe in You

will reach these customers, what it will take (in terms of resources) to get the job done, and why the organization or venture capitalist should believe in the management team and/or the entrepreneur. The formal process for assessing a business venture and its business plan has been deferred until the closing chapter in this textbook. This is intentional, in that conducting such an analysis requires a full understanding of the marketing, operations, and finance fundamentals that are covered in upcoming chapters. For now, it is important to understand the importance of planning and the core business focus of transitioning an idea into a formal business start-up.

> Upon reading a business plan, you should be able to determine who the customer is, why the business will be successful in reaching these customers, how the business will reach these customers, what it will take (in terms of resources) to get the job done, and why the organization or venture capitalist should believe in the management team and/or the entrepreneur.

Franchising: One Way to Mitigate Risk

Over the past several decades, one of the most popular start-up business models has been the franchise. Just what is a franchise? It is a business model under which business owners share a common brand and operate through a defined business framework. Why are franchises so popular? For many new entrepreneurs, the franchise (in theory) provides a proven way to launch and manage a business. At their core, "best of class" franchises provide their franchisees (the purchaser of the franchise) with brand recognition in the marketplace, a proven turnkey operating plan, prelaunch and ongoing owner and staff training, purchasing power through economies of scale, regional and/or national marketing support, and new product development and operating technique improvement R&D. Starting a new business is a risky venture. The idea behind franchises is that this risk is reduced when compared to going it alone. Many entrepreneurs do not have the time, the financial resources, or the expertise to develop all aspects of the business formula required for success. Developing profile and awareness, for example, can take months and/or years for new business ventures. The franchise model ideally will bring to the new business owner immediate profile and awareness. Operating as a franchise, however, does not come without a price. Most franchise models require the business owner to pay an initial franchise fee (often several thousands of dollars) at the time of purchase, as well as ongoing royalties for the use of the franchise name and business model. Contributions to a national marketing fund are also quite common. As an example, A&W, Canada's second largest hamburger chain, requires its franchisees to pay an initial franchise fee of $50 000 (for a 20-year agreement) as well as royalties (called service fees) of 2.5% of net sales and a contribution to the A&W Advertising Fund of 2.5% of net sales. In addition to these fees, the franchisee must pay for the cost of the business. Investment in a full-service, freestanding A&W restaurant is in the $950 000 to $1.4 million range. Franchisees need to demonstrate unencumbered access to equity of at least $350 000 in order to qualify as a business owner. Unique to A&W is their Urban Franchise Associate Restaurant program, which offers millennials and young entrepreneurs an opportunity to operate an A&W restaurant with an initial capital investment of $125 000 to $150 000.[8] Tim Hortons' current weekly royalty fee is 6% of gross sales, and its monthly advertising fund contribution for franchisees is 4% of gross sales. Currently, a Tim Hortons franchise costs are in the $500 000+ range. This includes a franchise fee of $35 000. Franchisees are expected to have unencumbered access to liquid assets of approximately $500 000, and a net worth of at least $1.5 million. Tim Hortons also reserves the right to have franchise agreements written for a 10-year period, with an a option to renew for an additional 10 years.[9]

The purchase of a franchise, however, does not mean guaranteed success. Prospective business owners need to recognize that due diligence still must be conducted for the local market to ensure that the size of the market is large enough and the competitive landscape is understood. The franchisor (the seller of the franchise model) must also be assessed in order to ensure that the level of support and expertise it is purporting to offer can actually be delivered. Finally, the franchisee needs to execute the business model in an efficient and effective manner, and meet customer expectations to be successful. Under a franchise agreement, it should also be understood that the freedom to deviate from the defined franchise model will most likely be significantly restricted. A&W Food Services Canada Inc., for example, does not permit franchisees to add items to the menu on their own. Menu items are set, and considerable market research and testing by the franchisor is required prior to the addition of any menu item. Franchisees should expect reduced control over products, services, operating hours and protocols, and advertising as part of their franchise agreement.

Franchise models are not for everyone. Each individual, based on an assessment of their skills and competencies, monetary capacity, and desire for control and creativity, will need to determine if this business model works best for them. For many, as indicated above, it is a desirable way to get into business while at the same time reducing the risk of going it alone. It is a personal decision. The marketplace is full of franchise opportunities. The question becomes whether it is the right way for you to become an entrepreneur.[10]

Web Integration

For more information regarding franchise business opportunities in Canada, Google "Canadian franchise opportunities" or visit the Canadian Franchise Association Web site at www.cfa.ca.

 Business IN ACTION

So, You Want to Start a Booster Juice

Booster Juice is an example of a great Canadian small business success story. The brainchild of two young entrepreneurs, Dale Wishewan and Jon

Amack, Booster Juice has grown from its humble beginning in 1999 to an international business with locations in Canada, the U.S., Mexico, the Netherlands,

© Tracy Harris

India, and Brazil. Through solid business planning and execution of its franchise-based operations strategy (business model), president and CEO Dale Wishewan (now a member of the Canadian Franchise Association Hall of Fame) has overseen the growth of Booster Juice, which now has almost 400 stores worldwide and, to date, has sold over 125 million smoothies (and counting). Although the product line was originally based on smoothies, the menu has grown to include juices, hot drinks, shakes, and food offerings such as paninis, wraps, quesadillas, and energy bowls. The smoothie line itself has been expanded to include high-protein smoothies, hardcore smoothies, and superfood smoothies, to name a few. Booster Juice also has expanded its revenue model to include "Grab n' Go" items such as whey protein powder, coconut water, KIND snack bars, Pumpkin Seed Crunch, protein and whey bars, and superfood yogurt blends.

Interested in opening a Booster Juice franchise? In doing so, you need to consider the underlying costs and resources that make up the development and execution of this franchise-based business model.

First, you will need to understand your asset-based expenditures. In this particular situation, these can be thought of as the costs of starting the business. You will need to pay an initial franchise fee ($30 000) to Booster Juice for the rights to use their name and for their involvement in assisting you in establishing your business, as well as an ongoing royalty fee of 6% of gross sales and a marketing fee of 3.5% of gross sales. You will also need to purchase the equipment to set up the business, and fund the additional one-time start-up expenses, such as beginning inventory, pre-opening business expenses, professional fees (accounting and legal, etc.), and leasehold-improvement expenses. Overall, depending on the site chosen, the style of store you have agreed to set up, and the geographic location of your operation, these expenses could total approximately $300 000 (CAD) or more. So what do you get for your investment? Booster Juice will provide its business expertise and refined business model which will assist you in your business plan development, store build, hands-on training, marketing and merchandising programs, and fully established operating and distribution logistics systems. In essence, a turnkey operation.

Once set up, you now have to run the business on a day-to-day basis. This means you need to sell your smoothies and the related menu items at a level sufficient to cover expenses. You also need to purchase the food and beverage items to create the smoothies and other menu offerings, and the packaging required to serve them. Add to this the labour required to serve your customers, as well as the business costs associated with running your operation—utilities, insurance, debt interest repayment (assuming you borrowed part of the money needed to set up the business), advertising, royalties to Booster Juice, and other miscellaneous operating expenses. Suppose these are estimated to run $350 000 on an annual basis.

This means that your Booster Juice business needs to generate approximately $386 000 of revenue per year (keep in mind that the first 9.5 cents on every dollar go to Booster Juice in the form of a royalty payment and market fee) just to cover your $350 000 cost base (excluding any desired return on investment by the owner). These costs need to be incorporated into your revenue model to ensure that the prices you set cover the costs of being in business. In looking at your menu, if the average amount a customer spends when visiting your Booster Juice is $7, then you need to have just over 61 000 customers per year to achieve the revenue stream of $386 000 that is necessary to cover your operating expenses, meet your royalty and marketing fee obligations, and make your debt interest payments (if you partially financed your business). This means you need 5000+ customers per month, or just over 1200 per week, or approximately 170 customers per day (assuming you are open 355 days per year).

Booster Juice franchise agreements are typically written for a 10-year period. Applicants are required to have a net worth of approximately $375 000, and access to approximately $110 000 in liquid assets. Ideal candidates possess prior experience in the QSR (quick service restaurant) industry and a good understanding of their local market.

Web Integration

Want to learn more about Booster Juice, its operations and franchise opportunities? Visit **www.boosterjuice.com**.

Financing Your Business Start-Up

As indicated above, the analytical process of conducting a formal venture assessment and valuation is discussed in the last chapter of this textbook. It is important, however, to recognize that a key need of business start-ups is access to capital (money). For many entrepreneurs, one source is using their own savings; another is obtaining capital through a willingness to pledge personal assets (wealth) as **collateral** for a business start-up loan. This might involve a second mortgage on a home, the pledging of a cottage as collateral against a loan, or the use of some other asset that possesses monetary value for collateral purposes.

But what if the would-be entrepreneur has a promising and potentially sustainable business opportunity, yet does not have the personal wealth, and therefore access to capital, to finance the start-up? In these situations, entrepreneurs will need to seek out other sources. Common sources of capital for new business start-ups include angel investors (family, friends, wealthy associates, etc.), venture capital firms, provincial and federal government start-up grants, government-backed small business loans, lines of credit, and partners via partnership and/or corporation structures (discussed more fully in the next section of this chapter). In addition to these traditional funding options, the Internet has enabled the development of crowdfunding as a potential source of start-up financing. **Crowdfunding** is the process of funding a project or business venture by raising money via an Internet-supported funding management platform. These sites typically provide entrepreneurs with the opportunity to raise the required capital from the monetary contributions of a large number of people. What is unique to this approach is that these contributors generally do not receive an equity stake in the business, but are considered "supply capital" in return for the product or service the start-up intends to offer. These contributions typically represent a pre-purchase on the part of the investor. Popular crowdfunding sites, at the time of this writing, are FundRazr, Kickstarter (see the Business in Action later in this section), ArtsFund, CHIMP (charities), and Vested.[11]

In Canada, crowdfunding service providers can be found at both the national level and the provincial level. Kickstarter Canada offers crowdfunding support across Canada, while Alberta-based ATB BoostR focuses on funding support for local Alberta-based businesses, and La Ruche emphasizes funding opportunities for Quebec City and its surrounding area. Crowdfunding can also focus on niche or selective markets, be

Collateral is an asset that an individual pledges as security toward a credit facility (loan); the individual agrees to forfeit the collateral in the event of an inability to repay the loan.

Crowdfunding is the process of funding a project or business venture by raising money via an Internet-supported funding management system.

they fashion, real estate, film, or social project development and change. As crowdfunding matures, we can expect a further expansion of these services.[12] Fundica connects entrepreneurs not only with funders, but also advisers. The site focuses on identifying for entrepreneurs potential sources of grants, loans, tax credits, and equity funding from private, municipal, provincial, and federal funders. The site also offers advisers an opportunity to market their services to entrepreneurs in order to facilitate the matching of entrepreneur needs with skilled and experienced professional services.[13]

Although on the surface crowdfunding appears very attractive, keep in mind that this approach often requires the would-be entrepreneur to organize and manage the start-up largely on their own. Crowdfunding also possesses the limitation that raising capital may take time, and may not generate the actual capital required. As noted above, taking out loans, second mortgages, lines of credit, or tapping into credit cards also represent potential access to capital for start-ups. The risk, of course, is that such actions result in entrepreneurs personally guaranteeing such loans and, in the event the business does not succeed, facing the repayment of such debt for many years to come. Angel investors and venture capitalists are attractive options, as they bring to the start-up capital that is equity-based versus debt-based. Entrepreneurs are, however, trading an ownership stake in the business—and, in some cases, majority control—for the capital needed to fund the start-up. For many entrepreneurs, relinquishing control of part of the business is a hard decision to make. What makes the decision easier is to think in terms of what the equity investment by the investor can, and should, bring to the table. In an ideal situation, there are five key benefits to seeking out an angel investor or venture capitalist. Drawing conclusions as to how many of these benefits such an investor can bring to the start-up can greatly assist in the decision-making process surrounding when to pursue an equity-based investment and how much of the ownership portion of the business to part with as part of the negotiation process. These five benefits are outlined in Figure 7.6.

FIGURE 7.6   **Five Benefits of Angel Investors or Venture Capitalists**

Advantage	Commentary	Strength of Contribution			
Capital	Current and future capacity for equity-based investments, free of debt repayment obligations.	Weak	Fair	Good	Excellent
Reputation and Credibility	Adds legitimacy to the business. Makes it easier for others to do business with the start-up.	Weak	Fair	Good	Excellent
Business Relationships	Has connections/ties to distributors, suppliers, bankers, customers, and potential partners.	Weak	Fair	Good	Excellent
Business Expertise	Possesses expertise in the sector or field which the start-up is pursuing.	Weak	Fair	Good	Excellent
Management Recruitment	Has access to the managerial expertise which the start-up will require as it grows and evolves.	Weak	Fair	Good	Excellent

Business IN ACTION

Kickstarter—Bring Your Creative Project to Life

What do an Oscar-winning film, a skateboard park in Philadelphia, a customizable watch, and a human-propelled helicopter have in common? The answer is

Kickstarter, an innovative platform for raising capital. The company was founded by Perry Chen, a former musician who, while working in New Orleans, grew

Used with permission from Mosaic Manufacturing

frustrated by his inability to draw talent to New Orleans to play because of managers who continually cited the high costs of travel. Chen began to wonder if there were not a way to get audience members to pledge to buy tickets in advance of the show to entice these musicians to come and play. Moving back to New York in 2005, Chen met Yancey Strickler, a music journalist, and Charles Adler, a creative director, and the three of them shared a common vision. Together they hired Web developers and advisers to get their idea off the ground, and officially launched Kickstarter on April 28, 2009. Kickstarter now has 93 employees and is headquartered in Greenpoint-Brooklyn, N.Y.

What Kickstarter offers entrepreneurs working in the creative industries (e.g., film, computer games, dance, publishing, technology) and living in the United States, United Kingdom, Canada, or seven other permitted countries, is a platform to "crowdsource" funding. Crowdsourcing is a new concept and refers to the act of generating funding or support from a large online community. Unlike in an IPO (initial public offering) on a stock exchange like the NYSE or the TSX, however, entrepreneurs on Kickstarter who crowdsource funds for their projects do not offer equity stakes in their enterprises. Instead, they might offer the product or artwork they are developing itself in exchange for capital. Anyone with an idea that meets Kickstarter's guidelines can show-case their project on Kickstarter using a stylish Web page and an explanatory video. They then solicit "pledges," from $1 up, with a funding target. If the funding target is reached, the project is funded; if it

is not, no money changes hands. It's an all or nothing enterprise. Since its inception in 2009, over 16 million people have backed a Kickstarter project, with over 51 million pledges provided totalling more than $4.2 billion. 160 000 projects have been successfully funded (estimated 36% funding success rate), with 342 projects raising $1 million or more, and more than 5500 raising $100 000 or more. The largest percentage of funded projects raise $10 000 or less (67%). Music, Film and Video, Games, and Publishing are the four top funded areas on Kickstarter. Kickstarter makes its money by charging successfully funded projects a 5% fee on the funds collected.

Kickstarter doesn't vet or curate projects; it simply serves as a platform to raise money. One can thus find weird and wonderful projects on Kickstarter. In 2014, over $13 million was pledged to the Coolest Cooler, a drinks cooler with a built-in ice crushing blender, waterproof Bluetooth speaker, and USB charger; over $6 million was pledged to PonoPlayer, an improved portable digital audio player that was spearheaded by Neil Young; and over $8 million went to developing the card game Exploding Kittens. Perry Chen must have also smiled when he saw fans crowdsource funds for a sold-out Foo Fighters gig in Richmond, Virginia.

The top-funded Kickstarter project as of February 2015 was Palo Alto, California–based Pebble Technology's Pebble Time (billed as an "Awesome Smartwatch—No Compromises"), which raised over $20 million from more than 67 000 backers. The Pebble Time watch featured a colour e-paper display, microphone, seven-day battery life, and was fully compatible with over 6500 existing Pebble apps and watch faces. Investors could choose their level of support and the corresponding benefit they would receive, given their investment, from Pebble Technology. Pebble Technology followed this initial project with a second watch (Pebble 2) in May 2016, raising an additional $12.8 million. Pebble Technology was sold to Fitbit in 2016 for an estimated $40 million. The Coolest Cooler (referred to above) was the second most funded Kickstarter project, raising $13.3 million in 2014, followed by the board game Kingdom Death Monster 1.5, which raised $12.4 million in November 2016.

Kickstarter launched its Canadian website in 2013. At the time of this writing (March 2019), there were 17 668 live Canadian projects on Kickstarter. Some of the fully funded projects, which raised over $1 000 000 CAD (as of 2017) include the following:

Product	Amount Pledged	# of Pledges
Revols—Premium Quick Custom-Fit Wireless Earphones	$3 374 513	10 569
Smart Parka—The World's First Complete Winter Coat	$3 257 695	8805
ZNAPS Adapter/Connector	$3 007 370	70 122
Helix—The World's Best Folding Bike	$2 262 621	1069
Luup Litter Box—The Best Cat Litter Box Ever Made	$1 178 504	14 333

LO4   Business Ownership Options

As was stated at the front end of this chapter, starting a business is often one of the most exciting decisions an individual, or group of individuals, can make. A key initial decision associated with the formation of a business is the type of legal structure to be utilized in order to enable the individual, or individuals, to commence business operations. In making this decision, five main factors will influence its final outcome. Although not meant to be all-inclusive, these factors are believed to be predominant influences in determining the type of legal structure to utilize in commencing business operations (see Figure 7.7):

1. Ease of business set-up and operation
2. The degree of control that an owner desires
3. The magnitude of risk that individuals are willing to take on
4. The capacity of individuals to provide the financial needs required
5. The anticipated skills required for success

FIGURE 7.7   Factor Analysis: The Legal Formation of a Business

FIGURE 7.8   **Business Ownership Options**

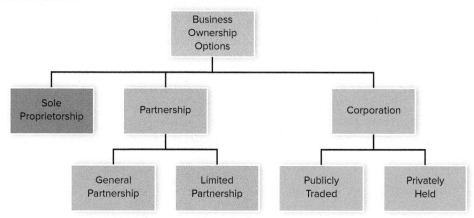

Ease of set-up relates to how easy it is to get a business up and running, and the various government regulations and required "filings" associated with a particular legal structure. The degree of control refers to the degree of ownership and level of decision-making authority that an individual (or individuals) desires within the business operation. The magnitude of risk refers to the level of financial, operational, and legal liability that individuals are willing to accept in owning and operating a business. Financial capacity refers to the financial resources that individuals have access to in order to invest in commencing business operations and supporting its ongoing cash requirements. A required skills analysis evaluates the degree of expertise that is needed to successfully manage the business against the skill set of the individual or individuals. Although these five factors are discussed in the context of commencing a business operation, it is important to note that a review of these factors will occur at several points during an organization's life cycle, as the business owners assess the needs within each of these areas and draw conclusions as to the capacity of the existing structure and ownership base to accept the risk and deliver the required resources and skills essential to sustaining the business operation. As the needs of the organization change, or the level of risk magnifies, the need to adjust the business organization's legal structure may be in the best interests of all those involved.

Using these five factors as a base for decision-making purposes, individuals can seek to form their business under one of three legal structures: a sole proprietorship, a partnership, or a corporation (see Figure 7.8). It should, again, be noted that commencing with one legal structure does not inhibit the ability of an individual, or individuals, to change the business structure in the future should it be in the best interests of the business organization.

As the needs of the organization change, or the level of risk magnifies, the need to adjust the business organization's legal structure may be in the best interests of all those involved.

Sole Proprietorships

For many, the **sole proprietorship** is the easiest way in which to commence a business. A sole proprietorship is the commencement of business by a single individual. In a sole proprietorship there is no real creation of a separate legal

Sole Proprietorship refers to a business that is owned by one person and that is initiated without a requirement to create a separate legal entity.

FIGURE 7.9   **Factor Analysis: Sole Proprietorship**

Factor	Summary Conclusions	Advantage	Potential Concern
Ease of Set-Up	Generally requires little more than registering the business name	✓	
Degree of Control	100% ownership and full decision-making control	✓	
Magnitude of Risk	Unlimited personal liability for risks associated with the business		✓
Financial Capacity	Limited to the financial resources of the sole proprietor		✓
Skills Required	Limited to the skill set and business competencies of the sole proprietor		✓

business entity. In essence, the individual and the business are one and the same. Business commencement generally takes place (it varies slightly by province) by registering your business, if in a name other than your own, and paying the required registration fee. In many cases, the name of the business is simply the name of the individual. If this is the case, most provinces do not require any formal registration at all. The debts of the business are also deemed to be the debts of the owner. Any income earned by the business is treated as the personal income of the owner. The key advantage of the sole proprietorship beyond the simplicity of the commencement of the operation is that the sole proprietor has 100% control of the business with regard to ownership and in making decisions relating to the business. A key risk issue is that the sole proprietor is 100% personally exposed to the liabilities incurred by the business. In the event that the business is unable to pay its debts (i.e., monies that it owes), the sole proprietor becomes personally obligated for such debts. A second concern with sole proprietorships is that the skill set of the business is limited to the skills possessed by the sole proprietor. For example, an individual who is skilled at building houses may not have the business acumen to successfully own and operate a residential or commercial real estate development business. Finally, sole proprietors are limited to their own personal capacity to invest and/or borrow money in support of the business organization. Those sole proprietors with limited financial capacity may find that they are unable to invest the necessary resources in the business organization in order to sustain it on an ongoing basis. Using our factor analysis approach (identified in Figure 7.7) in considering the legal formation of a business, the sole proprietorship can be summarized as shown in Figure 7.9.

> The key advantage of the sole proprietorship, beyond the simplicity of the commencement of the operation, is that the sole proprietor has 100% control of the business with regard to ownership and in making decisions relating to the business.

Partnerships

Partnership is a business organization that is formed by two or more individuals.

Recognizing some of the limitations of sole proprietorships, individuals desiring to undertake the formation of a business often opt to take the route of a **partnership**. A partnership is a business organization that is formed by two or more individuals. Although we often think of partnerships as being two partners, it is important to note that many partnerships have more than two partners. Legal and accounting firms are a good example of this, with a number of these firms possessing many partners. Although you don't technically have to have a **partnership agreement** to commence a business partnership in Canada (the partnership act of the province where the business is located may rule that a business is a partnership on the basis of its structure), it is highly recommended that such an agreement be developed and put into force at the time of inception of the business. Creating a partnership agreement ensures that the expectations of each partner, and the details of how the partnership is going to work, are fully understood by all partners involved. The partnership agreement also outlines the percentage of ownership that is attributed to each partner. As with a sole proprietorship, partnerships are not separate legal entities when it comes to liability and taxation. Income earned and liabilities incurred by the partnership are treated as personal income and personal liabilities to each of the partners. Business income or losses pass through the partnership and are reported on each partner's personal income tax return. In the event that the partnership itself is unable to pay its liabilities, these then become the personal obligations of the partners. Partnerships also carry the obligation of what is called **joint and several liability**. This means that each partner could be liable for the total debts of the partnership if other partners are unable to pay their portion of a partnership's obligations. As can be inferred from the name "partnership," individuals often choose to initiate this form of business formation as it enables the partners to jointly share the risk, jointly contribute the dollars needed to fund the business (thereby enabling a greater level of financial capacity than partners could provide on a stand-alone basis), and take advantage of the combined skills and competencies of all partners involved. An additional concern relating to partnerships is the sharing of ownership and decision-making control. This can be especially disconcerting in small partnerships with two or three partners. Differences of opinion on strategic direction, commitment to the business, or competencies in operating the business can, and often do, occur. To protect from this type of discord impacting the business, many partnership agreements include a **buy–sell agreement**. Using our factor analysis approach to considering the legal formation of a business, a partnership can be summarized as shown in Figure 7.10.

> Creating a partnership agreement ensures that the expectations of each partner, and the details of how the partnership is going to work, are fully understood by all partners involved.

Partnership Agreement is a written agreement among the partners that outlines the expectations of each partner and details how the partnership is going to work.

Joint and Several Liability refers to the liability obligation of partners as the result of a legal contract. Partners can be held individually liable for their share of the obligation (several), or fully liable for the full obligation (joint) in the event that the other parties to the agreement are unable to pay their obligations.

Buy-Sell Agreement is a written agreement among the partners that details the sale by one partner and the purchase by another of the business interest of the selling partner.

FIGURE 7.10 Factor Analysis: Partnership

Factor	Summary Conclusions	Advantage	Potential Concern
Ease of Set-Up	Easy to set up; however, the development of a partnership agreement is highly recommended. A time delay may result, and legal fees will most likely be incurred.	✓	
Degree of Control	Ownership and decision-making control is divided among partners, in accordance with the partnership agreement.		✓
Magnitude of Risk	Unlimited personal liability (joint and several) exists for risks associated with the business.		✓
Financial Capacity	Financial resource capacity is expanded to include the capabilities of all partners.	✓	
Skills Required	Skill set and business competencies are expanded to include the capabilities of all partners.	✓	

Our discussion above has been largely focused on what are termed "general" partnerships, where all partners are active in the business and share the full business risk associated with the organization. It is important to mention that another type of partnership arrangement does exist; this is called a **limited liability partnership (LLP)**. A limited liability partnership is a partnership that is made up of both general partners (at least one) and limited (passive) partners. Limited partners are individuals who contribute equity capital (money in exchange for a percentage of ownership) to the organization, but are not actively involved in the management of the business operation and have minimal control over daily business decisions. Given this minimal business involvement, the partnership agreements associated with LLPs clearly stipulate the limitations of the liability exposure of these limited (passive) partners to the value of their investment. The general partner(s) assume(s) the full liability exposure on behalf of the partnership. Limited liability partnerships are commonly found in the real estate sector, where large sums of capital are required for development purposes but the day-to-day management responsibilities can be delegated to a small management team.

Limited Liability Partnership (LLP) is a partnership that is made up of both general partners (at least one) and limited (passive) partners.

Corporations

The formation of a **corporation** results in a marked change in the legal status of a business organization. Unlike sole proprietorships and partnerships, which are not viewed as separate legal entities, a corporation is just that. By virtue of its business definition, a corporation creates a distinct legal entity separate from its owners. This distinct, separate legal entity is established by the process of **incorporation**. In Canada, this can be done at the provincial level, which enables the business to legally operate in a given province, or federally, which enables the business to operate throughout Canada. A key advantage in incorporating federally is that you are able to use the same business name in all provinces. It should be noted, however, that federal incorporation is more expensive to set up, and requires additional paperwork over and above that found at the provincial level. In addition, incorporation brings with it requirements associated with corporate governance. A **board of directors** will need to be established, officers of the corporation elected, minutes of meetings kept, and resolutions associated with business decisions approved and documented.

Corporation is a business entity that, legally, is separate and distinct from its owners.

Incorporation is the legal process of setting up a corporation.

Given the commentary above, it can be rightfully assumed that the incorporation process will result in a longer time frame to get a business up and running, as well as a higher cost to do this. Although the cost of incorporation varies by province, and between provincial incorporation and federal incorporation, it can be assumed that the cost of the incorporation process will be in the hundreds, if not thousands, of dollars. So, why incorporate if it is so much easier to just open up a sole proprietorship or to form a partnership? First, forming a corporation protects the organization's owners (shareholders) by limiting their liability. As a separate legal entity, the liabilities of the corporation do not automatically transfer to the owners in the event that the corporation is unable to pay its bills. This, in itself, is a very attractive feature of a corporation. Second, ownership rights are clearly defined and are based on the percentage of stock owned by its owners. Third, the ability to issue shares of stock as a means of raising additional cash (capital) for the business organization is unique to the corporation. In addition, business organizations need to be incorporated in order to be eligible for many federal government programs, and to take advantage of tax incentives relating to capital gains exemptions and small business deductions. The corporate tax rate, for those business organizations that are earning profits, may also result in a lower total tax obligation than if the business were left as a sole proprietorship or partnership. Having said this, incorporation does require the filing of a tax return on the part of the

Board of Directors is the term for the governing body of a corporation, comprising individuals chosen or elected to oversee the management of the organization; an appointed or elected body of a for-profit or not-for-profit corporation that oversees and advises management on issues challenging the organization on behalf of its stakeholders and shareholders.

FIGURE 7.11   **Factor Analysis: Corporation**

Factor	Summary Conclusions	Advantage	Potential Concern
Ease of Set-Up	More cumbersome to set up. A search needs to be conducted of the corporate name (to verify its availability). Articles of Incorporation need to be created, and incorporation documents need to be filed. It is, initially, the most expensive form of business set-up. As a separate entity, incorporation requires the filing of a separate tax return for the corporation, as well as other annual reporting requirements. Governance set-up and procedural requirements also exist.		✓
Degree of Control	Ownership is based on the percentage of shares in the corporation owned by an individual.		✓
Magnitude of Risk	As the corporation is a separate, legal entity, the liabilities of the corporation are limited to the corporation itself.	✓	
Financial Capacity	Financial resource capacity is expanded, as the corporation has the ability to issue shares of stock to raise capital. The corporation can also borrow money in its own name.	✓	
Skills Required	Skill set and business competencies are expanded to include the capabilities of all shareholders, and/or a professional management team.	✓	

corporation, and then including income received from the corporation (dividends), by its owners, on their personal income tax returns, where it could be subject to additional taxation. Again, using our factor analysis approach to considering the legal formation of a business, a corporation can be summarized as shown in Figure 7.11.

> Because it is a separate legal entity, the liabilities of the corporation do not automatically transfer to the owners in the event that the corporation is unable to pay its bills.

As noted in Figure 7.8, there are two main types of corporations that students need to familiarize themselves with—private corporations and public corporations. **Private corporations** are business organizations whose ownership is privately held. This means that the shares of the corporation are not publicly traded and are not available to the general public for purchase. As an example, assume that a business located in Montreal, Quebec, is incorporated in that province as a private corporation. The Province of Quebec would assign this business a provincial corporate registration number; let's assume that it is Quebec 9647-0500. The articles of incorporation would identify that shares have been issued to the owners involved in this private corporation, reflective of the percentage of ownership attributed to each. These shares, however, are not available for sale to just anyone. As a private corporation, the selling of the shares would be a private transaction between the current owner of the shares and a potential purchaser. The articles of incorporation may restrict just how shares may be purchased and offered for sale. For example, there may be an obligation to offer existing shareholders what is called "first right of refusal" on the shares to be sold before a shareholder can seek an outside buyer. In a private corporation, the shares do not trade on one of the public exchanges as publicly traded companies do. This results in greater difficulty in establishing a price for

Private Corporations are corporations whose ownership is private. The shares of stock of the corporation are not publicly traded.

Public Corporations are corporations whose shares of stock are traded on at least one stock exchange or are publicly available in the over-the-counter market.

IPO (Initial Public Offering) refers to the initial sale of stock, by a corporation, through a public exchange.

Exchange is an organization that facilitates the trading of securities, stocks, commodities, and other financial instruments. Exchanges provide a platform for selling these financial instruments to the public at large.

OTC (Over-the-Counter) refers to stocks being publicly traded through a dealer network versus an exchange.

these shares, and, potentially, the selling of these shares, than that experienced with the selling of shares relating to a public corporation.

Public corporations are corporations whose shares of stock are initially issued via an **IPO (initial public offering)**, and whose shares are then traded on at least one stock **exchange**, or are publicly available in the **OTC (over-the-counter)** market. Public corporation shares, once issued, are then considered to be publicly held. Unlike the private corporation, whose share price is difficult to value due to the fact that the shares are not publicly traded, the share value of publicly traded corporations is set as the result of daily trading activity on these shares by the marketplace (public) at large. Publicly traded corporations also have significantly more regulatory and periodic information filing requirements that they need to abide by. These requirements are set out by the securities commission that oversees the exchange the company is trading its shares on. In Canada, securities exchange governance has been established at the provincial level. In Ontario, for example, this commission is referred to as the OSC, or Ontario Securities Commission, which administers and enforces the security legislation of the province of Ontario. In Alberta, it is the Alberta Securities Commission. In Quebec, it is the Autorité des marchés financiers (AMF). Within the United States of America, a single federal regulatory agency has been established for this purpose: the U.S. Securities and Exchange Commission, or SEC.[14]

LO5 Legal Ownership Evolution

As stated at the beginning of this chapter, the decision on which type of legal approach to take when forming a business will depend on a number of factors, five of which have been presented in our factor analysis summary of each of the three legal options discussed (sole proprietorship, partnership, and corporation). For many individuals, commencing business operations is easiest via the establishment of a sole proprietorship. As the business moves from its initial embryonic phase and begins to grow and mature, its cash requirements, as well as the potential liability exposure, may necessitate a revisiting of the initial legal formation. As an example, the need for additional cash necessary for investment into the business in order to support growth may result in the need for a sole proprietor to take on a partner, or to incorporate in order to sell shares of stock to venture capitalists or venture capital companies. Let's use the example of Lululemon Athletica Inc. to illustrate this evolutionary process. Keep in mind that although Lululemon Athletica's growth led to a particular path in terms of legal formation and transition, other companies have taken different paths with equal success. Lululemon Athletica Inc.'s path of business formation and evolution is illustrated in Figure 7.12.

Most Canadians are aware of Lululemon Athletica Inc. and its yoga-inspired apparel line built around a value proposition of healthy living. Lululemon, with annual sales now exceeding US$3 billion, is already one of Canada's great business success stories and is poised to be one of Canada's next great global brands. Things were not always this way at Lululemon Athletica. As discussed in a Business in Action vignette in Chapter 3, Lululemon founder Dennis (Chip) Wilson commenced business operations, on his own, in 1998. Wilson, as owner, was successful in growing the business through a combination of business credit, cash he personally invested into the business, and profits generated by the business. This business approach served Wilson well initially, as he stretched his brand recognition and opened additional store locations. He recognized, however, that in order to gain access to the level of investment required to significantly grow Lululemon Athletica, financial resources beyond his personal capacity would be necessary. With this in mind, Wilson restructured Lululemon Athletica Inc. as a private corporation in 2005, and successfully sold shares of stock in his business to private investors. Two of the most noteworthy

FIGURE 7.12   **Lululemon Athletica: Evolutionary Path**

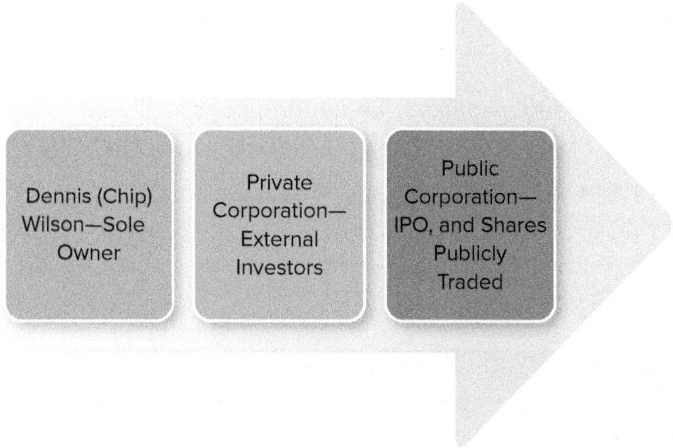

Dennis (Chip) Wilson—Sole Owner

Private Corporation— External Investors

Public Corporation— IPO, and Shares Publicly Traded

private investors were the Boston-based venture capital firms Advent International Corp. and Highland Capital Partners. These two companies invested approximately US$195 million in Lululemon Athletica Inc., for a significant minority (estimated at 48%) ownership stake in the company. In addition to the capital investment, the two firms also brought to Lululemon Athletica Inc. a wealth of new business competencies to complement the skills that Chip Wilson possessed. Yes, Wilson had to give up some decision-making control of Lululemon Athletica Inc. and saw his ownership stake decrease, but the additional financial capacity and skills, along with better management of the expansion risk being undertaken, made the shift in business structure worthwhile. As Wilson indicated publicly, when commenting on the equity infusion being provided by Advent International Corp. and Highland Capital Partners, "We like the Advent/Highland group because of whom they have brought to the table. The expertise of the board and management will ensure that we are successful in the U.S. and worldwide." With this new influx of cash, Lululemon Athletica Inc. continued its successful growth path. In 2007, seeing additional opportunity to expand and grow, Lululemon Athletica Inc. made a decision to further restructure from a private corporation to a public corporation. This transition was highlighted by the launch of its IPO (initial public offering) and the listing of Lululemon Athletica Inc. shares on both the Toronto Stock Exchange (TSX, listed as LLL) and the NASDAQ (listed as LULU). The issuance of these additional shares of ownership in Lululemon Athletica Inc. enabled the company to raise approximately US$320 million, thereby providing the additional capital needed to finance the company's future growth aspirations. The 2007 IPO was ranked the third best IPO offering in the United States that year (out of 177).[15]

Again, the example of Lululemon Athletica Inc. was intended to provide an illustration of how the evolution of the business, and the changing needs of the organization, can result in shifts in the legal structure behind the business operation. As business owners and managers, we need to continually be aware of the financial capacity of our business, the liability exposure, the risks being incurred, and the skill sets necessary for success. Using these factors as a basis for a business review, we can then make forward-thinking adjustments as to how we operate our business in order to ensure its ongoing success. The need to raise capital to fund future needs can, and often does, play a key role in this decision-making process. The remainder of this chapter focuses on providing some insight into where, and how, managers utilize internal and external financial resources in order to fund their growth strategies and maintain their financial stability. Most of our discussion will pertain to corporations, as the flexibility of the capital structure within these organizations provides us with the best framework for discussion. A macro-based discussion relating to not-for-profits is also provided, as there are some unique differences in the sources of cash between for-profit organizations and not-for-profits (NFPs).

> As business owners and managers, we need to continually be aware of the financial capacity of our business, the liability exposure, the risks being incurred, and the skill sets necessary for success.

 Business IN ACTION

Sequoia Capital

Have you ever wondered how businesses such as AdMob, Apple, Cisco, eHarmony, Electronic Arts, Google, LinkedIn, Oracle, PayPal, Yahoo, YouTube, and Zappos got started? Yes, it takes great ideas, savvy entrepreneurs (Steven Jobs, Stephen Wozniak, Larry Page, Sergey Brin, etc.), and the ability to create the business structure to effectively design, develop, and communicate the solutions (products and services) to the marketplace to meet the needs of the targeted customers. It also takes money. The amount of money that a business will burn through in its initial start-up phase, and in moving the organization to breakeven point, can be staggering. It can take years and cost millions of dollars. So, where do entrepreneurs get the cash to sustain a business until its revenue is sufficient to cover its costs? Well, one option is to get venture capital companies, such as Sequoia Capital, to invest in them. In exchange for an equity stake in the business (percentage of ownership), firms such as Sequoia Capital invest the required thousands, or millions, of dollars necessary to get these young but potentially lucrative upstarts off the ground. We say lucrative because, in return for this investment, the venture capital company will expect the market value of the business it invests in to grow, thereby enabling it to get a solid return on its investment when, and if, it chooses to sell its share of the business. Sequoia Capital specializes in venture capital funding in business sectors such as energy, financial services, health care services, Internet, mobile, outsourcing services, and technology

markets. The organization, like other venture capital firms, seeks to collaborate with the founders in a way that enables these entrepreneurs to successfully launch and sustain their businesses. By collaboration, Sequoia Capital provides more than just money. They also provide access to seasoned professionals and managers who provide much-needed guidance and expertise to the development of the business idea and the launch of the business into the marketplace. Sequoia Capital has three rounds of business financing that entrepreneurs can apply for. The first is "seed" funding, which is designed to assist in getting the business off the ground. Sequoia typically invests $100 000 to $1 million in such start-ups. Yes, Sequoia is selective, but this selectivity has enabled it to successfully move forward to additional rounds of funding approximately 75% of these stage-seed companies. The second round of funding is what is called "early stage" funding. This funding seeks to assist business ideas that have gained traction in the marketplace and now need the necessary financing and support to build and sustain the business model and its supporting structure. Sequoia Capital typically invests between $1 million and $10 million in this stage into the selected companies that it chooses to support. The third stage of funding is "growth stage" funding. Typically, with investments in the $10 million to $100 million range, this stage of funding is focused on assisting these companies with the necessary capital to expand their markets, make necessary acquisitions, grow the depth of competencies and expertise, and prepare for the launch of the organization's

IPO. Although these might be typical funding levels, Sequoia is not hesitant to invest at higher levels in situations where the opportunity justifies the risk. As commented on below, Sequoia has recently written cheques in the $300+ million range, and has publicly stated that it would consider potential investments in the $750 million to $1 billion range. Companies funded by Sequoia Capital (founded, in 1972, by Don Valentine) now account for more than 20% of the value of the NASDAQ. Recent funding announcements by Sequoia Capital include investments in the direct-to-consumer beauty company Glossier ($100 million), delivery service upstart DoorDash ($400 million), tech-enabled storage company Clutter ($200 million), and content online platform Reddit ($300 million). Other past investments include Aruba Networks, HubSpot, Trulia, Tumblr, Kayak, and WhatsApp. With more than 1200 venture investments, and worldwide exposure in China (making up approximately 50% of its current portfolio), India, Israel, and the United States, Sequoia Capital thinks of itself as the entrepreneur behind the entrepreneurs. In total, Sequoia has raised over $14.6 billion across 20 funds. The dollars raised and the investments made have resulted in the companies that have formed its investment portfolio to create public market share value in excess of $3.3 trillion USD. Oh, and by the way—all of the companies listed in the opening sentence of this Business in Action feature received start-up funding from Sequoia Capital.

© Photo Edit/Alamy

Web Integration

For more information regarding Sequoia Capital, visit **www.sequoiacap.com**. On Twitter, Sequoia Capital is available @sequoia, or search for Sequoia Capital on Google.

A Note Pertaining to Not-for-Profits

Just as for-profit entities need to seek out new business opportunities in order to grow their companies, so too do not-for-profits. Historically, many not-for-profits have relied on external funding sources, such as government, foundations, and granting agencies, to cover their operating expenses. For foundations, reduced returns on principal invested have resulted in a reduction in the dollar amount of support that they, in turn, are able to provide. Faced with budgetary deficits coupled with taxpayers demanding minimal increases in taxes, governments are reducing or withdrawing support in many non-core service areas. Transfers to non-government granting agencies are also being reduced. The end result is that not-for-profits are being increasingly challenged to create new revenue streams and business opportunities. Management teams, largely focused on administrative efficiency and service delivery, now find themselves challenged to become increasingly entrepreneurial if they are to survive and grow. A good example of this entrepreneurial transition is a recent agreement between Sunnybrook Health Sciences Centre, located in Toronto, and Sanofi-aventis, a major pharmaceutical player. Researchers at Sunnybrook have created a breakthrough compound that could help millions of people afflicted with diabetes. The agreement provides Sanofi-aventis with exclusive rights to commercialize a compound, called Vasculotide, that is designed to treat chronic wounds, a major threat to diabetics. The licensing fee, paid in the form of royalties, will return to Sunnybrook Health Sciences Centre much-needed dollars to support continued research and to fund patient care.[16] Other not-for-profits, such as the Salvation Army, the March of Dimes, and the Cerebral Palsy Association of Canada, have developed retail thrift stores as a mechanism for generating revenues to support their organizational missions and financial requirements. As has been stated earlier, the balancing act for not-for-profits seeking additional revenue through the sale of products and/or services is to accomplish this without being perceived as abandoning their mission, and without causing the for-profit sector to challenge their not-for-profit status, and the tax shield that it provides, due to perceived unfair competitive practices. Absent of the ability to seek private-equity investment, and challenged by heightened competition among NFPs for a dwindling pool of philanthropic dollars, not-for-profits increasingly need entrepreneurial ideas and concepts if they are to ensure the long-term sustainability of their organizations.

Management Reflection—
The Launch Decision

As stated earlier in this chapter, the idea of starting one's own business has tremendous appeal to many individuals. The feeling of being your own boss can be second to none. Having said that, the physical, emotional, and financial stress that it places upon an individual and their family can be challenging to say the least. An important aspect of assessing a business opportunity is the understanding of the market risk and the level of financial commitment the new business will require. Developing a strong feeling for the initial capital requirements at the time of business inception, and the ongoing required cash infusions needed to become cash flow positive and

FIGURE 7.13   **Market/Opportunity Pyramid**

Can the management team make it happen?

Is the business system aligned and properly structured?

Are the market and financial characteristics strong enough to result in success?

Is the customer fully understood?

Is there a true market need and is the timing right?

reach the breakeven point, are essential analytical elements to determining whether a business opportunity can attain the revenue levels required to sustain itself. Entrepreneurs need to ensure that they possess the capacity to provide the level of capitalization needed to ensure its formation and operational liquidity and solvency. Financial risk assessment alone, however, does not constitute a formal venture analysis. Investors and/or business analysts must look beyond the numbers and fully analyze other health and performance metrics. Reviewing the product development process, assessing customer connection tactics, critically evaluating the acumen of the management and/or entrepreneurial team, and identifying the specialized assets and employee skill sets needed for success are all fundamental to this analysis.[17] Investors and creditors also need to assess the operational capacity of the infrastructure being put into place in order to determine if the financials being projected can actually be realized via the business model being developed. For entrepreneurs, the key is not only to recognize opportunity, but also to place this in the context of the external market dynamics within which it will operate, and assessing the people skills on board to seal the deal and drive its execution. The core decision to proceed will, ultimately, come down to whether the idea being presented can achieve sufficient scale to ensure short-term initial success and longer-term sustainability. A tool to assist in the conclusion of this initial launch or don't launch decision is what is termed the market/opportunity pyramid (see Figure 7.13). If the response to the five questions posted in the pyramid is yes, then a launch decision would appear to be the likely conclusion reached.

Chapter Summary

The purpose of this chapter is to provide students with initial exposure to the key characteristics that successful entrepreneurs possess. Also provided is an understanding of the challenges to which new business start-ups need to respond as they seek to gain traction in the marketplace and procure the required capital funding (investors and/or creditors) to support the realization of their business's vision. As is noted in the chapter, new business start-ups and business expansions both contain an underlying element of risk. A key requirement of any entrepreneurial initiative is to understand the level of risk (both financial and personal) and to seek ways to mitigate and manage such risk. The development of a business plan and an understanding of the key pivot or inflection points the entrepreneur will face are fundamental to this process. Investors and creditors use such a plan and the inherent planning sequencing within it to determine whether the management team possesses the skills and acumen to successfully launch and grow the business.

An additional key component of a business's evolution is the determination of the underlying legal structure that the organization will form itself around and evolve toward. The chapter provides students with a base-level understanding of the different legal structures that business owners can utilize when establishing their organizations. Specifically, three different legal structures were reviewed: sole proprietorship, partnership, and corporation. These legal structures were discussed in terms of the advantages inherent within each, as well as some of the potential concerns that owners need to be cognizant of as they choose an initial legal structure for their new business. Included within this discussion was the recognition that choosing one legal structure type does not preclude the business owner from changing to another structural option in the future. In fact, many organizations modify their legal structure as they move through their individual life cycle. This may be predicated on the inherent advantages and potential concerns associated with each legal structure, or the direct result of the need to tap new sources of capital to further fund the organization's growth.

The chapter closes with a note pertaining to the role of venture analysis in the not-for-profit sector, and a closing management reflection on the key components that form the decision-making process leading up to a business venture launch decision.

Developing Business Knowledge and Skills

Key Terms

entrepreneur *p. 248*

venture capitalist *p. 251*

cash flow positive *p. 253*

breakeven point *p. 253*

inflection points *p. 254*

collateral *p. 261*

crowdfunding *p. 261*

sole proprietorship *p. 265*

partnership *p. 266*

partnership agreement *p. 267*

joint and several liability *p. 267*

buy–sell agreement *p. 267*

limited liability partnership (LLP) *p. 268*

corporation *p. 268*

incorporation *p. 268*

board of directors *p. 268*

private corporations *p. 269*

public corporations *p. 270*

IPO (initial public offering) *p. 270*

exchange *p. 270*

OTC (over-the-counter) *p. 270*

Questions for Discussion

1. What is meant by the acronym MERFS? What do each of these key characteristics of successful entrepreneurs mean to you? (LO1)

2. What are the five key fundamentals that investors and creditors will want validation of as they assess the potential success of a business start-up or venture? (LO2)

3. What key factors need to be taken into consideration when assessing the possibility of taking on an angel investor or venture capitalist as part of your new business start-up? (LO2)

4. What are the key conclusions which you would like to reach as a result of reviewing a business plan? (LO3)

5. Why is franchising such an attractive business start-up option? How does the franchise assist in the mitigation of risk? (LO3)

6. What are the three primary legal forms of business ownership? What are the advantages and disadvantages of each? (LO4)

Question for Individual Action

Assume that you are considering opening a College Pro painting franchise in your home town this summer. Using the six phases of new venture assessment as a guide, prepare a business plan for this potential new venture. Be sure to focus on both market risk and financial risk analysis.

Team Exercise

Choose a recent successful technology start-up. Assess this organization against the core fundamentals explained in the chapter section titled "The Business of Entrepreneurship." What, in your mind, has made this start-up so successful? Is it the quality of the management team? The uniqueness of the product/service offering? Did they catch existing competitors sleeping? What about the market? Was it a creative "niche market" play? Are they a disruptor in the broader market? What do you feel is their underlying competitive advantage? Be prepared to present your analysis and conclusion to the class.

Case for Discussion

Sasha Foods

Sasha Wong and her partner, William Lee, have always had a desire to get into business for themselves. Sasha's parents, entrepreneurs in their own right, have owned a successful specialty food market in their Greater Vancouver neighbourhood for several years since immigrating to Canada. Having worked in her parents' business for a number of those years (where she also met William), Sasha has developed a good understanding of the business management complexities associated with even this small an operation. Sasha and William's plan is to open a wholesaling company, called Sasha Foods, which will specialize in importing high-quality, gourmet Japanese sauces and foods. Sasha and William have both spent considerable hours researching the local marketplace and have determined that the growing Asian market in the Greater Vancouver area represents a tremendous opportunity. Unlike the current North American brands of soya and teriyaki sauces, and rice noodles and cakes (as examples), Sasha and William intend to offer their customers authentic sauces and related food products imported directly from Asia. Their plan is to offer these products through their own store-front location, as well as through specialty and gourmet retail locations (such as Sasha's parents' store) in British Columbia. William also visualizes an opportunity to provide these products to the growing Asian restaurant industry, which now makes up a significant portion of the dining landscape in Vancouver, as well as developing an ecommerce site for across Canada sales. For Sasha and William, the question is where to begin. Some preliminary market research has been completed. The desire to proceed appears to make sense given the data collected and analyzed—but, where to start? What types of decisions need to be made to move Sasha Foods from a concept to a reality?

Preliminary Market Research Information

• Asian Ethnic & International Foods annual sales estimate (Canada)	$250 million
• Asian Ethnic & International Foods annual sales estimate (Greater Vancouver, B.C.)	$25 million
• Estimated annual growth rate—Asian Ethnic & International Foods (General)	16%
• Estimated annual growth rate—Asian Gourmet Ethnic Foods	8%
• # of registered ethnic and international food importers for Asian food in Canada	40
• # of registered "gourmet" ethnic and international food importers for Asian food in Canada	5
• Percentage of Vancouver-based Asian food sales that are non-gourmet	85%

Primary Customers

• Immigrants from Asia/Pacific countries now residing in Vancouver

• White-collar urban professionals who live and/or work in the downtown Vancouver core

• Upscale Asian restaurants in Vancouver

Potential Distribution Focus

- Gourmet and specialty Asian food outlets

- Selected organic and ethnic-based grocery stores

- Direct delivery

- Ecommerce

Questions

1. Create a vision and mission statement for Sasha Foods.

2. Develop a list of questions that you think Sasha and William need to consider further in determining whether to launch this venture. Remember, the "devil is in the details."

3. Create a list of key risks and/or barriers that you think may impact the success of Sasha and William's venture.

4. As a potential angel investor, what would be the key determinant for you in concluding whether you should invest in Sasha and William's business venture?

CHAPTER 8

Developing Your Business Structure and Culture

LEARNING OBJECTIVES

This chapter is designed to provide students with:

LO1	Knowledge of the core components associated with designing a business system
LO2	An understanding of the key decision-making areas that establish an organization's framework and strategy execution
LO3	An exposure to the underlying factors associated with creating an organization's operating structure
LO4	An understanding of the important role an organization's culture plays in influencing its business system and business plan execution
LO5	An understanding of the key criteria that determine the management approach needed to guide the business
LO6	An overview of restructuring and its key success metrics

Snapshot

What to Expect in This Chapter

This chapter provides students with insight into the core characteristics associated with business system design, the outcome of which provides the formal framework for successful execution of the tactics required to meet the organization's overall objectives. The content emphasized in this chapter includes the following:

- Business System Design
- Developing the Organizational Framework
  - Structure
  - Culture and Environment
  - Management Approach
- The Concept of Restructuring
- Management Reflection—The Importance of Business System Design

 Business IN ACTION

Inclusion and Diversity—It Does Make a Difference

Can hiring people of varying ages, genders, ethnicities, religions, and world views truly make a difference? Does having an inclusive culture within your business where individuals are respected and appreciated allow you to be more effective and innovative? Research is saying YES in response to both of these questions. McKinsey & Company, one of the world's most prestigious global consulting firms, released a January 2018 research study titled "Delivering through Diversity." An extension of prior research launched in 2015 ("Why Diversity Matters"), this research effort, based on a data set of more than 1000 companies covering 12 countries, looked at the relationship between the relevance of inclusion and diversity and its impact on the financial results of organizations. Two specific financial metrics were used in this analysis: profitability (measured by average EBIT, or earnings before interest and taxes), and value creation (measured as economic profit margin). In addition, McKinsey also studied extensively the inclusion and diversity efforts of 17 companies that represented all major regions of the world as well as multiple industry sectors. In a nutshell, McKinsey

was looking to determine whether the integration of inclusion and diversity into a business culture would aid in the achievement of an organization's overall growth and profitability objectives. In this regard, McKinsey concluded the following:

- A definitive statistical correlation exists between more diverse leadership teams and financial outperformance. This further reinforced the initial findings found in the 2015 study.

- Companies in the top 25% with respect to their integration of inclusion and diversity in leadership roles were 21% more likely to outperform other companies on profitability and 27% more likely to have superior value creation.

- Although gender inclusion was important, performance was further benefited by those companies that fully embraced ethnic/cultural diversity. In fact, companies in the top 25% that did this were 33% more likely to have industry-leading profitability.

- The highest performing companies in terms of both profitability and diversity had more women in revenue-generating roles than in supporting staff roles.

- Those companies in the bottom quartile (bottom 25%) based on their integration of inclusion and

Bloomberg via Getty Images

diversity in leadership teams were 29% less likely to generate above-average profitability when compared to all the companies studied.

So just what is it that drives this relationship between I&D (inclusion and diversity) and performance? As a result of the two studies mentioned above, McKinsey has concluded that companies that effectively integrate I&D into their workplaces are better able to attract top talent, improve customer relationships, enhance decision making, and heighten employee satisfaction—all of which leads to higher levels of commitment, productivity, and performance.

To deliver true impact through I&D it is important that CEOs and C-suite leaders embed the integration of the concepts of inclusion and diversity into their human resource processes and that such actions and activities cascade their way throughout the organization's hiring approach and practices. They must also look to link these core inclusion and diversity requirements to key performance metrics, and structure their organizations in a way that fully benefits from the intended outcomes of their I&D policies and procedures. To be successful in this manner requires companies to make the education of their management teams as to the need and benefit of I&D integration core to their training approach. There also needs to be a formalized structure whose responsibility it is to create and uphold the communication channels with respect to inclusion, celebrate and share the benefits of diversity, and communicate the goals and progress that inclusion and diversity initiatives have contributed toward. Building an inclusive and diverse culture is no easy task and does require a major investment of time and money on the part of many companies. The benefits, however, speak for themselves. Hiring, training, and retaining employees is a major expense for businesses. The effort should result in companies benefiting from such hirees in terms of the ideas, skills, experience, and engagement they bring to their jobs. Why not get the greatest benefit possible from employee relationships? I&D does just this. The more inclusive and diverse the workforce, the broader the net is cast in terms of innovative solutions to the challenges facing an organization and the objectives it is trying to achieve.

Web Integration

To learn more about the McKinsey & Company 2018 study related to inclusion and diversity, visit **https://www.mckinsey.com /business-functions/organization/our-insights/delivering-through-diversity**.

LO1   Business System Design

When we think of a business system, four key components should come to mind for the seasoned manager. You can think of these as the cornerstone to the structural foundation of a business, how it operates, and how its tactical execution is tied to its strategic plan. These components, when properly designed, aligned, and developed, ensure the successful execution of a business strategy.[1] These components are as follows, and are illustrated in Figure 8.1:

- Organizational structure, culture, and management approach
- Control systems to manage strategic intent
- Mechanisms for effective talent management
- Operational processes and market support and alignment

FIGURE 8.1   **Business System Design**

Organizational Structure, Culture, and Management Approach relates to the formal framework around which the business system is designed and how such a structure directs and influences collaboration, the exchange of knowledge, the communication and sharing of ideas, and the work environment surrounding the accomplishment of tasks and the meeting of responsibilities (the focus of this chapter).

Control Systems to Manage Strategic Intent defines the managerial evaluation and control processes utilized to determine the success of the organization in meeting its strategic and operational goals and objectives. This would include financial management systems, along with the establishment of key success metrics relating to productivity, market share growth, and asset performance, to name a few. It also refers to the formalized communication tools used to disseminate critical information up, down, and across the organization. These control systems are designed to guide managers and employees during the integration of business-level strategies in support of the overall corporate-level vision and mission.

Mechanisms for Effective Talent Management refers to the decision-making hierarchy, the delegated span of control within an organization, and the allocation of position power within it (discussed in this chapter and further supported by Chapter 9).

Operational Processes and Market Support and Alignment focuses on the processes and initiatives needed to support and direct product/service transformation within the organization, the creation of the value proposition applicable to such products/services, and the distribution, marketing, sales, and service in support of these products/services. These operational and market support processes are commonly referred to as the **value chain**. The various components that make up the value chain are discussed in detail in Chapters 10 through 12.

An organization's business system needs to be designed and developed in a way that ensures the organization functions on a day-to-day basis in a manner that maintains solid alignment between the strategic intent of the organization

Value Chain is the term for the processes and initiatives needed to support and direct the product/service transformation within the organization, the creation of the value proposition applicable to such products/services, and the distribution, marketing, sales, and service in support of these products/services.

and the activities taking place in support of this intent. As briefly illustrated above, this need to maintain alignment between the organization's strategy and structure is fundamental to the successful achievement of its goals and long-term vision. With this in mind, the balance of this chapter focuses on demonstrating how managers design an organization's structure, influence its culture, and define its decision-making approach in order to provide the framework for accomplishing this task.[2]

> An organization's business system needs to be designed and developed in a way that ensures the organization functions on a day-to-day basis in a manner that maintains solid alignment between the strategic intent of the organization and the activities taking place in support of this intent.

 Business IN ACTION

Aligning Strategy and Organizational Structure

Back in Chapter 6, Developing a Business Strategy, we saw that business growth and profitability is predicated on two core elements: a well-directed and positioned strategy, and the efficient and effective tactical execution of that strategy. So how does this relate to organizational structure? For an organization to effectively execute its strategy, its structure must be developed and remain in alignment in a manner that provides the necessary support. Organizational structure provides employees with critical guidance relating to decision-making and work flow optimization. A well-aligned organizational structure ensures optimal communication across the organization, maximizes employee productivity, and inspires innovation and creative problem solving.

Conversely, poorly developed and/or aligned organizational structures often result in confusion in roles relating to accountability and responsibility, breakdowns or missing links in the coordination of business functions, a silo mentality and its resulting failure to share ideas, and heightened performance issues due to inefficient evaluation and/or monitoring practices. Without a formal organizational structure, employees may find that they do not know where to go for answers in response to

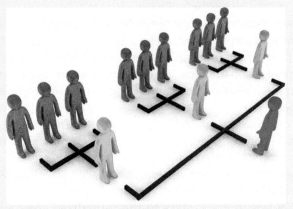
© Miskolin/Dreamstime.com/GetStock.com

critical situations that may arise in the course of doing business.

Properly developed organizational structures create the interactive web around which departments and individuals interact. The structure, by its nature, should also offer checks and balances as to the decision-making process relating to the allocation and deployment of company resources. It should effectively reinforce the interaction of employees and managers in a way that not only ensures operational efficiency and effectiveness, but also maintains and enhances employee cultural interaction and overall organizational morale.

When developing or adjusting an organization's formal structure, managers should think about the following questions:

- Does it enhance and/or reinforce the desired level of coordination and communication among individual employees, work units, departments, and divisions?

- Does it provide the required flexibility for the organization to respond to technological innovation and/or market-based disruptions that may impact long-term success?

- Does it reinforce the company's strategy for growth, talent optimization, and resource allocation and deployment?

- Does it enhance and appropriately facilitate the responsibilities of the company's management team in planning, organizing, leading, controlling, and developing?

- Does it enhance and/or maintain the critical relationships associated with the company's customers, suppliers, partners, and broader external stakeholders?

The importance of organizational structure lies in its ability to facilitate the optimal delivery of the organization's business model to the marketplace in a manner that motivates its talent (workforce) and offers clear and concise direction and instruction on where and how to act, interact, and compete. In understanding this, why is it that so many organizational structures seem to create barriers to success versus facilitating it? Organizational structures become misaligned for a number of reasons. First there is inertia. We simply continue to do business a certain way because we have always done it that way; the company does not evolve the structure at the same rate as company growth or change occurs. Second is the concept of "empire building." Managers and individuals become increasingly resistant to change as such adjustments may impact their influence and importance within the organization. Third, technology can act as a barrier to change. The tendency often is to constrain changes to an organization's structure around the existing technology infrastructure that supports the business. Fourth occurs when the organization's strategy has changed, resulting in the structure no longer supporting the company's new vision and delivery intent. Fifth is a disconnect between what the company wants to achieve, how its reporting communicates results, and how its incentives compensate for results generated. Short-term objectives can often act as barriers to long-term growth and change when the two become misaligned.

Organizational structure should not be thought of as a static component within the organization's business model. As with its other components, organizational structure should be viewed as a fluid piece to the execution puzzle. When change is required, changes should be made. The goal is to ensure that the structure is in alignment with the strategic vision and the organizational objectives set forth by the organization's senior management team and its board of directors. Like steering a ship, it is one thing to know you are off course and the adjustments that are required to get back on course. It is another thing to implement the necessary changes to ensure the course correction is made. This means communicating to the crew, ensuring that accountability and responsibility is given to a specific individual(s), and seeing that the required actions and follow-up take place. The organizational structure provides the mechanism for formalizing this process.

Developing the Organizational Framework $\quad$ LO2, LO3, LO4, LO5

When developing the organization's framework, managers should take into consideration three key questions:

1 What is the best *structure* that will develop, connect, and maintain relationships with our current and anticipated customer base and ensure the effective and efficient design, development, and delivery of our products/services to the marketplace?

2 What *culture or environment* is needed to deliver and reinforce the market position we are striving to achieve (as outlined in our business strategy) and facilitate the development and maintenance of high-performance work units and systems within our organization?

3 What *management approach* do we feel will best support the activities and interactions required within the organization to successfully achieve the goals and objectives defined in our strategic plan?

These questions can be visualized as three spheres around which the development of an organization's framework, which will ultimately guide its business system and model, will be created (see Figure 8.2).

As Figure 8.2 illustrates, the spheres representing each of these areas overlap. This is intentional in that each area influences the others with respect to the development of an organization's framework and the consequences realized. The end result is the creation of a framework that provides the backbone as to how the organization will facilitate the delivery of its operational plan and, ultimately, its vision and mission.

Structure

Structure is the formal framework around which tasks are organized and responsibilities allocated within an organization.

As noted above, **structure** relates to the formal framework around which tasks are organized and responsibilities are allocated within an organization. As managers, we need to view the requirements of our business in meeting the expectations of our customers and determine the best structural approach to take in order to support and accomplish this. Behind this decision is the concept of customer "touch points." In designing structure, we need to think about how we interact with customers, and design the organization's framework in a way that best facilitates these interactions and ensures the highest level of responsiveness to meeting the needs of the individuals or businesses who buy and use our products. We must also realize that the design and development of a structure should not be thought of as being static (i.e., a one-time event), but rather requires ongoing monitoring to ensure it continues to meet the needs of the organization as it evolves and grows (or contracts). What is recognized as an acceptable structure for a new or emerging single-product-focused company may no longer apply as the organization grows to two, three, or more product/service offerings, adds additional divisions focused toward unrelated markets, expands geographically, or utilizes an acquisitions approach toward growing its business. Structures also

FIGURE 8.2 Developing an Organization's Framework

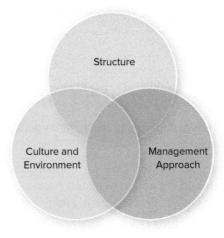

need to be assessed against changes occurring in the marketplace to ensure they remain pertinent to maintaining our connection with defined target markets, respond to competitive pressures, support stakeholder and/or shareholder expectations, and, where applicable, meet compliance or legal requirements. Structure is also about driving efficiency and effectiveness. Regardless of the focus of our strategic intent (premium price, low cost, niche market player), our structure must ensure we deliver our products/services to the marketplace in a manner that is superior to the competition. Our structure is a core component of the framework behind how this is accomplished.

> Managers need to realize that the design and development of a structure should not be thought of as being static (i.e., a one-time event) but rather requires ongoing monitoring to ensure it continues to meet the needs of the organization as it evolves and grows (or contracts).

Types of structure As indicated above, the structure of an organization most likely will change over time as the organization evolves and its strategic goals and objectives change. Efficient structures will reflect the best framework for a company at a given point in time. Structures are fluid in that as needs and conditions change, so too must structures. Having said this, many organizations have a tendency to follow a generalized structure development path as they flow through their life cycle. In their infancy stage, organizational structures tend to be fairly flat and simple. If you think of an entrepreneur launching a new business, in many cases the number of employees and the managerial decision-making structure will be fairly straightforward (owner and a few employees; no formal hierarchical structure). As the organization grows, there may be a need for better controls to maintain efficiency and effectiveness. In this situation, the organization may shift to a functional structure, where it is departmentalized around specific tasks such as marketing, sales, manufacturing, service, engineering, finances, and HR. As the organization grows further, there may be a perception that the company can be better managed if it reorganizes around specific customer categories, with each category acting as a separate value cell or operational unit. The rationalization might be that this will enable the teams assigned to a specific type of customer to more fully concentrate and specialize on the products or services applicable to this defined customer base, with the end result being improved connections and interactions with the specific customer category assigned to them. Within each customer category, marketing, sales, manufacturing, and service may be dedicated to a single purpose (the product(s) they are involved in), whereas other areas of the organization, such as finance and HR, may remain centralized depending on the size and desired outcomes of the organization. As the organization continues to evolve similar product lines may materialize, resulting in a desire to restructure around product lines or divisions. Also, organizations may possess multiple business interests through acquisitions or new market development. This may result in organizations structuring their operations almost as separate businesses, often referred to as strategic business units (SBU). Transitioning from a regional player to a national or international player may also result in organizations structuring their businesses geographically. Figure 8.3 provides a sample of one possible evolutionary path an organization's business structure framework could follow. It should be noted that this is simply an illustration, as organizations often will combine components from each type to develop the customized business system approach that they feel best meets the needs of the organization, is most responsive

FIGURE 8.3   **Sample: Structural Evolution**

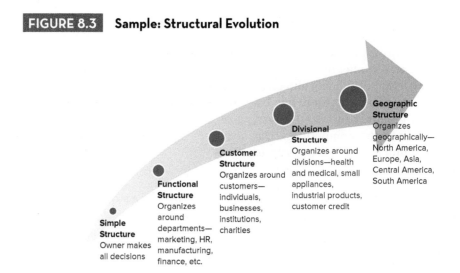

to their customer and stakeholder requirements, and maintains a culture of innovation and opportunity development. Figure 8.4 provides a simplified example of each different type of structure noted above.

The structures discussed thus far have been largely traditional in their nature and have emphasized some form of departmentalization as a core component of their framework for development. It should be recognized that such structures may not be viewed as the best approach or natural evolution for all companies. Departmentalized approaches to structure seem to fit best for traditional organizations where some aspect of task specialization is present. In this situation, the grouping of jobs into departments seems to make logical sense from the perspective of efficiency and effectiveness as well as ease of managerial control. In some companies or industry sectors, however, task specialization and the need for departmentalization may not

FIGURE 8.4   **Types of Organizational Structures, Simplified**

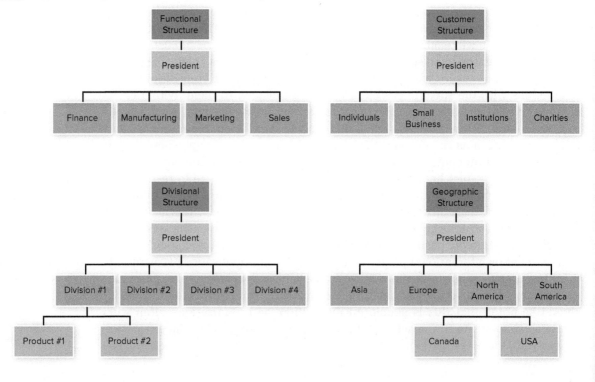

FIGURE 8.5   Matrix-Style Organizational Structure, Simplified

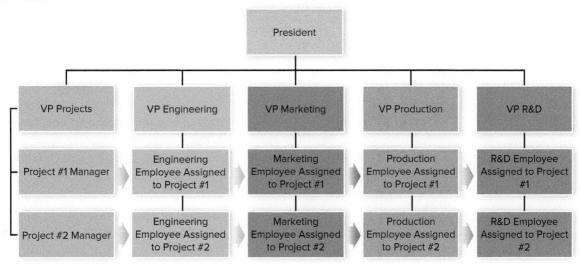

be the best organizational structural approach. A good example is companies or industries where project management makes up a predominant component of the organization's operations. In these situations, employees from various departments need to work jointly, in a cross-functional environment, on a project or specific initiative for a defined period of time. An example of an organizational response to such a situation would be a matrix-style structure. A matrix organizational structure takes into consideration that individuals will have specific expertise related to defined departmental areas. The difference, however, is that this expertise can be considered fluid in that different types of expertise may be needed for each project the organization currently has on the go. In this situation, the organization defines project managers who then draw on the resources and expertise of various departments to successfully complete the projects designed. Engineering firms, construction companies, and large project-driven organizations are the types of companies that are more likely to consider a matrix-style approach to organizational structure. Figure 8.5 provides an example of a matrix-style organizational setup.

Although our focus up to this point has been on largely traditional structural frameworks, the arrival of the digital age and its accompanying technologies is having dramatic impact on the evolution of organizational structure. The increasing mobile freedom technology brings has enabled individuals to demonstrate the ability to work effectively from virtually any location. The Business in Action vignette focused on the "virtual" organization offers insight into the rise of this increasingly acceptable structural model, and the impact it has on our ability to effectively manage an organization whose structure, contrary to traditional thought, is absent any physical framework.

Business IN ACTION

Virtual Organizations

The rise of the digital age has resulted in a significant rethinking of the way that organizations perceive the composition of their organizational structure. The Internet, satellite communications, mobile devices, cloud-based services, enhanced computer networking, and information communication platforms have enabled organizations to develop virtual structures—in contrast to the traditional structures, with formalized offices and locations, we have historically

FIGURE 8.6   **Characteristics of Virtual Organizations**

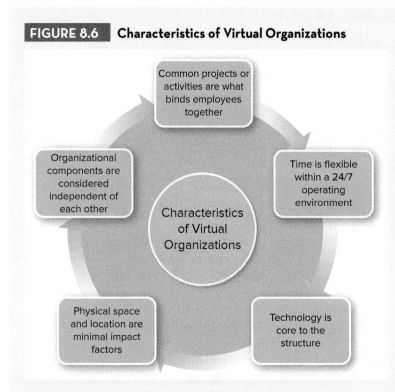

created as a basis for conducting business. This technology-based evolution has resulted in organizations that can operate virtually from anywhere and at any time.

By definition, a "virtual" organization organizes itself around communication technologies and capabilities rather than physical domain features (see Figure 8.6). Its existence is predicated on the principle that individuals who are part of the organization or who interact with it can conduct business from any location, and can maintain the collaborative relationships fundamental to conducting work as a result of a formally established communication network and support protocols. See Figure 8.7 for a sample virtual organization structure.

FIGURE 8.7   **Sample—Virtual Organization**

Miskolin/Dreamstime.com/GetStock.com

Proponents of virtual organizations point toward a number of perceived advantages they believe underscore the value of conducting business virtually. First is the cost savings advantage that virtual organizations offer over traditional organizational structures. Virtual organizations eliminate or significantly reduce expenses relating to real estate, office space, and utilities. By their very nature, they can also choose to focus on specific geographic areas for certain business components, where employee competency levels are high but comparative wages are low (India, as an example). Second, again by its virtual nature, the ability to have employees work from practically anywhere enables the organization to seek out global talent, rather than being restricted to a specific geographic region. Third, virtual teams, in the absence of bureaucratic decision-making structures, are felt to be able to respond more quickly to changing market conditions, and to benefit from shortened development cycles. The absence of bureaucracy is also seen to result in higher levels of productivity by employees, which ultimately leads to higher profits. Finally, the virtual nature of the business enables organizations to quickly expand into and leverage new market opportunities, due to the absence of a need to create significant physical asset infrastructure which is often part of a traditional business model ramp-up.

Detractors of virtual organizations point to the fact that although physical asset requirements are reduced, the increased costs of maintaining and enhancing technologies negate a significant portion of the savings found when measured against traditional business models. They also point to the lack of collaboration and potential conflict that could occur due to cultural, time-zone, and societal differences between globally based employees. There is concern that social isolation resulting from the lack of in-person interactions can impact productivity. Communication with customers and strategic partners can also find itself strained at times due to the lack of nonverbal communication reinforcement cues such as voice, eye contact, and body language. Finally, and most notably, a key concern with virtual organizations is the managerial challenge of overseeing remotely located employees, in many cases across large geographical distances. Communication clarity, performance evaluation, and training and coaching are all challenging managerial requirements in a virtual setting.

Are virtual organizations here to stay? The answer is a definitive yes. Technology is rapidly reducing the size of today's market environment. Global competition requires organizations to be able to respond more quickly than ever before to new opportunities and shifting customer trends and needs. Flexibility and agility, the cornerstones of virtual organizations, simply deliver faster and more efficiently on these two business fundamentals. The major challenge lies in ensuring that individuals responsible for managing within such environments are able to adjust their communication and interactive style in a way that enables the development of a positive and fully supportive business culture, even within a virtual setting.

So what is the best way to structure your organization? The response to this is that it depends on a number of factors. The organization's size, geographic dispersion, range of business undertakings, task specialization requirements, general nature of its work, ability to leverage communication and interactive technology, and perceived best way to connect with customers all will influence how an organization structures its work responsibilities and its management decision-making process. It also has been emphasized that structures are not static, and that organizations will revisit and modify their structures throughout their evolution. Periods of growth—whether the result of acquisition, current product growth, or new market opportunity development—as well as periods of organizational contraction due to economic or financial challenges, or simply a need or a desire to be more efficient and effective, can all result in substantial changes in the appearance and framework of an organization. Organizational structures can, and should, be thought of as almost a customization of the manner in which an organization perceives it is best able to manage its business system and deliver its products/services to the marketplace. The ability to create a more efficient and effective structure, and to create stronger customer relationships, can result in a competitive advantage in the marketplace. The creation of these structures often results in a hybrid use of components of the various structural options highlighted above.

Organizational structures can, and should, be thought of as almost a customization of the way an organization perceives it is best able to manage its business system and deliver its products/services to the marketplace.

Building blocks of structure Recognizing that the need to revisit an organization's current structure can be influenced by external and internal factors, the reorganization of a business's structure generally focuses on some or all of the building blocks illustrated in Figure 8.8: customer intimacy, work efficiencies, and degree of departmentalization.

Customer intimacy refers to ensuring the structure an organization designs and puts into place is built on interactions and connectivity to customers in order to meet their expectations for contact, service, and support. As organizations grow, the tendency can be to build structure more around internal efficiencies and practices versus ensuring that such structures are designed to support the value proposition around which products and services are sold. Managers must ensure that customer "touch points" (i.e., mechanisms for interaction) are fundamental to structural development and alignment. For example, if a decision is made to facilitate customer sales and support via a Web site, then the site must be designed to ensure ease of use and maximization of benefit to the customer. The outcome is to develop a framework for customer connection and intimacy that encourages and rewards customers for doing business with the organization, thereby encouraging heightened frequencies of purchase (repeat business) and maximizing the "per interaction expenditure" by customers while creating a potential barrier to competitors desiring to attack the organization's customer base.

Work efficiencies refers to the need for the organization to fully analyze the type, number, and responsibilities of the various positions within the organization and align these to the tasks required to support the design, development, marketing, distribution, and sale of the organization's products and services in the most efficient and effective manner possible. This analytical assessment could include such initiatives as re-engineering fabrication and assembly processes, reviewing continuous improvement tactics, assessing packaging and shipping procedures, defining new uses and modifying existing uses of technology within the workplace, determining human resource allocations to various products/services, implementing quality assurance protocols, and redefining specific task requirements and responsibilities on a position-by-position basis. A key outcome of work efficiency evaluation is the desire to create core competencies within the organization that will enable it to compete more effectively in the marketplace and that will ideally result in a sustainable competitive advantage.

> **Customer Intimacy** is the term for the interactions and connectivity that organizations seek to foster with their customers in order to meet their expectations for contact, service, and support.

> **Work Efficiencies** refers to the alignment of the tasks required to support the design, development, marketing, distribution, and sale of an organization's products/services in the most efficient and effective manner possible.

FIGURE 8.8   **Building Blocks of Organizational Structure**

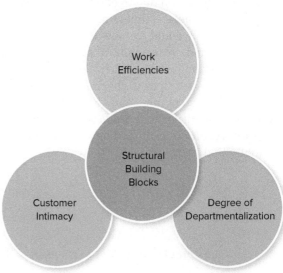

Departmentalization refers to dividing the organization's work units into defined functional areas. This type of division would take into consideration the specific skill sets needed for the employees involved and the tasks/responsibilities to be completed. The degree of departmentalization is generally driven by efficiency and effectiveness outcomes. By grouping employees into defined functional areas the organization is striving to centralize the tasks involved, thereby creating synergies within the department with the end result ideally being the maximization of efficiency and effectiveness. A common example of departmentalization is found within functional structures where organizations create defined departments, such as finance, engineering, manufacturing, and marketing. Often-listed advantages of departmentalization include the sharing of tasks, economies of scale resulting from the centralization of tasks, ease of managing due to the narrowly defined skill focus, and greater control over the quality of work being produced. Disadvantages that need to be recognized are that departmentalization can lead to a "silo mentality" where decisions are made in isolation of other organizational needs, reduced cross-organizational communication, loss of the organizational "big picture" or vision by employees, and a tendency to focus on internal priorities versus external customer, market, and stakeholder needs.[3]

> **Departmentalization** refers to the process of dividing the organization's work units into defined functional areas.

Business IN ACTION

The Importance of a Strong Corporate Culture

So, what exactly drives organizational results? Is it the level of research and development (R&D) spending an organization undertakes? Is it the specific strategy the organization pursues? What about operational efficiency and effectiveness? Yes, all of these elements contribute to the success of an organization, but what truly drives results is the underlying culture present within an organization. Why is this the case? Before responding to this question, let's review some recent research results by Booz & Company relating to global innovation and R&D spending. According to Booz & Company research, no statistically significant relationship exists between financial performance and innovation spending (R&D). In fact, a number of companies significantly outperform their competitors on a broad range of performance metrics (such as revenue growth, profitability growth, shareholder returns, etc.) despite spending less money on R&D (Apple, for example). How does this happen? The reason, according to Booz & Company and shared by a number of other researchers and analysts, is that culture matters. It is the organization's culture that makes the difference. This is not to imply that strategy, innovation

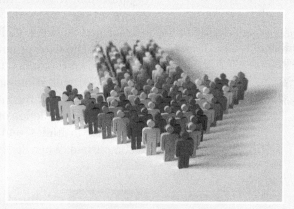

© Mike_kiev/Dreamstime.com

spending, and operational efficiency don't matter. It is just that they are dependent upon the alignment of an organization's culture to these goals.

Simply put, culture can be most easily thought of as the way that your organization does business. It is the company's DNA, the unique identifier of the underlying values that, as an organization, you bring to the marketplace. What is important for companies to realize is that their success is dependent upon their internal culture, because it is the culture that decides how employees will interact at the workplace, as well as outlining the specific policies that will guide employees in their interactions with customers and channel and supply partners. A culture that extracts the best from its team members and that creates healthy relationships among employees is considered fundamental to a company's overall success.

In a poll of the Global Innovation 1000 (the top 1000 innovative companies), Booz & Company found that successful companies share two common underlying cultural attributes. The first is a strong identification with the customer and an overall orientation toward delivering a positive customer experience. The second is a passion and pride in the products and services the company offers. Additional attributes felt to be important toward developing a positive corporate culture were respect for the technical talent and knowledge employees possess; an openness to new ideas from customers, suppliers, and other industry-related sources; a culture of collaboration across functional areas and regions; a sense of personal accountability by employees; and a tolerance for mistakes.

Developing and maintaining a successful culture requires attention and detail. Cultures are not developed overnight, but evolve one decision and interaction at a time. They are also the result of a consistent and deliberate nurturing of the fundamental values business founders and managers deem essential to communicate across their stakeholder community. Yes, achieving strategic objectives is important, but equally important are the behaviours and actions your organization takes and accepts in getting there.

Culture and Environment

Culture defines how the individuals within the organization behave and how the organization as a whole will react to both internal and external challenges and stimuli.

While organizational structure can be thought of as the skeleton and muscles of the organization, where a framework is developed for supporting the day-to-day processes and activities, the culture of the organization can be thought of as its conscience and its heart. **Culture** defines how the individuals within the organization behave and how the organization as a whole will react to both internal and external challenges and stimuli. Culture can be thought of as the manner in which all the layers of the organization interact with each other (see Figure 8.9). It reflects the behavioural aspect of the internal processes and procedures the organization uses to facilitate the completion of tasks and the management of outcomes. It is the underlying values, attitudes, and interactive relationships that govern how work is to be accomplished. When developing the framework for an organization, managers need

FIGURE 8.9   **Cultural Interconnectivity**

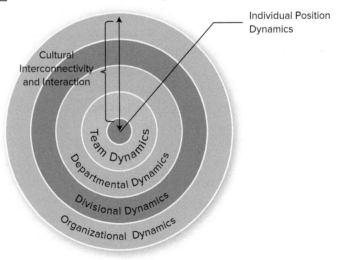

to take into consideration the environment within which they want employees to work, the norms or behaviours they desire to reinforce, and the interactive and interconnectivity opportunities they desire to incorporate into the decision-making and task completion process.

> While organizational structure can be thought of as the skeleton and muscles of the organization, where a framework is developed for supporting the day-to-day processes and activities, the culture of the organization can be thought of as its conscience and its heart.

Managers also need to recognize that immigration and the interconnectivity of the global marketplace will bring individuals from a variety of cultural backgrounds into contact with each other, both within and outside of the workplace. This cultural diversity impacts not only how individuals interact, but also how individuals perceive authority, how they negotiate solutions to problems or challenges, how they view decisions (long-term versus short-term), how gender influences perceptions of authority, and their overall view of structure and hierarchical constraints and parameters. One of the leading authorities in assessing the influence of culture on structural efficiency and strategy execution is Professor Geert Hofstede of Maastricht University. His cultural dimensions model (see Figure 8.10) outlines five key dimensions that managers need to assess as they evaluate the impact of cultural interaction both within and outside of their organizations. Hofstede's widely used model provides managers with a good starting point to assess changes to their organizational culture as the organization evolves and as the interconnectivity with different global cultures grows.[4]

Web Integration

Want to learn about the cultural dimensions model and Geert Hofstede's work? Visit **www.geert-hofstede.com**, or Google "Hofstede cultural dimensions model."

FIGURE 8.10   **Hofstede's Cultural Dimensions Model**

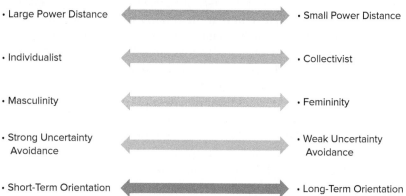

- Large Power Distance ⟷ • Small Power Distance
- Individualist ⟷ • Collectivist
- Masculinity ⟷ • Femininity
- Strong Uncertainty Avoidance ⟷ • Weak Uncertainty Avoidance
- Short-Term Orientation ⟷ • Long-Term Orientation

Source: Geert Hofstede, Gert Jan Hofstede, Michael Minkov, "Cultures and Organizations, Software of the Mind," Third Revised Edition, McGraw-Hill 2010, ISBN 0-07-166418-1. © Geert Hotstede B.V., quoted with permission.

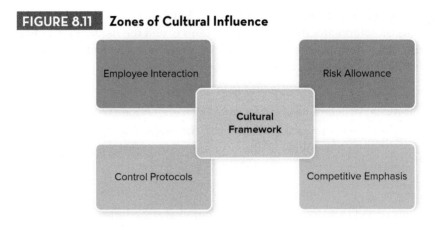

FIGURE 8.11   **Zones of Cultural Influence**

With a focus on the internal culture, managers can, in a sense, set the tone and seek to develop a measure of control over the environment within which the organization operates daily. They do this by defining the type of culture desired in advance of implementing organizational framework modifications. This is accomplished by defining behavioural norms and boundaries around four fundamental zones (see Figure 8.11).

Employee interaction refers to the level and style of interaction that occurs among employees and between work units and their management teams. It defines the participatory nature of the work environment, the sense of teamwork that is fostered within the organization, and the commitment of the management team toward supporting and developing each employee's skills and capabilities.

Risk allowance refers to the degree of entrepreneurship that is embedded into the organization. It is the extent to which the environment allows and encourages risk taking and flexibility in making decisions, supports innovation and innovative ideas, and rewards creativity in the workplace.

Control protocols refers to the rigidity or flexibility associated with the application of, and adherence to, rules, policies, and procedures within the organization. It is the degree of rigidity, order, and uniformity that is embedded within the organization, and the overarching emphasis on work conduct defined by efficiency and effectiveness protocols. Financial systems, quality control systems, and reward systems are examples of control protocols developed by an organization to oversee and direct operational performance.

Competitive emphasis refers to the extent to which the organization rewards and reinforces goal achievement, emphasizes competitiveness (internal and external), and defines its success on the basis of market superiority. This can also be thought of as the degree of passion that the organization communicates to its employees (and the frequency of such communications) relating to organizational successes and achievement of performance benchmarks. This also includes the effective use of logos and other visual representations by the organization in order to create a profile and define its market uniqueness.

The key with respect to this cultural framework is to develop a culture that passionately pursues the attainment of the vision and the mission of the organization.[5] This cultural framework becomes the underlying fabric of the organization and governs the connectivity of each individual employee to the organization and its "raison d'être." Organizations that will benefit from a positive work culture are those that enable the flow of information horizontally as well as vertically, and that resist the development of silos by creating protocols that involve team dynamics and cross-functional decision making, information transparency, the sharing of vision and mission, and the belief in employees as assets versus an expense. The same can be

Employee Interaction refers to the value-creating skills an organization's employees bring to the marketplace. The success of many businesses lies with the specialized skills that exist within its labour force.

Risk Allowance refers to the degree of entrepreneurship that is embedded into the organization.

Control Protocols refers to the rigidity or flexibility associated with the application of, and adherence to, rules, policies, and procedures within the organization.

Competitive Emphasis refers to the extent to which the organization rewards and reinforces goal achievement, emphasizes competitiveness (internal and external), and defines its success on the basis of market superiority.

said of setting and communicating expectations. Employees who understand the expectations placed on them and who perceive such expectations, although challenging, as doable and realistic will challenge themselves to achieve these heightened levels of performance. This assumes, of course, that these expectations are provided in an environment and culture that celebrates such successes and ensures employees have the resources needed to succeed.[6]

The key with respect to this cultural framework is to develop a culture that passionately pursues the attainment of the vision and the mission of the organization.

Business IN ACTION

Tony Hsieh, CEO Zappos

Want to learn how to create a great company? Tony Hsieh, CEO of Zappos, fervently believes it's all about creating a great culture. In fact, Tony's philosophy is built around the belief that if you get the culture right, then the other key elements, such as delivering great customer experience, creating a strong brand image, and communicating a passion for the organization's products and services, will just happen naturally. For Tony, it does not really matter what you sell that makes a company successful. It is more about how you deliver your products and services to the marketplace, and what you do for your employees along the way. Take Zappos as an example. The company sells shoes, clothing, handbags, luggage, and assorted men's and women's accessories—not really a unique product line for any player in the retail space. So how is it that Hsieh was able to build Zappos into an ecommerce success story, generating over $1 billion in sales? In Tony's mind, it is all about building the business around 10 core values that all employees within the organization are committed to. These 10 core values are as follows:

1. Deliver WOW through Service

2. Embrace and Drive Change

3. Create Fun and a Little Weirdness

4. Be Adventurous, Creative and Open-Minded

© Aurora Photos/Alamy

5. Pursue Growth and Learning

6. Build Open and Honest Relationships with Communication

7. Build a Positive Team and Family Spirit

8. Do More With Less

9. Be Passionate and Determined

10. Be Humble

In delivering on these core values, Zappos employees know that both the speed at which customers receive online orders and the service they experience are fundamental to building repeat business and to spreading the word. Understanding this, Zappos places its emphasis on ensuring its entire business model and underlying structure is designed to provide unparalleled customer service. Core to this is the belief that only items that are physically stocked in Zappos fulfillment centres (warehouses) will be made available for sale to customers. Add to this a commitment to provide the absolute best selection of shoes in terms of style, colour, size, and width, and you can sense the importance the company places on exceeding customer expectations.

Tony Hsieh understands that as ecommerce and the digital age evolve and mature, the growth in online retailing is where future opportunity lies. He also understands that customers will seek out those companies that offer the best service and the best selection. It is his vision for Zappos to be that online store. In this vein, Zappos made the decision, in 2009, to join the Amazon.com family. The acquisition by Amazon, however, did not mean that Tony's tenure as CEO and his dream of making Zappos the online retail store of choice came to an end. Contrary to this, Zappos still operates independently from Amazon, and Tony is still at the helm. Yes, the structure has evolved and changed as Zappos has grown and has become part of the Amazon family. In fact, in 2010 the company initiated a significant restructuring, breaking itself into 10 different semi-autonomous businesses with the intent to create even closer connections to its customers. The focus on culture, however, has not changed. What has also not changed is the belief that culture starts at the top. Hsieh firmly believes that in the hiring process cultural fit is as important a decision factor as skill set—if not more important. What brings passion out in people is the environment within which they work. Hiring people with the right

values and beliefs means that they too will hire individuals with these same values, thereby further developing and ingraining the culture within the organization. This is where the true strength of the organization lies. For Tony, it is simple. You cannot have deeply engaged customers (75% of Zappos sales are from repeat customers) without deeply engaged employees.

Now, some may remember that Zappos did attempt to expand its operation by shipping to Canada (2008), only to exit a brief time later (2011). If the company is so unique at delivering on its customer experience, why was the venture into Canada not successful? In analyzing the situation, Zappos found that the experience it delivered to customers in the U.S. could not be replicated in Canada. The Zappos product selection in Canada was limited due to restrictions associated with its distribution agreements with brands it carried in the U.S. The company simply was not permitted to sell all of the brands it carried in Canada. Second, delivery speed and free shipping and free returns were both hampered by Canada/U.S. customs and logistic constraints. In short, accepting orders and shipping to Canada could not be handled in a way that met the Zappos definition of service and customer experience. The inability to replicate the Zappos experience in Canada not only led to dissatisfied customers in Canada, but also was impacting the internal culture of the organization. The underlying conflict that occurred between the values around which the company built its business and the constraints it faced in attempting to deliver on this to the Canadian market was simply insurmountable. In this situation, preservation of the culture and its underlying core values superseded the desire to broaden the company's North American reach.

Management Approach

As part of our discussion on developing an organizational framework, we also need to direct our focus toward defining (in broad terms) how the organization will be managed and the hierarchical structure that will be used to communicate the managerial process to employees. As you will see, the managerial approach really is reflective of the conclusions reached with regard to structure and culture. This includes decisions on the centralization or decentralization of managerial decision-making authority and responsibility, the extent of responsibility that various managerial positions will oversee (referred to as span of control), the coordination of the work effort that is considered most efficient to effectively direct the operational and market support processes

FIGURE 8.12   **Key Management Approach Criteria**

within the organization, and the nature of the specific tasks that individuals within the organization accomplish on a day-to-day basis. Figure 8.12 illustrates the core criteria that ultimately will influence an organization's managerial approach.

Managerial hierarchy refers to the number of levels of management deemed necessary to effectively manage the organization, and the sequential ranking of the managerial positions in relationship to one another; this hierarchy is often referred to as the "chain of command." It will be driven by the structural design of the organization (functional, geographic, customer, product focus). The number of layers of management will ultimately determine how tall or flat the organization is (see Figure 8.13). In general, the larger and more complex the organization, the more layers of management are required to effectively manage it. The key to hierarchy development,

Managerial Hierarchy refers to the number of levels of management deemed necessary to effectively manage the organization, and the sequential ranking of the managerial positions in relationship to one another.

FIGURE 8.13   **Tall versus Flat Organizations**

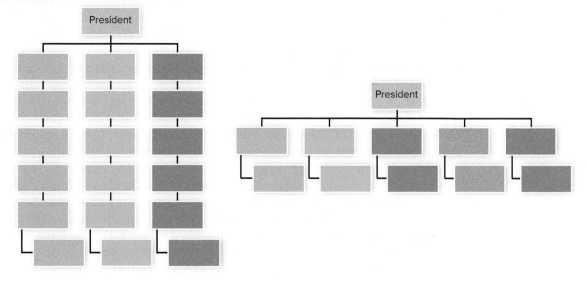

however, is where to position decision-making control so that the organization can effectively respond to the needs of the marketplace it serves in a manner that enables "management acumen" to be viewed as a competitive advantage. It is for this reason that organizational structures are continually being assessed and reassessed, as ineffective design can lead to poor or uninformed decision making.

Decision-making control refers to the level of responsibility and decision-making authority that is transferred to each specific managerial position. Again, structure will influence this, but so will the confidence that top-level management has in its lower-level managers to effectively make decisions that will benefit the organization. Decision-making control, in essence, reflects the location of organizational authority. Will it be centralized or decentralized? Centralized authority generally retains managerial control and decision making at the top of the organization. Supporters of centralized approaches believe that this results in the greatest efficiency and ensures that decisions are made in a consistent manner across the organization. They also argue that a centralized approach better ensures that the organization's operating plan remains aligned with its strategic objectives and vision. Opponents to a centralized managerial approach argue that this results in lower-level managers feeling less empowered and therefore reluctant to make decisions. This can result in a slower response to customer needs, lower morale among such managers, and heightened organizational conflict due to the inability to respond to day-to-day planning, organizing, and directing requirements. Many also believe that this approach inhibits the development of lower-level managers, resulting in long-term negative impact to the organization's overall health. A decentralized managerial approach is believed by its proponents to provide the organization with a quicker response mechanism to internal and external issues, stronger developmental outcomes, higher morale levels for lower-level managers, and less overall organizational conflict as decisions are made on the spot. As with any situation there are opponents who express concerns about such a managerial approach, pointing to the potential for inconsistency across the organization as various managers will interpret policies and procedures differently. They also point toward the increased risk of poor decisions due to some managers lacking experience or the information needed to make a fully informed decision, as well as loss of control over business operations as decisions may not be made in alignment with the overall corporate strategy and operating plan.

Span of control refers to the number of subordinates a manager will have reporting to him/her (see Figure 8.14). The span of control is generally determined by an analysis of the position's breadth and complexity of responsibilities, the degree of day-to-day interaction with subordinates, and the experience, expertise, and capabilities of both the individual in the position and those who report to them. In general, the more the manager has to be involved in the day-to-day interactions of an area of responsibility, and the more complex the tasks associated with the responsibility assigned, the narrower the span of control will be.

Coordination of the work effort refers to the grouping of tasks and the facilitation of collaborative efforts among departments that must occur within the organization (and in interacting with its broader ecosystem) to ensure its products/ services are designed, developed, produced, packaged, and distributed in a manner that successfully reaches the desired markets, and that customer connectivity and intimacy are achieved and their benefits maximized. This coordination of work effort will have a significant impact on the managerial hierarchy (or chain of command) that an organization puts into place, as well as the span of control associated with each managerial or supervisory position created. Work effort coordination also assesses the nature of the work that needs to be accomplished, and seeks to identify the most efficient processes for accomplishing such work. Decisions relating to process standardization or customization, production protocols, cross-functional project team formation, job rotation, training initiatives, and new technology deployment

FIGURE 8.14 **Span of Control**

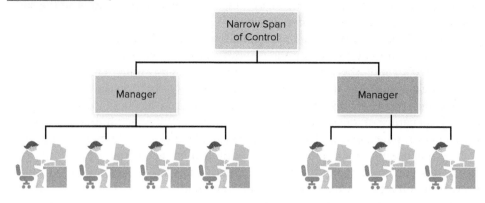

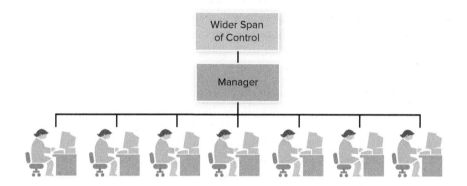

are but a few of the decisions that would fall under work coordination analysis. The determination of whether to consider outsourcing, via partners, versus in-house manufacturing or support processes is another possible decision area relating to the coordination of work effort. A good illustration of the importance of the coordination of work effort lies in the complexity of tasks associated with the manufacturing of commercial airplanes. The Chinese state-owned manufacturer Comac is attempting to break into the narrow-body passenger aircraft sector largely currently dominated by Boeing and Airbus. Given the growing demand for aircraft globally (it is estimated that China will need 9000 such aircraft over the next 20 years), along with the related positive technology-based economic spin-off for the economy at large, China has identified this market sector to be critical to its future growth. This requires China, via Comac, to build an aerospace industry literally from scratch. To do so requires a staggering number of business decisions extending across the entire business model and its underlying value chain (discussed in more detail in Chapter 10). The coordination of work effort is simply mind-boggling if Comac is to reach the level of manufacturing sophistication and the economies of scale essential for success. Comac will need to coordinate the development of an entire industrial chain to build the aircraft and the related hardware and software technologies. It also needs to create the supporting R&D centres to facilitate the planning, design, and development of aircraft and software; to devise the maintenance training and support methodologies required once planes are in the air; to determine the extent of interaction with various partners such as United Aircraft Corporation (Russia), General Electric & Boeing (USA), and Safran SA (France), to name a few, and with approval-related aviation regulatory agencies across the globe such as Transport Canada and the FAA (USA); to develop its marketing team and supporting staff teams fundamental to customer interaction, quality assurance, and safety assurance—not to mention the physical asset base essential to support it all. Adding to this complexity is the need to do all of these things in parallel (that is, at the same time) versus a gradual step-by-step process.[7]

Nature of the work refers to the specific tasks that need to be accomplished at the individual job level within the organization. Are we manufacturing a product? Are we a retail operation that purchases finished products and then resells them to customers? Are we a service industry, such as an investment bank, a real estate brokerage firm, or a charitable entity focused on serving the homeless? Assessing the nature of the work means defining what tasks are required in order for us to meet the needs of our customer base, whether such customers are other businesses, consumers, or a combination of both. It then means determining the best way to develop our response to the need identified. Again, we can use the Chinese aircraft manufacturer Comac an example. The management team at Comac will need to assess what exactly needs to be done at each level of the organization, and within each position, to ensure that Comac reaches "best of class" status with respect to quality, fuel efficiency, safety, and overall aircraft value. The team will also need to continuously reassess how Comac will interact with customers, regulatory agencies, employees, suppliers, partners, investors, and financial institutions, to name a few.

Implementing the managerial approach Effective managers are continually looking to build culture, structure, and supporting relationships around the underlying need to integrate teams and plans with the organization's overall goals and objectives. The objective in making decisions relating to this is to foster within the organization a culture of functional and technical excellence, create a collaborative environment of teams and people working together, improve the quality and sustainability of products, and create a decision-making process that delivers the operating results expected by its shareholders as well as stakeholders. As managers, we look to accomplish this by defining the needed managerial approach and building the framework for achieving the stated strategy utilizing the core components noted above. General managers and C-level managers need to think beyond today's fires and seek to define how the business system is going to be developed and adjusted to continually meet the needs of the organization's customers and stakeholders. A core fundamental aspect of this is a regular review of the organization's structure and its management decision-making approach. As strategies change, so must the business system framework required to ensure the successful execution of the revised strategic direction (see Figure 8.15).

Nature of the Work refers to the specific tasks that need to be accomplished at the individual job level within the organization.

FIGURE 8.15   **Management Approach Process**

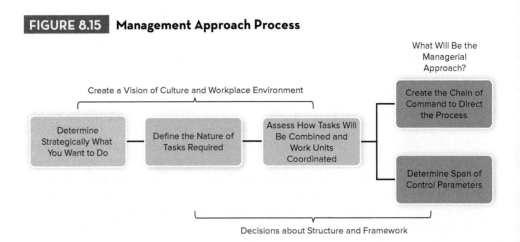

General managers and C-level managers need to think beyond today's fires and seek to define how the business system is going to be developed and adjusted to continually meet the needs of the organization's customers and stakeholders.

Decisions relating to structure and framework are derived from an assessment of the nature of the tasks required and the most efficient and effective grouping of these tasks to maximize the efficiency and effectiveness of the organization and meet its strategic objectives. As such an assessment takes place, it is important for managers to also visualize the culture and work environment they feel will best enable the talent within the organization to respond to the challenges such strategic objectives bring. With these two areas defined, managers can then determine the managerial approach that best fits the alignment of the structure to the organization's objectives and creates the culture and work environment envisioned as being fundamental to the achievement of the current objectives and the organization's long-term vision and mission.

Business IN ACTION

Microsoft—Restructuring for the Future

So what do you do when the underlying core business fundamentals around which you have built your business will no longer apply going forward? That was the critical question facing Satya Nadella after he took over as CEO of Microsoft in 2014. The company's success—upon which it built its legendary dominance of the personal computing software market—was largely driven around a market ecosystem where the personal PC was king. Looking forward, Nadella fully understood that this would not be the case, as technology was rapidly shifting toward a market environment built around cloud-based technologies and applications, mobile-based methodologies, and productivity shifts driven by data analytics and artificial intelligence. In this new environment, the Windows operating system, around which the personal computing industry was built and operates, will play a diminishing role going forward as alternate application and software approaches will fundamentally change the industry. The same goes for the hardware side. Microsoft's Surface, for example, although making some headway in the mature PC market, will also find a diminished role as the marketplace shifts toward virtual reality, augmented reality, server-based cloud environments, and other types of computing devices.

Asia File/ Alamy Stock Photo

To realign the company with the significant market shifts commented on above, Nadella is completely restructuring the way that Microsoft does business. Divisions focused on devices and software for businesses are being combined in order to provide a complete "one stop" service approach to these clients. The Windows division, once a stand-alone entity, is being moved into the operation built around the Azure cloud software, reflecting the company's business shift toward cloud services. The Windows device team has been amalgamated into the Office software team, which now provides client services relating to laptops, tablets, the Office suite of software, email, and Skype. All these moves are designed to provide Microsoft with a unified, plat-form-driven approach to both customer support and product/service development.

Benefits surrounding the significant change taking place are driven by a desire to create a closer relationship with customers, whether it be in terms of reinventing business productivity processes, building a leading-edge cloud-based platform for supporting client operations, or creating a more productive personal computing environment for a customer's employees. The idea driving all of this, as noted by Nadella, is to "empower every person and every organization on the planet to achieve more." Internal benefits, equally important when restructuring an organization, are felt to be a more cooperative versus resource competitive environment within Microsoft between divisions and product categories, and a renewed sense of purpose and mission for the company's entire employee base.

Change continues at Microsoft, and its slowness to respond to market shifts did result in a loss of momentum and market opportunities sacrificed to the likes of Apple, Amazon, and Google, to name a few. The company, however, appears to be back on track, and in reinventing itself looks to be in a much better position to compete going forward.

The Concept of Restructuring

LO6

Restructuring addresses the need to change an organization's business system or desired position in the marketplace, or to make fundamental changes to the way an organization does business.

Often, when browsing the business section of a newspaper or a Web site, we come across an article about a company that has announced a **restructuring** initiative. For many, the questions that come to mind ask what restructuring is, and what the rationale is for an organization to initiate such an exercise. Restructuring generally occurs when companies recognize a disconnection to their intended strategy as a result of disruptions that have occurred either internally or from the external marketplace. Recognizing that a change to their business system or their desired position in the marketplace is required, organizations decide to make fundamental changes to the way in which they do business. This often is driven by a desire to change the formalized structuring around which a company's activities, resources, and workforce have been grouped. Restructuring an organization can be in response to such activities as an immediate need to reduce costs, a longer-term need to redirect the organization's business efforts due to a fundamental shift in the demand for the products/services they offer, competitive pressures, a change in customer behaviour, technology obsolescence, or bankruptcy. Having said this, restructuring does not have to be a reactive business decision, nor is it solely focused on downsizing, or retrenchment, due to liquidity or solvency issues challenging an organization (although we tend to hear more of such situations via the media). Although these are valid reasons for initiating a restructuring strategy, restructuring can be due to positive circumstances, such as significant growth, the launch of new products or services, the acquisition of a company, or a future anticipated move in the marketplace by the organization. Figure 8.16 provides a summary of typical reasons for restructuring to occur. Ultimately, the goal of any restructuring initiative should be to increase the value and the long-term health of the organization.

> Restructuring generally occurs when companies recognize a disconnection to their intended strategy as a result of disruptions that have occurred either internally or from the external marketplace. Its goal, ultimately, is typically focused on improving performance and/or stimulating innovation.

FIGURE 8.16   Typical Reasons for Restructuring to Occur

- Reorganization of operations to reduce costs
- Response to a shift in customer behaviour
- Refocus of an organization's efforts regarding key products and/or account relationships
- Integration of new technologies that significantly change operating protocols
- Creation of more efficient and effective outcomes resulting from the interaction of an organization's workforce
- Divestiture of a portion of the organization (product line, subsidiary, etc.)
- Acquisition or merger by the organization
- Enhancement or more effective leveraging of an organization's competitive advantage
- Significant transformation of the business's underlying business model

When thinking about restructuring, managers should focus on three common elements to the plan: structural design, execution, and communication.

- **Structural design:** The first element is the structural design of the restructuring plan. What changes or adjustments to the organizational structure will be required to successfully achieve the desired objectives of the restructuring plan? What impacts to our culture are anticipated? Are significant changes being implemented that will fundamentally change our chain of command and managerial decision-making process?

- **Execution:** What will the restructuring process look like? What are the various phases to the plan that will need to be implemented? Is this simply a subtle change as a result of challenging the status quo in order to maintain or enhance the organization's competitive position, or is this a significant and drastic move as a result of very real and significant market disruptions? Will the restructuring process severely disrupt the organization's business operations? If so, what is the intended strategy to help keep business flowing?

- **Communication:** What is the communication plan? How are we going to communicate the restructuring to the various stakeholder groups impacted? Have we definitively tied the restructuring plan to the revised organizational strategy to ensure a full understanding of the rationale for the action? How can we minimize negative impact to morale and preserve our employee culture if such an impact is perceived to exist?

A key determination in the success of a restructuring initiative lies in the extent of the change the organization is undertaking. In general, restructuring single, isolated business processes or initiatives is easier to implement, with a higher probability of success. For example, the desire to restructure the fabrication process of a single product via enhanced technology application is easy for a managerial team to focus on and guide to its completion. The risk of implementation gets considerably greater, and the probability of success lower, as the degree of change required, the broadness of the change focus, and the length of time to completion all increase. Figure 8.17 provides an illustration of the risk and complexity impact on the probability of success for a restructuring effort.

Keep in mind that to be successful at any restructuring effort an organization's management team must remain focused on the objectives desired, get actively involved in the transformation process, and commit with the staying power required

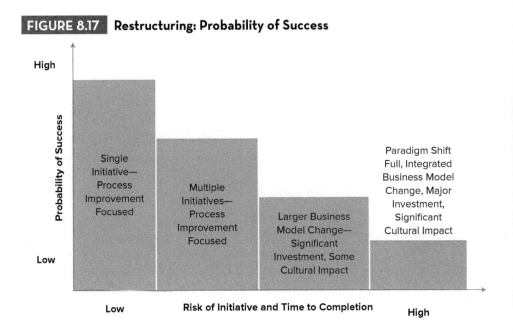

FIGURE 8.17 **Restructuring: Probability of Success**

to see the project to its successful completion. Prioritization and sequencing of what needs to be accomplished, the amount of change needed to ensure that the desired results are achieved, a full understanding of the learning curves for staff involved, and an accurate sense of the time and investment requirements needed are all fundamental success metrics to achieving the desired organizational goals.[8]

> To be successful at any restructuring effort an organization's management team must remain focused on the objectives desired, get actively involved in the transformation process, and commit with the staying power required to see the project to its successful completion.

Management Reflection—The Importance of Business System Design

Managers need to recognize the important role that an organization's business system structure and its culture and work environment play in the accomplishment of its business strategy. The structure, culture, and managerial approach fundamentally influence the flow of communication, the level of collaboration, and the efficiency and effectiveness of the work being performed. Structure and culture are what forms the backbone of the organization. It is the formalized process through which tasks within the organization are aligned with the strategic objectives of the company, and are executed in support of this stated strategy. The development of the "chain of command" or managerial hierarchy directly influences the speed with which decisions are made, the approval processes required to make things happen, and the responsibility and accountability levels within the organization. As managers, we need to take the time to plan this hierarchy in a manner that drives efficiency and effectiveness, but that also creates a culture and work environment that energizes our workforce, encourages the sharing of ideas, fosters innovation and creativity, eliminates bureaucracy, and articulates the organization's vision and mission.

The development of the chain of command or managerial hierarchy directly influences the speed with which decisions are made, the approval processes required to make things happen, and the responsibility and accountability levels within the organization.

Chapter Summary

This chapter focuses on the importance of the organizational framework in the design of a business system and in the execution of a business strategy. The chapter outlines the key components of the organizational design process: the development of an organization's formal structure, the impact of culture and the environment on the efficiency and effectiveness of an organization, and how the managerial approach will, ultimately, influence and support the activities and interactions that are occurring within the business. The chapter also seeks to familiarize students with the different types of organizational structures companies can utilize to develop and direct work processes and tasks, and the building blocks managers should review when determining the structural approach to be utilized. An important component of this process is the determination of the managerial approach that the organization as a whole will implement and the key factors that will influence this decision. The chapter ends with a discussion of the concept of restructuring and the relationship of the extensiveness of the change and the amount of time required for the redesign process.

Developing Business Knowledge and Skills

Key Terms

value chain *p. 283*

structure *p. 286*

customer intimacy *p. 292*

work efficiencies *p. 292*

departmentalization *p. 293*

culture *p. 294*

employee interaction *p. 296*

risk allowance *p. 296*

control protocols *p. 296*

competitive emphasis *p. 296*

managerial hierarchy *p. 299*

decision-making control *p. 300*

span of control *p. 300*

coordination of the work effort *p. 300*

nature of the work *p. 302*

restructuring *p. 304*

Questions for Discussion

1. What are the four key components that are used to formulate the design of a business system? (LO1)
2. In developing an organization's framework, what three questions should be utilized to drive the development process? How are they interrelated? (LO2)
3. In your opinion, what are the key criteria for determining the type of organizational structure a business should evolve toward? (LO3)
4. More and more, researchers and analysts continue to emphasize the importance of culture in determining the overall level of success organizations achieve.

What is it about culture that, ultimately, enables it to exert such influence? As a manager, how do you influence the cultural fabric of an organization? (LO4)

5. Discuss the five key criteria that are used to determine the managerial approach an organization develops to guide its decision-making process. How are these combined to form a process for finalizing the intended managerial approach? (LO5)

6. What is restructuring? When thinking about restructuring, what three common elements should managers focus on to ensure that a successful restructuring takes place? (LO6)

Question for Individual Action

Revisit the Business in Action associated with the concept of virtual organizations. Assume that the company you have just been hired to work for operates largely on the basis of a virtual organizational structure. What are some of the key challenges you will need to work through in becoming a new employee of a company based on a virtual organizational structure? Now, place yourself in the position of a supervisor of a new employee within this same setting. What methodologies or approaches do you feel you would need to put into place to ensure that the new employee becomes a productive member of your team?

Team Exercise

Using annual reports, company presentations (see company Web sites), and a broader Internet search, analyze three or four leading publicly traded Canadian companies and draw conclusions as to the focus of their organizational structure. What does their organizational setup (i.e., their org charts) tell you? What does their current formal structure look like (functional, product-focused, customer-focused, matrix, etc.)? How do their structures enable them to better serve their customers and maintain their advantage in the marketplace? Do you see any underlying flaws in their organizational setup that may cause challenges going forward?

Case for Discussion 1

Restructuring at Club Athletica

Tony J. Condie, president (and owner) of Club Athletica, is in a bit of a dilemma. His organization has grown considerably over the last three years, and a real opportunity exists to significantly expand the business operation and become a major player in the delivery of fitness services within the community of New Bedford. The dilemma, however, is how he should restructure his organization to continue to meet the needs of his current customer base and effectively manage his business while taking advantage of these new opportunities.

New Bedford is a municipality of 200 000 residents just outside of Toronto. The municipality is predominantly made up of white-collar occupations, with heavy emphasis on government and university-related services. There is a newly evolving biotech industry within the municipality as well. The community is considered to have slightly above-average incomes and is projected to grow at a rate of 9% per year for the next five years.

As part of his five-year plan, Tony is focused on growing his business through the establishment of additional Club Athletica locations. This will enable Club Athletica to provide programs and services that are convenient and in close proximity to the various geographic sectors within the city. With its current facility centrally located, the plan is to open two additional locations in the southeast and northwest sections of New Bedford. Both areas are expected to realize significant population growth over the near term.

Success, however, does not come without its share of challenges. Tony's current Club Athletica location has doubled its membership over the past couple of years, causing considerable strain on the facility and his management team. Tony, as the owner, continually finds himself directing day-to-day facility issues and operations. It seems that he is constantly putting out operational fires, acting as the IT "go to" person, and responding to customer concerns personally. This already leaves him with little time for strategic planning and new site development. With his previously publicly announced commitment to open his two additional facilities over the next 12 months, locations leased, and marketing beginning to ramp up, a sense of the loss of control is beginning to creep into his mind. Clearly, the current organizational structure is not set up to handle a multi-site operation. The focus to date has been on a single-site operation, with responsibility accountability as shown below:

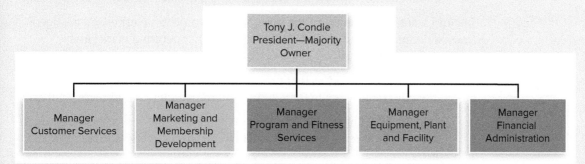

Tony has reached the following conclusions regarding the anticipated expansion of Club Athletica:

- Although smaller in size than the current facility, the two new locations will essentially offer the same services as his existing Club Athletica location (fitness centre, group fitness classes, personal training, water massage therapy, tanning, and temporary child care services for children of members using the facility).

- Facility cleaning, membership services, program requirements, and maintenance issues will exist at all three locations and must be accounted for.

- Membership access must be transparent at all locations. Club Athletica members should be able to access any of the three facilities seamlessly, and see consistency in the delivery of services and programs regardless of which facility they are in.

- Current server and software systems will need to be reassessed and upgraded. A key requirement will be the implementation of a new member management software system that can track member usage and provide other key membership data and statistics for all three locations.

- Administration services and marketing will be housed at the central location for all three facilities, as will IT and other core support services.

In addition to the new locations and the operational issues associated with them, Tony also recognizes that he needs to spend more time out in the community, networking and increasing the profile of Club Athletica. After all, generating new business, soliciting new organizations for corporate memberships, and creating better prospecting links requires face-to-face interaction on the part of the business—and Tony knows and understands that this is what he does best. In addition, it is rumoured that new competitors may be popping up in the area given its population growth and attractive demographics. So much to think about—so little time!

With all this in his mind, Tony knows that a redesign of the way he conducts business and of his current organizational structure is required. The current functional structure (as shown above) just doesn't seem to make sense given all the changes that will take place in the upcoming 12 months and the need to create a stronger image and profile for Club Athletica. The private investors backing Tony, all true supporters of the Club Athletica concept, are reminding him, however, of the need to maintain control over unnecessary expenditures during this expansion. They do, however, recognize the need for additional employees if the growth is to be properly managed. Unsure where to begin, Tony has asked you and your team to review his current situation and provide him with some initial thoughts, and assist him by outlining a process that he can follow in redesigning his organization.

Questions

What recommendations would you make to Tony and Club Athletica? Specifically:

1. Identify what you believe are the three to five key decision criteria Tony needs to consider in redesigning Club Athletica's current operating model and organizational structure.

2. Develop a simplified process that you would recommend to enable Tony to fully assess the core requirements for a successful transition to a multi-site location.

3. Assuming you could hire two additional managerial positions, what would they be? How would you redesign the organizational chart to reflect these new additions?

Case for Discussion 2

Leadership and Change at Microsoft

The following case should be read and assessed in conjunction with this chapter's Business in Action: Microsoft—Restructuring for the Future.

Since assuming the role of CEO at Microsoft Corporation in 2014, Satya Nadella has focused the organization's strategy on cloud computing and artificial intelligence (AI). His aim is to position Microsoft as an ally in large-scale digital transformation, enabling clients to leverage what he calls tech intensity, "a fusion of cultural mindset and business processes that rewards the development and propagation of digital capabilities that create end-to-end digital feedback loops, tear down data silos, and unleash information flows in order to trigger insights and predictions, automated workflows, and intelligent services."[9]

For Nadella and Microsoft, the initiatives undertaken and the organization's overall strategic focus seem to be working. Microsoft closed 2018 as the most valuable company in the world by market capitalization (share value times number of shares outstanding). Since then, it has been an ongoing battle with Amazon, Apple, and Alphabet for this title.

With new technologies including AI, IoT (Internet of things), and digital business models now being rapidly adopted by companies across many business sectors (mainstream adoption), the size of the global IT market is expected to increase from $2 trillion (USD) to $4.5 trillion over the next decade.[10] Microsoft believes it is well-positioned to exploit this opportunity.

Judson Althoff, Executive VP, Worldwide Commercial Business at Microsoft, told an audience at a recent Citi Global Technology Conference that the firm's approach to winning in the technology sector is built around three primary drivers:

- Microsoft's core business model, which unlike Amazon's, precludes Microsoft from competing with its customers;

- The 'trust factor' that ranges across not only an increasingly open technology strategy but also business policies stating that the data created by business customers is the property of those business customers, and not of Microsoft; and,

- Microsoft's end-to-end creation of hybrid technologies that allow customers to move seamlessly from the cloud to on-premises technology.[11]

Adapted from speech by Judson Althoff, EVP of Worldwide Commercial Business at Microsoft; Citi Global Technology Conference September 6, 2018.

Althoff explained Microsoft's role this way:

"So much of what we do with customers in the cloud today and at the edge," he said, "is about really transforming their business—and so classically what would have been thought of as COGS, not related to IT, is digitizing. And so when we look at an opportunity for a large retailer, grocer, in their stores to help them keep food fresh, it's not about the servers we might sell them in the back of the office, or the PCs that we might sell them in the front of the office. It's everything from the sensor to the sensor fabrics to the large data stores to the AI capabilities that help them reason over supply-chain management for fresher foods."[12]

Of course, having a compelling solution in an attractive industry means little if the organization does not have the ability to execute. That is where Nadella comes in.

Nadella joined Microsoft in 1992, moving from the role of Executive VP of Microsoft's Cloud and Enterprise group to the role of CEO in 2014. He replaced Steve Ballmer, a larger-than-life figure at Microsoft, who succeeded Bill Gates as CEO in 2000.

Over time and prior to Nadella at the helm, observers had seen the culture at Microsoft shift from its innovation-driven early days to one challenged by bureaucracy, politics, and a high level of internal competition.[13] The organization, in essence, was perceived as having become lethargic and content to rely on its past success and stable of products as the driver of future performance. This reliance on the past, and the inertia resulting from it, is what had resulted in Microsoft's loss of overall market-shaping momentum and its overall market-leader position.

Accordingly, one of Nadella's key tasks in assuming the CEO role at Microsoft was to reset the culture, making it "a people company instead of a product company."[14] The effort to shift the corporate culture at Microsoft is grounded in the idea of a growth mindset and a focus on learning. To create change, Nadella, leveraging the scholarship work of Stanford psychology professor Carol Dweck, inspired the organization to adopt a conviction that new ideas and new capabilities, supported by hard work, good strategies, and accepting input from others, are fundamental to future growth. As Chris Capossela, Microsoft's CMO, stated, in reflecting on the transformation process undertaken by Nadella, "We went from a culture of know-it-alls to a culture of learn-it-alls," and "Everything we do now is rooted in a growth mindset."

Two high-profile activities showcasing the culture change at Microsoft are One Week, an annual gathering where employees work, either in person or remotely, on projects outside of their day-to-day activities, and Hackathon, the largest private coding and new idea marathon on the planet. In 2018, as an example, more than 18 000 Microsoft employees and stakeholders across 400 cities and 75 countries came together to solve problems and advance ideas relating to technology as well as to broader social challenges, such as how Microsoft technology could be used to assist in managing a large-scale disaster. "The hackathon is most notable, though, for what it reflects about its host," according to a recent article about culture change under Nadella. "In many ways, it's a microcosm of all the ways Microsoft has changed since Nadella has taken over: thousands of employees from across different departments, working together to experiment, learn, and build. No longer is Microsoft an amalgam of warring city-states, competing for resources and recognition."[15] To date (since its inception 5 years ago), more than 40 000 people have participated in Hackathon.

In Canada, Microsoft's growth in the Nadella era is reflected by the recent announcement of the firm's new state-of-the-art headquarters in Toronto. Microsoft expects to move to the new Bay Street location in 2020. The firm also manages an innovation hub in Vancouver, an R&D facility in Montreal's AI hub, data centres, and a network of regional sales offices.[16]

Questions

1. Given Microsoft's strategic focus, why was it important for Nadella to reset the corporate culture at Microsoft?

2. Why do you think it made sense to choose a Microsoft insider to succeed Ballmer? What were the potential risks of this decision, should the right insider not have been promoted?

3. What do you think of some of the steps Nadella has taken so far? What do Nadella's actions state about the importance of visionary leadership when initiating cultural change?

CHAPTER 9

Managing and Leading the Organization's Talent

LEARNING OBJECTIVES

This chapter is designed to provide students with:

LO1	An appreciation for considering employees as assets rather than expenses
LO2	An appreciation for the fundamentals needed to create a positive work environment
LO3	An overview of the motivational tools that are key for managers
LO4	An understanding of the competencies a manager must possess to be successful in managing talent
LO5	An understanding of the internal and external challenges managers face in managing talent

Snapshot

What to Expect in This Chapter

This chapter focuses on managing and leading an organization's talent. The content emphasized in this chapter includes the following:

- The Importance of Talent
- The Employee Transformation Process
  - What Constitutes a Great Company?
  - What Makes for a Great Job?
  - Compensation and Lifestyle Influences
- The Motivational Tool Kit
- Managing Your Workforce
  - The Core Management Challenge
  - Skills Successful Managers Must Possess
  - Understanding Your Power Base
  - Determining the Culture/Structure Balance
  - Managing in a Unionized Environment
  - Inclusiveness, Diversity, and Employment Equity
  - Triggers of Performance Erosion
  - The Danger of Short-Term Pressures
- Leadership/Management—Today, Tomorrow, and Beyond
- HR Management in the Small Business Setting
- Management Reflection—Finding the Right Balance

 Business IN ACTION

The War for Talent

For many of the world's global business players, the war for executive talent is heating up. Over the upcoming decade, one of the most defining issues that will challenge organizations across all business areas is the acquisition and retention of highly skilled managerial staff and supporting talent. Whereas companies in the past have benefited from a large management and talent pool of baby boomers in their 30s and 40s, this age group has now moved into their 50s and 60s, with retirement shortly to follow. Organizations are already feeling the pinch, as companies are finding in their search for executive talent that the marketplace is becoming increasingly crowded. Globalization has added to this in that the competition for talent not only lies with businesses in

Digital Vision/Getty Images

close proximity, but in reality, the world. Recruitment efforts are extending well beyond the traditional boundaries of cities, provinces, states, and countries.

Recent statistical research shows that there will be no growth in the age 45–64 segment of the population over the next 20 years, with the percentage of total population for this age category actually decreasing by 2.5%. Add to this the fact that the surge of women—who historically have provided employment expansion opportunities for the marketplace—has peaked, thereby further tightening the available labour pool. McKinsey & Company has commented on the fact that skilled worker shortages—estimated at as much as 45 million workers in developing economies and 95 million in fully advanced economies—could be the reality of company workforce challenges as early as 2020. Attitudes of executives have also changed, as more university graduates, MBAs, and young business professionals are looking for opportunities with smaller upstart companies where the risk/reward opportunity (excitement, flexibility, ability to impact, financial and equity-based rewards) is believed to be sufficiently more attractive from a career perspective. Today's younger managerial professionals are also much more "job mobile," viewing their careers as bridging several organizations and opportunities versus staying with a single business organization for their career duration. For organizations in need of top-level management talent to guide and grow their business, this declining supply of talent is further compounded by the need for even more sophisticated skill sets in the managers

they do manage to recruit and retain. Today's global marketplace is demanding managers with significantly greater global exposure and acumen, strong leading-edge technology competencies, multicultural management experience, and entrepreneurial skill sets needed to keep organizations innovative and at the forefront of the industries within which they compete. As Chambers, Foulon, Handfield-Jones, Hankin, and Michaels stated in their article "The War for Talent," organizations will be increasingly challenged to define and redefine their employee value propositions in order to communicate to prospective employees why they should come work for them rather than the company next door. The challenge then becomes how to develop these employees once recruited, and how to continue to challenge them in a way that results in success for them and for the organization, thereby retaining their talents for the benefit of the organization for the long term. This challenge goes beyond simply the concepts of higher pay and a few additional perks or privileges. It is much more embedded in the psychological and sociological relationships that form a core part of the work environment. Companies that truly understand this are redefining how their organizations are designed, how recruitment and retention activities are structured, and how to continuously innovate their talent relationships in a way that maintains a balance with the rate of change occurring in the HR arena.

The Importance of Talent

In very broad terms, the opening chapters of this textbook have attempted to create a sense as to the overarching role of C-level managers, general managers, and small business owners with regard to managing their respective organizations. This overarching role can be thought of as encompassing four broad areas of responsibility: market assessment and strategy development and execution; business model design, development, and implementation; financial resource management (discussed in later chapters); and the fourth, discussed in this chapter, attracting, retaining, and managing talent. Recognizing that all four areas are important and, in many ways, interconnected, the objective of this chapter is to discuss the pivotal role that the organization's talent plays in directing its strategy, capital, and financial resources and business system components in order to achieve excellence in operational performance.

To provide some additional insight, let's assume you are getting ready to embark on a trip. Initially, you must define where you need to go—just as a business, in its strategic development process, needs to define the company's overall business direction. The *market assessment and strategy development* responsibility involves determining a destination, choosing a route, and providing a GPS to ensure you stay on track. The *business model design and development* responsibility involves determining the type of vehicle to be used, deciding whether to use your own vehicle or rent a vehicle, arranging pre-trip maintenance, booking hotels, and purchasing maps and tickets. The *financial resource management* responsibility involves establishing a budget, allocating the required financial resources to ensure the monetary needs of the trip are met, and ensuring financial obligations incurred during the trip are covered. Finally, the *talent* responsibility involves driving the vehicle, interpreting the route and GPS directions, ensuring the schedule is maintained, and arriving at the destination as planned. As you can recognize from this simple illustration, although the strategy direction is defined, the financial resources are provided, and the system is developed to meet the trip's requirements, it still comes down to the "talent" to ensure the trip is completed successfully. Herein lies the importance of an organization's human resource complement, or what is called its talent. An organization's success is only as good as the management team that leads it and the talent that executes the strategy and is responsible for delivering on the key success metrics. Knowing this, then, why does it appear that so many organizations still view their managerial staff and employees as an expense line on the income statement rather than as an asset similar to the capital and financial assets that appear on their balance sheets? The answer appears to be that too many organizations think of their talent as a consumable versus strategic resource—and, therefore, manage it on the basis of short-term needs—versus as a core strategic component and integral part of the organization's long-term strategy. As managers, we need to recognize our employees are a core area from which we can develop and leverage a sustainable competitive advantage, and design and implement human resource recruitment and development strategies in a way that makes them an integral part of the strategic planning and execution process.

Business IN ACTION

Creating an Employer Brand

Organizations spend billions of dollars each year promoting their brands to customers like you and me. The development of a brand and the image it portrays are felt to be fundamental to the success of the organization and our perception of the quality of the products/services offered. While there is no argument that the design, development, and reinforcement of a brand is critical to the overall marketing success of an organization (think Apple, Google, Coca-Cola, etc.), so too is the development of an organization's brand as an employer.

Mark Bowden/Monkey Business Images

As the chapter-opening Business in Action highlighted, the "war for talent" is only going to accelerate going forward. This means that the need for organizations to recognize their image as an employer is becoming as important as their external image to the marketplace. Unfortunately, this is not the case in many work environments, as the workforce (talent) is often viewed as an expense line item

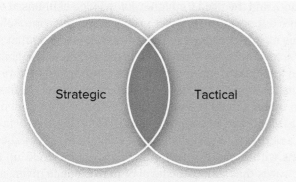

versus an asset. A recent Gallup State of the Global Workplace (U.S.-based) recently reported that up to 85% of employees do not view themselves as engaged or actively engaged in the workplace, with resulting losses in productivity being quantified as an estimated $7 trillion.

So how do you create an "employer brand"? The answer to this lies in viewing your human resource activities through two lenses. The first is from a strategic perspective, and the second is from a day-to-day interactive (or tactical) view.

Strategically, building an employer brand involves three key fundamentals. First, the organization needs to think, plan, and design the type of culture it wants to deliver to its employees, and be prepared to communicate this to both current and future employees. Second, it needs to view the hiring of employees in the same manner as it looks to sell its products/services to the marketplace. This means thinking about the employee relationship in the same light as a customer relationship, and creating an interactive thought process that looks to nurture this relationship and provide an exceptional employee experience. Third, the role of HR needs to be fully embraced as a critical component of strategy development, removing prior preconceived notions of employees as "cost-centred." Decisions relating to strategy need to be reflected in the perception of, and decisions associated with, the ability to attract and retain the required talent.

On the tactical side, it is all about the day-to-day interaction with employees and the inclusion of their thoughts and talent in a way that creates and reinforces engagement in the organization's success. This engagement process can include (but is not limited to) focus group discussions with employees

relating to their jobs and the work environment, employee satisfaction surveys, training managers to have effective performance development conversations, auditing current performance evaluation systems to ensure that they are fair and equitable, and developing a valid and reliable promotion system and process that ensures individuals being promoted into managerial ranks possess the necessary skills to deal with the managing of people. Today's employees (talent) are looking for a company that offers an engaging and rewarding experience. They are looking for purpose, career development opportunities, training, and the opportunity to make a difference. Many see their work lives and personal lives as being interconnected, and view their job as a core aspect of their identity.

Building an employer brand is not something that happens overnight. If done correctly, however, it can create a sustainable competitive advantage for companies not only in their war for talent but also in their overall strategic and operating results. When compared to the performance of companies in the bottom 25% of their respective market sectors, statistical evidence by Gallup has demonstrated that those top-tier companies that get performance management right benefit from significant improvement in customer satisfaction (+10%), productivity (+17%), sales revenue (+20%), and profitability (+21%) as a result.

Building an employer brand is dependent on getting a company's employee engagement formula right. It begins with an understanding of where you are and a solid vision of where you want to be. This generally means fixing the current shortcomings of the HR process in place, and transforming these processes and culture in a way that creates high levels of engagement and performance. Companies know that survival and growth stem from innovation and new ideas. Ideas stem from people. So too does execution on innovation. To acquire and retain the best people requires being a leader in the development of a talent asset perspective with your workforce. In other words, it requires a consistent and continuous commitment to an outstanding employer brand at the same level as is required to develop an outstanding marketing brand.

Demographics, globalization, and the need for higher-knowledge skill-based employees are requiring us to take a longer, more "asset versus expense" approach to our human resource team. This means defining human resource objectives that are in line with business objectives, and targeting talent at all levels within the organization for skill, knowledge, and capability improvement as an opportunity to raise operational productivity, sales, and profits. A key component of this asset-based approach to human resource management is recognizing that managers need to spend more time on talent development; managers need to focus their efforts on coaching and providing feedback to employees, ensuring that a culture of collaboration and communication exists within the organization, effectively addressing underperformance, providing rewards that reflect the level of performance given, and investing in the resources needed in order for all to be successful in their work endeavours. It is hoped that, once you have read this chapter, you will gain some insight into how managers can successfully respond to the challenges of managing their human resources team.

> Managers need to spend more time coaching and providing feedback to employees, ensuring that a culture of collaboration and communication exists within the organization, effectively addressing underperformance, providing rewards that reflect the level of performance given, and investing in the resources needed in order for all to be successful in their work endeavours.

LO2 The Employee Transformation Process

Organizations spend a tremendous amount of time and money on attracting, developing, motivating, and retaining their employees. In keeping with our aim to view each employee as an asset versus an expense, as managers we should seek a return on our investment in each employee just as we look to achieve a return on the investments we make in technology, equipment, buildings, and so on. To receive this anticipated return means that we need to view and treat our human assets in the same way we would treat our other capital and financial assets. Assume, for example, we are looking to purchase a new piece of equipment for our organization. In making the purchase decision we will determine the type of equipment needed, develop the specifications the decision should be based on, assess the different purchase options, choose the equipment to be purchased, determine the level of support needed to maintain this equipment, and ensure it is being properly used. We will also need to make periodic investments in the equipment to maintain its efficiency, consider other uses that make sense for the equipment, and plan to retain the equipment for as long as it continues to contribute to the organization's operating productivity, sales revenue generation, and overall profitability.

The same approach should be fundamental to decisions involving our human assets. We should first determine the need within the organization that we are trying to solve and develop a set of specifications that identify the specific skill set required to fill the position. Then, we should determine the type of individual best suited to filling the need, recruiting and selecting a preferred candidate from a list of applicants. Once this person has been hired, we must

© Wavebreakmediamicro/Dreamstime.com/GetStock.com

provide orientation, training, and skill support development to the new employee, seek to maximize the individual's potential through periodic or ongoing investment in new or existing skill development, look to enrich the employee's experience through additional opportunities for contribution to the organization, and evaluate and provide feedback on the employee's overall productivity and contribution to the sales and profitability of the organization. Just as capital assets have a life cycle, so, too, do employees. The key as managers is to maximize the length of this life cycle for as long as the benefits to the organization continue to accrue in terms of productivity, sales revenue generation, and profitability. Success in this regard means that employees feel valued and are given the opportunity to grow and excel in the areas of responsibility and accountability applicable to them, and are rewarded in a manner that they feel is commensurate with their commitment.

As with investment decisions relating to equipment or a building, the recruitment and development of human resource assets requires a significant upfront investment on the part of an organization. It also recognizes that there will be a period during which the investment in the employee will exceed the productivity value of that employee. Figure 9.1 provides a simplified overview of the transformation process that an organization incurs in moving an employee into the organization and then to a fully productive level.

With few exceptions, employees do not simply walk in the door on their first day of work and instantly contribute to the organization at 100% of their productive potential. A significant amount of time and money is invested by the organization in attracting the preferred candidate, hiring this individual, and then transitioning the new hire into the organization and into the specific position. This investment takes the form of costs associated with:

- preparing the job specification or job description
- identifying the type of candidate required and advertising and recruitment (agency fees, etc.)

FIGURE 9.1 **Employee Transformation Process**

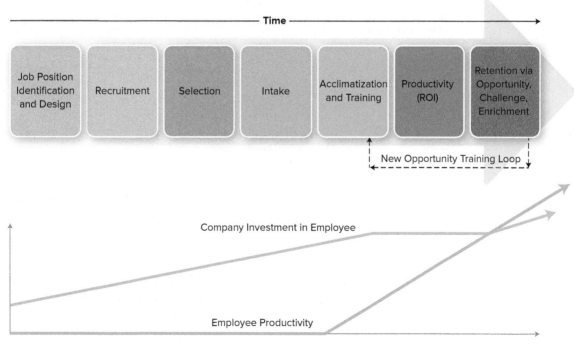

- interviews and aptitude or behavioural testing (if required)
- travel, relocation, and job acclimatization, such as orientation and training
- hiring bonuses and other job-related expenses

Keep in mind that once the prospective employee is hired, wage and benefit costs are incurred as well. Recruiting top-level managers can take months and can require an investment of several thousand dollars on the part of the organization. Once the employee is in the position, time also has to be allowed for the individual to understand the organization's culture, its decision-making structure and process, its customer base, and the operational processes driving its products and services. It is not unusual for this acclimatization and training period to extend from six months to the first full year that an employee is with an organization.

This discussion demonstrates that each employee hired represents a considerable investment on the part of the hiring organization. As managers, it is essential that we think through the process and plan for hiring an employee in the same way that we look to purchase equipment and other valuable organizational assets. In addition to this investment attitude, we also need to consciously think in terms of what will be required to ensure the new hire becomes productive and remains of value by making a contribution toward meeting the organization's vision and mission. As managers, a major part of ensuring our organization reaps the benefits of its employees' productivity lies in our ability to effectively manage our workforce and invest in them the time, energy, and financial resources that will enable them to effectively perform their jobs. This means that, as managers, we need to provide the motivation, rewards, and environment to move our employees up the productivity curve to a point where their contribution results in a positive return on the investment we have made in them, and that will provide, on an ongoing basis, the incentive and desire to maintain such productivity levels (see Figure 9.2). We must also recognize that a failure to provide the right work *environment, rewards,* and *recognition*-based incentives (ERR) will heighten the probability of employee defection (turnover), thereby forfeiting any potential return on our investment and requiring us to spend new dollars to attract new employees to take their place.

FIGURE 9.2   **Productivity (Contribution) Curve**

FIGURE 9.3   **Creating a Positive Work Environment**

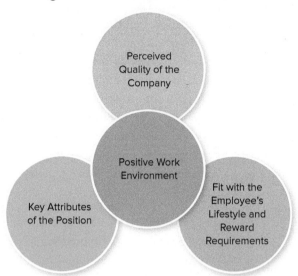

Managers need to provide the required motivation, rewards, and environment to move employees up the productivity curve to a point where their contribution results in a positive return on the investment the organization has made in them and that will provide, on an ongoing basis, the incentive and desire to maintain such productivity levels.

So, just what does it take to create a work environment that encourages employees to reach and maintain high levels of productivity? The remaining parts of this chapter try to provide some guidance for managers with respect to this question. The answer lies in our ability, as managers, to deliver a work environment that leads each of our employees to conclude that they work for a great company, they have a great job, and the reward system offered meets their compensation and lifestyle expectations (see Figure 9.3).[1]

 Business IN ACTION

Gokhan Cifci—Rewarding Staff for a Job Well Done

A challenge for any new restaurant in any city lies in trying to break through the clutter and create an eating experience that gets noticed and develops a strong enough customer following to enable the restaurant to survive and flourish. After all, the restaurant business has one of the highest rates of first-year failures of any industry sector. Add to this the fact that Kingston, Ontario is home to Canada's highest number of restaurants per capita, and the situation only becomes more challenging.

For Gokhan Cifci, however, the challenge was one that he was more than up to. Gokhan, who opened Tango Nuevo in July 2013, knew that for his restaurant to be a success his staff needed to deliver a unique and service-best experience to patrons. He also knew that in order for staff to fully commit to delivering his vision they needed to be part of the process both in terms of objective identification and strategy execution. Rolling into 2014, Gokhan did just that. At the beginning of the year, he and his team of 24 full- and part-time staff met and set out goals for the year. This included both financial goals for the restaurant, as well as a target of seeing Tango Nuevo rank in the top five in terms of restaurant reviews in Kingston. Gokhan realized that this was not going to be an easy goal to reach given that his restaurant, at the time, was less than one year old; that the industry, by its very nature, is staffed by predominantly part-time staff; and that staff turnover has always been a major concern. He did, however, commit to his team that if these goals were met he would close the restaurant for a week and take everyone to Cuba.

Although he was new to the world of business start-ups, what Gokhan did understand—and what can be a lesson for all of us—were two key fundamentals. First was thinking through the type of individuals he needed to have on his team. Finding staff who were willing to work hard was part of this requirement; the other part was to build a team culture in a way that the individuals on the team complement each other and collaboratively achieve the goals set. The second key to his success was in making the employees he did hire feel appreciated. Employees want to know that they are doing their job well and their hard work and efforts are being noticed. In addition to ensuring they knew they were appreciated, Cifci made it a point to update his staff on the restaurant's progress throughout the year in terms of the goal set in January. He also continuously reminded them to have their passports ready, as achievement of their goal meant that everyone would spend a winter week in Cuba.

True to his word, Cifci closed Tango Nuevo for one week in January 2015 and took his staff to Cuba. In all, 16 employees, along with boyfriends, girlfriends, and some customers, enjoyed the fun in the sun. Those employees who were unable to go to Cuba received cash bonuses. Cifci even invited back an employee who had left the team midway through 2014 but contributed to the restaurant meeting its goals.

A key additional insight gained from this experience goes beyond simply rewarding staff for a job well done. The week in Cuba also served as a team-building exercise where staff got to know each other better, and became re-energized for 2015 and the new goals they would now aspire to reach. So where does Gokhan Cifci go from here? His May staff meeting, where the 2015 goals were to be revisited and objectives finalized, was also slated to include a similar incentive. The incentive itself is only part of the formula. We should all look to recognize the importance of our talent in the same way that Gokhan does. In doing so, we will all better understand what it means to create a high-performance team.

What Constitutes a Great Company?

As the saying goes, everyone loves a winner. The same holds true regarding our choice of where to work. Employees like to be part of a winning team. This does not necessarily mean the company has to be the biggest competitor within its industry. It really refers to the fact that employees need to believe the organization is perceived as an industry leader or a challenger and innovator within the market segments that it serves. This could be at the international, national, regional, or local level. For many employees, their work environment is a major aspect of their overall life. Employees like to feel that the organization they work for offers exciting challenges for the future, possesses values that are in line with their own thinking, is composed of talented people all working toward a well-defined goal or vision, is recognized within the industry and the community as an innovator and strong performer, is led by a high-quality management team, and provides an acceptable level of job security for its workforce. As managers, it is important that we recognize this fundamental underlying requirement and seek to communicate to our employees the victories and the positive attributes of our company in a way that instills pride in being part of the organization.

What Makes for a Great Job?

Although attracting and retaining individuals who want to work for a great company is essential, ensuring that the job we are asking them to do challenges them and fits into their career aspirations is a second key component of keeping individuals at optimal performance levels. For managers, this means that we need to meet the expectations of employees on three levels. First, it is important that we communicate to employees how their job fits into the big picture of the organization overall and contributes to the mission and vision of the organization. Employees need to understand how they fit in if they are to view their job as being meaningful—each employee, no matter whether they are the CEO of the organization or a front-line server dealing with customers on a day-to-day basis, must have a sense as to the purpose of their work in delivering the organization's mission. Second, employees need to feel that their current position provides challenges commensurate with their background and skill set. Great jobs offer employees opportunities for advancement, the ability to grow through job enrichment or job enhancement, and the ability to take on a sense of ownership and accountability for the work being performed. Third, employees need to perceive a good fit with their immediate supervisor or boss. Employees value feedback and interaction with their managers. They are looking for approval, praise, and recognition of a job well done, as well as positive, constructive criticism delivered in a professional manner when corrections to their performance need to be communicated. They are also looking for their managers to respect them, trust them, set expectations that will realistically challenge them, provide the appropriate level of resources, and remove barriers that stand in the way of their ability to perform their work. Two-way communication via establishing objectives and sharing performance expectations is essential to a culture and an environment where employees can excel.

Compensation and Lifestyle Influences

The final component of creating an environment for optimal productivity within a workforce, and for attracting and retaining employees, is the establishment and communication of a reward system that meets their compensation and lifestyle needs. Recognizing that compensation levels are limited by the financial capabilities of an organization, employees fundamentally need to perceive that the organization's compensation system is equitable in its underlying performance/reward framework. In other words, organizations need to ensure that inequity within their reward system, driven by internal and external comparisons, does not result in employees feeling undervalued or unappreciated. Recognizing the difference between high and low performers and ensuring that poor performers are not unfairly rewarded at the same levels as high performers is an important component of the internal equity assessment process. Keep in mind that, although we think of compensation largely in terms of salaries or wages, compensation also encompasses bonuses, such as signing bonuses, longevity bonuses, and performance bonuses; long-term incentives, such as stock options; employee benefits, such as life and health insurance; and pensions or retirement plans. An additional component to establishing a high-performance work environment is the requirement for employees to recognize that their organization understands and respects their need for a balanced lifestyle. The ability to provide flextime options, meaningful and valued fringe benefit options, performance-based financial incentives, acceptable levels of stress, a manageable work pace, opportunities for advancement, developmental programs for personal and job-related growth, and recognition reward systems all work to create an underlying framework for positive performance.[2]

> High levels of employee performance are directly related to employees' belief that they work for a great company, have a great job, and enjoy a reward system that meets their compensation and lifestyle expectations.

Business IN ACTION

Creative Ways to Reward Employees

Canadian companies, along with companies worldwide, are learning more and more that building a highly productive workforce staffed by happy and highly motivated people can be accomplished in many ways. Although stock options, performance bonuses, and regular wage increases are still important, business leaders and their boards of directors are finding that supporting lifestyle balance and providing day-to-day reinforcement that employees are valued can result in far greater returns in terms of work performance, employee retention, and active company loyalty. Although these "new-style" benefits come with a price tag, for many companies the return they receive from their workforce far exceeds the cost. So, just what are some of the more creative ways that Canadian organizations are using to attract, retain, motivate, and meet the needs of their workforce? Well, here are just a few of the many creative benefits currently being offered.

Purdy's Chocolatier of Vancouver awards production and warehouse employees points based on their input into how to improve operations. These points can then be redeemed for a variety of benefits ranging from coffee cards to paid days off. The company also provides employees with on-site massage therapy sessions for only $20 per hour. SAP Canada Inc. provides employees with maternity top-up, tuition subsidies, and share matching. The company also offers an "Autism at Work" program whose focus is

© Justmeyo/Dreamstime.com/GetStock.com

on developing the special talents of individuals who have autism; SAP is committed to having people with autism comprise one percent of their workforce globally. Allstate Insurance of Canada offers its employees one of Canada's most generous flexible work-life programs. The program includes formalized and ad hoc work from home programs and fitness club discounts among its benefits. ATB Financial of Edmonton, Alberta offers its employees "buy and sell" options on vacations. Employees can exchange up to one week of vacation for more benefit credits, or use their benefit credits to purchase additional vacation time.

Mountain Equipment Co-op of Vancouver supports its staff with onsite yoga classes, shower facilities for bicycle commuters, and a private nap room for breaks during the day. The company also has an employee lending program for computers, bicycles, and boats. Marriott Hotels of Canada Ltd. provides significant room discounts to workers and their immediate families (children, parents, and grandparents) when travelling for vacation and leisure purposes. The discount becomes 50% greater during the holiday season for employees travelling for non-work-related reasons. McDonald's Restaurants of Canada Ltd. provides employees with an eight-week paid sabbatical in addition to their regular vacation for every 10 years of continuous service.

Companies also are seeing increased value in assisting employees with personal development goals. Loblaw Companies Limited provides both online and in-house training programs, and offers tuition subsidies (up to $1200 per year), subsidies for professional designations, and career planning advice. The company also allows students and new graduates to gain work experience via co-op placements and paid internships. Other Canadian companies, including Ivanhoé Cambridge Inc., National Bank of Canada, Novotel Canada, and OpenRoad Auto Group Ltd. offer similar types of programs.

Not all perks or benefits are financially related. Many creative ideas are designed to enable workers from all levels to participate in company decision making and to ensure that the organization's mission and vision are effectively communicated to employees. Other benefit approaches seek to acknowledge and support the interconnectivity between work and an employee's personal life. Some of the more unique approaches by Canadian companies include the following. At Frima Studio, a Quebec-based video game developer, employees are given the opportunity to pitch game ideas in a *Dragons' Den*-style competition. Successful pitches result in employees being freed from their usual daily tasks one day per week to develop ideas. Vancouver's ACL Limited maintains a formal Bring Your Kids to Work policy to help parents manage child care emergencies. Hatch Ltd. (Mississauga, Ont.) has a similar program for its employees. Digital Extremes Ltd. (London, Ontario) has a commercial kitchen and dining room at head office with full-time staff who prepare healthy meals daily and special treats on Friday. K&S Potash Canada GP (Saskatoon, SK) provides employees with 40 hours per year to be used to handle family appointments,

© Don Denton/The Canadian Press

elder care, or personal time. 3M Canada dedicates a development month each year for its employees. The month focuses on interactive online training, virtual workplace instructor-led sessions, videos, and panel discussions.

In addition to the examples noted above, many Canadian companies are active in supporting employee initiatives relating to the social well-being of the communities where they are located. Island Savings Credit Union of Duncan, B.C., has provided more than $1 million to family-focused initiatives through its community investment program. Keg Restaurants Ltd.'s "Keg Spirit Foundation" has raised more than $10 million since 2001 in support of over 300 youth-focused charities. Geo. A. Kelson Company Limited matches all charitable donations raised by employees,

Great Ways to Reward Employees without Spending $$$	
	"How To" Activities
Use your words	Verbal and written (notes, etc.) reinforcement
Flexible hours	Freedom with responsibility
Acknowledge effort	Even if the results are not fully successful
Keep it meaningful	Allow people to showcase their talents
Create a culture of success	Invest in your team
Communicate the larger picture	Share vision, information, results, accomplishments, and challenges
Offer open houses	Enable family members of employees to share and understand an employee's work
Publicize results	Communicate accomplishments to others
Say thank you	Show appreciation

and each employee is eligible to receive a company donation in support of their favourite charity.

Given the turbulent economic times we have recently experienced, companies are also seeking to provide their employees with reassurance that they are valued and that concerns relating to job security and downsizing will be handled in a manner that communicates to employees the importance of their contributions to the company's success. A number of companies, such as NuStar Energy, have initiated no-layoff policies. Others, where layoffs are necessary, are offering heightened severance packages and enhanced outplacement support services.

For smaller companies, and those with less financial capacity, some of the perks described above may not be possible. This does not mean, however, that employees cannot be recognized for a job well done. Creative ideas used by companies to reward their employees include employee car washes, morning fruit baskets, subsidized gym memberships, wellness fairs, community volunteer days, and subsidized lunch days. The CEO of Canadian company Digital Extremes donated one month of his salary so that one of his employees could afford home renovations to ensure accessibility for a loved one who lives with disabilities. The company is also an ongoing supporter ($150 000 in 2017) of Covenant House Toronto (shelter and care for homeless and trafficked youth). And, as described in a previous Business in Action feature, Gokhan Cifci closed his Kingston restaurant for a week and took his staff to Cuba because the restaurant hit its previous-year financial and performance objectives.

As you can see, the diversity of programs and services being used to reward employees reaches far beyond simple salary or wage-based compensation. As managers, it is important to take the time to observe and interact with our employees to learn how we can better support both their work environment and their individual development. Creativity is at the core of developing potential reward and recognition instruments, with the ultimate goal being the desire to develop and maintain an environment that values its employees within the organization in which we manage.[3,4]

LO3   The Motivational Tool Kit

On a day-to-day basis, a manager's main task within an organization is to develop a productive workplace. This means making decisions associated with both the strategic objectives and tactical plans within their area of responsibility. With regard to

FIGURE 9.4   **Motivational Tool Kit: TALENT**

- Trust and Respect
- Approval, Praise, Recognition
- Lead By Example
- Enrichment
- Negotiation Skills
- Treasure

human resource decisions, managers need to individually motivate each worker, as well as collectively motivate the team that they oversee. Gone are the days of using punishment and coercion as methodologies for driving productivity from a workforce. Today's managers need to recognize that high-performance teams and productive employees are the result of an environment of collaboration, cooperation, positive reinforcement, competent leadership, and effective communication. Creating a positive and productive work environment is not always easy, but there are some fundamental things that managers can, and should, keep in mind when looking to work with, enhance the productivity of, and motivate their employees. These can be thought of as your motivational tool kit and are easily remembered by the acronym TALENT (see Figure 9.4).

T = Trust and respect One of the key attributes of great work environments is that they are developed on the underlying principle of trust and respect. Employees value managers and companies that trust them and respect their views and opinions. A recent survey by the McKinsey & Company revealed that trust between a company and its employees is a key attribute of a dedicated workforce.

A = Approval, praise, and recognition Often cited as one of the most important motivators, employees respond positively to praise and recognition for a job well done. Managers should not underestimate the role that regular, positive feedback plays in maintaining a high-performance work unit. Recognition of a job well done heightens levels of employee satisfaction in the workplace and is a key driver of employee retention. It should be noted that recognition does not always have to be monetarily focused. Research has demonstrated that praise and commendation, attention, and opportunities for new challenges are as strong a motivator as money. In fact, a recent McKinsey survey concluded that three non-cash motivators—praise from immediate managers, attention from leaders, and a chance to direct projects—were as effective a motivator as three leading money-based motivators (performance cash bonuses, increase in base pay, and stock options).

L = Lead by example Employees expect their managers to lead by example. The willingness of managers to work side by side with employees, as part of the team, to get the job done results in employees building stronger bonds with these managers and having greater respect for them.

E = Enrichment Employees often value the opportunity for new work experiences and additional challenges. Enriching the opportunities for individual growth on the job will result in a more productive and higher-skilled workforce. When such enrichment opportunities can be offered, this also reinforces the respect that the organization has for an employee, recognizes the skills that the employee possesses, and reinforces the value that the employee provides in assisting the organization with meeting its mission and vision.

N = Negotiation skills Negotiation skills refers to a manager's ability to deliver two key areas of support to their employee base. The first has to do with a manager's ability to orchestrate, on behalf of their team, the removal of barriers, the acquisition of resources, and the enhancement of processes that will enable the team to achieve the level of performance needed to accomplish the stated goals and objectives. This means creating an environment that supports success. The second support area is the ability of managers to effectively communicate to their employees the desired level of expectations for each individual, as well as the team overall, in a manner that reinforces an environment of collaboration, accountability, and interdependence.

T = Treasure Employees are motivated by financial incentives that are directly related to work performance and levels of productivity. Performance-based cash bonuses and other creative financial incentives are valued by employees as long as they are felt to be equitable, realistic, and achievable. It should be understood, however, that financial incentives by themselves are not as strong a motivator as the other tools within TALENT. For individuals who are satisfied with their compensation levels, additional short-term bursts of financial rewards may result in only short-term bursts of additional productivity. Another key concern with financial incentives lies in their "sustainability." Once given, removal of such rewards due to market pressures, economic downturn, or company solvency and liquidity issues may actually act as a demotivator rather than a motivator. It should, however, also be noted that, in general, insufficient monetary rewards cannot be fully compensated for by good human relations activities on the part of managers.

 Business IN ACTION

Evolution of Motivational Theory

Today's views on how to motivate employees and develop productive work environments are the result of significant research and contributions by many over the past 100+ years. Modern practices have evolved from a number of published works by some of the foremost business thinkers. Frederick Taylor, often referred to as the "father of scientific management," published a leading study of productivity analysis in 1911 titled "The Principles of

Scientific Management." For Taylor, it was all about studying workers to find the most efficient ways of doing things, and then teaching other employees these same techniques.

Abraham Maslow conducted a series of studies on human behaviour between 1939 and 1943 that resulted in what is now known as "Maslow's hierarchy of needs." Maslow's work found that employees, based on their individual situations, are motivated by varying types of needs, beginning with the most basic (physiological and safety) and evolving toward more intrinsic needs, such as love or belonging, self-esteem (recognition and appreciation), and self-actualization (self-development, creativity, and job satisfaction).

H. Armstrong Roberts/Getty Images

In the 1960s, two additional important studies were released regarding motivation and workplace performance. Frederick Herzberg provided valuable insight into what managers can do in the workplace to motivate employees. Herzberg's work sought to divide factors influencing work performance into two categories, hygiene factors and motivational factors. Hygiene factors focused on the work environment and were found to be factors that did not necessarily motivate, but when they were absent or not adequately provided would result in worker dissatisfaction and, therefore, lower levels of performance. Hygiene factors were found to be general working conditions, policies and administrative procedures, salary, job security, organizational structure, and type of supervision. For Herzberg, true motivational factors were directly related to what makes people happy and what will result in higher levels of work performance. Herzberg found that true motivational factors were related to achievement, recognition, interest in the task being performed, responsibility given, and potential for advancement. A second study during this same time period, by Douglas McGregor, examined theories relating to individual behaviour in the workplace. In his "Theory X and Theory Y" McGregor concluded that managerial attitudes toward their workforce directly influenced performance and productivity. Theory X managers believe that workers have an inherent dislike for work, dislike responsibility, are motivated solely by financial rewards, and need to be threatened or coerced in order to be productive.

At the opposite end of the continuum are managers who have a completely different set of assumptions. Theory Y managers believe that people like work, will commit themselves without coercion or punitive outcomes toward objectives that they are challenged by, will accept and seek responsibility and accountability for their work, and are motivated by a variety of rewards beyond monetary compensation. McGregor concluded that, where possible, implementation of Theory Y attitudes by managers lead to higher levels of productivity, because workers will contribute more to an organization if they are treated as responsible and valued employees. Conversely, an unsupportive atmosphere at work generally leads to lower levels of productivity and higher levels of employee turnover.

In his 1967 publication titled "The Human Organization," Rensis Likert examined the different types of leadership styles within organizations. Likert concluded that in order for an organization to achieve maximum profitability and to have good labour relations and high levels of productivity, organizations need to make optimal use of their human resources. Recognizing that organizations have different structures and are guided by different managerial styles, Likert identified that organizations that have confidence in their employees, provide them with the opportunity for input and participation in the goal-setting process, give them true responsibility for the attainment of those goals, offer them a cooperative environment, and communicate with them regularly, receive in return the highest levels of employee performance. Victor Vroom offered managers the "expectancy theory," which theorized that the amount of effort an employee exerts on a given task is directly related to the outcome desired and the reward to be received. Employees will be much more motivated to initiate and successfully complete a task if the expectations are such that the employee sees a meaningful outcome for the effort.

As can be expected, ongoing research continues into what it takes to motivate people in the workplace. Additional theories continue to be offered, all designed to enable organizations to improve the overall productivity and performance of their workforce. Today's marketplace and work environment is significantly different than the world that Frederick Taylor and Abraham Maslow experienced. Global competition, and changes in attitudes toward work and life, all have resulted in shifts as to what it takes to manage in today's complex, fast-paced society. Although our workforce needs and desires have changed, one thing has fundamentally remained constant. As managers, we need to continually view our human resources talent as a core asset to the organization and to encourage their active participation in the decisions relating to the goals and direction the organization is striving toward. If you would like more information on motivational theory, conduct a Google search for "employee motivation."

LO4   Managing Your Workforce

Managing a workforce in today's complex business setting requires a diverse skill set. Managers need to be able to engage employees, build consensus, develop and execute strategy, anticipate and remove productivity barriers, enhance operational efficiencies, and manoeuvre their way through increasingly complex regulatory, environmental, and legal environments. On a daily basis, managers need to figure out what to do despite increasing uncertainty in an ever-changing global economy, and the ever-growing enormous amounts of relevant information that today's technological and data-mining tools place in front of them. To be able to successfully organize, develop, direct, and lead their team, managers themselves need to fully understand the direction the organization is pursuing and the key competitive advantages it hopes to bring to the table as it seeks to acquire and retain customers. They then need to be able to take this information and develop a road map for success, as well as a framework for ensuring that objectives are met, and communicate this effectively to their employees. Once the direction is set and the road map established, managers then need to be able to monitor the progress being made via the benchmarks they have developed and make the appropriate corrections to keep the effort on track, thereby ensuring that objectives are met. Knowing what needs to be done and how to do it is one thing. To succeed in carrying out these tasks, managers need to be able to transcend this analytical assessment of what needs to be done and "lead" employees in ensuring the goals and objectives are accomplished in a manner that exceeds customer expectations and outperforms competitive rivals. Managers must also be realistic in the current competencies and capabilities of their team and take the time to identify employee skill gaps that may prevent the team from accomplishing both current and anticipated future initiatives. With the identification of skill gaps, managers must then embark upon the appropriate skill-development strategies to ensure these gaps are closed, thereby providing their team with the best possible chance of success. Figure 9.5 outlines these key areas of workforce management focus.[5]

FIGURE 9.5   **Workforce Management Focus**

Determine the managerial style needed to achieve the results (Lead)

Understand what needs to be done and the outcome that needs to be achieved (Plan)

Use performance metrics to keep the effort on track and focused on the overarching objective (Direct)

Identify the focus of the effort and procure and allocate resources in response to it (Organize)

Identify the competencies and capabilities the team needs to improve and initiate such improvements (Develop)

To be able to successfully organize, develop, direct, and lead their team, managers need to fully understand the direction the organization is pursuing and the key competitive advantages it hopes to bring to the table as it seeks to acquire and retain customers.

The Core Management Challenge

In the prior discussion we focused on the key role of managers, this being their role in planning, organizing, developing, leading, and directing organizational efforts and the individuals who work for them. So, just how do managers convert these concepts to practical application? Figure 9.6 offers some insight into this.

In reviewing Figure 9.6, we see that what managers obviously are looking for is to guide and attain the required level of company performance. To do this requires that they create a positive reaction across all employees as to what needs to be accomplished. It is this individual reaction that will determine if company performance expectations are met. Individual reaction is predicated on three key items: the tools (resources) employees have at their disposal, the ability of the organizational structure to support their work efforts, and the underlying culture, decision process, and managerial approach that oversees the transformation process. If any of these three key items are lacking or misaligned, then

© Emerger/Dreamstime.com/GetStock.com

FIGURE 9.6   **Managing the Organization**

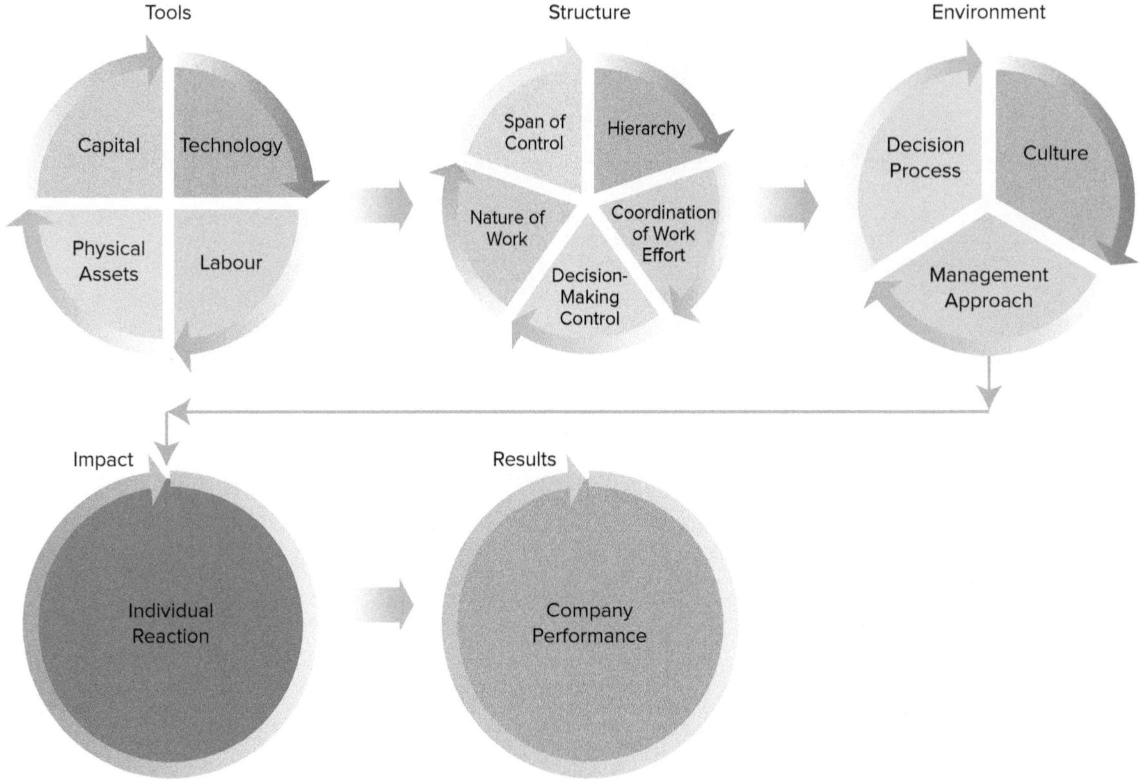

the individual reaction of employees will be impacted and company performance will, ultimately, be compromised. Given that we have already discussed the underlying tools (resources) needed to successfully execute strategy, as well as the importance of structure in establishing the framework around which work is done, our focus for the remainder of this chapter lies in how we, as managers, can create a positive environment for our workplace talent. This entails not only how we manage the evolution of our culture, but also how we interact with each employee we encounter. It means understanding not only what motivates employees (as discussed earlier in this chapter), but also how our managerial style can, and will, influence reaction and performance. It also requires us to recognize the potential pitfalls which we can fall into and which can effectively derail even our best efforts for providing an engaging and highly supported work environment.

Skills Successful Managers Must Possess

To be successful in their planning, organizing, developing, directing, and leading endeavours, managers must recognize that their skill set needs to encompass four key competencies. These critical skills are what separate high-performing managers from lower-performing individuals (see Figure 9.7). It should be noted that of the four key skill sets identified, three have to do with communication and employee interaction.

- **Conceptual skills:** As noted above, managers need to be able to visualize, understand, and communicate the big picture. This means describing to their employees how their work and their efforts contribute to the overall success of

FIGURE 9.7   **Managerial Skill Set**

the organization. They need to be able not only to create a vision of a "killer strategy" for the company to pursue, but also to develop and manage the underlying structure and culture required to achieve it. The ability to continually reinforce this positioning message to their team is critical to the ongoing maintenance of high levels of productivity.

- **Leadership skills:** Strong leadership skills are fundamental to successful managers. Leading means being able to build continuous momentum within your workforce, and building a system that encourages innovation, creativity, and can survive beyond a single individual (succession management). Leadership is all about inspiring others to achieve identified levels of expectations. Successful leaders—via maturity, energy, charisma, intuitiveness, empathy, and controlled emotion—will frame the culture of their organization or work unit. Leadership is all about accepting responsibility when things do not go well (which Jim Collins refers to as "confronting the brutal facts"), and sharing credit when success is realized. A fundamental characteristic of great leadership is the willingness to place the organization's needs above those of the individual. Great leaders trust their team and are not afraid to have their ideas challenged. Strong leaders also demonstrate a true passion for their team and their company, and communicate an underlying desire to be the best at whatever they undertake.[6]

- **Technical and analytical skills:** Simply put, to be successful managers must have a solid understanding of the work that needs to be accomplished. This is essential to be able to identify the relevant issues that need to be addressed, barriers that need to be removed, and performance metrics that need to be achieved if the organization's goals and objectives are to be met. Managers may not be required to understand every facet of an employee's work responsibilities, but they need to have a technical understanding of the core fundamentals of the positions that they are overseeing if they are to be successful in coaching, mentoring, and supporting an employee's work effort. The ability to recognize operational inefficiencies and ineffectiveness is directly related to the technical knowledge one has of the processes being undertaken and the analytical ability to assess the individual steps within such processes. Managers need to take the time to learn the core fundamentals of the positions they supervise. An often overlooked source of organizational conflict is the lack of managerial competency to develop and guide the process a work unit is expected to follow, and to appreciate the complexity of tasks that employees are challenged by on a day-to-day basis.

- **Human relations skills:** The ability to communicate expectations in an engaging, motivating, and collaborative manner is key to successful management. Successful managers understand that their role is to develop and motivate their HR asset. Daily interaction means responding to the needs of their employees in a manner that reinforces the fundamentals laid out in the acronym TALENT (see Figure 9.8).

Understanding Your Power Base

An additional fundamental to strong human relations is the recognition, by managers, of which power base to use when interacting with their employee team (see Figure 9.9).

FIGURE 9.8   **Leadership/Management Side of Interacting with Talent**

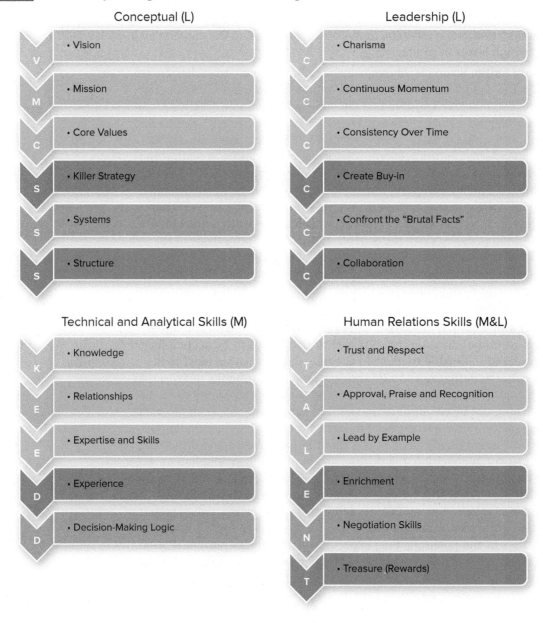

Conceptual (L)

- Vision
- Mission
- Core Values
- Killer Strategy
- Systems
- Structure

Leadership (L)

- Charisma
- Continuous Momentum
- Consistency Over Time
- Create Buy-in
- Confront the "Brutal Facts"
- Collaboration

Technical and Analytical Skills (M)

- Knowledge
- Relationships
- Expertise and Skills
- Experience
- Decision-Making Logic

Human Relations Skills (M&L)

- Trust and Respect
- Approval, Praise and Recognition
- Lead by Example
- Enrichment
- Negotiation Skills
- Treasure (Rewards)

FIGURE 9.9   **Manager's Power Base**

> The ability to communicate expectations in an engaging, motivating, and collaborative manner is the key to successful management.

Managers have at their disposal two bases of power. The trick is to know when to use each of them in order to ensure that interactions with employees build a culture and environment of collaboration and professionalism, yet enable the manager to meet the needs of the organization in terms of organizing and directing the task(s) at hand. The two key power bases of a manager are personal power and position power. **Personal power** is the power that a manager possesses as a result of their leadership competencies. It is the ability to motivate, facilitate, demonstrate empathy, and collaborate with staff in order to meet organizational expectations. **Position power** is the power that a manager legitimately holds due to the title they have within the organization. This power is derived on the basis of expertise, legitimacy of rank, the ability to control rewards and resources, and the requirement to assess performance. Let's take an example to illustrate the effective use of each. Suppose a manager has been informed, by his supervisor, that sales of the product line he manages have really taken off. Although delighted with the success, the manager realizes that this unanticipated growth will result in the existing complement of staff having to work additional hours (overtime), including weekends, for the next two to four months until HR can recruit, select, and intake additional employees to meet current and anticipated future demand. Recognizing that this will affect upcoming vacation schedules and lifestyle activities for his team, the manager will need to ask his staff to work with him in resolving this issue in a manner that meets organizational expectations and recognizes the imposition the situation will cause to their personal lives. To approach this on the basis of position power, mandating (without employee input) how the situation will be handled could result in a significant negative impact. The manager would be better suited to approach this on the basis of personal power, and collaborate with his staff to find a solution that best meets their needs and ensures the organizational objectives are met. In a second situation, assume that an employee's performance is below expectations and that prior efforts to coach the employee have resulted in little to no performance improvement. The manager is now faced with placing the employee on formal notice that their performance is in need of improvement, otherwise additional consequences will occur. In this situation, the manager is best suited to approach the meeting and discussion on the basis of position power, and provide the employee with a straightforward discussion of the issues and potential outcomes of the performance deficiency. The position power enables the manager to communicate that her responsibility for the performance of the entire team and each individual team member necessitates the formality of the discussion. It

Personal Power is the power that a manager possesses as a result of his/her leadership competencies. It is the ability to motivate, facilitate, demonstrate empathy, and collaborate with staff in order to meet organizational expectations.

Position Power is the power that a manager legitimately holds due to the title he/she has within an organization. This power is derived on the basis of expertise, legitimacy of rank, the ability to control rewards and resources, and the obligation to assess performance.

should be noted here that the manager, in utilizing this power base, should focus on the behaviour correction required, dealing only with the issues that have manifested themselves. The discussion should be handled in a professional, courteous manner, absent any unrelated personal references toward the employee as an individual/person.

Leadership styles and effective management strategies are, ultimately, driven by the power base that a manager perceives as necessary in overseeing their responsibility within an organization. The style can also be influenced by the nature of the tasks being performed, the organizational culture, the centralization or decentralization of decision making that occurs, and the capabilities and experience of the workforce itself. In general, managers who exhibit participative, managerial decision-making approaches, and who understand the decision factors influencing the power base from which to determine where, and how, to approach a situation, are believed to produce more effective results from a motivational, collaborative, and performance perspective.

> Leadership styles and effective management strategies are, ultimately, driven by the power base that a manager perceives as necessary in overseeing their responsibility within an organization.

Determining the Culture/Structure Balance

Reflecting back on Chapter 8, and the concept of organizational structure and its underlying culture, a key responsibility of managers is the formation and guidance of cultural development. Culture, and the engagement of employees at work, is without a doubt one of the most challenging issues managers must contend with as they look to create a dynamic, innovative, and high-performing workforce. What was originally considered an HR problem—the need to engage employees in meaningful work, coordinated by a strong leadership team, and integrated within a strong collaborative team-based environment—is now a key requirement of all managers to create. The key to making decisions relating to the culture/structure balance that will result in the optimal workplace environment is to determine the mix of collaboration, autonomy, and centralized decision-making control required given the tasks to be completed and the management approach to be deployed. Figure 9.10 offers some insight into this process. In thinking about culture and the tasks required, managers are constantly balancing the concepts of participation, flexibility, and interactiveness on the part of employees with the need to formalize decision-making responsibility, process efficiencies and standardization, and overall accountability. Added to this is the fact that, as noted in Chapter 8, workforces are becoming increasingly virtual and on-demand—an environment that requires a willingness, at some degree, to adjust formalized structures in a way that allows for individual autonomy and decision making in support of customer-centric business models.

In this regard, it is essential for managers to assess the three points shown on the culture/structure decision triangle (see Figure 9.10) and determine where the ideal lies. Finding this "sweet spot" can be interpreted as creating a balance between the desired level of employee interaction and the amount of risk allowance managers are comfortable transferring to employees. This is offset by the control protocols that management feels need to be in place and the degree of competitiveness it wants to create among divisions, departments, or work units within the organization.

FIGURE 9.10 Culture/Structure Decision Triangle

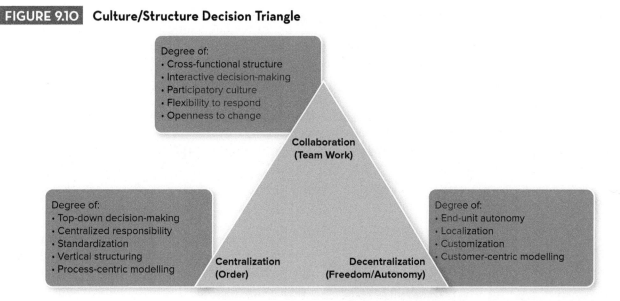

Degree of:
• Cross-functional structure
• Interactive decision-making
• Participatory culture
• Flexibility to respond
• Openness to change

Collaboration
(Team Work)

Degree of:
• Top-down decision-making
• Centralized responsibility
• Standardization
• Vertical structuring
• Process-centric modelling

Degree of:
• End-unit autonomy
• Localization
• Customization
• Customer-centric modelling

Centralization
(Order)

Decentralization
(Freedom/Autonomy)

What is making this increasingly challenging for leaders and managers alike is the fact that the way in which people interact, coupled with the changes in what truly motivates individuals at work, is facing true disruption, much in the way that markets are. Added to this disruption is the potential disconnect between what will yield business results in the near-to-mid-term and what is essential for long-term success. Most managers today are measured on the basis of business results, with less emphasis placed on the ability to generate and maintain a strong and enduring culture. Yet employees are increasingly looking for meaningful work, development, and advancement opportunities, and true engagement in the work environment. It is almost as if we need to think of employees as customers rather than workers, and approach them in a manner that creates a unique bond of loyalty and commitment. For strategies to be properly executed the culture needs to be aligned in such a way that business results are achieved, but also so that employees are truly engaged, thereby driving the highest level of TALENT results out of everyone. As a manager, one has to decide just what type of culture, and its corresponding structure, enables the company to achieve both of these objectives. There is an old saying: "Culture eats strategy for breakfast." As managers we need to determine the best combination of collaboration, centralization, and autonomy in order to engage workers and truly integrate them into our culture.[7]

Managing in a Unionized Environment

Perhaps one of the most challenging environments to manage within is that of a unionized environment. This statement is not intended to imply that the challenge of a unionized environment is one fraught with conflict and animosity between management and the union(s) representing the organization's workers. It is much more about ensuring that as a manager within such an environment we take the time to fully understand the **collective bargaining agreement** (labour contract) governing the workplace (see Figure 9.11), and the underlying procedures for dispute resolution that have been agreed to by both parties, including those related to **grievances**, **mediation**, and **arbitration**.

Collective Bargaining Agreement is a legally binding document that defines the policies, procedures, and protocols both the company and its union have agreed to with respect to the regulation of workplace conditions for a defined period of time.

Grievances are complaints raised by an employee.

Mediation is the process by which management and the union invite a third party to assist in the resolution of a dispute.

Arbitration is the settling of a dispute by a third party, whose decision is considered to be binding on both parties to the dispute.

FIGURE 9.11   **Understanding the Collective Bargaining Agreement**

- Know the rights of both employees and management, as outlined by the contract.

- Recognize the key provisions and hot spots that continually surface from the collective agreement and build a plan as to how to effectively respond to them.

- When faced with employee concerns or grievances, employ the appropriate actions that support the integrity of the collective agreement (mediation, arbitration, etc.). Where possible, include specific references to provisions within the collective agreement that form the basis for your decision.

- Understand the role of the union steward, and build an environment of trust and collaboration between management and the union's representatives.

- Set clear and definitive expectations in a way that promotes high levels of performance, offers feedback, and motivates workers.

© Yurolaitsalbert/Dreamstime.com/GetStock.com

Union Steward (Shop Steward) is a representative of the union who works in ensuring that employee interests, as outlined by the collective bargaining agreement, are respected by the company and its management team.

Unionized environments do not change the fundamental requirement of managers, that being the need to establish a solid working relationship with their employees. Encouraging discussion, listening carefully to employees, and demonstrating strong communication skills remain the cornerstone of effective human resource management. Critically important within this process is to be sure that all employee interactions are approached in a fair and equitable manner and that disputes are resolved quickly and fairly. In addition to employees, however, managers must also learn to interact and recognize the responsibilities of the **union steward (shop steward)**. Union stewards are representatives of the union and work in ensuring that employee interests, as outlined by the collective bargaining agreement, are respected by the company and its management team.

In managing in such an environment, managers are advised to focus on three key conclusions driven from the collective agreement (see Figure 9.12).

First, it is important for managers to understand the degree of flexibility they have in assigning work to their employees. This applies to the ability not only to adjust or interpret a job description, but also to bring in new ways of working and initiate cross-training or task rearrangement or modification. The allocation of overtime, the use of temporary workers, and the adherence to seniority rules are other examples of flexibility parameters governed under the contract.

FIGURE 9.12   **Three Key Conclusions—Collective Bargaining Agreement**

Second, managers need to be sure to understand the communication channels and protocols agreed to when delivering information to the workforce. Negotiated agreements may stipulate specific situations where information must be communicated through official union representatives versus directly to employees. There may also be requirements when union representatives, such as the union steward, must be present when interacting with employees.

Third, managers need to buy in to the concept of the union as a partner in obtaining the organization's strategic objectives. Problem employees requiring disciplinary action, business challenges, and competitive issues are but a few of the situations where strong working relationships between the union and the organization can be used to overcome what may seem to be insurmountable obstacles.

The fact that workers organize should not automatically result in managers perceiving that the organization is now facing an adversarial environment. One key benefit of a negotiated collective bargaining agreement is that the rules and regulations governing employee actions, benefits, and protocols are clearly defined. If managers take the time to understand the agreement governing their work environment, then the boundaries of worker engagement, being known, become much easier to work with. Unions, like managers, want the organization to succeed, and want their workers to contribute to the competitive capabilities of the company. Yes, wages and benefits are one focal point of unions, but the desire to create job security and support the personal development and growth of its workforce are fundamental to its existence. These goals can be achieved only through a joint partnership approach with the company and its management team.[8,9]

Inclusiveness, Diversity, and Employment Equity

The Canadian Human Rights Act, and the Canadian Human Rights Commission that supports the legislation, outlines measures that managers are required to follow to ensure people from four underrepresented populations (women, Aboriginal peoples, persons with disabilities, and members of visible minorities) are treated fairly and reasonably. Further, employers seeking to do business with the federal government, and who have more than 100 employees and whose work with the government exceeds $1 million,[10] are required to commit to an agreement to implement employment equity and demonstrate on a regular assessment basis that such policies exist and are actively executed within their organizations. Employment equity in this situation means demonstrated policies that provide fair and reasonable access to employment for underrepresented populations in a manner that is transparent and non-discriminatory, and reasonable efforts to ensure that full representation from the designated groups is occurring.

The Employment Equity Act: Underrepresented Groups

- Women
- Aboriginal peoples
- Persons with disabilities
- Members of visible minorities

The Canadian Charter of Rights and Freedoms provides that every person is equal before and under the law, and this is supported by additional federal law recognizing that in some situations, particularly those relating to employment opportunity, preference is and should be given to historically disadvantaged groups. This preference is considered to be non-discriminatory in the eyes of the law, and reflects the need for companies and their management teams to design, develop, and implement programs, plans, or arrangements that seek to prevent or reduce disadvantages relating to underrepresented groups.[11]

As managers, we have a duty to accommodate persons from these employment groups and ensure that we provide the levels of accommodation and support required to enable these individuals to perform the daily tasks associated with their jobs. For you and me in managing our workforce this may mean that we need to revisit the underlying facilities associated with work locations; establish or revisit selection, promotion, and performance evaluation practices and policies to ensure they do not contain inherent biases relating to future promotion and retention; and review merit and pay-raise policies to demonstrate equal and fair assessment practices are implemented and adhered to. Best practices also include ensuring that job postings, candidate searches, hiring committee composition, interview approaches, and hiring decisions are free from underlying inherent biases that place these groups at a disadvantage. This would involve recognition that nontraditional or nonconventional experiences should be viewed as valid options for demonstrating expertise, and that the need for accommodations to the work environment should not be viewed negatively as part of the hiring decision. Our society is more diverse than ever before. Women are more fully engaged in the workplace and have more than adequately demonstrated their ability to successfully manage at the highest levels. Discriminatory practices that existed in the past have resulted in unfair and unreasonable biases being applied against underrepresented groups. As managers, it is imperative to understand moving forward that such discriminatory practices must be corrected and that true value exists in the benefits diversity and inclusion bring to decision-making processes at all levels of the organization.

Triggers of Performance Erosion

Much of this chapter has focused on defining what employees are looking for from organizations today and how we, as managers, can motivate employees to higher levels of work performance. Equally important is for us to understand that we can quickly erode high-performance work units or teams through the actions that we, as managers, exhibit on a day-to-day basis. In this regard, it is important for new managers to realize that there are four main triggers of performance erosion.[12] These are as follows (see Figure 9.13):

1. **The mediocrity of lip service**—refers to the disconnect between what management says is important for company success and what it actually focuses its efforts on. For example, management may communicate that its focus is to drive and support innovation and new product development as critical to its current and future success. Even having said this, however, management fails to allocate the necessary resources and assets to support truly innovative work and/or new product development. Instead, it allocates resources aimed at reducing costs and or seeking operational efficiencies. For employees, the disconnect becomes a basis for disengagement and disillusionment. What employees thought was the underlying structural and cultural focus is in reality something completely different.

2. **Managers who lack focus**—refers to situations where managers continually change what the organization is working toward. The end result is that a strategic or tactical execution can never be fully carried out to completion, as the strategy to be focused on changes and the tactical methodology for getting there is repeatedly revised. Employees simply are unable to gain traction in solving problems, responding to challenges, or taking advantage of opportunities, as management overly reacts toward

FIGURE 9.13 **Triggers of Performance Erosion**

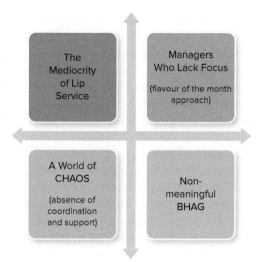

short-term pressures or flavours (i.e., "flavour of the month") as a basis for setting priorities.

3 **Managers create a world of chaos**—refers to the inability of managers to effectively integrate and coordinate the cross-functional activities within their companies. Think of it as the right hand not knowing what the left hand is doing, and vice versa. An example of this occurs when sales managers make promises to clients that are beyond the capabilities of the operations unit to deliver upon, and then look for some miracle to occur that will deliver the product/service to the client as promised. The end result is a failure to execute in a way that reinforces customer satisfaction and loyalty, and that instead generates internal conflict and chaos as the organization now expends significant non-productive activity fighting the self-induced crisis and massaging clients due to the lack of coordinated effort on the part of the full team.

4 **Non-meaningful BHAG ("big hairy audacious goals")**—refers to the fact that goals set by management are abstract in a way that employees of the organization cannot translate into actionable tactics and daily work priorities. Either goals are too broad in scope or too numerous to prioritize, thereby resulting in a clear lack of direction to the talent-base of the organization. It is imperative that managers communicate with distinct clarity what the organization wants to accomplish and that they do so in a way that enables employees to see it from their perspective. For goals to be meaningful, the view from the top must match the view from the bottom up. Employees want to see how their work fits into achieving the vision and mission of the organization.

Keeping these key triggers of performance erosion in mind on a daily basis is critical to ensuring that employees within the organization remain engaged and focused on the execution-based tasks at hand. Employees must understand their sense of purpose and be able to measure their progress. To be successful at this, they must recognize consistency and clarity in what needs to be accomplished and how it fits into the success of their company.

The Danger of Short-Term Pressures

As discussed earlier, managers are continuously being challenged by market uncertainty and what appears to be an endless and diverse supply of potentially relevant information that can influence the direction and implementation of business goals and objectives. In today's corporate environment, the challenge to drive toward higher levels of productivity and continually increase performance efficiency and effectiveness targets seems to never end. For managers, it is all about time management and responding to the latest internal and external pressures. This constant pressure to meet shareholder expectations and monthly, quarterly, and current-year operating targets has a tendency to shift managers into a short-term focus mode. The danger of this pressure is that it causes managers to shift away from their five fundamental zones of effort (planning, organizing, developing, directing, and leading) and concentrate on the three that are designed to most efficiently respond to such short-term pressure (planning, organizing, and directing). When this shift to short-term pressure occurs, the areas of leadership and development—two fundamentals of long-term strategic and operational health—often get relegated to a lower priority, while a third area, planning, focuses more on immediate operational plans, which may lose their synergy with the organization's overall strategic plan and long-term vision. The potential near-term impact of this short-term management approach, referred to as "short-termism," is the following:

- Organizations tend to decrease their emphasis on talent management strategies.
- Organizations and their decision-making processes have a tendency to become "siloed," with a reduced emphasis on collaboration and information sharing.
- Company investment decisions tend to be dominated by immediate short-term financial results and shareholder return expectations.
- Talent development costs are viewed more as an operational expense than a capital investment.
- HR actions tend to be more "knee-jerk" driven, hiring only at the last minute and where absolutely necessary, as such hiring is viewed as a potentially profit-reducing expense.
- Absence of career and competency development is viewed as a near-term requirement; that is, as a tactical issue versus a strategic issue.

Although economic pressures may legitimately require an organization to think in terms of the immediate future (due to solvency or liquidity problems), a number of firms fall into this trap, again, due to the perceived need on the part of the management team or its board of directors to continually exceed shareholder/investor expectations in the immediate term. The long-term consequences, however, given this movement away from protecting the investment in the talent component of an organization, can result in failure over the longer period to develop the competencies in their staff and their management team to meet the strategic requirements of the company going forward. For many, the end result of this short-term focus is that managers do not spend enough time on talent management strategies, and that these strategies become no longer aligned with the organization's long-term business strategy. This "short-termism" loop and the consequences of this type of decision-making attitude are illustrated in Figure 9.14.[13]

The constant pressure to meet shareholder expectations and monthly, quarterly, and current-year operating targets has a tendency to shift managers into a short-term focus mode.

FIGURE 9.14   **Short-Termism Loop: Impact to Talent Development**

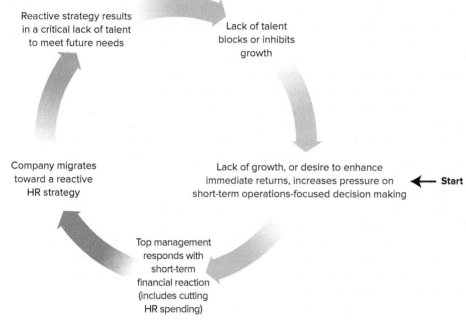

The de-emphasis of long-term goal setting and talent development initiatives can, and often does, result in heightened organizational conflict. If short-termism permeates an organization for an extended period, the end result can be myriad disruptors, all of which can cause an organization to drift away from its intended goals and objectives. Incompatible goals due to **silo mentality** can arise among what are meant to be cross-functional units. The staffing resources needed to get the job done and meet the increasing complexity of the tasks required can become insufficient, and the managerial competencies needed to guide the organization forward can become lacking. In responding to this challenge, managers must resist the temptation to become predominantly focused on meeting and exceeding short-term expectations, and recognize that, while important, these results need to be balanced in consideration of the long-term health of the organization. Shareholders, for example, are but one component of our stakeholder base. Customers, suppliers, employees, and other parties connected to our organization all need to have their expectations met as well. Successful firms do just that—they balance the needs of all stakeholders, and manage the organization in a manner that not only ensures its survival today, but also protects its long-term competitiveness and sustainability going forward.

Silo Mentality refers to managerial decisions that do not take into consideration the cross-organizational impact that such decisions will have.

Leadership/Management—Today, Tomorrow, and Beyond

LO5

> Strategy is 5% planning and 95% execution. Execution is 5% technical and 95% people.

In the prior sections of this chapter, relating to managing your workforce, our focus has been on discussing the underlying skill sets that managers must develop and possess in order to be successful in planning, organizing, directing, developing, and guiding the organization. We also identified the sources of power (personal and positional) that managers can utilize in the course of motivating and challenging their workforce TALENT. When we get right down to it, however, a manager's fundamental responsibility lies in the ability to positively transform the organization as it journeys toward the achievement of its vision. In this vein, the core tasks of managers lie in the art of decision making and in their ability to engage others within this decision-making structure. This requires strong leadership skills, not only in terms of choosing the right path, but also in the underlying process initiated to determine such a path. This takes us right back to our discussion in Chapter 1 relating to visionary leadership, and the need to inspire your workforce to pursue a shared goal and then create a culture that encourages them to identify with it and achieve it.

Ted Turner, founder of CNN, was observed saying that, "Life is a game and money is how we keep score."[14] From a purely investment/return perspective, Turner may be correct. One can and should argue, however, that there is more to the game of business than simply the monetary outcome. For managers, the key outcome that should be strived toward, in addition to the monetary objectives, is validation that we earned the respect of our peers and employees in the process of pursuing these goals. Astute business people focus on four key criteria around which organizations are built: vision, innovation, strategic thinking, and social responsibility. They also understand that not every problem can be solved immediately, and that collaborative interaction, investigation, and information validation are essential components to making the right choices in the course of both tactical and strategic decisions.

Although some may take the position that the underlying traits of leadership have not changed (the need to motivate, engage, excite, create direction, etc.), the dynamics of today's global marketplace have created a whole new set of underlying skill requirements and personal challenges. The velocity of market convergence, disruption, and emerging-economy development have accelerated the pace of innovation, shortened product life cycles, and resulted in companies and brands becoming obsolete at astonishing rates. The end result is that leadership and the accompanying decision-making skills associated with it require stronger risk management, negotiating, and interpersonal and collaborative competencies than ever before. Add to this the fact that today's markets never sleep; the global marketplace has resulted in 24/7 leadership. This impacts today's leaders in three fundamental ways. First is the tremendous scrutiny that now takes place, from various stakeholder communities, as a result of the information technology revolution underway. Blogs, Twitter feeds, 24-hour news channels, and social media have resulted in CEOs and leaders having to face literally instant critiques and questioning of the decisions they make and the actions their organizations undertake. Second, the rigour of managing across multiple time zones and enhanced geographic differences requires a stamina level and a schedule complexity not seen before. Add to this the cultural and social sensitivities of a global marketplace, which require leaders to be much more understanding and knowledgeable of cultural differences and the required empathy needed to develop and maintain organizational stability and linkage. Third, the degree of uncertainty and volatility in markets requires leaders to recognize that prior experiences and historical success may no longer be the formula upon

© Hermintomo/Dreamstime.com/GetStock.com

FIGURE 9.15   **Managing in the 21st Century**

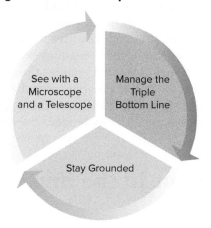

which to make future decisions. It also requires an acceleration of the decision-making process as windows of opportunity open and close faster than ever before. In managing in such an environment, leaders must learn to balance the confidence and security of past success with the need to listen, seek a wider range of input, and provide increased empowerment to others. CEOs and leaders can no longer do it on their own. They need the expertise, judgment, and buy-in of their team in order to be effective in navigating through today's turbulent markets and maintaining calm and focus within their organizations. So what can leaders do to better prepare themselves for the increasing complexity and challenges brought on by today's global market environment and technological revolution? In an article titled "Leading for the 21st Century," McKinsey & Company offers the leaders of tomorrow three sound pieces of advice (shown in Figure 9.15 and adapted for brevity in the following discussion).

1 **See with a microscope *and* a telescope.** The microscope analogy refers to the need for leaders to drill down and ensure they fully understand the challenges and decision ramifications of managing in today's increasingly scrutinized and critiqued environment. In a similar vein, the telescope imagery signifies that in today's rapidly changing markets, managers must be increasingly cognizant of the trends, challenges, disruptions, and opportunities appearing on the horizon.

2 **Manage the triple bottom line—recognize that decisions cannot be made in isolation.** Managers are recognizing more and more that external factors and stakeholders are gaining greater leverage toward influencing the strategic and tactical decision-making process within companies. Government's involvement in the marketplace, given the impact of the financial crisis and subsequent slower economic growth, de-leveraging requirements, and high unemployment level challenges, is considered by many to be at an all-time high. Add to this the increasing pressures associated with societal expectations relating to corporate social responsibility, and one quickly realizes that decisions can no longer be made in isolation of the broader public arena. Managers must think across all components of the triple bottom line (people, planet, profit) as they implement strategy and execute tactics across the globe.

3 **Stay grounded.** Given our rapidly changing market environments, managers are facing increasing pressures to anticipate and proactively control an ever-increasing number of variables now impacting the long-term viability of the companies they manage. Crisis management, which used to be the exception, now seems to be an almost everyday event in

the lives of many executives. Staying grounded during such crises requires significant maturity, focus, stamina, and leadership. The ability to adhere to the saying "never let them see you sweat," and to manage in a world of chaos, complexity, and pressure, requires increasing psychological, sociological, and methodical decision-making skills. CEOs and managers must bring to the table a skill set that enables them to appropriately assess such situations and establish a sequential controlled response in a way that calms the organization, prevents decision-making paralysis, and enables it to proceed with overcoming such challenges.[15]

HR Management in the Small Business Setting

The HR issues for entrepreneurs and small business managers are the same as those that face much larger organizations. Entrepreneurs and small business managers must still determine how to motivate their workforce, inspire them to commit to the organization and seek to excel, and create recognition and compensation systems that encourage high levels of productivity, retain employees, and ensure equity and fairness to all. Having said this, the challenge for small business owners and entrepreneurs is that all of this often has to be done without the support of a fully established HR department—in reality, many entrepreneurs and small business managers *are* the HR department. Constantly challenged by day-to-day market and financial risk pressures, entrepreneurs and small business managers often relegate the establishment of formal HR policies and procedures to the back burner, always intending to deal with them but rarely finding the time. It is important for these individuals to understand two important fundamentals in this regard. First, given their size and lack of personnel in the HR area, a mistake that entrepreneurs and small business managers often make is trying to apply large-business structures to their small operations. The key is to keep it simple. Entrepreneurs and small business owners should seek to use mechanisms that are sustainable and that can be applied consistently with little bureaucratic infrastructure. Second, in establishing their approach, entrepreneurs and small business managers should look to develop strategies toward those performance factors that represent the best win/win outcomes for them and their employees: compensation, benefits, training, flexibility and work balance, and a feeling of inclusion. Note that promotion and advancement does not appear in this list—this is not because they are not valued, but because, in many small business settings, the opportunity to reward in this fashion may be limited. If they are available, then they certainly should be added to the list. The idea, just as with large businesses, is to create a positive work environment. Small business employees want to understand the owner's vision, and often are a great resource of ideas for greater cost efficiencies and growth opportunities. Entrepreneurs and small business owners should seek to tap in to their employees in this way. Employees in many small business settings often look for greater responsibility. In fact, one recommended strategy for delegating is for the small business owner to identify five things that routinely consume their time and assign those tasks to a dependable and competent employee. Entrepreneurs and small business owners who can succeed in delegating can find their day-to-day operational load lightened, thus allowing greater time for planning and developing growth and profitability initiatives. Compensation can be an issue when trying to retain employees, but many small business owners and entrepreneurs have found that retention bonuses (say, at three, six, and nine years) have been an effective mechanism for developing staying power with employees and providing positive reinforcement for a job well done. Others have found that profit sharing also yields positive benefits. Operating a small business is all about getting personal with your employees, and communicating both the good and the bad in a collaborative manner. Employees who understand the business as a whole are more likely to demonstrate increased accountability and responsibility, take initiative, and seek to protect the business owner's investment. In small business, culture is everything. If nothing else, entrepreneurs and small business owners need to create a fun, team-based place to work. In today's market, young professionals are looking to entrepreneurship and small companies more and more as an exciting career choice. For owners of small businesses, this represents an opportune time to receive maximum benefit from the knowledge and skill set that these highly qualified employees can offer. The trick is for entrepreneurs and small business owners to fully leverage these critical skills in a way that encourages these individuals to excel, and create a sense of ownership in them via a reward system that places value on their contribution.[16]

> Employees who understand the business as a whole are more likely to demonstrate increased accountability and responsibility, take initiative, and seek to protect the business owner's investment.

Management Reflection—Finding the Right Balance

Managers must interact with their workforce in a manner that builds continuous momentum, inspires high levels of performance, ensures an understanding of the work to be accomplished, and creates "buy-in" on the part of employees to the vision and goals of the organization. To accomplish this, managers have to operate on a number of different planes—leading by example; organizing or creating an environment that fosters collaboration and guides the process; and empowering their staff, enriching their experiences, and creating mechanisms that assure accountability and responsibility for the work or tasks assigned to each staff member. They also need to provide support mechanisms and provide feedback to ensure employees understand what is expected of them. Creating and maintaining a positive work environment requires a consistent, methodical approach on the part of managers. It begins and continues to develop with each interaction a manager has with staff. Getting off on the right foot is fundamental, but so is genuinely striving to ensure that employees feel valued and are regularly recognized for their accomplishments. Although not meant to be all-inclusive, Figure 9.16 provides a checklist for effective talent management that managers can refer to in order to ensure the environment within which they manage is a positive one for the individuals who work under them.[17]

Managers are constantly being challenged with finding the right balance in setting strategy, operating the business, and designing and developing the organization's asset and resource base. A critical component of this process is determining where, and how, to make the best use of the organization's talent assets in a manner that provides an advantage in the marketplace and meets or exceeds customer and stakeholder expectations. To create a truly productive and efficient workforce, managers need to recognize that employees are as important an asset as the equipment and infrastructure used within the business. A key component to

FIGURE 9.16   **Checklist for Effective Talent Management**

✓ Do my employees know and understand the organization's vision and mission?

✓ Do my employees know and understand what is expected of them?

✓ Do my employees have the tools to do the job right?

✓ Am I providing each of my employees the opportunity to do his/her best every day?

✓ Have I provided each of my employees with the opportunity to learn and grow?

✓ Do I provide each of my employees with regular feedback as to how they are doing?

✓ Do I provide my employees with coaching and mentoring, when needed, to ensure that they meet the expectations asked of them?

✓ Do I ask my employees for their opinions prior to implementing changes that will impact their work productivity and performance?

✓ Have I provided my employees with opportunities to make friends at work?

✓ Have I sat down with each employee recently and provided them with a formal performance appraisal on how well they are doing their job?

✓ Do my employees believe that I truly care about them?

talent asset management is the creation of a work culture that encourages collaboration and cooperation among employees and the management team. Cross-functional communication, open dialogue on problem solving, recognition of work well done, and the willingness to accept responsibility and accountability for individual actions form the foundation of such a high-performance culture. As a manager, it is your ability to lead by example, as well as to develop your team's competencies, that will mark your success. Planning, organizing, and directing your team is fundamental to your success as well. The key is to communicate what you want your team to focus on and achieve, and then provide the culture and environment to ensure that each member of the team has the tools and the opportunity to succeed.

> As a manager, it is your ability to lead by example, as well as to develop your team's competencies, that will mark your success.

Chapter Summary

This chapter was designed to provide you with an overview of the managerial requirements associated with managing and leading an organization's talent. Fundamental to this was a focus on defining the skills and competencies that managers must possess in this regard. To be successful, managers must be able to plan, organize, develop, direct, and lead their employee talent. To truly motivate their workforce, organizations and their management teams must develop a relationship of trust and respect, recognize efforts on the part of their staff and offer praise, enrich their work experience through new opportunities and challenges, lead by example, exhibit strong negotiation skills both with employees and on their behalf, and provide them with acceptable levels of compensation and rewards. Managers also must be able to conceptualize how an employee's work fits in with the overall vision and mission of the company. They must be able to exhibit strong leadership skills to motivate their work units to higher levels of performance and productivity, provide support via strong technical and analytical skills, and possess strong human relations skills in interacting with employees on a day-to-day basis.

The chapter also provides an overview of the ongoing challenges and pressures managers will face in leading their staff and in managing their areas of responsibility. Critical to this is to recognize the dangers associated with short-termism and the potential loss of strategic direction and long-term organizational health that can result from such a mentality. In closing, managers need to recognize three fundamental requirements to their work. They must establish direction, mobilize action, and develop their teams to successfully meet the expectations of the organization, its customers, and its stakeholders.

Developing Business Knowledge and Skills

Key Terms

personal power *p. 335*

position power *p. 335*

collective bargaining agreement *p. 337*

grievances *p. 337*

mediation *p. 337*

arbitration *p. 337*

union steward (shop steward) *p. 338*

silo mentality *p. 343*

Questions for Discussion

1. So, you're the boss. Now what? Assume you have just been promoted to a managerial position. What key thoughts and actions would you reflect on in order to develop and maintain a highly productive workforce? (LO2)

2. Compensation by itself is not believed to be a strong long-term motivator of employees. Why is this? Conversely, why can't the other motivational tools found in the acronym TALENT fully compensate for insufficient compensation levels in the workplace? (LO3)

3. What are the four critical skills that separate high-performing managers from low-performing individuals? In your mind, which of these skills is most important? Why? (LO4)

4. What are the three key understandings managers need to assess when determining their relationship with the union, representing workers, as a result of a collective bargaining agreement? (LO4)

5. Why should organizations and managers be wary of the short-termism loop? What is its potential long-term impact on talent development? (LO4)

Question for Individual Action

Think about an employment situation you have been part of recently. In reviewing this company and its formal and informal setup, can you identify potential areas where structures, policies, practices, or programs created inequities for you or members of underrepresented groups? In your mind, are these barriers more related to culture or to structure? What actions would you recommend to enable the company to begin to overcome such obstacles to underrepresented groups?

Team Exercise

As a team, meet and discuss what you believe young professionals such as yourselves are looking for from an employer as you leave your post-secondary education and venture into the workforce. Look beyond salary and wages and seek to describe what you feel will be the true motivators for you to excel within an organization. What about retention? What will keep you with an employer? Do you see yourself wanting to work for multiple employers over your career? If so, then why? Prepare a presentation summarizing your views and opinions and share this with your class.

Case for Discussion 1

CFP Inc. (Organizational Redesign)

Matt Wilson, co-owner and president of CFP Inc., a growing technology sensor component company, realizes that CFP is at a crossroads. The business, which opened in 2002, has grown from operating out of a small garage in Surrey, British Columbia—with Matt, his wife, Sarah, and his brother Robert as its sole employees—to a $12-million operation with 45 full-time and 25 part-time employees. The business plan up to this point has been well executed, developing a strong customer base made up of a number of loyal (if finicky) customers across North America who need a variety of sophisticated sensor applications. With Robert's engineering and design expertise, Sarah's office management skills, and Matt's strong business acumen (MBA class of 1999), managerial responsibilities for critical aspects of the business have been effectively distributed among these three principal owners.

The strong business growth, intensifying global competition, and ever-increasing customer demands for smaller, more complex, and higher-performing sensors are causing Matt, Sarah, and Robert to feel increasingly stretched. Almost 100% of Robert's time is consumed with design, prototype development, and related R&D projects. The design team, which he also oversees, has grown to 10 employees. Sarah is consumed, on a daily basis, with human resource issues, payroll and administration requirements, customer and supplier interactions, and ever-increasing government regulations (tax compliance, health and safety, etc.). As more and more of CFP Inc.'s customer base lies outside of Canada, international shipping considerations, USMCA (formerly NAFTA) compliance, and paddling through the enhancements to the "Buy America" legislation and its complex Canadian-exception rules eat into her valuable time as well. Like Robert's R&D department, the administration area has also grown, taking on four full-time and two part-time employees to assist with the continually growing workload. Add to this the learning curve associated with the newly installed financial management computer system and, well—you get the picture.

Matt, too, is feeling the pressure. Although technically the company president, Matt, up to this point in time, has largely played the role of a general or operations manager. Matt and his team of managers (five in total) oversee the operations, marketing and sales, customer service, and plant and facility aspects of CFP Inc.'s business system. Growth of the operation has resulted in the manufacturing area moving to a two-shift operation, covering 16 hours per day. Customization of plant equipment seems to be occurring almost every quarter, as Robert and his team seek to keep CFP Inc.'s customers happy with leading-edge sensor solutions. Add to this the required technology applications that need to be continually introduced in order to improve efficiencies and effectiveness and remain competitive with Asian manufacturers, and the constant search for suppliers that can meet CFP Inc.'s sharp tolerance and performance expectations. Beyond manufacturing, Matt is also dealing with salesforce and dealer development, and the increasing customer support requirements that growing businesses like CFP Inc. face as a result of their success.

All of this has been fairly manageable but things are set to change again, which is resulting in the need to reassess how the business will be managed going forward. As part of the recently completed planning-cycle process, which CFP Inc. initiated in 2018, the company decided to take advantage of what was viewed as a great growth opportunity in Brazil. CFP Inc., supported by Export Development Canada, recognized a real demand for a complex sensor application in Brazil's emerging petrochemical manufacturing, automotive, and aerospace sectors. Following six months of negotiations, the deal has now been finalized, and the potential to double the size of CFP Inc. over the next two to four years has gone from an idea to a reality. With such a major initiative under way, Matt knows that his time will be totally consumed with getting the Brazilian operation up and running. Robert will also need to be heavily involved, as his unique, patented sensor design is core to the entire business arrangement. Both Matt and Robert will be spending a large chunk of their time in Brazil interacting with, and supporting, their newly acquired Brazilian customers. Matt and Robert both know that, as good as Robert's initial leading-edge design is, modifications will need to be made once prototypes and actual product implementation take place. This time requirement means two things: Matt can no longer oversee the existing operation on a day-to-day basis, and Robert will need to transfer the day-to-day supervision of his R&D team to someone else. Sarah, in addition to overseeing the administration area, is transitioning into the role of CFO (chief financial officer) for CFP Inc., overseeing all financial management responsibilities. In addition, a significant number of employees will need to be hired, beginning in as little as three to six months, to meet not only the growing North American demand but also the volume requirements anticipated from Brazil.

At a meeting of the three principals (Matt, Sarah, and Robert) and their advisory board, it was concluded that the time had come to hire a COO (chief operating officer) who could manage the operation, thereby allowing Matt and Robert the time and focus necessary to ensure the Brazilian deal is a success. The only remaining question coming out of this meeting was just what type of person they should be looking for, and whom this person should be.

Questions

CFP Inc. has turned to you for an answer to the question of what type of person they should be looking for. Develop an overview of the characteristics of the type of individual CFP Inc. should find to fill the position of COO. What types of skills does he/she need to possess? Based on this list of skills, where would you place your emphasis? What are your top two prioritized competencies that this individual must possess? Why did you choose these?

Case for Discussion 2

Sodexo: Building an Inclusive Culture

Sodexo is considered to be one of the world's leading providers of food services. Headquartered in Paris, France, its management team presides over a global "quality of life services" organization with revenues in excess of €20.4 billion. Other categories of activity under Sodexo's business model include facilities management, workplace and technical services, benefits and reward services, and personal and home services. Services are delivered by over 460 000 employees across more than 70 countries including Canada.

Culture is central to the organization's strategy. Indeed, Sodexo believes its core values of service spirit, team spirit, and spirit of progress help to set it apart from the competition. In Sodexo's own words, each of these components to culture consists of the following:

Service Spirit

- Clients and consumers are at the center of everything we do.

- To serve them well on a daily basis, we have to demonstrate our availability and responsiveness, to anticipate their expectations and to take pride in satisfying them.

- Sodexo has become a global company, but we remain locally-focused; our managers in the field are true entrepreneurs, close to their clients and empowered to make decisions.

Team Spirit

- It is an absolute need in all of our operations, our business units and administrative offices, as well as in our management committees.

- Each person's skills combine with other team members' knowledge to help ensure Sodexo's success.

- Teamwork depends on the following: listening, transparency, respect for others, diversity, solidarity in implementing major decisions, respect for rules and mutual support, particularly in difficult times.

Spirit of Progress

It is manifested through:

- Our will, but also the firm belief that one can always improve on the present situation.

- Acceptance of evaluation and comparison of one's performance, with one's colleagues in the company or with one's competitors.

- Self-assessment, because understanding one's successes as well as one's failures is fundamental to continuous improvement.

- A balance between ambition and humility.

- Optimism, the belief that for every problem there is a solution, an innovation or some way to progress.[18]

In addition to the comments noted above, the company is also committed to assessing its success against a comprehensive CSR (corporate social responsibility) road map it calls "Better Tomorrow 2025," an initiative that defines what Sodexo sees as its obligations to individuals, communities, and the environment.[19] Sodexo's commitment to CSR is not merely lip service or "greenwashing." Its commitment to

CSR and the corresponding achievements realized in this area have been recognized publicly by its inclusion on the *Fortune* list of World's Most Admired Companies, the Dow Jones Sustainability Index, the FTSE4Good Index, and the DiversityInc Top Companies for Diversity.[20]

In Canada, Sodexo has also been recognized as one of Canada's Top Employers for Young People, one of Canada's Best Places to Work for LGBTQ, and has been consistently recognized as one of Canada's Best Diversity Employers by Mediacorp.[21]

It is this commitment to inclusion and diversity that has truly been a major factor behind the culture at Sodexo. Five employee-led communities of practice form the core focus of advancing Sodexo's commitment to diversity and inclusion (D&I) on a global basis:

Gender: Sodexo's focus on gender balance, gender equity, and an inclusive culture is driven by its SoTogether Advisory Board. The board comprises 28 women and 7 men from 17 nationalities and focuses on five primary areas: leadership development, communication, gender networks, HR processes, and flexibility.

Culture and Origins: Sodexo's Global Taskforce on Culture and Origins focuses on building a culture of inclusion across four primary areas: First Nations, local minorities, refugees, and religions.

Disability: Through DisAbility Voice, Sodexo has a target of 100% of its workforce having access to programs with people for disabilities globally by 2025.

LGBTQ: The firm's Global Pride Group's mission is to "elevate awareness and nurture an inclusive culture for all LGBTQ employees, allies and community members." Supporting activities are undertaken by 11 Pride networks globally.

Generations: Respect for the value that each generation brings to Sodexo—both the institutional knowledge of long-serving employees and the progressive outlook of new employees—is driven by programs such as reciprocal mentoring.[22]

These commitments are supported in Canada by such initiatives as the firm's recent "Open-Up" campaign that is working to raise awareness of invisible disabilities such as autism and ADHD, partnership and training programs for Indigenous groups, its Women in Leadership and Learning (WiLL) program, and a subgroup called Women in Facilities Management that promotes women in STEM careers.[23]

Sodexo employs over 13 000 people in Canada, working with 185 clients across 233 sites. Client sectors include corporate, education, healthcare, energy and resources, senior living, and sports and leisure.[24]

Questions

1. Sodexo describes its mission in the following way:

"Every day, our 420,000 employees across the world work together to:

- Improve the Quality of Life of all those we serve. We strive to design On-site Services and Benefits and Rewards Services (formerly Motivation Solutions) that improve people's well being, process efficiency and infrastructure reliability and quality. We are also gradually introducing Personal & Home Services.

- Contribute to the economic, social and environmental development of the cities, regions and countries where we operate. We demonstrate this commitment every day by employing tens of thousands of people locally at our sites worldwide and contributing to their fulfillment and career development.

- We have also developed a blueprint for the Group's corporate responsibility called Better Tomorrow 2025. Our Better Tomorrow 2025 commitments help us continue our journey to make life better for individuals, communities and the wider world. These commitments focus on the difference we can make and challenge us—and all of the organizations we work with—to do more."[25]

How does Sodexo's commitment to diversity and inclusion support the firm's mission? Can Sodexo derive competitive advantage from its approach to culture?

2. U.S.-based Aramark is one of Sodexo's primary competitors. It is a Fortune 200 organization with a primary focus on food service and facilities management. It operates with approximately 270 000 employees across 19 countries. Like Sodexo, Aramark has been named as one of *Fortune*'s World's Most Admired Companies and recognized as one of the Top 50 Companies for Diversity and one of the best places to work for LGBT equality.[26]

Why do you suppose both companies are working so hard to develop progressive, inclusive cultures? Does the information about Aramark change your answer to the question about competitive advantage in #1 above?

PART 3

CHAPTER 10

The Marketing Challenge

LEARNING OBJECTIVES

This chapter is designed to provide students with:

LO1	An understanding of the purpose of marketing
LO2	Recognition of how marketing is linked to strategy
LO3	Knowledge of the importance of positioning in the formulation of marketing strategy
LO4	An appreciation of the importance of marketing research, segmentation, and targeting in the marketing process
LO5	A base-level exposure to where, and how, marketers seek opportunities for new product/ service ideas, development, and growth
LO6	An awareness of how an organization's marketing team seeks to influence customers and create loyalty for the products these customers buy

Snapshot

What to Expect in This Chapter

As identified by the learning objectives, this chapter focuses on exposing students to key concepts associated with the role of marketing within an organization. The content emphasized in this chapter includes the following:

- Marketing's Purpose
- Marketing's Link to Strategy
- The Concept of Positioning
- Segmentation and Target Marketing
  - Marketing Research: A First Step in the Segmentation Process
  - Transitioning Segmentation Analysis to Target Marketing
- Marketing's Challenge
  - Need Identification
  - Understanding the Consumer Decision-Making Process
  - Responding to Needs: Value Proposition Development and Communication
- A Note Pertaining to Not-for-Profits
- Management Reflection—Back to Strategy

Business IN ACTION

Facebook and YouTube: Still the Social Network Industry Leaders

The age of social media marketing is fully upon us. To not be thinking in terms of the development of a social media marketing campaign for your business or organization is literally unheard of in this day and age. The critical question today, however, is not "Should we invest in a social media campaign?" but rather, "Which communication channel will enable us to best deliver on our marketing communication strategy?" As of this writing, Facebook and YouTube, despite an increasingly crowded digital platform market, remain the social media sites of choice.

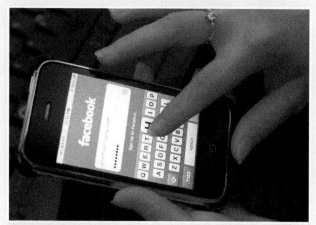

AFP/Getty Images

Facebook now possesses more than 2.3 billion monthly active users (MAUs) globally, of which an estimated 1.5 billion log on daily, with approximately 1.1 billion doing so via their mobile devices. On average, its Like and Share buttons are viewed across an estimated 10 million Web sites daily. A new Facebook profile is created roughly every five seconds. Broaden this to include Facebook's subsidiaries of WhatsApp, Instagram, and Messenger, and the estimated number of users interacting via the Facebook family rises to 2.7 billion, with more than 2 billion using at least one Facebook service daily. In this regard, Facebook (#1), Facebook Messenger (#3), WhatsApp (#4), and Instagram (#5) are four of the top five ranked social media platforms (YouTube is #2), with Facebook accounting for approximately 85% of all social media Internet traffic (Figure 10.1). Facebook is also the #1 network for small business social media campaigns, followed by Instagram and YouTube.

YouTube estimates that as many as 9 billion people globally are active users (1.9 billion MAUs) of this

FIGURE 10.1   Top Social Media Sites in 2019

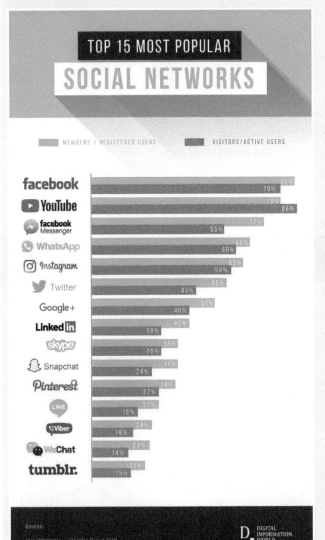

Source: Used with permission of Digital Information World, https://www.digitalinformationworld.com/2019/01/most-popular-global-social-networks-apps-infographic.html, January 1, 2019. (Facebook logo) Used by permission of Facebook, (Twitter logo) Used by permission of Twitter, (LinkedIn logo) Used by permission of LinkedIn Corporation © 2015, (Pinterest logo) Used by permission of Pinterest, (Google logo) Used by permission of Google, (Tumblr logo) Used by permission of Tumblr.

social media Web site. Unlike Facebook, however, the majority of users on YouTube are individuals who have not registered with YouTube with respect to formally setting up a membership account. Still its presence in the market is impressive (#2 search engine), particularly with the 16- to 24-year-old demographic.

As social media marketing continues to grow and mature, the critical component for businesses will be how to most efficiently deliver the message in a way that will resonate with its user base. For Facebook and YouTube the evolving trend at this stage lies in the ability to deliver live video content to the masses. Since Facebook released its "Going Live" service there have been more than 3.5 billion live videos uploaded to this platform. Its sister company, Instagram, has also seen a significant rise in video viewing, with double-digit growth occurring annually. Shifting back to YouTube, the company now has over 300 000 paying YouTube TV subscribers, and its entertainment content in the 18- to 49-year-old demographic now reaches more people than any of the major networks or cable broadcasters. As an example, 96% of teens online in the United States watch YouTube videos. A key business benefit of videos lies in their ability to educate and/or assist in offering solutions to problems facing individuals across all demographics. YouTube, for example, estimates that 70% of its viewers look to the platform to assist them in solving a problem, with 70% of its content being viewed on mobile devices.

Although on top today, Facebook and YouTube need to continually meet the needs of their users and the business and social organization customers currently tied to their platforms. As with any industry, the market is fluid and the underlying dynamics are continually shifting. Globalization, along with the continual further segmentation of the market along specific demographic or behavioural patterns, will challenge the dominance of these current social media leaders. Up-and-coming social media sites such as Houseparty, Kik, Vero, Musical.ly, Steemit, along with expanded capabilities from such established platforms as LinkedIn, Pinterest, WeChat, and Snapchat, will lead to further potential fragmentation in this segment.

As noted at the beginning of this Business in Action, as managers the question is not whether we should consider social media as a core component to our overall marketing strategy. It is much more about which platform will provide us with the highest penetration potential to the primary customer groups we serve and what is the best approach to do this. For the rival social media platforms, being relevant today may not mean being relevant tomorrow. Just as businesses need to keep their products and services relevant to the solutions required by current and prospective customers, so too do social media platform providers. For Facebook and YouTube, it is all about continuing to embed themselves in today's social fabric as the "go to" sites for information and needs solution. For their rivals, it is all about positioning their platforms in a way that outperforms the ability of Facebook and YouTube in reaching designated customer groups and effectively communicating their ability to do so.

Marketing's Purpose

When you think of the word "marketing," what comes to mind? For most people, it refers to the development and delivery of an advertising or media campaign. While this is indeed a part of the marketing process, the development and delivery of an advertising or media campaign is often the last step in the development and delivery of a marketing strategy. The marketing process (discussed in more detail later in this chapter) begins long before the advertising strategy is developed and delivered to the targeted customers. It is really a much broader process that encompasses assessing market dynamics, identifying needs and solutions, and determining what price to charge. It also encompasses ensuring that customers have access to the product through the development of distribution channels and options, and delivering the communication message in order to create awareness and preference for the products/services that an organization is offering to its existing, and potentially new, customers. Having said this, what is the purpose behind the development of a marketing strategy? In its simplest context, the purpose of **marketing** is to design, develop, and communicate value. Value in this context refers to the ability of an organization to communicate, to existing and potential customers, why its product/service offering meets the needs of these individuals and businesses, and why it should be judged superior to those of competitive alternatives.

Marketing is the process through which organizations design, develop, and communicate the value of their products and/or services.

In its simplest context, the purpose of marketing is to design, develop, and communicate value.

Let's look at two fundamental principles associated with customer behaviour that will, hopefully, highlight the importance of this value-based approach to understanding the purpose of marketing.

Principle #1 Customers don't buy products or services—they buy solutions to problems or needs.

Principle #2 Customers will not pay more for a product if they can get a similar product for less.

Assuming agreement with these two fundamental principles underlies the challenge and, therefore, the purpose of marketing. The greater the ability of an organization to deliver to its existing and new customers solutions to their problems or needs that are interpreted to be of higher quality, uniqueness, importance, or convenience, the greater the product/service's value becomes to these customers. This perceived difference in value is what truly differentiates a company's products/services from those of its competitors. This differentiation can then be used to create a preference for the organization's products/services over those of its competitors, thereby resulting in loyalty and commitment for its products, its brands, and the organization in the marketplace. This value does not always have to be tangible; for example, based on functionality. Value, real or perceived, can equally be based on intangible attributes such as peer acceptance, status, emotional benefits, pride of ownership, brand commitment or loyalty, and so on.

A customer's value relationship with an organization can, in many ways, be summed up as the overall experience that the customer has when interacting with an organization. Keeping this "value" purpose in mind, let's now take a look at the role of marketing within an organization and how the development and execution of a successful marketing strategy will assist the organization in meeting its business objectives, its long-term vision, and the organization's intended mission.[1]

> The role of marketing is to determine who desires a given product/service, what is important to them in making this decision, how the company should position its solution relative to rivals, and how to communicate and deliver the value the customer desires.

LO2 Marketing's Link to Strategy

It goes without saying that marketing is a critical component associated with the successful execution of an organization's strategy. Largely perceived as the communications link between an organization and its marketplace, marketing is fundamentally responsible for connecting customers to the products and services offered by an organization, and reinforcing the needs and desires that are being satisfied. This means understanding the six R's of marketing: the *right need* to pursue, the *right solution* to offer, the *right value proposition* to position the organization's products and services around, the *right methodology for delivery*, the *right price to charge*, and the *right communication message* to use.

In developing an organization's marketing strategy and ensuring its alignment to meeting the objectives of the overall corporate and business-level strategies that it supports, marketers need to be able to demonstrate an effective response to six core challenges (see Figure 10.2). These six core challenges can be framed into a series of six questions that marketers must be able to answer in order to assess the viability or success of the potential of a product and/or service offering. The six questions are as follows:

1. Do we understand our targeted customers' needs and desires?
2. Do we believe that our current or anticipated product and/or service represents a viable solution to the targeted customers' needs and desires?
3. Can we create a value proposition that positions our product and/or service as the best solution to our targeted customers?
4. Is there an existing or potential viable distribution model for delivery of our product and/or service to the marketplace in a manner that effectively reaches our targeted customers?
5. Can we support the product and/or service and its delivery to the marketplace at a price point that is attractive to the targeted customer and that allows us to be profitable?
6. Can we develop and deliver to the targeted customers a communication message that will attract these buyers to our product and/or service?

FIGURE 10.2   **Core Challenges of Marketing**

You will notice that the term "targeted customers" has been used within each of these questions. This is because within a given marketplace not everyone will be interested in our product/service offering, or, if interested, will be able to afford it (or desire to purchase it) at the price point we have established as being necessary to ensure that our business model is profitable. The concept of targeting customers and its relationship to the mechanics of segmentation are discussed later in this chapter.

To be successful in the execution of its overall strategy, an organization must be successful at both the product strategy level and the business strategy level. Marketing is integral to this success. Properly positioned products, combined with a superior (in terms of effectiveness) marketing effort, lead to organizational profitability and growth (see Figure 10.3). This, in turn, leads to the achievement of product and/or service objectives that support the achievement of business objectives and, ultimately, organizational objectives and the company's overall vision and mission (see Figure 10.4). Properly positioning a product and/or service is the focus of this chapter, while the execution of a superior marketing effort via the development of the elements that make up a product and/or service's marketing mix is the focus of Chapter 11.

FIGURE 10.3   **The Marketing Formula**

FIGURE 10.4   **Marketing's Impact on Strategy**

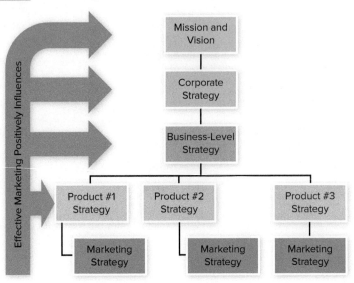

To be successful in the execution of its overall corporate strategy, an organization must be successful at both the product strategy level and the business strategy level.

LO3   The Concept of Positioning

As alluded to throughout this textbook, a key fundamental associated with the development of an organization's business strategy is how it will position its brand, products, and/or services in the marketplace. Figure 10.3 (the marketing formula) goes one step further and definitely states that in order to execute a successful marketing strategy a management team must establish an effective and well-defined market position. So, what are we referring to when we talk about positioning? The easiest way to think about the concept of **positioning**, according to social marketer Francois Legarde,[2] is to think about it as being the place in the consumer's mind that you want your organization's brand, products, and/or services to own. When potential purchasers think about solving a particular need, we want them to think about the brand, products, and/or services that we offer and the benefits that will accrue to them by selecting our offerings over those of our competitors. Positioning is all about developing a unique, credible, sustainable, and valued place in the minds of our customers. It is how we distinguish ourselves from our competitors in the marketplace. Market position can be built around product and/or service features and attributes, functional and/or emotional benefits, or cultural values. Brands, products, and/or services that are well positioned automatically come to the consumer's mind when making repeat purchases, or seemingly float to the top of the purchase potential list when customers are thinking about making a first-time purchase. For example, if you were considering purchasing a 55-inch flat-screen television, what would be your three first choices of retail locations to visit in order to purchase this TV? For many Canadians, the response would include prominent multi-channel retail businesses such as Best Buy, The Source, Walmart, Costco, and The Brick. This is because all are well-positioned in the minds of a majority of consumers as possessing the brands and products, supported by the necessary services, to result in a positive purchase experience. Online retailers such as Amazon.ca, Dell. ca, and TigerDirect.ca may also slide into this preferred purchase order. Similarly,

Positioning refers to our ability to develop a unique, credible, sustainable, and valued place in the minds of our customers for our brand, products, and/or services.

FIGURE 10.5   Positioning to Win

Successful Positioning Objectives

- Communicate the solution effectively to the targeted customers
- Understand the market to be served
- Understand the customers to be targeted
- Deliver the solution in a way that is superior to competitors

Tim Hortons has firmly established itself as the market leader in Canada in the "to-go" coffee beverage category, in part due to its positioning strategy of aligning its brand to being "truly Canadian."

> Positioning is all about developing a unique, credible, sustainable, and valued place in the minds of our customers for our brand, products, and/or services.

In order to effectively position our brand, and the products and/or services that we attach to it, marketing managers need to be successful in the attainment of four key objectives (see Figure 10.5).

A key requirement associated with effective positioning is the development and validation of marketing research relating to both market dynamics and customer needs. As will be discussed later in this chapter, this involves conducting analyses relating to competitors, customers, potential market segments, and internal competencies in order to determine where, and how, the organization will position its brand, products, and/or services. In closing, positioning is built around a value proposition that clearly differentiates an organization's brands, products, and/or services from those of its competitors and, based on a solid understanding of market fundamentals, effectively delivers on the identified target customer's needs. Critical to this process is the ability to establish in the minds of our targeted customers that the price/quality relationship of our offering is superior to that of our competitors, and results in customers concluding that our solution best meets their needs.

Business IN ACTION

D-Wave Systems Inc.—Positioning within a Specialized Niche

Founded in Vancouver in 1999, D-Wave Systems Inc. continues to gain increasing traction within a very specialized computing niche. When we think of computers, we often think of laptops, tablets, and smartphones, which make up the bulk of society's computer requirements. Despite the incredible capabilities of today's consumer-based computers and their accompanying electronics, there is still a field of complex problem solving that even today's supercomputers are unable to respond to. It is within this niche that we find D-Wave. Backed by over $160 million in venture funding, D-Wave is focused

Used by permission of D-Wave Systems Inc.

on the emerging field of quantum computing, and on developing the technology necessary to solve high-value commercial and scientific problems. Examples of such complex problem-solving areas include cancer research, anomaly detection, searching for exoplanets, complex mission planning, and systems optimization. Potential customers include universities, government defence and laboratory facilities, bioscience, big data, and energy and geoscience companies.

A leader in this field, D-Wave's products are considered to be some of the most advanced quantum computers in the world. Exploiting quantum mechanics, and building systems around qubits (which can be 1 and 0 at the same time) versus bits, the complexity and intelligence behind its systems will enable quantum algorithms to solve problems far too complex to be solved today. Its latest system, scheduled for release in 2020, is its D-Wave 5000-qubit quantum computer, which will utilize a 5000-qubit quantum processor, fuelled by its new-chip topology technology that has been branded as "Pegasus." The company has also expanded into related cloud services, enabling developers to develop and run open-source applications on its quantum computers. Part of this expanded service includes the ability of companies to purchase processing time directly through D-Wave, thereby enabling these institutions to crunch through large masses of information and complex calculations absent of the major investment required to purchase complete systems on their own. For D-Wave, the evolution of its service support, coupled with its industry-leading technology, has enabled the company to deliver what it believes is the most connected commercial quantum system in the world.

Although quantum computing is still regarded as being in its introductory phase, the potential for quantum computing offers considerable opportunity. As of this writing, D-Wave has installed more than $50 million worth of quantum systems at customer sites, and its client list includes such world-class companies as NASA, Lockheed Martin, Google, Los Alamos National Laboratory, and the Oak Ridge National Laboratory, to name a few. The company has been granted over 160 patents and has published over 100 peer-review papers in leading scientific journals.

Used by permission of D-Wave Systems Inc.

Although work still needs to be done to fully bring quantum computing into the broader business market, the potential benefits of this emerging technology are enormous. The optimization problem approach of quantum computing enables problem solvers to bring into the equation numerous domains relating to the decision-making process at levels not seen before. This should enable users to reduce costs, save time, accelerate innovation, and realize better decisions. Areas from which significant benefits could be derived include transportation modelling, air traffic control, communication systems, healthcare diagnostics, and creating and testing scientific hypotheses. Early applications associated with quantum applications include machine learning, pattern recognition, cyber security, image analysis, financial analysis, bioinformatics relating to cancer research, traffic flow, manufacturing processes, and Internet marketing.

The D-Wave mission is to unlock the power of quantum computing to solve the world's most challenging problems. Specific areas of focus relating to this mission lie in the fields of science, engineering, modelling and simulation, health care, financial analysis, logistics, and national defence. Investors backing D-Wave include (but are not limited to) such well-known venture capital organizations and start-up support organizations as Kensington Capital Partners, PSP Investments, GrowthWorks, In-Q-Tel, Goldman Sachs, Bezos Expeditions, and BDC.

Web Integration

To learn more about D-Wave Systems Inc., visit their Web site at **www.dwavesys.com**.

Segmentation and Target Marketing

LO4

Successful companies recognize that they cannot be all things to all people. Attempting to provide a standardized product to the entire marketplace often results in failing to meet the needs and expectations of customers seeking a specific value or benefit from a product or service. To avoid taking this average approach to the market, successful marketers focus on trying to identify particular segments within the market and then delivering products/services specifically aligned with meeting the needs of customers within these segments. For example, as part of its initial launch strategy Porter Airlines focused on meeting the needs of business passengers travelling into and out of Toronto, considered by many to be the commercial capital of Canada. Porter Airlines intentionally based itself at Billy Bishop Toronto City Airport, located approximately five minutes from Bay Street and downtown Toronto. Given this close proximity, business travellers could leave the downtown core and be on board their flights, initially to Ottawa and Montreal, in less than 45 minutes. Expansion further extended Porter's reach to include New York, Boston, Washington, D.C., and Chicago, along with the majority of central and eastern Canadian business cities such as Quebec City, Halifax, Thunder Bay, Moncton, Windsor, and St. John's. Porter also chose to fly Bombardier-built Q400 turboprops fitted with leather seats and extra leg room, and offered free wine and snacks on board, again delivering meaningful additional benefits to its targeted market segment. The company also owns the terminal at Billy Bishop Toronto City Airport as well as a majority of the landing and gate slots, thereby creating initial barriers of entry to its competitors Air Canada and WestJet, both which at the time serviced the downtown core via Pearson International Airport (Air Canada now flies out of Billy Bishop as well), located a significant distance away and considered by many business travellers to be far less convenient.[3]

Marketing Research: A First Step in the Segmentation Process

As noted above, a core ingredient for success in business is to understand the needs of our current and potential customers and then to deliver on these needs in a manner that is superior to our competitors. Critical to this is the development and utilization of marketing research in determining how best to respond to the needs of a targeted market segment. The concept of market segmentation recognizes that "one size does not fit all." This means that we need to define the best way to segment the market, and determine how this **segmentation** will result in an improved

Segmentation refers to determining the best way to divide the market in a manner that will result in a better understanding of potential customer needs, interests, preferences, attitudes, and behaviours.

probability that we can be successful in targeting a given segment and marketing our products and/or services to these potential customers.

> The concept of market segmentation recognizes that "one size does not fit all."

The development of marketing research information that we can use in determining which segments to target can be thought of as coming from two sources:

1 Primary sources; and

2 Secondary sources.

Primary Sources of Information are those that an organization develops or utilizes to generate information specific to the organization and the products and services it offers.

Primary sources of information are those that an organization develops and/or utilizes to generate information specific to the organization and the products and services it offers. Examples of primary sources of information are customer surveys; customer input via social media sites such as Facebook, tweets from Twitter users, and company Web sites; focus groups that we establish to test and/or obtain comments on existing products and services or new product concepts; formal test marketing initiatives; and behavioural observations. As an example, a manufacturer of ice cream may use a focus group to taste and rate new flavours prior to launching these flavours into the marketplace. McDonald's may choose to test new menu items in a limited geographic area to determine overall customer acceptance and to receive feedback with respect to taste and quality. Organizations, more and more, are using Facebook and other social media to gather customer information relating to the market segments they are pursuing. Whereas focus groups may provide organizations with a better understanding of the value of their product or service, the sample size is quite small. Social media networks enable marketers to monitor comments, opinions, and results from a much larger sample. These sites also enable marketers to get a much earlier and stronger sense of trends occurring in the marketplace. Reviewer blogs provide information on the strengths and weaknesses of product releases. Behavioural and attitudinal trends can also be monitored and better understood as a result of assessing the commentary and "chat" occurring among specific demographic groups.

Secondary Sources of Information are those that already exist and are available at no cost or on a fee basis; managers use these information sources to conduct research and draw conclusions.

Secondary sources of information are those that already exist and are available at no cost or on a fee basis; managers use these information sources to conduct research and draw conclusions. Examples of secondary information would be researching the Statistics Canada Web site to gather demographic information (age, gender, family, income, households) about a particular geographic area; reviewing various media options to better understand current and forward-occurring social and cultural trends; accessing Conference Board of Canada information relating to national economic trends; conducting generic information searches via Google or Bing; undertaking information searches of competitors via company Web sites, annual reports, or third-party commentary; and evaluating product test results from third-party testing organizations (Consumer Reports, CNET, etc.) and blogs of identified experts in a particular field.

In tying marketing research to segmentation, marketers and managers will strive to create a profile of the customers within the various segments identified within a market. This profile is often developed around a combination of four core characteristics:

1 Demographics—age, gender, income

2 Geographic clustering—location, reach

3 Psychographics—lifestyle, status, ego, emotion, tastes, trends

4 Behavioural—use, buying patterns

FIGURE 10.6   **Segmentation**

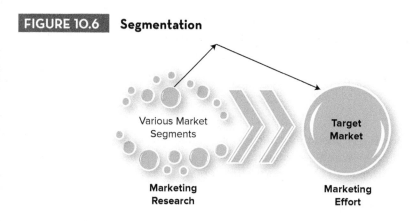

This information is then used to help determine which segments to target and in the facilitation of the response to three fundamental questions that will, ultimately, drive the marketing effort (see Figure 10.6):

1 What are the key decision criteria that potential and/or existing customers use in determining which product(s)/service(s) they will buy?

2 What is the priority or ranking of these criteria? Is there any one criterion that will predominantly influence the purchase decision?

3 How can we best position our product/service offering to align most closely to meeting these key decision criteria used by our sought-after customer base when measured against our competitors?

Transitioning Segmentation Analysis to Target Marketing

Utilizing marketing research to assist in better understanding the marketplace and how it is segmented enables marketers and managers to determine which segments are the most attractive recipients to the marketing message that the organization intends to convey and, ultimately, those prospective customers that represent the highest probability of buyers for the products and/or services being offered. This evolution from market assessment to target marketing forms the front end of what is called the marketing process (see Figure 10.7).

FIGURE 10.7   **The Marketing Process**

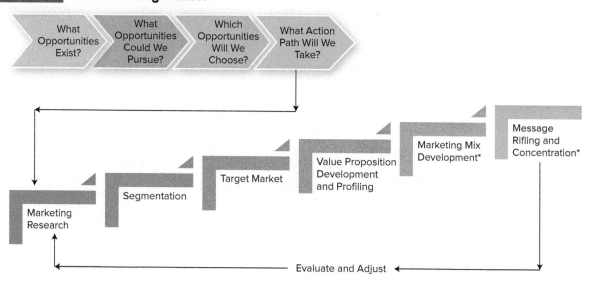

*Marketing Mix Development and Message Rifling and Concentration are covered in Chapter 11.

Utilizing marketing research to assist in better understanding the marketplace and how it is segmented enables marketers and managers to determine which segments are the most attractive recipients to the marketing message that the organization intends to convey.

Target Marketing is the process whereby organizations determine which market segments represent the strongest clustering of potential customers who are most likely to purchase the product and who have the capacity to do so.

Target marketing is leveraging the information acquired during the research and segmentation process and determining which market segment(s) the organization feels is/are its primary or best opportunity for penetration and sales success. By defining target market segments, the organization can develop its value proposition around those decision criteria that the customer values the most, thereby tailoring the product and/or service offering to best meet the needs of the target market identified and the customer profile created. Target marketing also recognizes that although a large portion of the market may be aware of our product and/or service offering, the ability, desire, or willingness to purchase it may lie with a much smaller percentage of the market. Target marketing enables organizations to focus on those potential customers who are most likely to purchase the product and who have the capacity to do so. This enables these organizations to concentrate their marketing resources on reaching these customers and tailoring their marketing message in a manner that presents their product and/or service offerings as the best solution to the potential customers' needs (see Figure 10.8).

An easy way to think about segmentation and target marketing is that segmentation determines the level of need that various clusters within the marketplace have with respect to a problem they face, and their viewing of an organization's product/service as a solution to this need (see Figure 10.9). By "need," we mean the overall desire to solve a problem and satisfy a want. Target marketing then looks at the segments exhibiting the greatest need (desire to solve the problem or satisfy the need), and looks to identify those segments with the greatest willingness to pay for the solution to the need—or, in other words, purchase the product or service. Marketing research will assist us in understanding what the "need" is. Segmentation defines the level of need, and target marketing defines those who will pay for the need. As marketers, understanding what the need is, who has it the most, and who is most willing to pay for it enables us to develop a value proposition that is tailored to offer our product and/or service as the best solution. This then enables us to create a communication message, which is rifled directly at the customer's reason for the need, along with the development and execution of a marketing mix strategy, thereby aligning our product/service as the ideal solution. The remainder of this chapter

FIGURE 10.8   **Segmentation Analysis to Target Market**

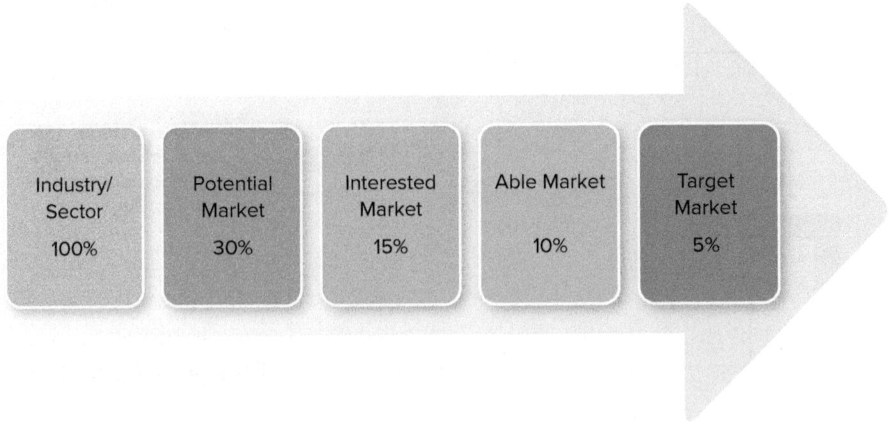

Industry/ Sector	Potential Market	Interested Market	Able Market	Target Market
100%	30%	15%	10%	5%

FIGURE 10.9   **"Need to Pay for the Solution to the Need" Approach**

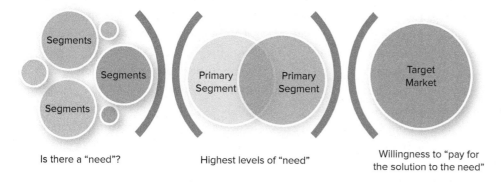

Is there a "need"?   Highest levels of "need"   Willingness to "pay for the solution to the need"

focuses on the additional tools needed to leverage the "pay for the solution to the need" process, with Chapter 11 focusing on communication message rifling and the marketing mix development and execution.

Business IN ACTION

3M Company

Ever wonder where the Post-it Note came from? It is just one of the many innovative products developed and marketed by 3M Company (Minnesota Mining and Manufacturing Co.). With more than 55 000 products offered to the marketplace, 3M seems to be everywhere. Scotch Tape—it's a 3M product. Thinsulate insulation—made by 3M. Ace bandages—again, 3M. Your iPhone—some of its components are made by 3M. Sandpaper—you guessed it: a 3M innovation. In fact, you can find 3M products embedded in a number of products found in automobiles, hospitals, offices, and your home. The company releases an average of 1000 new products per year. Revenue in 2018 was US$32.8 billion, of which approximately one-third of it came from new product modifications and new products for new or existing markets. In 2018, 3M was listed as #97 on the *Fortune* 500 list of the largest companies in the United States.

Established in 1902, 3M has evolved around a business model focused on innovation and new product development. For 3M, a key fundamental performance metric is to have at least 30% of its revenue produced by new products launched within the last five years. To achieve such performance benchmarks, 3M needs to have a continuous flow of new

Bloomberg via Getty Images

products in its development pipeline. This requires a culture of innovation and an R&D budget to support it. 3M does just that. In 2018, approximately 8100 members (9%) of its workforce were focused on R&D, where the company spent more than $1.8 billion on R&D (approx. 5.8% of sales) and estimates the generation of more than 3000 patents. Critical to this emphasis on new product development and R&D results is the allowance of its R&D scientists to use 15% of their time to pursue ideas on their own. The results are new and innovative ideas spread across such business areas as infection prevention, abrasives, adhesives, and imaging.

3M technology is behind what enables us to have brighter traffic signs, better-gripping golf gloves, and micro-needles that could soon replace hypodermics, thereby lessening the pain associated with the delivery of medicines. At 3M, it is not so much about creating the "next big thing," but about creating hundreds and hundreds of solutions per year to the little things that its customers need and value. A key aspect of this development is the need to effectively market these products through its sales and distribution channels. This requires a significant and well-executed marketing effort. Backed by its strong brand recognition, 3M works closely with its customers to identify new product opportunities in its existing core businesses. It also means exploring new business opportunities in areas such as renewable energy, water infrastructure, and mobile digital media, to name a few. 2019 is a benchmark year for the company in that all new product introductions must comply with its new Sustainability Value Commitment. This commitment focuses on reusability, recyclability, energy, waste, water savings, responsible sourcing, and the corresponding need to improve air quality, reduce greenhouse gas emissions, and improve worker and healthcare patient safety. The company has also received a variety of awards relating to employee satisfaction in the U.S. and Canada, establishing itself as one of the best companies to work for in North America.

Web Integration

Want to learn more about 3M Company and its strategy and marketing focus for the future? Visit **www.3m.com**.

Business IN ACTION

Loblaw Companies Limited—Repositioning Its Brand

For almost 100 years, Loblaw Companies Limited has been an iconic player in the Canadian grocery sector. Not generally immediately thought of as an innovator, and operating in what many consider to be a slow-cycle industry (groceries), Loblaw Companies Limited continues to surprise and transform itself. In doing so, the company has demonstrated that even well-established brands in mature industries can continue to prosper and that innovation is not simply the domain of high-tech start-ups.

Over the past few decades Loblaw Companies Limited, under the umbrella of parent company George Weston Limited, has demonstrated a continual emphasis on reinventing where, and how, it does business. The company's President's Choice brand is a leader in in-house (private) label marketing. Its Joe Fresh line, launched in 2006, demonstrated that grocery operations can successfully expand beyond the

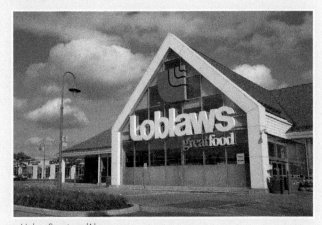
© Helen Sessions/Alamy

product line constraints of food and beverages. Its acquisition of Shoppers Drug Mart in 2013 effectively combined Canada's largest grocery store with the country's #1 pharmacy operation, thereby expanding its grocery, health, and beauty products, and especially its PC brand, immediately to an additional 1200-plus store locations, many of which are already located in every major centre across Canada.

So what is next for Loblaw Companies Limited? With its national reach firmly in place, one of the company's next moves is to further elevate the PC brand in the eyes of consumers. For Loblaw this is all about shifting from a product-focused brand to that of a lifestyle brand. Much in the way that Tim Hortons has been successful in creating an emotional tie between its brand and Canadians, Loblaw hopes to do the same thing with its President's Choice brand and with the perceptions Canadians have with respect to Loblaw. To do this the company will shift its advertising focus from marketing products to content marketing that focuses more on storytelling and connecting the brand to the mainstream "foodie culture." A major focus of this rebranding will be using social media and analytics in a way in which Loblaw Companies Limited is able to predict trends occurring within the food sector, both nationally and regionally, and assist customers in participating in such trends through the use of Loblaw products and services. Pursuant to this, Loblaw spent 2018 building out its digital marketing strategy, investing in technology that it states will improve customer adoption and overall customer satisfaction. A good example of this execution lies in the development and roll-out of its PC Express "click and collect" pick-up service. The program is now available in over 670 Loblaw, Shoppers Drug Mart, and GO transit locations. Loblaw's has indicated that the service is only 10 minutes away from an estimated 75% of Canadians. The integration of the PC Optimum rewards program across its banners (Loblaw, Shoppers Drug Mart, Provigo, Atlantic Superstores, Maxi, No-Frills, etc.), along with expanding the program beyond Loblaw companies (e.g., Esso), has also been fundamental to its rebranding shift, and has enabled Loblaw to data-mine the

© Steve Leonard

purchase and behaviour patterns of over 18 million members. 2019 marks the launch of its app, which the company hopes will enable it to further connect with members, providing online deals to food, apparel, and beauty items, thereby delivering additional value and drawing additional traffic to its banners.

Loblaw also understands that food in Canada is experiencing a renaissance, with Canadians becoming much more food savvy and desiring more information and insight than ever before into where their food is coming from. In recognition of this, Loblaw is purposely positioning itself as a company best able to respond to and support this trend. For example, the company has partnered with Google Inc. to build a "food pulse index" that will track online conversations about food and publish and update the results on a regular basis. Such trends will then translate into new product development and integration into its operations.

With the marketplace becoming more competitive than ever, Loblaw knows that it needs to be better at anticipating and meeting the needs of customers than ever before. By creating this higher level of closeness to its customers through conversing with them about what they want, versus telling them what to buy, Loblaw hopes to create a unique bond with customers that will ensure the company's products and services meet their expectations both today and beyond.

Marketing's Challenge   LO5, LO6

As indicated in Figure 10.2, marketers within an organization must respond to six core challenges. Within each of these challenges is a multitude of tasks that, if executed properly, will lead to the effective positioning of the product in those market

FIGURE 10.10   **Marketing Challenge: Need Identification**

segments the organization intends to serve. With a base-level understanding of positioning, segmentation, and target marketing in place, let's now begin the process of assessing these challenges in more detail.

Need Identification

Need identification focuses on assessing opportunities that exist within the marketplace for our current and potential (soon-to-be-launched) products and/or services. It means attempting to identify untapped or unmet needs within the marketplace and leveraging our R&D capabilities to develop products and/or services that will meet such needs. It also means looking at our current portfolio of products and/or services and deciding where opportunities exist that will enable us to maximize their revenue and profitability potential (via the product/opportunity matrix). Finally, need identification considers whether our emphasis should be on new customer acquisition, further leveraging relationships with existing customers, or a combination of the two (see Figure 10.10).

When we think about need identification, we can assess the marketplace we are reviewing in two fundamental ways:

1. Where do opportunities exist?

2. What market dynamics present themselves in the segments we are considering?

Seeking out opportunities that enhance the success of the products/services we offer or that identify untapped needs in various market segments furthers the achievement of the organization's overall strategy and is a fundamental role of marketing. As managers, we need to recognize that such opportunities can come from a variety of sources. To assist managers in analyzing the various potential options for further revenue and profitability growth, Igor Ansoff developed a growth strategy opportunity identification model called the Ansoff matrix. This matrix is more widely known today as the product/opportunity matrix (see Figure 10.11). Within this matrix, Ansoff suggests that managers should focus their analytical review in four areas when assessing market opportunity:[4]

1. Market penetration opportunities

2. Product/service development opportunities

3. Market development opportunities

4. Diversification opportunities

FIGURE 10.11   **Ansoff Matrix (Product/Opportunity Matrix)**

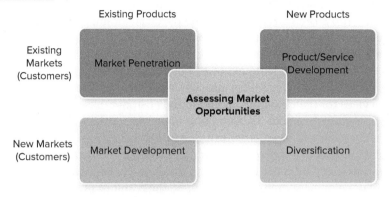

Source: Ansoff Matrix, QuickMBA Strategic Management, www.quickmba.com/strategy/matrix/ansoff, July 2010; www.ansoffmatrix.com; www.vectorstrategy.com.

Market penetration opportunities focus a manager's attention on growing the sales revenue of the organization's existing products through its existing customer base. This means seeking ways to (a) get its existing customers to purchase the organization's products/services more frequently, or (b) increase the average transaction revenue per purchase at the time when these customers are buying. For example, according to past comments by Canadian Tire, more than 50% of Canadians shop at Canadian Tire at least once per month, while 40% shop there once per week. Statistics Canada's estimated population of Canada in 2019 was 37.4 million. Assuming this is still the case,[5] this means that an estimated 18.7 million Canadians shop at Canadian Tire once per month, and that 14.9 million Canadians shop at Canadian Tire once per week.[6] Assuming that when they visit Canadian Tire Canadians spend an average $20 per visit, Canadian Tire can potentially increase its annual retail sales by an estimated $3.84 billion if it can get the additional 10% (50% – 40%) of these Canadians who shop at Canadian Tire once per month (3.74 million) to shop there once per week. Likewise, if Canadian Tire can improve its average transaction revenue per customer (basket size) from $20 to $25 across the 40% of Canadians who shop there weekly (14.9 million), then Canadian Tire could increase its revenue by an estimated $3.87 billion. Market penetration opportunities are all about trying to increase one's market share from an existing market and/or driving a greater "share of wallet" of existing customers each time they spend. To be successful with such strategies, an organization's marketing team must develop ways that will stimulate the additional frequency of purchase (and/or repurchase) or provide incentives for customers to increase the share of wallet they are willing to spend with the organization. Incentives to encourage customers to purchase larger quantities of a product, trade discounts to acquire premium shelf space in order to make products more visible, advertising initiatives focused on stimulating renewed product/service interest, and rebates, coupons, and other sales stimulation initiatives are just some of the many weapons that organizations will use to create additional demand for their products and services.

New product and/or service opportunities focus a management team on identifying and developing new products/services for the existing markets within which it competes, and/or the existing customer base that it serves. For example, a retail operation that sells gas fireplaces makes a decision to develop an annual preventive maintenance program for the fireplaces it has sold, and looks to sell this additional service to its existing customer base. Businesses such as Best Buy and Staples develop and sell to their customers extended warranty programs designed to cover the various electronic products these customers purchase. Walmart, recognizing an opportunity to better serve its existing market and customer base, shifts to a Supercentre format that results in Walmart adding a fully integrated grocery store operation into its retail concept. A potato chip manufacturer decides to make a bean dip under its own brand name and market this in conjunction with its chips. Apple Inc. created its iTunes and App Store sites to support the purchase of music and applications by users of its iPad and iPhone products. Its product portfolio has been further expanded via its creation of new products/services such as Apple Pay and Apple Card. For many companies, a critical part of the ongoing marketing and organizational strategy process is their investments into R&D for the purpose of creating new products and services for their existing and potential customer base. This chapter's Business in Action vignette about 3M Company underscores the value of new product and service development to an organization's long-term success.

Market development opportunities focus a management team on identifying and cultivating new customers for the existing products an organization currently offers. Market development opportunities can be the result of product line extensions of existing products designed to capture new customers via **segmentation stretch**, or simply finding new uses for existing products that attract previously uninterested customers to purchase an organization's existing product. General Mills saw the potential for additional sales of its Cheerios cereal to additional similar but different market segments by adding variations of the original Cheerios product offering. Confident in its brand name and in its ability to retain existing Cheerios customers, General Mills has repositioned Cheerios toward that of a more health-focused cereal (whole-grain oats, lowers cholesterol), and introduced additional brand extensions such as Multi-Grain Cheerios, Banana-Nut Cheerios, Yogurt Burst Cheerios, and Berry Burst Cheerios. In initiating brand and/or product extension strategies to stretch a product/service offering across wider market segments, managers need to consider two key points. The first has to do with **cannibalism**. Managers need to determine whether any sales volume erosion has occurred to the existing product/service offering, and, if so, whether this volume decrease is offset by the newly launched extended brand's sales gains. The marketing team also has to be careful about sending mixed messages when marketing a similar product toward similar but distinct segments (kids, families, adults). Second, when accompanied by a repositioning shift, marketing managers need to ensure that **customer desertion** to a competitive offering does not occur due to the change in brand or product communication message focus. In addition to stretching a product's reach through brand extension strategies, marketing managers can also seek to uncover new uses for existing products and services. The ability to successfully transition a product toward multiple uses can open new significant sales opportunities for products/services. Arm & Hammer Baking Soda, a product produced by Church & Dwight Co. Inc., has recognized considerable revenue growth due to the many additional uses for this product beyond simply baking. As far back as 1927, Church & Dwight began communicating the personal healthcare potential of Arm & Hammer Baking Soda for bath, body, and teeth. As a result of the tremendous success of its "baking soda in the refrigerator and the freezer" campaign, 1972 marked a significant shift in the way that baking soda was perceived by both customers and the company. This new view of the various solutions that baking soda offered to cleaning and maintenance problems within the household produced a variety of market opportunity spin-offs. Utilizing a brand extension strategy, Church & Dwight has broadened Arm & Hammer Baking Soda's positioning around that of an economical, gentle, and environmentally safe cleaning, deodorizing, and medicinal product.

Segmentation Stretch refers to expanding the focus of a product/service to similar and related market segments that share a positive affinity for the product/service offering.

Cannibalism is the reduction in sales of an existing product/service due to the launch of a new, similarly targeted product/service offering.

Customer Desertion occurs when customers move to a competitive offering due to a change in brand or product communication message focus.

Web Integration

To view a historical timeline of the evolution of this popular product's market development strategy, visit **https://www.armandhammer .com/about-us.**

Diversification opportunities focus managers on assessing opportunities that lie outside the organization's current products and/or services, and represent the creation or development of new markets served by new products/services. In many cases, diversification opportunities represent new business initiatives by an organization. Diversification could be the result of natural organic growth by the organization, or could be due to an acquisition. Diversification opportunities could be in related or unrelated areas of current market and business expertise. Apple's original business premise was focused on manufacturing and marketing computers. Apple has since diversified, organically, into the music distribution industry and into the smartphone industry as a catalyst for further growing the organization. Spotify, predominantly known as a music streaming business, acquired two companies in 2019, Gimlet Media and Anchor, as catalyst for moving it beyond music and into the audio-related podcast market.[7] Facebook has embarked on a significant acquisition strategy in order to gain access to a variety of technologies relating to social media and networking and mobile applications—all markets that the organization sees as critical to its long-term growth strategy. Instagram, WhatsApp, and Oculus VR are examples of recent acquisitions designed to provide Facebook with access to the technological expertise and products/services needed to continue to expand its reach in the rapidly growing social network market.[8] The Tata Group of Companies (India) is one of the most widely diversified organizations in the world. Tata has business operations spanning seven different market sectors: information technology and communications, engineering products and services, materials (steel and composites), services (hospitality, real estate, financial, insurance), energy (oil and gas), consumer products (watches, jewellery, automobiles), and chemicals (pharmaceuticals, fertilizers).[9]

Utilizing Ansoff's matrix is just one of a number of interrelated steps in determining what and where opportunities exist in the marketplace and which ones are best to explore and pursue. Additional key steps involve conducting marketing research to identify the fit between potential market needs and the products and/or services that we intend to offer, determining whether this identified opportunity is substantial enough to meet financial and market share performance expectations and current and anticipated competitive activity in the targeted segment, and assessing the resource and capability requirements needed to effectively deliver on the identified opportunity.

 Business IN ACTION

Vector Media

Located in Ottawa, Vector Media is one of Canada's leading independent media planning and buying agencies. Offering a wide range of services to its clients, Vector Media excels in the areas of paid media strategy development and execution. The company also offers its clients ongoing services and insight relating to an increasingly complex media landscape that not only covers the traditional media options, but also looks to leverage, on behalf of clients, the rapidly changing and expanding digital marketplace.

Guided by two fundamental principles—1) you don't have to be big to be good, and 2) media is the new

Used by permission of Vector Media

creative—Vector Media and its partner organization The Marketing Works have been serving national, regional, and local clients for over 20 years. A key area of specialization for this organization lies with clients who provide services and experiences that are large-ly intangible in nature. This requires Vector Media to craft media strategies that are focused more on the experience than a specific product. The company excels in both business-to-business and business-to-consumer categories. Current and recent clients, to name a few, include Export Development Canada, Canadian Association of Petroleum Producers, Lone Star Group of Restaurants, Canadian Arthritis Society, Canadian Internet Registration Authority, and Brookfield Renewable Energy. The company also specializes in programmatic media buying, which is the automation of digital media buying on industry-defined platforms (displays, video, mobile, etc.) that integrates real-time ad performance with consumer digital behaviour data in order to deliver the right message, at the right time, and in the right place.

As an advertising consultancy and agency, Vector Media's approach is to assist its clients in using paid media as a strategic tool for building brand awareness, and realizing a strong return on invest-ment for the media spends incurred. The company also assists organizations with in-house marketing and media units to plan and execute social media campaigns, as well as manage the transactional side of media activities that have been selected in pursuit of a client's specific marketing objec-tives. The company's "sweet spot" for success, so to speak, lies in serving clients who are not big enough to warrant the serious attention from the big multinational advertising agencies, but whose needs and required levels of experience lie beyond their in-house units, or local agencies with limited range and depth.

Web Integration

Want to learn more about Vector Media and tap into their marketing blogs? Visit their Web site at **www.vecmedia.com**.

Understanding the Consumer Decision-Making Process

As stated above, a critical aspect of marketing is the identification of needs that ex-ist in the marketplace to which an organization can respond. Equally important, however, is ensuring that we understand why potential customers purchase a par-ticular product and/or service, and how they determine, out of a number of competi-tive offerings, which product/service to buy. Significant marketing effort is allocated to understanding this critical question of why and how people buy.

> A critical aspect of marketing is the identification of needs that exist in the marketplace to which an organization can respond.

The buying process[10] In making a decision to buy, potential customers will fundamentally go through a four-phase process (see Figure 10.12). The length of time spent within each stage of this decision-making process will be dependent upon the potential customers' familiarity with the product/service, the various alternatives offered in the marketplace, whether it is a first-time purchase or a repeat purchase, and the level of financial commitment associated with the transaction.

For marketers, a key fundamental requirement in developing the marketing strategy for an organization's products/services is to devise the positioning

FIGURE 10.12   **Consumer Decision-Making Process**

strategy and marketing mix tactics (discussed in detail in Chapter 12) that will enable its products/services to occupy the dominant position in the minds of potential customers as they enter into, and transition through, this decision-making process. As marketers, our goals with respect to this decision-making process are the following:

- Be at the top of the potential customer's purchase list as they enter into the decision-making process, and reinforce and support the purchase of our product as the potential customer transitions to the point of purchase.

- If we are not at the top of the potential customer's purchase list during the initial consideration of purchase alternatives, then our goal is to disrupt the potential customer's predetermined list of viable purchase alternatives in a way that creates awareness and preference for our products and/or services.

- Assuming that we have won the battle for the initial purchase, reinforce and support the customer in a way that encourages them to develop a loyalty and commitment to our product, thereby making future purchases almost automatic with little consideration of alternative products and/or services being offered by our competitors.

Figure 10.13 provides an illustration of the influence and impact associated with this decision-making process with respect to the three goals identified above. It illustrates a situation where the potential customer is looking to make an initial purchase of a product and/or service, or is making a repurchase where no loyalty has been generated to a previously purchased product and/or service. As such, the potential customer is open to considering, or can be influenced to consider, alternatives available in the marketplace. As marketers, this non-loyal situation means that we (as well as our competitors) have the opportunity to disrupt the potential customer's predetermined purchase choice at several key points in the decision-making process (noted by the starbursts). We can disrupt this process and, ideally, influence the potential customer to purchase our product and/or service through the use of a number of different marketing tools.

FIGURE 10.13   **Consumer Decision-Making Process: The Marketer's Goals**

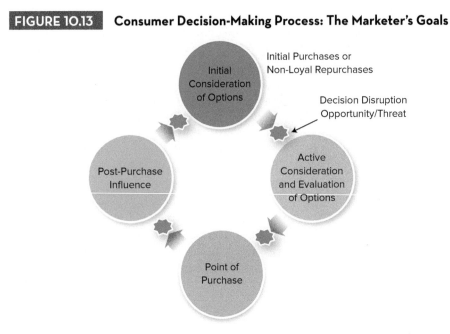

Examples of these tools, which can be referred to as the marketer's tool box, are as follows (see Figure 10.14):

- Company-driven marketing techniques
- Consumer-driven marketing techniques
- Channel support and interaction techniques

Let's use an example to illustrate the way that marketing works to influence the customer decision-making process. Assume you are in the market to purchase a new digital camera; the question you face involves which brand to purchase. Your initial thought is to consider a Canon camera, because your current, although somewhat dated, camera is a Canon. Recent advertisements, however, have led you to consider stepping up to a DSLR camera versus a simple "point-and-shoot" digital camera. The Canon EOS 80D immediately comes to mind. However, you have also taken note of recent advertisements for Nikon and Olympus cameras, brands you also have heard

FIGURE 10.14   **Marketer's Tool Box**

Category	Tools of the Trade
Company-Driven Marketing Techniques (Digital and Traditional)	Advertising Sales Promotion Publicity Point of Purchase Displays Dedicated Sales Force
Consumer-Driven Marketing Techniques	Internet Searches Product Reviews Peer Recommendations Analysts' Blogs and Vlogs Social Media Web Sites and Commentary
Channel Support and Interaction Techniques	Dealer Incentives Point-of-Purchase Discounts Channel Member Training Exclusivity Arrangements Salesperson Recommendations

good things about. Jumping onto various Web sites and reading a number of product reviews and "best buy" lists expands your options to include cameras by Fuji, Panasonic, Sony, and Casio (a brand you initially did not consider). A good friend of your parents owns the Canon EOS 80D and reminds you of the need to purchase additional lenses depending on the type of pictures you want to take. Although the EOS 80D takes great pictures and is a definite step up over regular digital cameras, the initial price point and the need to purchase supplemental lenses leads you back to considering point-and-shoot digital cameras. With this in mind, this same friend makes you aware of the Canon PowerShot SX730 HS, which has 40× optical zoom capabilities and is highly regarded by industry bloggers and "best pick" reviewers. Armed with this information, and desiring the extended zoom option, you revisit the Internet, seek ideas and comments through Facebook, and reduce your potential purchase list to four cameras: the Canon PowerShot SX730 HS, the Sony Cyber-shot WX220, the Panasonic Lumix ZS70, and the Olympus TG-5. Now, where do you buy the camera? You decide to visit Best Buy, Staples, Costco, and Henry's to gather more information, as well as revisiting Amazon.ca to further check out reviews and compare prices. At Best Buy, the sales representative provides additional information on each camera and also informs you that Canon currently has a special promotion that allows you to trade in your current Canon camera to receive a discount on the purchase price of the Canon PowerShot SX730 HS. Reinforced by the sales representative that the camera is an excellent option, you decide to purchase the Canon PowerShot SX730 HS. The familiarity of the brand, your prior experience with a Canon product, confirmation by reviews that it is a solid performer, and the trade-in discount promotion led you to this conclusion.*

In addition to illustrating the various influences that will occur throughout this decision-making process, there is another key point associated with marketing: the need to effectively manage and positively reinforce the post-purchase phase of the decision-making process. Effective marketing does not end at the point of purchase. Considerable emphasis is placed on the post-purchase period, which is where true customer loyalty and commitment is developed. This is important for three reasons:

1 Customers need immediate and ongoing reinforcement that the purchase they made was the right one. Reinforcing the purchase decision, particularly decisions that require a significant financial commitment, is fundamental to developing customer loyalty and commitment.

2 For many purchases, particularly business-based purchases, ongoing servicing and training may be core aspects of the buying decision. The quality of such support services is, in many cases, as important as the initial purchase.

3 Satisfied customers tell others about the quality of the products and services that they purchase and use. Active referrals from current customers assist us in broadening our customer base.

> Marketing does not end at the point of purchase. Considerable emphasis needs to be placed on the post-purchase period, which is where true customer loyalty and commitment is developed.

As marketers, we need to realize that having current customers repurchase our products/services is fundamental to building the scale we need in order to sustain our organization. It is critical to develop within our customer base a level of loyalty and commitment

---

*The choice of the Canon PowerShot SX730 HS as the product to be purchased is for illustration purposes only. The author is not stating that this brand and model is superior to any of the other brands and models mentioned.

FIGURE 10.15   **Consumer Decision-Making Process: Maximum Customer Loyalty**

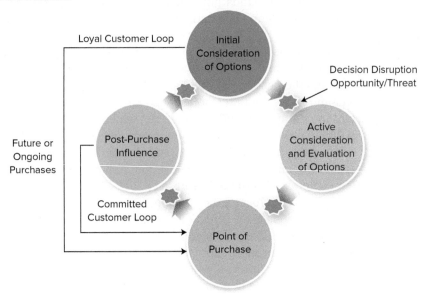

to our products/services that moves our customers to skip the initial stages of the customer decision-making process at the time of repurchase and go directly to the "purchase" phase, repurchasing our product/service without considering other competitive alternatives. Figure 10.15 illustrates this ideal position of maximum customer loyalty.

For marketers, the challenge is a continuous need to reinforce and reward our existing customers, thereby minimizing customer desertion (customers leaving us) while attempting to continually attract new customers in order to further grow our customer base (see Figure 10.16). Growing the company is all about reinforcing to our current customers that we offer the best value proposition in the marketplace, while attempting to disrupt the purchase patterns of potential customers by getting them to actively consider our products and/or services as viable options and, ultimately, purchase them to meet their needs or solve their problems. To effectively accomplish this, we need to understand which market segments are closely aligned to having their needs solved by our products/services, and target those with the ability to transition their "need" into "paying for the solution to the need." Then, in understanding their decision-making process, we must best position our value proposition in a way that results in the purchase of our products/services instead of competitive offerings.

FIGURE 10.16   **Growing the Customer Base**

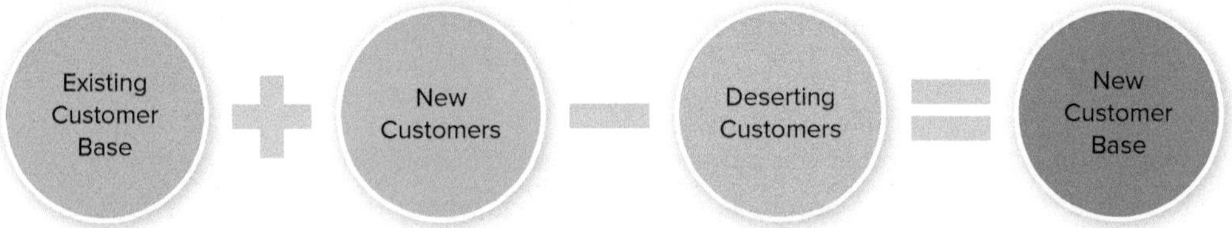

Existing Customer Base **+** New Customers **−** Deserting Customers **=** New Customer Base

Responding to Needs: Value Proposition Development and Communication

The role of marketing, as reinforced throughout this chapter, is to communicate the **value proposition** for an organization's products/services as the "best" solution to the needs of a targeted market of prospective customers (Figure 10.17).

Value Proposition is a statement that summarizes whom a product or service is geared toward and the benefits the purchaser will realize as a result of using the product or service.

FIGURE 10.17 **Value Proposition Composition**

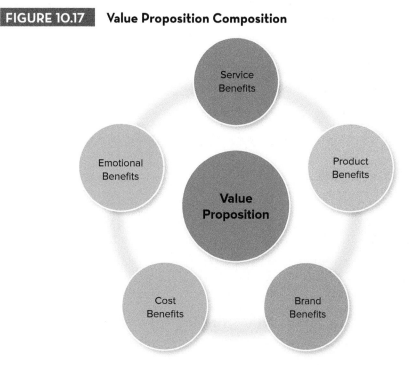

Marketers also look to communicate to the purchaser how the product or service differs from competing products or services offered in the marketplace. For example, suppose you decide to purchase a tablet. The question for you is which product to purchase; the marketplace offers a number of competing choices. You could purchase an Apple iPad Pro or iPad Air, Samsung Galaxy Tab S4, Lenovo Tab 4, Microsoft Surface Pro, Azus ZenPad 3S 10, or one of the models offered by other companies, such as Dell, Google, Huawei, Amazon, HP, etc. Your decision will be influenced by the benefits (real and perceived) the products offer versus the price being charged. Your decision may also be influenced by the nature of the communication message and its overall focus. Again, keep in mind that is important to understand that value propositions are not driven strictly by tangible or functional product benefits. In fact, many of the reasons why products or services are purchased have little to do with the actual product itself, but more with the perceived benefits the product or service offers. The following equation is often used to describe the core elements of a value proposition.

Value Proposition =

Service Benefits + Product Benefits + Brand Benefits
+ Cost Benefits + Emotional Benefits

Companies develop value propositions for the purpose of communicating to customers how their products/services are different and the important benefits that they offer.

The strength of a particular value proposition is the perceived sum of the company's ability to deliver in each area noted within the value proposition equation versus the strength of its competitors' value proposition equations measured across these same benefit areas. This is then measured against the price being charged for the product, thereby creating a perceived price/quality relationship in the mind of the potential purchaser.

FIGURE 10.18 Price/Quality Relationship

Quality Perception

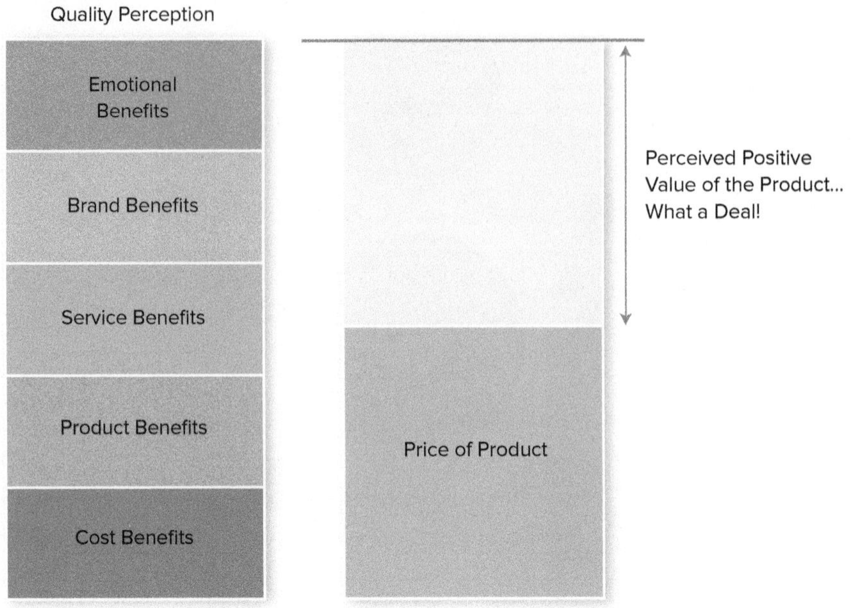

For customers, the end result of this value proposition comparison is the conclusion as to (a) which product/service offerings best meet their needs, and (b) which is the best value for the price paid. Figure 10.18 provides a visual characterization of this price/quality relationship assessment process. For companies, the emphasis is on driving as large a positive gap as possible between the real or perceived benefits a product/service offers versus the price paid. This gap illustrates the strength of the "wow" factor (what a deal!) in the relationship between your product and its price.

Going back to our tablet example, the current market leader in this marketplace is the Apple iPad. Why? Because customers have concluded that the tangible product features (touch screen and other interfaces, video capabilities) along with the brand benefits (Apple's brand strength), the support services (such as iTunes and the App Store), the overall ease of use, and the peer affiliation of owning an iPad make it the preferred choice. Simply stated, for the significant portion of the market segment interested in tablets, Apple's value proposition is deemed to be the best choice for the greatest number of customers.

So how does one go about creating a value proposition statement? Figure 10.19 illustrates the fundamental questions to which a value proposition must respond.[11] Successful value propositions are geared toward highlighting the key decision criteria purchasers believe to be most important, and communicate how the product or service best responds to these needs.

Recognizing that the entire organization needs to deliver on the value proposition, marketing's role is to create and communicate this message to targeted customers and to continuously reinforce the product and/or service offering's ability to deliver on this message. This means that marketers must have a full understanding of who their customers are, why they buy, and how they buy. They also must recognize what aspects of the buying process require the use of which marketing techniques in order to ensure that the value proposition is effectively delivered and that the value message is reinforced. Recent work by McKinsey & Company[12] on the impact of the various tools within the marketer's tool box (Figure 10.14) has shown that the need for effective marketing strategy goes beyond simply a strong company-offered media campaign. The need to respond to consumer-driven marketing techniques and channel support point-of-sale techniques grows in importance the farther the potential customer moves through the decision-making process (see Figure 10.20).

FIGURE 10.19   **Sample Positioning Statement Template**

PART 1 OF THE STATEMENT

For . . . .   (the target market)

Who want . . . .   (the consumer need)

Our products or services are . . . .   (demonstration of the solution)

Which feature . . . .   (key benefits provided)

PART 2 OF THE STATEMENT

Unlike . . . .   (our main competitors)

Our product provides . . . .   (key points of differences)

As supported by . . . .   (what makes our differences possible)

And protected by . . . .   (why the competition cannot easily overcome it)

Source: Courtesy of K. Wong, Queen's University.

FIGURE 10.20   **Impact of Influencers**

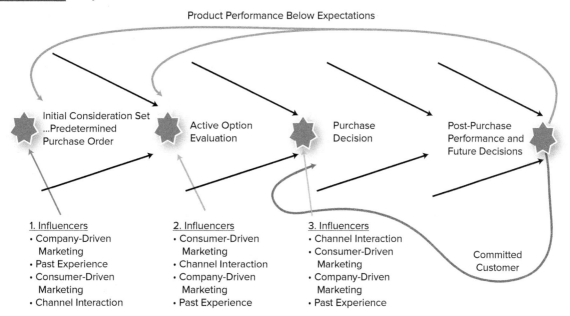

The need to respond to consumer-driven marketing techniques and channel support point-of-sale techniques grows in importance the farther the potential customer moves through the decision-making process.

A Note Pertaining to Not-for-Profits

Just like for-profit entities, not-for-profit organizations need to create and sustain demand for the products and services they offer. Equally important, they must be able to communicate, as core to their marketing process, the value that the mission and vision of the organization has to the community and a broader set of stakeholders. For not-for-profits, this concept of social marketing needs to ensure that the organization becomes fully rooted as a valuable resource to the community it serves, and is seen as a valued benefit in a way that encourages individuals, businesses, and government(s) to support the delivery of such products and services through philanthropy, membership or program fees, or budgetary commitment. The vitality of the not-for-profit organization is predicated on positioning itself as the preferred provider of products and/or services, and in meeting the needs of its user base in a way that generates loyalty, empathy, and commitment to the cause the not-for-profit aspires to respond to. As an example, the Humane Society of Canada works to protect dogs, cats, horses, birds, rabbits and small animals, livestock, lab animals, wildlife, and the environment.[13] Its local community-based affiliates offer services relating to caring for injured, abused, and homeless animals, finding homes for such animals, promoting responsible pet ownership, organizing spay and neuter programs, undertaking emergency animal rescues, and providing education services relating to animal care.[14] To be effective in this work, the Humane Society needs to create a position in the community as the preferred delivery agency for such services, and to create the necessary profile and awareness to generate the dollars needed in the form of fees for services rendered, donations, government support, contractual arrangements, and so on. Not-for-profits, like for-profit entities, need to recognize, as well, that not all individuals, businesses, and organizations will need, appreciate, or respond to their mission and/or vision. The concepts of marketing research, segmentation, and target marketing are equally important to the not-for-profit in determining which services to offer, where and how to deliver such services, and how best to tap into the various private philanthropic, public and private grant, and government funding opportunities vital to their success.

Management Reflection—Back to Strategy

When considering the potential of a market segment, marketing managers need to consider five fundamental factors that Kenneth Wong, a leading marketing strategist at Queen's University in Kingston, Ontario, refers to as the "mission critical factors" associated with marketing strategy. These five factors are outlined in Figure 10.21.

These five critical factors are fundamental to ensuring that the marketing strategy is linked with an organization's overall strategy, vision, and mission. By understanding marketing's role as a key component in our ability to execute strategy, in conducting such an analysis managers can validate that the marketing effort will be aligned with the organization's strategy and that the structure of the organization

FIGURE 10.21   **Market Dynamics: Critical Factors**

- Market Clarity and Stability
- Customer Analysis
- Competitor Analysis
- Competitive Advantage Analysis
- Culture and Business System Analysis

Source: Adapted from Kenneth Wong, Queen's University.

will be appropriately directed to ensure its successful execution. The alignment of marketing's effort to an organization's strategy can be fully assessed through the response to the following questions:

- **Market clarity and stability:** Will things stay right within this market long enough for us to fully implement our intended marketing strategy and achieve our targeted financial goals? Are there external pressures, political influences, industry innovations, or competitive responses that will close the perceived window of opportunity prior to the successful execution of our strategy? Is there clarity and stability in the market segment(s) we intend to pursue?

- **Customer analysis:** Are we marketing our products/services to the right set of customers? In other words, have we identified the primary market segments that have the greatest need and will be receptive to our product/service offerings?

- **Competitor analysis:** Have we analyzed our competitors and their respective positioning strategies? Do we understand and can we anticipate their competitive actions and responses?

- **Competitive advantage analysis:** Have we identified the right competitive advantage around which to position our product? Has this perceived advantage been validated via marketing research and/or some other objective basis?

- **Culture and business system analysis:** Do we have the right culture, capital capacity, and business system to support our intended positioning strategy and marketing effort? Can we deliver on what marketing intends to communicate to the targeted market segment(s) in terms of needs solution, benefits, services, and features?[15]

Chapter Summary

This chapter is designed to familiarize students with the fundamentals needed to develop a marketing strategy for an organization. Critical to this process is recognizing the purpose of marketing and understanding the role it plays in influencing the execution of an organization's corporate and business-level strategy. A major emphasis within this chapter is recognizing the importance of segmentation and target marketing as central to the marketing process. Knowing which segments of the market will be most receptive to the products and services being offered is key to the success of any business. The chapter also attempts to provide students with guidance on where organizations can look for new growth opportunities, and on understanding the customer decision-making process and how this will influence the development of an organization's communication and positioning strategy. A central focus of this discussion is on understanding the components that make up the marketer's tool box, as well as recognizing the importance of how these various marketing elements impact value proposition development. The chapter closes with a discussion relating to positioning not-for-profit organizations, as well as with a "management reflection" that synthesizes the critical factors driving marketing strategy execution. Understanding the five big questions that marketers need to ask when formulating marketing strategy is the key outcome of this closing discussion.

Developing Business Knowledge and Skills

Key Terms

marketing *p. 359*

positioning *p. 362*

segmentation *p. 365*

primary sources of information *p. 366*

secondary sources of information
   p. 366

target marketing *p. 368*

segmentation stretch *p. 374*

cannibalism *p. 374*

customer desertion *p. 374*

value proposition *p. 380*

Questions for Discussion

1. What are the six core challenges that marketers must be able to respond to when assessing the viability or success of a product or service offering? (LO2)

2. What is the importance of positioning with respect to marketing and the development of a marketing strategy? (LO3)

3. What is the difference between segmentation and target marketing? How does marketing research influence this process? (LO4)

4. What are the predominant tools that make up the marketer's tool box? How are these tools used within the consumer decision-making process? (LO5)

5. What constitutes a value proposition? How is this different from simply communicating the core functionality of a product and/or service? (LO6)

6. How is marketing a not-for-profit organization different from marketing a for-profit entity's products and services? How are they similar?

Question for Individual Action

A recent article in *Retailing Today* commented on a study that concludes millennials (20- to 35-year-olds) are not loyal to fashion brands. It indicates further that 45% of those surveyed indicated there is nothing brands can do to reverse this trend. Do you agree with this conclusion? What does this say about the importance of value proposition development? If you were managing a fashion brand what actions would you consider to reverse this trend?

Team Exercise

Choose a not-for-profit organization in your community. Based on your research and resulting understanding of the mission and vision of this not-for-profit, create a social networking positioning campaign for the organization. Where and how do you believe it should concentrate its social networking effort? What market segments should it target? How should it judge the success of this initiative? What other key positioning initiatives would you recommend in addition to the social marketing effort?

Case for Discussion

New Brand Thinking: P&G Wants Your Laundry

Procter & Gamble (P&G) has always wanted to sell you products like Tide, Gain, Bounce, and Downy. Now, the consumer packaged goods (CPG) powerhouse wants to do your laundry for you as well.

Founded in 1837 in Cincinnati, Ohio, P&G is one of the largest CPG companies in the world. Major categories within its product portfolio include beauty (19%), grooming (10%), health care (12%), fabric and home care (32%), and baby, feminine, and family care (27%). Total annual revenue was in excess of $65 billion (USD) for the most recent fiscal year (2018), with approximately 44% of revenue derived from its North American operations (Canada, the United States, and Puerto Rico).[16]

Given its history and dominance in soaps and detergents (P&G has been marketing Ivory soap since the late 19th century and Tide since 1947), the firm's interest in the dry-cleaning category should come as no surprise. The dry-cleaning market is large and somewhat fragmented. Revenues in the United States alone are in the neighbourhood of $9 billion (USD) annually. While broader trends such as environmental concerns, casual work wear, and the rise of fast fashion may each have a negative effect on demand, dry cleaning is also positively affected by the business cycle. That is, demand for dry cleaning services tends to rise as per capita disposable income rises.

The company launched P&G Dry Cleaners in 2010 and now has over 125 locations in the U.S. The facilities are operated primarily by franchisees. Services include dry cleaning; wash, dry, and fold; alterations and repairs; and care for special fabrics and special types of goods including wedding dresses and household items and bedding. Other elements include drop-off and pick-up through drop-boxes and designated lockers, and a car-side valet service.[17] The locations are supported by over 700 lockers in apartment buildings, retail stores, and other locations. There are also over 20 installations of Tide University wash, dry, and fold services on U.S. campuses.

In February 2019, Procter & Gamble announced the consolidation of its various laundry services under the Tide Cleaners banner, and signalled ambitious plans to grow the business to over 2000 drop-off locations within the year.[18]

Ed Zurga/Bloomberg via Getty Images

"Tide Cleaners is going after urban millennial and Gen Z consumers—who often have little love or capacity for doing laundry—by expanding its pickup-and-delivery laundry service nationally and making one of the biggest direct-to-consumer plays ever for a Procter & Gamble Co. brand," *Advertising Age* said at the time.[19]

The organization believes urban millennials and Gen Z will be receptive to Tide Cleaners, given that they are already committed to outsourcing basic tasks such as grocery shopping and even transportation.

"The time people spend on chores is decreasing, and there's less and less consumption happening at home," Sundar Raman, VP of P&G North American Fabric Care said. "The market for out-of-home laundry is just as big as for in-home, and growing faster."[20]

Advertising agency Saatchi & Saatchi created a video with the tagline "Life, Not Laundry" to support the expansion. The supporting integrated marketing communications effort will be largely local, in keeping with the direct-to-consumer nature of the business.

"Now for the first time Tide will have a name and face for people interacting with the brand," Raman said, "not just a bottle on the Walmart shelf."[21]

Questions

1. Tide is one of P&G's "billion dollar brands" and perhaps the most important brand in the company's largest category, fabric and home care. Is stretching the brand into cleaning services worth the risk?

2. P&G did not have any plans initially for expansion of the concept beyond the United States. If you were, however, to develop a high-level marketing plan (target segment, positioning, integrated marketing program) for the introduction of the service in Canada, what would it look like?

CHAPTER 11

Understanding the Marketing Effort

LEARNING OBJECTIVES

This chapter is designed to provide students with:

LO1	Familiarity with the key marketing mix elements that make up the four pillars of the marketing effort
LO2	An understanding of the importance of intrinsic value proposition attributes in the formulation of an organization's product and/or service differentiation strategy
LO3	Exposure to the four key fundamental factors that will impact the setting of price for an organization's products and/or services
LO4	An awareness of the key decision-making factors that will influence the type of distribution and delivery system an organization develops for its products and/or services
LO5	An appreciation for the marketing process associated with the development of the communication message applicable to an organization's product and/or service offerings
LO6	A base-level exposure to the intricacies of the product life cycle
LO7	An introduction to portfolio management

Snapshot

What to Expect in This Chapter

As identified by the learning objectives, this chapter focuses on exposing students to key concepts associated with the execution of marketing strategy. The content emphasized in this chapter includes the following:

- Four Pillars of the Marketing Effort
  - Product Strategy: Value Proposition Attributes versus Product Attributes
  - Pricing Strategy: Return on Sales Maximization
  - Distribution Strategy: Connecting with Customers
  - Communication Strategy: Communicating the "Fit"
- Managing a Product's Life Cycle
  - Managing across the Life Cycle
- Managing a Product Portfolio
- A Note Pertaining to Not-for-Profits
- Management Reflection—Managing the Marketing Effort
- Appendix—Advanced Topics Relating to Pricing

Business IN ACTION

The Battle for Cloud-Based Gaming Heats Up

As the various chapters of this textbook point out, the execution of a company's business strategy is built around its ability to effectively deliver its products and services to the targeted market sectors as solutions to the needs of its current and prospective customers. Part of this process entails the development of a marketing mix (discussed this chapter) with activities that reflect the interconnectivity of decisions made with respect to pricing, market connectivity (distribution), communications, and product/service offerings. This, of course, cannot be made in isolation of rivals seeking to deliver solutions to customer needs in the same markets within which a given company competes. Although we often perceive that the logical winner in a given market sector is the company with the best product, this is not always the case. The winner typically is the company that develops its marketing mix components in a way that enables its value proposition (discussed in Chapter 10) to be viewed as being superior to that of rivals and can develop and execute its customized business model in a manner that creates the purchase conversion necessary for success.

A good example of where we are seeing a looming major battle for market share and growth capture—and, hence, marketing mix development requirements—lies in cloud gaming. Some of the biggest technology players, including Sony, Google, Microsoft,

Bloomberg via Getty Images

and Amazon, have targeted the cloud gaming industry as a significant business opportunity and are rapidly positioning themselves for disruption and market share acquisition as the convergence of technology across multiple platforms continues. January 2019 saw Google announce its cloud-gaming service called Stadia, with plans to enable the streaming of games to go directly from its server farms to smartphones and related mobile devices, TVs, and computers. Microsoft's entry, called xCloud, announced in March 2019, offers cloud gaming as a complementary addition to its Xbox gaming portfolio. Microsoft envisions xCloud as a platform that not only will offer more ways to interact with your Xbox, but also will enable users to seamlessly connect to their smartphone, tablet, or other connected devices. The idea is to transition the full effect of traditional gaming onto mobile devices and to enable gamers to pick up where they left off with games as they move from one device to another. No longer will content be PC or specific hardware constrained, thereby offering the more than 2 billion plus gamers globally the opportunity to interact as

never before. Chinese tech giant Tencent is another big player betting on this market sector. Tencent, in March 2019, announced its entry into this market space with its cloud gaming service called Start. As with the other players, Tencent is promising to make high-quality gaming available on any device at any time. Already an online gaming provider, Tencent believes that its experience and existing content in this sector will enable it to generate a fast-mover advantage over rivals. It adds to this its strong position in Asia, where the race for 5G application has a leading edge, and where the market opportunity appears to be greatest. Then there is Amazon, which reportedly is expecting to enter this market, and which brings global server capabilities and significant customer reach that offer other strategically advantageous ways of winning in this market sector.

Experts seem to agree that main-market cloud-based gaming remains a few years away, but traditional gaming manufacturers such as Sony, Microsoft, Nintendo, EA, etc. need to be prepared for

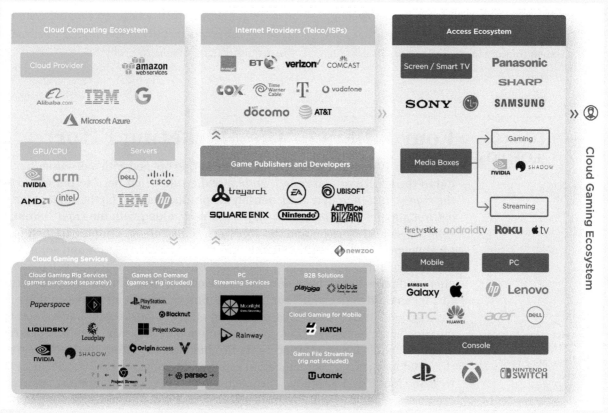

Used by permission of NewZoo Games & ESports Analytics

significant disruption and potential profit volatility relating to their existing stand-alone gaming portfolios. Also, being the dominant player today does not mean that you will remain the dominant player going forward. Critical to success is the ability to execute across a company's marketing mix, offer a value proposition to the marketplace that is superior to rivals, and create, manage, and execute on a supporting business model. In this regard, execution is not going to be a breeze. Cloud-based gaming play requires the rapid movement of significant data and images at lightning speed (we are talking milliseconds). This, in the minds of many, will need 5G networking and device capabilities. 5G is coming, but the build-out of infrastructure will take time. Also, just because a game is now available in the cloud does not mean that active gamers will automatically transition to it. Companies have to think about the value-added services they can offer and the unique experiences they can create. Pricing also comes into play. Can a cloud-based business model be monetized? What will this look like (subscription-based, pay-as-you-go, etc.)? Can the return on invested capital required to build out the supporting technology infrastructure be realized and, if so, how long will it take to generate the returns? Then there are privacy issues relating to multiple users interacting

in a single environment, as well as regulatory issues governing trade and intellectual property practices across the global business environment. All of this needs to be built out around a complex collaborative business relationship among cloud computing ecosystem providers, Internet providers, cloud gaming service experts, game publishers and developers, and system access players (media box, mobile, console, PC, smart TV, etc.).

The potential opportunity within cloud-based gaming appears to be such that the companies identified above, plus a whole host of others, are prepared to make significant investments in this market arena. Winning in this marketplace is dependent upon a management team's ability to create and execute the right marketing mix approach. Vital to this undertaking will be the need to win over influencers, attract core gamers to create momentum, and deliver not only quality content, but also a supporting infrastructure that will enable users to perceive the value proposition as truly delivering a unique and pleasurable experience. The key link lies in the fluid integration of the delivery model with the business model in a way that will enable the required infrastructure and support systems to be at cost points that will enable pricing to attract the required scale to ensure profitability.

Four Pillars of the Marketing Effort

LO1, LO2, LO3, LO4, LO5

In Chapter 10, our analysis relating to marketing opened with a discussion pertaining to the six R's of marketing: understanding the *right need* to pursue, creating the *right solution* to that need, getting the product backed by the *right value proposition* and the *right methodology for delivery*, along with the *right communication* messaging strategy and the *right pricing strategy*. Chapter 10 then focused on concepts, models, and tools relating to need identification and solution positioning, including a preliminary discussion on value proposition development. This chapter directs its attention toward the remaining four R's, and the marketing effort focus needed to ensure our organization's success in an increasingly competitive market environment. This marketing effort is most easily understood as the creation and execution of an organization's **marketing mix**, comprising strategic and tactical decisions relating to its product/service offerings, pricing, distribution, and marketing communication efforts and approaches. Historically referred to as the four P's of marketing (product, price, place, and promotion), the ability to create and integrate these four decision areas into a unified marketing approach can be more effectively thought of as the "four pillars to the marketing effort." It should be noted that the term "promotion" has since been replaced with the word

Marketing Mix refers to an organization's strategic and tactical decisions relating to its product/service offerings, pricing, distribution, and marketing communication efforts and approaches.

FIGURE 11.1   Four Pillars of the Marketing Effort (Marketing Mix)

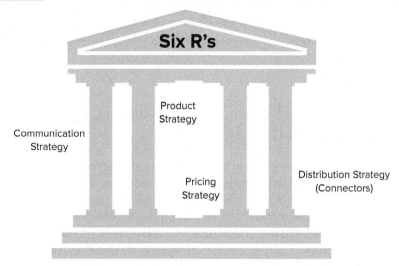

"communication," and the term "place" has been replaced with the word "distribution," meaning the channels used to ensure that the product is accessible to purchasers. Distribution is now further evolving toward being referenced as "connectivity" given the market digitization and ecommerce evolution taking place. These changes have been made to more accurately reflect today's marketing approach, which goes far beyond simply promoting products and/or services at bricks and mortar locations (see Figure 11.1).

In creating our marketing mix via these four pillar components, our effort is on developing, demonstrating, and communicating to our current and potential customers why our product is the best solution to their need, and then ensuring that it is available for customer acquisition through a convenient delivery option (bricks and mortar location, online, etc.) and at a price point that represents the best price/quality trade-off. Assuming that our marketing research, segmentation, and target marketing analysis is accurate, an effective marketing mix effort should result in achieving a definitive "fit" between our product/service offering and the needs of our potential customers. Traditionally, marketing textbooks and marketers have been trained to think of the marketing mix around four concepts: product strategy, pricing strategy, distribution strategy, and company-managed communication strategies. Although valid in terms of a company-centric approach, an alternate view is to think of a successful marketing effort as including these areas, but to design it and build it with a more customer-centric slant (see Figure 11.2). Let's take a look at each of these areas in order to explain the value of this different approach to creating a marketing mix.

FIGURE 11.2   A Different Way to Think about the Marketing Mix

Traditional	Revised
Product Strategy	Value Proposition Attributes
Pricing Strategy	Maximize Return on Sales
Distribution Strategy	Connect with Customers
Communication Strategy	Communicate "Fit"

Assuming that our marketing research, segmentation, and target marketing analysis is accurate, an effective marketing mix effort should result in achieving a definitive "fit" between our product/service offering and the needs of our potential customers.

Product Strategy: Value Proposition Attributes versus Product Attributes

When one thinks of product strategy, one has a tendency to focus his/her concentration and efforts on the tangible attributes of the product or service an organization is offering. Although valid in that such attributes (functionality, packaging, component makeup, etc.) are important and necessary decision-making areas relating to product and/or service offering design, this potentially hard or somewhat tunnelled vision of what the product and/or service strategy is all about may result in marketers failing to develop and leverage other essential and core-differentiating attributes. As was noted in Chapter 10 (as well as Chapter 1), viewing the product strategy as that of value proposition attributes brings into play a considerably broader range of attributes that can be used to more fully align the organization's offerings to the needs of the target market and create greater opportunity for differentiation. Creating a value proposition strategy broadens the focus to include such additional items as branding, emotional bonding, peer acceptance, and post-purchase service support. The product strategy essentially becomes the overall "experience" that the customer has with the product and the organization offering it. When combined with the functional, packaging, and component attributes, this results in a much stronger differentiated message to communicate to potential customers. When thinking about product positioning and product strategy, the key is to think about how the product and/or service offers to the customer the best solution in the face of competitive alternatives. As an example, companies that are positioned as premium-price players in a market segment may find their customer base being attacked by a low-price, low-cost competitor. This can be especially troublesome if the competitor offering's tangible product quality is comparable to that of the premium-price player. However, by offering a total solution package that combines financing options, a higher level of service support, stronger technical expertise on the part of its sales representatives, specialized or customized product options, longer warranty periods, a reputable brand name, and strong product reliability, the premium-price player can, in many cases, retain its competitive edge. The important takeaway is that in viewing product strategies via value proposition attributes, the focus of the marketing team shifts from simply "building a better mouse trap" to creating positive performance gaps between the company and its competitors in such a way that even if the tangible mouse traps become of equal quality, other differentiators have been created that continue to create preference for the organization's products and/or services (see Figure 11.3).

Viewing product strategies as the development of value proposition attributes shifts the marketing team's focus from simply "building a better mouse trap" to creating positive performance gaps between the company and its competitors.

Viewing product strategies through value proposition attributes can often result in the discovery of new market space as well. The ascension of Netflix and the demise of Blockbuster (and other video-rental stores) can be largely attributed to

FIGURE 11.3   **Value Proposition Strategies**

```
  ┌──────────────┐
  │  Tangible    │
  │  Product     │
  │  Attributes  │
  └──────────────┘
                        ┌────────────────────┐
        +          →    │ Develop Positive    │
                        │ Performance Gaps    │
                        │ Over Competitors    │
  ┌──────────────┐      └────────────────────┘
  │ Intangible   │
  │ Product      │
  │ Attributes   │
  └──────────────┘
```

Netflix's recognition of the core value proposition–based solution to the customer's need, that being the core attribute of convenience (streaming and, initially, physical home delivery). Rather than focusing on building a strategy whose predominant focus is strictly around titles of movies, Netflix chose to build a product/service strategy around the concept of the ease of convenience of acquiring the product. The company continues to build out its value proposition, and therefore its value-added distinction, by adding additional benefits such as original content and a growing library of titles, while maintaining an affordable pricing structure that appeals to a broad market sector. Thinking in terms of value proposition attributes gets marketers to look at the product across a number of different potential advantage points (see Figure 11.4).

The power of brands Name recognition is one thing, but a brand name that communicates and epitomizes positive performance attributes that are judged to be superior to those of competitors is huge in today's competitive market environment. Companies spend millions of dollars on creating brand image, and rightly so. A brand that carries emotional ties and strong intrinsic value into a value proposition greatly improves the chances for its success. Strong brand names communicate quality, reliability, product consistency, and peer acceptance in many market sectors. When we think of snowboards, the brand name Burton comes to mind. Images of coffee, in Canada, immediately bring up Tim Hortons and Starbucks. Think of online shopping, and Amazon is often top of mind. So, just what makes a brand so powerful? The answer lies in the ability of the brand to move its customer

FIGURE 11.4   **Value Proposition Attributes**

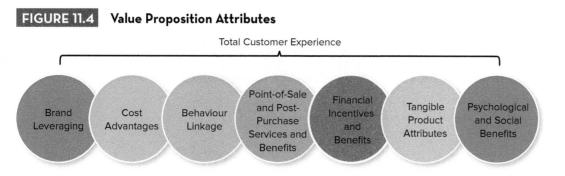

FIGURE 11.5   **Brand Ladder**

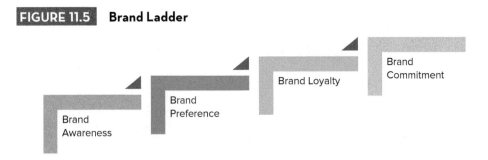

market beyond simply awareness of the brand itself to a level of commitment that is unmatched by competitors. Truly successful brands, which add power to a company and/or its products and services, are those that have evolved to the top end of the brand ladder (see Figure 11.5).

> Truly successful brands, which add power to a company and/or its products and services, are those that have evolved to the top end of the brand ladder.

Predetermined Purchase List refers to the ranking of products/services that purchasers develop for all the options available when making a purchase decision.

Brands that have reached the "brand commitment" level on the ladder have an active and loyal customer base that continually places the brand at the top of their **predetermined purchase list**, resulting in their immediate migration to the purchase decision without further consideration of alternate competitive options. One way to visualize this would be to think of a person so committed to Starbucks coffee that they are willing to drive past several Tim Hortons and Second Cup outlets in order to find the nearest Starbucks location. Brands seldom command this type of allegiance overnight. It is a level that is obtained over time and is the result of the organization continually meeting and exceeding its customers' expectations across all value proposition components. In many cases, to achieve such a relationship level with their customers organizations must successfully connect with them on three levels: product attributes, benefits, and emotional ties (see Figure 11.6).

FIGURE 11.6   **Brand Success**

Brands that have reached the "brand commitment" level have an active and loyal customer base that continually places the brand at the top of their predetermined purchase list.

Brand awareness is often gained as organizations communicate, and the market accepts, that the brand offers distinctive features that set it apart from its competitors. The movement up the ladder toward brand preference and brand loyalty results in customers using this brand and, recognizing the benefits from it, choosing to repurchase the brand and concluding that its benefits (versus those of competitors) are such that a relationship to the brand is formed. Brand commitment evolves as ongoing use results in the brand becoming an automatic response when the need for this product or service presents itself. The decision to purchase is automatic, and the belief toward substitute brands is that they simply will not result in the same level of satisfaction. In essence, the brand has created an emotional or psychological link with the customer in such a way that the intrinsic value of the brand is transferred to the customer as a result of using the brand. As an example, the General Motors brand Cadillac historically has focused its marketing efforts toward creating an emotional tie or bond with customers with the implication that ownership of a Cadillac is directly correlated with business success. (Yes, you are constantly the last one to leave the office. Yes, you are the "go to" person when decisions need to be made—and, yes, you shoulder the major responsibilities within the organization. As you look out your office window, however, at the last car remaining that evening in the employee parking lot, it is yours, and it is a Cadillac. You have truly made it.) Keep in mind that perception is reality when it comes to brands. Think of Toyota and how many people perceive the brand to represent quality. Think of Apple; the brand communicates innovation and a seamless platform ecosystem across all of its devices. The ability to transition a brand from awareness to commitment is all about delivering the value proposition in a way that demonstrates distinctiveness and creates emotional and psychological ownership with customers as the proven solution to solving their needs. Again, this means going beyond the core tangible attributes of a product and tapping into the emotional "psyche" of the customer in terms of attributes such as style, ego, status, peer pressure, and lifestyle affiliation, to name a few. Tim Hortons' "truly Canadian" theme-based brand affiliation is at the heart of its marketing success and is an excellent example of how to create an emotional bond with an organization's customer base.

The ability to transition a brand from awareness to commitment is all about delivering the value proposition in a way that demonstrates distinctiveness and creates emotional and psychological ownership with customers as the proven solution to solving their needs.

Business IN ACTION

Canada's Most Admired Brands

In today's market environment, organizations are recognizing more and more the importance of brand distinction as being fundamental to long-term success.

Having said this, in today's world of social media, instant communication, and heightened connectivity, never before has greater exposure of a brand to the impact of managerial decisions and actions existed.

What has taken a company decades to develop can be tarnished in seconds in today's technologically connected world—just ask Tim Hortons, VW, Uber, Pepsi, or even the Food Network's Paula Deen. As managers, our decisions and interactions can and do significantly influence the perception of a brand. How we interact internally and externally, given social media's depth and market strength, is under scrutiny more so than ever before. The marketplace and our stakeholders view a brand as a fundamental communication vehicle relating to an organization's purpose, as well as its stand on important societal issues, in addition to the product/service value proposition its has historically represented. In this light, it is important to no longer view brands through the single lens of customer satisfaction, strictly based on the experience relating to a product or service, but much more broadly through the lens of a company's reputation—a complex integration of social conscience, honesty, and transparency, in additional to physical and/or intangible needs satisfaction.

Having said this, which brands currently stand out in the minds of Canadians? This response does vary, depending on whether we are focused on customer feedback, perceived quality surveys, brand reputation surveys, or overall financial performance as a result of strong market position anchored by an underlying brand strength. It also varies with market demographics and behaviour patterns with respect to generational differences. Leger, in its annual Corporate Reputation study, has ranked Canada's top 10 most admired brands rolling into 2019 as shown in Figure 11.7.

This ranking, compiled from over 30 000 responses, is based on underlying brand attributes that communicate a sense of fairness and doing the right things when it comes to interactions with customers, partners, and society at large. As shown above, Canadian Tire was recognized as Canada's most admired brand at the close of 2018, beating out Google, which had held that position for the last four years. Respondents identified Canadian Tire's giving back to the community (Jumpstart program), along with its perception of inclusivity and its attachment to Canadian values as communicated in its First Skate campaign, as key reasons for pushing this company to the top spot. Respondents also felt that Canadian Tire's new Triangle reward program's flexibility, along with its close local

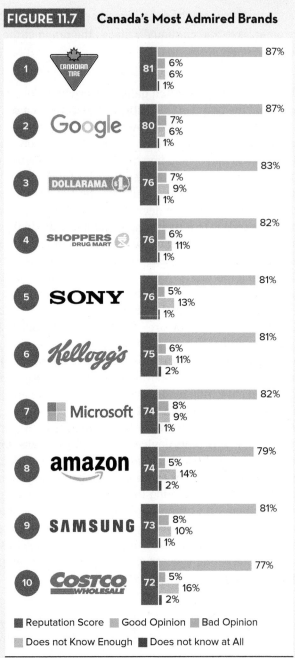

FIGURE 11.7   Canada's Most Admired Brands

		Reputation Score	Good Opinion	Bad Opinion	Does not Know Enough
1	CANADIAN TIRE	81	87%	6%	6% / 1%
2	Google	80	87%	7%	6% / 1%
3	DOLLARAMA ($1)	76	83%	7%	9% / 1%
4	SHOPPERS DRUG MART	76	82%	6%	11% / 1%
5	SONY	76	81%	5%	13% / 1%
6	Kellogg's	75	81%	6%	11% / 2%
7	Microsoft	74	82%	8%	9% / 1%
8	amazon	74	79%	5%	14% / 2%
9	SAMSUNG	73	81%	8%	10% / 1%
10	COSTCO WHOLESALE	72	77%	5%	16% / 2%

■ Reputation Score   ■ Good Opinion   ■ Bad Opinion
■ Does not Know Enough   ■ Does not know at All

Courtesy of Leger 360 and taken from *Leger 2019 Corporate Reputation Study.*

community attachments, were representative of a customer-driven company. Tim Hortons, a perennial top-five brand, rebounded rolling into 2019 to #33. The company, which had been #4 in 2017, fell sharply to 50th in 2018, following a tarnishing of its image as a result of negative market perceptions relating to some franchisee clawbacks of employee benefits and break allowances in order to offset increases to the minimum wage in Ontario, as well as negative publicity relating to disputes between franchisees and corporate owner Restaurant Brands International. VW (emissions scandal) and Pepsi (Kendall Jenner) also were working toward recovery mode following brand-tarnishing actions, although full restoration of a brand image following its tarnishing does take time.

As noted in the opening comments of this Business in Action, not all demographics share the same conclusions. In Leger's 2018 most admired company survey (Figure 11.8), millennials had a slightly different view of Canada's most admired companies (2019 differences were not available at the time of this writing). For this demographic, the overall determination of an admired brand demonstrates a slightly different set of conclusions relating to perceptions of corporate social responsibility, honesty and transparency, innovation, quality of products and services, and financial success.

Companies that, according to Leger, were not held in high esteem (in terms of admiration) and therefore finished in the lower quartile of the survey included

- Hyundai
- Labatt
- Pfizer
- RE/MAX
- Telus
- Keurig
- Cascades
- Starbucks
- Lowe's
- CIBC
- Reitmans Canada Ltd.

Starbucks, as an example, was still rebounding from customer dissatisfaction of its handling of a gaffe with its annual Christmas drink cup, while CIBC was still in the midst of repositioning itself following its parting of ways with PC Financial.

Individual lessons can be learned from all of the companies represented in this list of Canada's most admired brands. For some companies finding themselves at the lower end of the survey, the results simply point to a need to more firmly position the brand beyond the product portfolio and look to offer strong ways to

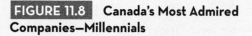

FIGURE 11.8 **Canada's Most Admired Companies—Millennials**

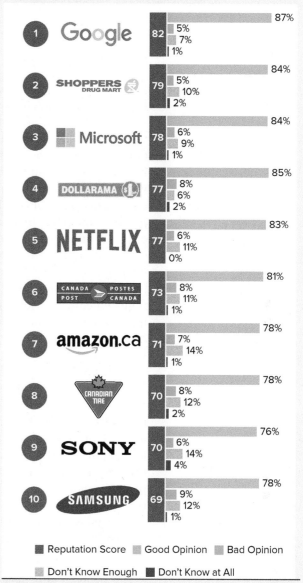

Courtesy of Leger 360 and taken from *Leger 2018 Corporate Reputation Study.*

identify the brand as important to the lives of Canadians and the way we view our culture and ever-evolving social expectations. Having said this, a common thread does run through the 10 "best of the best" companies listed above. That thread is a recognition that success lies beyond simply having a great product or service. Success lies in the combination of a customer-centric business model, built around a unique story, supported by a positive and collaborative workplace culture and a strong commitment to corporate social responsibility and to the communities within which they operate.

Web Integration

Want to learn more about Canada's most admired brands, and see exactly why and how companies are ranked? See **https:// leger360.com/white-papers/legers-reputation-study-2019-ranking/**.

Pricing Strategy: Return on Sales Maximization

Is business all about obtaining the largest market share? Should a company's pricing strategy be solely based on undercutting our competitors in order to get the sale? Does our pricing strategy truly reflect the value of the products and services we offer? Does the strategy support our brand and the positioning behind our value proposition? These are just some of the several questions that will challenge marketers and managers when it comes to pricing the products and services their organizations offer. In the face of a growing global marketplace, companies are being challenged across many sectors with a relentless downward pressure on price. Increasing competitive intensity and product substitutability, coupled with the rapidity of technological innovation and change, continues to contribute to this downward pressure. This, coupled with the constant challenge of "expense creep," places additional pressure on organizations to maintain and protect their operating margins. Upward pressure on capital costs, HR costs, R&D requirements, market development costs, and process development costs, to name a few, all contribute to this upward pressure on an organization's cost base. As managers, we can respond to this ongoing pressure in one of two ways (see Figure 11.9).

Our ability to respond to this globalization trend fundamentally comes down to how well we can differentiate our products and services from our competitors' products and services in the markets we are serving. The ability of our marketing mix to demonstrate and communicate this to our target markets is, and will be, a core component of our success. In situations where we are unable to truly differentiate our products and services, price will become a major point of comparison and, therefore, a core decision-making criterion as to which product and/or service is chosen by potential customers. The ability to effectively differentiate ourselves will enable us to minimize price as a major point of comparison, thereby reducing its influence on the decision-making process (see Figure 11.10).

> The ability to effectively differentiate ourselves will enable us to minimize price as a major point of comparison, thereby reducing its influence on the decision-making process.

FIGURE 11.9   **Responding to Price Pressures**

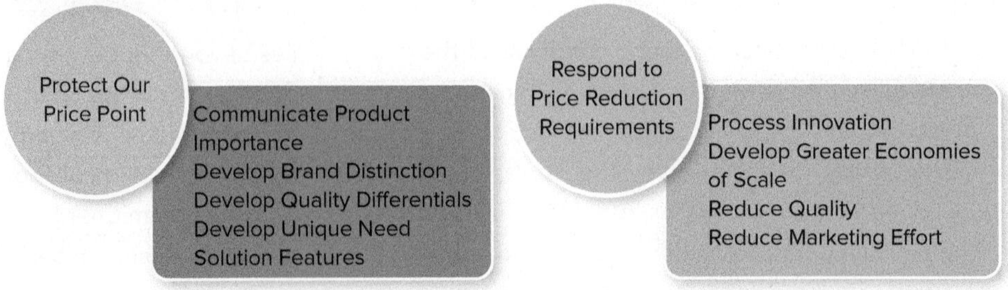

Protect Our Price Point
Communicate Product Importance
Develop Brand Distinction
Develop Quality Differentials
Develop Unique Need Solution Features

Respond to Price Reduction Requirements
Process Innovation
Develop Greater Economies of Scale
Reduce Quality
Reduce Marketing Effort

FIGURE 11.10   Influence of Price–Purchaser Decision Criteria

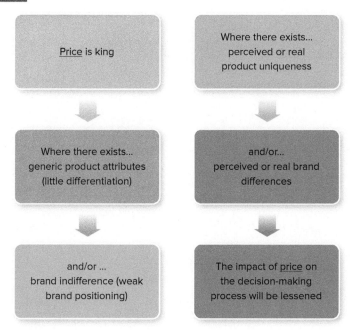

Managing the pricing process Determining what price to charge is critical to the execution of the marketing strategy and to the overall success of the marketing effort. Pricing involves considering a number of factors and requires solid knowledge of both internal and external influences. Internally, managers and marketers must fully understand the cost base of the organization and the margins that are needed in order to ensure that the price being charged is sufficient to cover the operating expenses and to support the investment needs of the organization. Externally, managers and marketers need to assess the competitiveness of their price against alternate product offerings, and against the willingness of the customer to "pay for the solution to the pain" at the price point being considered. When thinking about pricing and what price to charge, four key fundamentals need to be assessed prior to finalizing a pricing decision. These are as follows (see Figure 11.11):

1 Fully identify the cost structure components of the product/service that the organization intends to offer to the targeted market.

2 Research and identify the cost structures of your major competitors, and the extent to which they intend to focus on price as a major point of comparison.

3 Analyze the **price elasticity** of the target market; that is, the change in demand that is anticipated to occur at various price points. An additional aspect of this is to understand the price range that consumers will conclude is acceptable for the product/service you intend to offer. A core fundamental is the ability to define the **consumer price threshold**: the maximum price point that the customer is willing to pay for your product or service.

4 Determine the degree of value proposition positioning strength that the product/service commands in the marketplace. This will enable marketers and managers to identify the premiums that can be allocated to the base pricing model given core differentiators such as brand strength, emotional ties, psychological attribute uniqueness, publicity initiatives, and other positioning-based communication message tactics.

Price Elasticity is the change in demand that is anticipated to occur at the various price points the organization is considering for its product and/or service.

Consumer Price Threshold refers to the maximum price point that the customer is willing to pay for a product or services.

FIGURE 11.11   **Key Fundamentals to Setting Price**

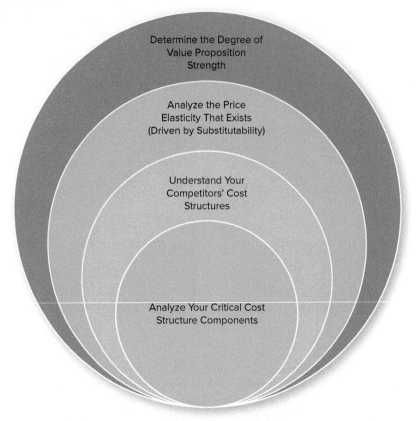

With information generated from analyses within the four areas noted above, managers will also need to consider the required margin that must be incorporated into the pricing structure in order to ensure that additional organizational-based expenditure obligations—such as debt repayment, equipment and capital asset replacement, inflationary cost pressures, product-line growth initiatives, and allowances for unforeseen contingencies—are factored into the pricing formula. Profit expectations, which should include acceptable returns on the investment made in the product within a defined **payback period**, also need to be taken into consideration.

As one can conclude, pricing is not an easy thing to do. For an organization, however, the setting of price is one of the most important components of the marketing process. Price reflects the cost that the customer must endure in order to acquire the desired product or service. It fundamentally impacts the perceived value of the product, as it is one-half of the measurement (the other being the value proposition being purchased) that the customer will use when determining if, and when, to buy, and which product or service to buy. For managers, the focus of setting price should be on the following questions: how can we maximize our return on sales on the product/service we offer in a way that ensures competitiveness, lies within our customers' acceptable price range, results in a recognized value advantage between our product/service and those of our competitors, and contributes to the long-term wealth of the organization?

Payback Period represents the length of time required to recover, or earn back, the cost of an investment.

> Successful pricing strategies seek to maximize the return on sales on the product/service we offer in a way that ensures competitiveness, lies within our customers' acceptable price range, results in a recognized value advantage between our product/service and those of our competitors, and contributes to the long-term wealth of the organization.

Business IN ACTION

The YMCA of Kingston—How Understanding Price Impacts Business Decisions

As indicated in the opening chapter of this textbook, the author served as the Chief Executive Officer of the YMCA of Kingston, Ontario, for 14 years. During this tenure, the YMCA of Kingston faced a crossroads with respect to its main facility (called Wright Crescent), which dated back to 1955. The focus was to decide whether the organization should build a new YMCA facility in Kingston or renovate the existing facility. At the time, construction costs for a new YMCA facility were estimated at approximately $12 million. Alternatively, the investment needed to modernize and expand the existing facility was placed at approximately $6 million ($2 million for required upgrades to HVAC and other infrastructure needs, and $4 million for a significant addition to its aquatics centre). The renovation approach, however, while enhancing the capabilities of the YMCA, would still leave it with a relatively old structure, one that would require further financial expenditures down the road. In deciding which direction to take, the board of directors hired a consulting firm to undertake a significant marketing research study relating to both the potential for membership growth as a result of building a new facility and the overall price elasticity (including consumer price threshold identification) for YMCA membership fees. Analyzing and drawing conclusions relating to the fee structure range was fundamental to ensuring

that the YMCA could pay the cost of debt associated with building the new facility. Financial calculations conducted by the management team at the time concluded that a monthly membership fee in the $60+ per month per adult member range would be required to support the cost of debt that would be needed to build a new facility and appropriately support its revised operating expense projections. The facility would need to attract a larger membership base in order to support this initiative as well. The conclusion reached by the consulting firm, based on its market analysis, was that the upper end of the price range for YMCA memberships in Kingston hit a price threshold at a price point significantly below the needed $60+ per month per adult member range. The price threshold was estimated to be $45 per month per adult member. At the time, the YMCA was charging approximately $35 per month per adult member. The research further concluded that there was little impact on demand elasticity between $35 and $45 per month per adult member, but at the $45 per month threshold demand dropped significantly. This information played a significant role in the decision of management and the board of directors that, based on the fundraising abilities of the organization, the cost of debt that would be incurred, and concerns over pricing at a point needed to ensure the future solvency of the organization, building a new facility was not feasible without significant risk. The board and the management team, in their wisdom, opted for an expansion of the existing facility, recognizing that the price point of $45 per month per adult member would be sufficient to enable this registered charity to undertake such an initiative without exposing the organization to significant financial risk. The enhanced facility, including a major addition to its aquatics centre, was opened to the public in the fall of 2008.

Used with permission from YMCA

Web Integration

For more information regarding the YMCA of Kingston and its services and facilities, visit www.kingston.ymca.ca.

Distribution Strategy: Connecting with Customers

The development of a distribution strategy is all about connecting with customers. Channels of distribution and the development of channel intermediary relationships fundamentally revolve around ensuring that customers have convenient and accessible ways of purchasing our products and/or services. What was once predominantly thought of as a "bricks and mortar" development process has been dramatically changed by the development of Web-based technology services. In establishing a distribution strategy, it is important for marketers and managers to think in terms of how and where customers will purchase our products/services, and then to create the linkage that allows them to do so. In establishing these connection links, a number of key decision areas will come to mind. These decisions are not made in isolation of each other, but are best thought of as an integrated decision process, with decisions across all three jointly determining where, and how, we believe customers will have the best access to our product coupled with the optimal level of sales support. These key decision areas are as follows (see Figure 11.12):

1 Direct, indirect, or mixed systems

2 Product/service delivery options

3 Degree of sales support

Direct Distribution refers to connecting directly with customers and handling the final sale of products and/or the delivery of services without the assistance of a channel intermediary.

Channel Intermediary refers to an organization that assists a company in the distribution and delivery of goods or services to its customers.

Direct, indirect, or mixed systems Direct, indirect, or mixed channel configurations (systems) refers to the amount of involvement and control an organization desires to maintain over the final sale of its products and/or services. **Direct distribution** implies that the organization intends to connect directly with its customers to handle the final sale of its products and/or the delivery of its services without the assistance of a **channel intermediary** (see Figure 11.13). Organizations tend to use direct distribution channels as a result of a belief that their product is better supported by dedicated, company-employed sales personnel, and/or that they can gain greater customer loyalty and greater "share of wallet" by dealing directly with the customer. Amazon.com's business model has been predominantly built around a direct distribution, Web-based model. In the cosmetics industry, Avon Products Inc. and Mary Kay Inc. both use direct sales personnel to sell their products and services to families across North America. Direct distribution approaches can also be the result of organizations believing that they can more effectively control the

FIGURE 11.12   **Channel Decision-Making Process**

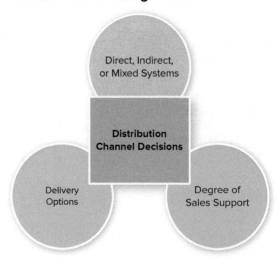

FIGURE 11.13   **Direct Distribution**

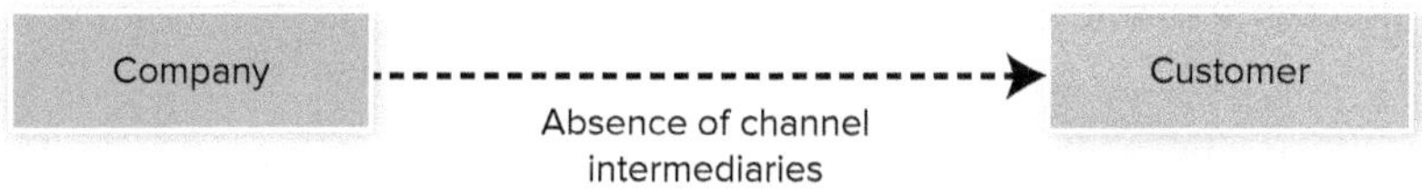

Company - - - - - - - - - - - - - - - - - - - ▶ Customer

Absence of channel
intermediaries

FIGURE 11.14   **Indirect Distribution**

Company - - - - ▶ Channel
Intermediaries - - - - ▶ Customer

Inclusion of channel
intermediaries

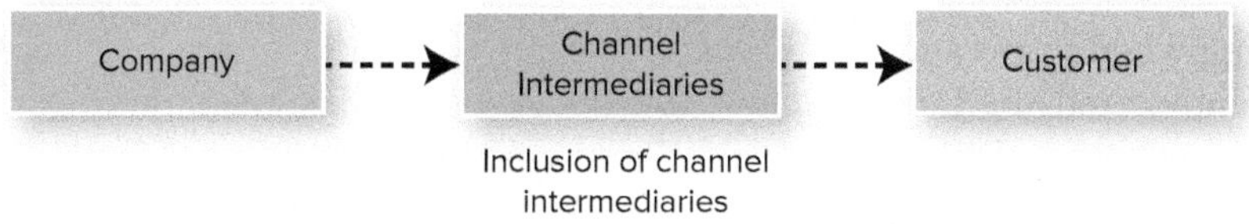

transportation and distribution costs associated with their products. In addition, organizations spearheading the creation of new market space and/or product areas may feel that a direct approach is necessary to effectively educate customers on the benefits of their products/services or new technologies. Direct distribution tactics can take into consideration single-customer contact points, or utilize multiple purchase option arrangements to facilitate the delivery of goods and services to customers.

Indirect distribution implies the use of a channel intermediary, such as a broker, wholesaler, or retailer, to facilitate the sales of an organization's products and/or services to the customer (see Figure 11.14). Organizations tend to use indirect distribution tactics as a result of the belief that significantly greater market reach and support can be provided by leveraging the expertise, locations, facilities, and experience of channel intermediaries. An example of an indirect distribution approach is an individual who desires to sell their home. In most cases, the homeowner will hire a real estate agent/broker to facilitate the sale and handle the transaction on their behalf. The ability to reach buyers and interact with them, along with the expertise and knowledge that a real estate agent/broker can provide regarding property valuation and the legal transactions associated with it, are predominant reasons why this approach is viewed by many as the preferred route to take. Indirect distribution is also used when an organization feels that customer familiarity with the use of the product is sufficient that a personal- or company-dedicated selling approach is not essential to the overall value proposition strategy, and/or when the cost of reaching customers is significantly higher than that incurred by using a channel intermediary. For many agricultural-based operations, the necessity of getting a product quickly from the fields where fruits and vegetables are grown to the supermarket aisles in urban areas requires the expertise of transportation and handling brokers and wholesalers. These channel intermediaries are experts in moving these products in a manner that minimizes costs and perishability. They also have the established contacts with a customer base that is ready to purchase these products and services, thereby providing a ready market for the products that these agricultural-based operations produce.

Mixed distribution systems incorporate both direct and indirect distribution options within their distribution strategy (see Figure 11.15). The ongoing development of Web-based models has resulted in more and more organizations viewing this distribution tactic as a preferred business model. The use of mixed distribution systems is not limited simply to the addition of Web sites. Tapestry Inc. (Coach, Kate Spade, Stuart Weitzman brands), maker of the famous Coach purses, sells its products in Canada both direct to customers via company-owned and operated stores, and via its Web site (www.coach.com). In the United States, however, in addition to

Indirect Distribution implies the use of a channel intermediary, such as a broker, wholesaler, or retailer, to facilitate the sales of a company's products and/or services to its customers.

Mixed Distribution Systems are distribution systems that incorporate both direct and indirect distribution options within their distribution strategy.

FIGURE 11.15   **Mixed Distribution**

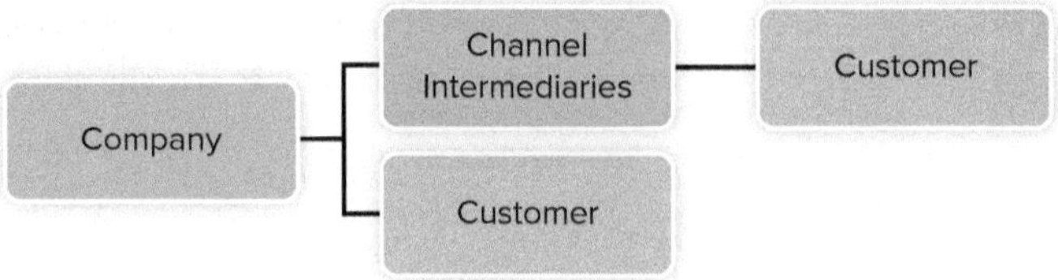

company-owned stores and its Web site, Coach Inc. sells these same products through select (authorized) indirect channel intermediaries (in this case, retail operations such as Nordstrom, Dillard's, Macy's, Bloomingdale's, and Lord & Taylor). Coach handbags can even be purchased online via Walmart.com, which has now shifted the focus of its website, much like Amazon, to be a purchase platform for other retailers (in addition to Walmart products and services). Dell Inc. originally sold its computers direct to customers through its online Web site and customer service centres. Dell has expanded its distribution strategy to a mixed distribution approach by making its computers available for purchase at Amazon.com, Best Buy, and Walmart.[1] Referring back to our example of Amazon and its initial direct distribution play, the company, as a result of its purchase of Whole Foods (USA) and More (India), has now expanded its original business model into a mixed distribution system with respect to grocery and related items, and its acquisition of PillPack[2] is viewed by some as entry into the pharmaceutical space beyond simply an online provider.

Product/service delivery options As stated earlier, the best way to think of the development of an organization's distribution strategy and its accompanying tactics is in terms of creating a methodology for "connecting" with customers. It is about getting your product or service to your customer at the right place and time and in a way that is truly convenient and seamless for the purchaser. This means that the organization needs to continuously assess its approach in terms of accessibility and convenience in addition to cost and distribution efficiencies. More and more organizations are adopting a distribution approach that seeks to maximize the options customers can use when purchasing a product or service. With Web-based strategies becoming more fully developed, technology advances pushing costs down, and customer buying trends exhibiting non-traditional behaviours, the addition of a variety of purchase opportunity options is becoming more and more necessary to maintaining customer interest and loyalty. A recent example of further adding flexibility and reach to a company's distribution strategy is the growing use of "pop-up" store locations. Pop-ups are a temporary use of physical or online retail space by a company in order to provide additional access to its goods and services. Pop-ups are often used by companies to test market opportunities in new locations in order to determine if sufficient demand for its products exists, judge the reaction to new products as part of a test market launch, expand market reach on a temporary basis during peak seasonal periods (Halloween, Christmas, etc.), reach new customers, generate a "get it while supplies last" purchase mentality, and educate customers on product features and uses. The concept of the pop-up store is generally driven by the desire to expand the customer base, create stronger brand awareness, and/or generate additional sources of revenue in locations not typically serviced by the company. Canadian-based Shopify.com has built its business model around being a pop-up online retail location for businesses looking to expand their market reach and leverage new revenue opportunities.[3]

Organizations that incorporate a number of different channel connections through which customers can purchase a product and/or service are undertaking a

multi-channel distribution strategy. The critical component to this approach, however, is the need to ensure that customers experience a seamless interaction with a company regardless of which option they choose to use to connect with a particular business. BOPIS (buy online, pick up in store) and BORIS (buy online, return in store) are two good examples of where such seamlessness needs to exist. Returns, as an example, represent a constant challenge for many companies expanding into online interactions. Returning products to online players not only represents a significant cost, but also can result in a significant negative impact on the overall customer experience and future loyalty if not handled conveniently and seamlessly. Amazon, as an example, has entered into a "returns agreement" with Kohl's department stores in the United States in order to create an additional convenience-based return option. Customers who desire to return a product to Amazon can simply drop the product off at Kohl's, which then handles the return transaction and ships the product back to Amazon. For customers, the expectation is that service will be excellent regardless of where, when, or how they want to purchase or return an item. For companies, the challenge is, as noted, to do this in a manner that controls costs while ensuring that customer needs are met and the customer experience is protected.

Degree of sales support within the channel In addition to considering the broad-level distribution approach to connecting with customers (direct, indirect, mixed) and the channel configuration to be used (product delivery options), managers must also think about the type of channel they believe will best support the customer during the buying process. A key decision associated with determining the type of channel system lies in determining the level of sales support that is needed for your product and/or service. Although customers care about the quality of the product and its price, a positive buying experience is what really drives value. A key part of this experience is ensuring that customers are supported in the selling process by channel intermediaries and at the point of purchase. The buying process, as discussed in Chapter 10, consists of four stages: need identification, information search, alternative selection, and the purchase decision. The distribution channel's maximum value lies in the stages of alternative selection and supporting the purchase decision (although it also supports the two initial stages, relating to need identification and information search). Determining how extensive a distribution channel to develop is, in many ways, directly related to the sales support required in educating customers on why the purchase of an organization's product and/or service represents the best solution to their needs. In general, the greater the complexity of the product, the greater the lack of familiarity with the product category by the customer, and the greater the price, the more important the sales support becomes at the time of the purchase. When assessing the types of channel relationships to pursue, managers tend to assess the best fit around the following channel relationship categories:

1. Intensive distribution arrangements
2. Selective distribution arrangements
3. Exclusive distribution arrangements

> Although customers care about the quality of the product and its price, it's a positive buying experience that really drives value.

   Intensive distribution arrangements seek to maximize product availability in the marketplace. Intensive distribution implies a desire by an organization to distribute the product and/or service through as many locations or channel outlets as is

Multi-Channel Distribution refers to the incorporation of a number of different channel connections through which customers can purchase a product and/or service.

Intensive Distribution is a decision by an organization to distribute the product and/or service through as many locations or channel outlets as is possible.

possible. The idea is to have customers see your product and/or service wherever they go. A good example of this lies with **convenience goods**, which are products and services that we use every day. Often, decisions to buy are based on convenience and availability in addition to brand loyalty and commitment. The desire to purchase a soda is a good example of this. Energy-boosting drinks can be found in retail stores, vending machines, grocery outlets, arenas, convenience stores, office building kiosks, and restaurants. As indicated, the advantage of this distribution approach is that it maximizes market penetration and offers tremendous potential for achieving significant scale. The risk for the organization is that it requires a significant financial commitment in inventory to achieve this broad-based availability. It also results in having the product handled by a larger number of distributors, many of whom are carrying a wide variety of products, a number of which are most likely in direct competition with the products/services the organization is trying to sell. This means that the ability and the willingness of the distributor to focus their selling efforts on our product are limited, as there is no focused commitment on our product/service offering.

Selective distribution arrangements narrow the breadth of access that products and/or services have in the marketplace. The decision to limit the extent of the reach could be based on the need for heightened sales support at the time of purchase. As an example, Sofame Technologies Inc. of Montreal limits the sales of its technologically advanced, energy-efficient heat recovery systems to a selected list of authorized dealers. These dealers are considered by Sofame Technologies to possess the necessary expertise and marketplace contacts to assist Sofame in the sale and support of its products. This decision could also be based on a desire to reinforce a brand name or a particular image for a product or service.[4] Going back to our Tapestry Inc. (Coach-branded handbags) example, this organization uses a selective distribution channel for the sale of its products. The purchase of a Coach handbag must take place at either a Coach Inc. retail location or at one of its authorized distributors (Nordstrom, Dillard's, Bloomingdale's, Lord & Taylor). You will not find Coach purses at physical bricks and mortar Walmart or Target locations. The physical set-up and focus of these retailers are simply not in line with the customer profile and image that Tapestry Inc. seeks to communicate to the marketplace. Selective distribution may also be based on geographic clusters, differentiation initiatives, joint ventures, and strategic alliances. Organizations using selective distribution arrangements do so because they believe their products or services will be better supported at the point of sale by these channel intermediaries. They also feel

FIGURE 11.A

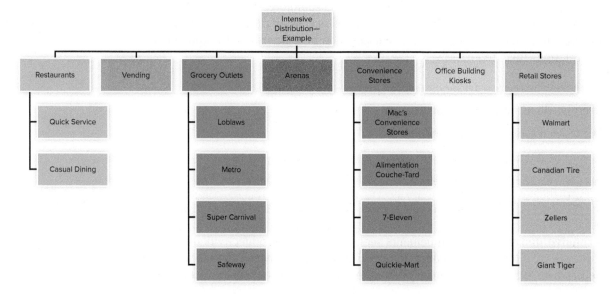

FIGURE 11.B

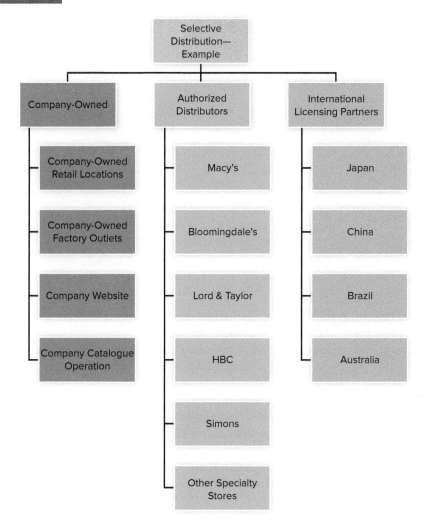

that they can retain a greater degree of control over how the product is priced, marketed, and sold. Finally, these same organizations, by offering an authorized dealer status, can contractually limit the number of competitive offerings that the channel member agrees to carry, thereby minimizing direct competition at the point of purchase for the product or service the organization is seeking to sell.

Exclusive distribution arrangements reflect a further focusing on the distribution of products through a single, authorized channel intermediary. For manufacturers of products, this means offering these products through only one market representative. As an example, Tesla electric vehicles can be purchased only at Tesla "in-person" showrooms or through its online purchasing platform. Organizations often use exclusive distribution arrangements when the selling process associated with their products requires the highest levels of support, or when the organization is attempting to break into new markets. Distribution exclusivity is also a key to franchise-based operations, where the franchisor agrees to provide to the franchisee a full business operating model governed by an exclusivity contract. As an example, M&M Food Market Inc. provides access to its operating model, and its products and services, only to contractually licensed franchisees. The benefit for organizations is that it is anticipated that awarding an exclusive distribution contract to a channel intermediary will result in a total commitment, or a higher level of commitment, by that intermediary. In general, exclusive distribution arrangements should also give the organization maximum say in how the product/service will be marketed and

Exclusive Distribution refers to a decision by an organization to offer its products and/or services through a single market representative.

FIGURE 11.C

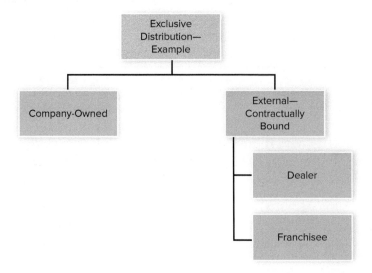

sold, and generally prohibit the channel intermediary from carrying competitive lines. The risk for the organization is that, should the exclusive distribution arrangement not result in the required level of sales success, then the organization may have few immediate alternate options to stimulate demand for the product, as contractual provisions may prevent the organization from terminating the relationship in the short term. For the channel intermediary, the benefit is that it can add to its portfolio a product/service that cannot be purchased elsewhere. Assuming that the product is well received by its target market, this can result in enhanced loyalty not only to the organization's brand, but to the channel intermediary as well. Initial forays into international markets are often undertaken via exclusive distribution arrangements with dealers, brokers, or other channel intermediaries.

Importance of channel intermediaries Although recent trends have seen many businesses shift their distribution strategies to Web-based, direct-reach sales options, managers and marketers should not underestimate the power and importance of channel intermediaries. Successful companies recognize that channel intermediaries are not simply an outlet for the sales of an organization's products and services, but rather are viewed as a key stakeholder and partner in the overall demand-generation and selling process. Channel intermediaries, when properly cultivated and incentivized, can become instrumental in building market share, shaping the product mix through key information gathering and feedback, forecasting demand, participating in and sharing the costs of sales and marketing efforts, educating customers, and acting as critical contacts at the front end of the organization's customer relationship model. In many situations, channel intermediaries bring to the market experience and expertise that the manufacturing and/or service company does not possess in-house. Significant risk mitigation can also take place through channel intermediaries, who commit to purchasing products and/or services in advance, and absorb the cost of unsold inventory once these products are purchased. Used effectively, channel intermediaries help make the connections with customers

Profit Leaks are inefficiencies within an organization's marketing mix that result in margin erosion and loss of profit.

more effective, assist in driving down costs, and help to identify **profit leaks**, thereby improving the overall performance of product and service–supplying organizations. The growth and market strength of Under Armour is a good example of a company that has benefited as a result of a strong distribution channel and market reach marketing strategy predicated on the use of channel intermediaries.

Successful companies recognize that channel intermediaries are not simply an outlet for the sales of an organization's products and services, but rather are viewed as a key stakeholder and partner in the overall demand generation and selling process.

 Business IN ACTION

Business-to-Business (B2B) Sales

The global financial crisis and subsequent recession have caused both sellers and buyers to reflect on their current business relationships. The trimming of human resources and the renewed emphasis on productivity maximization have challenged employers, on both the buying and the selling ends, to do more with less. Add to this the upward cost pressure currently being felt across sales and distribution channels due to ever-climbing transportation expenses, and the pressures to improve efficiency and effectiveness initiatives have never been greater. Competitive intensity, coupled with the need to grow or at least maintain profitability in the face of declining or stagnating sales volume, has resulted in a significant shift in business models across the globe. The end result is that the way in which businesses interact with each other in the B2B (business-to-business) setting is fundamentally changing. For the selling organizations in this value chain relationship, it means trying to provide heightened levels of customer service in the face of tighter and scarcer resources. For the buying organizations, it means seeking out solutions that will enable them to create and sustain competitive advantages in the face of waves of competitive turbulence.

The above commentary is meant to reflect on the fundamental question that is occurring in sales-based organizations today: How do we continue to grow our sales revenues when the business customers we work with have seen theirs flatten? Do we simply try to take sales away from our competitors who are also serving this same client base, or can we develop a more productive and solution-based relationship with this client base, thereby advancing the needs of both our and their organizations? The answer

lies in responding to both of the challenges noted by these questions. To accomplish this, we need to understand better than ever before what our customers want and need. Then, we need to make sure that our salesforce delivers this better than any of our competitors. Recent research by McKinsey & Company has identified the following trends in the relationships between buyers and sellers. First, buyers are becoming increasingly demanding and are, more and more, looking for customized solutions to the challenges they are facing. Second, these buyers are asking sellers to accept more risk and provide greater monetary allowance and benefits, particularly with respect to significant purchase commitments. They are also requiring that these sellers maintain an ongoing relationship presence with these contracts, providing ongoing support, expertise, and value. Finally, customers are looking for solutions, not simply products and/or services. They expect sellers to provide higher levels of expertise at the front end of the sale to ensure that the benefits the buyers hope to achieve are realistic and realizable.

For sellers, these increasing requirements on the part of buyers result in the need to restructure the sales approach to meet these needs and keep profitability objectives obtainable. To do this, sellers must consider three key responses to the heightened demands of customers. First, selling organizations need to commit to long-term training initiatives for their staff to ensure that sales representatives are capable of meeting the expertise requirements of customers. If this is not feasible, then organizations need to develop "pools of expertise" that sales representatives can draw on when needed. Second, selling organizations need to do a better job of assessing the forward profitability potential of each client, and adjust their selling efforts accordingly. Buying organizations, whose potential for future sales is greatest, should be allocated higher levels of salesforce commitment. Finally, as buyers are becoming more accustomed to enhanced technologies, sales organizations should make better use of technology-based sales techniques such as Web conferencing tools, video conferencing, online order platforms, and telephone-based technical support (versus the continuous and costly pressures of meeting face to face). More than ever, customers are willing to accept simple, fast, and inexpensive transaction vehicles, as long as the level of support is there and they see savings derived from these mechanisms reflected in an organization's pricing going forward.

Sales representatives must also pay closer attention to the forward-thinking strategies of their customers in order to anticipate and position the organization toward upcoming sales opportunities.

In closing, selling organizations must align themselves with what customers perceive to be important in maximizing the selling experience, while managing the process in a way that enables the achievement of profitability objectives. This needs to be accomplished without sacrificing the perceived level of commitment the organization has to its customer base. Stronger assessment of customer value, technology options, and required levels of in-house expertise are core to this process.

Communication Strategy: Communicating the "Fit"

Message Rifling is a focused message, driven by a well-defined and developed value proposition, that is targeted specifically at a defined audience.

The fourth pillar of the marketing effort is an organization's communication strategy. Often thought of as advertising and promotion, this marketing mix element involves significantly more than just the development of a media-based message. The key fundamental of this pillar is that the communication strategy needs to demonstrate the "fit" of the value proposition developed as the best solution to the needs of the target market being focused on. Communication strategy development takes the information discussed in Chapter 10 (segmentation, target market selection, customer profiling and positioning) and embodies this within a focused message, driven by a well-defined and well-developed value proposition and targeted specifically at a defined audience (see Figure 11.16). This is referred to as **message rifling**.

FIGURE 11.16   Communicating the "Fit"

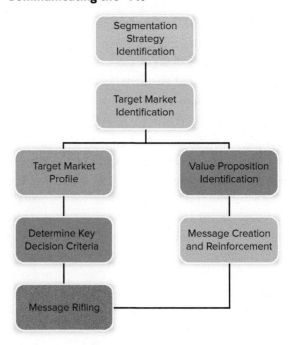

FIGURE 11.17 **Marketer's Tool Box**

Category	Tools of the Trade
Company-Driven Marketing Techniques	Advertising Sales Promotion Publicity Point-of-Purchase Displays Dedicated Sales Force
Consumer-Driven Marketing Techniques	Internet Searches Product Reviews Peer Recommendations Analysts' Blogs and Vlogs Social Media Web Sites and Commentary
Channel Support and Interaction Techniques	Dealer Incentives Point-of-Purchase Discounts Channel Member Training Exclusivity Arrangements Salesperson Recommendations

Message rifling is all about making sure that you are communicating the right product/service value proposition components, to the right audience, at the right time, via the right message mechanism. As managers, we have a variety of communication options. Message communication can be via company-based media programs, direct marketing efforts, channel incentives to stimulate sales support via our channel partners, and third-party initiatives such as product reviews, blogs, and publicity-based initiatives designed to draw positive attention to our offerings. These options were discussed in Chapter 10, and form what has been identified as the marketer's tool box (shown again in Figure 11.17). These communication options are best thought of as tactical tools designed to deliver on the overall marketing effort being implemented for a particular product/service value proposition.

> Message rifling refers to making sure you are communicating the right product/service value proposition components, to the right audience, at the right time, via the right message mechanism.

The development of the marketing communication strategy is really the commencement of the selling process. As was mentioned above, the key is to determine how to link the strategy for the products and services being offered to the marketplace in a manner that enables us to get targeted potential customers to listen to our message and to build a relationship with them, which results in their adoption of our products and/or services. This means we need to think about the best approach to personalizing the relationship, while showing them how our products/services will solve their needs. In developing a communication strategy, managers must think about four key questions:

1. Do we understand why these customers need our products and/or services?

2. Do we understand the level of knowledge that our customers possess concerning the products and/or services we are asking them to purchase?

3 Do we understand who the actual decision maker is when making such a purchase?

4 Are we able to clearly define, in simple terms, what makes our products/services different?

By answering these four questions, we can then use this information to determine where and how best to apply our marketing budget to create awareness for our products and/or services, build interest in them, explain what customers will receive for the purchase, and reinforce the conclusion that our offering is the best fit for solving their need. Armed with this information, and based on our understanding of the buying process, we can finalize decisions on whether we should pursue targeted potential customers through social media, traditional media channels (TV, radio, print media), direct marketing (online, telemarketing, and other offline options), event sponsorship, publicity and public relations tactics, trade shows, merchandising and point-of-sale options, Web-based channels, packaging, or a combination of the above.

Growing importance of social media as part of the communication strategy   As discussed in Chapter 10, consumers move through a multi-stage process when determining which products and/or services to purchase. Historically, this process has led marketers to believe that their efforts should be in two specific areas: creating brand awareness, and swaying purchasers to buy. This meant emphasizing traditional advertising approaches and selling incentives at the point of purchase, in what many interpreted as a "hard sell" environment. Today's customers, armed with access to almost unlimited information via digital and Web-based resources, are looking for marketers to engage them in the buying process, not dictate to them what they should buy. Developing the communication strategy in support of products and/or services today, given the power of the digital environment, means shifting the emphasis to a much broader marketing mandate. This would include:

1 Coordinating communication activities in a way that engages the customer through an increasingly Web-based information and social-network-driven purchase decision.

2 Creating interest in the brand in a way that enables the customer to personalize a relationship with the brand and, hence, act as an ambassador for it.

3 Recognizing the need to create and manage access to an increasing demand for content relating to the products and/or services being offered, the distribution channels being used, and the promotions being offered.

4 Increasing the emphasis on selective utilization of social media and third-party Web-based options in a way that ensures targeted potential customers are reached.[5]

To illustrate the impact that social media is playing in the execution of marketing communication strategies, we take a brief look at some significant findings relating to both the well-known social media engines (Twitter, Facebook, YouTube) and the power of blogs. In a recently published case study, "Social Media Opportunities for Public Companies, Case Study: Players Network, Inc.," New Media Plus—an organization that provides real-time solutions for social media, Web development, graphic design, and online advertising—provided the following insights into the dramatic impact that social media is having on the way customers search for, stay informed about, and buy products and services:

- Studies have shown that people who follow companies and their brands on Facebook and Twitter are more likely to purchase products or services from those companies. They also are more likely to recommend those companies to their friends. More than half of those surveyed indicated a greater willingness to buy a product they follow, and over 60% indicated a willingness to recommend brands that they follow to others.

- The primary reasons why users follow a brand on Facebook are (a) to receive discounts and promotional information for the brand, (b) to identify themselves as customers of a particular brand or company, (c) to draw others to the brand, and (d) because doing so is fun and entertaining.

- Individuals in fully developed countries in Europe, North America, and Asia spend, on average, more than four hours per month watching YouTube videos. Canadians, for example, watch an average of 4.4 hours of YouTube videos per month.

- Companies that blog are found to have more visitors to their Web sites and create more inbound links to their Web sites. Blogging also results in more indexed pages in support of company products, services, and brands.

To place these findings in perspective, let's look at the current level of activity relating to the Internet and social media. Recent estimates of global Internet use as of March 2019 are discussed below.[6]

- The number of Internet users globally is estimated at over 4.3 billion:

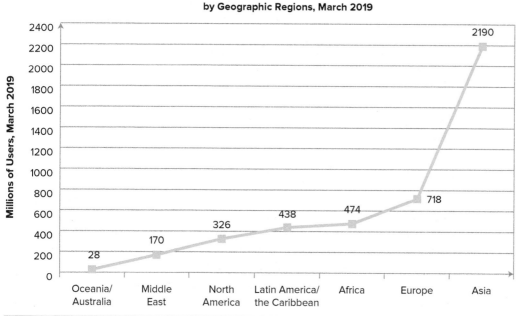

Internet Users in the World by Geographic Regions, March 2019

Sources: Data taken from Miniwatts Marketing Group, Nielsen Online, International Telecommunications Union, and GfK.

- Penetration rates for Internet accessibility now exceed 56% globally, with North America (89%) and Europe (81%) having the highest penetration rates.

- The number of mobile subscribers worldwide now exceeds 5 billion.

- In Asia and Africa, over 50% and 35% of the population, respectively, is now online:

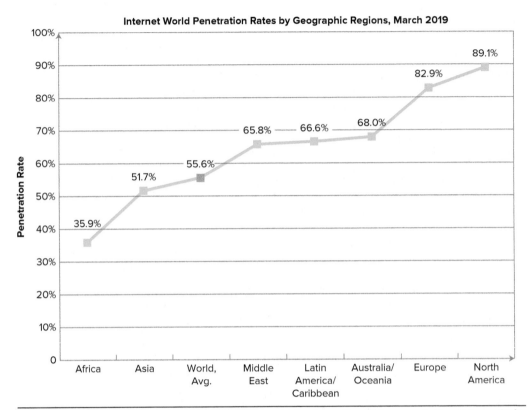

Internet World Penetration Rates by Geographic Regions, March 2019

Sources: Data taken from Miniwatts Marketing Group, Nielsen Online, International Telecommunications Union, and GfK.

As pointed out in the opening Business in Action vignette in Chapter 10, there are currently more than 2.7 billion participants using Facebook services. It is estimated that there are more than 300 million blogs. Over 1.8 billion people, in more than 90 countries, use YouTube monthly and over 600 million hours of video content are uploaded daily. There are an estimated 320 million active tweeters, offering an estimated 500 million tweets per day or 200 billion tweets per year.[7] A recently illustrated example points to the power of the reach of social media networks. A university student, on break at his parents' home, had a disagreement with his mother over cleaning his room. The disagreement centred on whether he should clean his room before the family's cleaning service arrived to clean the house. The mother felt that the room should be tidied up. The student disagreed, indicating that if he were to clean the room, then what would be the value of having a cleaning service. The student, in frustration, decided to post the question on Facebook, asking for comments as to whether it made sense to clean his room prior to the arrival of the cleaning service. The student received hundreds of thousands of responses to this query from all over the world, some in support of the student and some in support of his mother's position. The point is simply that other communication vehicles could not generate such activity, on a global scale, in such a short period of time.

The conclusion to be drawn is that social media marketing, if managed properly, can create reach for an organization and can build loyalty for its products and services in a way never before seen. The most prominent newspapers in the world cannot claim anywhere near the reach of Facebook and Twitter in terms of numbers of subscribers. The key to remember, however, is that despite its tremendous reach, social media marketing requires a strategy, just as any other business decisions need to be made with strategy in mind. Effective social media marketing requires identification of established objectives and evaluation measurements against quantifiable performance metrics. Even before the development of such objectives, companies need to realize that venturing into social media marketing requires a significant commitment. Content has to be frequently updated to ensure that it stays

FIGURE 11.18   Social Media Success Factors

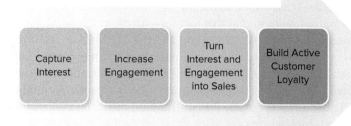

relevant; failure to do so will lead to customer desertion and dissatisfaction. Commitments also have to be made around site and blog monitoring to ensure that relevant data generated by the social media sites used are collected and incorporated into current and future business decision making. When used correctly, social media marketing can provide significant benefits to the organization across a variety of fronts. Companies today are using social media marketing to improve customer relations, inform customers of product promotions and sales, provide coverage for events the organization is participating in, reinforce advocacy of issues understood to be of importance to its followers, monitor customer perceptions of new product releases, assess competitive actions, notify investors of upcoming information releases, and protect and reinforce the organization's reputation. Undertaking social media marketing, like anything else, does not mean automatic success. Managers must recognize its value and its limitations. For social media marketing to be successful, it needs to accomplish four critical things (see Figure 11.18):

1 Capture interest among general Internet traffic

2 Increase customer engagement with the organization

3 Turn interest and engagement into sales

4 Build active customer loyalty

Take Tim Hortons as an example. Tim Hortons launched its Facebook page in 2009; today, it is one of Facebook's most popular Canadian-based sites, with more than 2.3 million fans.[8] This means that approximately one in every 14 Canadians using Facebook is linked to Tim Hortons. The site encourages Tim Hortons customers to post comments on what they love about Tim Hortons. For Tim Hortons, it is a new relationship-building approach to marketing, one that gives the company a unique way to engage with customers. Instead of talking at its customers, it is talking with them. Social media is a venue to gain information and learn about customer likes and dislikes, as well as get responses on key purchase-based decisions. For instance, did you know that past analysis has shown that 67% of Tim Hortons' Facebook followers order a large or extra-large coffee, and that 25% of these customers visit Tim Hortons more than twice per day? Forty-nine percent of these same customers visit Tim Hortons at the start of the day, and 31% order a double-double when they stop in. Why Tim Hortons? More than 55% of the respondents to the Facebook survey on the Tim Hortons site indicated that it is the special taste of the coffee that keeps them coming back. Information like this, from an organizational perspective, is valuable for inventory, staffing, and general operational purposes. Tim Hortons is now expanding its Facebook presence by purchasing ads on Facebook, or what Facebook likes to refer to as "engagement units." Tim Hortons hopes that this combination of a site presence supported by an advertising campaign will assist in growing sales and further building customer loyalty.[9]

Lululemon Athletica's Facebook site, with more than 2.1 million fans, provides customers with an opportunity to comment on upcoming designs, stay up to date on Lululemon events, offer inspiring stories to others, and get the latest news on yoga and fitness tips and trends. Like the Tim Hortons site, Lululemon's site is all about creating the special bond with customers that will enable the organization to create strong brand commitment and active loyalty—all of which results in customers becoming ambassadors for the organization and the products and services it offers.[10]

Returning to our general discussion concerning communication, marketing communication strategies are designed to support the specific objectives an organization has established for a defined business period. These objectives could be focused on building market share, improving the profitability of the current volume, educating customers on product/service benefits, creating profile and awareness, reinforcing brand preference and commitment, supporting point-of-sale initiatives, enhancing the organization's reputation, and delivering post-purchase reinforcement of purchase decisions. Communication tactics form a vital part of this strategy, as their fundamental goal is to effectively deliver the message to the marketplace, thereby defining and reinforcing the purpose of such objectives. A critical aspect of the communication effort lies in its support of the execution strategies in place as a product and/or service, positioned by its value proposition, moves through its life cycle.

Business IN ACTION

The Emergence of Omnichannel Marketing

More and more in retailing and marketing literature we are presented with the term "omnichannel." The question being asked by many is how this term is different from other marketing buzzwords such as multi-channel distribution, direct and indirect channels, and/or extensive distribution. After all, they all seem to refer to some aspect of the channel of distribution an organization will develop and execute within in order to deliver its products and services to the marketplace.

The difference lies in the focus of the management actions and decision making the term *omnichannel* represents. Multi-channel distribution, direct and indirect channels, and extensive distribution are marketing terms built around a historical operations-based, product-centric view of how we get the right product to

the customer at the right place and time. Omnichannel refers to the continuity of the customer experience in interacting with a company. By the nature of the term itself, *omni* implies an understanding of all things. With respect to marketing, it implies that organizations need to strategically create a customer-centric environment in a way that enables customers to have a continuous and consistent experience across all formats and devices. The customer experience needs to be created in such a way that there is seamless integration across mobile, Web-based devices and bricks and mortar platforms. It also implies that what used to be a one-way communication, closed-loop system, where a company controls the buying environment, has now become a two-way communication, open-loop system, where customers, via technology, are able to jump across all brands and conduct direct comparison of products and services on the fly. It is this technology revolution that is shifting the emphasis of marketing strategy even further from the traditional model of service delivery, and even beyond the simple engagement of social media, to a model that focuses on the continual relationship between media and messaging, and fully embeds data-sharing relating to product research, product and purchase selection, and payment platforms into a seamless marketing mix.

Omnichannel marketing recognizes the significant shift in consumer power that has occurred as a result

of the technological advances evolving in the market-place. With this new technology has come new rules for marketers to work with. These new rules can be summarized as follows:

1. Customers are seeking seamless environments—this means that regardless of their information and purchase approach, whether it be via cell phone, tablet app, Web-based inquiry, in-store visit, or a combination of the above, the experience should be continuous and similar in nature.

2. Customers can engage any product, from any company, at any time. This means that the buying process often does not start or end with a visit to your company. Instant comparisons, via NFC technology, etc., with competing products and services can, and will, occur. A recent study published by Bazaarvoice (ROBO—Research Online Buy Offline) showed that 82% of smartphone users consult their phones on purchases they are considering while in a physical store, and more than 45% of potential customers read online reviews prior to finalizing a purchase.

3. A purchase journey may not be made across a single device; it may result in multiple visits across multiple devices. As an example, a customer may add a product into a company's "shopping cart" via the company's Web site but, for a variety of reasons, not buy it. The product should, however, still be in the customer's shopping cart should they re-access the purchase process via a mobile device or tablet-based app.

4. Overdependency in a single channel emphasis (bricks and mortar, etc.) may result in untapped potential in another, and/or lost sales to rivals offering a truer omnichannel experience.

5. Data are everywhere; the question is how to gain the best insight and foresight from the data collected. The better we understand our customers' decision-making process, the better we can build our systems to meet their needs. Examples of areas that omnichannel data initiatives can focus on include (but are not limited to):

   • Shifts in customer sentiment toward brands and products

   • Shifts in product interest and price sensitivity

   • Increasing and/or declining engagement among some or all of an organization's customer base

   • Listening events ranging from webinars and user groups to social media activities (Twitter, LinkedIn, Facebook)

   • Shifts in Web behaviour

   • Engagement with bloggers, etc.

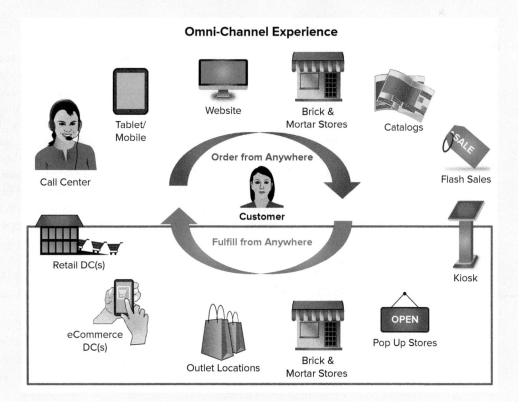

Omni-Channel Experience

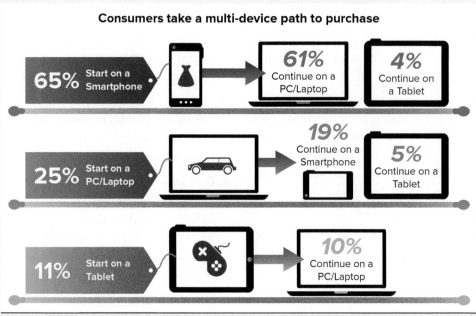

Consumers take a multi-device path to purchase

65% Start on a Smartphone → **61%** Continue on a PC/Laptop   **4%** Continue on a Tablet

25% Start on a PC/Laptop → **19%** Continue on a Smartphone   **5%** Continue on a Tablet

11% Start on a Tablet → **10%** Continue on a PC/Laptop

Source: © Marketo Inc., Used with permission by Marketo Inc.

In closing, omnichannel marketing, when effective, shapes the marketing experience and personalizes it to the customer. In analyzing customer behaviour via clicks, interactions, and the collection of underlying data, effective marketers can mould the experience and reinforce it in such a way to stimulate interest, preference, and purchase for the products and services being offered. To state the ongoing evolution in simplistic terms, omnichannel marketing ultimately looks to fulfill two goals: the ability for customers to order products and/or services from any device, and the ability of companies to fulfill such requests from any point within their distribution models.

LO6   Managing a Product's Life Cycle

The lives of products and services, like companies, are defined by what is called a life cycle. The length of this life cycle and the success that a product or service has within it is determined by both the success of the positioning strategy designed for the product/service and the successful execution of its marketing effort (marketing mix). Traditionally, products that have achieved some initial level of success will transition through five specific stages of life during their life cycle: development, introduction, growth, maturity, and decline (see Figure 11.19). Although most textbooks on this subject start the product life cycle at the introduction stage and, therefore, define the cycle as having four stages, the initial stage of development is included here because it does reflect a significant risk to the organization in terms of both resource consumption and financial commitment. The development stage refers to the steps associated with the creation of a new product/service. This includes the development of an idea or concept; the assessment of its feasibility to be commercialized; the development of a physical prototype (if a product); an analysis of its market potential via focus groups (customer and channel partner), surveys, or third-party testing; resource allocation approval; test marketing; and pre-launch communication initiatives.

Figure 11.19 illustrates a traditional product life cycle. It is traditional in that all five stages are defined and that the revenue and profitability curves reflect a standard growth model where the product, once developed, is introduced to market and, after a period of time, gains market acceptance with its targeted

FIGURE 11.19   **Traditional Product Life Cycle**

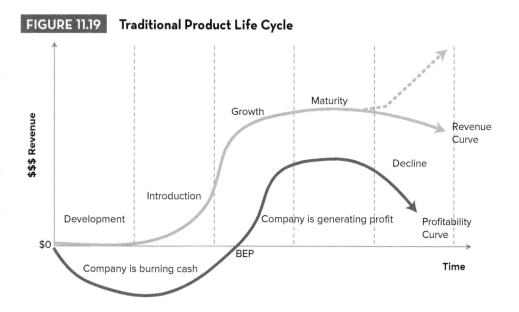

customers. This is then followed by a period of growth where more and more customers become aware of the product and become more familiar with the product
and its benefits. Assuming that the marketing strategy is effective, demand for
the product begins to accelerate significantly. This increased demand and accelerated product adoption rate enables the product to generate sales sufficient to
cover its operating expenses (identified as the BEP—breakeven point), followed
by initial profitability (BEP is discussed in more detail in later chapters). As first-
time customers continue to purchase the product, coupled with repeat purchases
of the product by existing customers, revenue continues to climb, resulting in the
product line becoming able to generate profits. Again, assuming success in this
manner, sales volumes will continue on an upward trend with improved profitability occurring as the product moves through this growth phase. Moving forward in
time, at some point the first-time buyers of the product will begin to decline in
number (because most people who desire the product have now purchased it),
thereby resulting in the sales growth of the product to slow and potentially flatten.
Demand for the product, at this point, can be thought of as being largely driven by
repurchase rates. The length of the maturity stage will be determined by our ability to stimulate repeat purchases and find additional pockets of new customers via
segmentation and target marketing techniques. Product innovation and enhancement, product-line extension strategies, market penetration tactics, and market
consolidation strategies are all examples of initiatives that can be employed in a
mature market to continue to lengthen this stage and maintain or enhance sales
and profitability strategies (see the dashed line in Figure 11.19). At some point, the
product will begin to experience a decline in sales. This could be due to product
obsolescence, a shift in customer needs and demand, or a combination of the two.
As the product progresses through this decline stage, a decision will need to be
made as to how long to support the product and when it would be appropriate for
the organization to divest itself of it.

The discussion above is for illustration purposes only. Not every product follows
the same path. Product life cycles, and the reason for their length and overall success, are influenced by a number of both controllable and non-controllable factors.
For managers, however, it is important to assess what a potential life cycle would
look like, and be prepared to make adjustments to the marketing effort and the overall product strategy once the life cycle is underway. In some cases, life cycles can be

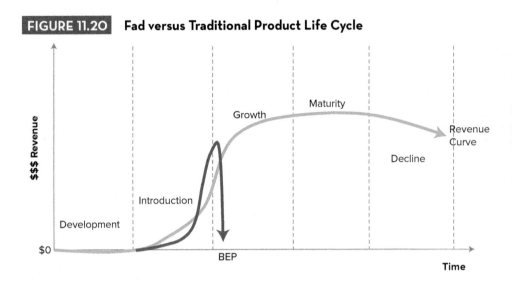

FIGURE 11.20   **Fad versus Traditional Product Life Cycle**

very short. In other cases, life cycles can extend over many years. As an example, consider the life cycle of a fad. In many cases, the overall duration of a fad can be thought of in months versus years. This is largely due to the fact that fads in general represent one-time purchases (little opportunity for repurchase). Given this, the life cycle of a fad may look more like that presented in Figure 11.20. Companies and their management teams who understand the nature of a product as a fad know not to invest heavily in capital infrastructure for the product, given that its lifespan will be very short.

Figure 11.20 could also illustrate the life cycle for a product that has had some early success in attracting first-time buyers but that does not live up to expectations, resulting in low to no repurchase rates as well as negative information being communicated to non-users, which results in diminishing first-time purchaser interest. A similar type of life cycle could also be an initial product offering (such as a variation of financial derivatives) that is forced to be pulled from the market due to governmental regulations or legislation resulting from concerns over negative risk consequences for the market at large.

Figure 11.21 illustrates a product that is enjoying a successful life cycle and then is suddenly rendered obsolete. This could be due to a new emergent technology, a significant shift in customer preferences and behaviour, or a combination of both. It

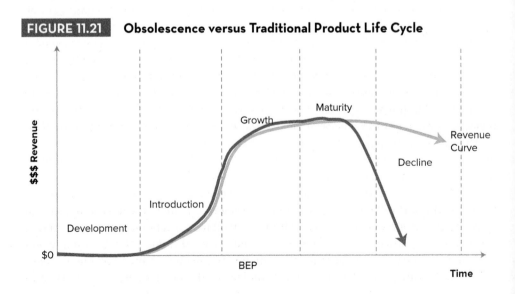

FIGURE 11.21   **Obsolescence versus Traditional Product Life Cycle**

FIGURE 11.22   **Life Cycle Outcomes**

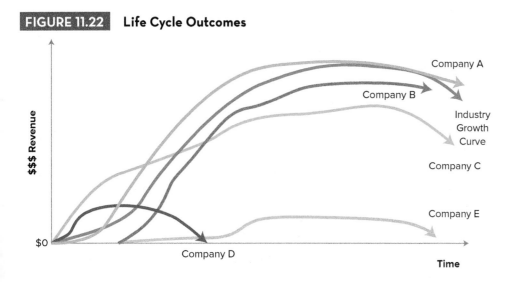

could also be the result of an unanticipated and uncontrollable risk trigger impacting the company and its industry. A good example of this would be the dramatic decline in the sale of music CDs as a result of the advent of disruptive innovators, such as Napster and Kazaa, and the downloading of music via similarly focused Web sites. We are also seeing the same life cycle degradation occurring with respect to the purchase of music downloads, as the market shifts toward music streaming via online services such as those offered by Spotify, Pandora, Amazon, Google, and Apple.

The ability to effectively position a product and execute a successful marketing effort will also significantly influence the length and success of its life cycle. Let's take the example of an emerging market, such as the market for smartphones. This industry represents a significant opportunity for a number of mobile phone manufacturers globally. Although many of these manufacturers may enter the market at early stages of market development, not all will be successful. Figure 11.22 provides some potential outcomes for companies involved in this market.

In Figure 11.22, five companies have entered our hypothetical smartphone industry. The orange line represents the industry growth curve for this period from the time of the initial emergence of this industry to the current date. As you can see, companies A, C, and D all entered the industry at its inception. Companies B and E entered a bit later. Company A has ended up being the industry leader, with its growth rate exceeding that of the industry. Company C initially looked to be the market leader, with a quick growth spurt early on, but then experienced a flattening of sales coinciding roughly with the time that Company B entered the market. Company D had some brief success early on, but then simply was unable to compete, and exited the market. Company B continued to show strength despite being a later entrant into the market, and has ended up #2 and a main market challenger to Company A. Company E, also a late entrant, never really did find a position in the marketplace that customers identified with and, as such, ends up being a marginal player.

Managing across the Life Cycle

Success within the life cycle of a product or service comes down to possessing an effective positioning strategy backed by a successful marketing effort formulated around a meaningful (in the eyes of customers) value proposition. As managers, we need to be able to sense the stage of development not only for our product/ service offering, but also for the industry itself. We also need to anticipate competitive actions, coupled with their potential for disruptive innovation, and shifts that can, and most likely will, occur in consumer preferences and/or behaviour. Life cycle management is all about knowing what the key success factors are within each stage (see Figure 11.23), and the potential triggers that will cue managers to the transition in focus that is necessary as the product/service offering shifts from one stage to the next. Having said this, managers also must take care that their

FIGURE 11.23   Managing across the Product Life Cycle

	Development	Introduction	Growth	Maturity	Decline
Marketing Objective	Viable product idea. Can be commercialized.	Customer acquisition. Grow market share and required scale. Properly position with primary target audience.	Customer acquisition and customer retention. Grow market share and required scale.	Customer retention and segmentation stretch. Defend market share, and/or seek to create new market space.	Harvest or milk the product. Treat it as a cash cow. Assess possibility to revitalize the product.
Marketing Effort	Test marketing. Pre-launch advertising and publicity. Establish initial channel partners.	Create awareness and profile. Meet expectations. Successful product launch. Define market position and key differentiators.	Create product and brand preference and loyalty. Reinforce early adopters' decisions to buy. Stress differentiation.	Reinforce brand and product differentiation. Increase market penetration and market development activities. Assess potential for product line extensions.	Data mine to determine most profitable customers. Maximize efficiency and effectiveness of expenditures.
Financial	Manage burn rate. Sufficient enough capital.	Manage burn rate. Get to breakeven point. Sufficient capital to cover operating expenses and launch needs.	Achieve break-even point. Sufficient capital to continue to support product and business system needs.	Maximize return on sales. Maximize the returns on additional incremental investment.	Maintain margins in the face of diminishing volumes. Assess attractive divestiture options.
Profits	Non-existent—no revenue stream	Generally, no profits early on.	Achieve profitability objectives.	Seek profit and ROI maximization.	Maintain profitability for as long as possible.
Competitors	First-to-market concerns. Protecting intellectual property.	Starting to emerge or are already in the market. Who has first mover advantage?	New entrants entering the market. Enhanced product offerings from competitors.	Watch for market consolidation. Assess risk of disruptive innovations.	Look for additional revenue opportunities as competitors exit the market.
Common Stage Transition Triggers	Concept can be shifted to working prototype. Focus groups (customers and suppliers) respond positively to idea. Test marketing meets or exceeds expectations. Pre-launch publicity and promotion generates interest.	Product launch occurs, signalling commercialization. Initial customer acquisition takes place.	Demand for the product accelerates, placing pressure on infrastructure capacity and operating margins. Competitive segmentation activities emerge.	Demand in core markets slows. Repurchase dependency heightens. Competitors further segment the market. Consolidation activity increases. Niche market activities increase.	Repurchase rates slow. Segmentation opportunities diminish. Some competitors exit the market. Consumer trends shift is readily apparent. Innovation opportunities become minimal.

actions do not result in a self-fulfilling prophecy. An example of this would be assuming that the marketplace for a particular product or service will soon decline due to the belief that because we are in a mature market, decline is inevitable. Given this belief, the managers then make decisions to pull back on supporting the product, thereby reducing the marketing effort and, ultimately, leading the product or service offering into decline.

> Success within the life cycle of a product or service comes down to possessing an effective positioning strategy backed by a successful marketing effort formulated around a meaningful (in the eyes of customers) value proposition.

 Business IN ACTION

Transportation—Cost Implications (Global Reach)

One only has to look back over the last 10+ years to see the significant impact that globalization has had on the competitive landscape of many commercial sectors. With the rise of the emerging economies (as discussed in Chapter 3), many organizations have sought to take advantage of the market and production-based opportunities that these economies have offered. The end result has been the ability to offer the global consumer more products than ever before at very attractive price points. Taking advantage of outsourcing and the comparative advantages that various countries across the globe offer, businesses have become experts in managing global supply chains. The efficiency and effectiveness of this model has resulted in the development of complex and highly sophisticated transportation systems predicated on cost efficiencies that enable products to be assembled across the globe and transported to customers at a lower cost than if the products were produced at home. This model, however, has been largely developed around the theory that the additional cost of transportation is more than offset by the savings achieved in labour and other direct product costs that result from producing abroad. The challenge going forward lies in whether this model will hold true in the face of rising standards of living in emerging economies, and the cost implications to transportation in light of ever-changing demand and supply issues. As an example, Air Canada estimates

that for every dollar increase in oil prices, its fuel costs increase by $25 million on an annualized basis. While oil prices have fallen dramatically over the recent past, long-term consensus is that the current environment of inexpensive oil will not continue indefinitely. Transportation costs impact the margins and profitability of companies at all levels of business activity. Emerging economies and their growth are expected to continue to place upward pressure on the cost of commodities. Add to this increased transportation costs to deliver such raw materials to their markets, and the end result is an already higher cost base at the front end of the manufacturing and/or assembly process. These costs then make their way through the distribution channel when transportation costs continue to impact an organization's overall cost base and, therefore, the price that needs to be charged to the final user. As the cost of oil rises, as an example, so, too, does the cost of gasoline, jet fuel, and other product categories that are petroleum based. The long-term upward trend in fuel prices will continue to impact trucking companies and their cost of doing business. Although there may be a willingness, perhaps, to absorb short-term increases to remain competitive, these trucking companies will ultimately be required to pass on these costs to buyers. Manufacturers and suppliers will continue to use technology and enhanced transportation modelling in an effort to offset this upward cost creep.

AFP/Getty Images

Don Hammond/DesignPics/getstock.com

Rising transportation costs also impact the buying capabilities of customers. The global marketplace is driven by the demand for goods and services, with the consumer accounting for a significant portion of this overall demand. Consumer-based goods companies, which are facing upward price pressure given transportation costs, also must recognize that these same cost pressures are being felt by consumers themselves, thereby impacting their propensity and their ability to purchase goods and services. With the price of oil, on a per barrel basis, expected to continue its long-term move upward as the global demand and supply relationship tightens, transportation costs will continue to be front and centre in the minds of managers and marketers, as well as consumers.

LO7   Managing a Product Portfolio

Up to this point, our focus has been on managing a single product. In many organizations, managers are responsible for the growth and financial solvency of an entire product portfolio. This could be with respect to a family of products marketed under a primary brand (Cheerios, Honey-Nut Cheerios, Multi-grain Cheerios), or a series of complementary products such as Frito-Lay snacks (Lay's, Fritos, Doritos, Tostitos, Cheetos, Sun Chips, Cracker Jack).[11] Each product needs to be evaluated and value propositions adjusted and repositioned through continuously focused and refocused marketing communication efforts. As managers, we need to make decisions on where to expand the investment in support of a particular product and/or product line, where to maintain a given level of investment, when to reduce investment (harvest), and, finally, when to divest ourselves of it. This means constantly assessing the market potential of the product or service that we are evaluating, making adjustments to its positioning in the market, and revisiting the marketing communication efforts in a way that reinforces or revitalizes the product and its brand, its awareness, preference, loyalty, and commitment. Portfolio management is all about making decisions on where to invest in order to improve the organization's market position going forward. As managers, one fundamental we can almost always count on is that the resource needs of the organization will exceed our ability to supply such resources. This means that, given the finite nature of our financial and physical resources, and the fact that our needs will exceed our supply, we will continually be pressed to define priorities on where to invest and grow the organization. Decisions relating to this will impact the various products and/or services within our portfolio. As managers, however, our responsibility lies in doing what is best to improve the overall performance of the organization versus any one individual product line. Trade-offs will, ultimately, have to be made. One approach to making decisions relating to where to invest, maintain,

FIGURE 11.24   **Assessing Future Product Potential**

		Strong	Weak
Future Market Potential	High	What should be done to further expand our scale and our returns, given our strong market position?	What can we do to change things? Will rebranding or repositioning get us back on track?
	Medium	Is there an opportunity to stretch or tap further into secondary markets to improve returns?	Can we improve "harvesting" or "niche" marketing results by increasing the efficiency and effectiveness of our marketing effort? If not, should we divest?
	Low	Should we simply seek to maximize the "cash cow" effect? Can the dollars being generated be better used elsewhere versus reinvested in this product?	Why are we here? Does divestiture mean that freed resources can be better used elsewhere?

Current Value Proposition Strength

harvest, and divest is called the growth/share matrix, made popular by the Boston Consulting Group. This business model suggested that, as a frame of reference in making portfolio management decisions, managers focus on the growth potential of a product relative to the product strength that it currently possesses in the marketplace. A variation of this model is presented in Figure 11.24.[12]

> Portfolio management is all about making decisions on where to invest in order to improve the organization's market position going forward.

Taking the core components of the growth/share matrix, the model presented in Figure 11.24 is designed to focus managers on the core cost/benefit trade-offs that need to be considered given the relationship between market potential and the current market position that a product's value proposition has within the marketplace. This revised model also recognizes that market potential may not always be categorized as high or low, but that a given, acceptable level of market potential may offer managers opportunities to further grow a product line and/or service opportunity via selective strategies. As managers, we need to recognize that growing markets require investment. The key question, however, lies in the return that such an investment can generate over the anticipated life of the product's life cycle. Similarly, products that have failed to achieve acceptable returns should be questioned, with the focus being on either correcting the situation via positioning and renewed marketing effort, or divesting of the product in order to reallocate the resources toward more profitable ventures.

A Note Pertaining to Not-for-Profits

As with for-profit entities, not-for-profit organizations (NFPs) must also be skillful in the execution of their marketing efforts. For not-for-profits, these efforts focus on both communicating the mission of the organization and stimulating and reinforcing the demand for the NFP's products and services. Of significant challenge for the NFP is to be successful in doing this without creating the perception that the NFP has abandoned its altruistic motives for financial purposes. Not-for-profits must also seek to make use of the same tools that for-profit entities use in the creation of their marketing mix. Social networks, focus groups, media-based advertising, and channel partner development are of equal importance in the NFP arena. Utilization of Facebook and other social media sites enables stakeholders to provide a real "voice" in support of the not-for-profit's efforts. Social media sites, organized by the NFP, provide a viable, low-cost opportunity for communicating the organization's community activities, and solicit requests for assistance on meaningful objectives organized by the not-for-profit. For the NFP, the key components for survival lie in the ability of the organization to achieve rootedness within the community and vitality through membership, philanthropic gifts, and the meaningful delivery of its services in support of its mission. To successfully accomplish this, the NFP needs to achieve the same outcomes as for-profit organizations with respect to brand recognition and a value proposition that is judged by its customers and users to be superior to those of other for-profits and NFPs competing for the same dollars. Sustainable business models, even in the not-for-profit sector, are built around the four pillars of marketing. The life cycle of an NFP is subject to the same market pressures as those of companies and products in the for-profit sector. Failure to communicate and deliver a meaningful solution to a need can result in the desertion of support from both monetary and altruistic stakeholders.

> Sustainable business models, even in the not-for-profit sector, are built around the four pillars of marketing.

Business IN ACTION

The Hospital for Sick Children—Marketing a Fundraising Campaign

Constructed in 1949, The Hospital for Sick Children (SickKids) was at that time the largest children's hospital in the world. However, although advances in medicine have been both dramatic and significant as time progressed, this has not been the case

JHVE Photo/Shutterstock.com

for the hospital's underlying infrastructure—its buildings, plant and facility equipment, and so on. As Dr. Mike Apkon, President and CEO of SickKids, stated, "Many of the world's top paediatric health experts work right here at The Hospital for Sick Children, but our facilities and infrastructure don't match the level of expertise of our people. Twenty-first century medicine shouldn't be held back by a 1949 building." The oldest parts of the hospital—now 70 years old—have ceiling heights that can't accommodate robotic technology or the weight of MRI machines, and key patient areas are cramped and lacking in infection control.

In response to the need to recreate one of the world's leading children's hospitals, in 2017 The Hospital for Sick Children, via its Foundation, launched the largest fundraising campaign in Canadian health care history. Backed by $570 million in donations and pledges, in October 2017 the SickKids Foundation publicly announced a $1.3-billion fundraising goal, entitled "SickKids VS Limits campaign." The five-year campaign is anticipated to be completed in March 2022.

The ultimate vision for the hospital is that of a state-of-the-art medical treatment and research facility, designed to support the latest advances in clinical procedures, optimize patient safety and infection control, and provide "best practice" family-centred care. The fully redeveloped campus will include building a new SickKids campus ($600 million), offering a fully supported environment enabling break-through paediatric health research ($600 million), and establishing partnerships for enhanced patient care ($100 million).

Organizations such as SickKids must clearly show the public at large that supporting the services they provide adds value to society and to donors' personal daily lives. In developing its marketing campaign, it was crucial that SickKids Foundation demonstrate the need for donors to step up to help reach the goal. This fundraising campaign therefore requires a well-developed marketing strategy. The campaign needed to drive urgency and grab the attention of new potential donors in a new and disruptive way. To communicate the fundraising campaign need requires a fully integrated marketing strategy and campaign supported by TV, digital, cinema, social media, print, and out-of-home (TTC billboards and streetcar takeovers). Critical to the launch of the campaign

was a two-minute video at the Toronto Maple Leafs home opener that articulated the need and, equally important, showed the SickKids brand was winning in the ongoing battle against the enemy—childhood illness.

The marketing campaign, developed in partnership with Cossette, the Foundation's marketing agency of record and OMD, their media agency of record, took the position that it would be more effective if it positioned SickKids as a high-performance brand. This would demonstrate to the public a winning brand deserving of support at all levels, as any gift would contribute to the achievement of tangible positive results in this epic battle. The campaign strategy and its corresponding activities resulted in Cossette taking home eight Cannes Lions awards in 2017, and in SickKids earning the 2018 Grand Prix and three Golds (Cause, New Brand Positioning, and Strategic Thinking) at the 2018 CASSIES award ceremony, among many others.

So how is the campaign doing? With more than 800 000 donors to date, SickKids is over halfway toward achieving its goal. It also was announced in October 2018 that the Government of Ontario would commit $2.4 billion in funding to construct the building shell of a new hospital, but that the hospital, via its $1.3-billion campaign, will need to provide all of the internal supporting infrastructure and research-related requirements. It is estimated that the transformation to a new hospital campus will take approximately 10 years to complete. Accompanying the children in the photo is Peter Gilgan, of the Peter Gilgan Foundation, who made a $100 million gift to the SickKids VS Limits campaign. A long-time supporter of SickKids (prior donations in excess of $40 million), the new patient care tower of the revitalized SickKids campus will be named the Peter Gilgan Family Patient Care Tower. Students interested in watching the two-minute kick-off video, or in becoming more knowledgeable about the efforts being undertaken by SickKids, can visit https://www.sickkidsfoundation.com.

Steve Russell/Getty Images

Management Reflection—Managing the Marketing Effort

The effective execution of an organization's marketing mix is one of the critical success factors that managers must focus on in their bid to ensure the immediate and long-term health of their organization. Profits and profitability come from satisfied customers who have received value as a result of their purchase experience. In planning an organization's overall strategy, and in executing the tactics associated with it, committed expenses often precede operating performance. Recognizing this, managers must be sure of the direction that the organization is taking in positioning its products and services and of the effective execution of its marketing effort. In many sectors in today's marketplace, the choices that customers have have never been greater. This explosion of choice has required organizations to further customize their product and/or service offerings in order to create uniqueness and improve the overall perception of the importance of their product in solving a customer's problem. Doing so, however, results in an even finer segmentation and target market slicing and dicing approach. Driven by this need to specialize in order to create enhanced differentiation, marketers and managers also increase the probability of error that the alignment executed will not yield the required success results. In many product and/or service categories, customer expectations are such that many believe the perfect solution to their needs and/or problems must exist. For managers and marketers, this results in a growing complexity of how to position and market. It also means that the ability to create brand profile, preference, and commitment are becoming more fundamental to the success in many product and service categories. Faced with an almost endless number of choices, customer decision making has become so overwhelming, in some cases, that those customers are often forced to default to the most familiar brand and/or the one that is most easily accessible. As managers, we need to recognize the demands that all of these interrelated pressures are placing on our ability to be successful in the delivery of products and services in the segments in which we are marketing. Being at the top of the predetermined purchase list at the time of the purchase decision is paramount to our success. For the customer, in some ways it may not matter whom they choose—as long as they choose. For us as managers, whom they choose is core to our sustainability and success. Our marketing mix needs to communicate why that choice should be us.

Appendix—Advanced Topics Relating to Pricing

With the emergence of the global marketplace and the ongoing explosion of online selling and buying, the challenges associated with pricing are greater than ever before. Whereas the marketplace at one time could depend on a relatively fixed price approach, where an initial price could be set and held for an extended period of time, pricing decisions today are more fluid and dynamic. Competitors are continually utilizing price as a weapon of competitive rivalry in order to gain awareness and drive demand for their products and/or services. Conversely, retailers are also looking to use price as a key component of a differentiation strategy that, as an example, could seek to establish a luxury-focused brand identity in the marketplace, thereby enabling organizations to drive greater margins from the sale of individual products/services. Volatility in transportation costs due to rapid changes in the price of fuel have resulted in industries, such as the airline industry, adopting variable pricing strategies that add surcharges to base prices in order to compensate for uncontrollable fluctuations in costs. With more companies doing business globally,

FIGURE 11.25 **Total Cost-Base Analysis**

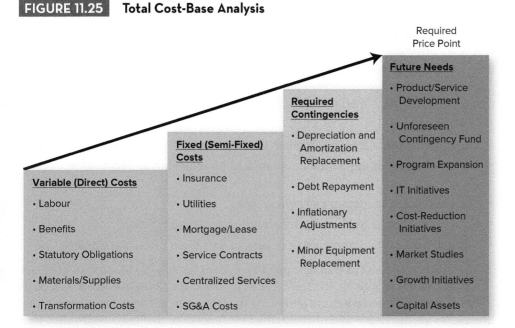

currency exchange rates, combined with market size (in international regions) and different environmental and other regulatory requirements, add further complexity to the pricing decision-making process.

With all this in mind, one can readily see that the art of pricing a product or service has become an almost customized process, for which one needs to consider the four fundamental impact factors identified in Figure 11.11: total cost base, effectiveness of marketing effort, value (real or perceived), and market price sensitivity.

As was also discussed earlier in this chapter, managers need to fully understand the costs associated with their organization's operations. In addition to understanding these fundamental operational requirements, managers also need to anticipate the required additional financial contingencies associated with the organization, as well as its future needs, to ensure that price points being considered adequately cover both the current and future organizational financial requirements (see Figure 11.25).

In terms of the required additional financial contingencies, managers need to think about the establishment of reserves sufficient to fund the replacement of equipment, plant, and facility, and other capital assets, due to wear and tear and obsolescence. Debt repayment requirements, and **expense creep** due to inflationary pressures, are additional factors that should be assessed and incorporated into a product or service's pricing formula. In addition to these known needs, future needs also must be analyzed. This could be focused on such items as product development through R&D investment, technology-based initiatives to enhance organizational processes, service systems or process support systems, market studies focused on new market opportunities, or other potential growth initiatives. It is important to understand that revenue is the result of price times quantity sold, and as such is the core source of the dollars that an organization has at its disposal. What it does not generate internally through the sale of its products and/or services will need to be secured externally (these concepts are discussed more fully in Chapter 13). Although it is recognized that the total financial needs of the organization generally cannot be generated internally, the operations of the organization are what will, ultimately, need to be used to repay the costs incurred, and the debt taken on, in support of organizational activities. This needs to be considered and assessed when determining price points for the various products and services offered by the organization.

Expense Creep refers to the tendency for expenses associated with the organization's various cost lines to rise due to inflationary pressures, union negotiated contracts, and so on.

As managers, we must also understand that pricing decisions cannot be made in a vacuum, focused solely on costs, but that external influences, competitive offerings, and customer expectations will all significantly influence the price at which we offer our products and services to the marketplace. Customers, in finalizing a product selection or a decision on where to purchase needed services, will assess the various options and determine which competitive offering they feel represents the best price/quality trade-off. This decision will be influenced by factors such as:

- The customer's ability or willingness to pay
- The preferences of the customer in terms of functionality and intangible "psychographic" benefits
- The importance of quality and performance
- Behavioural issues, such as the regularity and intensity of use
- The number of direct alternatives or options available in the marketplace

This purchase process (as was discussed in earlier chapters) is based on a comparison of the value proposition being offered by the organization against that of its direct competitors, and a determination, by the customer, of the product/service that best meets his/her needs and provides the best functional and perceived value. Recognizing this as a core fundamental to the purchase decision process, managers need to ensure that the price they set meets the needs of the organization with respect to covering its costs and driving the required profit margin (organization's incentive to sell). They must also, however, match this with the price that provides customers with an acceptable incentive to buy (see Figure 11.26).

Pricing decisions cannot be made in a vacuum. External influences, competitive offerings, and customer expectations will all significantly influence the price at which we offer our products and services to the marketplace.

The ability of an organization to effectively differentiate itself from its competitors via uniqueness, quality, or importance can mitigate the use of price as a weapon of competitive rivalry by its competitors. Marketing effectiveness, focused on brand, product, or use differentiation, can be fundamental to enabling an organization to

FIGURE 11.26   Pricing Incentive

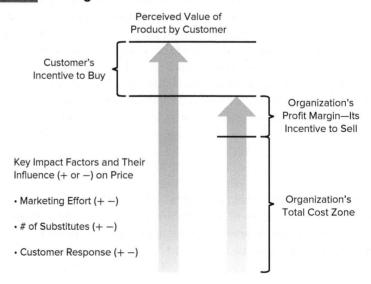

FIGURE 11.27   **Pricing: Marketing Effectiveness**

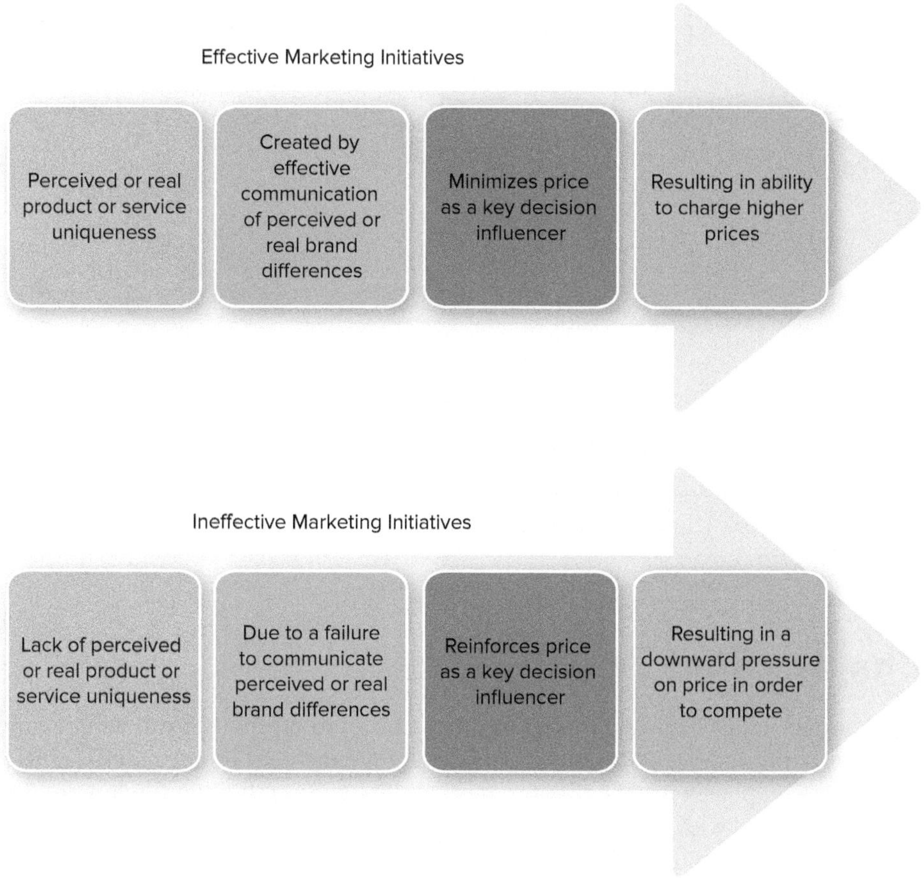

Effective Marketing Initiatives

| Perceived or real product or service uniqueness | Created by effective communication of perceived or real brand differences | Minimizes price as a key decision influencer | Resulting in ability to charge higher prices |

Ineffective Marketing Initiatives

| Lack of perceived or real product or service uniqueness | Due to a failure to communicate perceived or real brand differences | Reinforces price as a key decision influencer | Resulting in a downward pressure on price in order to compete |

achieve stronger margins through premium pricing strategies that buyers accept as valid "value" reinforcement. The absence of such effective marketing messages can, and often does, result in price becoming a more critical decision criterion on the part of purchasers (see Figure 11.27).

As has been previously noted, the pricing process, on an ongoing basis, remains a challenging aspect of management's responsibility. It is, after all, the root from which revenue is generated. By clearly identifying the profit objectives of the organization, and more fully understanding its cost base and the external impact factors that will influence price, managers can more effectively price products and services in a way that reinforces the firm's overall strategic positioning in the marketplace and maximizes the value proposition the organization offers to its customers. Once price is set, the process does not end. Ongoing assessment of profitability, costs, and competitive conditions is required to continually ensure that market reaction to the pricing strategy in place maintains the necessary balance between the needs of the organization and meeting the expectations of its customer base (see Figure 11.28).[13]

By more fully understanding the cost base of an organization and the external impact factors that will influence price, managers can more effectively price products and services in a way that reinforces the firm's overall strategic positioning in the marketplace and maximizes the value proposition the organization offers to its customers.

FIGURE 11.28   Pricing Process

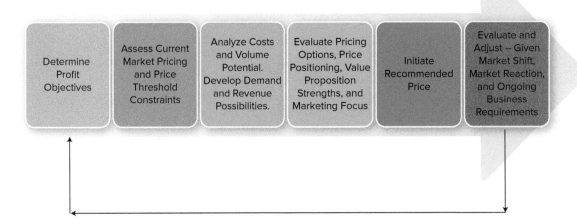

Chapter Summary

This chapter focuses on understanding the marketing effort that we, as managers, will need to direct in order to ensure a successful execution of our marketing strategy. A core emphasis in this chapter is on understanding the key fundamental elements associated with developing our value proposition, price position, distribution approach, and communication tactics, which are critical to the success of products and services associated with our organization. The recognition of the importance of brand power, as well as the influence of price on the purchase decision-making process, is a key component of this discussion. The distribution tactical discussion is supported by commentary associated with channel selection requirements and the integration of sales support and channel intermediary decision-making involvement in the product/service delivery process. The chapter also revisits the concept of the "marketer's tool box" from Chapter 10, adding to this discussion the integration of these tools with the concepts of segmentation, target marketing, customer profiling, and value proposition development into a rifled communication message, which results in the product and/or service being offered as the best "fit" for responding to a customer's needs. The chapter then transitions into a discussion of the key stages of a product or service's life cycle, and how we, as managers, can and should manage this process, defining the key objectives to be achieved within each stage and cueing us to the required tactical marketing shifts that will influence our success. An extension of this discussion is a broadening of our responsibilities to actively assess, on an ongoing basis, the overall market potential of our entire portfolio of products, drawing conclusions as to where to invest, expand, maintain, retrench, and divest, depending on overall current product strength and future market potential. The chapter closes with a note relating to the importance of not-for-profits to recognize that the four pillars of marketing (marketing mix) are fundamental to their success as well, along with the importance of maintaining their balance between altruistic mission requirements and the economic realities of financial stability and sustainability.

Developing Business Knowledge and Skills

Key Terms

marketing mix *p. 392*

predetermined purchase list *p. 396*

price elasticity *p. 401*

consumer price threshold *p. 401*

payback period *p. 402*

direct distribution *p. 404*

channel intermediary *p. 404*

indirect distribution *p. 405*

mixed distribution systems *p. 405*

multi-channel distribution *p. 407*

intensive distribution *p. 407*

convenience goods *p. 408*

selective distribution *p. 408*

exclusive distribution *p. 409*

profit leaks *p. 410*

message rifling *p. 412*

expense creep *p. 431*

Questions for Discussion

1. What are the four pillars of marketing? How do these pillars (marketing mix elements) combine to create an organization's marketing effort? (LO1, LO2, LO3, LO4, LO5)

2. The average supermarket can offer 40 000+ items to its customers. A quick look at the market can identify as many as 90 different types of shampoos and almost 100 different varieties of toothpaste. One manufacturer of orange juice has over 20 different varieties itself. What does this say about the importance of branding in today's marketplace? (LO2)

3. What are the two primary ways in which managers can seek to respond to the globally driven downward pressure on price? Of the two, which do you feel is the more effective? Why? If your answer is "it depends on the situation," then what key positioning indicators would determine which route you would take? (LO3)

4. What are the four key fundamental factors that managers need to assess when determining what price to charge for an organization's products and/or services? (LO3)

5. The distribution of products and/or services can impose upon an organization some of its largest transaction costs. How do channel intermediaries assist in reducing these costs for manufacturers and suppliers? (LO4)

6. What do you believe are the key marketing objectives that managers need to focus on within each stage of a product and/or service's life cycle? Given your response, where would you focus your marketing effort in order to ensure that these identified objectives are met? (LO5, LO6, LO7)

Question for Individual Action

Choose a product or service that was recently introduced into the marketplace, but was then pulled from the market by the company. Why did the company cease offering this product and/or service? Based on your knowledge of marketing, what, in your mind, was the fundamental reason for this product or service failure? Was it due to poor positioning, an ineffective execution of the marketing mix, or a combination of the two? Be prepared to present your analytical findings to your fellow classmates.

Team Exercise

As a team, identify a not-for-profit organization in your city or town that you have some familiarity with. Research its current use of social marketing media in communicating its mission and message to its community stakeholders. How effective do you believe its social media approach is? What recommendations would you make to this NFP to improve its use of this communication tool? Create a fundraising idea for this NFP and provide an outline as to how you would implement a social media marketing campaign in support of it. Prepare a presentation outlining your fundraising idea and the social media campaign that you have developed in support of it.

Case for Discussion

Omnichannel—The New Normal at Nordstrom

In 2014, U.S.-based fashion retailer Nordstrom entered the Canadian marketplace, opening its first store in Calgary's Chinook Centre. Since then, the company has opened stores in Toronto's Eaton Centre, Yorkdale Shopping Centre, and Sherway Gardens, as well as Ottawa's Rideau Centre and Vancouver's Pacific Centre. The entry of these full-line stores was followed by four Nordstrom Rack stores, one each in Toronto, Ottawa, Edmonton, and Calgary. In testing the Canadian market, Nordstrom maintains plans to expand to other centres in Canada over the coming years as part of its Canadian growth strategy.

Founded in 1901, Nordstrom carries a wide range of mostly upscale brands in the women, men, kids, home, and beauty categories. While many retailers have been struggling to adjust to life in the convenience and digital economy, Nordstrom has moved steadily to provide multiple opportunities for consumers to interact with the brand both via physical locations and online ecommerce websites. Nordstrom's current product portfolio consists of the following:

Zhi Qi/Dreamstime.com

- *Full-line stores*: Nordstrom operates 122 full-line, bricks and mortar stores in the United States and Canada.

- *Nordstrom Rack stores*: The off-price division (brands are offered at 30–70% off retail) operates 244 bricks and mortar stores.

- *Nordstrom.com*: Customers from over 95 countries can purchase from the full-line Web site.

- *Nordstromrack.com*: If they prefer, customers can complete their Nordstrom Rack purchases digitally.

- *Hautelook.com*: Nordstrom's members-only shopping site offers discounts of 50–75% from retail through flash sales and limited time events.

- *Jeffrey Boutiques*: The luxury boutique, acquired by Nordstrom in 2005, operates in New York, Atlanta, and Palo Alto.

- *Clearance stores*: Nordstrom operates two "Last Chance" clearance stores in Phoenix and Chicago.

- *Trunk Club Clubhouses*: Customers interact digitally with stylists to assemble curated trunks of clothing that are shipped directly to their doors. Customers can also use the Trunk Club styling services through bricks and mortar locations in Boston, Chicago, Dallas, Los Angeles, New York, and Washington.

Although there has been an ongoing perception that bricks and mortar retail is dying, Nordstrom in particular continues (at least, to date) to prove such critics wrong. The secret sauce for Nordstrom's success has been a growth strategy focused on key moves in two distinct areas: ecommerce and "off rack." As stated by former company president Blake Nordstrom, "We invested early in our omni-channel capabilities integrating our inventory across our stores and online over a decade ago. This has enabled us to serve customers in multiple ways. Today we have more than 60 combinations in which merchandise is ordered, fulfilled and delivered." The company was also one of the first players in the women's apparel discount sector, opening its first Nordstrom Rack location in 1973, with over 70 locations by 2010 (compare this to Macy's just opening its first off-rack location in 2015).

The early digital push by the 100-year-old-plus firm enabled it to realize significant gains across its various channels and, at least initially, weather the digital storm that has disrupted retail over the past several years. As an example, in 2018 Nordstrom online sales were already 25% of total sales revenue, well beyond the online presence of rivals such as Macy's, Kohl's, and JC Penney, with sales revenue of 30% coming from digital sales for its full-price business. Another key to its success has been its strategic focus to leverage its online presence (via the Nordstrom app) to increase traffic to its physical store locations. Nordstrom's "reserve online and try in store" is now available in over 50 locations across North America, and the company also offers curbside pickup. Its integrated digital and physical omnichannel platform has enabled it to have 85% of its online returns being made at a Nordstrom store. Its online presence is also further leveraged by its Nordy Club loyalty program, which now has over 9 million members and whose members represent 56% of Nordstrom's sales revenue. The company also makes extensive use of both online and physical pop-up shops to maintain its connection with customers and drive higher rates of frequency of purchase.

Nordstrom.com has 700 million annual site visits offering expanded selections in key brands and categories. Over time, about one-third of its off-price customers cross-shop in its full-price business. In addition, Nordstromrack.com and HauteLook have both rapidly evolved into billion-dollar banners. In 2017 they accounted for 18% of off-price sales and had new customer growth of 45%. Its not just the online presence, however, that has led to Nordstrom's success. It is also the strategic execution of its omnichannel strategy. The company has invested heavily to modernize its platform and increase its speed and agility to continuously enhance its ecommerce product content, navigation simplicity, and overall ease of use.

Most recently, the retailer has been experimenting with a merchandise-free concept it is calling Nordstrom Local. Starting with three locations in Los Angeles, services at the merchandise-free shop include:

- Buy online and pick up in store

- Onsite alterations

- Reserve online and try in store

- Curbside pickup

- Personal stylists and Trunk Club

- Easy returns and exchanges

- Easy returns to any online retailer

- Gift wrapping

- Tuxedo rentals (partnership with The Black Tux)

- Basecoat manicures

- Dry cleaning

- Grab and go food

- Barber (partnership with Baxter of California)

- Cobbler

- Complimentary beverages

- Goodwill donation drop-off

Make no mistake about it, conventional retailers such as Nordstrom are being threatened not only by Amazon, but also by the dramatic rise of more niche direct-to-consumer brands. At the same time, while the consumer decision journey clearly begins online these days, most transactions are still ultimately accomplished in a bricks and mortar setting. Omnichannel, then, is the new normal. For Nordstrom to continue to grow and thrive in this disruptive environment requires a constant willingness to change as market dynamics continue to evolve. Despite its early success as a fast mover in the digital environment, its long-term success is still predicated on its ability to distinguish itself in the face of growing competition. Nordstrom, known for its excellent customer service, will have to continue to outperform. Likewise, its product selection, cur-

Lester Balajadia/Shutterstock.com

rently focused on beauty and footwear, along with women's apparel, will need to continue to demonstrate "best of breed" from a service perspective in a way that makes Nordstrom a destination for these products and services. Nordstrom has also been busy revamping its market approach in order to develop and maintain its "connectivity" with millennials. In addition to the pop-up shops noted above, the company has also been partnering with up-and-coming fashion brands Madewell, Topshop, and Bonobos, as well as launching Nike concept shops. The company is continually seeking ways to create and reinforce its upscale, dynamic shopping experience via the integration of high-touch, digitally driven methodologies.

Questions

1. What is your impression of Nordstrom's omnichannel efforts to date? Given the continual decline in mall traffic, where Nordstrom is predominantly focused, can the company continue to shine and grow its revenue line via its current omnichannel strategy?

2. Ken Worzel, Nordstrom's chief technology officer (CTO), has stated, "If we don't get customer service right, no amount of technology or whiz-bang features will be enough." Is Ken right in this conclusion?

3. What about millennials? Given the disruptive forces occurring in today's retail sector, along with the changing shopping habits of millennials, do you feel Nordstrom can develop a preferred position with this age group?

4. Overall, has Nordstrom developed a defensible market position? What additional recommendations would you offer to the company going forward to improve growth capabilities that are not already being implemented by the company?

CHAPTER 12

Technology, Analytics, and Operations Management

LEARNING OBJECTIVES

This chapter is designed to provide students with:

LO1	An understanding of how operations management fits into an organization's overall business system
LO2	Recognition of the key areas of responsibilities of operations managers
LO3	A description of the primary and support activities that make up an organization's value chain
LO4	Exposure to the core managerial decision-making areas that reside within an organization's operations cycle
LO5	An understanding of the importance of establishing quality standards and embedding these within the culture of the organization
LO6	An overview of operations management for small businesses

Snapshot

What to Expect in This Chapter

As identified by the learning objectives, this chapter focuses on managing an organization's operations and supply chain. The content emphasized in this chapter includes the following:

- Operations Management: Fitting Into the Big Picture
- Responsibilities of Operations Managers
- The Organization's Value Chain
  - Value Chain Analysis: Primary Activities
  - Value Chain Analysis: Support Activities
- The Operations Cycle
  - Process Management
  - Supply Chain Management
  - Product/Service Management
  - Information Technology–Based Operational Analytics
- Establishing Quality Standards
- Operations Management in Small Businesses
- Management Reflection—Operational Success

Business IN ACTION

The Big Data Revolution Is Here

In reviewing the history of business, certain pivotal points have dramatically changed the way business is conducted. First there was the Industrial Revolution, which transformed our commerce arenas from an agricultural-based market environment to an industrial-based market environment. This was followed by transformative trends such as automation and globalization. Today, we are on the verge of one of the most transformative business events ever experienced: the "big data" revolution.

Organizations today have access to more data than ever before. Utilizing powerful analytical modelling, supported by artificial intelligence (AI) and machine-based learning methodologies, organizations are becoming more capable of integrating their data knowledge across multiple business functions and teams. Big data has enabled many companies to generate competitive advantages relative to rivals in areas such as customer service capabilities and improvements, operational expense reductions through efficiency and effectiveness initiatives, enhanced speed to market with products and services that capitalize on the latest customer trends, and disruptive business models that have reshaped the entire way companies within industries conduct business. In fact, an overriding concern among C-suite executives involves perceived threats from data-driven, highly agile companies that leverage data and analytics

Haywiremedia/Shutterstock.com

NicoElNino/Shutterstock.com

to aggressively compete in markets in ways never before dreamed of by a market sector's current incumbent companies. Whether it be the tech giants (Apple, Amazon, Google, Facebook) or other smaller but dynamic business start-ups, business cultures that have built their business models around leveraging the power of analytics continue to upset industries and derail historical market leaders at rates faster than ever witnessed before.

Imagine the business potential possibilities if you could...

- Predict the lifetime value of a customer by measuring their future purchase potential.

- Develop a prediction model that accurately verifies how likely a particular customer is to make a purchase.

- Map a customer's entire digital ecosystem, influencers, and digital behaviour.

- Predict exactly what a company needs to do to maximize its full revenue growth potential.

- Pinpoint the digital sites that have the greatest influence on a brand's competitive potential and space.

These are but a few of the potential outcomes being worked on and acted upon by analytically innovative companies. Whether it be improving the customer experience, identifying emerging trends, mitigating supply chain risk, targeting new customers, developing cost-efficient scalable and repeatable operational and research-focused processes—big data and the analytical capabilities associated with it is fundamentally changing the way decisions are being made and strategic pivots are being orchestrated.

As you read through this chapter and its underlying focus on creating efficient and effective business operations, think beyond the traditional approach to manufacturing and marketing and look to draw key conclusions relating to the creative use of the data being acquired, accumulated, and mined. Think in terms of how this can be leveraged into valued outcomes that drive competitive advantage and can lead to creating true distinctive capabilities that will enable you not only to personalize and customize interactions with current and prospective customers, but also to create a culture that will continually look toward applying advanced analytics and machine-learning processes to support more efficient decision making across an organization's entire operation.

Rawpixel.com/Shutterstock.com

LO1   Operations Management: Fitting Into the Big Picture

Based on your readings of prior chapters, you should be getting a sense as to the importance of developing a business system within the organization and ensuring that this system is aligned properly to the business's strategy, vision, and mission. Chapter 6 focused on the framework for developing this strategy, and Chapters 8 and 9 emphasized the importance of developing the formal business structure,

FIGURE 12.1   Business System Components

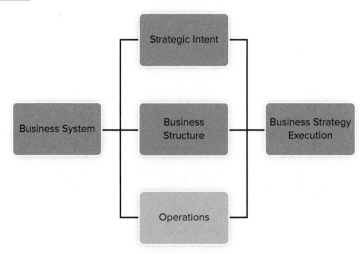

culture, employee productivity initiatives, and decision-making hierarchy—or, in summing up all of these items, the framework to direct and control it. For a business to truly be successful, a third fundamental component to its business system must be present: the organization must develop and maintain efficient and effective operational processes that deliver to the marketplace the products or services the organization offers. Successful organizations understand the interconnectivity of strategy, business structure, and operations, and seek to ensure that all three are integrated into the decision-making process and that structure and operations are aligned and in support of the organization's strategic goals (see Figure 12.1).

> Successful organizations understand the interconnectivity of strategy, business structure, and operations, and seek to ensure that all three are integrated into the decision-making process and that structure and operations are aligned and in support of the organization's strategic intent.

When we visualize the interconnectivity of these three business system components, we should conclude the following:

- Strategy is what we want to accomplish.
- The business structure should provide the controls and the formal communication and responsibility framework that will guide the organization as it seeks to realize its strategy.
- Operations are understood to be the actual processes employed, which, when combined with the utilization of the organization's capital assets, enable strategic outcomes to be actualized.

These three components and the corresponding actions that take place within the operations area result in getting the right product or service to the right customer at the right place at the right time for the right price. Keep in mind that the decisions we as managers make are focused on developing customer interactions and selling our products and services (see Figure 12.2). As an example, this is exactly what the Canadian banks and financial institutions need to think about as they consider where, how, and to what extent their strategies will need to be adjusted in response to tech-savvy fintech companies, online mortgage providers, and digital credit card providers (to name a few), all of whom are seeking to disrupt components of their overall product portfolio.

FIGURE 12.2   **The Big Picture**

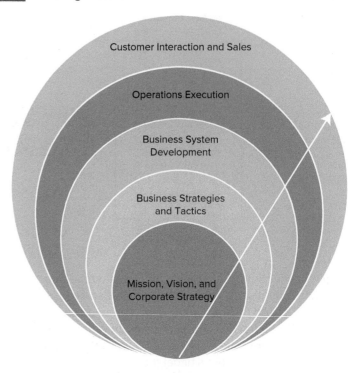

As stated in earlier chapters, successful businesses look to establish within their business systems competitive advantages that enable them to deliver their products and/or services to their targeted market segments in a manner superior to that of the competition. These advantages could be the result of more effective market positioning and brand strength; more effective use of analytics and artificial intelligence (AI) methodologies as well as hardware technology and process advantages; or leveraging pure cost advantages due to economies of scale, lower labour or production costs, and so on. What will ultimately create these advantages for an organization within its competitive market environment is the ability of the management team to transfer such strategic intent through the decision-making structure and into the effective execution of operational processes. This is the domain of operations management—*the execution of operational tactics in support of business strategy.*

> Successful businesses look to establish within their business systems competitive advantages that enable them to deliver their products and/or services to their targeted market segments in a manner superior to that of the competition.

LO2   Responsibilities of Operations Managers

Operations Management is the effective design, development, and management of the processes, procedures, and practices embedded within an organization's business system for the purpose of achieving its strategic intent.

Operations management is all about the effective design, development, and management of the processes, procedures, and practices embedded within an organization's business system for the purpose of achieving its strategic intent. In broad terms, the mandate of today's operations management team can be thought of as encompassing four broad categories of responsibility (see Figure 12.3). The intent of the operations management team is to design and develop such processes, procedures, and practices in a way that takes into consideration time requirements

FIGURE 12.3 **Operations Management: Areas of Responsibility**

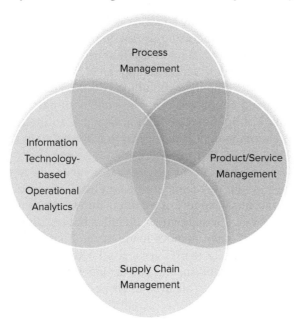

associated with getting products/services to the market. In addition, decisions need to be made relating to the quality/cost trade-offs that are designed to support the value proposition being communicated to the target market by the marketing team via the organization's marketing mix strategy. It is important to recognize that the areas of responsibility identified in Figure 12.3 overlap, as there is a definitive inter-connectivity between decisions made within each of the areas noted.

- Process management
- Supply chain management
- Product/service management
- Information technology–based operational analytics

Process management is the design and development of the work flow and connectivity of the operational requirements (processes) needed to ensure that an organization's products and services are efficiently produced and effectively delivered to the marketplace. Process management looks at the specific tasks that need to be accomplished by the organization and orders or sequences them to result in the most effective and efficient work flow. It is similar to the development of blue-prints or schematics associated with building a structure or outlining a work flow. As indicated above, this process development and task sequencing is assessed with respect to time, quality, and cost requirements and constraints. A key out-come of process management decision making is the determination of how the transformation process for products and services will be designed. It also looks at what equipment and structures will be used to ensure that the transformation max-imizes efficiency and effectiveness objectives and is aligned with the organiza-tion's market position and the related communication message. This may result in an assembly-line approach, a fully automated technology-manufacturing process making extensive use of robotics, or a handcrafted, customized approach to the fabrication or finishing of products and services. A further discussion of process management factors occurs in the next section of this chapter, which relates to the value chain.

Supply chain management refers to the management of the flow of materials and/or products, information, and costs through the front end of an organization's

Process Management is the design and development of the work flow and connectiv-ity of the transformation re-quirements (processes) needed to ensure that an or-ganization's products and ser-vices are efficiently produced and effectively delivered to the marketplace.

Supply Chain Management is the management of the inter-dependencies among suppli-ers, manufacturers, and distributors; it seeks to de-velop the terms and condi-tions that will enable all parties to efficiently and ef-fectively meet their obliga-tions to one another due to their business relationships.

value chain. It includes interactions such as the purchase of materials from suppliers and the coordination of just-in-time (JIT) inventory practices. It also considers the warehousing and distribution logistics required to move finished product from the organization's manufacturing or distribution facility to its channel partners, who ultimately sell the product to its final users (customers). Supply chain management is all about relationship management. It is the management of the interdependencies among suppliers, manufacturers, and distributors. It also seeks to develop the terms and conditions that will enable all parties to efficiently and effectively meet their obligations to one another due to their business relationships. Supply chain management is discussed in more detail in the next section of this chapter.

Product/service management refers to the variety of activities that commence with the design and development of potential new products in R&D and extend to the post-purchase support of products and services now in the hands of customers. Product/service management includes supporting product modifications, enhancements, and other changes made throughout the product's life cycle. It also involves the decision trade-offs associated with quality and cost. Decisions relating to functionality, durability, and performance are just some of the factors that need to be assessed within this area of responsibility. Product/service management decisions are made in close cooperation with the organization's R&D, marketing, and engineering departments. Consumer wants and preferences must be identified, and decisions jointly made prior to the product/service management team incorporating them into the design or redesign of a new or current product. Product/service management decisions also consider competitor product/service adjustments that are known to be "in development" or that have been presented to the marketplace, as well as emerging technologies that potentially could disrupt a marketplace. Product/service management decisions also focus on assessing the cost base of a product by analyzing its various components and determining which features need to remain, to be added, and to be removed or modified.

Information technology–based operational analytics refers to the assessment of historical data along with observations and conclusions relating to the inclusion of predictive data into the decision-making process. This is supported and acted upon via applications of machine-based learning, AI, and other analytics-based methodologies in a way that enables the operations management team to actively manage the organization's current and future needs in four distinct areas: 1) work flow optimization and technology-based efficiency and effectiveness planning, 2) monitoring of customer and market behaviour in order to predict future trends and needs and uncover business opportunities, 3) enhanced service support via data-based knowledge management and methodology application, and 4) intelligent forecasting, again based on data-based analytics, in order to enhance the scheduling accuracy of the various tasks and processes the organization undertakes in the delivery of goods and services to the marketplace.[1] As with the other key responsibilities, the use of information technology–based operational analytics will be discussed in more detail later in this chapter.

As demonstrated by this initial discussion of the responsibilities associated with operations management teams, the decision-making focus is quite broad and highly interconnected not only across the four areas identified above, but also in the sense that it requires considerable collaboration and communication across the entire organization. Let's now drill deeper into the realm of the operations management team by analyzing the process flow that will occur, to some degree, within all organizations, and how the supporting capital asset base and business structure are integrated to form a cohesive business system.[2]

Product/Service Management refers to the variety of activities that commence with the design and development of potential new products in R&D and extend to the post-purchase support of products/services now in the hands of customers.

Information Technology–Based Operational Analytics refers to the assessment of historical, as well as predictive data in a way that enables the operations management team to actively manage the organization's current and future operational needs.

The Organization's Value Chain

LO3

Keeping the discussion relating to operations management simple is, in itself, a difficult task. The evolution of technology and data-based decision making, when combined with the emergence of heightened competition in global and domestic markets and the increasing efficiencies driven from specialization, is resulting in increasingly sophisticated ways in which we produce, market, and deliver products/services to the marketplace. Techno-savvy production processes, warehouse and distribution logistical software, sophisticated material procurement analytical methodologies, extensive market segmentation and granulation supported by analytics, and enhanced outsourcing and offshoring strategies all make for increasingly complex operations management arenas. To try to maintain some order to our discussion, and to gain a full appreciation of the complexity of the interconnectivity across the organization, our focus will be on tying this discussion to a business concept called *value chain analysis*.

The value chain is a business concept that was first proposed by Michael Porter of the Harvard Business School in 1985, in his book *Competitive Advantage: Creating and Sustaining Competitive Performance*. At the centre of Porter's value chain model is the underlying principle that managers should seek to make decisions across the chain's activity areas in a manner that contributes positively to the overall value of the products or services being produced or offered. By "value," it is implied that the benefit a decision would deliver to the product or service would outweigh the cost associated with it, thereby enhancing its value. The idea behind using this model is to get managers to think about how to plan their work, schedule the required activities, determine the most efficient allocation of resources, and execute those activities in a way that maximizes the value of the process. This maximization of value can be in the form of cost efficiencies, or it can be in the form of high quality standards, customization or product uniqueness, or high performance standards (to name a few). Again, the key is to think in terms of adding value that cannot be easily duplicated or mimicked by the competition in order to create a sustainable competitive advantage inherent within the activities the organization undertakes. To illustrate this concept, think of the release of Apple's iPhone X. The iPhone X, in actuality, is a collection of glass, metal, and electronic parts and components that on their own represent little value (strictly with respect to the individual components) to the iPhone customer. According to the research firm IHS Markit (as part of a broader Bloomberg report), the estimated the cost of the iPhone X (parts and manufacturing, as of November 2017) was approximately US$370.25. Of this $370.25, the touch screen was the most expensive component, costing an estimated $110.00 per phone. Coming in at just under under $17.00 per phone was the facial recognition scanner, with other components and manufacturing costs making up the balance.[3] Apple's initial retail price for the iPhone X was US$999 (base model). This means that, for the finished product, Apple is generating a 63% gross profit margin from the sale of each unit (1 – 370.25/999). Keep in mind that Apple still has other expenses that must be recovered from this $999 selling price (marketing, research and development, distribution, and general sales, service, and administration expenses). The point is that as part of its overall value chain process, from which the value proposition materializes, Apple is able to command a significant price increase over the core costs of the components it is using in the manufacturing of the iPhone X because of the value that the iPhone X represents to the final consumer. This is the root concept of value chain analysis (value maximization), and one that often can be best assessed by asking the question, "What is it that we must do to deliver maximum value to our customers?" In defining the key success metrics associated with this response, we should then tailor our value chain initiatives to execute the required tactics, processes, and methodologies essential to achieving **value maximization** in the eyes of our customers.

Value Maximization refers to maximizing the benefits (price/quality comparison) that an individual or set of customers will realize as a result of using a product or service.

At the centre of the value chain model is the underlying principle that managers should seek to make decisions across the chain's activity areas in a manner that contributes positively to the overall value of the products or services being produced or offered.

Value Chain Analysis: Primary Activities

In managing our value chain, we as managers must look at the connectivity between two key areas of business system (company-centric side of the business model) activity. These two areas are called primary and supporting activities. **Primary activities** relate to the specific activities through which the development and transformation of a product or service occurs as it is produced and delivered to the marketplace. These areas (which may or may not occur in all organizations) are as follows, and are shown in Figure 12.4:

- Inbound logistics
- Operations
- Outbound logistics
- Marketing and sales
- Customer service

Primary Activities relate to the specific activities through which the development and transformation of a product or service occurs as it is produced and delivered to the marketplace.

Inbound logistics refers to the management of supplier relationships relating to those parts and/or components, or finished products, that are brought into the organization in order to manufacture finished products for delivery to the marketplace. Again, using our iPhone X example to illustrate a manufacturing setting, this would relate to the scheduling, shipping, and temporary warehousing of the glass, metal, and electronic parts and components. For a retailer purchasing finished goods—for example, a shirt from Thailand—this would relate to the coordination of the shipping and delivery of these shirts to the retailer's warehouse, and their temporary storage until they were shipped out to retail sites around the country.

Inbound Logistics refers to the management of supplier relationships relating to those parts and/or components, or finished products, that are brought into the organization in order to produce finished products for delivery to the marketplace.

Operations refers to the manufacturing and/or product change processes set up to ensure that the final product the organization is manufacturing or handling is ready for the marketplace. In our iPhone X example, this would be the manufacturing process used to combine the various parts and components into an actual iPhone X. For a retailer purchasing a finished product—again, for example, a shirt from Thailand—this may mean packaging the product and attaching the required labels

Operations refers to the manufacturing and/or product change processes set up to ensure that the final product the organization is manufacturing or handling is ready for the marketplace.

FIGURE 12.4   **Value Chain: Primary Activities**

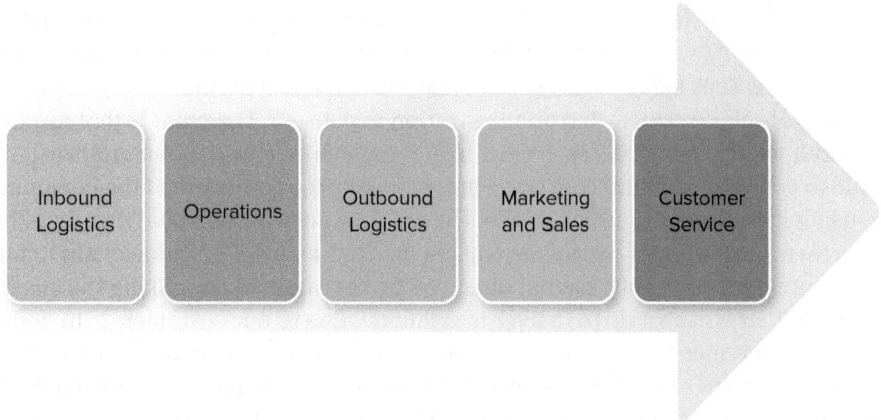

| Inbound Logistics | Operations | Outbound Logistics | Marketing and Sales | Customer Service |

Source: Adapted from Michael Porter—Value Chain Analysis.

to ensure that it meets information regulations specific to Canada, and/or branding the shirt under their company's name. Operations decisions would include process application, labour, and production management activities.

Outbound logistics refers to the distribution activities required to get the right product to the right place at the right time. This means getting the finished product to the customer via a distribution channel that is accessible, convenient (in terms of the customer's ability to purchase), and able to minimize stockouts and other sales impediment factors that could result in customers shifting to an alternate provider. Outbound logistics decisions focus on warehouse needs, distribution, and inventory management activities, as well as on transportation and routing activities. In the case of the iPhone X, outbound logistics refers to decisions and activities relating to shipping the iPhone X to Apple's own stores, determining other retailers that will be authorized to sell the product (when a decision is made to broaden the distribution), and delivering the product to them. The same holds true for the sale of finished products through retailers. Outbound logistics also manages the warehousing, inventory, and transportation logistics for these organizations. The Business in Action vignette relating to Walmart is a good example of this.

> **Outbound Logistics** refers to getting the finished product to the customer via a distribution channel that is accessible, convenient, and able to minimize stockouts and other sales impediment factors.

Marketing and sales refers to those activities that create profile and awareness for the organization's products, services, or brand(s), and the benefits derived from the acquisition and use of such products or services. Referring back to Chapter 1 and our discussion relating to the creation of a value proposition, it is the role of marketing to effectively communicate the benefits of the products and services being offered in a manner that creates preference for, and commitment to, the organization's products and services on the part of its customer base. Advertising, sales promotion, packaging, and point of sales communication, as well as contributing to decisions relating to distribution channel selection and setup, all form a part of marketing and sales activities. One of Apple Inc.'s core strengths is its brand strength and the ability of its marketing and sales departments to leverage this strength, and the emotional tie that individuals have to the brand. Apple Inc.'s ability to communicate the uniqueness of its products and the high levels of satisfaction derived by users of its products are fundamental to its success.

> **Marketing and Sales** refers to those activities that create profile and awareness for the organization's products, services, or brand(s), and the benefits derived from the acquisition and use of such products or services.

Customer service refers to the support provided to customers before, during, and following the purchase process. Customer service can be thought of as technical support, repair support, warranty service work, installation, replacement parts management, upgrading options, and customer training, to name a few. A key desired outcome relating to customer service is to maintain and, where possible, enhance the value of the product/service purchased by the customer. Achieving this can result in high levels of customer satisfaction, which translates into customer loyalty and commitment. When effectively implemented, these activities can result in active customers who recommend others to your company, as well as strong customer loyalty that minimizes the potential of customer desertion to competitors.

> **Customer Service** refers to the support provided to customers before, during, and following the purchase process.

Viewing the primary activities (inbound logistics, operations, outbound logistics, marketing and sales, and customer service) together as a chain should allow you to visualize the interconnectivity among process management, supply chain management, and products/services management. Operations management teams need to look at the types of processes to initiate in order to smoothly manage the inflow of materials and the transformation of such materials into finished goods, followed by the outflow of such products and services from the organization. The ability to design, develop, and effectively implement these processes in a way that is superior to those of its competitors can enable the organization to achieve a significant and sustainable competitive advantage in the marketplace. Management must then seek to optimize the relationships with its supply chain (inbound logistics, operations, and outbound logistics) partners. The development of strong supplier and distributor relationships is invaluable to the organization. Suppliers and distributors assist the organization in understanding market trends and shifts, maintaining a watchful eye on competitive innovation, and ensuring that cost control management practices are put into place throughout the supply chain in order to maintain competitive pricing strategies. Finally, while these two areas are being actively managed, the operations team must also look toward the future, designing, developing, enhancing, and maintaining the various products and services being offered to the marketplace.[4]

> The development of strong supplier and distributor relationships is invaluable to the organization with regard to understanding market trends and shifts, maintaining a watchful eye on competitive innovation, and ensuring that cost control management practices are put into place throughout the supply chain in order to maintain competitive pricing strategies.

Business IN ACTION

Walmart—A Lean, Keen Operating Machine

Walmart is #1 (again), according to *Fortune* magazine. For an unprecedented 10th time in 12 years, Walmart (WAL MART STORES INC.) sits on top of the *Fortune* 500 ranking of U.S. businesses (based on sales volume). With sales exceeding US$500 billion, Walmart has been either #1 or #2 in revenue each year for the past decade. With 11 300 stores operating under 59 different names, in 27 countries, along with 10 ecommerce Web sites around the world and employing a workforce exceeding 2.2 million employees, Walmart serves more than 275 million customers per week. What makes Walmart so great? The company is founded on three basic principles: respect for the individual, service to its customers, and striving for excellence. It is this third principle that has resulted in Walmart becoming the lean, keen operating machine it is today. At its roots, founder Sam Walton created a culture that was never satisfied that prices were as low as they could be, or that quality

was as good as the customer expected. This culture continues to drive Walmart today, as it relentlessly pursues continuous improvements to its operations in the search for more efficient and cost-effective ways to bring to the marketplace the goods and services that its customers desire. A key component of this strategy has been to develop a sustainable, competitive advantage within its supply chain. Few, if any, companies in the world are more effective at moving goods and services through the front end of the value chain (supply chain) than Walmart. Walmart has effectively combined technological sophistication and innovation, transportation modelling, inventory management efficiencies, and global buying power given its economies of scale to evolve its operations into the largest retail organization in the world. For Walmart, the operation's focus is straightforward. The company continuously develops and applies a wide range of innovative merchandising approaches. Its regional hub–based distribution model, utilizing cutting-edge inventory management processes, efficiently handles hundreds of thousands of cases of merchandise each day. Its sophisticated computer system automatically transmits order replenishment information to many of its suppliers, saving time and money. This same system, via its inventory tracking model, also keeps Walmart on top of the changing buying patterns of its customers, thereby enabling it to quickly modify its product offerings. Walmart's buyers, backed by its tremendous buying power, work closely with its supplier network to develop and support partnerships that enable this retail giant to meet its (and its customers') expectations of quality.

Web Integration

Want to learn more details about Walmart's supply chain efficiencies? Google Walmart supply chain management, or visit www.walmart.com.

Value Chain Analysis: Support Activities

Although one might get the impression that the primary activities noted above form the basis of the responsibilities of operations managers, it is equally important that these managers recognize and effectively manage—collaboratively, with the rest of the organization—the support activities needed to ensure the strategy execution is a success. **Support activities** are those areas within the organization that are not directly associated with the actual processes the organization uses to produce products and/or deliver services; these activities, however, are integral parts of the support structure the primary activities rely on to successfully execute strategy (see Figure 12.5). Some examples of support activities include:

- The IT department, which will collaborate with the operations department on the development and application of new technologies and analytics-based methodologies in support of the value chain process.

- The research and development and engineering departments, which primarily focus on new product development, existing product enhancement, and process design and development.

- Human resource management, which assists in recruitment, employee development, and support services for employees.

- Other supporting departments such as finance, accounting, legal, and environmental safety.

> **Support Activities** are those areas within the organization that are not directly associated with the actual processes the organization uses to produce products and/or deliver services but that are an integral part of the support structure the primary activities rely on to successfully execute strategy.

The successful execution of the primary activities of the organization is facilitated by the organization's support activities.

The Operations Cycle

LO4

The initial part of this chapter dealt with identifying where, and how, operations management teams fit into the overall business system that an organization has developed to successfully deliver its products and/or services to the marketplace. The broad concept of the flow of activities within this business system has also been

FIGURE 12.5   **Value Chain: Support Activities**

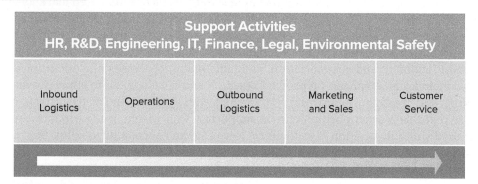

Source: Adapted from Michael Porter—Value Chain Analysis.

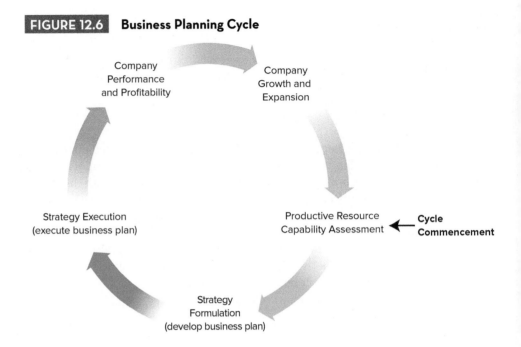

FIGURE 12.6   **Business Planning Cycle**

illustrated utilizing the value chain as a basis for this discussion. With this in mind, we turn our attention toward how operational tactics are integrated into the organization's overall strategy. We will also more fully define where operations managers spend their time and effort on a day-to-day basis.

Going back to Chapter 6 and the development of a business strategy, an organization will need to determine and confirm its mission and vision. This information, combined with a resource and capability assessment and market assessment, is then formulated into a business strategy. The strategy is then executed with the intention that strong market performance and profitability will follow, thereby meeting the company's current strategic expectations and maintaining the course toward the fulfillment of its vision and mission. As discussed in Chapters 1 and 6, this process is outlined in what has been defined as the business planning cycle (see Figure 12.6).

Why mention this again? Because a key area of responsibility with regard to the strategy execution phase of the planning cycle lies with the operations management team. Operations managers need to understand the strategic intent of the organization and, using this information, translate it into the action plans that will drive the execution of the organization's strategy. A key component of this process is to take the information derived from this strategy review and implement it through what is called the **operations cycle**. The operations cycle is the alignment of the operational tasks within an organization by its management team in order to meet the strategic outcomes defined in the organization's business strategy (see Figure 12.7).

For example, if the organization's intent is to focus on differentiated markets via the development of feature-rich products and services and communication of uniqueness and value-added benefits to customers, then the operations cycle within the organization needs to reflect this. This would imply an operations cycle that possesses flexibility and customization, and high-quality processes and operations. It also includes an emphasis on product research and development to stimulate innovation and creativity, and strong relationships with suppliers and distributors to ensure that this market position can be supported. Conversely, if the organization's desired strategic position is to focus on low price and acceptable quality, then the operations cycle will more likely place an emphasis on **process standardization** and **process simplification**. This requires a focus on process research and innovation versus product research and innovation, highly centralized material

Operations Cycle is the alignment of the operational tasks within an organization by its management team in order to meet the strategic outcomes defined in the organization's business strategy.

Process Standardization is the design and utilization of common platforms and common task sequencing to produce/develop a variety of products or services.

Process Simplification is the design and utilization of a minimum number of tasks when developing products and/or services.

FIGURE 12.7 **Operations Cycle**

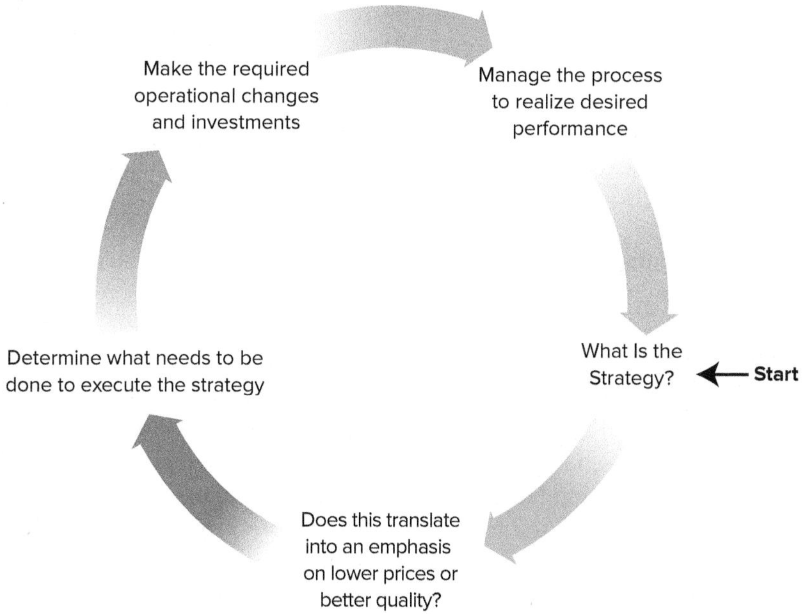

procurement to maximize economies of scale, and a focus on capital investment that drives ease of manufacturing design and execution.[5] Figure 12.8 provides an outline of the alignment between strategy and operational execution.

> Operations managers need to understand the strategic intent of the organization and, using this information, translate it into the action plans that will drive the execution of the organization's strategy.

With the operating cycle as a framework, operations managers must now delve into how best to respond to the specific objectives that have been formulated with the organization's strategic plan. This means that they need to determine how best to execute the operating cycle, taking into consideration their spheres of responsibility

FIGURE 12.8 **Strategy and Operational Alignment**

Strategic Intent	Operations Management Focus	Operations Application Focus
Low Cost/Low Prices	Tight cost control Structured organization Tight process supervision Meeting volume-based targets	Process standardization Process simplification Economies of scale Technology intensive Low-cost distribution R&D process improvement focus
Differentiated Strategy/ Higher Prices	Focus on quality vs. quantity Emphasis on culture of collaboration and communication Greater allowance for creativity and self-achievement Emphasis on defining and adding value to products	Higher labour skills Stronger emphasis on creativity skills Strong tie-in with marketing Strong R&D product development focus Strong partnership approach with distributors

Source: Used with permission of Kenneth Wong.

(refer back to Figure 12.3): process management, supply chain management, product/ service management, and information technology–based operational analytics.

Process Management

In terms of process management, operations managers have four core decision areas that need to be examined (see Figure 12.9). These are as follows:

1 Process design, layout, and execution

2 Materials management

3 Facility design and layout

4 Capital asset evaluation and acquisition

Process Design, Layout, and Execution refers to the as-sessment and implementation of the tasks necessary to get the required work accom-plished, and how such tasks will be grouped and se-quenced to ensure that the most efficient and effective processes are utilized in the production of products and/or services.

Process design, layout, and execution refers to the assessment and imple-mentation of the type of tasks needed to get required work accomplished, and how such tasks will be grouped and sequenced to ensure that the most efficient and effec-tive processes are utilized in the production or delivery of products and/or services. Depending on the nature of the industry and the work required, this could include fabrication processes, assembly processes, quality assurance processes, clerical and administrative support processes, internal and external transportation processes, en-vironmental initiatives, and hazardous waste handling processes. Decisions will need to be made, as well, as to how the flow of work will be sequenced and what steps must be initiated into the process to ensure that quality, timing, performance, and service expectations are met. Other decisions could be related to the flexibility re-quired, the technology to be used, and the level of human interaction at various points throughout the process. As an example, one decision could be determining if the greatest output efficiency would be one based on a fixed process approach, where the process being developed is focused on one product line only, versus a flexible production approach capable of handling more than one product but recognizing that

FIGURE 12.9   **Process Management: Key Decision Areas**

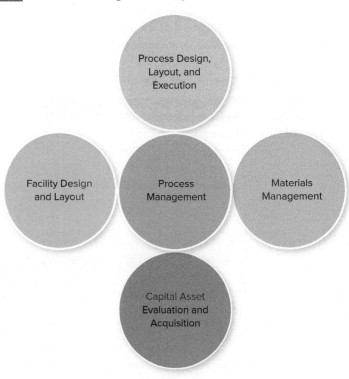

FIGURE 12.10   **DICE: Process Design, Layout, and Execution**

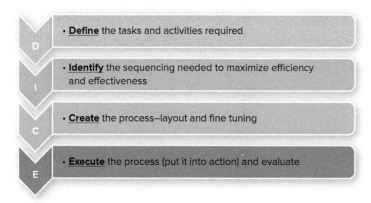

- **Define** the tasks and activities required
- **Identify** the sequencing needed to maximize efficiency and effectiveness
- **Create** the process—layout and fine tuning
- **Execute** the process (put it into action) and evaluate

retooling time and other factors may add additional costs to the work flow process. In general, a good way to think of process design and layout is to view it as a flow-chart, or as the analysis of a road map. Visualizing the work flow needed, and using process management software, tools, and models, managers will define not only a starting point for the various tasks required, but also an ending point, which results in the product/service getting to the right place at the right time and to the right customer in a manner that meets the organization's strategic positioning and financial performance objectives. This means defining the work that needs to be done, identifying the task sequencing that will result in the most efficient and effective work flow necessary to accomplish the required transformation, creating this work flow, and then executing and continuously evaluating the performance results. An easy way to remember the key fundamentals associated with process design, layout, and execution is by the acronym DICE—*define, identify, create,* and *execute* (see Figure 12.10).

> Process management decisions will need to be made as to how the flow of work will be sequenced and what steps must be initiated into the process to ensure that quality, timing, performance, and service expectations are met.

To illustrate the DICE process, let's consider the Toyota Production System (TPS). The TPS Concept exhibit provides a broad-level overview of the TPS concept[6] and illustrates the end results of a DICE analysis. After defining the tasks required and determining their sequencing, Toyota created its TPS process. Now fully implemented, Toyota's operations management team monitors and manages the system, assessing its overall efficiency and making ongoing decisions relating to continuous improvements in order to maximize its effectiveness and contribute to the achievement of the organization's overall business strategy.

Although we have focused our discussion of process design largely on the development of continuous-process work flows, short-term or outcome-specific project management analysis can also form a critical component of operations management responsibility in many business sectors. These would include areas such as engineering and commercial real estate development and construction. Project management can also relate directly to new product development and the launch of a new product or service. As with continuous process layout methodologies, business design technology software tools and models exist to assist managers with these critical project management tasks. Two commonly used project management tools are the **PERT chart** and the **Gantt chart** (see Figures 12.11 and 12.12). Both PERT charts and Gantt charts are project management tools that offer a decision-making framework to assist managers in estimating the time, money, and people required to develop and execute

PERT Chart is a scheduling methodology that focuses on task sequencing and the identification of the critical path of steps that will most greatly impact the ability to complete a project, and the length of time needed for completion.

Gantt Chart is a methodology used to schedule the steps associated with a project and the time required to complete each step.

TPS Concept

Jidoka
—Highlighting/visualization of problems—

Quality must be built in during the manufacturing process!

If equipment malfunction or a defective part is discovered, the affected machine automatically stops, and operators cease production and correct the problem. For the Just-in-Time system to function, all of the parts that are made and supplied must meet predetermined quality standards. This is achieved through jidoka.

1. Jidoka means that a machine safely stops when the normal processing is completed. It also means that, should a quality/equipment problem arise, the machine detects the problem on its own and stops, preventing defective products from being produced. As a result, only products satisfying quality standards will be passed on to the following processes on the production line.

2. Since a machine automatically stops when processing is completed or when a problem arises and is communicated via the "andon" (problem display board), operators can confidently continue performing work at another machine, as well as easily identify the problem's cause to prevent its recurrence. This means that each operator can be in charge of many machines, resulting in higher-productivity, while continuous improvements lead to greater processing capacity.

Just-in-Time
—Productivity improvement—

Making only "what is needed, when it is needed, and in the amount needed!"

Producing quality products efficiently through the complete elimination of waste, inconsistencies, and unreasonable requirements on the production line. In order to deliver a vehicle ordered by a customer as quickly as possible, the vehicle is efficiently built within the shortest possible period of time by adhering to the following:

1. When a vehicle order is received, a production instruction must be issued to the beginning of the vehicle production line as soon as possible.

2. The assembly line must be stocked with required number of all needed parts so that any type of ordered vehicle can be assembled.

3. The assembly line must replace the parts used by retrieving the same number of parts from the parts-producing process (the preceding process).

4. The preceding process must be stocked with small numbers of all types of parts and produce only the numbers of parts that were retrieved by an operator from the next process.

Source: "Toyota Production System," created from data found at ihttp://www.toyota-global.com/company/vision_philosophy/toyota_-production_system/.

a business project. PERT (Program Evaluation and Review Technique) charts focus on the identification and dependency relationships of the tasks required, along with the recognition of the critical components of the project that must be completed at given points in a project's life, which if not understood and managed will result in project delays. PERT charts are often referred to as critical path analysis. PERT charts are generally thought to deliver greatest value to a project at its inception; that is, identifying—before a project begins—the critical activities and time duration for each task. Gantt charts provide similar but generally more detailed information than that provided by PERT charts, and focus more on the management of the project once it has begun. Gantt charts generally focus on the identification, tracking, and management of the more specific tasks and activities associated with the broader critical activities initially identified in the PERT chart associated with a given project. They typically reflect a specific schedule of completion for scheduled tasks, and are generally supported by benchmarks relating to dates and completion percentages at specific points in time. PERT and Gantt charts can be thought of as methodologies to define and

FIGURE 12.11 **Example PERT Chart**

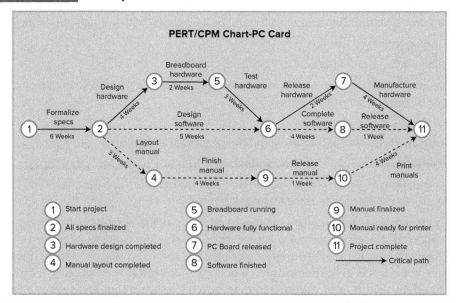

Source: RFF Electronics, RFF Flow5 Professional Flowcharting, www.rff.com/sample_pert.htm, May 2019.

detail the design and development of the work flow for a project, in order to effectively manage its completion and the underlying resources and time requirements relating to the identified project. Both offer a visual view of the time lines and activities required to complete a given project or task, thereby offering all involved a broad macro-level picture of the work to be done. An abundant variety of software programs are available to assist managers with creating both PERT and Gantt charts (Workzone, Clarizen, Smartsheet, and NetSuite are a few examples).

FIGURE 12.12 **Example GANTT Chart**

[Project Name]
[Company Name]

Project Lead: John Doe
Today's Date: 2/24/2009 (Tue)(vertical red line)
Start Date: 1/5/2009 (Mon)

WBS	Tasks	Task Lead	Start	End	Duration (Days)	% Complete	Working Days	Days Complete	Days Remaining
1	**Task Category 1**	John	1/03/09	3/17/09	74	80%	52	59	15
1.1	Sub Task		1/03/09	1/20/09	18	100%	12	18	0
1.2	Sub Task		1/21/09	2/19/09	30	95%	22	28	2
1.3	Sub Task		1/22/09	2/09/09	19	95%	13	18	1
1.4	Sub Task		2/10/09	3/18/09	37	50%	27	18	19
2	**Task Category 2**	Jane	3/01/09	5/11/09	72	13%	51	9	63
2.1	Sub Task		3/01/09	3/17/09	17	50%	12	8	9
2.2	Sub Task		3/01/09	3/17/09	17	30%	12	5	12
2.3	Sub Task		3/18/09	4/25/09	39	0%	28	0	39
2.4	Sub Task		4/15/09	5/12/09	28	0%	20	0	28
3	**Task Category 3**	Bill	4/25/09	8/01/09	99	0%	70	0	99
3.1	Sub Task		4/25/09	5/11/09	17	0%	11	0	17
3.2	Sub Task		5/12/09	5/28/09	17	0%	13	0	17
3.3	Sub Task		5/29/09	7/04/09	37	0%	26	0	37
3.4	Sub Task		7/05/09	8/02/09	29	0%	20	0	29

Source: Gantt Chart Template for Excel by Vertex42.com.

Materials management refers to the management of the inputs required in order to develop the products or services the organization is intent on delivering to the marketplace. Materials management could be associated with inputs/items such as:

- components for assembly purposes
- parts for repair and maintenance of products sold
- raw materials, such as molten aluminum for the fabrication of transmission casings or pistons for automobiles
- hazardous waste disposal
- sanitary practices for the safe handling of food at restaurants
- regulation compliance for the handling of goods such as prescription drugs
- the handling of fully finished goods that the organization has purchased with the intent of reselling such items through its retail outlets

As you can sense, materials management and process management are quite interconnected. Materials management refers to the specific tasks associated with the handling of materials, while process design, layout, and execution detail how this handling of materials is to be orchestrated within the full work flow of the organization.

Facility design and layout refers to infrastructure layout and related facility components that will be required to house and support the processes noted above. Key decisions in this area of operations management responsibility include decisions relating to production **capacity**, plant, facility, and/or retail locations, warehousing, storage, and other similar decisions. Walmart, as an example, uses a regional hub approach to supporting its various store locations. As Walmart builds and opens new stores, it also has to consider how it is going to support the stocking and restocking of these stores through its distribution system. This means that further expansion plans associated with Walmart go beyond individual store selection and require a larger, regional expansion approach.[7] Similarly, Shoppers Drug Mart, in launching its newly designed stores, had to make a significant number of decisions relating to the square footage allocation of its newly expanded departments (cosmetics, convenience foods) and what each of these store areas was going to look like as part of its process of attracting customers. Toyota Motor Company, in building its Canadian manufacturing facility in Woodstock, Ontario, had to make decisions relating to the size of the facility and the types of vehicles to be built there. The plant, announced in 2005, took approximately three years to build, with the first vehicle rolling off the assembly line in December 2008. Designed to build Toyota's RAV4 sports utility vehicle, the plant was built with an annual production capacity of 270 000 vehicles. Economic conditions in 2008 resulted in production initially being limited to approximately 75 000 vehicles annually, but since then the plant has been operating at close to full capacity (approx. 250 000 vehicles). Recent announcements (2019) have indicated that production at this plant (and its sister plant in Cambridge, Ontario) will be reduced by 10% going forward for the near term. Although one of the primary producers for Toyota of its RAV4 for North America, the Woodstock plant was not successful in getting the nod from Toyota to build its RAV4 hybrid for all of North America (it will still build them for Canada). The production of this hybrid vehicle has been shifted to a plant in Kentucky (USA), where additional excess capacity was available (due to the discontinuation of Toyota's Venza model and slower than expected Camry sales) and there was a need to increase capacity to keep that plant operating efficiently. Toyota has indicated that both Woodstock and Cambridge are being considered for new vehicles currently under design.[8] Decisions relating to capacity, plant size (footprint), and plant layout often have to be made years in advance, based on estimated sales forecasts given anticipated market conditions. Building too little capacity can result in not being able to meet customer demands, which presents an opportunity for competitors to move in to the market and steal market share. Too much capacity, particularly if production processes limit the ability to change what is being produced (i.e., fixed assembly lines), can result in idle plant and equipment, which ties up dollars and can negatively impact the organization's cost structure (hence the need to shift production, in Toyota's case to Kentucky). In addition to size considerations, efficiency planning is an essential part of facility design and layout decision making. The flow of materials through the facility and the sequencing of tasks must be considered when determining the look and layout of a facility. In retail operations, facility design can relate to decisions such as product positioning on shelves, the movement of products within a store to reflect seasonal or promotional sales initiatives, and the ambiance of the retail location to reflect a theme or contribute to the uniqueness and appeal of a particular brand or product line.

> Decisions relating to capacity, plant size (footprint), and plant layout often have to be made years in advance, based on estimated sales forecasts given anticipated market conditions.

Capital asset evaluation and acquisition refers to an assessment by the operations management team of the state of current capital assets and a determination as to their applicability to meeting the needs of the organization. Obsolete equipment must be replaced or modernized. New technologies need to be acquired and implemented. Plants, facilities, and equipment that are no longer needed should be divested of. As the organization changes and evolves, so, too, do its capital asset requirements. Managers must continuously assess the operational capabilities resulting from the capital assets available, and determine what to retain, what to invest in, what is missing and therefore needs to be acquired, and what is no longer necessary and therefore can be sold off or discarded. Over the past several years, all three North American automobile manufacturers (GM, Ford, and Chrysler) had to make tough decisions about which brands to keep, which vehicles to keep producing, and which plants will continue as central to the production process. GM, for example, has eliminated the Oldsmobile, Saturn, and Pontiac brands. Ford shuttered its Mercury division, and announced in 2018 that it would cease manufacturing and phase out selling sedans for the North American market (Mustang being one exception). Its North American model focus will lie with SUVs and trucks, particularly hybrid versions of these vehicles, going forward. These types of decisions have resulted in the closing of many plants, the elimination of hundreds of dealers, and the early retirement or termination of thousands of employees. The decisions relating to which plants to close and which brands to eliminate were the result of assessing the organization's strategic intent, conducting a resource and market assessment, and then evaluating the efficiency, effectiveness, and competitiveness of the capital asset infrastructure at various plant locations. These factors determined which assets to keep and which assets to sell or discard.

Capital Asset Evaluation and Acquisition refers to an assessment by the operations management team of the state of current capital assets and a determination as to their applicability to meeting the needs of the organization.

Business IN ACTION

AI—Assisting Our Response Capabilities in Emergency Situations

Imagine the destruction of an earthquake of significant magnitude striking in the centre of a heavily populated area in the middle of the night. Or think about a hurricane, such as those that have hit the southern United States in recent years (Florence, Maria, Michael, Andrew, Katrina). The 2017 hurricane season in the United States, Mexico, and the Caribbean was the most costly

Darryl Dyck/Bloomberg via Getty Images

on record, resulting in an estimated $200+ billion in damages. Consider massive wildfires, such as those that have devastated towns in Alberta (Fort McMurray) and California (Paradise). The 2016 Fort McMurray wildfire burned approximately 1.5 million acres, destroyed more than 2500 homes, and had estimated damage costs just under $4 billion. The 2018 Camp Fire in California killed 85 people and destroyed more than 18 000 structures. We can add to our mental list other major disasters such as floods, tornadoes, droughts, tropical storms, and tsunamis.

As global warming impacts our planet, natural disasters are becoming more frequent and more damaging. Since 1970 the number of disasters worldwide has more than quadrupled, to an estimated 400 per year. Since 1980 there have been 219 climate disasters in the U.S. alone which have damage costs in excess of $1 billion, resulting in total losses from these exceeding $1.5 trillion. But the list does not necessarily stop there, nor are disasters simply contained to North America. Infectious disease epidemic outbreaks and human-made incidents such as violent mass trauma (community violence, terrorism) and ecosystem disruption (oil spills, nuclear and chemical incidents), constantly challenge our global ability to respond to and manage the underlying physical, mental, and emotional needs and outcomes relating to them.

Emergency service and response management teams are constantly assessing how they can improve their response to and management of natural disasters. Shifting weather patterns, heightened storm and record rainfall activity, aging populations, increasing political unrest, and urban sprawl and development all are adding to the underlying complexity of doing just this. In an effort to better predict potential disasters and respond when actual disasters strike, these emergency service and response management teams are increasingly turning to artificial intelligence (AI) and machine-based learning methodologies. Some of the ways in which AI is being used in support of emergency response efforts include the following:

- AI techniques relating to image recognition and classification can be used to immediately assess damage and overall impact as these visual and/or heat-mapped images come in from satellites and other sources. AI methodologies can immediately filter images to recognize the most impacted areas, thereby enabling a more focused relief effort response.

- Unlike 911 emergency services, which are voice-call constrained, AI methodologies, via mechanisms such as voice-to-text and audio and picture-based analysis technologies, can quickly assess such information or emergency requests and draw conclusions on critical response areas, thereby accelerating time-sensitive emergency response.

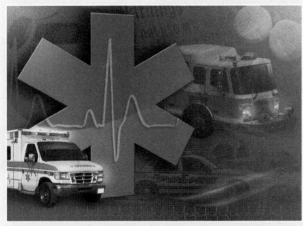

Haywiremedia/Shutterstock.com

- AI methodologies can also provide immediate information broadcast across a variety of sources and technologies as a mechanism for quickly and accurately communicating vital information to people within the impacted areas. AI methods such as chatbots, emergency alert bulletins, and so on can also be used to handle informational requests (lost loved ones, displacements, etc.) coming in from outside the impacted area and, when attached to databases relating to the disaster, offer credible and valid information to those inquiring about potential victims, emergency shelter locations, or organized meeting site protocols.

- On the predictive side, AI and machine-learning methodologies are being used to predict the potential impact and magnitude of an event before it occurs, thereby enabling disaster-relief organizations to anticipate and supply impacted areas in advance, and arrange critical response command and communication centres in near proximity to the impact zone. AI software has been successful in predicting which storms are likely to result in significant physical disaster or, based on data analysis, anticipate the directional spread of infectious diseases.

- When coupled with drones and other robotic units, AI methodologies can offer significant insight into assessing the pending actions relating to real-time behaviour and movement not only of the disaster itself but also of the people within the impact zone.

These are but a few examples of how AI and machine-based learning methodologies and techniques, coupled with today's technological advances, are assisting our ability to respond to emergency disasters, whether natural or human-made. As AI continues to evolve, we can anticipate that the use and importance of this beneficial technological advance will assist us in improving both our predictive capabilities as well as our response competencies and overall success. Although this Business in Action feature offers one insight into the power of AI and machine-based learning, its benefit to all of us is not limited to just emergency response. AI methodologies are becoming critical in other areas such as hospital emergency room triage, cancer and other disease identification, social media monitoring relating to community violence and terrorism activities, and climate change impact modelling, to mention a few. Overall, although concerns may exist as to its use from a privacy perspective, AI can and will add significant value in how many services are positively provided to our global population going forward.

Web Integration

Want to learn more about the use of AI in the support of emergency services? Visit https://datasmart.ash.harvard.edu/news/article/three-emerging-technologies-improve-emergency-management.

Supply Chain Management

As indicated earlier in the chapter, supply chain management refers to the management of the flow of materials and/or products, information, and costs through the front end of an organization's value chain. This means planning, sourcing, and delivering the required components, parts, or products purchased for resell to the organization, and then delivering the finished products to the marketplace either through business-to-business relationships (B2B) or business-to-customer (B2C) sales locations. An additional function of supply chain management—and one that

FIGURE 12.13   **Supply Chain Partners**

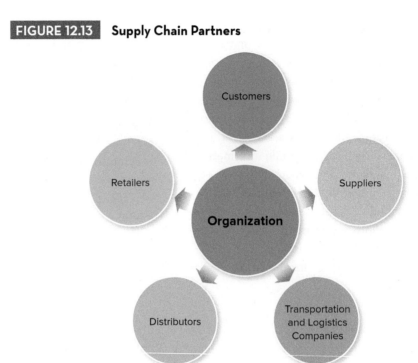

is often overlooked—includes the development of a responsive network for dealing with defective merchandise and/or unsold items (excess inventory), if these are to form part of the organization's customer service strategy. For an organization, a key aspect of supply chain management is an understanding of the various partners the organization will need to interact with to ensure that it successfully develops the network needed for the efficient flow of goods and services into and out of the organization. Figure 12.13 provides an overview of some of the key partners that need to be included in an organization's supply chain network.

When we think about supply chain management we are referring to the development of the supply chain structure and the accumulation of the necessary information needed to make effective supply chain decisions. Examples of activities that form a core part of the planning mode are shown in Figure 12.14.

For simplicity purposes, we often view supply chain managers as having the following three overarching responsibilities (see Figure 12.15):

1 Supply chain planning

2 Supply chain operating execution

3 Supply chain performance evaluation

Supply chain management refers to the development of the supply chain structure and the accumulation of the necessary information needed to make effective supply chain decisions. Examples of activities that form a core part of the planning mode are:

- Making decisions relating to outsourcing of various supply chain functions versus keeping such activities in-house.

- Assessing the various software and ecommerce services that will be required to effectively manage supply chain tasks.

- Analyzing sales forecasts to determine appropriate product quantities to purchase.

Supply Chain Management is the management of the interdependencies among suppliers, manufacturers, and distributors; it seeks to develop the terms and conditions that will enable all parties to efficiently and effectively meet their obligations to one another due to their business relationships.

FIGURE 12.14 **Supply Chain Management Responsibilities: Planning Mode**

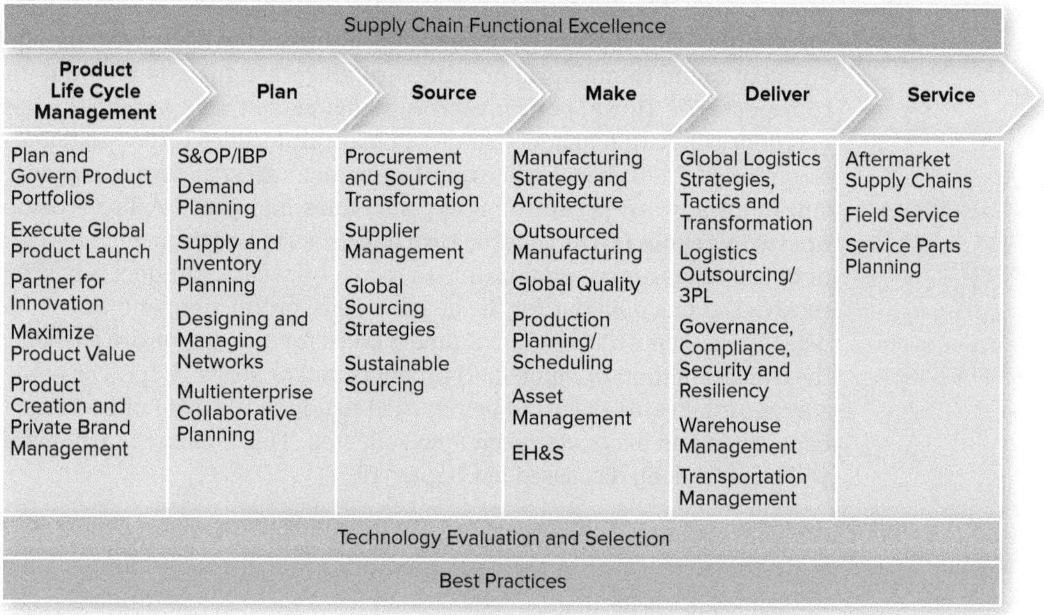

Supply Chain Functional Excellence
Product Life Cycle Management
Plan
Source
Make
Deliver
Service
Plan and Govern Product Portfolios
Execute Global Product Launch
Partner for Innovation
Maximize Product Value
Product Creation and Private Brand Management
S&OP/IBP
Demand Planning
Supply and Inventory Planning
Designing and Managing Networks
Multienterprise Collaborative Planning
Procurement and Sourcing Transformation
Supplier Management
Global Sourcing Strategies
Sustainable Sourcing
Manufacturing Strategy and Architecture
Outsourced Manufacturing
Global Quality
Production Planning/ Scheduling
Asset Management
EH&S
Global Logistics Strategies, Tactics and Transformation
Logistics Outsourcing/ 3PL
Governance, Compliance, Security and Resiliency
Warehouse Management
Transportation Management
Aftermarket Supply Chains
Field Service
Service Parts Planning
Technology Evaluation and Selection
Best Practices

Source: Taken from Gartner Inc., http://www.gartner.com/resources/262900/262988/262988_1_hr.png.

- Designing the transportation and warehouse networks to effectively manage the flow of products through the organization's value chain.

Supply chain operating execution refers to the execution of the specific tasks necessary to ensure that key performance results are achieved. This would include activities such as the management of inventory levels, efficient utilization of the organization's transportation fleet, effective use of technology systems in place, accurate and timely invoicing and collection, ensuring that products reach the market in a timely fashion, and the achievement of the required manufacturing quantities to meet the expectations of retailers and other product distributors.

Supply chain performance evaluation refers to the critical outcomes that the supply chain must achieve in support of the organization's overall operating

Supply Chain Operating Execution refers to the execution of the specific tasks necessary to ensure that key performance results are achieved.

Supply Chain Performance Evaluation refers to the critical outcomes that the supply chain must achieve in support of the organization's overall operating performance.

FIGURE 12.15 **Supply Chain Management Responsibilities: Overarching**

Supply Chain Planning
Supply Chain Operating Execution
Supply Chain Performance Evaluation

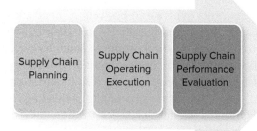

performance. Two critical outcomes in this regard are (1) maximum utilization of the capital asset base, and (2) minimization of the time involved within the cash operating cycle. Maximization of the capital asset base has been alluded to earlier in this chapter. This represents the focused desire, on the part of the supply chain management team, to minimize unnecessary and wasteful expenses due to inefficient transportation flows, poor inventory management and warehouse inefficiencies, and poor capacity management due to inaccurate sales forecasting and demand interpretation. Inefficiencies in capital asset and infrastructure management often result in an upward pressure on expense lines and profitability erosion. The **cash operating cycle (COC)**, also known as the cash-to-cash cycle, refers to the amount of time it takes for an organization to recover the cash (product is sold and money is received) it has paid out for the development, production, and distribution of products. It represents the amount of time it takes for money you are spending to finance the transformation of inputs into products and/or services (process flow across the stages of the value chain) to be returned to you in the form of cash once sales have been made and accounts receivable collected. This concept (cash operating cycle) will be more fully discussed in Chapter 13.

> In general, the shorter the cash operating cycle, the more quickly the organization is getting back the cash it has expended on producing its goods and services and, therefore, the less the organization needs to rely on cash reserves or short-term debt financing to cover the costs of the expenditures incurred.

The idea behind supply chain management is to assist the organization in reducing its cost base, thereby offsetting market pressures toward lower prices. It does this by trying to make the most effective use possible of the dollars it must invest, and by striving to maximize the financial performance of the organization through superior management of inventories, warehouses, transportation fleets, distribution networks, and sales forecasting methodologies. This means ongoing assessment and analysis of sourcing and procurement practices, labour allocation, distribution processes, inbound and outbound warehouse practices, inventory management practices, and supplier payment options, to name a few. The core idea is to provide the right products and/or services to the market at the right time, at the lowest supply chain costs possible.[9]

Product/Service Management

As identified earlier in this chapter, one of the spheres of responsibility of operations managers is their collaborative involvement (with R&D, marketing, and engineering) in the design and delivery of existing product enhancements, as well as new products/services. As markets evolve and customers' needs, expectations, and attitudes change, organizations will continually review their existing product portfolio to determine where to enhance existing products, launch new products, or invest in emerging opportunities and/or technologies that will spur future product/market opportunities. In assessing the organization's current business planning cycle and its overall longer-term strategy, operations managers play a key role in determining the ability of the organization to execute changes to the existing product line and/or develop future products and services. Discussions relating to product/service management opportunities are generally focused around three specific areas: existing product/service changes, new product opportunities, and long-reach opportunities (see Figure 12.16).[10]

Cash Operating Cycle (COC) refers to the amount of time it takes for an organization to recover the cash (product is sold and money is received) it has paid out for the development, production, and distribution of products.

FIGURE 12.16   **Product/Service Management Focus**

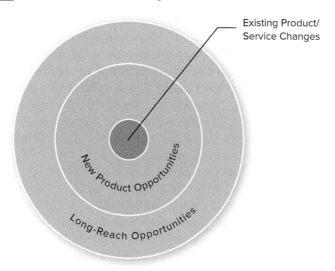

Existing Product/
Service Changes

New Product Opportunities

Long-Reach Opportunities

These three areas are as follows:

- Existing product/service changes
- New product opportunities
- Long-reach opportunities

Existing product/service changes relates to the existing products and/or the existing level of services offered to the marketplace within which the organization currently competes. Decisions associated with this area of operations management relate directly to the product modifications or enhancements that are deemed necessary from a competitive perspective (such as component input changes, feature/benefit modifications, level of service support, and stocking of replacement parts). It represents an assessment of the current value of an existing product within the market it currently serves, and the additions, adjustments, or deletions required to enhance or maintain its current position (or to successfully reposition it). The laundry product Tide, for example, has gone through a number of evolutions since its debut in 1943, all with a focus on defending and growing its market leader position in the laundry detergent market. The years since 1943 have seen Tide evolve, through powder, crystal, and liquid product offerings, to its current availability of product choices, such as compact powder (puck), quick stick (Tide to Go), and target market options such as Tide with Febreeze, Tide Stain Release, and Tide Washing Machine Cleaner.[11] Apple's iPad, the recognized industry leader in the tablet market, has been the recipient of continuous innovation and upgrades as Apple seeks to drive ongoing revenue and profitability from this particular product offering. Again, existing product/service adjustments can be thought of as core enhancements or changes that are deemed necessary because they are fundamental to maintaining the product/service's competitive position, meeting its revenue and profitability objectives, or improving its overall appeal in the marketplace.

New product opportunities refers to the development of new products for market opportunities that exist today and for which research has concluded there is near-term revenue potential. Amazon's development of the Alexa assistant and its related ecosystem support devices (Echo, etc.) not only provides Amazon with immediate new revenue derived from the sale of Alexa-related devices, but also offers an additional connectivity mechanism with Amazon customers, thereby enabling the company to generate additional revenue from the broader Amazon portfolio of products and services that have now become more easily accessible via having Alexa in your home. Recognizing that products, ultimately, will have a defined life, companies as part of their product portfolio assessment process will look for new market opportunities via new products and/or services aligned with current or emerging market needs as an ongoing critical component of their strategic planning process.

Long-reach opportunities refers to the investment in, and development of, new product research for potentially emerging markets of the future. The intent of these types of R&D decisions is to develop leading-edge technologies and/or products and services that will enable the organization to obtain "first mover advantage" when, and if, these markets emerge. Examples include prescription drug research and development; electric car battery development; space travel, exploration, and servicing; and hydrogen fuel cell technology development. An additional example of investments in long-reach opportunities is occurring at Apple Inc. and Google Inc.; R&D dollars are being spent by these two companies today on emerging technologies that will, hopefully, supply these companies with their products of tomorrow. Both are currently experimenting with the development of electric vehicles with the intent of entering this market, as the emphasis of product development in this sector moves from transportation functionality to entertainment and smart technology–driven (driverless cars) benefits and features. The marketplace remains uncertain, so investments may not materialize into actual product opportunities. The need exists, however, to focus on such emerging markets if companies like Apple and Google are going to maintain their market leader position in the target segments they serve.

 Business IN ACTION

Limelight Platform—Redefining the Experiential Marketing Business Model

With the proliferation of mobile devices and increased online connectivity diversifying media delivery and consumption, companies have recognized that they must look beyond traditional one-way media channels (print, radio, television) to communicate value to potential consumers more effectively. Experiential marketing is a form of advertising that circumvents the passive one-way communication of traditional advertising by creating an immersive consumer experience that engages the most human senses possible. In this way, the experience is used as a means to form a memorable and emotional connection with the consumer so that it may be leveraged to generate sales and consumer brand loyalty.

One method used by organizations to generate these brand experiences for consumers is to include them in memorable events and engagements. Mercedes-Benz, for example, hosts events to showcase their upcoming automobile inventory and invites consumers to attend not only to view the products offered by Mercedes-Benz, but also to experience what the Mercedes-Benz luxury brand offers. However, the logistical complexity of staging and marketing brand events often requires companies to enlist experiential marketing agencies to assist in their strategizing, development, and execution.

Limelight (formally part of Immersion Media), based in Toronto, is one such example of an agency that specializes in the experiential space. At its inception, clients were initially paying Immersion Media to develop engaging experiential events and accompanying digital assets, such as a branded Web site or mobile device application, to assist in the leveraging of said events. While this business model is effective for multiple company events of the same calibre, Immersion Media's founders recognized that extensive resources and coordination across numerous company departments and outsourced components were required every time clients requested new branded apps and Web sites for an upcoming event. Moreover, there was a distinct lack of consolidation in data collection from an experiential campaign, requiring

Used by permission of Limelight Platforms Inc.

laborious and prolonged analysis that made it difficult to quantify the return on investment (ROI) for a specific event. To make the development of digital assets and subsequent analysis of events more efficient for clients, Immersion Media (as it was known at the time) created an internal software program called Tembo that contained all of the digital and analytic attributes necessary to design, market, and analyze an event in a fully customizable, drag-and-drop template. It was then that Immersion realized they had innovated a technological solution to solve not just their clients' need for greater control of digital asset production, marketing, and event analytics, but also the needs of all agencies and brands that are generating experiences live or online. Immersion redefined their business model as a result, shifting sole focus away from providing agency services and spinning Tembo off into an expanded stand-alone corporation called Limelight Platform.

The developers at Immersion Media founded Limelight Platform Inc. in 2014 to provide an event-marketing software service that satisfies the needs of experiential marketing managers by fusing the specialized components of experiential marketing into a singular, streamlined process. Without any knowledge of computer coding, Limelight users can easily develop, market, and analyze digital assets (automated emails, Web sites, mobile applications, etc.) for their experiential events with the software's fully customizable, branded, drag-and-drop content management system. A great advantage of this system is that it returns flexible digital asset control back to experiential content managers while reducing time, costs, and expended labour. Data, the cornerstone of marketing ROI, are also collected from every step of Limelight's marketing process and consolidated in real time on a singular

dashboard display where they are easily accessible to the Limelight user. Furthermore, Limelight's software is entirely application program interface (API) agnostic with front-end and back-end plug-in capability—meaning user-designed digital assets and the data they collect can be integrated easily within customer relations management (CRM) programs already used by companies to target consumer leads more effectively, and generate a greater ROI of their experiential marketing campaigns. All of these benefits culminate into seamless event organization, management, and analysis. For example, rather than outsourcing the development and design process to an experiential agency, experiential managers of Mercedes-Benz utilized Limelight's software to design, market, and manage an aforementioned Mercedes-Benz vehicle launch event, creating automated email marketing invites and follow-ups, a branded Web site for event attendees to RSVP, and an onsite mobile application that allowed managers to manage the guest list and collect attendee data at the event itself.

In closing, Limelight Platform is a true disruptor in the experiential marketing industry because it allows users to quickly create branded digital assets for their events at a fraction of the cost and effort of an agency, while collecting data on the effectiveness of these digital assets to determine an exceptional ROI for their efforts. The company has tapped into start-up accelerators Incubes and Accelerprise to provide financial and management support as it looks to expand nationally across Canada and internationally around the globe. Limelight now operates an office in Rocklin, California in addition to its Toronto office. Key Limelight Platform clients include BMW, Porsche, GM Canada, Hyundai, MolsonCoors, Allstate, Scotiabank, and Progressive, to name a few.

Information Technology–Based Operational Analytics

Information technology–based operational analytics focuses on two common elements in support of the operations management decision-making process:

1 Combining software and machine-learning methodologies with operations infrastructure and technologies to improve the design, creation, transformation, delivery and servicing of goods and services to the marketplace, and

2 The utilization of data, analytics, and business-value dashboards to gain critical insights, thereby enabling companies to improve customer service, create greater efficiencies in the execution of operational processes and protocols, and mitigate supply chain and broader operational risks.

In this regard, think about information technology–based operational analytics as the full integration of the power of the Internet, data-collecting software, machine-learning methodologies, and the physical movement of goods and services, ultimately ending with the customer with performance being assessed on the basis of excelling in the delivery of the total customer experience. In looking to keep things simple, analytics backed by reliable and credible data conclusions enables companies to make decisions in four key ways:

- The generation of insights not previously recognized or understood that will enable us to reduce our costs to serve.
- The recognition of new and/or better approaches to capturing long-term revenue and enhancing customer loyalty.
- An understanding of the critical behaviour activities fundamental to improving overall customer satisfaction.
- The identification of methodologies to improve overall performance and an understanding of the benefit of such impact, if implemented, versus the cost of implementation.

In short, analytics enables us to unlock, predict, optimize, and validate key business findings, thereby enabling the company to maximize its full economic potential (Figure 12.17).

Traditional operations management responsibilities focused on the transformation of goods and services through the front end of the value chain: inbound logistics, transformation processes (manufacturing, production), and outbound logistics. The new wave of operations management responsibilities adds to this the requirement to respond to the growing expectations of customers for reduced delivery times, and heightened and engaged interaction via social media and other Web-based tools. This is where the power of analytics comes into play. Analytics enables management teams to respond to heightened competitive environments and increasingly demanding customers by assisting in the development of work flow optimization, technology-based automation (artificial intelligence and machine-based learning methodologies), monitoring customer and market behaviour, enhanced service support, and intelligent forecasting and enhanced scheduling accuracy. The ability to harness the power of analytics is what enables companies to recognize where and how they can change in order to generate the greatest positive impact on their customer relationships and underlying financial results. This, of course, is predicated on the ability of the company to develop and successfully mine the data available via the technical tools and intellectual processes at its disposal. It also requires a management mindset and

FIGURE 12.17   **Power of Analytics**

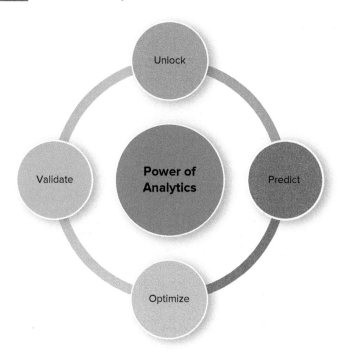

organizational culture that will take the insights generated and apply this knowledge to its business model and underlying value chain. Figure 12.18 provides some insight into the variety of ways that analytics is being used across the value chain to aid management in making decisions about where and how to compete.

FIGURE 12.18   **Value Chain Analytics**

Managing the Value Chain via Analytics & AI Methodologies

Financial KPI Tracking & Evaluation Analytics

• HR Management Workforce Analytics
  (Retention, Performance, Promotion)
• HRM Peak Period Staffing

MIS, IT, HRM, Fin and Acct., Legal, Admin

R&D (Engineering) ↔ Inbound Logistics — Transformative Processes — Outbound Logistics ↔ Marketing, Sales & Service

AI and Analytics-based
Product Design
Methodologies
R&D Expenditure
Management and
Optimization
Advanced Analytics &
AI Methodologies
Testing
AI Topic Research
Evaluation and
Assessment

• Inventory Management Optimization
• AI automated Process Methodologies & Analytics
• Facility Management Analytics
• Predictive Quality Assessment Analytics
• Supply Chain Partner Analytics & optimization
  analysis
• Procurement Transaction Analysis Analytics
• Economic Order Quantity Optimization
• AI and Analytics-based product design methodologies
• Operational KPI Tracking and Evaluation Analytics

• Customer Behaviour
  Analytics
• Marketing Mix Analytics
• POS Transaction Analytics
• Weather Analytics
• Seasonality Analytics
• Granulation & Segmentation
  Analysis
• Social Media Sentiment
  Analysis
• Predictive Sales Analytics
• Marketing KPI Tracking &
  Evaluation Analytics

AI = Artificial Intelligence
POS = Point of Sale
KPI = Key Performance Indicator

Source: Adapted from Michael Porter's *Value Chain.*

FIGURE 12.19   **Driving Business Results from Analytics**

Hindsight	Insight	Foresight
After-the-fact information and reporting	Understanding cause and effect relationships within a specific business context	Predicting business trends and transforming business systems in anticipation of such trends
Intuition-driven decision making—check results	Some data insight embedded into decision making (generally operational) Fair to good integration of customer data and online data; enhanced near-time decision inclusion	Capabilities to integrate structured and unstructured data into decision making are in place Able to create a single view of the customer Heightened ability to make decisions in fact-based environment
Focus is on improving business intelligence	Focus is on improving business performance	Focus is on redefining the business model

Source: Created from data provided at EKNResearch.com.

Probably the most important benefit of information technology-based operational analytics is the fact that it enables organizations to shift from a reactive business model that fills orders to a model that proactively manages the business and, in predicting customer needs, can deploy resources in a way that best fills these needs. As organizations evolve toward analytical-based decision-making models and improve their competencies relating to it, heightened use of analytical methodologies enables the company to move beyond harnessing the value of historical information assessment (hindsight) to that of creating critical insight and even advanced foresight into its predictive and prescriptive analytical models and supporting methodologies (see Figure 12.19). This enhanced ability to forecast demand, predict business trends, better understand customer behaviour, and anticipate market shifts enables organizations to quickly adjust business factors such as inventory to meet growing customer demand, restructure transportation models to more accurately deliver goods and/or services to customers, and build out distribution support in a manner that meets the growing need for instant servicing—a growing mentality when, armed with smartphones and other mobile devices, customers are looking for the delivery of products and services at faster rates than ever before. In short, these heightened capabilities enable a company to refine its business model, via critical insights derived from its analytical capabilities, faster, more efficiently, and more effectively than rivals, thereby driving competitive advantage in the markets it serves.

So, just how does an organization successfully implement an information technology–based operational analytics program? According to Gartner, one of the world's leading information technology research and advisory companies, a key to this is to view the organization's business model in a new way (see Figure 12.20).

The intent of this model is to encourage organizations to conduct a digital technology assessment of their current business model in order to better understand the impact new technologies are having on their business, to identify issues and opportunities in the current business model that technology might address, to assess how innovation is disrupting their current business and its underlying ecosystem, and to look for innovation implementation opportunities to better meet the needs of customers.[12]

Ideate	Reflecting on and rethinking the way that decisions are made
Create	Reviewing the way that products are manufactured and delivered into the marketplace
Engage	Mapping the way that customers interact with the organization, and searching or seeking out new and more meaningful ways of adding engagement to this process
Offer	Assessing analytics and data in order to more quickly recognize and better understand trends impacting the product portfolio
Monetize	Understanding how value is being exchanged (pricing and payment) and determining new ways of offering products and services to the marketplace
Learn and Change	Reassessing the way that the organization learns, assesses itself, and executes change

The end result of the assessment of the organization's business model, via this technology lens (Gartner model), is to enable companies to better integrate technology into their operations management processes via digital technology integration mapping (see Figure 12.21).

Digital technology integration mapping simply asks four key questions relating to how technology is and/or should be used in our operation. These questions are as follows:

- Enhance—where and how should our current technology be upgraded?

- Add—what new technologies should we integrate into our operating ecosystem?

- What existing technologies should be maintained?

- What technologies are now obsolete and need to be removed from the operating environment?

FIGURE 12.20   Gartner Business Model Assessment Framework

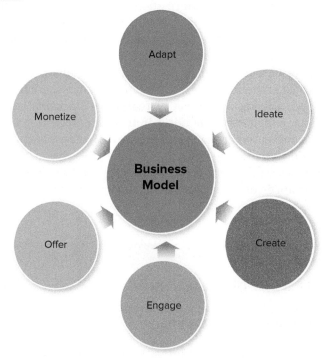

Source: Taken from Gartner Inc.
http://www.gartner.com/resources/273000/273028/273028_2_hr.png.

FIGURE 12.21   Digital Technology Integration Mapping

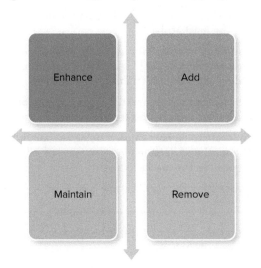

The role of big data and analytics in the operations decision-making process will only continue to heighten as time passes by. With more data streaming at businesses than ever before, the importance of uncovering the insights hidden within these data is what will separate the top performers from all others. Unlike the decisions of the past, which were largely based on instinct, experience, and preconceived notions, information technology–based analytics offers managers fact-based insights in real time, thereby enabling organizations to achieve higher levels of operational efficiency than ever before. Business process optimization, infrastructure and asset efficiency improvements, reduced costs, and improved service levels are but a few of the many benefits the use of such data is bringing to businesses large and small.[13] Add to this the ability to predict upcoming trends, risks, and opportunities, and one can quickly see why investments in analytics-based technologies are accelerating at an unprecedented pace.

In closing, the incorporation of information technology–based analytics into operations management has fundamentally changed the way that companies are doing business. Gone are the days where organizations would initiate a sales campaign and/or launch a new product and then look to assess results based on **lagging indicators** (outputs measured after the fact) such as revenue, profitability, net new customers, sales lead conversion rate, etc. Today, managers are interacting with the process much more quickly as a result of real-time data being collected and assessed. These data, in generating **leading indicators** (activities and actions that can be tracked or measured at the front end), reveal almost instantaneously how well the organization is executing its strategy. This enables the management team to move beyond the descriptive question of what happened to more predictive questions of what will happen or is happening, why did it happen, and what we should do in response to the results being realized.

Lagging Indicators are outputs measured after the fact (such as revenue, profitability, net new customers, and sales lead conversion rate).

Leading Indicators are activities and actions that can be tracked or measured at the front end, revealing almost instantaneously how well the organization is executing its strategy.

Business IN ACTION

Desire2Learn—Pioneering Innovative Methods in eLearning

D2L (Desire2Learn), a leading global educational software company based in Kitchener, Ontario, was founded by John Baker in 1999. The idea came to him as part of a class project. As an engineering student at the University of Waterloo, John was challenged to come up with a question no one had asked before.

His question was, "How can we use technology to dramatically transform and improve learning?" One of the solutions that D2L developed was Brightspace, an integrated learning platform. This unique learning-environment technology is being used by over 1200 schools, universities, and businesses around the world. In Canada, 30% of higher education and K–12 schools use the software, and Brightspace's market share overall is estimated at 13% of the North American market (an estimated 3.6 million enrollees). Brightspace facilitates course management and e-learning, which in turn has allowed courses to be scaled and personalized in ways that were unimagined 15 years ago.

Used by permission of D2L Corporation

Used by permission of D2L Corporation

In 2015, *Canadian Business* published "How the 'Netflix of Education' Is Using Big Data in the Classroom," naming D2L one of Canada's most innovative companies. There are other companies that offer learning platforms. What makes D2L stand out and be more competitive is how it uses analytics and the data available from its user base. Just like Netflix can predict whether someone will like a movie, Brightspace can offer additional insights into how a student will progress in a course, based on assessing their current performance and overall activity focus.

Given a student's transcripts, D2L can use a predictive algorithm based on the data collected from students over the past 15 years to predict the student's letter grade in a course before the course even begins. D2L is confident the algorithm can do this with over 90% accuracy. However, Brightspace takes these analytics one step further. Brightspace can then use those data to customize the student's learning experience in the course to increase the chances of a positive outcome.

Another innovation D2L is exploring is using gaming as a teaching tool. Game-based learning allows teachers to design games that complement their course material.

The games mimic online games, with avatars and awards to interest and incentivize students. In a trial at Mohawk College in Hamilton, Ontario, use of game-based learning increased course completion rates by 25%.

At the course level, a teacher can use D2L to see which students have completed which activities. Cross-referencing these data with the results attained by the students will allow the teacher to modify the activities and the content of the course to produce better results. At the program level, student data can be analyzed to ensure student activities are varied throughout the program to support different learning styles.

D2L continues to be at the forefront of evolving technology focused on enhancing the learning experience of students. The organization aspires to improve the learning of every learner, regardless of geography or ability. The organization's fundamental belief is that everyone should be able to teach and learn the way that they want to. It is focused on ensuring that everyone has access to the best possible learning opportunities, enabled by the best teaching and utilizing the best that technology has to offer.

Web Integration

To learn more about D2L, visit **www.d2l.com**.

LO5   Establishing Quality Standards

As one can see, the role of the operations management team is complex and challenging. With the rapid change in technology, the ongoing maturing of the global market, and the influx of new competitors from all parts of the world, operations managers must seek to design, develop, implement, and manage processes vital to the successful execution of an organization's strategy. A key part of this challenge is to continually protect and, in many cases, enhance the quality of the products and services being offered in the face of constant downward pressure on price. This means that operations managers and their teams must work to continually improve the efficiency and effectiveness of the organization's operations cycle, while at the same time striving to reduce the costs incurred in doing so (see Figure 12.22). A key weapon in this ongoing challenge to preserve quality and maintain the product standards expected by customers in the face of pressure to reduce costs lies with the organization's culture and the development of performance standards. Operations managers know that the ability to establish within the organization a culture focused on preserving quality and maintaining product consistency is fundamental to maintaining a competitive advantage in the face of intensifying competition. Managers also recognize that their ability to supply their products to customers in B2B settings is predicated on their capability to meet consistent and measurable quality standards. With an increasing focus on specialization and automation, finished goods producers rely on their suppliers to deliver consistent (quality) parts and components for integration into their production/transformation processes. Operations and supply chains are becoming truly global, with manufacturing partners and suppliers performing more and more of the transformation work on the products and services sold by many companies. Legal, environmental, ethical, and social responsibility issues are impacting the operations of organizations more extensively than ever before.

FIGURE 12.22   **Quality Impact Factors**

A key weapon in this ongoing challenge to preserve quality and maintain the product standards expected by customers in the face of pressure to reduce costs lies with the organization's culture and the development of performance standards.

In response to this, organizations and their operations management teams are implementing behaviour-directed methodologies designed to assist in the control of consistency and quality standards within the organization. For many, **ISO (International Organization for Standardization)** certification is an essential first step in ensuring that they meet the expectations of their customers. The ISO has developed more than 18 000 standards relating to the manufacturing and supplying of products and services. Its focus is to make the manufacturing of products and services safer, more efficient, and more socially responsible. Its work results in customers benefiting from knowing that manufacturers have conformed to international standards relating to reliability and quality. By achieving ISO certification, manufacturers agree to adhere to the product and process specification requirements and criteria in the manufacturing of products and services within their industry classification, and to use a common technological language in their communication with suppliers and customers. ISO standards cover a wide range of industry sectors, such as agriculture, construction, engineering, manufacturing, distribution, and information and communication technologies, to name a few. The ISO's best-known categories of standards cover general management practices and quality standards (ISO 9000 series) and environmental management standards (ISO 14000 series).[14]

> **ISO (International Organization for Standardization)** is the world's largest developer and publisher of international standards.

Web Integration

Want to learn more about ISO certification? Visit **www.iso.org**.

Although ISO certification is a good first step for many organizations, particularly in the manufacturing and distribution sectors, organizations often look to develop a culture of quality (beyond ISO compliance) in order to achieve a sustainable competitive advantage over their competitors. Toyota's development of TPS is a good example of an organization developing standards to guide its operations-based processes and to embed within its culture a sense of discipline toward uncompromising quality. Alan Mulally's Ford One program (highlighted in Chapter 8) is another example of attempting to shift the cultural attitude within an organization toward quality. Other companies have turned to developed methodologies such as Six Sigma and TQM to assist in redefining cultural attitudes toward quality and to significantly upgrade their quality performance results. **Six Sigma** is a methodology that focuses on a philosophy of total improvement. It seeks to integrate within an organization's culture an organized approach for the analysis of processes, with the intent of minimizing (and eliminating) the occurrence of defects—which, ultimately, impact the quality of the products/services being delivered to the marketplace and the costs incurred in their creation. Based on a methodology of DMAIC (define, measure, analyze, improve, control) for existing operations, or DMADV (define, measure, analyze, design, verify) for new operations, Six Sigma analyses guide managers to map the processes being used within the organization, align these with customer needs, and then seek to improve or develop such processes and implement the necessary controls for maintaining the heightened (required) quality levels. Although historically best suited for situations where quantitative data are available and defect rates can be measured, the Six Sigma approach has been extended to non-quantitative situations as well. Developed by Motorola Inc. in the 1980s and made famous by General Electric (under CEO Jack Welch), Six Sigma has resulted in significant savings for

> **Six Sigma** is a methodology that focuses on a philosophy of total improvement.

many companies across a wide variety of manufacturing sectors. Six Sigma gets its name from its statistical orientation of deviation from the mean. Attainment of Six Sigma represents a situation where the manufacturing processes being employed are virtually free of defects (3.4 defects per 1 million chances). An easy way to think of Six Sigma is that better processes, with lower defect rates, mean lower costs, which results in improved profit margins.[15]

TQM (Total Quality Management) is a broad-based approach to managing quality within the organization.

While Six Sigma focuses on the specific processes within an organization, **TQM (total quality management)** can be viewed as more of a broad-based approach to managing quality within the organization. TQM can be thought of as a management system that seeks to assimilate the concept of quality improvement across the entire organization. TQM challenges the organization to be customer focused and to strive for total employee involvement to ensure that quality (in the delivery of products or services) is fully integrated as a core component into the organization's strategy, processes, and communication messages. Similar to Six Sigma, TQM looks for managers to implement quality improvement initiatives on the basis of facts and on the utilization of analytical thinking in determining ways to become more efficient and effective. TQM also directs its emphasis on the processes used within the organization to interact with customers. The focus of quality improvement needs to be in those areas of the organization that influence the quality perception at known critical customer touch points.[16]

Web Integration

Want to learn more about Six Sigma and its use in today's marketplace? Google Six Sigma methodologies.

Six Sigma and TQM are but two of the many approaches organizations and their operations management teams can initiate to improve and maintain heightened quality levels. For example, BPR, or business processing re-engineering, focuses on how organizations transform production and manufacturing processes to improve the way that people work. In reality, companies often take components of the various models offered and use them to formulate their own customized approaches to managing quality through their manufacturing and/or service-based delivery processes. Toyota's TPS approach is, again, an excellent example. Regardless of the path chosen or the methodology selected, managers need to recognize that certain core fundamentals will determine their overall degree of success. These fundamentals can be summarized as follows (see Figure 12.23):

- Quality initiatives, such as those described above, are successful only if they are accompanied by strong management support and commitment.
- To be successful, quality initiatives must be supported by a well-structured approach and deployment process. This needs to include clear identification of the roles and responsibilities of those involved. Specific, measurable, actionable, and controllable objectives must be identified.
- Quality initiatives must be viewed as requiring a team-based approach. Involvement, input, rewards, and recognition must be shared with all involved.
- The progress and results of the initiatives must be effectively communicated to all involved. The sharing of knowledge and successes is fundamental to developing a quality-focused culture.

Web Integration

Want to learn more about TQM and how to incorporate it into the workplace? Google TQM or total quality management.

FIGURE 12.23   **Successful Quality Initiative Implementation**

Operations Management in Small Businesses

Operational efficiency and effectiveness is one of the predominant challenges facing the small business owner. Possessing, in many cases, limited resources and expertise, small business owners often do not have the abilities or the financial capabilities required to take full advantage of the technologies and practices available to maximize the cost-effectiveness of their businesses. Also, lacking the depth and functional expertise of full-time operations management professionals, small business owners must generally seek to tackle the intricacies of operations management while attending to the broader business issues (sales, finance, HR, and so on). A small, generally more transient employee base also limits their ability and desire to commit significant financial resources into the training and education of what are perceived to be non-critical business positions. With all of these challenges noted, just how does a small business owner seek to tackle the need to create as efficient an operation as is possible? The answer to this question lies in the fact that, although limitations do exist, the small business owner can incorporate many of the key characteristics of successful operations management. Small business owners should look to understand customer expectations and translate this into processes designed to support customers at the key interaction touch points where the business and customers connect. Small business owners should also think in terms of product consistency, striving to deliver consistent experience with each customer interaction. A key component of this process is to determine what skills are fundamentally required at the point of customer contact and seek to ensure that employees are recruited, trained, and educated to support this interaction. Small business owners should also take the time to plan their business layout. A good way to do this is to walk through every step associated with the process of delivering products and/or services to the customer and then design the layout and process in support of this. Taking the position of the customer and working backwards through this process is an eye-opener for many small business owners and professionals. Finally, small business owners need to be careful not to make operational decisions "on the fly," but rather based on facts and via a systematic, analytical process that ensures the changes or adjustments being made enhance service and do not negatively impact the delivery of service in other areas. For many small business owners, a key to success is communication of the business strategy and effective communication of how operational areas are linked to this plan. Often feeling alone, small business owners should seek to involve their employee team in discussions relating to facility layout, process planning, and service delivery changes. Employees "in the trenches" of the day-to-day operations can often provide positive and constructive ideas on how to improve services and/or make better use of technology. The additional benefit is the sense of involvement they will get from such discussions and the motivational impact the process will have on their future work effort.

Management Reflection—Operational Success

More and more organizations understand that the battle to develop sustainable competitive advantages lies at the front end of the value chain. The need for efficient and effective transformation processes and supply chains can, and will, dramatically influence the ability of an organization to compete in today's global marketplace. The ability of marketing to build brand differentiation is dependent upon the consistent and effective delivery of quality products and services at price points that customers are willing to pay for the value received. To be successful in meeting customer expectations and in contributing to the organization's overall value proposition, operations managers must develop the deep functional expertise and the general business skills needed to develop and manage the processes and methodologies required for competitive purposes. They must also understand and seek to eliminate those costs within their operations that do not add value to the products or services being offered. Decisions relating to this cannot be made in isolation of others. Operations managers need to integrate a cross-functional approach to their decision making that includes internal stakeholders, such as sales, marketing, customer service, and finance, to name a few, as well as external stakeholders, particularly supply chain partners and distribution channel representatives. This collaborative and cooperative approach is vital to ensuring that decisions made within one area of the transformation and distribution process do not negatively impact other areas. Finally, organizations must tailor their operations to the needs of their customers, ensuring that the expectations of these customers are met, and that the right product is delivered to the right place at the right time for the right price.

To be successful in meeting customer expectations and in contributing to the organization's overall value proposition, operations managers must develop the deep functional expertise and the general business skills needed to develop and manage the processes and methodologies required for competitive purposes.

Chapter Summary

The focus of this chapter is on acclimatizing students to the responsibilities of operations managers. The chapter begins with a discussion of the important role operations management plays within the organization's business system and in the execution of the organization's business strategy. The role of the operations manager is discussed, as are the four areas of responsibility associated with this position: process management, supply chain management, product/service management, and information technology–based operational analytics. This is followed by an analysis of the value chain, including the identification of the primary activities and support activities associated with it. With this broadened understanding of the role of the operations management team provided, the chapter then focuses on an overview of the key decision-making areas that operations managers will face on an ongoing basis. These include decisions relating to process, materials, facility layout, asset management, and supply chain planning, execution, and performance monitoring. In addition to this, a commentary is offered with respect to the importance of establishing quality standards for an organization and embedding these into its culture. This discussion includes references to ISO certification, the use of Six Sigma and TQM methodologies, the identification of quality impact factors, and the managerial competencies required for the successful implementation of quality initiatives. The chapter closes with a brief discussion of the challenges facing small business owners and their use of operations management tools and techniques, as well as a final reflection on what managers need to understand in order to initiate successful operations management strategies and tactics.

Developing Business Knowledge and Skills

Key Terms

operations management *p. 444*

process management *p. 445*

supply chain management *p. 445*

product/service management *p. 446*

information technology–based operational analytics *p. 446*

value maximization *p. 447*

primary activities *p. 448*

inbound logistics *p. 448*

operations *p. 448*

outbound logistics *p. 449*

marketing and sales *p. 449*

customer service *p. 449*

support activities *p. 451*

operations cycle *p. 452*

process standardization *p. 452*

process simplification *p. 452*

process design, layout, and execution *p. 454*

PERT chart *p. 455*

Gantt chart *p. 455*

materials management *p. 458*

facility design and layout *p. 458*

capacity *p. 458*

capital asset evaluation and acquisition *p. 459*

supply chain management *p. 462*

supply chain operating execution *p. 463*

supply chain performance evaluation *p. 463*

cash operating cycle (COC) *p. 464*

lagging indicators *p. 472*

leading indicators *p. 472*

ISO (International Organization for Standardization) *p. 475*

Six Sigma *p. 475*

TQM (total quality management) *p. 476*

Questions for Discussion

1. What is meant by the term *operations management*? What are the four main areas of responsibility that decisions relating to operations management revolve around? (LO1)

2. What are the four key decision areas associated with process management? How are they interconnected? (LO2)

3. What is the major focus of supply chain management? What are the primary areas of responsibility of supply chain managers? (LO2)

4. How are information technology and analytics changing the role of the operations management team? (LO2)

5. What is the underlying principle behind the value chain business model? Describe the primary activities that make up the value chain and how they are integrated with support activities in order to allow organizations to effectively manage the design, development, and distribution of products and services. (LO3)

6. What is meant by the operations cycle? How does it integrate with an organization's business planning cycle? (LO4)

7. What are the key factors that impact quality within an organization? How do managers successfully manage quality implementation initiatives? (LO5)

Question for Individual Action

Interview a small retail business owner in your town about how they manage their operation. Who makes decisions regarding facility layout? How are these decisions made? What about inventory management? How are decisions made regarding what products to buy and how far in advance the products must be ordered? What factors influence the types of products they carry? What about warehousing? How much of their facility square footage is allocated to inventory storage?

Team Exercise

In the 1980s, Motorola Inc. developed what is known today as the Six Sigma methodology. Recognizing its value in managing quality and in reshaping a culture focused on quality, General Electric adopted Six Sigma as a major component of its operational strategy. Since then, a large number of major corporations across the globe have adopted Six Sigma. As a team, prepare a presentation that traces the origin of Six Sigma and provide an overview as to how this methodology works. Be sure to discuss how Six Sigma is implemented within an organization. Also develop two or three success stories from organizations that have implemented Six Sigma and that demonstrate the cost savings realized. Think about this in terms of a cost/benefit trade-off.

Case for Discussion 1

Martinette Packaging Limited

Martinette Packaging Limited currently operates five packaging facilities (plants) across Canada (see Table 12.1). These plants package frozen fruits and vegetables which are then sold to major retailers such as Loblaw Companies, Metro Inc., and Sobeys Inc. Fruits and vegetables are purchased from six cooperatives in the U.S. These cooperatives are located in the states of California, Alabama, Texas, and Florida (also identified in Table 12.1).

TABLE 1.1

Martinette Packaging Facilities	Cooperative Collection Locations
Laval, Quebec	Sacramento, California
Belleville, Ontario	Bakersfield, California
Regina, Saskatchewan	San Antonio, Texas
Calgary, Alberta	Montgomery, Alabama
Burnaby, British Columbia	Jacksonville, Florida
	Ocala, Florida

A specialist in fruit and vegetable packaging, Martinette Packaging Limited understands the critical nature of getting its fruits and vegetables to its plants as soon as is possible in order to preserve freshness and minimize spoilage and perishability. Product is picked at the optimal point of the harvesting season by the cooperatives in order to maximize flavour and nutritional components, which if not flash frozen quickly, compromises product quality and impacts key customer relationships. Transporting in a climate-controlled environment is fundamental to maintaining the freshness of the product while in route to processing plants. Even short delays can compromise product quality. Relationships with customers have been considered to be excellent, as Martinette Packaging Limited has established a reputation for product quality and consistency with its buyers and has also demonstrated "industry best" service records in terms of meeting order deadlines and volumes. Although a well-entrenched industry player, buyers have consistently demonstrated a willingness to develop and create alternate channels for fruit and produce product lines if prices from suppliers continue to rise.

Up to this point in time, Martinette Packaging Limited has transported the purchased fruits and vegetables via its own trucking company, Martinette Transportation Inc. The current monthly transportation costs associated with this operation, handled by its trucking subsidiary, average $265 000 per month. Martinette Packaging Limited has, however, seen these costs rise by an average of 7% to 10% annually as a result of union-negotiated labour contracts, maintenance expenses, increased customs and duty costs, and increased fuel costs. It is anticipated that this upward pressure on costs will continue for the foreseeable future (next three years).

The company recently hired Ace Consulting, a transportation consulting firm, to review its subsidiary's operation in order to determine if additional cost efficiencies could be realized. Martinette Packaging Limited is being pressured by its retail buyers, particularly one that represents 50% of their business, to reduce costs, as downward pressure on price resulting from an intensive competitive market sector is impacting margins across the retail sector. In finalizing its analysis, Ace Consulting surprised management by recommending that Martinette Packaging Limited consider selling its trucking subsidiary and outsourcing its transportation operation to a select group of private contractors. Based on Ace Consulting's preliminary interviews with qualified contractors, and utilizing current fuel prices, Martinette Packaging could save an estimated $250 000 to $300 000, per year, over the three-year period.

Private contractors interviewed by Ace Consulting would be willing to sign a three-year contract, locking in rates for the three-year contract period. Contracts, however, would stipulate that prices charged would be adjusted to reflect a fuel surcharge should fuel prices rise more than 10% during the contract period. Also lying outside of the contract would be surcharges for lost time for drivers due to congested driving conditions, construction work on highways, and seasonal weather disruptions. The projected cost savings also assume that contractors would be able to contract with other businesses for transportation loads to fill their trucks, should the shipment sizes being transported by Martinette Packaging represent less than 85% of load capacity. Worth noting as well, however, is that situations where Martinette's shipments represented less than 70% of load capacity, and where additional business could not be generated to fill a given truck, a partial load surcharge would also be applied. Given the operational geographic radius that most trucking companies focus on, Ace Consulting estimates that five to six different trucking operations would be involved in transporting the fruits and vegetables from the cooperatives to Martinette's packaging facilities.

Martinette Transportation Inc., a wholly owned subsidiary of Martinette Packaging Limited, was established in 2004. Since its inception, the operation has grown from a single small refrigerator/freezer truck to one that owns and operates 12 full-size state-of-the-art refrigerator/freezer transports. The average age of its fleet is 5 years. Ace Consulting estimates that selling the assets of this subsidiary would result in an estimated net inflow (following repayment of truck loans for vehicles in the fleet) of $2 million. Ace Consulting has also indicated that a ready buyer is available to purchase the assets of Martinette Transportation Inc., should the parent company decide to sell.

If Martinette Packaging Limited decides to sell its subsidiary, employee severances would have to be paid. These are estimated to be in the $300 000 to $400 000 range. The company also has to be cognizant of the potential impact of the sale on other parts of the organization (morale, etc.), as well as potentially straining the relationship with its other employee unions. Still, the estimated savings could go a long way to protect Martinette Packaging Limited's own margins in the face of increased pressure from its buyers to reduce prices.

Questions

As a member of Martinette Packaging Limited's management team and/or its board of directors,

1. What key questions would you want answers to?

2. What risks do you foresee in proceeding with the transition to outsource this activity?

3. Do you consider the shipping component of this operation a critical activity, or a supporting activity to what the company does?

4. Would you proceed with Ace Consulting's recommendation?

Case for Discussion 2

Operations Management at Winnipeg's Price Industries

Winnipeg's Price Industries is a Canadian success story in the air distribution business. Founded in 1946 as primarily a sales organization, Price Industries is now a powerhouse in the industrial air distribution HVAC (heating, ventilation, and air conditioning) market, with 38% market share in the United States and 49% in Canada. While air distribution materials may be perceived as commodities, Price Industries chooses to set itself apart with a focus on service and customer experience.

"The basis of our success lies in taking care of our customers and our people—everything we do is about service," the privately held organization says in its vision document.

Price Industries identifies the key elements of its vision this way:

- Service Culture—A profound service orientation permeates everything we do at Price.

- Delivery Excellence—We provide short lead times and reliable, on-time delivery.

- Easy to Do Business—We make it simple and easy to do business with Price.

- Product Innovation—We invest continuously and relentlessly in product innovation.

- Technical Support—We provide the best and deepest technical support and application engineering in the industry.

- Custom Applications—We welcome specials and custom designs for unique requirements.

- People—We are diligent in hiring the "right" people. Our people share and embody our values.[17]

To drive research and development at speed, the company's design engineering leverages technologies including CAD 3D software and CFD analysis, data acquisition, and instrumentation. The work is also supported by Price Research Centre North (PRCN), an expansive R&D facility in Winnipeg. In addition to supporting innovation in both commodity and niche products, the facility allows customers and users such as engineers, contractors, and architects the opportunity to interact with Price Industries products in a range of operating conditions. Price Technical Centers (PTCs) in Atlanta and Phoenix also provide hands-on product displays and the opportunity to learn about the company's products and services. The Winnipeg location has a Price Mechanical Tech Centre to accomplish a similar function.

On the manufacturing floor Price strives for process improvement, investing in both capital equipment and in the training and development of its people. This includes a commitment to lean manufacturing. Price's manufacturing leadership team comprises acknowledged industry experts with a deep understanding of lean manufacturing techniques. The company invests heavily in educating everyone in the organization on these techniques, and encourages everyone to put them to use on the shop floor every day. All plants have obtained ISO 9001:2015 certification.

Logistics are underpinned by a four-plant, three-location distribution system with hubs in Winnipeg, Atlanta, and Phoenix, allowing it to access most major North America markets in one trucking day. "That makes the supply chain—my job—very challenging because I can't stock 100 per cent of everything that any customer might order," says Kelly Singleton, Price's purchasing manager. "We have many variations of products and offerings to suit each of our customers' unique requirements. The goal is always to deliver the perfect order while providing exceptional customer service." Logistics and distribution are also supported by the integration of a number of systems, including the Price Shopfloor Information Management System (PRISIM), the organization's bar coding system.

Customers and users are supported by a range of software tools, such as *All-in-One for Engineers* and *Room Designer*, and free access to the *Price Engineer's HVAC Handbook*. Price also has an established network of sales representatives to support the overall operation and its customer base.

Questions

1. Identify and discuss two or three components of operations management you see in action at Price Industries.

2. How does Price pursue alignment between strategic intent and operations management focus? How might you use the value chain to support your answer?

PART 4

CHAPTER 13

Understanding Business Finances

LEARNING OBJECTIVES

This chapter is designed to provide students with:

LO1	An understanding of the five fundamental components of financial analysis
LO2	Knowledge of the key components associated with the revenue model
LO3	An understanding of cost-base analysis and the ability to calculate an organization's breakeven point (BEP)
LO4	Exposure to the concept of margin management
LO5	An overview of the various sources of funds available in supporting an organization's cash needs

Snapshot

What to Expect in This Chapter

As identified by the learning objectives, this chapter focuses on exposing students to the basics associated with capital and financial markets. The content emphasized in this chapter includes the following:

- The Fundamentals of Financial Analysis
- The Revenue Model
- Cost Structure and Cost Drivers
  - Variable versus Fixed Costs
  - Breakeven Point Analysis
- Margin Requirements
- Cash Operating Cycle
- Capitalization Requirements
  - Sources of Funds
- Putting It All Together
- A Note Pertaining to Not-for-Profits
- Management Reflection—The Need for Capital
- Appendix—Advanced Topics Relating to BEP, Pricing, and Revenue Model Management

Business IN ACTION

Assent Compliance—Securing Equity Capital Funding

As this chapter comments on, one of the key pillars of a financial strategy for for-profit companies is the ability to raise equity capital. For many businesses, the financial requirements associated with launching and/or expanding their business operations is predicated on having the financial capacity to do just that. As will be discussed both in this chapter and in Chapter 15, venture capitalists and venture capital organizations play an important role in supplying the capital needs of many blossoming business operations. The events of 2018, as an example, offer insight into this equity-raising market in Canada. According to the Canadian Venture Capital & Private Equity Association (CVCA), there were 165 VC (venture capital) deals in Canada as of fourth-quarter 2018, totalling $1.3 billion in equity funding. One of the beneficiaries of this venture capital sector is Ottawa-based Assent

Compliance, a recognized leader in supply chain data management and SaaS solutions that help organizations collect and manage supplier data, meet regulatory and internal requirements, and promote transparency across their supply chains. The company, in Q4 2018, secured one of the year's largest funding deals in Canada, receiving $161 million (CAD) in funding. Investors in this company now include venture capital organizations such as New York's Warburg Pincus, BDC Capital, Greenspring Associates, Open-Text Enterprise Apps Fund (OTEAF), and Volition Capital.

Assent's business model focuses on providing companies (particularly multinationals) with cloud-based solutions via its Assent Compliance Platform, which supports business decision making and operations management relating to supply chain risk management and government regulatory compliance. The emphasis lies in the company's ability to leverage

Courtesy of Assent Compliance

leading-edge technologies and extensive supply chain expertise to assist these companies with the efficient collection of supply chain data with a focus on business risk exposure relating to product compliance, corporate social responsibility and vendor management, as part of the overall product development and manufacturing processes. This enables customers operating in an SaaS environment to manage their data in ways that enable them to protect their brand, increase market accessibility, and reduce operational and financial risk.

Warburg Pincus, the leading venture capital firm backing Assent Compliance ($161 million CAD investment), specializes in software domain and related technology incubation. The company views Assent Compliance's supply chain data management expertise and its niche market specialization, which it can offer further assistance in cultivating, as having real potential for continued rapid growth. This significant investment by Warburg Pincus is the third round of funding Assent Compliance has received in the past three years. The company raised $20 million (CAD) in 2016, and $40 million (CAD) in 2017. Assent Compliance now has over 500 employees across four continents and is becoming the partner of choice for mid-market and enterprise-level companies globally who are in need of support to navigate the evolving regulatory environment at home and abroad, manage third-party supplier data, and meet their corporate responsibility goals.

The Fundamentals of Financial Analysis   LO1

The ability to analyze and draw conclusions regarding the financial integrity of an organization is fundamental to understanding both its current situation and the strategic and tactical planning decisions going forward. At its broadest level, this analysis looks to draw conclusions across five key areas. As illustrated in Figure 13.1, these five areas are:

1. Revenue model
2. Cost structure and cost drivers
3. Margin requirements
4. Cash operating cycle
5. Capitalization requirements

FIGURE 13.1   **Five Key Areas of Financial Analysis**

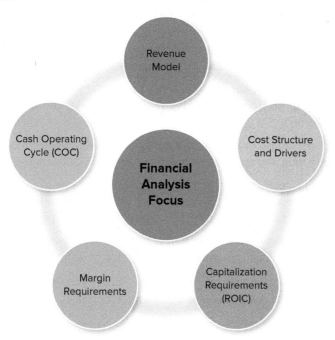

Assessing these five areas enables you and me, as managers, to draw some fundamental conclusions as to how the organization generates its revenue and the current trajectory of this important financial component (are sales increasing or decreasing), as well as where and how dollars are spent in support of this revenue-generation process. Our major mechanism for this analysis is to review and interpret the trends occurring within the financial statements (discussed in Chapter 14), which are prepared by the organization's finance team, against the targets the organization sets as part of its planning process. In terms of our approach relating to this financial assessment process, let's begin with a brief overview of these five key areas, recognizing that each will be covered in more detail both later on in this chapter, as well as in the chapters that follow. The intent of this chapter is not to illustrate the reporting of the financial information that each area focuses on, but to offer an explanation of the underlying importance each area brings to the financial analytical process. In offering this explanation first, it is hoped that the understanding of the actual statements themselves (presented in Chapter 14) will be made easier.

LO2 The Revenue Model

When we think about the revenue model, we are focusing on how the organization generates sales and, ultimately, the dollars that flow into its coffers through the delivery of its products and/or services to the marketplace. In simple terms, it can be thought of as the dollars generated as a result of the following equation:

$$\text{Per Unit Selling Price} \times \text{Quantity Sold} = \textbf{Sales Revenue}$$

Although simplified in this fashion, analysis of the revenue model does become more sophisticated as we seek to draw both current as well as longer-term conclusions relating to the financial health of the organization. As an example, the following list of questions illustrates the key components of this analytical process, and demonstrates the underlying complexity of revenue model analysis:

1 Which products within our portfolio are seeing increases in revenue? Likewise, which products are seeing decreases?

2 How much of our revenue is reliant on a single product? If we have one product, we know that we are 100% reliant on the success of this single product for all of our revenue. If we have multiple products, then what percentage of revenue comes from each product?

3 Are sales predominantly driven as a result of selling to new customers, or existing customers? What is the sales contribution of each?

4 If we are relying on repeat sales for a product, what is the frequency of purchase for our products? Is it daily, weekly, monthly, annually, every three years, and so on?

5 Are we dependent upon a small percentage of our customers for most of our sales? If so, who are they and are sales from these customers increasing or decreasing?

6 Is the selling price of our product being pushed down due to increasing competition? Are we able to manage selling price reductions through contracts and/or other mechanisms, thereby protecting further selling price declines?

7 What about average revenue per customer transaction. Are we able to increase this by bundling, packaging, or regrouping the way that we offer products and services?

The list of questions can go on and on depending on the nature of the products and/or services we sell. The important takeaway here is that, as managers, we need to analyze the underlying trends impacting our revenue model and draw conclusions as to whether these trends will assist us in growing revenue, or seeing a reduction in our revenue.

In our Chapter 1 discussion of the business model, of which the revenue model forms one component, we used Microsoft as an example. Let's return to Microsoft to illustrate how market trends are impacting its revenue model. A big part of Microsoft's revenue has historically been driven from sales of its Windows operating system to PC manufacturers. In thinking about this aspect of its revenue model and the revenue equation of Selling Price × Quantity Sold = **Sales Revenue**, we can see that there are two potential factors that will impact whether revenue will grow or decline within this operating division. First, a reduction in the demand for PCs that use the Windows operating system will result in a potential decline in revenue. This is actually happening worldwide as unit sales of desktops, laptops, and tablets have been on a downward trend since peaking in 2014.[1] This reduction in quantity sold directly impacted Microsoft's overall sales performance, as overall revenue was relatively stagnant from 2015 to 2018 given this drop in PC-related sales of Windows and Office products, despite growth in its cloud and service divisions.[2] The "selling price" part of the equation can be used either to offset this reduction or further contribute to the downward pressure on sales. If Microsoft is able to increase the price to PC manufacturers for its Windows and Office software then it may be able to hold its revenue constant despite a reduction in volume. If it is forced to keep price the same or lower then this will further impact its revenue outcome. In this particular situation, Microsoft was able to adjust its ASP (average selling price) upward a bit, thereby reducing the overall impact of the unit sales volume reduction.

Sales Revenue = Per Unit Selling Price × Quantity Sold

Figure 13.2 provides a further example of the analysis we could do with respect to better understanding the revenue model. In this figure, the XYZ Corporation, which manufactures electronic sensors, has a product portfolio that is made up of four products (products A, B, C, D). This figure, via three charts, illustrates the revenue for each of these products for the period 2016 through 2018. In this regard, we can see the movement of sales revenue for each product, as well as recognize the overall revenue contribution each product makes to the total sales revenue generated.

Specifically, with respect to XYZ, a quick analysis enables us to recognize the following conclusions relating to the revenue model's performance.

• Total revenue for XYZ Corporation has grown from $126 000 in 2016 to $154 000 in 2018, a 22% increase over the three-year period. Revenue has fallen, however, between 2017 and 2018, from a high of $160 000 000 to $154 000 000, a decrease of 4%.

• Products A and B represent 45% and 34% of revenue, respectively. The two combined generate 89% of XYZ's total revenue.

• Product A has experienced the greatest increase in sales revenue, growing from $43 000 000 to $70 000 000 over the three-year period, an increase of 163%. Product B has also seen a slight upward tick in sales, although sales between 2017 and 2018 are unchanged.

• Products C and D have both experienced a decline in revenue. Product C's revenue has dropped from $25 000 000 in 2014 to $19 000 000 in 2015, a 24% decrease. Product D's revenue has decreased each year over the three-year period, with the current revenue of $13 000 000 being just 65% of 2016 revenue.

Revenue is just one component of the overall financial assessment process. Revenue also is not profit, as up to this point in time the costs associated with delivering these products to the marketplace have not yet been taken into consideration. On the surface, however, with respect to the XYZ Corporation, the upward trend in sales revenue is largely the result of product A, as products B, C, and D have seen sales either stagnate or decrease. In managing the XYZ Corporation, key questions we

FIGURE 13.2   Revenue Model—XYZ Product Comparison

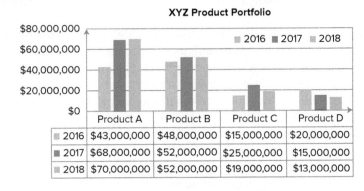

XYZ Product Portfolio

	Product A	Product B	Product C	Product D
2016	$43,000,000	$48,000,000	$15,000,000	$20,000,000
2017	$68,000,000	$52,000,000	$25,000,000	$15,000,000
2018	$70,000,000	$52,000,000	$19,000,000	$13,000,000

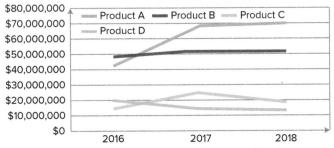

XYZ Product Portfolio

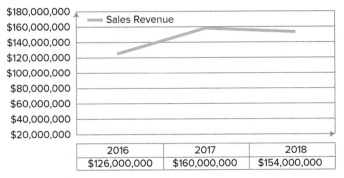

Sales Revenue

2016	2017	2018
$126,000,000	$160,000,000	$154,000,000

would be asking, given the information provided, would focus on both why product A is experiencing such a robust increase in sales, and whether this is sustainable, as well as why we are seeing such lacklustre sales revenue performance in our other three product lines. Are the revenue stagnation and/or reductions being experienced by products B, C, and D the result of downward pressure on price or a reduction in unit volume (quantity sold)? Let's use product C as an example of this relationship among price, quantity, and revenue (see Figure 13.3).

In 2016, assume the selling price of product C was $21.00 per unit. The number of units sold was 714 286, resulting in revenue of $15 000 000.

In 2017, in an effort to further grow its marketing position, XYZ Corporation dropped selling price for product C to $19.00 per unit. It was successful with this growth initiative, growing its volume (quantity sold) to 1 315 790 units, resulting in revenue increasing to $25 000 000.

In 2018, new market entrants have increased the competitive intensity of the marketplace. XYZ Corporation, however, was reluctant to cut its price in response to the entrance of lower-price rivals into its segment. Holding to the $19.00 per unit price reduced the quantity sold to 1 000 000 units, resulting in revenue dropping to $19 000 000.

FIGURE 13.3 **Price/Quantity Impact**

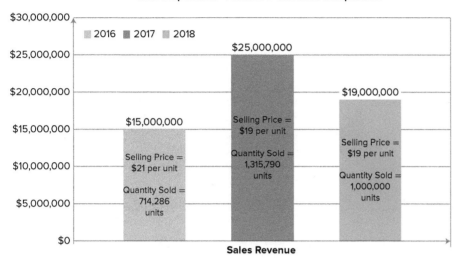

XYZ Corporation—Product C—Revenue Composition

- 2016 - 2017 - 2018

$15,000,000
Selling Price = $21 per unit
Quantity Sold = 714,286 units

$25,000,000
Selling Price = $19 per unit
Quantity Sold = 1,315,790 units

$19,000,000
Selling Price = $19 per unit
Quantity Sold = 1,000,000 units

Sales Revenue

Business IN ACTION

Apple—Where Does Its Revenue Come From?

As products are developed, are introduced to the marketplace, mature, and then are replaced by emerging technology, the revenue from such products varies from quarter to quarter and year to year. The challenge for companies is to keep growing in the wake of shifts that are occurring within the marketplace and that, ultimately, impact the current and future revenue streams of the products and services they offer.

Take Apple Inc. as an example. The company reported first-quarter earnings (Oct.–Dec.) for its 2019 fiscal year, and despite declines in overall iPhone sales (largely attributed to China) the company still produced a record earnings per share (EPS) of $4.18. Apple recorded revenue of $84.3 billion (USD) for this quarter, with net profit of $19.9 billion (USD). So where did this revenue come from? Apple's largest source of revenue continues to be its Products Division, generating

© laurentiu iordache/ Alamy Stock Photo

$73.4 billion. Its Service Division made up the other $10.9 billion in revenue (up 19% over the prior year). Sales of the iPhone continue to represent the lion's share of revenue, generating an estimated 62% of the company's revenue during this quarter. Apple's iPad (8%), Mac sales (9%), and services (13%) made up the other core revenue components.

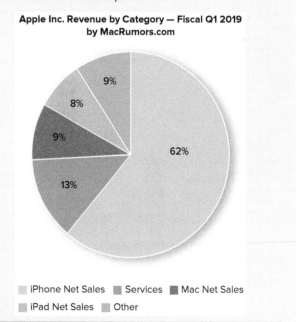

Apple Inc. Revenue by Category — Fiscal Q1 2019 by MacRumors.com

- iPhone Net Sales - Services - Mac Net Sales
- iPad Net Sales - Other

9%
8%
9%
13%
62%

Source: Used by permission of MacRumors.com, https://www.macrumors.com/2019/01/29/apple-1q-2019-results/.

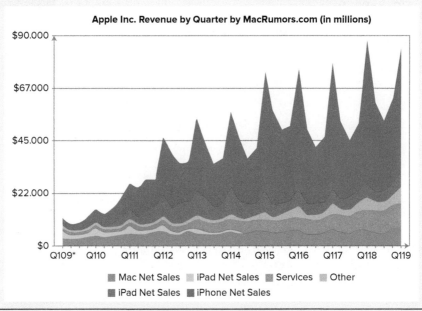

Apple Inc. Revenue by Quarter by MacRumors.com (in millions)

Legend: Mac Net Sales | iPad Net Sales | Services | Other | iPad Net Sales | iPhone Net Sales

Source: Used by permission of MacRumors.com, https://www.macrumors.com/2019/01/29/apple-1q-2019-results/.

Apple did see a revenue increase during this quarter for Macs, wearables, home devices, and iPads, while experiencing, as noted above, an approximately 15% decline in iPhone sales. As the second chart shows below, Apple revenue does vary from quarter to quarter, with first-quarter sales in any given fiscal year generally providing the strongest revenue results. Apple's second-quarter forecast for 2019 was to see revenue decline to just under $60 billion.

The 2019 revenue and profitability picture at Apple continues to build on the success of its core products, while demonstrating its ability to tap into new sources of revenue as existing products mature. Service-related items such as Apple Pay, Apple TV, wearables, Apple Card, etc. are anticipated to be the new revenue drivers for the near future. A look back at Apple's 2018 full-fiscal-year results sees Apple's total annual revenue at $265.6 billion, with $164.8 billion coming from iPhone, $18.3 billion from iPad, $25.2 billion from Mac, and $57 billion from services and related products.

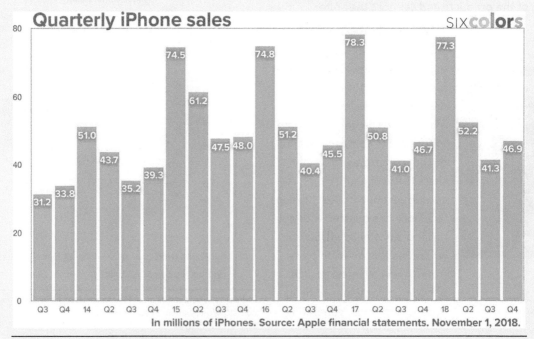

Quarterly iPhone sales   SIXcolors

In millions of iPhones. Source: Apple financial statements. November 1, 2018.

Source: Courtesy of Jason Snell/sixcolors.com.

Cost Structure and Cost Drivers   LO3

In simple terms, an organization's cost base is made up of the total costs associated with delivering the organization's products or services to the marketplace. A good way to think about the composition of this cost base is in terms of all the costs (across all value chain components) an organization incurs as it manufactures, distributes, markets, and sells products to other businesses or to consumers such as you and me. Let's return to our sample illustration of the XYZ Corporation, a manufacturer of electronic sensors, which, following fabrication, are sold to other businesses that then place these sensors into finished products that are sold to the marketplace at large. In this example, the cost base of the XYZ Corporation would be made up of the various costs identified in Figure 13.4.

As managers, we need to understand the cost structure within each of these areas. This enables us to fully understand the costs incurred in producing and supporting each sensor, a critical requirement in determining, ultimately, what price to charge for the sensors we are manufacturing. In addition to recognizing the costs incurred within each of these areas, we also need to determine whether these costs are directly involved in the manufacturing process (called direct or variable costs) or whether they are operational support costs (indirect, fixed, or semi-fixed costs) that exist because we are in business, but that are not directly tied to the creation of the product (in this case, our sensor). Figure 13.5 provides an easy formula for analyzing an organization's cost base.

In analyzing the composition of an organization's cost base we, as managers, hope to identify two fundamental conclusions:

1 The percentage of our costs that are considered to be direct or variable costs versus the percentage that are considered to be indirect (fixed or semi-fixed).

2 The cost areas (if any) that make up a significant percentage of our overall cost base.

FIGURE 13.4 **Cost Base: XYZ Sensor Organization**

FIGURE 13.5 **Computing the Total Cost Base**

Variable versus Fixed Costs

Variable Costs (Direct Costs) are those costs that are directly tied to the manufacturing of a product or the delivery of a service depending on the type of business being assessed.

As noted above, **variable costs** (also referred to as direct costs) are those costs that are directly tied to the manufacturing of a product or the delivery of a service depending on the type of business being assessed. Common examples of variable or direct costs are the cost of materials that are used in the manufacturing of a product, the direct labour costs associated with this transformation process, and distribution costs associated with getting the product to the right customer at the right place at the right time. In the manufacturing of electronic sensors by the XYZ Corporation, as an example, the variable or direct costs associated with the manufacturing and distribution of these sensors could include the following:

- The cost of the components that are used in the sensor (memory chips, power supplies, switches, relays, motion detectors, etc.)
- The cost of the labour needed to manufacture and/or assemble each sensor
- The cost of the packaging each sensor is shipped in
- The shipping costs associated with delivering the sensors to the customer

A good way to think about variable costs, in terms of our electronic sensor example, is that in the event that we ceased manufacturing sensors these costs would disappear. If we no longer manufactured sensors, we would have no need to purchase the components, hire people to assemble them, or incur shipping costs, because we would no longer be selling them.

Fixed Costs (Indirect Costs) are those costs that, although not directly tied to the manufacturing of a specific product or the delivery of a specified service, nonetheless exist as a result of conducting our business and operating our company.

Fixed costs (also referred to as indirect costs) are those costs that, although not directly tied to the manufacturing of a specific product or the delivery of a specified service, nonetheless exist as a result of conducting our business and operating our company. Examples of fixed or indirect costs—which a business must account for in its cost base and must, therefore, ensure are incorporated into its pricing strategy—are insurance, utilities, interest expense on debt, and administration costs. An additional uniqueness of fixed costs is that these costs represent an expense that is, for the most part, uncontrollable in the near term. This means that managers have little ability to change the amount of the expense. As an example, if you sign a five-year lease for a building that obligates you to lease payments of $5000 per month, then you have little ability to modify this monthly payment during the lease period regardless of the success of your business. The amount owed during the lease period ($5000/month) is, in essence, fixed. Another type of indirect cost that should be assessed is called *committed costs*. These are costs that the organization commits itself to within an operating year, and that often are spent in advance or at the front end of a manufacturing/sales cycle. Examples of a committed cost would be the marketing costs associated with launching a new product or service, advertising expenditures designed to further promote a product or service, software technology upgrades within a given year, and research and development costs that the organization has committed to spending. When analyzing an organization's fixed or indirect cost base, think in terms of the equation shown in Figure 13.6.

With an understanding of the types of costs we are looking for, organizations will now seek to build an understanding of their cost base. This is accomplished by working through the various zones within an organization's value chain and determining the cost composition of each. A good way to think of this is in terms of a

FIGURE 13.6   **Computing the Indirect Cost Base of an Organization**

ladder, with each rung of the ladder representing a cost zone. By working through these areas and identifying the cost structure within each, we can identify the total costs that an organization will incur in delivering its products and/or services to the marketplace (see Figure 13.7).

Using XYZ Corporation's product C as an example, and given the discussion we just had relating to costs, let's build a cost ladder for this product (see Figure 13.8). Assume the following costs for product C for 2018:

Design and Development Costs	$ 850 000
Supplier and Logistics Costs (material costs)	$ 7 600 000
Plant and Manufacturing Costs	$ 5 500 000
Distribution Costs	$ 500 000
Marketing and Sales Costs	$ 2 100 000
Admin. and Plant Overhead Costs	$ 800 000
Total Costs	$17 350 000

Going back to our original equation, which states that Variable Costs + Fixed Costs = Total Costs, we can also get a pictorial feel for what our total cost base looks like at various production and sales levels (see Figure 13.9). As the following section will illustrate, it is important to understand this relationship, as it does impact the

FIGURE 13.7   **Cost Ladder**

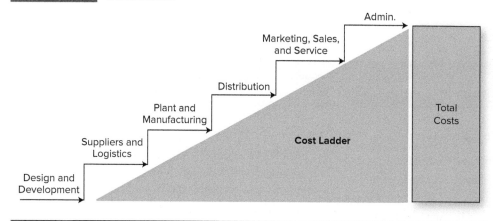

Source: Based on *The Definitive Business Plan*, Richard Stutely, 2nd Edition, Prentice Hall, 2007.

FIGURE 13.8   **Cost Ladder—XYZ Corporation, Product C**

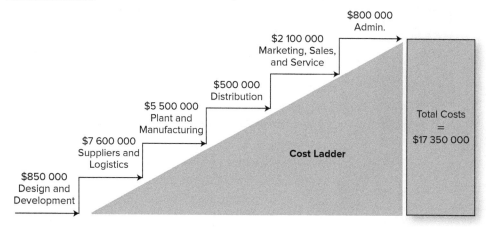

Source: Based on *The Definitive Business Plan*, Richard Stutely, 2nd Edition, Prentice Hall, 2007.

| FIGURE 13.9 | **Total Cost-Base Composition** |

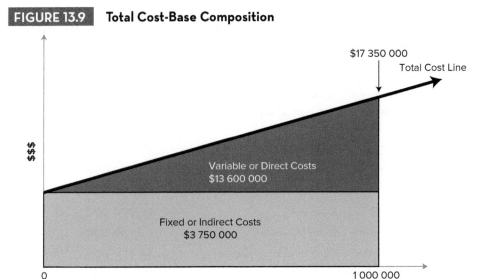

degree of control that a management team has over its cost base. Understanding an organization's cost base is essential in determining the required pricing strategy that will be utilized in the marketing of a product and its corresponding impact on profit.

> Understanding an organization's cost base is essential to determining the required pricing strategy that will be utilized in marketing the product and its corresponding impact on profit.

Business IN ACTION

What Is the Best Way to Cut Costs?

As one would anticipate, a large percentage of companies have focused on cutting costs as a way to protect profitability in the face of the financial crisis of 2008, the recession of 2009 and 2010, and the slow revenue line recovery that has occurred over the last five years. With

© Thomas Barwick/Getty Images

a number of industry sectors just getting back to the revenue levels they were seeing prior to this recent recessionary period, the need to assess cost allocations in order to maintain operating profits has become almost a quarterly standard operating procedure for many senior-level executives. With this in mind, and recognizing that almost all companies will need or desire to cut costs at some time during their life cycle, the question becomes what is the most effective way to do so. The answer is to enter into cost-cutting discussions with a mindset that ensures cost-cutting decisions and tendencies remain aligned with the organization's overall strategy. Although it may be easier, in the perceived interest of fairness and equity, to indicate that cost reductions should be made across the entire organization at an agreed-upon rate (say, for example, 10%), such an approach and action generally does not result in the most effective support of the organization's strategic intent. The key to cost cutting is to ensure that actions focused on reducing the cost base of the organization do not impact the sources of value (called value cells) that the organization relies on to compete in the marketplace. In the McKinsey & Company article "A Better Way to Cut Costs," authors Dennis Layton and Risto Penttinen suggest that there is a best-practice process organizations can follow when considering cost-reduction tactics. This approach advises managers, when restructuring, to be sure to restructure with the future of the company in mind. This means thinking about the current business model and its applicability to the future, as defined by the organization's strategy. This will result in the decision-making process focusing on the applicability of the structure to support the critical value chain processes in those areas of the organization that are core to its revenue generation future, and to ensure that resources are not depleted from these areas. It also means, when considering cuts to what is perceived to be the "fat" of the organization, to, again, ensure that the cuts made do not erode productivity standards or accountability, or eliminate vital processes, functions, or activities, especially within value cell zones. Managers need to think in terms of eliminating redundancies, low-value activities,

and management layers in a way that does not impede the ability of the organization to remain competitive. Finally, cost-cutting should be built around the concept of building capabilities, not destroying them. Decisions need to focus on redirecting resources to reinforce and enhance the organization's strengths and, where weaknesses do exist, to reduce resource allocation initiatives in a way that makes sense and does not jeopardize the organization's overall competitive ability. This process means that managers need to determine where they foresee future potential gain and marketplace strength, and build the organization around these value centres (cells). It goes without saying that cutting costs is never easy. For managers, however, developing such decisions around the organization's strategy and clearly articulating the link between cost cuts and resource reallocation, and communicating this to the organization's employee base, will enable such cuts to be better understood and accepted. The results of such an approach should also better position the company for the future than would be the case with an across-the-board "cuts" approach designed to have everyone share the same level of pain.

Breakeven Point Analysis (BEP)

A critical outcome of analyzing an organization's cost base is taking this information and utilizing it to determine the level of revenue required for the organization to break even. The **breakeven point (BEP)** is the level of sales revenue or volume required for the organization to cover all of its costs. It is most easily thought of as that point where the total revenue of the organization equals its total costs, resulting in a profit of $0 (see Figure 13.10).

For managers, the breakeven point is considered to be the minimum acceptable position for the business in the short term. Operating below the breakeven point means that the organization is operating in a loss position and, therefore, would need to draw upon its cash reserves and/or access to external cash resources (debt financing or equity financing) in order to assist in covering its expenses. If the organization did not possess sufficient cash reserves, and did not have access to additional cash from external sources, the end result could be insolvency and business closure. Operating at breakeven point does mean that total costs are being covered. It also means, however, that the organization is not making a profit. This lack of profit could result in the organization not generating future cash reserves and resources to cover such things as equipment replacement, new product development, and other strategic

Breakeven Point (BEP) refers to the point where total expenses = total revenue. The income statement, which takes into consideration actual cash expenses as well as non-cash expenses, results in profit = $0.

FIGURE 13.10   Breakeven Point

Minimum Acceptable Position for the Short Term

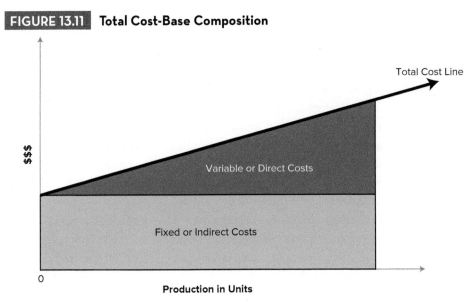

FIGURE 13.11   **Total Cost-Base Composition**

initiatives deemed essential to the long-term sustainability of the organization. Businesses, of course, need to earn current-period profits and sustain ongoing profitability in order to ensure their long-term success. The ability for managers to understand the sales volume(s) it takes to reach breakeven is an important part of the process of setting profitability objectives. Computing an organization's BEP is a two-step process:

• Step #1 is to estimate (within a degree of decision-making credibility) an organization's costs, and determine the nature of these costs (variable or fixed costs).

• Step #2 is to take this cost analysis and incorporate it into the breakeven point formula in order to effectively calculate the BEP for the organization. Keep in mind, again, that BEP is that point where total sales revenue equals total costs.

Looking back to earlier in this chapter, and with reference to our initial discussion of cost-base analysis, we attempted to define what the cost base for a given organization would look like. This was initially shown in Figure 13.9, and is repeated below as Figure 13.11.

> Breakeven point (BEP) is considered to be the minimum acceptable position for the business in the short term.

Breakeven point analysis takes this information and adds to it the anticipated revenue of the organization, based on its intended selling price, for the volume of units to be manufactured and sold. The point where the revenue from the sales of the products (units) offered to the marketplace equals the total costs (variable costs + fixed costs) associated with producing these products (units) is the breakeven point, as illustrated in Figure 13.12.

On the graph shown in Figure 13.12, the BEP is illustrated for a fictional company and production situation. At BEP, the volume being produced and sold by the organization, at its current selling price, is sufficient to cover its costs. Volumes of production above this point would yield a profit (assuming that they were sold), while volumes and sales below BEP would mean that the organization is not generating enough revenue to produce a profit for the firm. This is due to the fact that the revenue flowing into the firm (represented by the sales revenue line) is insufficient to cover all the costs (variable and fixed) that the firm is incurring as a result of being in business.

Calculating BEP in units   Computing BEP is relatively easy once the costs of the organization have been determined and the allocation between variable costs (direct

FIGURE 13.12 **Breakeven Point (BEP)**

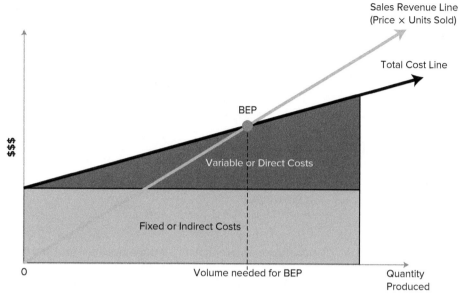

costs) and fixed costs (indirect costs) is understood. Whether the BEP calculation seeks to develop the breakeven point based on the number of units that need to be produced and sold or based on the total amount of revenue that needs to be generated is often determined by how the costs are best understood by the organization's management team. If costs are generally looked at on a per unit basis, as one would usually find in manufacturing operations, then calculating BEP in units may be the easiest approach. If costs are best understood as a percentage of sales revenue, then calculating BEP in dollars makes the best sense. The intent is to illustrate both approaches. We will, however, start with the formula calculation that provides BEP in units.

For illustration purposes, let's again go back to our sensor manufacturer. Assume that the XYZ Corporation is a manufacturer of electronic sensors. Its management team wants to know how many sensors need to be produced and sold to cover the total operating costs of the XYZ Corporation's latest product, called product E. The management team, in assessing the total costs of this product line for the XYZ Corporation, has determined the following:

Material costs (components) per unit	$ 10.00
Labour costs per unit	$ 9.00
Packaging costs per unit	$ 1.11
Shipping costs per unit	$ 6.34
Total variable costs (direct costs) per unit	$ 26.45

The fixed or indirect costs have been calculated and determined to be:

Plant overhead (utilities, insurance, service contracts, maintenance, etc.)	$ 500 000
Administration costs (payroll, accounting, IT, etc.)	$ 2 000 000
R&D costs	$ 500 000
Marketing costs (promotions, advertising, branding, etc.)	$ 1 500 000
Interest expense on debt	$ 500 000
Total fixed costs (indirect costs)	$ 5 000 000

XYZ Corporation intends to sell its sensors to a variety of high-end, advanced technology manufacturers, who then incorporate these sensors into their finished products. XYZ Corporation's average selling price (ASP) for this product category of sensors is $34.00 per unit. The question is how many units XYZ Corporation must produce and sell in order to break even (keep in mind that BEP is where profit equals $0).

The BEP formula is as follows:

$$\text{BEP (Units)} = \frac{\text{Total Fixed Costs}}{(\text{Selling Price per Unit} - \text{Variable Costs per Unit})}$$

$$\text{BEP (Units)} = \frac{\$5\ 000\ 000}{\$34.00 - \$26.45} = 662\ 252 \text{ units}$$

In order for the XYZ Corporation to break even, it must produce and sell 662 252 units at an average selling price of $34 (see Figure 13.13).

Once the BEP (in units) is determined, the BEP (in $$$) can easily be calculated by multiplying the BEP (in units) by the selling price. In this situation, the required revenue needed to break even would be 662 252 × $34 = $22 516 568.

If XYZ Corporation fails to sell at least 662 252 units at an average selling price of $34.00 per unit, it will suffer an operating loss. If it can produce and sell more than 662 252 units at an average selling price of $34.00 per unit, then it will enjoy an operating profit.

Keep in mind that selling prices and costs do not remain static, but change over time. This means that managers need to continually reassess their breakeven position in order to understand how changes to their cost structure or to their selling price will impact BEP. As an example, assume that, due to price increases in the cost of components and agreed-upon wage increases to employees, the variable cost (direct cost) of producing its product E sensors increases to $29.00 per unit. How does this impact BEP?

FIGURE 13.13   XYZ Corporation: BEP (Units)

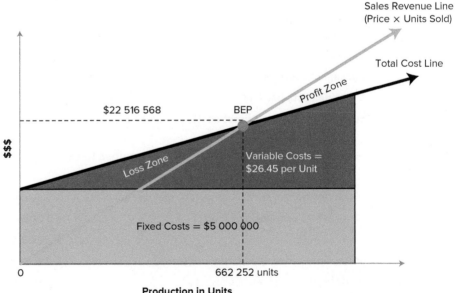

$$BEP \ (Units) = \frac{Total \ Fixed \ Costs}{(Selling \ Price \ per \ Unit - Variable \ Costs \ per \ Unit)}$$

$$BEP \ (Units) = \frac{\$5 \ 000 \ 000}{\$34.00 - \$29.00} = 1 \ 000 \ 000 \ units$$

In order for the XYZ Corporation to break even, it must produce and sell 1 000 000 units at an average selling price of $34. Given this change, the required sales volume needed to break even would be 1 000 000 × $34.00 = $34 000 000, or an additional $11 483 432 in sales revenue.

Managers need to continually reassess their breakeven position in order to understand how changes to their cost structure or to their selling price will impact BEP.

What if competitive price pressures force XYZ Corporation to reduce its selling price, resulting in an average selling price (ASP) of $33.50? Going back to our original example of variable costs of $26.45 per unit, the revised BEP in this situation would be:

$$BEP \ (Units) = \frac{Total \ Fixed \ Costs}{(Selling \ Price \ per \ Unit - Variable \ Costs \ per \ Unit)}$$

$$BEP \ (Units) = \frac{\$5 \ 000 \ 000}{\$33.50 - \$26.45} = 709 \ 220 \ units$$

In order for the XYZ Corporation to break even, it must produce and sell 709 220 units at an average selling price of $33.50.

Again, once the BEP (in units) is determined, the BEP (in $$$) can easily be calculated by multiplying the BEP (in units) by the selling price. In this situation, the required sales volume needed to break even would be 709 220 units × $33.50 = $24 113 480.

Figure 13.14 shows the movement in BEP based on the two changes we just discussed (an increase in variable costs and a change in the average selling price).

FIGURE 13.14 **XYZ Corporation: BEP Comparison**

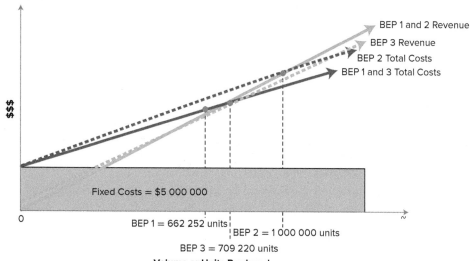

Calculating BEP in dollars ($$$) In some situations, in servicing their customers companies provide such a wide variety of products and services that it is unrealistic to compute BEP on a per unit basis. In this situation, these organizations, based on their cost analysis process and their business model, may be in a better position to compute BEP, initially, on the basis of total sales revenue ($$$). A good example of an industry that would likely assess BEP on this basis is the restaurant industry. Let's assume you are the manager of a coffee shop called the Coffee Mug. As the manager, you and your team have just recently completed a cost analysis of Coffee Mug's cost base. The results are as follows:

Variable (Direct) Costs as a % of Revenue	
Food costs	32%
Labour costs	33%
Paper and supply costs	7%
Franchise royalty	6%
Advertising fund contribution	2%
Total variable costs	80%

Fixed (Indirect) Costs	
Lease $	$40 000
Insurance	$ 2 500
Utilities	$20 000
Professional fees	$ 1 500
Building overhead	$10 000
Interest on debt	$ 14 000
Total fixed costs	$88 000

To compute the BEP (in $$$) for Coffee Mug, the formula used is slightly different. The BEP formula in this situation is:

$$\text{BEP \$\$\$} = \frac{\text{Fixed Costs}}{1 - \text{VC\%}}$$

$$\text{BEP \$\$\$} = \frac{\$88\ 000}{1 - .80} = \$440\ 000$$

In this situation, we are indicating that 80% of each $1 of revenue received is consumed in the variable costs of delivering the product and services to the customer. This leaves only $0.20 of each dollar left over to pay for the fixed costs, which total $88 000. The organization (Coffee Mug) would need to generate $440 000 in sales in order to cover all of its costs. If it generates less than $440 000, it will suffer an operating loss. If its sales exceed $440 000, it will enjoy a profit.

As a manager, you will most likely be interested in understanding what this means in terms of the number of customers you would need to serve annually, weekly, daily, or hourly in order to achieve this required sales volume of $440 000. An analysis of your operation determines that customers, on average, spend $4 per visit to your Coffee Mug. Given this, you would need 110 000 customers annually to break even. This could be further broken down to 2115 per week (assuming 52 weeks), or 302 per day. If you were open 10 hours per day, you would need, on average, 30 customers per hour, or approximately 7.5 customers every 15 minutes.

As with the XYZ Corporation, noted above, if Coffee Mug incurs higher than anticipated costs, it will result in its BEP being moved upward. As an example, assume that Coffee Mug's material costs increase to 35%, instead of 32%. This will increase the variable cost percentage to 83%. This movement will result in BEP being revised to:

$$\text{BEP \$\$\$} = \frac{\text{Fixed Costs}}{1 - \text{VC\%}}$$

$$\text{BEP \$\$\$} = \frac{\$88\ 000}{1 - .83} = \$517\ 647$$

A 3% erosion (increase) in the variable cost base of the organization results in the organization needing an additional $77 647 ($517 647 − $440 000) in revenue to break even (cover its costs).

As was indicated earlier, breakeven point is an important metric for companies to compute and understand. The simple formulas shown above can be further modified to identify key profit objective points, as well as revenue levels required not only for achieving a given profit objective, but also for ensuring that the financing costs of a business are covered. These more advanced BEP calculations can be found in the Appendix at the end of this chapter.

> BEP is used to identify the level that sales revenue has to reach in order to cover the total operating costs of an organization.

Margin Requirements

LO4

With respect to managing a company, **margin** is a term that relates to the relationship between revenue and costs. As will be illustrated in more detail in Chapter 14, where the statement of comprehensive income (income statement) is introduced, the word "margin" represents the portion of an organization's revenue that is left over after paying for an identified level of costs. Assume that a company has sales revenue of $1 million. To create this revenue, it incurred variable costs, in the form of product manufacturing and assembly costs, of $650 000. This would leave a gross profit margin of $350 000, or 35%. If fixed and/or indirect costs totalled $300 000, this would then leave an operating margin of $50 000, or 5% when compared against the sales revenue generated of $1 million. Again, the concepts of gross profit margin and operating margin will be covered in more detail in Chapter 14 as part of the discussion relating to the statement of comprehensive income. What is important to understand now is that managers will set target margin percentages as a way of assessing the overall efficiency of a business operation. Using the XYZ Corporation as an example, let's go back and take a look at product A, whose revenue for 2018 was $70 000 000. With respect to this product, let's assume the following:

Margin represents the portion of an organization's revenue that is left over after paying for an identified level of costs.

Sales Revenue	$70 000 000
Variable Costs (Cost of Goods Sold)	$49 000 000
Indirect Expenses (Marketing, Overhead, etc.)	$16 000 000

We would compute the gross profit margin for product A as ($70 000 000 − 49 000 000)/$70 000 000, or .30. This means that for each dollar of revenue product A brought in $0.70 was spent on producing the product, leaving $0.30 left over to pay for all other expenses. If the other expenses amounted to $16 000 000 as noted above, then the operating margin would be computed as ($21 000 000 − $16 000 000)/$70 000,000, or .05. This means that after all expenses were paid, product A's operating margin was 5 cents per dollar of revenue.

These margins are a key indicator of the overall operating efficiency of an organization. As noted above, managers will look to set margin targets and then view actual results against these targets. The ability to meet targeted expectations is an important part of the financial management assessment process. Not only are results measured against current-year targets, but they are also measured against prior-year performance in order to determine if the organization has been more or less effective in the delivery of its goods and services into the marketplace. Let's take a quick look at Wal-Mart Stores Inc., the largest retailer in the world, in this regard. For its fiscal year ending January 31, 2018, Wal-Mart Stores Inc. recorded revenue of $500.3 billion (USD). Its total operating expenses were $478 billion (USD), leaving operating income of $22.2 billion (USD); $22.2 billion (USD) divided by $500.3 billion (USD) equals .044, which we then interpret as an operating margin of 4.4%. This means that for each dollar of revenue Wal-Mart Stores Inc. took in, it generated a profit of $0.044.[3] Assume now that operating inefficiencies resulted in Wal-Mart Stores Inc.'s operating margin being reduced to 3%. This 1.4% reduction in operating margin means that of the $500.3 billion (USD) in revenue, Wal-Mart Stores Inc.'s operating income would be only $15 billion (USD). A 1.5% reduction in operating margin has cost the company an estimated $7.2 billion (USD). Assuming its margin fell to 3%, if Wal-Mart Stores Inc.'s target operating margin was 4.4%, then the company would want to know what resulted in the 1.4% reduction that occurred, resulting in the operating income of the company being less than targeted. Again, the intent here is to introduce you to the concept of margins, with Chapter 14 providing an enhanced understanding of this important metric via the formal discussion of financial statements.

Business IN ACTION

Dollar Stores—Rise of the Ultra-Low-Cost Player

For many of us, low-cost players such as Walmart, Giant Tiger, and Costco first come to mind when we think of where to find consistent low prices. But in today's market, with a number of consumers looking to economize as much as possible, the "dollar store" has emerged at the top of the consumer priority list. Although the dollar store concept has been around since the 1950s, it was the financial crisis and recession of the mid-2000s that brought on the boom years for dollar stores. By establishing themselves as ultra-low-cost players in an ever-increasingly bargain-seeking economy, the two major U.S.-based dollar stores, Dollar General Corporation (2018 revenue of $23.4 billion), and Dollar Tree, Inc. (2018 revenue of $22.2 billion), plus Canadian leader Dollarama (formerly Rossy, with 2018 revenue of $3.26 billion),

undercut entrenched low-cost players and captured greater market share in the process. The result has been explosive growth across the United States and Canada,

© Tracy Harris

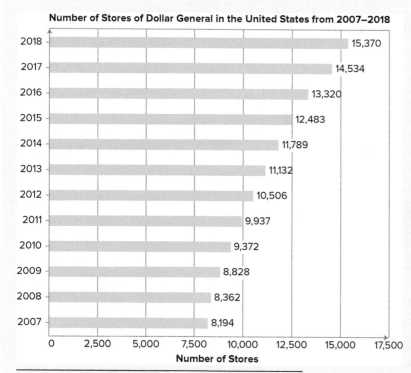

Number of Stores of Dollar General in the United States from 2007–2018

Year	Number of Stores
2018	15,370
2017	14,534
2016	13,320
2015	12,483
2014	11,789
2013	11,132
2012	10,506
2011	9,937
2010	9,372
2009	8,828
2008	8,362
2007	8,194

Source: Data obtained from Dollar General and Statista.com.

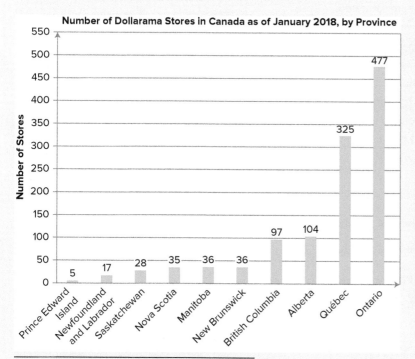

Number of Dollarama Stores in Canada as of January 2018, by Province

Province	Number of Stores
Prince Edward Island	5
Newfoundland and Labrador	17
Saskatchewan	28
Nova Scotia	35
Manitoba	36
New Brunswick	36
British Columbia	97
Alberta	104
Québec	325
Ontario	477

Source: Data obtained from Dollarama and Statista.com.

with the total number of Dollar General stores (see chart below) almost doubling during the period between 2007 and 2018. Dollar Tree Inc. stores (Family Dollar and Dollar Tree) now total over 13 000 stores as well. Like its U.S. counterparts, Dollarama has also seen ongoing growth, having opened over 1100 stores across Canada

at the end of 2018. Same-store sales, a key measure of retailer health, increased steadily for these ultra-low-cost players during this decade build-out, while big-box discount retailers like Walmart experienced multiple years of overall revenue growth stagnation.

Ultra-low-cost retail players originally targeted low-wage earners with their bargain prices for household necessities (think toothpaste, detergent, paper towels) and thousands of other low-cost items. Their main customers initially were women who headed up households, typically picking up a couple of items between weekly trips to big-box retailers like Walmart. But in recent recessionary and income-stagnant times, ultra-low-cost players are finding their largest growing segment lies with more affluent households. In what has been dubbed "new consumerism," saving is fashionable again as wealthier households are looking to cut costs in the face of an uncertain financial future, expanded household debt levels, and rising housing prices. Ultra-low-cost organizations also offer consumers exceptional convenience by providing consistent and predictable prices on national brand products, all in a store that is far easier to navigate than a big-box discount retailer. These ultra-low-cost players are able to maintain their slim net profit margins by occupying smaller store footprints in less premium locations. Combined with low wages and a small number of staff, selling items for a dollar really adds up. Ultra-low-cost players do not necessarily have the best quality products, but they offer exceptional value for items where quality is a less important factor. Their final-sale, no-returns business model approach also contributes to a lean operating structure. The industry's initial pricing model of one low price ($1) for everything in the store has evolved as well. Inflationary pressures, coupled with the opportunity to stretch upmarket, has seen the industry

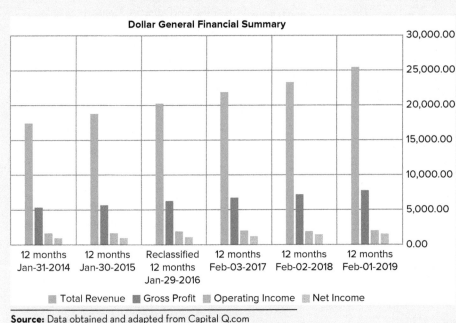

Dollar General Financial Summary

Legend: ■ Total Revenue ■ Gross Profit ■ Operating Income ■ Net Income

Source: Data obtained and adapted from Capital Q.com

Canada in the years ahead, threatening entrenched Canadian ultra-low-cost players like Dollarama Inc. Dollarama, however, is not planning to cede any retail share to its American counterparts. Backed by private-equity partner Bain Capital L.P., the company plans to continue its focus on North America, grow its product lines and price points, re-emphasize its $1.25 or less priced items, increase its Canadian location footprint, and expand internationally (Central America being an initial target area).

expand beyond the $1 format. As of 2018, for example, Dollarama had expanded its product line to include seven price points, ranging from $1 to $4.

As the North American market becomes more saturated, continued growth simply via adding stores may not be possible. Recognizing that a key driver of managing costs and protecting profitability lies in developing greater economies of scale, consolidation within the industry has occurred and most likely will continue to occur. 2014 saw an aggressive bidding war between Dollar Tree and Dollar General for Family Dollar and its $10 billion of annual revenue. Dollar Tree, the smallest of the three players prior to the bidding war, succeeded in its desire to acquire Family Dollar (for $9.1 billion USD). Today, Dollar Tree has over 200 stores across Canada, and is looking to continue expanding throughout

Going forward, the sector remains optimistic of its growth potential. Unlike a majority of higher-priced rivals, ecommerce and the increased pressures of a technology-driven world have yet to significantly impact this sector's growth trajectory—although in January 2019 Dollarama did launch an online site for customers desiring to purchase items in bulk. Will this remain the situation five to ten years from now? The answer remains uncertain, but this type of remarkable growth is impressive, particularly at a time when many Canadian retailers are struggling or exiting the market entirely.

Leading Dollar Stores in Canada as of January 2018, by Store Count

Store	Number of Stores
Dollarama	1,160
Dollar Tree	224
Dollar Store with More	114
Great Canadian	106
Buck or Two	43

Cash Operating Cycle

Cash Operating Cycle (COC) refers to the amount of time it takes for an organization to recover the cash (product is sold and money is received) it has paid out for the development, production, and distribution of products.

The **cash operating cycle (COC)**, also known as the cash-to-cash cycle, refers to the amount of time it takes for an organization to recover the cash (product is sold and money is received) it has paid out for the development, production, and distribution of products. It represents the amount of time it takes for money you are spending to finance the transformation of inputs into products and/or services (process flow across the stages of the value chain) to be returned to you in the form of cash once sales have been

FIGURE 13.15   **Cash Operating Cycle**

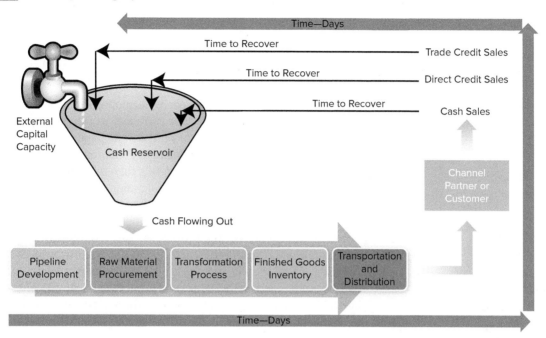

made and accounts receivable collected. Figure 13.15 illustrates a simplified cash operating cycle. In general, the shorter the cash operating cycle, the more quickly the organization is getting back the cash it has expended on producing its goods and services and, therefore, the less the organization needs to rely on cash reserves or short-term debt financing to cover the expenditures. An additional generalization associated with cash operating cycles is that the longer it takes for a company to produce its products, move them into the market, have them sold, and receive the revenue from them, the more expensive the cost of producing these products will be. In business, time is money.

> In general, the shorter the cash operating cycle, the more quickly the organization is getting back the cash it has expended on producing its goods and services and, therefore, the less the organization needs to rely on cash reserves or short-term debt financing to cover the costs of the expenditures incurred.

Understanding this cycle is critical in assessing the working capital or cash needs of an organization. The longer it takes, the more the organization is going to have to rely on its own cash reserves or external credit facilities, such as a line of credit, to ensure that it maintains an appropriate liquidity position. Economic downturns, product obsolescence, slow-paying customers—all impact an organization's cash operating cycle and the length of time it takes to get its initial product-based cash expenditures back.

To calculate an organization's COC, take the number of days a product spends in production and in inventory (called DIO, or days inventory outstanding), add to this the number of days it takes to receive money from the customer (called DSO, or days sales outstanding), and subtract from this total the number of days you take to pay your suppliers (called DPO, or days payable outstanding).

$$\text{Cash Operating Cycle (COC)} = \text{DIO} + \text{DSO} - \text{DPO}$$

As an example, let's assume that it takes Automaker Inc. 85 days to procure and receive the required auto parts, manufacture an automobile, and transport the automobile to a dealership. It takes another 38 days for the product to be sold to the customer (or for the dealer to pay Automaker for the automobile). Automaker Inc. pays its suppliers, on average, every 30 days. Automaker Inc.'s cash operating cycle would be computed as follows:

$$\text{Automaker Inc.'s COC} = 85 \text{ days} + 38 \text{ days} - 30 \text{ days} = 93 \text{ days}$$

It takes Automaker Inc. 93 days to receive its money for the sale of its automobiles. This means that Automaker Inc. must have sufficient working capital to fund the organization's cost base during this period of time, as it is paying its suppliers on a 30-day basis, paying employees bi-weekly, and incurring other operating expenses during this time. Should its automobiles take longer to sell, then this will elongate (and therefore deteriorate) the cash operating cycle, requiring additional working capital in order to meet Automaker Inc.'s operating expenses. In general, companies will work to shorten this cycle to as few days as possible, keeping in mind the extent to which such policies will impact the attractiveness of their products. This reduces working capital requirements and minimizes the risk that inventory will become obsolete and harder to sell. Comparing the cash operating cycle on a quarter-by-quarter basis, or a year-by-year basis, will enable managers to recognize and proactively deal with changes to the flow of cash into and out of the organization, and to the additional working capital requirements the organization will need to ensure its liquidity position is not compromised.

LO5 Capitalization Requirements

One of the core responsibilities of a manager is to assess the financial resource requirements of an organization and determine how those needs are going to be met. This means that managers need to review the **capital structure** of their organization and make decisions as to how the organization is going to finance its operations and what will be the mixture of use of the different sources of funds it will have at its disposal. A key component of this analysis will be to manage the debt/equity ratio (discussed in more detail in Chapter 14), which provides managers with an understanding as to how much debt the organization has incurred, or is willing to incur, in financing its operations, and whether this has added significant negative risk to the organization's financial stability.[4]

Capital Structure refers to an organization's mixture (use) of debt, internal cash reserves, and external equity-based investments in financial support of operational activities.

Sources of Funds

In general, for-profit organizations have three sources of funds available to them (see Figure 13.16). These sources of funds are as follows:

- Funds derived from operations
- Funds obtained via credit facilities (debt)
- Funds obtained via equity financing

Funds derived from operations Funds derived from operations refers to two internal sources of funds that managers can look to in order to fund current and future activities within an organization. These two internal sources of funds are:

- Current-year operating profits
- Retained earnings

Operating Profits equal total revenue minus total operating expenses.

Current-year **operating profits** (or operating surplus, in the case of not-for-profits) are the excess dollars that organizations have generated, and have at their disposal, during the current operating period as a result of their business activities after their current expense obligations have been paid. It can be best understood as total

FIGURE 13.16   **Sources of Funds**

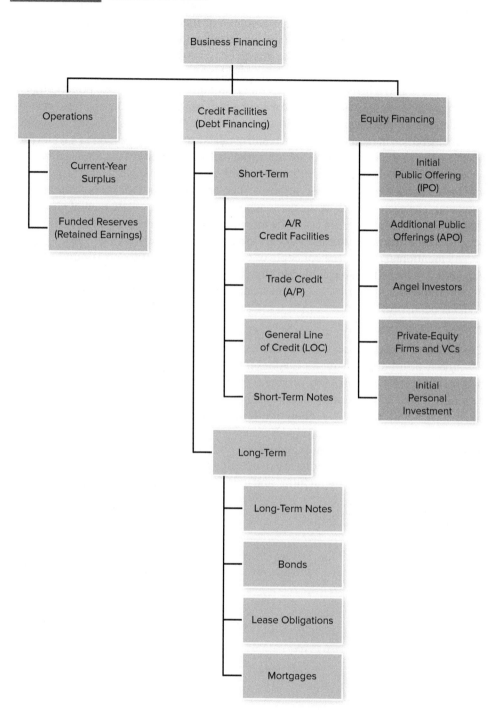

revenue minus total operating expenses during a defined period of time (i.e., month, quarter, or year). The organization's statement of comprehensive income (income statement), discussed in Chapter 14, which reflects operating results for this defined period of time, identifies the profit that the organization has realized from its operations. This profit, unless paid out to investors/shareholders, becomes an immediate source of new capital for an organization, which it can then choose to reinvest in support of future growth opportunities, enhanced R&D exploration, or the acquisition and/or replacement of equipment in support of the organization's activities.

Retained earnings represents the dollar amount of net earnings that an organization has accumulated over the history of its operations, and that it has chosen to hold within

Retained Earnings refers to the dollar amount of net earnings accumulated over the history of an organization that it has chosen to hold within the organization.

the organization (not pay out to investors/shareholders). Identified under the owners' equity section of the statement of changes in financial position (balance sheet), discussed in Chapter 14, retained earnings becomes a source of funds for the organization to draw upon in the event of operating losses during a given period, or in the event that additional investment needs to be made into the organization (growth, R&D, equipment replacement, acquisitions, and so on). Retained earnings will also be used to compensate for operating losses occurring in a given year. An important caution to identify, at this point, is that although retained earnings is considered a source of capital, managers need to also view the cash position of the company (found on the balance sheet) to be sure that the dollar amount identified in retained earnings is still available to the organization in a liquid form (cash, near cash). The ability to draw from prior earnings, which is what retained earnings represents, is based on the belief that the prior earnings remain within the organization and have not been used for other purposes, thereby diminishing the cash position of the company. The cash position of the company, as reflected on the statement of changes in financial position (balance sheet), is the most accurate recognition of the capacity of the organization to draw on its cash reserves to fund its current and future needs.

As mentioned above, the concepts of current-year operating profits and retained earnings are more fully explained in Chapter 14. At this point, it is important to understand that the operation itself represents a viable source of cash as long as it is, and has been, profitable.

Credit facilities (debt financing) Credit facilities refers to debt that an organization has taken on in support of its business activities. It represents the organization borrowing money or receiving products or services on a credit basis from another organization or individual(s). Credit facility arrangements provide the borrowing organization with access to money that it normally would not have access to, under the stipulation that it will be paid back over a defined period of time, or on a definitive date. The repayment terms may include an obligation to pay interest on the money borrowed as well. Credit facilities are generally viewed as falling into one of two debt categories: short-term credit facilities and long-term credit facilities (see Figure 13.17).

Credit Facilities is a general term that describes the variety of loans that could be offered to a business or a country.

FIGURE 13.17   **Credit Facilities**

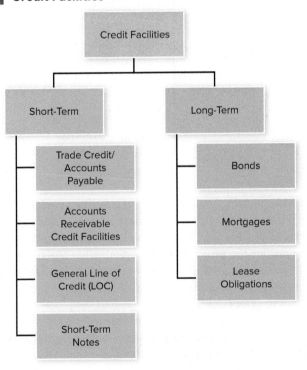

Credit facilities are a type of debt financing. With debt financing comes a legal obligation to pay both the interest on the debt, if applicable, and the debt principal, when due, regardless of the organization's financial position.

Short-term credit facilities **Short-term credit facilities** refers to debt obligations that an organization takes on for a short period of time, generally one year or less. Typical categories of short-term credit include trade credit, borrowing against the organization's future flow of accounts receivable, borrowing against a general line of credit the organization has established, or borrowing on a short-term-note basis (i.e., borrowing a specific sum of money for a specified period of time—three months, six months, one year). Trade credit, for example, is used when the organization orders products or receives services from another organization but payment for these products or services is deferred until a later date (e.g., "30 days to pay"). These are commonly referred to as the **accounts payable** of the organization, and are found under the current liabilities section of the statement of changes in financial condition (balance sheet), discussed in Chapter 14. Credit facilities relating to borrowing against the future inflow of **accounts receivable**, or against a **line of credit**, relate directly to the cash operating cycle and the managing of the cash flow needs of the organization. A line of credit (LOC) is a credit facility that gives the organization immediate access to a predetermined sum of money at a specified interest rate. Pre-approved through a lending facility, the line of credit provides the organization with the ability to draw on this account to meet frequent, short-term capital needs. As an example, if the cash flow of the organization is such that its cash receipts and accounts receivable collections may not be sufficient in time to meet a payroll obligation, then the organization could borrow the money to meet its payroll obligation through its line of credit and then pay off this short-term borrowing when the accounts receivable are collected and/or excess cash is accumulated. Short-term notes are obligations that an organization agrees to as a result of borrowing a defined sum of money for a fixed period of time (one year or less). Short-term notes are commonly written for periods such as one month, three months, six months, or one year. Organizations with short-term borrowing requirements make use of this type of credit facility in order to cover the cost of short-term projects, quarterly seasonal fluctuations in their business, bridge financing for longer-term projects, or other definitive short-term borrowing needs. These notes may be secured with **collateral**, or, assuming a strong credit rating on the part of the company, could be lent without a formal collateral requirement (i.e., secured versus unsecured notes).

Overall, short-term financing, and its integral support of the cash operating cycle, is a common activity with most organizations. The particular type of short-term financing undertaken will vary by organization and business sector. An understanding of the amount of short-term credit (debt) that an organization has taken on can be achieved by analyzing the current liability section of the organization's statement of changes in financial position. Credit facilities defined as short-term are expected to be repaid by the organization during the current operating year and are a key factor in assessing the liquidity of a company.

Credit facilities defined as short-term are expected to be repaid by the organization during the current operating year and are a key factor in assessing the liquidity of a company.

Long-term credit facilities **Long-term credit facilities** represent debt that an organization obligates itself to repay over a time frame that exceeds one year in

Short-Term Credit Facilities refers to debt obligations that an organization takes on for a short period of time, generally less than one year.

Accounts Payable refers to money owed by an organization to its suppliers and other short-term service providers.

Accounts Receivable refers to money owed by customers of the organization for products or services that the organization has delivered to such customers, but has not yet received payment for.

Line of Credit refers to an arrangement with a lending institution that provides an organization with a pre-arranged borrowing ceiling (maximum) that the organization can draw on at any time, and in any amount, up to the agreed-upon limit.

Collateral is an asset that an individual pledges as security toward a credit facility (loan); the individual agrees to forfeit the collateral in the event of an inability to repay the loan.

Long-Term Credit Facilities represent debt that an organization obligates itself to repay over a time frame that exceeds one year.

duration. As with short-term credit facilities, these debt obligations may or may not include an interest expense obligation; although, with long-term credit facilities, it is likely that such a **cost of borrowing** will apply. Examples of some of the more common long-term credit facilities that organizations tend to utilize in procuring borrowed capital for infusion into their operations are bonds, mortgages, long-term notes, and lease obligations. The amount of cash required to build the capital asset infrastructure needed to compete would be beyond the scope of many organizations if long-term financing capabilities, through the use of credit facilities, were not part of their funding mix. The costs, as an example, of the plant and facility investments required to build manufacturing facilities in the automotive, aerospace, and technology sectors can run into the millions of dollars. Long-term credit arrangements enable organizations to construct such facilities by providing the needed dollars up front and then allowing the organizations to repay these debt obligations over the useful lifespan of the capital assets that the debt has funded. For plant and facility capital assets, this could be periods of 15, 20, or 25 years or more. Given the importance of this source of funding, let's briefly look at some of the more common long-term credit facility options used by organizations.

Bonds A **bond** (also referred to as a fixed-income security) is a credit facility by which an organization (corporations, governments) borrows money for a stipulated period of time. In return for the use of these funds, the organization promises to pay the holder of the bond an agreed-upon amount of interest at regular intervals (generally semi-annually) during the period of time for which the funds are borrowed. At the end of the stipulated period of time, the organization borrowing the money agrees to repay the full amount borrowed (bond principal or face value). A number of different types of bonds are available in the marketplace (treasury, convertible, step-up, put bonds).

Although bonds are considered a credit facility (debt instrument), the purpose of a bond for many organizations is to raise capital for the firm. The dollars raised from the issuance of a bond are often used to provide an organization with the capital necessary to build infrastructure, fund acquisitions, or provide new working capital to the organization for the purpose of developing and growing the business.

Mortgages A **mortgage** is a credit facility that is backed by real estate collateral (generally, the real estate that the mortgage underwrites) and that sets forth a defined schedule of periodic payments for the full repayment of the debt owed, plus interest, over a defined period of time.

Long-Term Notes A **long-term note** refers to a credit facility under which an organization borrows a stipulated amount of money, for a defined period of time (which exceeds one year), and with a defined interest rate schedule (fixed or variable). Long-term notes are similar in their setup to that of a mortgage (defined repayment terms), except that they are generally written for a shorter time duration. Long-term notes can be underwritten either with or without a collateral requirement (secured or unsecured).

Lease Obligations Lease obligations that cover periods in excess of one year are considered long-term debt obligations of an organization. **Lease obligations** represent a legal obligation to pay a service provider with an agreed-upon amount of money, via a defined periodic payment schedule over an identified period, in return for the use of property, equipment, or some other service. At the end of this period, provisions may or may not be included in the lease to provide the organization with an opportunity to purchase the asset that has been leased. If such a provision does exist, lease buy-back provisions, along with a residual value formula computation to be used in determining the purchase value of the leased asset, generally at the end of the lease term, will be fully defined within the lease agreement. For many organizations, leasing represents a preferred option over the outright purchase of an asset. Leasing enables the organization to minimize the upfront cash outlay for equipment and other assets, and ensures that the organization stays current with the latest technology. As an example, assume that ABC Industries is in need of a high-capacity, high-speed, multi-functional photocopy, printing, and scanning unit to support its marketing and administration departments. After reviewing the potential options with distributors of a variety of brands and models, ABC Industries settles on its preferred choice. The cost of this photocopy, printing, scanning, and document-sorting machine is $63 000. ABC Industries can either choose to purchase the unit outright, or enter into a five-year lease agreement offered by the manufacturer. The lease agreement enables ABC Industries to pay $3000 down, and then make monthly lease payments based on the $60 000 remaining balance on the machine, plus a financing/leasing cost of 9%. These payments would be made for 60 months (five years). Based on the $60 000 remaining balance, with a financing/leasing cost of 9% for a period of 60 months, the monthly payments would be $1245. The total cost of the machine at the end of the five-year period would be $77 700 ($3000 + ($1245 × 60)). At the end of the lease period, assuming that there is no desire or opportunity to purchase the unit, the machine is returned to the manufacturer. In leasing, the person or organization that owns the land, equipment, or property is called the lessor. The person or organization that rents the land, equipment, or property from the lessor is called the lessee. Again, it is the recognition of the legal obligation to pay, under the lease agreement, that results in the requirement to recognize it as a liability of the organization.

Impact of Credit Facilities The ability to utilize credit facilities to assist with financing the cash operating cycle, and with enabling organizations to develop and grow their capital asset base, is a major reason for the creation of the incredible global business marketplace that we have today. This ability to secure access to significant amounts of capital, at reasonable costs of borrowing, is what enables companies to utilize the capital assets acquired to generate revenues and investment returns that exceed the cost of borrowing. The risk to organizations that take on debt is that, by utilizing credit facilities, these organizations are adding to the size of their fixed-cost base. Both the principal and interest payments associated with the various credit facilities tapped will need to be made, regardless of whether an organization's sales increase, remain unchanged, or decrease. The addition of this debt will also modify this same organization's breakeven point, as additional sales will need to be realized in order to pay for the costs associated with servicing and retiring this debt. As managers, in making decisions to utilize debt financing (credit facilities) as a source of funds for our business, we must ensure that the repayment obligations associated with the credit facilities undertaken do not jeopardize the liquidity and solvency of our organization. Debt, in the absence of revenue enhancement or cost reduction, results in nothing other than an increase to the cost base of the organization. Knowing this means that we need to be careful on how, and when, we use debt as a mechanism to fund the growth and/or expansion of our organization. This discussion of debt, and the concern associated with the amount of debt an organization should undertake, is meant to be an introduction to this topic. Chapter 14, Financial Statements Structure and Interpretation, expands upon this topic to ensure that students have a good base-level understanding of the role of credit facilities and the advantages and risks associated with the concept of **debt leverage**.

Debt Leverage refers to the use of debt to finance an organization's capital asset base.

As managers, in making decisions to utilize debt financing (credit facilities) as a source of funds for our business we must ensure that the repayment obligations associated with the credit facilities undertaken do not jeopardize the liquidity and solvency of our organization.

Equity financing options Up to this point, we have discussed two ways in which an organization can meet its capital requirements. The organization can obtain capital for reinvestment purposes from profitable current and/or past business operations. The organization also can utilize credit facilities as a way to assist in financing its cash operating cycle and in raising the needed capital to meet its development and growth requirements. The third way in which an organization can raise capital is through the procurement of equity financing. Depending on its legal structure (sole proprietorship, partnership, corporation), an organization will have access to private equity and/or public equity funding options (see Figure 13.18).

Private Equity refers to equity capital that is obtained by an organization from private sources (not through one of the public exchanges).

Private equity is equity capital (money) that is obtained by an organization from private sources (not through one of the public exchanges). Examples of private equity include the equity contribution to the business by the owner(s), family, friends, or some other initial backer (commonly referred to as an angel investor), private-equity firms, or venture capitalists. Private-equity investment opportunities are available to sole proprietorships, partnerships, and corporations. Private-equity investments can be either a direct monetary investment into the company (for sole proprietorships and partnerships) or monetary investments as a result of the

FIGURE 13.18 **Equity Options**

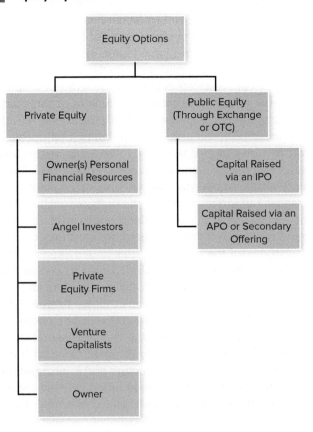

issuance (sale) of **stock** (for corporations). Regardless of the situation, equity-based investments into an organization represent the acceptance of an ownership stake in the business in exchange for the capital invested. Reflecting on the evolution and growth of Lululemon Athletica Inc., private-equity investments into this company included the personal investments made by Chip Wilson, potential early start-up capital from family and/or friends, and the private-equity firms Advent International and Highland Capital Partners. Sequoia Capital, highlighted in a Chapter 7 Business in Action feature, is also an example of an organization that provides private equity to businesses.

Public equity refers to equity investments in an organization by investors as a result of the purchase of publicly traded shares (stock) due to an initial public offering (IPO) or an additional public offering (APO), also referred to as a **secondary offering**. Proceeds from the sale of these shares are often used to provide the necessary capital to assist in the expansion of the business, build and/or update asset and infrastructure requirements critical to operation of the business, pay down or eliminate debt, or provide additional working capital in support of the business operation (see the Business in Action feature "What Is an IPO?"). Public-equity investment opportunities are limited to corporations.

Recently completed high-profile IPOs include the 2018 IPO (largest direct listing) by Spotify (SPOT), which created a value for the company of $9.2 billion, and the 2017 Snap Inc. IPO that placed the initial valuation of that company at $33 billion.[5] Recent successful Canadian IPOs include Shopify (2015), which raised $131 million, and 2017 Canadian IPOs by MedReleaf Corp. (TSX.LEAF—$80 million), ERO Copper (TSX.ERO—$110 million), Jamieson Wellness Inc. (TSX.JWEL—$300 million), Fairfax Africa Holdings Corp. (TSX.FAH.U—$151 million), and Titan Mining (TSX:SI—$50 million). Some of Canada's largest IPOs since 2000 include Kinder Morgan Canada's IPO of $1.75 billion, Sun Life Financial, which raised $1.89 billion, and Hydro One, which raised $1.83 billion in the equity market. In total in 2017 there were 27 IPOs initiated in Canada, raising an estimated $5.2 billion (CAD), up significantly from 2016 which saw only $466 million raised in the Canadian IPO market. IPOs in Canada raised an estimated $3 billion in 2018, and in first-quarter 2019 raised approximately $750 million on behalf of Canadian companies looking to expand their business operations.[6]

A recent example of an upcoming secondary offering is that of private-equity company Bain Capital, which owns just under 60% of Canada Goose's outstanding shares. Bain Capital, along with CEO and President Dani Reese, announced the selling of 10 million additional shares in November 2018.[7] Based on Canada Goose's share value as of this writing ($66 per share), this additional share offering could raise as much as $660 million. Fiera Capital, in March 2015, also completed a secondary share offering of 9 083 000 shares, raising $114 445 800. The purpose of this secondary offering was to assist the National Bank of Canada in maintaining its ownership position in Fiera Capital, and to enable it to invest in the development of product distribution and commercial business relationships between Fiera and National Bank.[8]

In discussing public-equity options, managers need to understand a couple of important points. First, a company receives the proceeds from the sale of stock only at the time of its initial issue and sale. After that, the trading (selling) of shares that occurs in the marketplace is between the owners of the stock (sellers) and the new purchasers (see Figure 13.19).

This means that managers and members of the board of directors, in consultation with the investment banking firm handling the initial sale, must determine whether the conditions are right for the launch of an IPO or a secondary offering, and if the asking price will be received from public investors. As an example, upstart Porter Airlines (Porter Aviation Holdings Inc.), based in Toronto, made a decision to

Stock is a security that represents a percentage of ownership in a corporation's assets, and entitlement to a pro-rata claim on earnings when released.

Public Equity refers to equity investments in an organization, by investors, as a result of the purchase of publicly traded shares (stock) due to an initial public offering (IPO) or an additional public offering (APO), also referred to as a secondary offering.

Secondary Offering refers to an additional public offering of an organization's stock for the purpose of raising new capital.

FIGURE 13.19   Public-Equity Offering: Cash Flow

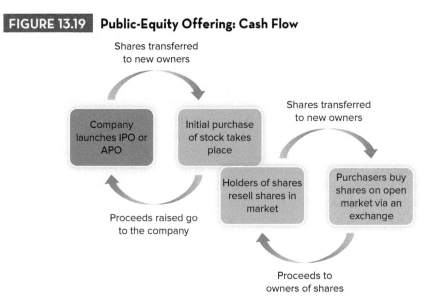

drop plans for an IPO in May 2010 due to the volatility and turmoil in the equity markets at that time. Robert Deluce, CEO of Porter Aviation Holdings Inc., indicated that it was prudent to defer the IPO until better market conditions existed that would enable Porter to get a better price for its shares. For Mr. Deluce and Porter Aviation Holdings Inc., the utilization of private-equity options may be a better route to take in the interim. Porter's IPO was initially priced at between $6 and $7 per share, and then revised to $5.50 per share, before it was pulled from the market. Investors were unwilling to pay this price for shares of Porter Aviation Holdings Inc. at that time. The company revisited its position in 2016 and again has deferred on launching an IPO, although Robert Deluce has indicated that an IPO is most likely inevitable looking into the future, at a time when Porter feels circumstances will permit a successful IPO result. This deferral decision was in part influenced by the inability of Porter Airlines to receive permission to fly jet aircraft (currently uses prop-based airplanes) from Toronto's City Airport. The company remains a private company at this time, financing its growth from internal as well as external private sources.[9]

Second, in considering an APO or secondary share offering managers must weigh the impact on the current share value of the organization's stock in the marketplace. Issuing additional shares of stock can result in **price dilution**, which means that the price of existing shares of stock will decline due to the fact that a larger number of shares (which represent ownership in the company) now exist. As an example, assume that the MTR Corporation currently has 10 million shares of common stock outstanding, and the price of these shares is $20 per share. This means that MTR Corporation has a **market capitalization value** (market cap) of $200 million ($20 × 10 million shares). If MTR Corporation makes a decision to offer an additional 5 million shares to the marketplace, this will have a downward impact on the price of the stock. This is because the number of shares outstanding (circulating in the marketplace) will increase to 15 million. In order for the market cap to remain at $20 million (assuming this is still a valid value for MTR), then the price per share will need to decrease to $13.34. Discounting potential upward movements due to improvements in MTR's cash position resulting from the share offering, the price of the stock will move (be diluted), from $20 toward a per-share value of $13.34. It should also be noted, with respect to secondary share offerings, that the additional money raised is typically applied to organization-based needs that are anticipated to improve the liquidity and/or performance of the company issuing these shares. These actions are intended to improve the organization's value in the eyes of current and potential investors, and its overall position in the industry sector within which it

Price Dilution means that the price of existing shares of stock will decline due to the fact that a larger number of shares (which represent ownership in the company) now exist.

Market Capitalization Value refers to the current market value of an organization. It is calculated by taking the number of shares outstanding multiplied by the current value of its shares.

competes. If successful, this action should enable the company issuing the shares to protect its share value against the price dilution to its shares due to the larger number of shares outstanding. The improved performance or financial position of the company would have an upward influence on share value, thereby offsetting some, or all, of the price dilution.

As you can recognize, the issuance of an IPO and/or APO (secondary offering) requires a great deal of thought on the part of the organization. As the organization receives only the proceeds from the initial sale of its shares, the business organization's managers, directors of its board, and the investment firm handling the issuance of the IPO or APO must all be confident that the timing and price point at which the shares are being introduced will result in the maximum benefit that the organization can expect to receive from the share issuance.

Stock Exchange is an exchange that provides a variety of services to investors, brokers, and traders, in support of the trading of stocks and other investment-related products and services.

Business IN ACTION

What Is an IPO and How Does It Work?

IPO stands for "initial public offering." The IPO signals to the marketplace that a business corporation is ready to go public, which means it is ready to provide general investors with the opportunity to purchase an equity stake in the business. It also means that the company's shares of stock will now be available for both purchase and sale, on a perpetual basis, across the **stock exchange** upon which the shares are listed. Examples of stock exchanges include the TSX (Toronto Stock Exchange), the NYSE (New York Stock Exchange), and the NASDAQ.

Used by permission of Twitter

Used by permission of Facebook

The purpose of the IPO is a simple one: to raise money. In an IPO, the founders of a company make a conscious decision to relinquish a portion of ownership in the company to external investors in return for capital. For the founders of the business, the IPO offers an opportunity to sell either a portion of the existing shares that have already been allocated to them through private equity investments in the business, or issue new shares in the company. In initiating an IPO, the founders of the business

need to determine three basic things associated with the IPO:

1. The desired amount of capital to be raised

2. The price per share the shares will be set at on the date the IPO commences

3. The number of shares to be offered to the public

Let's use the 2013 Twitter IPO as an example to illustrate how an IPO evolves (simplified). First, Twitter's board of directors, investor representatives, and management team needed to determine how much capital they wanted to raise for the company and/or return to their founding investors. For Twitter, this was estimated at $1.8 billion to $2 billion. Second, working in conjunction with an underwriter (or syndicate of underwriters), which in the case of Twitter was Goldman-Sachs, the company determined a legitimate selling price for the shares. For Twitter, the initial target price for its shares (based on the recommendation of the underwriter) was set at $26 per share. Needing to raise $1.8 billion, with a share price of $26 per share, required the issuance of 70 million shares ($1.8 billion/$26). The founders then determined how many of their existing shares they may be willing to sell, with the remainder of the shares (if any) being issued in the form of new shares. Again using Twitter as an example, assume the company had issued 500 million shares to private equity investors. These investors decide to release 10% of these shares as part of the IPO. This would equal 50 million shares. That means the other 20 million shares required to make up the total issuance of 70 million shares would be new shares the company would authorize issuance of.

Determination of the share price is a critical component of the IPO process, as once the shares commence trading (people begin buying or selling) the share price will move (up or down) in the open market. This will ultimately affect the actual amount of money the company receives. In the case of Twitter, the share price rose to $45 once shares were available to the public; this meant the IPO would raise $3.15 billion versus the targeted $1.8 billion to $2 billion. Does Twitter get all of the money? In this case, the founders would receive the proceeds for the shares they released (50 million × $45 = $2.25 billion) and the company would receive the proceeds from the new shares released (20 million × 45 = $900 million).

Keep in mind that, as noted above, share prices do change (based on supply and demand fundamentals) once shares begin trading on an exchange. This will impact the amount of capital an IPO ultimately generates. In the case of Twitter, the IPO exceeded the targeted amount of capital desired. In the case of Facebook's IPO the opposite happened. At the commencement of its IPO launch, shares of Facebook began trading at $38 per share. Shares initially rose to $42 per share, only to drop to $28 per share a few days later. This means that those who purchased shares at the IPO peak price of $42 per share saw the value of their investment drop by 34% ($28/$42) in roughly one week's time. Keep in mind, however, that as shown above, share price is not static. It is constantly in motion, depending on the current and anticipated future performance of a company. Having said this, the share price of Facebook has dramatically increased since its IPO launch. On April 11, 2019, as an example, shares of Facebook were valued at $178.13. An individual who purchased 1000 shares of Facebook at the peak of its initial IPO share value ($42) would have invested $42 000. Holding those 1000 shares to April 11, 2019, would see that investment valued at $178 130, or a financial gain of $136 130 (assuming that these shares were sold on this day to another investor). Referring back to our Twitter example above, Twitter's share value on April 11, 2019 was $34.67. The individual who purchased 1000 shares of Twitter at the peak of its IPO share price ($45) would have invested $45 000 to acquire those shares. On April 11, 2019, at a share price of $34.67, the investment value would have declined to $34 670, or a current loss position of $10 330.

Again, however, keep in mind that once the shares are issued the movement in their price does not impact the company's original dollar amount received from the issuance of these shares. The company receives its dollars based on the price paid by the investors at the time of the IPO.

Putting It All Together

As managers, we will most likely end up using a combination of all three funding sources in order to meet the needs of our cash operating cycle and our capital asset development requirements. Decisions relating to funds generated from internal operations will focus on how much of the current profit being generated should be used today and how much should be reserved for the future (transferred to retained earnings). It will also be influenced by the need, or desire, to return a portion of the profits to owners as a reward for their investment in our organization. Depending on the type of operation we are managing, we will most likely make use of a number of short-term credit options (trade credit being a primary example), as well as consider using longer-term options to support capital asset acquisition and development. With credit comes the risk of leverage. The biggest impact of leverage is that, when we are in a loss situation, the impact on liquidity and solvency magnifies, as we still have to meet our interest and principal repayment options. Although lenders may work with us in the short term, they will not tolerate repayment postponement indefinitely and, in a worst-case scenario, could initiate legal action against us, thereby further crippling the organization's ability to survive. Equity financing represents a viable way to generate capital externally for the organization. It does, however, require consideration of the long-term impact to the organization, particularly for its current owners, in terms of ownership dilution, loss of control, and the potential for decisions becoming more and more influenced by the need to meet investor ROI requirements. Equity financing is also predicated on the fact that the organization has the potential to be profitable, and that the future growth potential results in the best use of an investor's capital. The end result is that, as managers, we need to consciously think about where and how to use and obtain capital. It is an essential part of our strategic plan. Each source of funds (capital) has its own advantages and disadvantages. Taking on too much debt, or becoming overextended on the credit side, can impact our future ability to meet financial obligations or obtain new capital when it is most needed. Although equity financing may appear attractive, we need to be conscious as to how this is going to impact the future direction of the company and decisions supporting the intended strategy. New owners, by virtue of their investment, will most likely have a say in how we do business going forward. Figure 13.20 provides a summary of the advantages and disadvantages of each of the sources of funds discussed in this chapter. Keeping these advantages and disadvantages in mind as we seek to provide the organization with the funds necessary for its success will assist us in maintaining a balanced approach to where and how funds will be procured and used.

FIGURE 13.20 Summary: Sources of Funds

Source of Funds	Advantage	Disadvantage
Funds from Operations	• No external funding source is required • No dilution of ownership occurs • No fixed repayment schedule • No interest payments	• Monies available may not meet the full needs of the organization • Uncertainty may exist as to the amount of money available now and in the future • Monies needed internally cannot be distributed to owners as a return on their investment
Credit Facilities	• No dilution of ownership occurs • Can provide large inflows of capital now, with payments spread out over long periods of time • Enables the organization to use someone else's money to fund organizational needs • Interest expense is considered to be an operational expense	• Requires full repayment, either on a periodic or lump sum basis • Obligations must be met, regardless of the financial condition of the organization • A cost of borrowing is incurred • Collateral is usually required—may restrict future asset use
Equity Financing	• Enables the organization to raise cash without the leverage concerns associated with debt financing • No repayment obligations • External funding source—does not place pressure on operations to fund organization's needs	• Dilutes ownership • If publicly traded—control lies with the owner of a majority of shares (51%) • Short-termism—management decisions may be impacted by shareholder investment needs

For most organizations, managers will tend to look first toward internal funds to compensate owners and to finance new investments. When such funds are not sufficient to provide the necessary capital to finance the required investments deemed critical for the organization's success, the tendency will then be to look toward debt financing, in combination with internal funds or on its own. As noted above, a key issue here will be the ability or capacity of the organization to handle the additional debt load being contemplated. Owners, managers, and boards of directors of for-profit organizations will, in most cases, resort to external equity financing only when it has been concluded that the other sources of funds (internal and debt financing) cannot be used to adequately fund the needs of the business.

A Note Pertaining to Not-for-Profits

Although similar to for-profit organizations in many ways, one of the key fundamental differences between not-for-profit (NFP) organizations and for-profit organizations lies in their capital structure. For-profit business organizations, as has been illustrated within this chapter, have essentially three sources of capital funding: (1) cash available from internal operations (current profit and retained earnings), (2) the use of debt financing via a variety of credit facility options, and (3) equity investments (private or public) that are acquired in exchange for an ownership stake in the for-profit business. Not-for-profit organizations can utilize cash available from internal operations, as well as debt financing via credit facility options. This does assume, however, that the NFP delivers its products and services for a fee and, therefore, has revenue-generation capabilities. It also assumes that the NFP has established credit and has sufficient capital assets that can serve as collateral on a loan. Both of these situations may not exist. Many NFPs do not generate revenue but rely on funding totally from outside sources, such as various levels of government. They are, in essence, expense-driven organizations, whose budgets consist solely of transfer payments to them for the purpose of delivering services to the community. Many others do not have a sufficient capital asset base to serve as a basis for collateral, or operate in a manner that enables them to utilize the same breadth of credit facility options available to for-profit entities. Assuming, however, that access to these first two sources of capital exists, where for-profit and not-for-profit organizations fundamentally differ lies in the ability to utilize equity investments as a way to fund an organization's sustenance and growth. As NFPs are not owned by individuals, but rather exist for the collective good of society, and are not permitted to accept equity investments in the business in exchange for an ownership stake, private- and public-equity options simply do not exist for these organizations. Recognizing this absence of a third source of capital, not-for-profit organizations are allowed to fundraise in support of their organization's activities and services (some restrictions may apply, depending on legal formation, location, and articles of incorporation). These fundraising initiatives may take the form of activities such as the direct solicitation for donations, the implementation of fundraising events (runs, walks, auctions, etc.), and the implementation of annual giving campaigns and capital campaigns for the purpose of raising funds in support of programs, activities, and/or capital asset acquisition, refurbishment, and maintenance. The Business in Action in Chapter 11 focused on The Hospital for Sick Children (SickKids) is a good example of the utilization of fundraising to keep a not-for-profit, charitable organization relevant in today's market environment, thereby benefiting society as a whole. The concept of **philanthropy** and the ability to accept donations—and, if registered charities, issue donation tax receipts to their donors—represents a core fundamental source of capital for many NFPs. The end result is that, although different, NFPs also have three sources of capital funding available (see Figure 13.21). Unlike their for-profit counterparts, NFPs in general will prefer to undertake philanthropic initiatives as a viable source of funds prior to exhausting current internal reserves or undertaking new debt financing.

Philanthropy refers to the receipt of funds from another person or organization for the purpose of using them to enhance the well-being of others.

FIGURE 13.21   **NFP Sources of Capital**

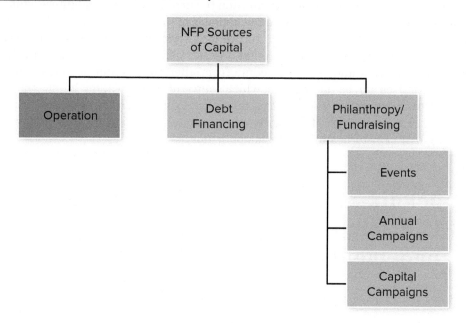

Managing the NFP requires the same type of decision-making skills and risk/reward trade-off analysis as is found in the for-profit sector. Managers need to assess the potential capital available from each of the three sources of funds that the NFP has at its disposal, and determine where and how to allocate these resources in order to achieve the NFP's mission and vision. In addition, managers of NFPs must recognize that although profit may be the *raison d'être* for for-profit entities, it is the achievement of the social mission and the delivery of its programs that represent an NFP's *raison d'être*. This implies that, in many cases, it is the distribution of wealth and benefits through the NFP's activities, even in the absence of generating a surplus, that must drive its management team's decision-making focus.

Management Reflection—The Need for Capital

With few exceptions, organizations have an ongoing thirst for capital. The need to fund new marketing initiatives, new products and services, new technologies, new equipment, new business locations, and the acquisition of the general capital assets required to make us more efficient and effective appears to be never-ending. With this insatiable appetite for capital comes the realization that decisions will need to be made on the best places or priorities to allocate this precious resource. The ability to acquire capital, either internally or externally, and effectively use it to generate new revenue sources—or higher levels of revenue from existing sources—can be developed into a definitive and sustainable competitive advantage. Access to capital means the ability to fund new initiatives and future growth. As managers, we need to recognize that capital access can come from one of the three sources discussed in this chapter. The trick, so to speak, is to make smart decisions on which source to tap for a particular initiative at a given time in order to maximize the benefit of the use of the chosen source of capital in a way that builds the long-term health of the organization. With this decision-making process comes an analysis of the various needs and desires of its internal stakeholders, as well as how to best position the organization to current external, and future, stakeholders. This process also requires a full analysis of the organization's cash operating cycle and an assessment of its future long-term financial needs. From this analysis comes a financial strategy that, in essence, defines for the organization where its capital is anticipated to come from, thereby enabling it to determine which initiatives will be funded from which source of funds. Without a full analysis in this regard, managers may find that they have exhausted a key source of funds, thereby restricting the ability to generate the capital needed to support the implementation of near-term and long-term opportunities.

Appendix—Advanced Topics Relating to BEP, Pricing, and Revenue Model Management

Using BEP to Understand Profit Objectives

As was indicated earlier in this chapter, BEP (breakeven point) is used to identify the level of sales revenue required in order to cover the total operating costs of an organization. It also has been noted that BEP should be considered the minimum acceptable position for an organization in the short run. The failure to achieve BEP will result in the organization requiring additional cash from other sources. Ongoing operating levels below BEP will eventually result in the organization becoming insolvent and possibly ceasing to exist.

Having said this, investors, shareholders, and management teams are not in business to break even. Expectations are that organizations will strive to achieve a defined level of profit in a given year, as well as ongoing profitability. For managers, understanding the level of sales activity (volume or revenue $$$) is fundamental to determining the feasibility of various profit objective levels and the determination of what profit objective the organization should strive for. The BEP formula can be modified in a manner that will enable the organization to see the sales volume requirements of such objectives.

> Investors, shareholders, and management teams are not in business to break even. Expectations are that organizations will strive to achieve a defined level of profit in a given year, as well as ongoing profitability.

Going back to the XYZ Corporation, our manufacturer of electronic sensors, let's revisit the original cost premise upon which the BEP calculation was based:

Material costs (components) per unit	$10.00
Labour costs per unit	$ 9.00
Packaging costs per unit	$ 1.11
Shipping costs per unit	$ 6.34
Total Variable Costs (direct costs) per unit	$ 26.45

The fixed costs were calculated and determined to be:

Plant overhead (utilities, insurance, service contracts, maintenance, etc.)	$ 500 000
Administration costs (payroll, accounting, IT, etc.)	$2 000 000
R&D costs	$ 500 000
Marketing costs (promotions, advertising, branding, etc.)	$ 1 500 000
Interest expense on debt	$ 500 000
Total Fixed Costs (indirect costs)	$5 000 000

Average selling price (ASP) per unit is $34.

Now, let's assume that, in addition to the costs noted above, the board of directors of the XYZ Corporation has challenged the management team to realize a profit (before taxes) of $4 million in the upcoming year. For management, the question becomes what sales volume is required in order to cover all of our costs and achieve a profit of $4 million. A simple modification to the BEP formula can calculate this for us:

The BEP + Profit formula is as follows:

$$\text{BEP} + \text{P (Units)} = \frac{\text{Total Fixed Costs} + \text{Profit}}{(\text{Selling Price per Unit} - \text{Variable Costs per Unit})}$$

$$\text{BEP} + \text{P (Units)} = \frac{\$5\ 000\ 000 + \$4\ 000\ 000}{(\$34.00 - \$26.45)} = 1\ 192\ 053 \text{ units}$$

The original BEP was 662 252 units. In order to achieve a profit objective of $4 million, XYZ Corporation needs to produce and sell an additional 529 801 sensors at an average selling price of $34.00 per unit (see Figure 13.22). Keep in mind that in the event that costs change, or the selling price is reduced, the numb er of units required to achieve this profit objective will change. As an example if, due to competitive pressures, the selling price is forced down to $33.50 per unit, the number of units that must be produced and sold to realize the $4 million profit objective will increase to 1 276 596 units (assuming that all costs remain unchanged).

FIGURE 13.22   **XYZ Corporation: BEP + P**

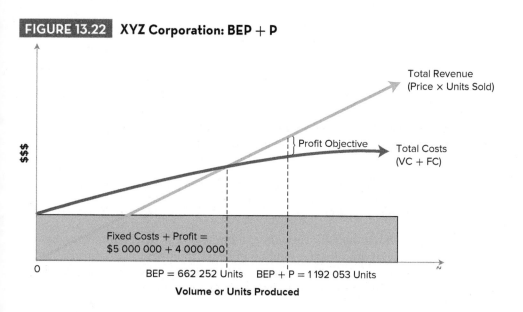

As with the BEP (in units) formula, we can also modify the BEP (in $$$) formula in order to recognize the total sales revenue needed to ensure we reach our profit objective. Going back to the Coffee Mug example, let's review the initial cost base assumptions, and then add a profit objective.

Variable (Direct) Costs as a % of Revenue	
Food costs	32%
Labour costs	33%
Paper and supply costs	7%
Franchise royalty	6%
Advertising fund contribution	2%
Total Variable Costs	80%

Fixed (Indirect) Costs	
Lease	$40 000
Insurance	$ 2 500
Utilities	$20 000
Professional fees	$ 1 500
Building overhead	$10 000
Interest on debt	$ 14 000
Total Fixed Costs	$88 000

Let's assume that the owner of Coffee Mug invested $400 000 to set up his franchise. Let's also assume that his objective was a 12% return on this investment annually. This would mean that the owner desires an annual net profit of $48 000 ($400 000 × .12). Modifying the BEP (in $$$) formula in the same manner as we did the BEP (in units) formula, the revised sales revenue required to break even and meet the desired profit objective would be as follows:

$$\text{BEP \$\$\$} + P = \frac{\text{Total Fixed Costs} + \text{Profit Objective}}{(1 - \text{Variable Costs \%})}$$

$$\text{BEP \$\$\$} + P = \frac{\$88\ 000 + \$48\ 000}{(1 - .80)} = \$680\ 000$$

The required sales volume needed to break even and achieve the profit objective would be $680 000. The original BEP (in $$$) was $440 000, so the Coffee Mug operation needs to generate an additional $240 000 in revenue if the owner is to achieve his desired 12% annual return on his investment.

Using BEP to Ensure That Full Cash Flow Needs Are Realized

Another way in which the BEP formula can be helpful is in determining what the sales revenue level requirement would be in order to cover the organization's full operating costs, meet its profit objective, and meet any principal repayment debt obligations that the organization is required to pay in the current year. As an example, let's go back to the Coffee Mug. Let's assume that the cost structure remains unchanged, as is, again, shown below. Let's also assume that the profit objective remains at 12% annually, based on the $400 000 investment by the owner.

Variable (Direct) Costs as a % of Revenue	
Food costs	32%
Labour costs	33%
Paper and supply costs	7%
Franchise royalty	6%
Advertising fund contribution	2%
Total Variable Costs	80%

Fixed (Indirect) Costs	
Lease	$ 40 000
Insurance	$ 2 500
Utilities	$ 20 000
Professional fees	$ 1 500
Building overhead	$ 10 000
Interest on debt	$ 14 000
Total Fixed Costs	$ 88 000

In addition, let's further assume that the owner borrowed $150 000, at 9.3% for 10 years, as a way to assist in financing his coffee shop start-up. This debt obligation would require an annual principal repayment in addition to the annual interest payment on the debt. Let's make this annual principal repayment obligation $15 000. Assuming that the owner wants all of these expenses to be paid for by the operation, and he still wants his $48 000 net profit (12% of $400 000), what is the required sales volume needed to support this?

$$\text{BEP \$\$\$} + P + \text{DRP} = \frac{\text{Total Fixed Costs} + \text{Profit Objective} + \text{Debt Repayment}}{(1 - \text{Variable Costs \%})}$$

$$\text{BEP \$\$\$} + P = \frac{\$88\,000 + \$48\,000 + \$15\,000}{(1 - .80)} = \$755\,000$$

For the owner, we can conclude the following based on our calculations:

- Operational BEP is achieved at a sales revenue volume of $440 000 (all operating costs are covered).
- Operational BEP and the profit objective are achieved at a sales revenue volume of $680 000.
- Operational BEP, the profit objective, and the loan repayment requirement are achieved at a sales revenue volume of $755 000.

In breaking this down, the owner can now track his annual, monthly, weekly, and daily sales volume to determine if his Coffee Mug is on track to deliver on the desired financial outcome. Assuming that he is open every day (365 days per year), he now knows that his daily sales need to be:

- $1205 to break even (BEP/365)
- $1863 to break even and realize his profit objective
- $2068 to break even, realize his profit objective, and fully pay the principal owed on the loan

    At an average sale per customer of $4, he also knows that he needs:

- 302 customers per day to break even
- 466 customers per day to break even and realize his profit objective
- 517 customers per day to break even, realize his profit objective, and fully pay the principal owed on the loan

Using BEP to Assist in the Setting of Price

Optimal price point pricing (cost-plus pricing) Another benefit of breakeven analysis is its value in assisting managers with understanding the optimal price to charge for products and services offered to the marketplace. Let's use an example with the AAPL Corporation, a manufacturer of smartphones, to illustrate how a derivative of the BEP formula can be used to determine where an organization, assuming total control of market factors, should price its product to ensure that all costs are covered and that its desired profit objective is met.

    Let's assume that AAPL Corporation plans to launch a new smartphone, called the SASS, into the Canadian marketplace. The SASS, which features touch-screen technology, single-key access to Facebook and Twitter, and access to current applications available through the AAPL App Store, is targeted toward the university student marketplace. In analyzing manufacturing and operating costs, AAPL's management team has concluded the following:

1. The direct costs associated with manufacturing the SASS have been estimated at $75 per unit.

2. The indirect costs associated with the SASS smartphone (plant overhead; selling, general, and administrative expenses; R&D expenses; interest on debt) for the first year of the product launch are estimated at $20 million.

3. The profit objective set for the SASS smartphone for the first year is $4 million.

4. The manufacturing capacity of the facility that will produce the SASS is 400 000 units in year one. Discussions with distributors (Rogers, TELUS, Bell, Phones R Us) indicate that, assuming it is a hit, the SASS will be able to sell all 400 000 units.

    Management's key initial question is what is the required selling price that AAPL will need to receive for the SASS smartphone in order for it to cover all of its costs and meet its targeted profit objective. This optimal price point can be calculated via the formula illustrated in Figure 13.23.

FIGURE 13.23   **Optimal Price Point**

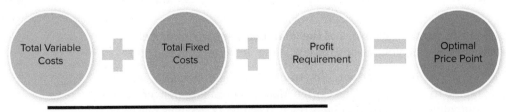

Quantity Produced and Estimated to Be Sold

In the case of AAPL, the optimal price point for the SASS smartphone would be calculated as follows:

Optimal Price Point (also referred to as Cost-Plus Pricing)

$$OPP = \frac{\text{Total Variable Costs} + \text{Total Fixed Costs} + \text{Profit Objective}}{\text{Quantity Produced and Expected to Be Sold}}$$

$$OPP = \frac{(\$75 \times 400\ 000\ \text{units}) + \$20\ 000\ 000 + \$4\ 000\ 000}{400\ 000\ \text{Units}}$$

$$OPP = \$135$$

The \$135 price represents the (optimal) price that AAPL will need to charge to ensure that it covers all of its costs and meets its desired first-year profit objective. For AAPL, this ideal or optimal price point needs to be assessed against a number of different factors. These would include, but not be limited to, the following:

- Is this price competitive with other similar competitive units and anticipated new competitive units in the marketplace?
- Is this price acceptable to our distributors, who, when adding their mark-up, will anticipate a strong and profitable addition to their product portfolio?
- Is this price point, and the corresponding mark-up that will be added to our product by our distributors, in keeping with our company and brand position in the marketplace?

Managers should not assume that the optimal price point is the only price point that can be used for a product as it enters the market. Often times, the optimal price point may simply be too rich for the market to accept, and/or may not be in keeping with the overall brand and pricing strategy of the company. It is meant to simply be one element of a full pricing discussion and plan. Trade-offs will have to be made. In some cases, the introductory price will need to be set low to stimulate interest and demand. In other cases, it will need to be set high in order to recapture the significant development costs associated with the product.[10]

Managers should not assume that the optimal price point is the only price point that can be used for a product as it enters the market.

Mark-up pricing and other pricing considerations Much of our discussion within this chapter has focused on manufacturing operations and the use of cost-base and breakeven analysis to ensure that the organization's pricing strategies are derived from a full understanding of their cost structures. Retail organizations that purchase finished goods with the intent of reselling these products also need to fully understand the costs incurred in the purchase and delivery of these finished products to the marketplace. As an example, assume that your organization purchases dress shirts from a manufacturer in Thailand for resale through your company stores. Although not technically manufacturing the shirt, costs are still incurred in importing the shirt to Canada, transporting it to the various retail outlets that the company owns, and maintaining and supporting its outlets. Going back to Figure 12.9, we are reminded that a very high percentage of our cost base is not directly related to the cost of the shirts, but to fixed or indirect costs associated with our operation's intent to resell the shirts in the Canadian market. When faced with a situation such as this, our focus is all about making sure that we price the shirt high enough to cover the total costs incurred by the organization and meet its profit objective. This means that we have to mark up the cost of the shirt to a level that ensures that full cost recovery and profit objectives are realized.

An easy way to initiate such a pricing approach is to utilize what is called **mark-up pricing** (also referred to as step-up pricing). To illustrate this process, let's assume the following cost structure:

Mark-up Pricing refers to the addition to the manufacturer's price that distributors add to the price of a product to ensure that their own direct and indirect costs are covered and that their profit margin is achieved.

Costs identified below are on a per-shirt basis	
Cost per shirt (purchase price from Thailand manufacturer)	$ 6.00
Transportation costs to Canada	$ 2.00
Import and customs fees for entry into Canada	$ 0.50
Port docking and unloading fees (Canadian port)	$ 0.50
Transportation charges to our regional warehouse	$ 1.00
Labelling and packaging costs under our brand	$ 1.00
Delivery and freight charges to retail outlets	$ 1.00
Total variable or direct cost per shirt	$12.00

As noted, the variable, or direct, cost of the shirt is $12. In addition to this cost, however, we must also cover the fixed, or indirect, costs of our organization. This would include marketing costs, general selling and administrative wages and expenses, warehouse plant and facility costs, leases and other business expense obligations (utilities, insurance, supplies, etc.) associated with our retail outlet operations, and the wages and benefits associated with our retail and distribution support staff. Let's make the assumption that this has been calculated by our finance department and requires a standard mark-up of 150% over the direct cost of the products that we sell. Our company's board of directors has also indicated that they are looking for management to deliver a 15% profit margin for the upcoming year. Both the additional indirect costs and the profit margin need to be incorporated into the pricing model in order to calculate a price that is sufficient to cover all of our company's expenses and yield the desired profit. An easy way to understand this retail pricing example is by viewing this pricing decision via a "step-up" process (see Figure 13.24).

As is shown in Figure 13.24, the mark-up pricing process results in the need for us to charge $34.50 for this shirt if it is to cover the 150% standard mark-up recom-

FIGURE 13.24   **Mark-up (or Step-up) Pricing Illustration**

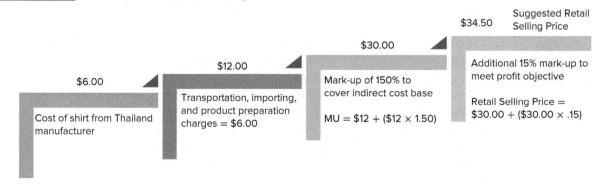

mended by our finance department, as well as the 15% profit margin being sought by our board of directors, as part of our organization's financial requirements for profitability and long-term solvency.

Keeping in mind the price consideration comments made with respect to optimal price point pricing, managers similarly need to assess the ability of the marketplace to accept the full results of a mark-up pricing calculation. Pricing decisions cannot be made in isolation of competitive price points and the willingness of the market to pay the price being offered. As an example, assume that you are interested in purchasing a refrigerator for your apartment or house. In assessing your options, you make a decision to check the prices of three retailers that offer the style and model of refrigerator you are interested in. During this search of these three retailers, you notice a price differential among the three. Why does this occur? This price differential could be the result of different cost structures of the three organizations. The cost structure differential could be the result of one retailer selling significantly greater volume than the others, resulting in its ability to purchase the product from the manufacturer at a lower price. It could also be the result of a more efficient business operation, which requires a lower mark-up to cover the organization's cost versus that of its competitors. It could further be the result of additional services that one competitor offers to differentiate itself from others. If not cost-related, the price differential could be the desire of one of the organizations to take a **price discounting** approach to drive market share or increase volume, or a **price skimming** approach, where the emphasis is on maximizing the profit margin on each of the units sold. This would be reflected in the profit margin objective attached to a particular product or service (see Figure 13.25). To further complicate the pricing process, some retailers may choose to incorporate **psychological pricing** (i.e., pricing at $33.99 versus $34.00) into their final price position, adjust prices for seasonality, provide **rebates**, coupons, or price reductions via temporary sales promotions, or offer customers quantity discounts should they buy certain amounts of the product.

> Pricing decisions cannot be made in isolation of competitive price points and the willingness of the market to pay the price being offered.

Price Discounting is a reduction in the price of the product with the intent to stimulate the sale of the product over a defined period of time.

Price Skimming refers to the utilization of a premium price strategy in order to maximize the margin return on the sale of each individual unit of a particular product.

Psychological Pricing is the utilization of pricing tactics that are designed to respond to the psychological tendencies of purchasers.

Rebates are a temporary price reduction offered on a product or service in order to stimulate sales. Rebates can be offered at the point of sale or on a deferred basis (example: mail-in).

FIGURE 13.25 **Mark-up Pricing Comparison**

Retailer	Cost of Refrigerator from Manufacturer	Retailer's Standard Mark-up	Profit Objective	Rebate or Sales Promotion Discount	Final Price to Customer
Retailer #1 High-End Retailer— fine furniture and appliances	$300.00	200%: includes free delivery, financing options, etc.	20%	$100.00 in-store rebate	$980.00
Retailer #2 Big Box Store— re-labels under own brand	$270.00 volume discount	160%: no frills—cash and carry only	10%	None	$772.20
Retailer #3 Specialty Appliance Store	$300.00	180%: trained staff, full installation, follow-up service, extended warranty	15%	10% discount	$869.40

Chapter Summary

This chapter focused on providing students with a base-level understanding of the different legal structures that business owners can utilize when establishing their organizations. Specifically, three different legal structures were reviewed: sole proprietorship, partnership, and corporation. These legal structures were discussed in terms of the advantages inherent within each, as well as some of the potential concerns that owners need to be cognizant of as they choose an initial legal structure for their new business. Included within this discussion was the recognition that choosing one legal structure type does not preclude the business owner from changing to another structural option in the future. In fact, many organizations modify their legal structure as they move through their individual life cycles. This may be predicated on the inherent advantages and potential concerns associated with each legal structure, or the direct result of the need to tap new sources of capital to further fund the organization's growth. Following this evolutionary business discussion, the chapter focused on communicating to students the three primary sources of funds that owners can utilize to access needed capital for their business organizations: funds derived from operations, financing through the use of credit facilities (debt financing), and equity financing. Each area is discussed in detail, with a focus on illustrating the various options available to managers within each funding source. This discussion also defines how the type of legal business structure impacts and/or influences the funding options available. A summary of the advantages and disadvantages of each of these fund acquisition options is also provided. The chapter closes with a note relating to the differences between for-profit corporations and not-for-profit organizations (NFP) with regard to the sources of funds available to an NFP's management team.

Developing Business Knowledge and Skills

Key Terms

sales revenue p. 489

variable costs p. 494

fixed costs p. 494

breakeven point (BEP) p. 497

margin p. 503

cash operating cycle (COC) p. 506

capital structure p. 508

operating profits p. 508

retained earnings p. 509

credit facilities p. 510

short-term credit facilities p. 511

accounts payable p. 511

accounts receivable p. 511

line of credit p. 511

collateral p. 511

long-term credit facilities p. 511

cost of borrowing p. 512

bond p. 512

mortgage p. 512

long-term note p. 512

lease obligations p. 512

debt leverage p. 513

private equity p. 514

stock p. 515

public equity p. 515

secondary offering p. 515

price dilution p. 516

market capitalization value p. 516

stock exchange p. 517

philanthropy p. 520

mark-up pricing p. 528

price discounting p. 529

price skimming p. 529

psychological pricing p. 529

rebates p. 529

Questions for Discussion

1. What are the five key areas associated with financial analysis that managers need to understand in order to keep their "fingers on the pulse" of the organization's finances? (LO1)

2. What key components do managers need to focus on in assessing an organization's revenue model and its underlying cost structure and drivers? How does the concept of margin management fit into this analysis? (LO2, LO4)

3. Do companies generate a profit at the breakeven point (BEP)? If not, what is the purpose of computing BEP? (LO3)

4. What are the three primary sources of cash (capital) for a for-profit organization? Is one more important than the others? As a manager, what approach would you take to determining how you would finance a new business investment? (LO5)

5. What is an IPO? How is it different from an APO (secondary offering)? (LO5)

6. What is the primary difference between for-profit organizations and not-for-profit organizations with respect to the sources of funds available to them? (LO5)

Question for Individual Action

Arrange an interview with the executive director or the chief executive officer (CEO) of a not-for-profit organization. Discuss with this individual the challenges they face in acquiring external funds to assist in the development and growth of their organization. What is their primary source of external funding? Do they have sufficient assets to enable them to utilize debt financing as a primary funding source? If so, what is their board of directors' position with respect to the use of debt financing? Prepare a brief presentation for your class highlighting the conclusions you have reached and the challenges you have uncovered as a result of your meeting.

Team Exercise

As a team, review two or three recently initiated IPOs. This may mean researching the prospectus for each IPO chosen in addition to analyzing the actual results realized. What were the fundamental reasons these companies gave for making the decision to become public corporations? What was the objective of each company in terms of the dollars forecast to be raised in the IPO? What was the money primarily going to be used for? Were these IPOs successful? Did the share value realized exceed the initial IPO expectations? Was the IPO withdrawn? If so, why? Prepare a presentation for the class that identifies the information developed on each of the IPOs assessed and the key conclusions reached.

Case for Discussion 1

Shaw Communications: The Perils of Debt

On May 3, 2010, Shaw Communications officially announced that it had purchased major portions of the recently restructured Canadian media giant Canwest Global Communications Corporation. The deal, with a value estimated at $2 billion, is a major part of the closing chapter on one of Canada's iconic business entities. For Shaw Communications, the purchase provides it with some of Canwest's most-coveted assets, its over-the-air and specialty television businesses, which include Canada's second largest television network, Global Television, and significant interests in a number of specialty television channels including the home and garden channel (HGTV). The deal, according to the official Shaw Communications announcement, was funded by the assumption of approximately $815 million of net debt that currently resides within Canwest, with the remainder of the purchase price provided in cash via Shaw's cash reserves and established credit facilities, and includes an approximately $65 million cash injection to enable its newly acquired interests in Canwest to emerge from bankruptcy. For Canwest Global Communications Corporation, it is the end of what has been a tumultuous decade. Determined to be an international player, Canwest Global Communications Corporation embarked on an ambitious acquisition strategy, which began in 2000 with its $3.5-billion acquisition of the *National Post* newspaper and other media-related interests from Hollinger Inc. This acquisition, combined with additional acquisitions and newly developed operations in places such as the United Kingdom, Australia, New Zealand, and Turkey, resulted in Canwest incurring debt in excess of $3 billion. This was then followed by the purchase of Alliance Atlantis, in partnership with GS Capital Partners, for $2.3 billion in 2007. The acquisition activity of the first seven years of the decade left Canwest Global Communications Corporation with just under $4 billion of debt and very little breathing room should its operations fail to generate the required revenue to support such a capital structure. For the Asper family (majority shareholders), and Canwest's CEO Leonard Asper, what then materialized was the "perfect storm." In an industry already threatened by changing consumer habits and a shift away from printed media for online information options, the financial crisis of 2008 and the recession of 2009 further accelerated the negative impact Canwest's debt position had on the organization's cash position, as advertising revenues in key divisions fell dramatically. The end result was that Canwest Global Communications Corporation was forced to seek bankruptcy protection under the Companies' Creditors Arrangement Act in October 2009. Following several months of negotiations that resulted in convincing a number of creditors to exchange their debt positions for equity positions, Canwest was still unable to demonstrate to remaining key creditors that a viable business model could be developed that would ensure that outstanding payments, as well as future payments, could be made. Senior creditors, led by Scotiabank and representing most of the major Canadian banks, which were owed approximately $950 million and whose debt was secured by the assets of the corporation, pushed to have Canwest broken up and sold in order to meet its debt obligations. In the early months of 2010, the bankruptcy court sided with these senior creditors, thereby resulting in a bidding process for Canwest's assets and the eventual sale of non-print media assets to Shaw Communications Inc. As indicated, Canwest's newspaper operations, including the *National Post*, are not part of the deal. The sale of print media assets remains subject to bankruptcy proceedings as of this writing, but this part of Canwest appears to be poised to emerge from bankruptcy as a separate legal entity supported by new ownership. This portion of what was once Canwest Global Communications Corporation is anticipated to operate under the name Postmedia Network Inc.

(Shaw Communications owns the rights to the Canwest name). For Canwest Global Communications Corporation, the situation that caused its demise was not that its operations were not profitable, but that they were unable to generate the required cash to meet the enormous debt obligations Canwest had committed itself to. At the time of the decision to commence with the selling of Canwest assets, it was estimated that Canwest owed more than $100 million in payments on the various lines of credit and loans that were still outstanding. It was also estimated that it owed more than $600 million to unsecured creditors.[11]

Questions

1. What lessons can be learned from the demise of Canwest Global Communications Corporation?

2. What does this case say about the risk associated with debt financing and the concept of debt leverage?

3. In seeking to expand through acquisitions, what risks are incurred when purchasing a business largely through debt financing?

4. If Canwest Global Communications Corporation's operations were profitable, then why was it forced into bankruptcy?

Case for Discussion 2

Palmero Jeans Inc.—Advanced BEP Analysis

With the presentation having just ended, Linda Martino, CEO of Palmero Jeans Inc., had a decision to make. Does she break with a longstanding vision that Palmero Jeans will be 100% made in the USA, and recommend to her board of directors that the company shift production of its jeans to Costa Rica? The decision, not to be taken lightly, is one that will fundamentally change not only the way the organization operates, but also how it positions the brand in an increasingly competitive marketplace.

Palmero Jeans Inc.

Established in 1976, Palmero Jeans Inc. is a manufacturer and distributor of high-end jeans wear, competing directly with the likes of Rock Star, Chip and Pepper, Dylan & George, Paper Denim, and Sass & Bide, to name a few. Focused on a California style, Palmero Jeans Inc. distinguishes itself with a vintage feel that is all about comfort. As their ad campaigns state, Palmero Jeans fit like a glove. Recently featured in *Teen Vogue* and on "Deals and Steals" (*Good Morning America, Canada AM, etc.*) and the Home Shopping Channel, Palmero Jeans Inc.'s "Superfine" collection has received rave reviews by jeans critics. Comments such as "they are so rad" and "these jeans are super cool" populate blogs and discussion boards serving this select and finicky niche market. A second line, called "Skinny Pockets," is focused toward a younger crowd, and emphasizes the perfect fit with fabrics that feel super soft. The tag line associated with the Skinny Pockets campaign is "Skinny Pockets are the jeans that you buy, wear, love, buy more, wear more, love more."

Market Dynamics

Although well distinguished in the designer jeans market, the situation at Palmero Jeans Inc. is not as bright and cheerful as the product line and its advertising suggest. For one thing, the market for designer jeans has taken a beating over the last two years, as the recession has negatively impacted demand and sales have declined. Considered by many to be a luxury good, the more mature shoppers are becoming much more discriminating in their brand selection and reluctant to part with their hard-earned dollars. Simply put, the consumer psychology is not so upbeat these days, with many buyers in this category playing more the part of "lookers" versus "buyers." In addition to the woes economic uncertainty brings, the market continues to see new entrants, both domestically and globally. New emerging brands, such as GRLFRND, Aires Arise, Lumier Garson, Jean Atelier, AGOLDE, Frame and Re/Done, further slice up what is already a niche specialty market. Add to this new entrants from Asia, such as R.Shemiste, SJYP, Fugian, Xian, and Nikesell, and the end result is a very crowded market where consumers have greater choice and prices are being forced down. Sure, an initial response, particularly with respect to the Asian brands, is that they are imitators versus true designer originals. Having said this, one has to admire the quality these brands possess and the unbeatable price points they are using to lure customers, particularly first-time buyers, to this product category. In particular, a Chinese manufacturer, Key2Fashion, has made significant inroads into the market in a very short period of time. Their success formula: cutting-edge design at a fraction of the cost. Key2Fashion just recently used a rash of celebrity endorsements from some A-list pop stars as a core part of its marketing platform associated with its major North American push.

At a Crossroads

For Linda, the stakes are high. Palmero Jeans Inc., a smaller industry player, is at a turning point. Historically a differentiator on the basis of product quality, technology has now enabled all manufacturers to produce their product lines at excellent quality levels. Yes, designs speak for themselves, but what customers are saying is that more and more companies are producing excellent fashion designs focused on competing segments of the market; the end result is that price, which was not considered to be a key purchase decision criterion, is becoming much more meaningful. In the short term, Palmero Jeans Inc. has responded with price decreases to ensure that fashion buyers remain committed to the brand, thereby protecting Palmero's relationships with its distribution channel members. These exclusive shop retailers have indicated, however, that other manufacturers, with lower price points, enable these retailers to expand their margins by buying low and selling high. Key2Fashion, in particular, has used this strategy as a way to ensure that their jeans receive significant shelf space in an increasingly crowded market. Recent announcements also point to both Levi Strauss and Lee further deepening their commitment to the designer market in pursuit of the younger demographic. This would place their products in direct competition with Palmero's Skinny Pockets line. Both of these companies moved jean production out of the United States a while back, with Levi Strauss now producing its products in Mexico, and Lee in India. Lee, in particular, is a potential threat for the Skinny Pockets product line, having recently signed a deal with a pair of famous vloggers to design and brand their new product offering.

Initial Analysis

Although Palmero Jeans Inc. has been committed to remaining a made-in-USA brand, Linda knows that an analysis needs to be conducted to determine whether the company should shift some, or all, of its manufacturing operations outside of the United States. Costa Rica's growing garment industry, its government's commitment to assist with the cost of building the manufacturing facility, and its close proximity to the United States all make it a viable option for consideration. Not wanting to change too much too soon, Linda's initial thought is to focus on a financial assessment for the Skinny Pockets product line (initially scheduled to be launched this year). As it has yet to be released, a shift in the manufacturing of this product is possible, as an initial short-run manufacturing process could be established at Palmero's Venice, California, plant until the manufacturing facility could be completed in San José, Costa Rica. This strategic shift might result in a reduction in projected profits in the initial year, but this should be more than offset with savings once the Costa Rican plant is up and running. Also mentioned is the possibility of delaying the introduction of Skinny Pockets into the marketplace until next year, giving the necessary time needed to build the Costa Rican plant and thereby maximizing the perceived cost advantage. Still, others on the Board of Directors seem adamant about keeping production in the United States given the short time that designer jean labels remain popular (the average is three years to peak, followed by one year of harvesting). The company is, after all, contemplating the commitment of $10 million to the development of a full-scale manufacturing operation in Costa Rica (the Costa Rican government is matching this investment at no cost to Palmero Jeans Inc.), with the intent of producing not only jeans, but also other fashion-related products at this new facility.

Before making a decision, however, Linda needs to at least get a feel for the financial numbers associated with this product line and the potential costs and benefits that could be realized if the manufacturing shift takes place.

Analytical Findings to Date

Linda has assigned you the task of analyzing the changes in the cost base that could be realized if a decision were made to relocate the manufacturing operation for the Skinny Pockets jeans line to Costa Rica. Associated with this, please note the following:

1. The annual costs, for the upcoming three years for the manufacturing of the soon to be launched Skinny Pockets product line at the current Venice, California, plant are as follows:

   a. Plant overhead, interest expense, and administration costs: $1 200 000 annually

   b. First-year labour cost per unit (pair of jeans): $15.00

   c. First-year material cost per unit (pair of jeans): $10.00

   d. First-year shipping cost per unit (pair of jeans): $3.00

   e. Union contract—cost of wage adjustment (employee raises) for duration of the product line's life: 3% per year (years 2 through 4)

   f. Anticipated material cost increases for the duration of the product line's life: 2% per year (years 2 through 4)

   g. Anticipated increase in shipping costs for the duration of the product line's life: 10% per year (years 2 through 4)

   Total production capacity of Skinny Pockets jeans at the Venice, California, plant: 200 000 pairs per year

2. The projected annual costs associated with manufacturing the Skinny Pockets product line at the San José, Costa Rica, plant are anticipated to be:

   a. Plant overhead, interest expense, and administration costs: $2 500 000 annually

   b. First-year labour cost per unit (pair of jeans): $4.00

   c. First-year material cost per unit (pair of jeans): $7.00

   d. First-year shipping cost per unit (pair of jeans): $6.00

   e. The workers in Costa Rica will be non-unionized and wages are expected to remain unchanged for the first four years of operations.

   f. Anticipated material cost increases for the duration of the product line's life: 2% per year (years 2 through 4).

   g. Anticipated increase in shipping costs for the duration of the product line's life: 10% per year (years 2 through 4)

   Total production capacity of Skinny Pockets at the San José, Costa Rica, plant: 360 000 pairs per year

3. If production is moved from the Venice, California, plant, it is assumed that the section of this plant being used to produce the Skinny Pockets product line will be closed and its employees will no longer be needed.

4. The initial pricing strategy for Palmero Jeans Inc.'s Skinny Pockets line is set for entry into the market at $48 per unit (pair of jeans). Feedback from distributors/retailers is already pointing toward the need for a more aggressive pricing strategy in order to be competitive with this demographic. It is entirely feasible that a price point of $38 per unit (pair of jeans), or even $35 per unit (pair of jeans), may need to be considered. This potential to move toward these lower price points will have to be considered as part of the decision-making process. Based on prior styles and designs, marketing anticipates the pricing curve to look like the following:

Skinny Pockets	Price per Unit (pair of jeans)
Launch Year (both locations)	$48.00
1 year later	$38.00
2 years later	$35.00
3 years later	$35.00

5. The board of directors has set a minimum annual return on the capital investment in a product line at 10%. With a $1.5-million investment in Skinny Pockets, this means that the annual profit to be driven from this line must be at least $150 000. This, too, needs to be part of the financial evaluation.

6. The marketing department, in conferring with key distributors and retailers, has estimated that first-year sales of the Skinny Pockets jeans line would be in the 125 000 to 165 000 units (pairs of jeans) range. Assuming that targeted sales projections are met, this could climb to between 200 000 and 300 000 units by its anticipated peak demand in year three. In fact, the following probability scale has been established by the marketing department in this regard:

Skinny Pockets	90% Probability	75% Probability	60% Probability
Year 1	125 000 units	150 000 units	165 000 unit
Year 2	150 000 units	175 000 units	200 000 units
Year 3	200 000 units	250 000 units	300 000 units
Year 4	180 000 units	160 000 units	125 000 units

Questions

1. Conduct a breakeven analysis (BEP) for the first three years of production for the Venice, California, plant and the San José, Costa Rica, plant. (*Hint*: Do not include the $10 million investment in the plant as an operational cost for this computation.)

2. Revise this BEP analysis to include the $150 000 annual profit from the Skinny Pockets product line as desired by the board of directors.

3. Based on the information provided in the case, your BEP analysis, and on business concepts learned to date, identify what you feel are the five most important decision criteria (think beyond BEP) that must be taken into consideration in making this decision. These criteria can be qualitative or quantitative.

4. In terms of a recommended strategic direction for the company, how would you rank the following options (1 = best to pursue, 3 = least attractive to pursue).

   a. Launch Skinny Pockets this year, with all three to four years of manufacturing taking place at the Venice, California, plant.

   b. Launch Skinny Pockets this year, with year 1 production at the Venice, California, plant, and years 2, 3, and 4 at the San José, Costa Rica, plant.

   c. Delay the launch of Skinny Pockets one year, and then produce all units at the San José, Costa Rica plant.

5. Explain why you chose the strategic action you identified as #1 above. Explain further why you thought that the action identified as #3 above was the least attractive to pursue.

CHAPTER 14

Financial Statements Structure and Interpretation

LEARNING OBJECTIVES

This chapter is designed to provide students with:

LO1	An understanding of the role financial statements play in assisting managers in managing their businesses
LO2	Exposure to the two types of financial transactions (operational and capital assets) that managers should track as part of their financial analysis
LO3	An understanding of the fundamentals of liquidity, solvency, efficiency, and capacity as they pertain to the financial assessment of a business
LO4	Exposure to the three primary financial statements (Statement of Comprehensive Income, Statement of Changes in Financial Position, and Statement of Cash Flows) that managers use in assessing the financial stability of an organization
LO5	An introduction to the use of trend, comparative, and absolute analytical tools as methodologies for interpreting the financial performance of an organization
LO6	A base-level insight into the role of forecasting and budgeting in the financial assessment process

Snapshot

What to Expect in This Chapter

As identified by the learning objectives, this chapter focuses on exposing students to the basics associated with financial statement analysis. The content emphasized in this chapter includes the following:

- The Role of Financial Statements
  - Two Fundamental Types of Business Transactions
- Liquidity, Solvency, Efficiency, and Capacity
- Three Primary Financial Statements
  - Statement of Comprehensive Income
  - Statement of Changes in Financial Position
  - Statement of Cash Flows
- Analyzing and Interpreting Financial Information
  - Ratio Analysis
  - Leverage Analysis
  - Trend or Comparative Analysis
  - Absolute Analysis
  - Forecasting and Budgeting
- A Note Pertaining to Not-for-Profits
- Management Reflection—Keeping Your Finger on the Pulse of the Organization
- Appendix—Computation of Ratios

Business IN ACTION

Assessing Financial Statements—A Key Requirement in Buying a Business

So you think you have found the perfect business to purchase. In order to determine if it is indeed the right purchase for you, it is important to conduct a due diligence assessment of the company's financial statements. This chapter, along with Chapter 13, is designed to assist you in understanding the fundamentals of the key financial statements which, once you understand, will place you on the path of doing just that.

Purchasing a business is a major, life-changing event for anyone. Making this decision requires potential purchasers to draw conclusions relating to a number of key areas in order to mitigate the risk of buying a business that is not quite what it appears to be. First it is important that prospective buyers understand the legal obligations of owning a business, as well as any obligations that are transferred to them as a

© Thomas Barwick/Getty Images

result of the purchase. Second is that prospective purchasers should conduct a full investigation of the competitive landscape. This includes understanding the numerous competitors your business will compete against, and should entail assessing the strengths and weaknesses, prices, and underlying cost structure of current competitors, as well as identifying potential new entrants into your business sector. Economic factors should also be assessed to determine how changes to market conditions, consumer confidence, technology disruptions, and so on will impact the future potential of your business, should you decide to proceed with the purchase. Third is to ensure that you fully understand the terms of lease transfers, intellectual property transfer (patents, trademarks, licences), and other anticipated rights to be passed on to you. Equally important is conducting a full assessment of the organization's major assets in order to determine that they are in good working order.

Fourth is to ensure you thoroughly check the financial stability of the organization. Astute purchasers will assess the content and verify the accuracy of the information presented in the organization's financial statements. Is the business generating enough money to cover its expenses, to meet future reinvestment requirements, and to allow you, the owner, to take a reasonable income from it? Are there new and/or anticipated current cost increases that need to be recognized and accounted for in your determination of a purchase price and the ongoing sustainability of the business? Do the sales records, bank statements, and expense journals reinforce the information presented in the statements being reviewed? What has been the rate of growth of profit, expenses, and sales revenue? Has the company been experiencing cash flow or debt repayment problems? Who are the key creditors and have they been paid on time? Will sales contracts remain legally binding on customers once the business is transferred to you? Is the owner selling because he/she has concluded that the prospects for the business are poor going forward? If you are borrowing money to purchase the business, can its current cash flow cover the additional interest expense payments and principal repayment terms you have agreed to? These are just a few of the many questions that financial statement analysis will bring to light.

© Torsakarin/Dreamstime.com/ GetStock.com

In analyzing the financial statements it is important to look at the trends the business is experiencing. As noted above, this will include whether sales, expenses, and profitability are increasing or decreasing. It is recommended that at least the past three years of financial statements should be used for this purpose. If five years are available, then a full five-year review offers even better insight into the company's track record. It is also important to assess in detail the most recent 12 months to further identify any immediate-term trends that may be impacting the business and may not have been noticeable in the recent past. Keep in mind that, although the historical statements offer some guidance as to the competitiveness of the business and how efficiently and effectively it was managed, you are purchasing the business based on its *future* performance potential. In this regard, a full forward-looking sales and cash flow forecast should form part of your analysis. This will ultimately result in the development of pro forma (projected) financial statements.

The value of financial statement analysis cannot be understated. The statements offer reflective insight into the effectiveness of a management team's decision-making and execution capabilities. They, in essence, provide one with the ability to keep a finger on the pulse of the organization. Yes, they are historical in nature; however, the underlying trends we can derive from their analysis offer significant insight into the future strength and competitive capabilities of an organization.

LO1, LO2 # The Role of Financial Statements

As has been discussed throughout this book, the role of the senior management team is to determine an organization's overall direction and then direct and manage the execution of the tactics and strategic thrusts that have been developed to ensure the organization achieves its vision and objectives. This requires the effective utilization of its assets, employees, capital, and management acumen so that its business system delivers a superior value proposition to its customers. Decisions are made across a number of key business areas—such as marketing, operations, business system configuration, and HR, to name a few—with the intent of meeting the organization's customer needs and expectations. So, how does a management team track the effectiveness of its decisions and product/service offerings with respect to growth, profitability, and asset productivity? This is accomplished through the analysis of its financial statements.

Analyzing and interpreting financial statements is what enables a management team to "keep its fingers on the pulse" of the organization. Financial statements keep managers up-to-date on the success of the organization's sales and marketing initiatives, and on the ability of the organization to control its costs and maintain its **gross profit margin** and overall **profitability margin** as it delivers its products and/or services to its target market.

> Analyzing and interpreting financial statements is what enables a management team to "keep its fingers on the pulse" of the organization.

Gross Profit Margin is the portion of an organization's revenue that is left over after the organization has paid the direct costs (wages, components, materials, etc.) associated with its products or services.

Profitability Margin is the portion of an organization's revenue that is left after all operating expenses associated with its products or services have been paid.

In analyzing the current financial situation of a company, managers generally rely on three primary financial statements: the statement of comprehensive income, the statement of changes in financial position, and the statement of cash flows (see Figure 14.1). These statements provide vital information to managers regarding an organization's current liquidity and solvency position, as well as its overall financial capacity to respond to opportunities and challenges that the organization may face in the near term. When assessed over a period of time, these financial statements also provide managers with information relating to the organization's overall growth and profitability trends, as well as its overall operating efficiency. It should be noted that while each statement is of value on its own, managers generate the clearest picture of what is happening within an organization by reviewing all three statements together and drawing conclusions based on the interconnectivity of the information generated from such a combined analysis. We will come back to discussing each of these statements in more detail, and also more thoroughly analyze the concepts of liquidity, solvency, efficiency, and capacity. Prior to doing this, however, it is important to understand the two fundamental types of business transactions that organizations will experience as they seek to grow their business and its overall profitability.

> In analyzing the current financial situation of a company, managers generally rely on three primary financial statements: the statement of comprehensive income, the statement of changes in financial position, and the statement of cash flows.

Two Fundamental Types of Business Transactions

Operational Transactions represent the flow of money within the organization that is directly related to day-to-day business dealings.

Managers are constantly making decisions—and reviewing the results of these decisions—regarding two fundamental types of business transactions: operational transactions and capital asset transactions (see Figure 14.2). **Operational transactions**

FIGURE 14.1   **Three Fundamental Statements**

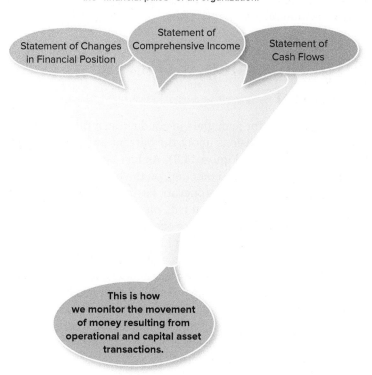

The three fundamental statements managers use to keep their finger on the "financial pulse" of an organization:

- Statement of Changes in Financial Position
- Statement of Comprehensive Income
- Statement of Cash Flows

This is how we monitor the movement of money resulting from operational and capital asset transactions.

represent the flow of money within the organization that is directly related to day-to-day business dealings. Revenue (generated as a result of selling goods and/or services) and reoccurring expenses relating to the manufacturing, distribution, and selling of such goods or services are primary examples of operational transactions. **Capital asset transactions** are decisions that managers make with respect to investment and divestment of capital assets (buildings, equipment, business subsidiaries) that may be needed, or are no longer needed, as part of the organization's business system. Although these are not directly related to the current year's profit for an organization, they do have an impact on its cash flow over the period

Capital Asset Transactions are the decisions managers make with respect to investment and divestment of capital assets (buildings, equipment, business subsidiaries) that may be needed, or are no longer needed, as part of the organization's business system.

FIGURE 14.2   **Two Fundamental Types of Business Transactions**

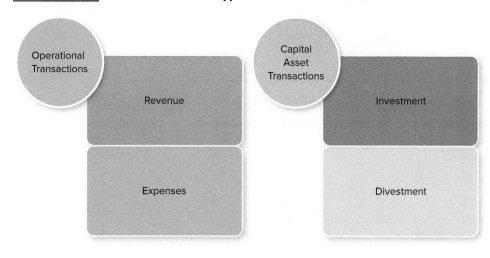

- Operational Transactions
  - Revenue
  - Expenses
- Capital Asset Transactions
  - Investment
  - Divestment

being analyzed. The discussion of the three financial statements identified above (statement of comprehensive income, statement of changes in financial position, and statement of cash flows) will provide further clarity on how operational and capital asset transactions impact an organization and its ability to earn a profit and ensure long-term sustainability.

LO3   Liquidity, Solvency, Efficiency, and Capacity

An important responsibility for managers in conducting a financial analysis of their organization is to draw conclusions about the current and future liquidity and solvency of the organization (see Figure 14.3). As has been noted in prior chapters, *liquidity* refers to the ability of the company, on the basis of the cash it has on hand and the cash it is generating within its operations, to meet its ongoing financial obligations. As an example, an organization will, on a monthly basis, have a variety of expenses that must be paid. Employees are expecting paycheques, suppliers are expecting payment for products/services provided to the business, and financial institutions are expecting that organizations will meet the repayment schedules associated with their credit facilities. In order to meet such obligations, businesses need to generate sufficient revenue from the sale of their products/services, or have sufficient cash on hand to cover such requirements until revenues can reach levels high enough to support these cash requirements. A liquidity assessment by a management team looks at these issues. Can the organization meet its current obligations both today and in the near term?

> An important responsibility of managers, when conducting a financial analysis of their organization, is to draw conclusions about the current and future liquidity and solvency of the organization.

Solvency refers to a longer-term assessment of the financial stability of the organization. Solvency focuses on the forward anticipated profitability of the firm, and whether the firm has or can acquire sufficient capital in order to remain in business. In addition to looking at liquidity issues noted above, solvency also takes into consideration future revenues, products/services under development, market position,

FIGURE 14.3   **Current and Future Liquidity and Solvency**

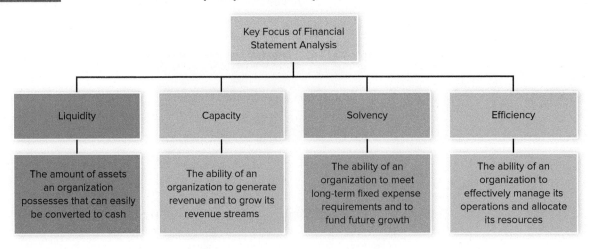

and the ability of the company to acquire additional capital resources if necessary. Solvency, in summary, refers to the ability of an organization to meet its long-term expense obligations and to profitably grow the company. An organization that becomes insolvent is unable to operate due to the lack of the necessary financial resources. For insolvent companies that are unable to find new sources of funding, the next step is generally closure and/or bankruptcy.

Efficiency refers to how effective the organization is in deploying its resources and managing its operational processes in the delivery of goods and/or services to the marketplace. Examples of efficiency measures would be how quickly we are collecting money owed to us from customers, how long it takes us to convert our inventory into sales, how productive our employees are, and how effective we are in utilizing our asset base and technology in generating sales for the organization.

Financial *capacity* is a general term that relates to an organization's cash reserves and borrowing power. Companies that have large cash reserves have the capacity to weather a downturn in the markets that results in a decrease in revenue. They also have the capacity (ability) to invest in research and development, launch new products, and initiate strong marketing plans. Companies that have valuable assets, and that have not taken on significant debt financing, also possess the capacity to borrow money in the event that they need to do so. As part of their strategic planning, managers look to assess the financial capacity of an organization in order to determine the amount of financial resources the organization has to work with. This will determine where and at what level the organization feels it can financially support its competitive position in the marketplace.

So, how do we get a read on the liquidity, solvency, efficiency, and capacity of an organization? We analyze and interpret its financial statements. The information provided within the statement of comprehensive income, statement of changes in financial position, and statement of cash flows provides us with valuable insight into drawing conclusions relating to these four assessment metrics.

> As part of their strategic planning, managers look to assess the financial capacity of an organization in order to determine the amount of financial resources the organization has to work with.

Business IN ACTION

Tying Financial Results to Executive Compensation

Although this chapter focuses on the analysis of financial statements and their utilization in managing an organization, managers must be careful not to become overly fixated on immediate short-term results to the detriment of the long-term health of the business. Positive short-term results are important in that they can build confidence in the management team's tactics and strategic thrusts. Positive short-term results also ensure that the organization maintains and/or improves its liquidity position and, at the same time, reinforces or delivers on the organization's longer-term direction. The risk, however, is that companies will become so fixated on the next set of financial statements that decision making may focus more on immediate bottom-line results than what is truly needed to protect, nurture, and grow the company's competitive edge for the future. The willingness to take excessive risks, or to trade growth opportunities, customer service advantages, and employee-based intellectual capital in order to achieve stronger near-term results, can compromise the underlying health of an organization.

A good example of where the lines become blurred between what is best for the company in the long term and what is pursued in the short term lies with the composition of executive compensation programs. Many such programs are tied to targets based on company profits or earnings. If not properly structured (e.g., an overemphasis on the short term), such compensation programs can lead to executives and employees pursuing goals that run contrary to the longer-term interests of shareholders and the broader stakeholder community. A prime illustration of the situation where this disconnect between compensation based on short-term results can impact the broader financial integrity of an organization was the 2008 financial crisis. Recognizing that uncontrollable external factors did play a role in the severity of the 2008 financial crisis, reflective analysis has led to the conclusion, by many, that compensation arrangements directly resulted in executives and employees taking excessive risks beyond traditional fiduciary levels deemed appropriate for financial institutions.

The underlying culprit in this situation was that instead of compensation programs providing incentives to avoid excessive risk, the programs in place within financial institutions actually encouraged and rewarded excessive risk taking, in many cases where the risk was not fully understood.

Equally disturbing are the significant "golden hellos" and "golden handshakes" that top-tier executives seem to receive either when coming onboard or in transitioning out of an organization. Many such bonuses within traditional top-tier executive compensation packages are not tied to performance and, as such, can generate considerable negative feelings toward organizations by both shareholders and employees. A general rule of thumb, dating back to the 1960s, is that CEO compensation should be benchmarked at no more than 20 times the pay of an average worker. Using U.S.-based CEO compensation as an example, in 2016 the spread between CEOs and the average worker had ballooned to an average of 376 times the pay of the average worker, significantly outgrowing the rate of employee pay increases. When stock options and other indirect compensation elements are added, CEO compensation rose by more than 800% between 1978 and 2016, whereas during this period the typical worker's wages rose 11.2% (reported by the Economic Policy Institute [EPI]).

Emerging popular thinking recommends that executive compensation packages migrate toward longer-term incentive plans, with a broader set of fully disclosed productivity metrics beyond profits and share price used for evaluation purposes. Managers, and the boards of directors that oversee them, need to learn how to balance the need to generate immediate returns with the need to protect and develop market-based competitive advantages that will ensure the long-term viability of the company, its products/services, customers, and other stakeholders. A key conversation surrounding this is the need to recognize that compensation programs have to go beyond the current overriding focus of near-term shareholder value and profitability and look to more broadly include the organization's obligations to its employees, customers, community, environment, and larger national and global concerns.

Three Primary Financial Statements

Statement of Comprehensive Income

A **Statement of Comprehensive Income** (Figure 14.4) is the financial statement that responds to the question of whether our business is earning a profit as a result of the sales we have made versus the expenses we have incurred in developing our goods and services and delivering them to the marketplace. This statement, which reflects a specific period of time (year, quarter, month), identifies the revenue we have received and then subtracts the expenses the business has incurred in generating such revenue. The residual amount remaining after all operating expenses have been deducted from an organization's revenues is profit. If expenses incurred exceed the revenue received, then the business would incur an operating loss for the period of time specified. Figure 14.5 outlines a typical (simplified) statement of comprehensive income format.

> **Statement of Comprehensive Income** is the financial statement that responds to the question of whether our business is earning a profit as a result of the sales we have made versus the expenses we have incurred in developing our goods and services and delivering them to the marketplace.

> The statement of comprehensive income reflects a specific period of time (year, quarter, month), identifies the revenue received, and then subtracts the expenses the business has incurred in generating such revenue.

In order to better understand what a statement of comprehensive income is telling us, we can break it down into its individual components as shown in Table 14.1.

FIGURE 14.4   **Statement of Comprehensive Income**

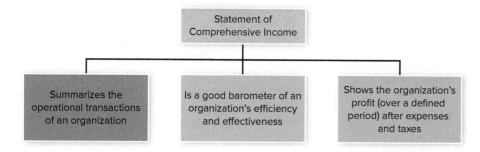

FIGURE 14.5   **Simplified Statement of Comprehensive Income**

	Sales Revenue	
Less:	Product Costs (COGS)	$$$$
Equals:	Gross Profit Margin	$$$$
Less:	General Operating Expenses	$$$$
Equals:	Earnings Before Interest and Taxes	$$$$
Less:	Interest Expense	$$$$
Equals:	Earnings Before Income Taxes	$$$$
Less:	Income Taxes	$$$$
Equals:	Net Profit or Loss	

TABLE 14.1

Sales Revenue	Reflects the dollar ($$$) amount that the organization has received as a result of selling its products and/or services. Revenue can be typically thought of as the sales that a company has made (less product or merchandise returns), and can be further broken down into the number of units an organization has sold multiplied by its selling price.
Cost of Goods Sold	Are the expenses that are directly incurred in the manufacturing of a product or the delivery of a service. As an example, if an organization were in the business of manufacturing and selling laptop computers, the cost of goods sold (product costs) involved would be the cost of the components used to build the laptop, the labour associated with assembling the laptop, and the packaging and delivery charges incurred to ship the laptop to the customer.
Gross Profit Margin	Is the difference between the total revenue that an organization receives and the direct expenses it incurs. Gross profit margin represents the amount of money left over from the sale of the organization's products and/or services, which can then be used to cover other business expenses and meet profit objectives.
General Operating Expenses	Are indirect expenses that an organization incurs and that must be paid from an organization's gross profit margin. General operating expenses include administrative expenses, general marketing expenses, and operational overhead (utilities, insurance, lease costs, maintenance costs, R&D costs, depreciation, etc.).
EBIT (Earnings Before Interest and Taxes)	Is determined by subtracting general operating expenses from gross profit margin.
Interest Expense	Is the interest payments that the organization is obligated to pay during a specified period on the debt that the organization has undertaken in order to finance its operations.
EBT (Earnings Before Taxes)	Is the amount of earnings the operation has produced prior to recognizing its federal and provincial income tax obligations.
Net Profit or Loss	Represents the firm's profit or loss from the sale of its products and/or services to its customers. This dollar amount is typically referred to as net income or net loss.

Statement of comprehensive income example: CAA Tronics Inc. Let's use the following example to provide an illustration of how a statement of comprehensive income is generated, and how the results can be interpreted.

CAA Tronics Inc. manufactures leading-edge electronic sensors that it sells through an established line of dealers. In reviewing its most recent 12 months' results, CAA Tronics Inc.'s management team has established the following revenue and cost information:

Sales

Quantity Sold	2 000 000 units
Selling Price	$32.00 per unit

Product Costs

Material Costs	$ 12.75 per unit
Labour Costs	$ 9.00 per unit
Distribution and Packaging Costs	$ 3.00 per unit

General Operating Expenses

Depreciation	$ 500 000
R&D Expenses	$4 000 000
General Marketing Expenses	$ 1 750 000
General Selling Expenses	$ 1 500 000
Administration Expenses	$ 1 050 000

Interest on Debt

Annual Interest Expense	$1 800 000
Corporate Tax Rate	25%

Utilizing the information noted above, the statement of comprehensive income for CAA Tronics Inc. for the year being assessed could be calculated as shown in Exhibit 14.1.

EXHIBIT 14.1

CAA Tronics Inc.
Statement of Comprehensive Income—20XX

				% Sales
Sales Revenue	(Selling Price × Quantity Sold) ($32.00 × 2 000 000 units)		$64 000 000	100%
Less:	Product Costs (also called Cost of Goods Sold)			
	Material Costs ($12.75 × 2 000 000 units)	$25 500 000		
	Labour Costs ($9.00 × 2 000 000 units)	$18 000 000		
	Distribution & Packaging Costs ($3.00 × 2 000 000)	$ 6 000 000	$49 500 000	77%
Gross Profit Margin			$14 500 000	23%
Less:	General Operating Expenses			
	Depreciation	$ 500 000		
	R&D Expenses	$ 4 000 000		
	General Marketing Expenses	$ 1 750 000		
	General Selling Expenses	$ 1 500 000		
	Administration Expenses	$ 1 050 000	$ 8 800 000	14%
EBIT (Earnings Before Interest and Taxes)			$ 5 700 000	9%
Less: Interest on Debt			$ 1 800 000	2.5%
Earnings Before Taxes (EBT)			$ 3 900 000	6%
Less: Income Tax Expense @ 25% (.25 × $3 900 000)			$ 975 000	1.5%
Net Income or Profit			$ 2 925 000	4.5%

FIGURE 14.6   **CAA Tronics Inc.: Statement of Comprehensive Income**

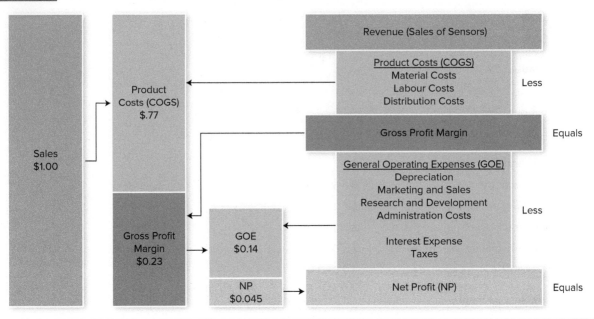

Source: *The Definitive Business Plan*, Richard Stutely, 2nd Edition, Prentice Hall, 2007. Used with permission.

As we can see from this example, CAA Tronics Inc.'s business operations generated $64 000 000 in sales in 20XX. This was the result of selling 2 million electronic sensors at a selling price of $32 per unit. CAA Tronics Inc. spent $58 300 000 on expenses in order to develop, produce, and distribute these units to its customers. Of this $58 300 000 in expenses, $49 500 000 was for product costs associated with manufacturing and distributing the product, while $8 800 000 was for general operating expenses (depreciation, R&D, marketing, selling, and administration). In addition, CAA Tronics Inc. was required to make interest payments on debt to its creditors in the amount of $1 800 000. This left CAA Tronics Inc. with earnings before taxes (EBT) of $3 900 000. Federal and provincial corporate income taxes amounted to $975 000, leaving CAA Tronics Inc. with a net profit of $2 925 000, or a 4.5% ROS (return on sales).

Another way to think about this is shown in Figure 14.6. Revenue represents 100% of the dollars flowing into the operation. In order to generate each $1 of sales, CAA Tronics Inc. incurs $0.91 in business expenses (variable costs of $0.77 and general operating expenses of $0.14). This leaves $0.09 to pay for interest expenses and taxes. Interest expense payments cost $0.025 (2.5 cents) per $1 of revenue, and taxes cost another $0.015 (1.5 cents) per $1 of revenue. The end result is that for each $1 of revenue received, CAA Tronics Inc. makes only $0.045 (4.5 cents) in net profit that it can then use to further improve the organization's financial and market position.

Key takeaways—statement of comprehensive income

Now that we have worked through the structure of the statement of comprehensive income, let's identify key takeaways that managers should keep in mind when assessing the information contained within it.

* The source of sales is as important as the sales amount.

* The key secret to making more money is to spend less money acquiring each additional dollar of sales.

* No sales = no revenue = no business.

- Total Revenue – Product Costs = Gross Profit Margin.
- Companies that are able to control product costs tend to have consistently higher gross margins.
- Without a competitive advantage, companies have to compete by lowering the price of the product or service they are selling; this damages gross profit margin.
- Gross profit margins by themselves do not guarantee profit. The three key killers to gross profit margins are high R&D costs, high selling and administration costs, and high interest costs on debt.
- If sales begin to fall, companies can quickly cut product costs. The challenge is how quickly they can cut committed, fixed, and semi-fixed expenses.
- The critical line in income statement analysis is EBT (earnings before tax); this defines the true level of earnings a company is realizing out of its operations.

Source: Adapted from Mary Buffett and David Clark, *Warren Buffett and the Interpretation of Financial Statements*, Scribner, 2008.

Statement of Changes in Financial Position

The **Statement of Changes in Financial Position** (Figure 14.7) is a financial statement that provides managers with an understanding of the resources the organization has at its disposal at a given point in time, and the financial obligations the business has incurred as a result of purchasing these resources. The title "Statement of Changes in Financial Position (Balance Sheet)" is reflective of the fact that the information being identified in this financial statement must adhere to the following accounting equation:

$$\text{Assets} = \text{Liabilities} + \text{Owners' Equity}$$

As in the equation above, the statement of changes in financial position is arranged into three areas: assets, liabilities, and owners' equity. The information contained within each of these sections of the statement of changes in financial position is outlined below.

Assets Assets represent the resources that the organization has at its disposal and that it can utilize in the generation of business activity and, ultimately, profit. Assets can be classified as either "current" or "non-current." Current assets are resources that organizations can convert to cash and/or consume, usually within a short period of time (i.e., one year or less). Examples of current assets are cash, marketable

Statement of Changes in Financial Position refers to a financial statement that provides managers with an understanding of the resources the organization has at its disposal at a given point in time, and the financial obligations the business has incurred as a result of purchasing these resources.

Assets refers to (1) the infrastructure and resource base of the organization; (2) the resources that the organization has at its disposal and that it can utilize in the generation of business activity and, ultimately, profit.

FIGURE 14.7   **The Statement of Changes in Financial Position**

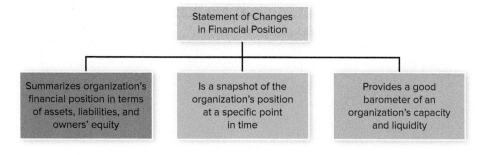

FIGURE 14.8   **Assets**

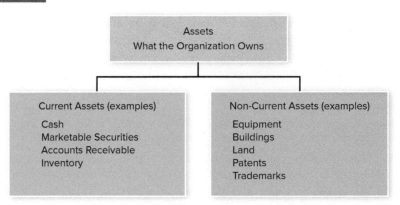

securities, accounts receivable, and inventory. Non-current assets are resources that are generally more fixed in nature, and typically represent the capital assets of the organization. Examples of non-current assets are plant and equipment, land, and the value of intangible assets such as patents or trademarks (see Figure 14.8).

Liabilities are the debts or financial obligations that an organization has incurred as a result of conducting its business.

Liabilities **Liabilities** are the debts or financial obligations that an organization has incurred as a result of conducting its business. As with the asset section of the statement of changes in financial position, the liability section typically separates such debts or financial obligations into those that are coming due in the short term (current liabilities) and those that extend into the future (long-term liabilities). A standard rule for current liabilities is that they are obligations the organization will need to pay within the current business year. Examples of current liabilities are accounts payable, trades payable, and short-term debt (such as a 90-day loan). Long-term liabilities are obligations that extend out beyond a one-year period. Examples of long-term liabilities are a 5- or 10-year loan, a mortgage on a building, or an obligation such as a 10-year bond (see Figure 14.9).

Owners' Equity represents the value of capital received from the owners of the business that is used to fund the start-up or ongoing operations of the business, as well as reflecting the value of the organization's retained earnings.

Owners' equity (or shareholders' equity) **Owners' equity** (Figure 14.10) represents the value of capital received from the owners of the business that is used to fund the start-up or ongoing operations of the business, plus the value of the organization's retained earnings. Generally, companies will retain a portion or all of their current-year profits in order to fund future growth opportunities, buy new equipment, purchase new buildings, develop new products, or to hold in reserve to cover

FIGURE 14.9   **Liabilities**

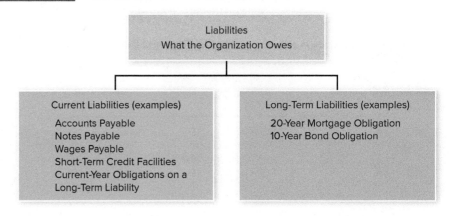

FIGURE 14.10   Owners' Equity

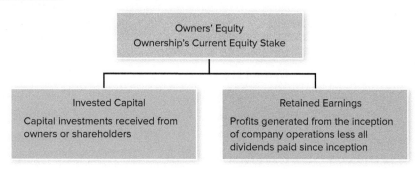

unforeseen contingencies. **Retained earnings** equals the profits generated since the inception of the company's operations, less all dividends paid since inception. An easy equation to help us remember the composition of owners' equity (also called shareholders' equity) is the following:

Owners' Equity = Owners' Capital Invested + Retained Earnings

The term "shareholders' equity" pertains to organizations that have issued stock as a basis of business ownership, with the capital invested reflecting the initial amount for which shareholders purchased their shares from the company.

Going back to our statement of changes in financial position accounting equation, Assets = Liabilities + Owners' Equity, we can see that, given the composition of the statement of changes in financial position, the following additional conclusions can be reached:

Liabilities = Assets − Owners' Equity
Owners' Equity = Assets − Liabilities

Knowing the relationships among each of these sections of the statement of changes in financial position is important for managers, because this understanding will assist in analyzing the liquidity, solvency, and financial capacity of the organization.

Statement of changes in financial position: CAA Tronics Inc. As with the statement of comprehensive income example shown earlier, let's review the financial position of CAA Tronics Inc. from the perspective of the statement of changes in financial position (Exhibit 14.2).

In reviewing CAA Tronics Inc.'s statement of changes in financial position for the current period, we can see that the organization has $12 900 000 in current assets (assets that could be, or will be, converted into cash in the near future). These are considered to be liquid assets in that they are cash or are relatively easy to convert to cash in the near term. The organization also has $42 000 000 of non-current assets, which consist of equipment, buildings, and land. The statement of changes in financial position also shows that CAA Tronics Inc. is constructing an additional capital asset, currently valued at $10 000 000 (construction in progress). This gives CAA Tronics Inc. a total asset base of $54 900 000.

CAA Tronics Inc. also is currently showing $36 800 000 in liabilities, which is made up of $5 800 000 in current liabilities and $31 000 000 in long-term liabilities. The owners' equity portion of the statement of changes in financial position shows that the owners have invested $9 000 000 in the business, and that, given its prior year's profitability, the organization has accumulated retained earnings totalling $9 100 000. Reviewing our

Retained Earnings refers to the dollar amount of net earnings accumulated over the history of an organization that it has chosen to hold within the organization.

EXHIBIT 14.2

CAA Tronics Inc.
Statement of Changes in Financial Position—20XX

ASSETS		LIABILITIES + OWNERS' EQUITY	
Current Assets		**Current Liabilities**	
Cash	$ 1 500 000	Accounts Payable	$ 2 500 000
Marketable Securities	$ 2 000 000	Wages Payable	$ 1 800 000
Accounts Receivable	$ 5 400 000	Taxes Payable	$ 975 000
Inventory	$ 4 000 000	Short-Term Debt	$ 525 000
Total Current Assets	**$ 12 900 000**	**Total Current Liabilities**	**$ 5 800 000**
Non-Current Assets		**Long-Term Liabilities**	
Equipment	$ 8 000 000	5-Year Note	$ 5 000 000
Buildings	$ 20 000 000	Mortgage	$ 16 000 000
Land	$ 4 000 000	10-Year Bond	$ 10 000 000
Construction in Progress	$ 10 000 000	**Total Long-Term Liabilities**	**$ 31 000 000**
Total Non-Current Assets	**$ 42 000 000**		
		Total Liabilities	**$ 36 800 000**
		Owners' Equity	
		Invested Capital	$ 9 000 000
		Retained Earnings	$ 9 100 000
		Total Owners' Equity	**$ 18 100 000**
Total Assets	**$ 54 900 000**	**Total Liabilities & Owners' Equity**	**$ 54 900 000**

accounting equation, Assets = Liabilities + Owners' Equity, we find that CAA Tronics Inc.'s statement of financial position for the period being reviewed does balance:

$$\text{Assets} = \text{Liabilities} + \text{Owners' Equity}$$
$$\$54\ 900\ 000 = \$36\ 800\ 000 + \$18\ 100\ 000$$

Key takeaways—statement of changes in financial position

As we did with the statement of comprehensive income, let's identify key takeaways managers should keep in mind when assessing the information contained within the statement of changes in financial position.

- In analyzing an organization's strengths, our focus should be on its working assets. These are the tangible assets the company uses to generate the products and services that it sells.
- As a general rule, companies that have lots of cash or near-cash equivalents, and little debt, are generally better positioned to work through growth stalls, economic storms, and industry disruptions.
- Low amounts of cash can indicate that a company has poor or mediocre business economics. Cash is not being generated as a result of the activities the company is pursuing.
- If a company is not making additions to its retained earnings, it is not growing its net worth.
- Depreciation is a real cost of doing business, because at some time in the future the asset will have to be replaced.
- The more debt a company has the more interest expense it has to pay.

Business IN ACTION

It Is All About Cash Flow

A key lesson for all managers to learn is that, from a financial perspective, running a business is really all about cash flow. The ability to effectively manage the inflows and outflows of cash within an organization, and ensure that ample cash is available when needed, is core to a business's success. It does not matter whether you are managing a small or medium-size business or a multinational firm generating billions of dollars of revenue: the underlying rule is that a business will continue to exist only if it consumes less cash than it brings in.

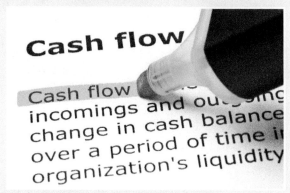

© Ivelin Radkov/Alamy

Revenue and profitability are important, but cash is what is critical to all businesses. It ensures that employees and suppliers are paid on time, and that money is available for investment into the business in order to take advantage of opportunities when they arise. A key element of this business fundamental is understanding the organization's cash operating cycle (discussed in Chapter 13) and recognizing where, and how, managers can look to manage the cash flow the organization is generating. Allowing receivable turnaround times to grow, as an example, means that the cash operating cycle gets extended out, as money from customers is taking longer to flow into the organization. An example of this occurred with a small Montreal-based business the author has worked with. The network development and service business was growing, with new clients coming on every month. Revenues were up, but the company always seemed to be short much-needed cash to meet its growing payroll and business-related expenses. An analysis of the situation discovered that accounts receivable turnaround times had increased from 30 days to well over 60 days. The problem did not lie with customers, but with the business actually producing and sending out invoices to its clients for work completed. This was often left to the end of the month, followed by customers taking the agreed-upon 30 days to pay. In some cases invoices were not actually produced until 45 or more days following the delivery of services to clients. In addition, the invoices were being manually prepared by two employees, and then mailed via traditional mail.

The solution? The company installed an electronic automated invoicing system. Once a job was completed, the service person completed the required billing information electronically and submitted it via a mobile device. The system then automatically generated an invoice for the client, which was reviewed for accuracy and electronically forwarded to the customer. Within three months of implementing the system, the company generated over $100 000 of additional cash simply due to reducing its accounts receivable turnaround times back down to 30 days. In fact, many clients paid within 10 days, taking advantage of a slight discount offered as an incentive. Within six months the accounts receivable turnaround time had fallen below 28 days.

Cash flow management is not just about managing receivables. Managers and business owners need to apply the same principles to all facets of their financial monitoring. Managing payables to minimize expense creep and to ensure that expenditure patterns and efficiencies are minimizing unnecessary cash outflows is fundamental to due diligence in cash flow management. This includes the close monitoring of prices, unit volumes purchased, services delivered, etc. Capital commitment decisions also need to be thought through fully, thereby ensuring that interest expense and principal repayment requirements can be properly budgeted for, and will not cause undue cash stress on the business.

Cash is king. In searching for operational efficiencies the standard response of managers is to cut costs. Focusing on cost reductions, however, typically generates only a certain amount of savings—and for companies that have been through cost cutting before, yields less and less benefit each time through the cost-cutting

© Feng Yu/Alamy

exercise. Managers and business owners are realizing that assessing cash flow practices can typically uncover significant savings opportunities and, when matched with efficiency-based solutions, can yield significant long-term cash flow benefits. Again, the author can point toward a business he has knowledge of. This organization was very lax in the collection of bad debt relating to the subscription services it offered. In a number of cases individuals continued to use the company's services despite having their payments returned for insufficient funds. Through the development and implementation of an account management system that actively tackled this issue, the business generated more than $75 000 of additional cash in the first 12 months. The company went on to share this success with other business owners within the franchise-style business organization, thereby recovering considerable dollars for other businesses as well.

Improving the cash position of a business is what ultimately generates wealth. Simply generating more revenue does not always generate more cash. It comes down to how efficient the company is in generating such revenue. Cash flow management recognizes that operational efficiencies through effective and ongoing cash management practices is what creates and grows the cash reservoir businesses fundamentally need in order to acquire and deploy the capital resources essential for long-term success.

Statement of Cash Flows

Going back to our initial discussion relating to financial transactions within an organization, we concluded that businesses will have two types of financial transactions: operational transactions and capital asset transactions. The statement of comprehensive income, as noted previously, provides us with a good understanding of the operational transactions that an organization incurs in its drive to create profitable growth. It must be understood, however, that organizations generate cash inflows and cash outflows beyond operational transactions. The purchase or construction of a building, the selling of additional shares of stock, and repayments of principal on loans are all examples of transactions that deal with the organization's capital assets. These transactions, which require monetary support in the same manner as those expenses being incurred on a statement of comprehensive income, also must be recognized within the managerial decision-making process. This is, in essence, the role of the **Statement of Cash Flows** (Figure 14.11). While the statement of comprehensive income provides insight into the operational transactions that are occurring within an organization, the statement of cash flows provides managers with a full understanding of the total movement of cash (from all sources) into and out of the business. Given this, many

Statement of Cash Flows provides managers with a full understanding of the total movement of cash (from all sources) into and out of the business.

FIGURE 14.11   **Statement of Cash Flows**

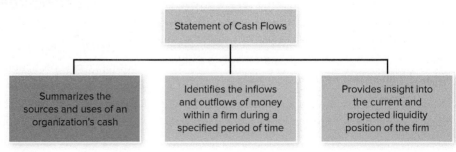

FIGURE 14.12   **Simplified Cash Flow Summary**

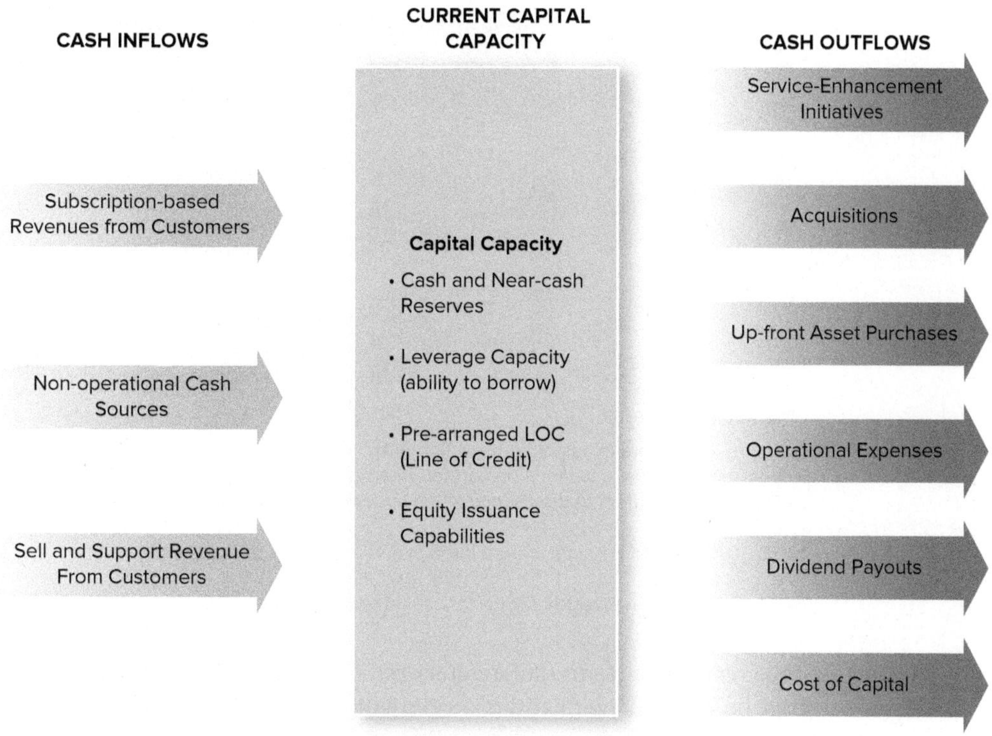

managers and analysts consider the statement of cash flows to be the best source of information relating to an organization's liquidity situation.

> Many managers and analysts consider the statement of cash flows to be the best source of information relating to an organization's liquidity situation.

Figure 14.12 offers some additional insight into the relationship between cash flowing into and out of an organization. In assessing the movement of cash within an organization we would want to take a look at the company's current capital capacity, as well as its major inflows and outflows of cash.

As illustrated in Figure 14.12, sources of cash could be from such items as revenue coming from services provided on a subscription basis or a sell and support basis, or additional cash coming from non-operations sources (sale of an asset, borrowing money, issuing stock, etc.). Cash outflows could be the result of investing in technology and/or other assets and initiatives associated with service enhancements, acquiring new assets, purchasing a competitor or supply-chain company, operational expenses, paying off debt, retiring shares of stock, and/or issuing dividends. This current movement (or flow) of cash is then measured against the overall capital capacity of the company in order to draw conclusions relating to the current liquidity position of company and its ability to fund projects and operations going forward. In drawing these conclusions we would look to try to identify tension or stress points within the organization that could be impacting our overall cash position. Examples of such tension or stress points are shown in Figure 14.13.

To further illustrate how the statement of cash flows benefits our understanding of managerial decisions relating to impacts on cash, let's take a look at the following example. Assume that Fit for Life Inc., a large health and fitness operation located in Toronto, decides to add an aquatics centre to its current facility. The anticipated cost of the aquatics centre is estimated at $5.0 million. As a result of unanticipated increases

FIGURE 14.13   Cash Flow Impact Factors (Blue) and Tension Points (Orange)

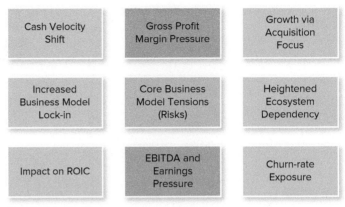

Terminology Ledger
- Churn Rate refers to customer desertion rate
- Ecosystem refers to reliance on partner organizations
- Cash Velocity refers to the change in the speed of cash flowing into the organization
- EBITDA refers to Earnings before interest and taxes, less depreciation and amortization
- ROIC is return on invested capital (or capital employed)

in construction costs, changes to the architectural drawings, and an enhancement of the services to be offered (versus those originally planned), the final cost of the aquatics centre totals $5.8 million. This additional $800 000 of capital represents an additional outflow of cash to the organization beyond the $5.0 million it originally planned to spend and had budgeted for. This $800 000 additional expenditure would not be picked up on the statement of comprehensive income, as it is not an operational transaction. It also may not be recognizable on the statement of changes in financial position, as it shows only aggregate amounts of the value of assets, not dollars being spent on assets as they are being built or acquired. You would have to check for differences in retained earnings levels or cash balances to pick up on this additional expenditure. Where this additional expenditure becomes immediately noticeable is in the statement of cash flows. It is this statement that shows the full impact of all cash-related decisions within an organization and, therefore, truly enables us to understand and sense what the cash position/situation of the organization is (see Figure 14.14).

With this preliminary discussion regarding cash flows in place, let's go back to our example of CAA Tronics Inc., and look at the impact of specific transactions on this company and its financial statements. In addition to the operating results shown on the statement of comprehensive income (Exhibit 14.1) and the statement of changes in financial position (Exhibit 14.2), assume that the following additional non-operational transactions took place in 20XX:

1. The $10-million 10-year bond now showing under the liabilities section of the statement of changes in financial position was issued in the current year.

2. The $10 million in "construction in progress" showing under the asset section of the statement of changes in financial position was spent in the current year.

3. The taxes shown as being owed on the statement of comprehensive income are deferred until the next period, and therefore do not actually have to be paid at this time.

4. Other non-cash items (such as changes to the levels of accounts payable and accounts receivable) netted out to be $100 000.

5. CAA Tronics Inc. repurchased 100 000 shares of company stock at $20 per share.

6. Principal repayment on the 5-year note and 20-year mortgage was $1 300 000.

FIGURE 14.14   **Simplified Statement of Cash Flows**

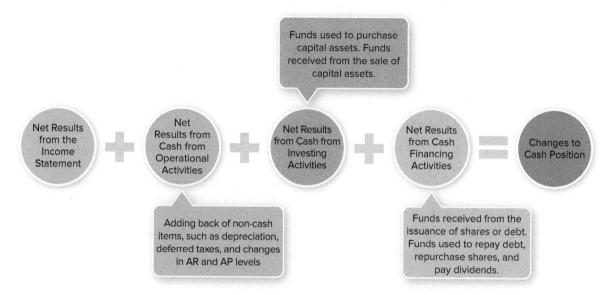

On the basis of this information, and using the information provided in Exhibits 14.1 and 14.2, we can create a statement of cash flows for CAA Tronics Inc. (shown in Exhibit 14.3).

EXHIBIT 14.3

CAA Tronics Inc. Statement of Cash Flows—Year 20XX		
Cash from Operational Activities		
Net Income (Deficit)	$ 2 925 000	(taken from Exhibit 14.1)
Depreciation	$ 500 000	(taken from Exhibit 14.1)
Deferred Income Taxes	$ 975 000	(taken from Exhibit 14.1)
Other Non-Cash Items	$ 100 000	
Net Cash from Operations	$ 4 500 000	
Cash from Financing Activities		
Repurchase of Stock	($ 2 000 000)	
Principal Payment on Debt	($ 1 300 000)	
Issuance of 10-Year Bond	$10 000 000	
Net Cash from Financing Activities	$ 6 700 000	
Cash from Investing Activities		
Construction in Progress	($10 000 000)	
Net Cash from Investing Activities	($10 000 000)	
Net Change in Cash Position	$ 1 200 000	
Cash, Beginning of the Period	$ 300 000	
Cash, End of the Period	$ 1 500 000	(reflected on Statement of Changes in Financial Position)

Net Change in Cash Position refers to the net movement in the cash position of the organization based on operating, financing, and investing activities.

When the **net change in cash position** is added to the beginning cash position of CAA Tronics Inc. from the prior year's statement of changes in financial position, this will equal the amount of cash shown for the current period. Assume that last year's cash balance on the statement of changes in financial position was $300 000. When this year's net change in cash position is added, the new cash balance on the statement of changes in financial position (Exhibit 14.2) equals $1 500 000.

Key takeaways—statement of cash flows

Some key takeaways managers should draw conclusions on with respect to their organization's use of cash include the following:

- Companies that have to make large capital expenditures just to remain in business will generally see a negative impact to their cash position over the long term.

- Too much debt maturing in a given year can lead to cash flow problems.

- Companies that have high development costs, heavy R&D investment requirements, accelerated depreciation schedules, continual retooling requirements, and high debt loads face long-term economic risk and potential cash shortages. The key question is, where will the money come from?

- Companies that have a high percentage of their cost structure associated with R&D, selling, general and administrative expenses, committed costs, and indirect costs such as depreciation and amortization are exposed to greater cash flow challenges in periods of economic downturn and/or industry disruptions.

Source: Adapted from Mary Buffett and David Clark, *Warren Buffett and the Interpretation of Financial Statements,* Scribner, 2008.

LO5, LO6   Analyzing and Interpreting Financial Information

Now that we have a better understanding of the information that is contained within our three primary financial statements (statement of comprehensive income, statement of changes in financial position, and statement of cash flows), let's take a look at how to further interpret this information when making business decisions and drawing conclusions relating to the financial health of the business. In conducting an analysis of an organization's financial health, our focus is generally in four specific areas:

1. *Ratio analysis*—the process by which we assess and interpret the relationships among the financial results shown on an organization's financial statements.

2. *Leverage analysis*—the process of assessing the impact of the amount of debt an organization has incurred in order to finance its asset base.

3. *Trend or comparative analysis*—whereby we look at trends occurring over time by analyzing financial statements across multiple time periods.

4. *Absolute analysis*—where we look at the specific dollar amount of financial resources available.

Only by utilizing all four methods are we able to get a true sense as to the financial position of the company and the overall direction of its financial health.

Ratio Analysis[1]

Ratio analysis is a primary tool that managers use to assess the financial health of an organization. **Ratios** seek to define the relationship between critical components of information found on the financial statements. Ratio analysis is really a driver for the development of questions to which the management team will seek additional information in order to effectively manage the organization. Managers are cautioned to realize that, although helpful, ratios by themselves are not always indicative of the financial health of the organization. This is why managers need to go beyond simply conducting such an analysis and generate key questions (relating to what is transpiring operationally) that will drive a more sound understanding of what is happening financially within the organization.

> Managers are cautioned to realize that, although helpful, ratios by themselves are not always indicative of the financial health of the organization.

Recognizing that ratio analysis can extend into a variety of analytical areas, managers fundamentally utilize ratio analysis to get a feel for the operational efficiency of the organization in four fundamental areas:

1. Profitability
2. Solvency and liquidity
3. Debt
4. Activity

These categories of ratios are discussed in general terms here, with the actual computation of the ratios identified within each of these categories shown in the Appendix located at the end of this chapter.

Profitability ratios **Profitability ratios** focus on assessing the amount of income the organization has earned in comparison to the operating activity that has taken place and the assets that have been used to support its income generation. Ideally, an organization will want to be as efficient as possible given the resources expended and the activities that have taken place. In general, the more efficient the organization is in its activities and its deployment of its assets the more profitable it should be (assuming revenues are sufficient to cover costs). Managers often will set target ratios for the organization as part of its planning process, and then compare the actual results against the targets to determine whether the organization is operating as efficiently as anticipated. Examples of profitability ratios often used by managers are as follows:

- Return on sales
- Return on assets
- Return on equity
- Earnings per share

Solvency and liquidity ratios As noted earlier in this chapter, when an organization is unable to meet its cash obligations in the short term, or becomes insolvent due to its inability to meet its cash obligations for the long term going forward, the end result

Ratios seek to define the relationship between critical components of information found on the financial statements.

Profitability Ratios focus on assessing the amount of income the organization has earned in comparison to the operating activity that has taken place and the assets that have been used to support its generation.

Solvency and Liquidity Ratios analyze the financial obligations that an organization has against its financial resources in order to determine whether the organization possesses sufficient capital to meet its upcoming needs.

can be bankruptcy and liquidation. Managers need to understand the amount of cash that will be required to meet their operating needs and financial obligations. **Solvency and liquidity ratios** assist in doing just this. By comparing financial obligations with the financial resources that an organization has, managers can determine whether the organization possesses sufficient capital resources to meet its upcoming needs. In this way, managers can anticipate cash shortages and/or excess cash positions versus being surprised by such events. Common solvency and liquidity ratios used by managers include:

- Current ratio
- Quick ratio
- Solvency ratio

Debt Ratios focus on the amount of debt an organization has taken on, the relationship of this debt value against its total asset base, and the ability of the organization to meet its debt servicing (payments) obligations.

Debt ratios **Debt ratios** focus on the amount of debt an organization has taken on, the relationship of this debt value to its total asset base, and the ability of the organization to meet its debt servicing (payments) obligations. Three common debt ratios used by managers are:

- Debt to asset ratio
- Debt to equity ratio
- Times interest earned ratio

Activity Ratios assist managers in assessing the efficiency and effectiveness of key components of an organization's operations.

Activity ratios **Activity ratios** assist managers in assessing the efficiency and effectiveness of key components of an organization's operations. By computing these ratios, managers can get a sense as to how effectively the organization is utilizing its asset base, whether changes in cash flow into and out of the organization could be negatively impacting its cash operating cycle, and how well capital is being utilized in support of the organization's strategic and tactical decisions. Recognizing that there are a variety of activity ratios at the disposal of management, some of the more common ratios are illustrated below. It should be noted that acceptable ratio levels do vary by industry, so it is important to assess the results of ratio analyses in comparison to the specific market environment within which the organization is competing. Two common activity ratios that managers utilize are as follows:

- Days receivable
- Inventory turnover

 Business IN ACTION

The Vulnerability of Leverage

As has been discussed in this chapter and the previous chapter, organizations need financial capital in order to grow and operate their businesses. This means looking internally at capital raised via business operations or existing within established reserves the organization has set aside, or externally via debt and/or equity financing. The question for many organizations involves identifying the best approach in accessing capital to meet the needs of the business. This decision, ultimately, falls to the senior management team and the organization's board of directors.

© ACE STOCK LIMITED/Alamy

The process of determining which pool of capital to tap is largely driven by a full assessment of the risk and return implications that each different source of funds offers and the total amount of funds required in order to take advantage of the opportunity identified. In terms of external funds, debt offers the advantage of using someone else's money to make investments aimed at improving the value of the organization and the underlying wealth of its owners (shareholders). With debt, however, comes a cost of capital (interest expense) and principal repayment that must be paid regardless of the financial outcome of the investments. Equity capital removes this cost of capital obligation, but dilutes ownership in the process.

In making the decision as to which way an organization should finance its capital needs, managers need to keep in mind two fundamental points:

1. The long-term strategic plan the organization is pursuing and the approach the organization wants to take in achieving this plan.

2. The degree of financial leverage the management team is willing to undertake in order to fund the capital requirements associated with the pursuit of the organization's vision and long-term strategy.

Financial leverage refers to the use of debt (credit facilities) in order to develop and/or acquire the working assets of a company. The theory behind financial leverage is that an organization uses borrowed money to increase its revenue and earnings, believing that the income being generated by the asset purchased

will be greater than the borrowing costs incurred by the company. The risk, of course, is that the opposite will happen; that is, that the income generated from the asset is less than the cost of borrowing.

The use of financial leverage varies by management team, by markets, and by industry sectors. There is no "one approach fits all" solution to determining where the optimal leverage point lies for an organization. Businesses where product life cycles are short, industry disruptions and/or convergence are occurring, or where technology rapidly changes operational processes and outputs are typically more prone to the risks of financial leverage than slow-cycle industries where companies are producing a consistent product line requiring little change. Having said this, excessive use of financial leverage has played a major role in the collapse of many historical "industry leaders," such as Blockbuster, Barnes and Noble, Hills Department Stores, and Canwest Global.

The retail sector offers a good case study relating to the risk associated with high leverage. Coming out of the recession of 2009 and 2010, the cost of debt was cheap and stock prices were depressed. Private equity companies, looking for opportunities to grow and magnify their returns to their shareholders, viewed retail as an opportunity to do just that. In this regard, a number of debt-funded acquisitions (called leveraged buyouts) within the retail sector were made. This resulted in these companies becoming heavily leveraged. Golden Gate Capital's acquisition of Payless, Sycamore Partners' acquisition of Staples, Bain, KKR, and Vornado's acquisition of Toys R Us, and Bain Capital's acquisition of Gymboree are but a few examples of the leveraged buyouts constructed during this time period. In all, there were just under 60 such acquisitions made by private-equity companies between 2011 and 2016. Of the 10 largest retail acquisitions made during this period, one-third of the companies acquired ended up in Chapter 11 bankruptcy (U.S.A.), with the most recent notable examples being Toys R Us, Payless, and Gymboree. Leveraged buyouts themselves may not be bad, as companies, after taking a company private, restructure it and then return it to the public stock market via a new IPO. The risk as noted above, of course, is that market conditions change and companies carrying high levels of debt with significant fixed costs of capital are unable to respond to it. The retail sector is, again, a lesson-to-be-learned example. Many of these private-equity companies did not anticipate the significant disruption now occurring within the retail sector, the magnitude of the Amazon effect, and the velocity with which consumers shifted to purchasing online. Positioned with largely bricks and mortar (physical store) business models, significant investments were—and still are—required to pivot to a full omnichannel model. For a number of these companies, their ability to make such investments is challenging as they already have high levels of debt on their balance sheets and, therefore, have limited capital capacity to make such investments.

Debt financing is attractive in that a company can use capital secured at a fixed rate in order to increase its return on equity (returns to its owners). With this, however, comes the risk of a potential increase in financial distress if the ability to service this debt (make the required payments) is jeopardized due to revenue declines, margin erosion, or other unforeseen and uncontrollable circumstances. In a

© Jackie2k/Dreamstime.com/ GetStock.com

worst-case scenario, bankruptcy, as we have seen in the retail sector, could be the only solution to situations where the debt is no longer manageable by the business. Managers and their boards of directors need to keep such risks in mind when contemplating debt financing. The key is to maintain a capital structure that has a sufficient degree of flexibility within it in order to navigate the uncertainty and potential volatility of the markets the company competes within.

Leverage Analysis

Leverage refers to the amount of debt an organization uses in order to finance its asset base.

As noted above and in the Business in Action feature "The Vulnerability of Leverage," **leverage** refers to the amount of debt an organization uses in order to finance its asset base. A firm with liabilities that represent a significant portion of its assets is considered to be highly leveraged. Depending on the profitability level of the firm, leverage can be interpreted as being either positive or negative. In profitable situations, where the EBIT of a firm is sufficient to cover its interest expenses, investors can realize higher percentage returns by employing debt financing to assist in the profitable growth of the organization. In situations where EBIT is not sufficient to cover the interest expense obligations of an organization, the loss the organization incurs will be greater than if leverage were not employed. The following scenario is meant to illustrate the positive and negative impact of leverage.

Benefits of leverage Assume that the ABC Corporation has total assets of $40 000 000. Now, assume two options associated with the creation of this asset base.

Option #1—ABC Corporation's asset base is created as a result of $40 000 000 being invested by its owners (shareholders).

Option #2—ABC Corporation's asset base is created as a result of $30 000 000 (borrowed at 6%) in debt financing and $10 000 000 in owner contributions.

Now, assume that the ABC Corporation's operation for the current year produces an EBIT of $4 000 000. With Option #1, because there is no debt there would be no interest expense; therefore, earnings before taxes would be the same: $4 000 000. Assuming a 25% tax rate, net income would be $3 000 000 ($4 000 000 – $1 000 000), and the return on equity (ROE), which is a measure of the return to owners (shareholders), would be as follows:

$$ROE = \frac{\text{Net Income}}{\text{Total Equity}} \quad or \quad \frac{\$3\ 000\ 000}{\$40\ 000\ 000} = 7.5\%$$

With Option #2, assume the same EBIT of $4 000 000. There is, however, $30 000 000 of debt, which requires the payment of interest expense totalling $1 800 000 (computed by $30 000 000 × .06). This means that EBT would be $4 000 000 – $1 800 000 = $2 200 000. Using the same 25% tax rate, the net income for ABC Corporation, in this situation, would be $1 650 000. With debt of $30 000 000, the total equity position of ABC Corporation's investors is $10 000 000. This means that the ROE for Option #2 would be:

$$ROE = \frac{\text{Net Income}}{\text{Total Equity}} \quad or \quad \frac{\$1\ 650\ 000}{\$10\ 000\ 000} = 16.5\%$$

Thus, by using someone else's money (creditors), investors in the ABC Corporation can improve their returns from 7.5% to 16.5%, or from 7.5 cents for each dollar invested to 16.5 cents for each dollar invested (see Figure 14.15).

Risks of leverage As shown above, leverage can benefit investors, assuming that sufficient net income is earned by the organization. What happens, however, in a situation where the organization does not earn a profit? How does this impact a firm that is using leverage as a mechanism for growing its asset base?

As will be illustrated, leverage comes with risk. If an organization chooses to use a significant level of debt financing, and the end result is an operating loss, the impact to investors would be greater than the loss that would have occurred had leverage not been utilized. Again, let's assess on the basis of a situation similar to that used above.

Assume the same two asset-base creation options as noted above:

Option #1—ABC Corporation's asset base is created as a result of $40 000 000 being invested by its owners (shareholders).

Option #2—ABC Corporation's asset base is created as a result of $30 000 000 (borrowed at 6%) in debt financing and $10 000 000 in owner contributions.

FIGURE 14.15   Benefits of Leverage

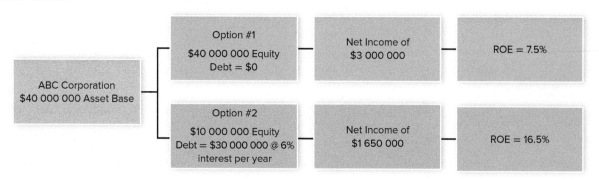

Now, assume that ABC Corporation suffers a loss (EBIT) of ($1 000 000). In Option #1, the negative ROE for investors would be (assume no taxes will be paid due to an operating loss):

$$\text{ROE} = \frac{\text{Net Income}}{\text{Total Equity}} \quad \text{or} \quad \frac{(\$1\,000\,000)}{\$40\,000\,000} = -2.5\%$$

In Option #2, however, the loss is much greater, as the ABC Corporation, in addition to an EBIT of ($1 000 000), would also still have to pay the interest expense on the $30 000 000 of debt, which amounts to $1 800 000. This brings the total operating loss to $2 800 000. Again, assuming that no tax payments would be required, the ROE to investors would be:

$$\text{ROE} = \frac{\text{Net Income}}{\text{Total Equity}} \quad \text{or} \quad \frac{(\$2\,800\,000)}{\$10\,000\,000} = -28\%$$

The greater losses, when assessed against a smaller equity base, result in a negative ROE of 28% to investors in the ABC Corporation (see Figure 14.16). In addition, as interest expense payments must be made, the ABC Corporation would either need to pay the interest expenses out of its cash reserves or seek some other external financing arrangement in order to ensure that it does not default on its debt obligations. As is illustrated, with debt financing comes an increased financial risk, particularly in situations where the organization is not driving operating margins sufficient to fund its debt obligations. As managers, we need to recognize this exposure and seek to utilize debt in a way that enhances the profitable growth of the organization versus exposing it to significant liquidity and solvency issues by carrying too much debt.

> Managers need to recognize this exposure and seek to utilize debt in a way that enhances the profitable growth of the organization versus exposing it to significant liquidity and solvency issues by carrying too much debt.

Trend or Comparative Analysis

Up to this point, we have been assessing financial statements and ratios based on a specific point in time. Although that information is valuable, to truly understand how an organization is doing managers often look to review current results against prior-year actual results and anticipated forecast results. We call this comparative

FIGURE 14.16   Risks of Leverage

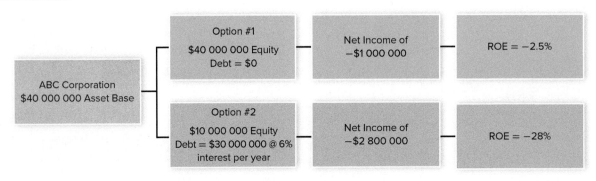

or trend analysis. By comparing financial statements and ratios against targeted objectives or against historical performance, we can draw some conclusions as to whether an organization's liquidity and solvency position are being improved or compromised, and whether the organization is improving its overall operating efficiency. Figures 14.17, 14.18, and 14.19 provide some examples of such an analysis.

Figure 14.17 illustrates the operating performance of BlackBerry Ltd. from 2014 to 2019. As one can see, it has been a challenging time for BlackBerry. The company has seen its revenue decline from a high of $6.8 billion (USD) in 2014 to $904 million for the year ending February 28, 2019 (BlackBerry's peak revenue was $19.9 billion in 2011). This dramatic drop in revenue has resulted in significant fluctuations in operating income, which was a negative $3.5 billion in 2014, to a negative $40 million as of February 28, 2019 (see chart A). This dramatic decline in revenue, coupled with

FIGURE 14.17   **BlackBerry Ltd.: Operating Performance ($$$ millions)**

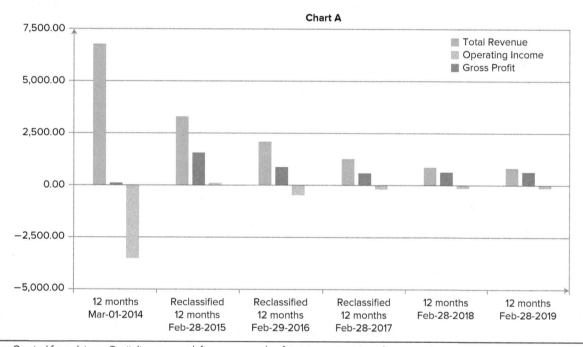

Source: Created from data on Capitaliq.com, googlefinance.com, yahoofinance.com, investopedia.com, reuters.com.

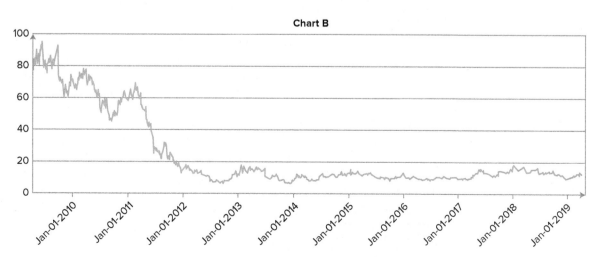

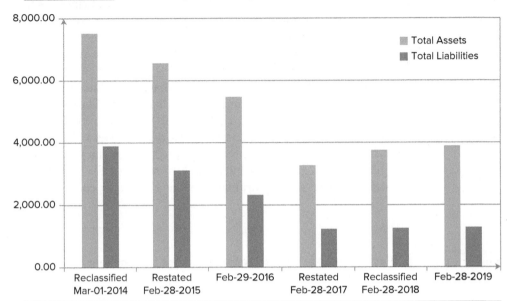

FIGURE 14.18   **BlackBerry Ltd.: Debt to Assets Relationship**

Source: Created from data on googlefinance.com, yahoofinance.com, investopedia.com, reuters.com.

significant business strategy shifts as part of its turnaround strategy, has resulted in considerable stress on the company's capabilities, and is reflected in the share price decline that took place in the early days of its loss of market position and has remained relatively weak since then (see chart B).

> By comparing financial statements and ratios against targeted objectives or against historical performance, we can draw some conclusions as to whether an organization's liquidity and solvency position are being improved or compromised, and whether the organization is improving its overall operating efficiency.

Figure 14.18 illustrates the debt to assets relationship for BlackBerry Ltd. for the period 2014 through 2018. Although free of long-term debt from 2011 through 2013, BlackBerry Ltd. had to take on $1.6 billion (USD) of debt in 2014 in order to maintain its liquidity and ensure its mid-term solvency. This was further increased to $1.7 billion (USD) in 2015, again supporting the near-term cash needs of the company as it struggled to turn the company around and regain position in a rapidly changing marketplace. The company also divested itself of non-core assets during this volatile period, shrinking its asset base from $13 billion in 2013 to $3.7 billion in February 2019. Although the relationship between debt and BlackBerry's asset base remains relatively low overall, we can conclude that as its asset base continues to decline (due to closing product lines or selling off assets) the capital capacity of the company will become more constrained (assets are the collateral for borrowing).

Figure 14.19 shows the overall comparative performance of BlackBerry for the years 2016 to 2019. As the company has migrated from a hardware producer to a software service provider, gross margin has significantly improved. With this shift, however, has been a reallocation of expenses from COGS (cost of goods sold) to operating expenses, which were only 38% in 2013 and now (2019) make up over 80% of the company's expenses.[2] As discussed in the Business in Action "BlackBerry—Reinventing the Business Model" in Chapter 1, the dramatic

FIGURE 14.19   **BlackBerry Ltd.: Profitability Ratios**

Blackberry—Margins (% of Revenue)	2016	2017	2018	2019
Gross Margin	43.5%	49%	73%	77%
Operating Margin	−21%	−.12%	−10%	−4%
Long-Term Debt to Asset	23%	18%	20%	17%
Operating Expense Percentage	65%	61.5%	83.5%	82%

transformation that CEO John Chen is guiding BlackBerry through is not something that can occur overnight. The company literally has completely reinvented its business model, which ultimately is reflected in the configuration and reporting of its financial results. As shown above, BlackBerry is a much smaller but leaner company. Its focus lies in new market development versus trying to compete in the handheld mobility space where it has clearly lost its market position and presence. The key challenge now is to get its operating income back to a positive situation. This will enable it to stop burning cash annually in support of the operation; its cash balance on its Statement of Changes in Financial Position–Balance Sheet decreased from $2.3 billion in 2016 to $916 million in February 2019, thereby enabling it to use more of its cash in support of revenue growth via acquisitions and/or organic new market development. John Chen is close to doing this, as, although negative, the losses at the operating income level have been significantly reduced and as of this writing the company is very close to achieving operational breakeven.

Managers will look to perform analyses across all ratio sectors (profitability, solvency, and debt), as well as analyzing activity ratios—such as inventory turnover, accounts payable turnover, and accounts receivable turnover ratios—in order to truly understand just how efficient their organization is and whether concerns regarding working capital and financing issues loom on the horizon.

A caution concerning ratio analysis It is important to recognize that, while ratio analysis provides many useful insights into the financial performance of an organization, ratios should not be the sole focus of the financial assessment process. As with any methodology, ratio analysis does carry with it some risks and limitations. Keep in mind that ratio analysis, by virtue of the method employed, focuses on single aspects of financial performance and, therefore, defines one performance dimension when many factors need to be, or should be, taken into consideration. As an example, computing an organization's sales growth rate from one year to the next may show solid growth overall, but excludes in the analysis the cost of capital that the organization expended to achieve this growth. The end result is that the cost of the sales growth may have exceeded the benefit. The same could hold true for a market-share calculation. Again, market share could have grown year-over-year, but at what cost? If volume is pursued at any cost, the additional market share gained could result in reduced earnings for the firm. EPS (earnings per share) could be going up, but this could be temporary and/or artificial growth in this metric. Managers may simply choose to cut or defer costs, repurchase shares, postpone projects, or take other short-term measures, all with the idea of producing greater immediate returns, which could compromise the long-term health of the organization. To compensate for this, a good guideline is not to look at a single ratio in isolation, but to view the business and its activities from a productivity, momentum, and profitable growth perspective, rather than simply the calculation of a series of ratios based on financial results. This shift in the assessment process enables managers to think of ratios as tools, not outcomes, and restructure their thought process toward questions such as Did our investments add value for our customers? Did the increased sales volume result in greater profitability for the organization? Is the return on the capital invested in support of a project sufficient to warrant the investment, and did the decisions we have made relating to where and how to compete result in gains in long-term shareholder wealth?[3]

> It is important to recognize that, while ratio analysis provides many useful insights into the financial performance of an organization, ratios should not be the sole focus of the financial assessment process.

Absolute Analysis

Ratio analysis and assessments of percentage changes in sales levels, margins, and other barometers of operating performance are sound assessment tools for managers to use when analyzing the efficiency, effectiveness, and financial health of an organization. We must, however, recognize that managers need to assess financial strength in absolute terms as well. Absolute analysis refers to an assessment of the actual dollar amount that organizations are generating and/or have at their disposal. As an example, doubling the cash balance on the statement of changes in financial position from $5000 to $10 000 is a 200% increase in the cash the firm has at its disposal. Although this sounds impressive, the amount is still only $10 000. Managers must look at the dollar monetary requirements that will be necessary to support the operation and determine whether such resources currently exist and/or are obtainable from outside sources (debt or equity financing). In addition, managers must assess their organization's financial capabilities against those of their competitors. This will enable them to determine where and how to compete, especially against much financially stronger opponents. As an example, let's take a look at four companies that are competing actively with each other for market share in the technology space (see Figure 14.20).

As we can see, all four companies have significant cash reserves from which to draw in the event of a need to invest in their organizations, fund new market opportunities, or weather revenue downturns that could result in operating losses. These significant cash reserves give Amazon, Apple, Google, and Microsoft greater capacity to develop products and services, make acquisitions, and invest in cutting-edge technologies that will enable them to further improve their operating performance, over the long term, when compared to many smaller rivals. This is one of the core reasons why these companies continue to dominate the technology space today. Looking at the social media space, Facebook Inc. as of December 31, 2018, possessed total cash and short-term investments of $41 billion (USD). Compare this to

FIGURE 14.20   Absolute Analysis: Cash on Hand ($$$ millions USD)

	Amazon (12/31/2018)	Apple Inc. (12/29/2018)	Alphabet Inc. (03/31/2018)	Microsoft Corporation (03/31/2018)
Cash on Hand	$31.7 billion	$44.7 billion	$16.7 billion	$6.6 billion
Short-Term Investments	$9.5 billion	$41.6 billion	$92.4 billion	$121 billion
Total Cash and Short-Term Investments	$41.2 billion	$86.4 billion	$109.1 billion	$127.6 billion

Twitter Inc., which on the same date held $6.2 billion in cash and short-term investments, and Snap Inc., whose cash and short-term investments were only $1.2 billion.[4] Clearly, Facebook Inc. possesses significantly greater liquid capital capacity then these two rivals when looking to make moves to further grow the company going forward (ideally, we would conduct a full working capital and leverage assessment to confirm this conclusion).

As managers, it is important to understand the absolute dollar values we have access to, the dollar amount of debt we owe, and the future potential dollars we believe the organization can generate. An understanding of our financial resources in absolute terms, when combined with ratio analysis and using comparative (trend) analysis, gives managers the best picture of the organization's health.

> As managers, it is important to understand the absolute dollar values we have access to, the dollar amount of debt we owe, and the future potential dollars we believe the organization can generate.

Forecasting and Budgeting

Up to this point, our focus has been on analyzing and interpreting actual but historical information relating to an organization's financial performance. Although this is a valuable and necessary process in managing an organization, so too is our ability to project forward anticipated results for the upcoming quarter, year, or planning cycle period. This process, commonly referred to as **forecasting and budgeting**, challenges management teams to anticipate what the organization's financial position will be, based on an analysis of a variety of factors. These factors could include (but are not limited to) external factors such as the economic environment, market conditions, emergence of new competitors, and new substitutes for the products and/or services we offer. Also considered would be internal factors such as new product launches, new technology applications, product discontinuation, new distribution channels, new uses for our products, new pricing requirements, and anticipated changes to our cost base. The importance of forecasting and budgeting is fourfold:

Forecasting and Budgeting refers to management's ability to project forward anticipated results for the upcoming quarter, year, or planning-cycle period.

1 Forecasting and budgeting require the organization to think about what is happening in the markets within which it competes and to determine how its various products and services will perform in the upcoming period.

2 Forecasting and budgeting set specific operational parameters for the various divisions and departments within the organization (and, therefore, the organization as a whole), and subsequently become operational targets that keep the organization on track in terms of operational efficiency and effectiveness.

3 Forecasting and budgeting require managers to make decisions related to resource allocation when measured against specific outcomes, thereby providing a process under which such scarce resources can be allocated toward those projects, initiatives, and products and services that are anticipated to yield the best results.

4 Forecasts and budgets become benchmarks/targets against which actual results can be measured, thereby enabling managers to make proactive decisions relating to reinforcing or correcting business activities and tactics in the event that actual results exceed or lag behind forecast or anticipated results.

One of the most difficult aspects of forecasting and budgeting lies in determining anticipated revenue streams. This becomes particularly more challenging in periods of economic retraction or volatility. The anticipated sustainability of revenue streams is an important part of the forecasting and budgetary process. The accuracy of sales forecasts underlies decisions relating to production, inventory management, and infrastructure spending. Decisions relating to cost adjustments that the company anticipates and competitive pricing pressures will influence the price the company will charge for its goods and services, and thus its sales revenue. Changes in customer needs, wants, and desires will also influence this. Companies must consider all of these things (and many more) when making predictions about what revenue will look like in the weeks, months, and years ahead. In essence, all decisions relating to the operation will stem from its sales revenue forecasts.

The company must then assess such sales levels against anticipated expenses to determine whether the company can meet the desired profitability and growth targets expected by its internal and external stakeholders. If such targets are not met, the organization must then seek to modify its cost base and/or find alternate revenue streams to ensure that sufficient cash flow is generated and that targeted profitability and growth projections are met. The forecasting and budgetary process can be visualized as per the diagram illustrated in Figure 14.21.

> The accuracy of sales forecasts underlies decisions relating to production, inventory management, and infrastructure spending.

Utilizing the strategic planning process and the various models at their disposal (Porter's Five Forces, PESTEL, SWOT), organizations will conduct an external assessment of how they believe their products and services will perform for the upcoming period. Based on this assessment, along with information derived from customers and distributors, organizations will quantify this anticipated performance into a formal financial revenue (sales) forecast. While this process is taking place, organizations will also assess their cost base and their various expense lines to determine changes that they anticipate will occur (wage adjustments, changes to the cost of goods sold, changes to indirect expenses such as insurance premiums, service contracts, etc.). With this analysis having taken place, the organization's management team will then proceed to the preparation of pro forma (projected) statements to determine the organization's anticipated profitability position. Additional financial resource requirements will be brought into

FIGURE 14.21   Forecasting and Budgeting Process

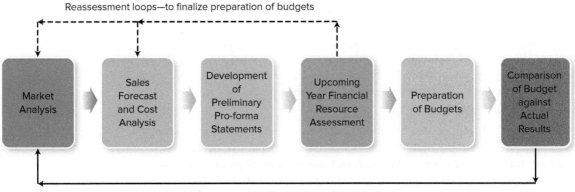

the picture (capital asset transactions, non-operational needs, etc.), thereby final-izing the full financial picture of the organization and resulting in the development of the financial budgets for the upcoming period. These budgets then become the benchmark against which the organization will measure its progress (actual ver-sus forecast results) for the period the budget covers. It should be noted that, as Figure 14.21 illustrates, the process will contain a number of situations where sales and expense forecast revisions and further financial analysis will be required. These are reflected in the reassessment loops shown in Figure 14.21. Information relating to the forecast versus actual results also becomes important for the next budgetary process and planning period.

A Note Pertaining to Not-for-Profits

Like for-profit entities, managers of not-for-profit (NFP) organizations need to dem-onstrate the same financial analytical skills as discussed above when managing the business side of their organizations. Liquidity, solvency, and efficiency issues are as important when managing an NFP as when managing in the for-profit environment. Having said this, in guiding the NFP it should be understood that there are some notable differences to the financial landscape that will impact the ability of the orga-nization's manager to respond to immediate and longer-term financial challenges. A good example of this lies in the statements of changes in financial position of many NFPs. Unlike for-profit entities, NFPs, by their nature, are unable to sell shares of stock or percentages of ownership. This limitation results in the inability to utilize equity financing as a key pillar in the development of their capital structure. In the absence of this, one could conclude that NFPs are limited financially to the dollars they can generate from their operations and in their ability to debt-finance. Many NFPs are not in the revenue generation business, and/or do not have a capital asset base of sufficient size that they could use as collateral for debt-financing purposes. So, how do these organizations generate the dollars needed to sustain their charita-ble and community-based mission? The answer lies in the receiving of grants, government subsidies, and private donations. For many NFPs, the ability to raise money via events, annual campaigns, capital (building) campaigns, and so on is an important part of their business strategy. Why mention it under the financial state-ment analysis section within this textbook? It is because these dollars often carry with them restrictions on their use—which can, and often does, limit an NFP man-ager's ability to respond to liquidity and solvency issues within the organization.

> Like for-profit entities, managers of not-for-profit organizations need to demonstrate the same financial analytical skills when managing the business side of their organizations.

When reviewing the asset portion of a statement of changes in financial position of an NFP organization, the key focus of our analysis is on the identification of such restrictions. Donations that have been raised for the renovation of a building, for example, will often be identified as being restricted, and therefore cannot be used for funding the day-to-day operations (salaries, administrative expenses, office sup-plies, etc.) of the NFP. Take a university as an example. The university may have significant endowments or bequeaths identified on its statement of changes in finan-cial position that have been set up for specific, restricted purposes. Despite this significant wealth, the university still has to raise tuition fees to cover its operating expenses, as these endowments are restricted in their use (e.g., to fund research,

FIGURE 14.22   NFP: Available Funds

purchase equipment, build new learning centres). Restricted funds are funds that have been designated for specific purposes. Although they may appear as a line item in the asset section of the statement of changes in financial position, managers have to be careful—for example, when computing ratios (such as the current ratio)—that such funds are not viewed as part of the organization's current asset base. This is because, although the organization has this money, it does not have the ability to use these dollars in the same way that a for-profit organization can manage its cash, near cash, and current asset base. In the NFP setting, the focus of the analysis is on what is termed "free and clear" available money. Simply put, this can be determined by taking the cash and near-cash assets of the NFP and subtracting any **designated restricted assets** (cash and near cash) in order to determine the true surplus funds available to management for the purpose of responding to the working capital needs of the NFP organization (see Figure 14.22).

Additional commentary in this regard is beyond the scope of this textbook. Just keep in mind that NFPs, although similar in their financial reporting, have significant and unique differences that require managers to assess financial liquidity, solvency, and efficiency from a different perspective. This, coupled with its unique financial mission objective (delivery of community needs versus profitability), results in a different application of the analytical tools needed for evaluating the success of the organization.[5]

Designated Restricted Assets are assets that have been earmarked for a specific purpose and that are not available for managers to support organizational operating needs.

Management Reflection—Keeping Your Finger on the Pulse of the Organization

Imagine trying to manage a business without having any sense of the financial results the organization is realizing. How would we know if the business decisions we are making are effective in achieving the business objectives set forth in our strategic plan? How would we know if top-line revenue is growing, or if profitability improvement initiatives have been successful? How would we know if we will have enough money next month or next quarter to meet the financial obligations that the organization will incur? Herein lies the importance of financial statement analysis. As was pointed out at the beginning of this chapter, managers must be comfortable in preparing, reading, and interpreting financial statements. The ability to do this enables managers to "keep their finger on the pulse" of the organization. Financial statement analysis is what cues managers to changes that are occurring within their organization's operations and with regard to its working capital requirements. Reviewing these statements provides us with tremendous insight into the liquidity, solvency, and financial capacity of an organization. The statement of comprehensive income provides us with crucial information regarding the operation. The statement of changes in financial position provides us with an understanding of the depth and strength of an organization's current financial capabilities, and the statement of cash flows enables us to sense whether the organization is generating or using cash, given its operations and capital asset transactions. Recognizing revenue trends, changes to operating efficiencies and profitability, and the breadth of our capital capacity are but a few of the key takeaways managers can derive as a result of their constant monitoring of the organization's financial statements. Actively monitoring these statements on a monthly, quarterly, and annual basis, as well as assessing comparative trends across operating periods, enables managers to truly understand their overall financial stability and potential.

Although looking at historical data is important, so too is our ability to utilize projected statements (called pro formas) to visualize what is going to happen looking forward. Assessing the results of the organization's financial performance, and proactively anticipating future results via forecasting and budgeting techniques, enables managers to effectively manage the financial needs of the organization and ensure that decisions relating to long-term profitable growth are identified and followed through with. Financial statement analysis should be thought of as a tool that, when mixed with a manager's assessment of the market environment within which the organization is competing, enables decisions to be made that contribute to the growth in the economic value of the organization and help it to achieve its vision and mission.

> Financial statement analysis is what cues managers to changes occurring within the organization's operations and with regard to its working capital requirements.

Appendix—Computation of Ratios

The following offers the computation of the major ratios identified in the ratio analysis segment of this chapter. The ratios identified and illustrated below are some of the most common ones used in interpreting financial statement performance. The calculations shown utilize the CAA Tronics Inc. statements illustrated in the discussion of financial statements within this chapter.

Profitability Ratios

Return on Sales (ROS)   The return on sales ratio identifies to managers the percentage of sales the company has generated that actually represent profit (net income) for the business. Utilizing information from the statement of comprehensive income, the return on sales ratio is calculated as follows:

$$\text{Return on Sales} = \frac{\text{Net Income}}{\text{Net Sales}}$$

If we use CAA Tronics Inc.'s statement of comprehensive income (see Exhibit 14.1), we can calculate its return on sales as follows:

$$\text{CAA Tronics Inc.'s Return on Sales} = \frac{\$2\,925\,000}{\$64\,000\,000} = 4.5\%$$

Another way of looking at this is that for every $1 in sales that CAA Tronics Inc. makes, it puts $0.045 (4.5 cents) in its pocket. The other $0.955 (95.5 cents) is consumed in covering its expenses and tax obligations. If the target for the year were an ROS of 6%, then CAA Tronics Inc. would have fallen short of its objective. Conversely, if the target were an ROS of 3%, then CAA Tronics Inc. would have exceeded its expectations.

Return on Assets (ROA) The return on assets ratio identifies the relationship of net income to the total asset base of the organization. This ratio reflects how productive the deployment of these assets was in producing income for the organization. ROA is calculated as follows:

$$\text{Return on Assets} = \frac{\text{Net Income}}{\text{Total Assets}}$$

Although not shown in the example that follows, return on assets is generally computed using the average total assets of an organization ((beginning assets + ending assets)/2). Sometimes managers and/or investors will add interest expense back into the net income figure in order to get a sense as to the return on assets prior to the cost of borrowing.

Again using CAA Tronics Inc. as an example, the ROA calculation would take the net income figure from the statement of comprehensive income (Exhibit 14.1) and divide it by the value of total assets found on the statement of changes in financial position (Exhibit 14.2):

$$\text{CAA Tronics Inc.'s Return on Assets} = \frac{\$2\,925\,000}{\$54\,900\,000} = 5.3\%$$

This ratio means that for each $1 of assets deployed by this organization, it generated $0.053 (5.3 cents) of net profit for the business. Organizations will then compare this ratio against previously defined targets and against industry standards to determine how effective their utilization of assets is.

The next two ratios, return on equity (ROE) and earnings per share (EPS), relate to the return investors will realize on their investment in the business.

Return on Equity (ROE) The return on equity ratio (ROE) computes the amount of net income that was earned on each dollar of invested capital provided by the business's owners (shareholders). This ratio is computed as follows:

$$\text{Return on Equity} = \frac{\text{Net Income}}{\text{Total Equity}}$$

Referring to CAA Tronics Inc.'s statement of comprehensive income (Exhibit 14.1) and statement of changes in financial position (Exhibit 14.2), the ROE for the current year would be computed as follows:

$$\text{CAA Tronics Inc.'s Return on Equity} = \frac{\$2\,925\,000}{\$18\,100\,000} = 16\%$$

As with the ratios noted above, this means that for each dollar of invested capital provided by owners (shareholders), the company generated $0.16 (16 cents) in net income. This would then be compared against forecast or targeted returns, as well as against the ROEs of competitors, to determine the use of invested capital and the attractiveness of the return when compared to other investment opportunities. Again, although not shown in this example, statement of changes in financial position items (such as total equity), within ratio computations, are often averaged over the period of time for which the calculation is being made.

Earnings per Share (EPS)   This ratio is calculated for corporations where shares have been issued and investors are looking to see what the return on their investment is for each share purchased. The earnings per share ratio reflects the return that individual investors would recognize for each share of stock that they owned. It should be noted that this does not mean that shareholders would actually receive this money, as the organization may not pay these dollars out but will most likely keep them in order to fund future capital needs.

$$\text{Earnings per Share} = \frac{\text{Net Income}}{\text{\# of Shares Outstanding}}$$

Let's assume that CAA Tronics Inc. currently has 8 000 000 shares of stock outstanding. This means that the organization has issued, and investors have purchased, these 8 000 000 shares. Again, using the net income from the statement of comprehensive income (Exhibit 14.1), we can compute the EPS for shareholders of CAA Tronics Inc:

$$\text{CAA Tronics Inc.'s Earnings per Share} = \frac{\$2\,925\,000}{8\,000\,000\text{ shares}} = \$0.365$$

In calculating the EPS for CAA Tronics Inc., we see that shareholders earned $0.365 (36.5 cents) per share. Because shareholders will own different numbers of shares, this is a useful way for an investor to determine the return on his/her individual investment.

Liquidity and Solvency Ratios

Current Ratio   One of the most popular ratios used in measuring the solvency and liquidity position of an organization is the current ratio. This ratio shows the relationship between an organization's current assets and its current liabilities. Remember that current assets are those assets that represent cash, near cash, or items that can be converted to cash in the short term (usually within the current operating period). Current liabilities are the financial obligations the organization must meet in the short term.

$$\text{Current Ratio} = \frac{\text{Current Assets}}{\text{Current Liabilities}}$$

Using CAA Tronics Inc.'s statement of changes in financial position (Exhibit 14.2), we can compute the current ratio for this business:

$$\text{CAA Tronics Inc.'s Current Ratio} = \frac{\$12\,900\,000}{\$5\,800\,000} = 2.22$$

What this means to CAA Tronics Inc.'s management team is that the organization has $2.22 in current assets for each $1.00 it has in current liabilities. For the management team, there is comfort in knowing that the organization has sufficient cash and near-cash resources to meet its current financial obligations. It should be noted, however, that what is an acceptable current ratio will vary by industry and by the length of an organization's business cycle (the length of time it takes to develop, manufacture, distribute, and sell its products/services). In some industries, a current ratio of 1:1 may be acceptable, while in others a much higher current ratio may be required. Maintaining a strong current ratio is a best practice for keeping an organization solvent and for meeting its liquidity needs.

Quick Ratio The quick ratio (also known as the acid test ratio) is a valuable ratio to use when an organization is really concerned about its current liquidity position. The quick ratio looks to remove from the current ratio calculation those assets that are not so easily converted into cash immediately and therefore would take time to generate cash from in the event of a need for immediate cash resources. These remaining assets, referred to as quick assets, are often limited to cash, marketable securities, and accounts receivable. These quick assets are then divided by the total value of current liabilities in order to determine an organization's ability to meet its current obligations strictly from its immediate cash position.

CAA Tronics Inc.'s quick ratio (again, using Exhibit 14.2) would be computed as follows:

$$\text{Quick Ratio} = \frac{\text{Cash} + \text{Marketable Securities} + \text{Accounts Receivable}}{\text{Current Liabilities}}$$

$$\text{CAA Tronics Inc.'s Quick Ratio} = \frac{\$1\,500\,000 + \$2\,000\,000 + \$5\,400\,000}{\$5\,800\,000} = 1.53$$

CAA Tronics Inc.'s quick ratio is 1.53, which means that it has $1.53 of quick assets for each $1.00 of current liabilities. This means that CAA Tronics Inc. is able to cover its short-term obligations from its existing cash and near-cash resources and still have some of these resources left over to meet other financial needs.

Solvency Ratio The solvency ratio is designed to assess the ability of an organization to meet its long-term financial obligations. This ratio takes an organization's net income, adds back depreciation (which is a non-cash transaction, and is found on the statement of comprehensive income; see Exhibit 14.1), and then assesses it against the total value of an organization's liabilities (see Exhibit 14.2).

$$\text{Solvency Ratio} = \frac{\text{Net Income} + \text{Depreciation}}{\text{Total Liabilities}}$$

CAA Tronics Inc.'s solvency ratio would be calculated as follows:

$$\text{CAA Tronics Inc.'s Solvency Ratio} = \frac{\$2\,925\,000 + \$500\,000}{\$36\,800\,000} = .093$$

An acceptable solvency ratio does vary by industry, but a general rule is that the ratio should be equal to or greater than .20. In this case, CAA Tronics Inc.'s solvency ratio is .093, which may indicate to management that the amount of debt that CAA Tronics Inc. has assumed is becoming significant and that additional use of debt may not be the most appropriate form of financing, as these obligations could lead to solvency and/or liquidity issues down the road.

Debt Ratios

Debt to Asset Ratio The debt to asset ratio assesses the relationship between the value of the debt that has been taken on by an organization and the value of its total assets. This lets managers and analysts know how much of the asset base of the organization has been created via debt financing. This identifies the amount of financial leverage the organization has assumed in order to build the company.

$$\text{Debt to Asset Ratio} = \frac{\text{Total Liabilities}}{\text{Total Assets}}$$

In CAA Tronics Inc.'s case, the debt to asset ratio would be calculated as follows (see Exhibit 14.2):

$$\text{CAA Tronics Inc.'s Debt to Asset Ratio} = \frac{\$36\ 800\ 000}{\$54\ 900\ 000} = .67$$

Based on the ratio as calculated above, CAA Tronics Inc.'s debt to asset ratio is .67. This means that for each $1.00 of assets purchased by CAA Tronics Inc., $0.67 (67 cents) was financed via debt. Acceptable debt ratios will vary by industry, but generally speaking, although some debt is acceptable, high debt to asset ratios worry managers and lenders alike. The higher the ratio, the more creditors own the business versus investors, and the more exposure the organization will have to solvency issues given the high costs of servicing such debt. The value of this debt ratio can also be an indicator of the risk attitude of the management team in that higher debt levels can imply a willingness to be more aggressive with respect to risk and a willingness to borrow money to fund business ventures.

Debt to Equity Ratio   The debt to equity ratio assesses the relationship between the amount of debt that has been taken on by an organization and the value of the equity position of its investors (shareholders). Keeping in mind the accounting equation, Assets = Liabilities + Owners' Equity, the debt to equity ratio calculates the amount of money an organization has borrowed in order to fund the creation of its asset base, against the amount of money that investors have provided.

$$\text{Debt to Equity Ratio} = \frac{\text{Total Liabilities}}{\text{Total Equity}}$$

In CAA Tronics Inc.'s case, the debt to equity ratio (also referred to as a leverage ratio) would be calculated as follows (see Exhibit 14.2):

$$\text{CAA Tronics Inc.'s Debt to Equity Ratio} = \frac{\$36\ 800\ 000}{\$18\ 100\ 000} = 2.03$$

Based on the ratio as calculated above, CAA Tronics Inc.'s debt to equity ratio is 2.03. This means that in building its asset base, CAA Tronics Inc. utilized $2.03 of debt financing for each $1.00 of capital provided by investors. In essence, CAA Tronics Inc. was leveraged a bit more than 2 to 1.

Times Interest Earned Ratio   When an organization takes on debt financing, it is promising to the lender that it will repay the lender both the principal borrowed and the interest charge incurred in borrowing the money. If an organization finds itself in unanticipated trouble, the lender's minimum expectation would be that the organization would at least meet its interest obligation on the debt it has taken on. The times interest earned ratio assesses the ability of the business to do just that.

Organizations make such interest payments out of their cash flow, and this obligation is typically budgeted to be taken out of revenues and the profit that is derived from the organization's business operations. The ratio, in essence, lets managers and analysts know if the organization is generating sufficient profit to meet its interest expense obligations. The times interest earned ratio is computed as follows:

$$\text{Times Interest Earned Ratio} = \frac{\text{EBIT (Earnings Before Interest and Taxes)}}{\text{Interest Expense}}$$

In computing the times interest earned ratio for CAA Tronics Inc., we would return to the statement of comprehensive income (Exhibit 14.1) to pick up the required information.

$$\text{CAA Tronics Inc.'s Times Interest Earned Ratio} = \frac{\$5\,700\,000}{\$1\,800\,000} = 3.16$$

The times interest earned ratio indicates that CAA Tronics Inc. can meet its current interest expense payments on its debt 3.16 times from the income that it is generating from its operations. The higher the number associated with this ratio, the more comfortable lenders are that at least the interest obligation associated with the debt will be paid. A low or negative number in this ratio could raise concerns about the organization's solvency position and its ability to service its debt.

Activity Ratios

Days Receivable The number of days it takes to convert accounts receivable to cash is an important piece of information for managers to understand. The ability to convert dollars owed to an organization into cash has a definite impact on the company's cash flow and cash operating cycle. Computing this ratio involves a two-step process. The first step is to calculate the average daily sales by an organization. This is accomplished as follows:

$$\text{Average Day's Sales} = \frac{\text{Net Annual Sales}}{365 \text{ Days}}$$

Once the average day's sales is computed, this number is then divided into the current amount of accounts receivable to determine an average collection period, which is called the days receivable:

$$\text{Days Receivable} = \frac{\text{Accounts Receivable}}{\text{Average Day's Sales}}$$

Using CAA Tronics Inc. as an example (see Exhibits 14.1 and 14.2), we can compute this as follows:

$$\text{CAA Tronics Inc.'s Average Day's Sales} = \frac{\$64\,000\,000}{365 \text{ Days}} = \$175\,342$$

The average day's sales have been computed to be $175 342. This number is then divided into the accounts receivable (shown on the statement of changes in financial position, Exhibit 14.2) to determine how many days it takes, on average, for accounts receivable to be collected from our customers:

$$\text{CAA Tronics Inc.'s Days Receivable} = \frac{\$5\,400\,000}{\$175\,342} = 30.79 \text{ days}$$

On average, it takes CAA Tronics Inc. 30.79 days to turn a dollar of receivables into cash. The organization would then benchmark this against its established policy, and measure it over time to ensure that the organization was not seeing an unnecessary lengthening of this period of time. Allowing the number of days receivable to increase could put short-term pressure on the organization's liquidity, as it would lengthen the cash operating cycle (cash-to-cash cycle) and require CAA Tronics Inc. to use more of its own cash to fund its operations until repayment is provided. Managers can perform the same type of calculation on key customer accounts to ensure that such customers are paying on time and there is not too much trade credit being lent to customers, thereby minimizing the risk of default. Companies desiring to speed up the payment process often provide slight discounts on invoice amounts to get customers to pay quickly (within 10 days), thereby improving the company's cash operating cycle.

Inventory Turnover The ability of a company to turn its inventory into cash is an important activity ratio to measure. Inventory represents products that have been paid for (either purchased as a finished good or manufactured) but have yet to be sold by the company and converted into sales revenue. The longer the inventory remains unsold, the greater the concern that the company will not be able to get its full selling price for it. Also, the longer it remains unsold, the greater the strain it places on the organization's cash flow. Managers therefore look to closely monitor the number of days products sit in inventory and the number of times the inventory is turned over in a given period. Two ratios that assist in assessing the financial aspects of inventory management are as follows:

$$\text{Inventory Turnover} = \frac{\text{Cost of Goods Sold}}{\text{Average Inventory}}$$

Let's assume that the cost of goods sold for CAA Tronics Inc. is as shown on its statement of comprehensive income (Exhibit 14.1), or $49 500 000. Let's also assume that the average value of inventory for the current period is $4 000 000. The inventory turnover ratio would be computed as follows:

$$\text{CAA Tronics Inc.'s Inventory Turnover} = \frac{\$49\,500\,000}{\$4\,000\,000} = 12.37 \text{ times}$$

This means that CAA Tronics Inc. is turning its inventory over 12.37 times, or a bit more than once per month. In fact, we can compute the actual number of days that the organization's products sit in inventory by conducting the following calculation:

$$\text{Day's Inventory} = \frac{365}{\text{Inventory Turnover}}$$

In CAA Tronics Inc.'s situation, this would be computed as follows:

$$\text{CAA Tronic Inc.'s Day's Inventory} = \frac{365}{12.37} = 29.50 \text{ days}$$

Chapter Summary

The focus of this chapter is to familiarize students with the importance of a manager's ability to analyze and interpret an organization's financial position. This is essential to making good decisions pertaining to how, and where, to deploy the organization's assets and financial resources. In support of this, the chapter provides students with an overview of the types of financial transactions that occur within an organization. The concepts of liquidity, solvency, efficiency, and capacity are also discussed as an essential part of assessing the financial condition of the organization and its ability to provide the necessary capital resources in support of its strategic plan. The chapter then provides an overview of the core components of the three primary financial statements—the statement of comprehensive income, statement of changes in financial position, and statement of cash flows—that managers analyze and interpret as a means for keeping their finger on the pulse of the organization. A further discussion is provided relating to the key ratios that managers calculate from the information presented on these financial statements, thereby enabling managers to draw conclusions relating to profitability, solvency, leverage, and operational efficiency. The use of trend and/or comparative analysis as a key component of this ratio analysis process is also discussed, as is the value in including absolute analysis as a core part of this managerial assessment approach. The importance of sales forecasting and budgeting forms part of this discussion as well. The chapter closes off with a note pertaining to a cursory overview of the differences between financial analyses of not-for-profit organizations and for-profit entities.

Developing Business Knowledge and Skills

Key Terms

gross profit margin *p. 542*

profitability margin *p. 542*

operational transactions *p. 542*

capital asset transactions *p. 543*

Statement of Comprehensive
   Income *p. 547*

Statement of Changes in Financial
   Position *p. 551*

assets *p. 551*

liabilities *p. 552*

owners' equity *p. 552*

retained earnings *p. 553*

Statement of Cash Flows *p. 556*

net change in cash position *p. 560*

ratios *p. 561*

profitability ratios *p. 561*

solvency and liquidity ratios *p. 562*

debt ratios *p. 562*

activity ratios *p. 562*

leverage *p. 564*

forecasting and budgeting *p. 571*

designated restricted assets *p. 574*

Questions for Discussion

1. What are the two fundamental types of business transactions? How are they interconnected and how can each type of transaction affect the other? (LO2)

2. What is the difference between solvency and financial capacity? How are the two interrelated? (LO3)

3. Which is more relevant in determining a company's well-being: activity ratios or solvency ratios? (LO4)

4. What are the advantages and disadvantages, to a business, of taking on additional leverage? (LO4)

5. Which is more relevant in interpreting and analyzing a company's financial position, ratio analysis or absolute analysis? What is the difference between the two? (LO5)

6. Why are forecasting and budgeting so important? What is the difference between the two? (LO6)

7. How is managing the financial resources of a not-for-profit organization different from overseeing a for-profit entity? In your mind, which is the more difficult to manage?

Questions for Individual Action

Situation I—Statement of Comprehensive Income Analysis

You have been recently assigned to the management team of the Econ Corporation, a manufacturer of external flash memory components. Senior management has asked you to prepare a projected (pro forma) statement of comprehensive income (income statement) for its core product, which it calls "SST." In discussing the release of this product, discussions with R&D, marketing, and operations have resulted in the following projections and cost estimates.

Revenue Projection	
Estimated Unit Sales (Demand)*	1 250 000 units
Selling Price per Unit	$36.00
Product Costs (COGS)	
Material Costs per Unit	$17.41
Labour Costs per Unit	$10.60
Inventory Carrying Costs per Unit**	$ 0.05
Operating Expenses	
Depreciation Expense	$ 1 133 000
R&D Expense	$ 850 000
Promotion Expense	$1 500 000
Sales Expense	$1 275 000
Administration Expense	768 000
Interest Expense Obligations	
Short-Term Interest Expense	$ 315 000
Long-Term Interest Expense	$ 684 000
Corporate Tax Rate	30%

*As SST has just been revised, the current inventory on hand is "0." All units must be manufactured.
**Inventory carrying costs is the cost for warehousing and shipping of units and is, therefore, applied against each unit.

Questions

1. Based on the information provided above, prepare a projected (pro forma) statement of comprehensive income for the component line "SST." Based on your projections, what is the anticipated **Net Income** for this product line?

2. Assume that Econ Corporation has 2 000 000 shares of stock outstanding. What is the projected **EPS** for Econ Corporation?

3. Assume that competitive pressures force you to reduce your selling price per unit by 10% ($32.40).

   a. What is the revised projected **Net Income** given this price reduction?

   b. What is the change to **Gross Profit Margin on a percentage basis**?

4. Go back to the original selling price of $36.00. Assuming that labour costs increase by 5% and that material costs increase by 3%, what is the revised projected **Net Income** in this situation?

Situation II—Statement of Cash Flows Analysis

The ABC Corporation is looking to assess the movement of cash flow within the corporation's recently completed fiscal year. A summary of the transactions that occurred is as follows:

- Net income for the current year totalled $2 500 000.

- Depreciation expense in the current year was valued at $500 000.

- Other non-cash items (such as changes to the levels of accounts payable and accounts receivable) netted out to be $100 000.

- An $11 000 000 investment in new plant and equipment was made in the current year.

- A $10 000 000 ten-year bond was issued in the current year.

- ABC Corporation repurchased 100 000 shares of company stock at $25.00 per share.

- Principal repayment on the 5-year note and 20-year mortgage totalled $1 200 000.

- The ABC Corporation's beginning cash balance was $2 200 000.

Questions

5. Prepare a summary statement of cash flows for the ABC Corporation.

   a. Identify its **Net Change in Cash Position** for the period.

   b. What **financial statement** will then be adjusted to reflect this change?

Team Exercise

As a team, go online and obtain the most recent annual reports for Nordstrom, Macy's, HBC, and TJX. Conduct an absolute analysis of these companies' statements of changes in financial position. Based on your analysis, which of these companies is best positioned to move forward in the retail department store market sector? What types of business decisions will these organizations have to make, and be able to make, as a result of your findings? Prepare a presentation of your research and analysis.

Comprehensive Exercise—Chapters 13 and 14

IGES Inc. and the "Enviro-Seal" Decision

IGES Inc. is considering the launch of a new product called "Enviro-Seal." Enviro-Seal is an innovative product, designed to meet and exceed the high temperature seal requirements necessary to comply with new North American regulations relating to emission control of very hot exhaust gases. The product is innovative in that its unique patent design provides a level of gas containment never before seen and will enable manufacturers to improve both their environmentally friendly marketing efforts and contribute positively to societal concerns regarding the release of carbon monoxide into the air. To date, all major automotive manufacturers have expressed an interest in obtaining access to this new product. General Motors is particularly interested, and has asked to meet with IGES Inc. to hopefully negotiate a deal for exclusive rights to the product. For Meshal Alanbar, CEO of IGES Inc., a key decision will be the price at which IGES Inc. will initially offer the product.

General Motors has indicated that higher prices will result in a lower order volume, as lower-end vehicle models, whose price points result in lower margins for manufacturers, can use a cheaper version of the Enviro-Seal product offered by two competitors. These cheaper versions will also meet North American regulations for the next two to three years. They do, however, result in more frequent repair issues, which historically have impacted the overall quality rating of the associated vehicles. A lower price for IGES's Enviro-Seal product could result in an expanded opportunity to move this product into the low end, in addition to generating the high-end market opportunity upon which the initial contract with General Motors could be executed.

Meshal has just wrapped up a meeting with his marketing and operations team assigned to the Enviro-Seal product. Based on marketing research, production analysis, and discussions with manufacturing representatives of the various automobile manufacturers, his team has presented the following to him in consideration of a final pricing decision.

Price per Unit	$250	$350	$400	$450
Projected Unit Sales	125 000	85 000	65 000	45 000

In addition, the following costs were presented to Meshal by his team:

Per unit manufacturing costs: $185.00
Selling, general and administrative (SG&A) support costs: $5 000 000
Required base-level tool and die costs, regardless of volume level: $1 500 000

Additional fixed tool and die costs required, which are based on volume, and supplemental to base-level tool and die costs are listed below. (Be sure to take these into consideration in your calculations, and to their related price points.)

Projected Sales Volume in Units	Additional Fixed Tooling Costs
125 000	$6 750 000
85 000	$4 500 000
65 000	$2 250 000
45 000	$2 250 000

1. Which price point yields the highest net operating margin (EBIT)?

   a. $250.00

   b. $350.00

   c. $400.00

   d. $450.00

   e. All prices yield a negative net operating margin (EBIT)

2. What is the **breakeven point (BEP), in units,** at a price of **$250.00**?

   a. 120 000

   b. 203 846

   c. 121 039

   d. 95 364

   e. 172 388

3. What is the **breakeven point (BEP), in dollars ($$$),** at a price of **$400.00**?

   a. 13 292 996

   b. 11 917 858

   c. 16 279 070

   d. 40 108 018

   e. 10 027 044

4. Assume that GM is willing to order **125 000** units. What is the **optimal price point (OPP)** required to ensure all applicable costs are covered and a profit (EBIT) of $3 000 000 is realized?

   a. $292.26

   b. $315.00

   c. $248.51

   d. $135.42

   e. $304.76

5. Assume that IGES Inc. will incur long-term debt of $4 000 000 in ramping up this product line. This credit facility will require an annual interest payment of $320 000, plus an annual debt principal repayment of $400 000. What is the new **optimal price point (OPP)**, at an order level of **125 000** units, that is needed to cover these additional annual expenditures (interest and annual debt principal repayment), all applicable operational costs, as well as return the previously mentioned profit (EBIT) of $3 000 000 to IGES Inc.?

   a. $320.76

   b. $356.69

   c. $254.51

   d. $310.76

   e. $298.26

6. Assume per unit manufacturing costs are increased by 10% to **$203.50** due to an unanticipated increase in material costs associated with the Enviro-Seal product. Competitive pressures result in IGES Inc. having to hold its price at **$250.00** per unit. What is the new **breakeven point (BEP)** in units for this product?

   a. 130 062

   b. 235 113

   c. 165 079

   d. 284 946

   e. 194 396

7. Using the revised per unit manufacturing cost of **$203.50**, what is the impact to net operating margin (EBIT) at a price point of **$400.00** and a projected sales volume of **65 000 units**, assuming all other costs remain unchanged (as per the initial assumptions)?

   a. No impact; net operating margin (EBIT) is unchanged

   b. Net operating margin (EBIT) increases by $1 202 500

   c. Net operating margin (EBIT) decreases by $1 202 500

   d. Net operating margin (EBIT) increases by $3 025 000

   e. Net operating margin (EBIT) decreases by $3 025 000

8. Assume your operations management team has developed a new process that will enable you to drop per unit manufacturing costs by 15% to **$157.25**. At a selling price of **$250**, and a projected sales volume of **125 000 units**, and assuming all other costs remain unchanged (as per the initial assumptions), what is the revised net operating margin (EBIT)?

   a. ($1 656 250)

   b. $1 656 250

   c. 3 202 800

   d. $6 452 800

   e. $4 952 800

9. Again, assume your operations management team has developed a new process that will enable you to drop per unit manufacturing costs by 15% to **$157.25**. At a selling price of **$250**, and assuming all other costs remain unchanged (as per the initial assumptions), what is the new **breakeven point (BEP) in units** for the Enviro-Seal product?

   a. 142 857

   b. 194 394

   c. 86 442

   d. 52 389

   e. 68 106

10. Assume that General Motors is willing to order **125 000** units. What is the optimal price point (OPP) required to ensure a profit (EBIT) of $3 000 000, given the reduction in per unit manufacturing costs to **$157.25** noted in question #8.

   a. $196.79

   b. $223.31

   c. $323.26

   d. $287.25

   e. $248.31

Answers: 1-c, 2-b, 3-c, 4-b, 5-a, 6-d, 7-c, 8-a, 9-a, 10-d

Case for Discussion

FLF Corporation

Based on the information provided, respond to the six questions asked about these financial statements.

FLF Corporation Comparative Statement of Comprehensive Income				
In Millions	2018-12-31	2017-12-31	2016-12-31	2015-12-31
Total revenue	7 208.77	7 691.64	7 175.96	6 128.84
Cost of goods sold	4 214.37	4 027.56	3 715.06	3 316.87
Gross profit	2 994.40	3 664.08	3 460.90	2 811.97
Selling/general/admin. expenses, total	1 410.84	1 537.95	1 367.14	1 073.21
Depreciation/amortization	778.24	700.33	629.63	560.63
Interest expense (income)	1 220.83	998.68	46.07	45.00
Other operating expenses, total	9.65	217.29	86.02	90.00
Total operating expense	3 419.56	3 454.25	2 128.86	1 768.84
Operating income	−425.16	209.83	1 332.04	1 043.13
Other income, net	87.94	4.44	15.04	18.43
Income before tax	−337.22	214.27	1 347.08	1 061.56
Income after tax	−337.22	171.42	943.02	743.09
Net income	−337.22	171.42	943.02	743.09

With respect to the statement of comprehensive income for the FLF Corporation, respond to the following:

1. Compute the gross profit margin percentage for the FLF Corporation for each of the four years shown. Has the gross profit margin percentage improved or deteriorated over the past three years? Explain what you think might be causing the changes observed.

2. Looking at the last four years, identify three other concerns that you would have about this organization's current operational performance. You may want to conduct some additional (profitability) ratio analyses to aid in your discussion.

FLF Corporation Statement of Changes in Financial Position				
In Millions	2018-12-31	2017-12-31	2016-12-31	2012-12-31
Cash and equivalents	295.64	416.12	452.94	377.93
Accounts receivable	459.07	519.29	481.38	463.30
Inventory	111.50	126.94	118.46	111.83
Total Current Assets	866.21	1 062.35	1 052.78	953.06
Property/plant	20 098.72	20 237.22	20 037.09	18 916.75
Goodwill, net	86.35	1 262.92	1 300.75	1 314.56
Intangibles, net	347.21	362.10	367.20	377.48

Equipment	4 642.86	2 482.73	1 280.69	931.15
Total non-current assets	25 175.14	24 334.97	22 985.73	21 539.94
Total Assets	**26 041.35**	**25 407.32**	**24 038.51**	**22 493.00**
Accounts payable	1 773.67	1 226.28	1 006.06	265.60
Notes payable/short-term debt	1 047.61	0.00	0.00	0.00
Total Current Liabilities	**2 821.28**	**1 226.28**	**1 006.06**	**265.60**
Long-term debt	12 856.58	11 175.23	12 994.87	12 355.43
Total Liabilities	**15 677.86**	**12 401.51**	**14 000.93**	**12 621.03**
Common stock	4 018.41	3 951.16	2 806.64	2 586.59
Retained earnings	6 345.08	9 054.65	7 230.94	7 285.38
Total Equity	**10 363.49**	**13 005.81**	**10 037.58**	**9 871.97**
Total Liabilities and Shareholders' Equity	**26 041.35**	**25 407.32**	**24 038.51**	**22 493.00**

With respect to the statement of changes in financial position for the FLF Corporation, respond to the following:

3. Compute the current ratio for the FLF Corporation for each of the four years shown. What has happened? What are the implications of these results for FLF?

4. Identify and explain the two things about the FLF Corporation's current financial position that concern you the most.

Using both statements...

5. Compute the solvency ratio and the times interest earned ratio for the FLF Corporation for each of the four years shown. What has happened? Again, what are the implications of this result for FLF?

6. Assume that you are a member of the board of directors of the FLF Corporation and that you have just reviewed these two statements. Identify three questions that you would ask the management team to respond to.

CHAPTER 15

Analyzing New Business Ventures

LEARNING OBJECTIVES

This chapter is designed to provide students with:

LO1	An understanding of the six phases of analysis associated with assessing business venture viability
LO2	An appreciation for the depth and scope of analysis required to fully understand a venture's market, operations, and financial risks
LO3	A recognition of the importance of assessing the estimated operational capacity of a new business against its projected revenue streams in order to validate the venture's capability of achieving its revenue objectives
LO4	An exposure to the entrepreneurial/managerial team characteristics required to successfully lead a new venture
LO5	An understanding of the personal challenges associated with starting a new business
LO6	An overview of the assessment and purchase process associated with acquiring an existing business

Snapshot

What to Expect in This Chapter

As identified by the learning objectives, this chapter focuses on exposing students to the basics associated with analyzing business ventures and new business opportunities. The content emphasized in this chapter includes the following:

- Analyzing Business Ventures
  - Market Analysis
  - Value Analysis
  - Financial Analysis
  - Operations Analysis
  - Management Competency Analysis
  - Contingency Plans or Exit Options
- Reality Check—The Perils of Starting a New Business
- Acquiring an Existing Business
  - Case Study—So You Want to Buy a Small Business
- A Note Pertaining to Not-for-Profits
- Management Reflection—The "Go or No Go" Decision

Business IN ACTION

Vanhawks—The Challenges of Commercializing a Great Idea

Back in 2011 Sohaib Zahid and Adil Aftab knew they wanted to start a business together, they just did not know what it was going to be. Zahid had developed a novel approach to the design of sports helmets through his sports medicine research, and Aftab had introduced carbon fibre to his existing wooden field hockey stick manufacturing business, Dita field hockey. An avid cyclist, Zahid soon recognized that in this world of increasingly interconnected transportation industries, the pedal-powered bicycle was one that had remained stuck in the past. So Zahid and Aftab set to work turning their idea of reinvigorating the archaic bicycle industry into action. Their focus? The creation of a cylindrical carbon fibre structure that would enable them to construct a lighter, stronger, and cheaper bicycle frame. Zahid also contacted his younger brother, Ali, and his friend, Niv Yahel, both technology gurus, to integrate sensor technologies into the bicycle frame and design an intuitive mobile application capable of collecting and storing the data

Used by permission of VanHawks

gathered by the sensors. The end result of this marriage of material and technology innovation was the creation of Toronto-based Vanhawks.

Their flagship product, the Valour, was marketed as the first ever connected urban commuter bicycle, which uses Bluetooth technology to sync the bicycle's data-gathering sensors to the Vanhawks mobile application. Users were to enter their destination into the app, which would then determine the quickest and safest route. This information was then synced with the bicycle, providing turn-by-turn navigation from LED lights built into the handlebars. Other features included handlebar vibration blind spot detection and ride metrics (speed, distance, calories burned, time).

The Vanhawks "smart" bicycle was and is a great idea—but, as many entrepreneurs are aware, having a good idea is not always a ticket to success, as demonstrated by the fact that 50% of new ventures fail within the first three years. Venture capitalists often comment that successful ventures start with great ideas, but a core understanding of market dynamics coupled with sufficient capital and experienced leadership are required ingredients for success. The Vanhawks team brought to the market what was felt to be a solution to a legitimate need and demonstrated the necessary visionary leadership at the onset of the business in entering this market. First, the Vanhawks team recognized the importance of capital, leveraging new external funding opportunities such as attaining $50 000 from start-up accelerator FounderFuel and using it to undertake the most successful Canadian Kickstarter crowdfunding campaign at the time, receiving $820 083 in 30 days. Second, the Vanhawks team understood the ever-increasing significance of operating efficiencies and quality adherence in the globalized business environment. They attempted to build out an operating model focused on keeping manufacturing costs low while preserving quality by leveraging their proprietary carbon manufacturing process, which they developed through partnerships with industry-leading bicycle and carbon fibre manufacturers in China and Taiwan. Their marketing campaign focused on demonstrating the critical importance of communicating the value of their product to the consumer through effective targeting, branding, and positioning, all the way down to their product names. For example, the Valour smart bike is intended to exemplify the Vanhawks mission of fighting against the personal transportation commute status quo. Zahid, at the time, described the Vanhawks organization primarily as a marketing company, whose role is not only to communicate the value of their smart bicycle, but also to connect with the customer on a deeper level by providing a memorable user experience. Finally, the Vanhawks team understood the significance of having a long-term vision. Their goal was to get enough Valours on the road to form a mesh network of users, with their embedded sensors providing route optimizations in real time. Through this online community, users would be able to tap in to data on potholes, closed roads,

Used by permission of VanHawks

and blocked lanes collected by other Valour riders to choose safer and smarter routes. Moreover, if one's Valour was stolen and another user happened to pass it by, a notification would be sent via the Vanhawks mobile app to alert the original owner of the bike's location. All this represented why the Vanhawks founders felt they had created more than just a bicycle company; they viewed themselves as an innovation company actively striving to revolutionize, or at least disrupt, the urban commute.

In continuing its quest, in spring 2015 Vanhawks was successful in raising an additional $1.6 million in venture capital funding essential to its strategy of penetrating European markets, where cycling is a popular mode of transportation. During this start-up phase they also looked to capitalize on what they viewed as an increasing adoption of cycling in North American cities.

So where is Vanhawks today? The company is still producing bikes, but the approach to the market and the structure of the company has changed considerably. Penetrating an existing market with established rivals is, by itself, a real

Used by permission of VanHawks

challenge for any entrepreneur. A value-added play that heightens the price point and looks to have potential purchasers rethink the way they perceive the product's use further adds to this challenge. Did Vanhawks fully understand the market? Perhaps, but the conversion of riders to this new concept will take time, and time requires money. In 2016, facing financial difficulty and struggling to deliver on the broader ecosystem it was trying to create, the company ran out of money. The idea of shaking up the bicycle industry via their broader ecosystem vision simply did not fully materialize. The perceived value of the disruption that they felt they brought to this market was not recognized or adopted by the scale of riders required for sustainable success. Does this mean that Vanhawks no longer exists? The company did shut down for a period of time in 2016, but Zahid's passion for the product lived on. The company was resurrected in 2017, rebuilding itself around an offline-online hybrid sales model, which enabled it to leverage experienced bicycle retail specialists and partners to sell its product (something the original solely online sales model did not do), and revamping the

ecosystem value proposition. This led to the company being acquired in 2017 by Concord, Ontario-based Warren Industries. Vanhawks now operates as a separate subsidiary of Warren Industries, and continues to build upon its new-found life and success. Warren Industries provides Vanhawks with those key additional ingredients required when one needs to truly build a sustainable business model—resources, insights, technology support, and operational experience.

This start-up still visualizes itself as evolving to become the operating system provider for the bicycle industry (think of them as the "android operating system" for this new emerging technology use). By rethinking the interface and the urban cycling experience beyond just the bike itself, Vanhawks sees itself as a best solution to an increasing number of bicycle users in cities around the globe. With Warren Industries supporting this vision, Zahid feels that Vanhawks remains poised to experience explosive growth. To date, Vanhawk bikes have riders in over 42 countries and have sold more than 1000 units (with an average selling price of $1500 per unit).

Chapter Overview

The purpose of this chapter is to synthesize the learning that has occurred over the first 14 chapters in this book. As managers or business owners, our core responsibilities lie with managing our business across three key areas: marketing, finance, and operations (see Figure 15.1), and building a business model that enables us to best meet the needs of our customers, thereby ensuring the sustainability of the business operation.

As discussed in Chapter 7, many of us have had aspirations of creating and growing our own business. In this regard Chapter 7 introduced concepts and fundamentals relating to entrepreneurship, the concept of business risk, and some ways to

FIGURE 15.1   **Three Key Areas of Business Management**

mitigate such risk. This chapter builds upon these concepts, as well as the models and tactics associated with marketing, finance, and operations. The chapter does this by presenting a working model for the assessment of a business venture— whether it be a new venture, expansion of an existing one, or the potential purchase of a going concern (business). It is hoped that in ending this book with this focus you will recognize how all of the fundamental concepts presented in the book come together, and that the skill set developed from this textbook and your course has successfully enhanced your understanding of business in a way that would enable you to effectively manage an upstart or existing business operation.

<table>
<tr><td>

LO1, LO2, LO3, LO4

Entrepreneur refers to a person who starts a business and is willing to accept the risk associated with investing money in order to make money.

</td></tr>
</table>

Analyzing Business Ventures

One of the most important skills a manager or **entrepreneur** can learn is how to analyze a business venture. Whether it is a new business opportunity or the expansion of an existing business's market space, the ability to assess the financial, operations, and market risk associated with such a venture is critical to the overall evaluation process. Recognizing that some level of risk will always exist, the analytical process associated with business ventures can be best thought of as a methodology for recognizing the degree of risk a potential business opportunity faces, and then, given this risk, assigning a "go or no go" to the project. This analytical process can best be described as a six-phase approach (see Figure 15.2), with each phase designed to assist in solidifying the final decision concerning the viability of the opportunity being assessed.

The six phases associated with venture analysis are as follows:

1. Market analysis
2. Value analysis
3. Financial analysis
4. Operations analysis
5. Management competency analysis
6. Contingency plans or exit options

A key emphasis within each of these areas is to try to define the certainty and therefore the probability of success of the venture in what is often a very uncertain and risk-laden environment. A key to this assessment approach lies in the search for and identification of "fatal flaws" that could potentially derail a venture in its early stages. Examples of fatal flaws can be inadequate pricing models, undercapitalization, weak

FIGURE 15.2   **Venture Assessment Fishbone Diagram**

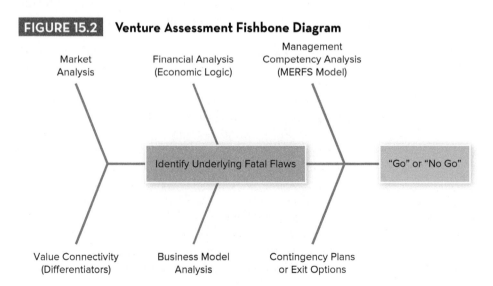

FIGURE 15.3 **Fatal Flaw Analysis**

management competencies, insufficient marketing research initiatives, poor understanding of industry configuration and market segmentation, or the absence of a
well-focused execution strategy (see Figure 15.3).[1] Identifying and understanding such
fatal flaws enables managers to determine whether such barriers can be overcome and
whether the risk associated with these barriers results in too much uncertainty to move
forward with the venture. The remainder of this chapter focuses on placing risk into
perspective and outlining the key analytical approach required within each of the
phases identified above, thereby providing managers and entrepreneurs with a blueprint for assessing the risk and potential success of a business opportunity.[2]

> A key to this assessment approach lies in the search for and identification of
> "fatal flaws" that could potentially derail a venture in its early stages.

Market Analysis

Market analysis is focused on the assessment of the risk and uncertainty associated
with entry into the targeted market space. In this assessment phase we are looking
to draw credible conclusions to the validity that the proposed plan will achieve the
market penetration anticipated and will obtain sufficient market reach and scale to
ensure the successful sustainability of the organization. Key success factors can
vary depending upon whether we are creating new market space as a first mover,
looking to compete as a new entrant in an existing market, or launching a product
line extension, thereby leveraging existing market competencies (see Figure 15.4).

Market analysis is all about assessing the legitimacy of the perceived opportunity
that the manager or entrepreneur sees for the organization. To legitimize this opportunity, we need to assess it in four ways (see Figure 15.5). First, we need to analyze the
current market environment. Is it the right time to enter into the market? Is the market's direction clear enough to ensure the sustainability of the venture, particularly in
the early stages? Does our PESTEL analysis reveal any significant barriers or

FIGURE 15.4   Market Analysis: Key Success Factors

First Mover—New Market	New Entrant—Existing Market	Extension—Existing Market
• Need/demand identification and alignment • Profile of need solution and company • Proper deployment of capital • Driver of the consumer adoption process	• Innovation • Superior customer relationship model to target market • Disruption of consumer adoption process • Proper deployment of capital in support of the business initiative	• New revenue generation opportunity • Degree of cannibalization • Validation of segmentation stretch opportunity • Degree of channel involvement in demand stimulation • Strength of brand extension • Proper deployment of capital

FIGURE 15.5   Four Key Metrics for Market Analysis

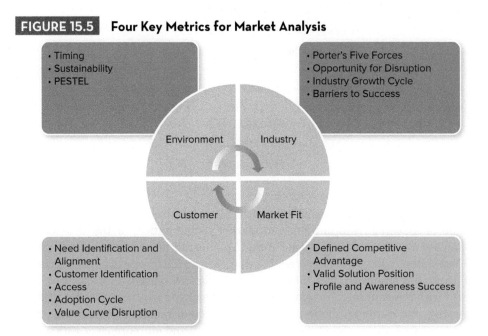

concerns that could impact our ability to succeed? Second, we need to look at the market sector or industry within which we will be competing. An assessment via Porter's Five Forces, coupled with a solid company-focused SWOT analysis and well-researched competitive analysis, should enable us to sense the overall future growth potential of the industry, and enable us to draw conclusions as to our overall company strength in comparison to that of our competitors. Third, we need to draw conclusions relating to the actual customers we hope to attract. What is the primary market for our product and/or service? Is the size of the segment we plan to attack large enough to achieve operational stability? Do we fully understand the profile of the customer we hope to acquire? What is the current adoption process for products and/or services such as ours? Do we really have a disruptive innovation that will lead customers to change their predetermined purchase order? Finally, can we conclude a true market fit? Do we feel that the products and/or services being offered provide a valid solution to the "pain" it is attempting to respond to? Will the proposed communication strategy deliver on the profile, awareness, and preference requirements that need to be achieved in order for our business to be successful? Can we conclude a definitive competitive advantage that we can build our positioning around?

Market analysis is all about assessing the legitimacy of the perceived opportunity that the manager or entrepreneur sees for the organization.

Business IN ACTION

Disney—Recognizing a Market Shift and Opportunity

Although much of this chapter is devoted to the development of a new business venture, existing companies, in assessing their current business models and market position, continuously look for new opportunities to grow their businesses. A critical component of this assessment lies in their ability to recognize disruptive changes in market demand and customer behaviour. The Walt Disney Company is doing this very thing. Disney, an entertainment powerhouse and the owner of ABC, ESPN, Marvel Entertainment, Lucasfilm, and Pixar in addition to its Disney-branded franchise (theme parks, Walt Disney Studios, etc.), recognizes the changes taking place in the way that you and I seek video-based entertainment. This is why in April 2019 Disney announced its intent to create a family-friendly streaming service (Disney+) in a bid to challenge Netflix's market-leader position. Disney recognizes that cable-based paid television, around which its ABC, ESPN, and related-network franchises are built, is seeing a slowing of consumer adoption as viewers, particularly millennials, shift to video-streaming options. In fact, 2018 marked a significant change in the entertainment sector as streaming services passed traditional pay TV services in terms of share of households in the United States.

Disney's ad-free, subscription-based service, anticipated to launch in November 2019, has been established with an initial monthly price of $7.50, or $70.00 for an annual subscription, well below

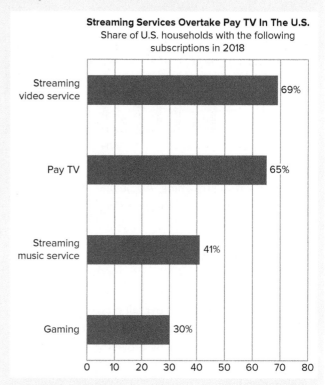

Streaming Services Overtake Pay TV In The U.S.
Share of U.S. households with the following subscriptions in 2018

Streaming video service	69%
Pay TV	65%
Streaming music service	41%
Gaming	30%

Netflix's current pricing structure of $8.99 to $15.99 (depending on the level of subscription purchased). Disney is investing a reported $1 billion+ in the development of its streaming service and supporting original programming and has set a target of 60 million to 90 million subscribers by the end of 2024. Although most definitely a force to be reckoned with, Disney does have to play catch-up to first-mover and industry leader Netflix. Now firmly established not only in the North American market but also internationally, Netflix's customer base continues to grow and the quality of its original programming, a core key to its success, continues to improve. To put things in perspective, Disney's initial foray into video streaming, Hulu, has a subscriber base of an estimated 25 million users and is expected to lose approximately $1.5 billion in fiscal year 2019. Netflix, which has been in existence now for 12+ years, has an estimated 139 million subscribers globally. Disney is not alone in its desire to penetrate what is clearly a market behavioural

canbedone/Shutterstock.com

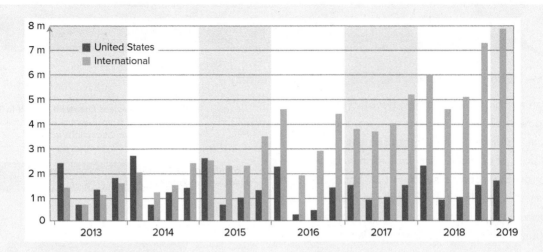

switch to video streaming. Apple and WarnerMedia both plan to launch video-streaming services in the upcoming near term.

An interesting twist to the story is the fact that Disney, up to the time of this writing, has been supplying Netflix with content (and receiving a licensing fee for it), thereby supporting its overall growth and market dominance. As part of its announcement, Disney indicated it no longer will be providing content to Netflix, giving up an estimated $150 million annually in licensing fees.

Disney understands that the critical component of the race for video-streaming customers lies in the ability to provide a wide breadth of content supported by quality original programming. It is here where Disney sees its competitive advantage. Backed by the largest "content vault" in the world, Disney's ability to supply hours upon hours of content is endless. In addition to its own content, in 2018 Disney purchased 21st Century Fox, gaining ownership of critically acclaimed movies such as *Avatar*. The company has also entered into agreements with Roku Inc. and Sony Corp. to distribute Disney content on streaming devices and gaming systems. The race is on, and it's one that Disney—backed by mega-titles such as *Star Wars, Monsters, Inc., Frozen, The Lion King, Black Panther*, and the Marvel Universe—intends to win.

Value Analysis

Although identified as a separate phase, the value analysis phase is closely integrated with the market analysis phase. In fact, the value analysis is really about fully understanding "market fit" and validating that we do have a definitive competitive advantage or uniqueness around which we can develop a positioning campaign. The ability to fully develop and communicate why your product and/or service is unique, why it is important in solving the target market's problems, and what its underlying value proposition strengths are will ultimately determine if customers will indeed adopt it. In short, we are really attempting to draw three conclusions from our value analysis:

1 Does the business plan demonstrate that we can create a customer habit of purchasing our product and/or service?

2 Does the business plan demonstrate that we can build an association with our targeted customer base and that our product and/or service provides a credible solution to their needs?

3 Does the business plan demonstrate that we can get customers to care more about our products and/or services than those of our competitors?

FIGURE 15.6	Value Analysis Litmus Test
Litmus Test Component	**Key Outcome**
Value Proposition	What is it? What makes it unique? Where is the value?
Target Market	Who is the primary target market? What does the target market look like? Do we understand the connection between the target market and the value proposition?
Customer Profile	How does the customer behave? Are there any unique characteristics we can leverage?
Key Decision Criteria	Why does this customer buy? Where is the decision-making weight placed? Is the value proposition properly aligned to this?
Target Message Development	What do we plan to say to catch and hold this customer's attention?
Communication Delivery	What is the plan for reaching the customer? Does this fit with the customer profile?

Chapters 10 and 11 of this textbook focused on the importance of being able to sense the core strengths of our value proposition and communicate them to our target audience. In assessing a business venture, we need to feel comfortable that the value proposition presented will achieve the three conclusions noted above. The way that we accomplish this is via the value analysis **litmus test** shown in Figure 15.6.

Litmus Test refers to a process or something that is used to make a judgment or draw conclusions about the acceptability of an opinion.

Value analysis focuses on fully understanding "market fit" and validating that we have a definitive competitive advantage or uniqueness around which we can develop a positioning campaign.

Business IN ACTION

Shopify Inc.—A Canadian Tech Success Story

The advent of convenient, low-cost Internet access has changed the way customers buy products. When assessing purchase decisions consumers now expect options for where and how to buy: in-store or online, pickup or delivery. To be successful in today's interconnected world, organizations need to be able to sell their products through as many channels as possible. In the past this was costly and complicated, requiring significant financial commitment and technical expertise on behalf of both the organization and the customer. Shopify Inc., a Canadian tech company based in Ottawa, recognized the potential of hassle-free online retail services and developed a streamlined and fully customizable commerce platform to capitalize on it. Although officially incorporated in 2004, Shopify's origins trace back to when it was a retail organization itself.

Used by permission of Shopify

In 2004, Shopify founder and CEO Tobias Lütke wanted to sell snowboard equipment online. He initially considered listing his products on various online marketplaces, but instead decided that he wanted to own his brand by selling goods to customers directly, thereby establishing meaningful customer relationships in the process. However, Lütke and his team found that existing ecommerce platforms were difficult to operate and restrictive in their design. These barriers, in his mind, prevented the ability to establish effective brand development, customer intimacy, and product management. A computer programmer by trade, Lütke figured that he could build such a tool himself. Armed with $450 000 in initial angel investments, Lütke and his team spent the next year and a half creating Shopify's customizable software. Their mission: to make commerce better and more accessible for everyone.

A Shopify subscription initially allowed users to create and manage an online store in order to sell their goods, from $29 to $179 a month. From the desktop or mobile device application dashboard, users could organize products, customize a storefront layout, accept credit card payments, and track and respond to orders. Built-in analytics tracked Web sales and progress in real time, thereby providing the opportunity to make strategic changes to sales campaigns on the fly.

With new rounds of venture capital investments in 2010 ($7 million), 2011 ($15 million), and 2013 ($100 million), Shopify began expanding its product offerings to provide users with the most comprehensive Internet-based distribution support and capabilities available in the market today. For example, Shopify Point-of-Sale (POS) gives users a card reader that allows them to run physical operations on an iPad in bricks and mortar or pop-up stores, and Shopify also enables its merchants to sell on social networks like Facebook and Pinterest. Notable advantages to Shopify's approach are its low-cost implementation, fast and secure order processing and payment, and reduced clutter in the client's Web-based workplace. Other Shopify features include search engine optimization, discount code generators, and social network integration. With so many social media users, social media integration is an incredibly useful way to increase exposure and sales. Shopify can even be used to sell products through a Facebook page.

Shopify has experienced meteoric growth since its launch in 2006. From a team of five working out of a local coffee shop to an employee talent base of over 3000 working in key market office locations across Canada and internationally, Shopify has used online and mobile software to effectively redefine commerce. In April 2015, Shopify announced its intent to file and initiate an initial public offering (IPO). The IPO was launched May 21, 2015 on the NYSE with an asking price of $17 (USD) per share. The stock closed at the end of the first day at $25.68 (USD), rising 51%

from its initial asking price and valuing the company at $1.9 billion (USD).

Fast-forward to 2019, and Shopify is now a multibillion-dollar company and has been recognized as one of Canada's Top 100 Employers. 2018 saw revenue for Shopify cross the $1 billion ($1.073 billion USD) mark. The company's share value is now (April 2019) at $219.62, and the market capitalization value of the company (# shares outstanding × share price), on this same date, exceeded $24 billion. As the company has expanded, so too has its client base. Initially focused on small and medium-sized businesses, Shopify's efficient platforms coupled with its significant market profile and reach have attracted larger brands such as Nestlé, The Brick, General Mills, Jamieson Natural Sources, Steve Madden, Nicole Miller, Kylie Cosmetics, Red Bull, and the Universal Music Group, to name a few. The company's ecosystem has also broadened, with partners and affiliates such as Intuit (accounting), Zendesk (customer service), and Klaviyo (marketing). The company now offers over 2500 applications through its Shopify App Store, theme designers through its Shopify Theme Store, and agency support via its Shopify Experts. Monthly recurring revenues from its subscription solutions have grown over 70% (compound annual growth rate) since 2012, and the company has consistently experienced net merchant revenue growth during this same period. The Shopify growth model is simple: the more merchants that join the platform the more gross monthly volume is generated, resulting in more channels, partners, and capabilities. Gross merchandise volumes through the Shopify platform now exceed $41 billion annually.

Looking to the future, Shopify remains confident in its ability to further grow its business model. Trends relating to self-employment, entrepreneurship, ecommerce growth, and consumerization of business interactions point toward continued growth both domestically and internationally. Machine learning capabilities and data-based analytics, driven by a huge database of billions of interactions with merchants and customers, offer additional revenue opportunities. The company also recently completed an additional share offering (December 2018), raising over $400 million in order to fund its upcoming growth strategies. Shopify currently supports an estimated 800 000+ businesses in over 170 countries.

Financial Analysis

Equally important to the task of understanding the market that the organization plans to attack, and the value proposition around which this attack is to be formulated, is the need to assess the financial requirements to support the business venture. This means taking the skills you learned in Chapters 13 and 14 and applying them to a financial analysis of the probability of success for the new venture being assessed. To be successful, managers and entrepreneurs need to develop a valid estimate of the capital needs of the organization, the length of time needed to ensure financial stability, and the cash requirements applicable to the cash operating cycle. Defining and understanding these base fundamentals will enable those conducting the analytical process to draw conclusions relating to the actual depth of the investment required, the expected returns on this investment, and the level of affordable loss that could be absorbed should financial projections not be met as anticipated. In conducting such an analysis, astute managers and entrepreneurs will assess the financial potential of a venture and, consequently, the risk/reward trade-off associated with it across five key financial analysis areas (see Figure 15.7).

> To be successful, managers and entrepreneurs need to develop a valid estimate of the capital needs of the organization, the length of time needed to ensure financial stability, and the cash requirements applicable to the cash operating cycle.

Demand and revenue model assessment As was discussed in Chapter 13, assessing the revenue model of a new venture is really about validating the legitimacy of where revenue is going to come from and how it will be generated. Keep in mind that

FIGURE 15.7 Focus of New Venture Financial Analysis

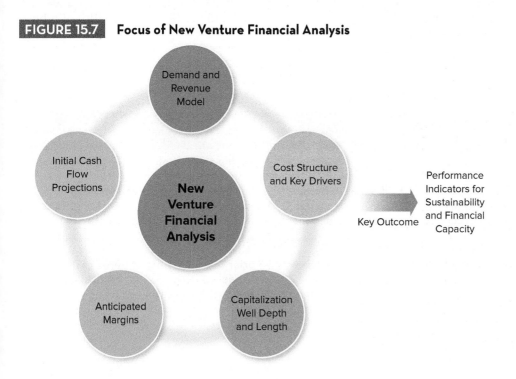

for new ventures, particularly new start-ups, demand begins at zero. The strategy for demand creation, therefore, forms a key part of the assessment of the revenue model, as without demand there is no revenue.

> Keep in mind that for new ventures, particularly new start-ups, demand begins at zero. The strategy for demand creation, therefore, forms a key part of the assessment of the revenue model, as without demand there is no revenue.

Revenue analysis focuses on the number of potential revenue streams the organization is adding, the sources of revenue within each stream, the initial size of these revenue streams, the growth potential of this revenue looking forward, the interdependency of this new revenue source on existing revenue sources (if they exist), and the price pressure that can be anticipated on the revenue streams identified (see Figure 15.8). In essence, we are trying to determine, with an acceptable degree of credibility, the initial demand and corresponding revenue inflow anticipated, its projected growth, and external forces that may impact such growth potential.

A good approach to drawing conclusions with respect to revenue is to develop a potential range of outcomes, thereby defining with a higher probability of confidence the upside and downside boundaries of the level of revenue anticipated. As an example, let's assume that the ZOOM Corporation is scheduled to launch its version of a tablet computer called the Scorebook. Let's further assume that marketing has developed its forecasts for this initial year, with ZOOM expecting to sell 4 million units (realistic forecast) at an average selling price of $450. However, ZOOM's management team, along with analysts, see upside sales potentially reaching 6 million units (optimistic forecast). On the downside, concerns exist that sales may be as few as 2 million units (pessimistic forecast). For ZOOM, the Scorebook, at an estimated average selling price of $450, will generate revenue of between $900 million and $2.7 billion, with an expected revenue stream of $1.8 billion achieved should the 4 million unit estimate be achieved. Being able to define the revenue sources and the anticipated revenue stream, particularly in the early stages of a new venture launch, is a first step in determining the financial viability of a business opportunity.

FIGURE 15.8   Key Financial Assessment Risk Factors

Revenue	Cost Drivers	Benchmark Requirements	Cash Flow Projections	Capitalization Well
• # of streams • Source(s) • Size of each stream • Growth potential of each stream • Interdependency of each stream • Price pressure on each stream	• Structure—fixed, semi-fixed, committed, and variable • Type—reoccurring vs. nonreoccurring • Key cost centres • Degree of control and market volatility • Source of competitive advantage • Built-in expense creep within each cost centre	• Point of positive cash flow • Breakeven point • GPM (gross profit margin) requirement and target • OM (operating margin) requirement and target • PM (profit margin) requirement and target	• Timing and size of cash inflows and outflows • Identify key impact factors on cash flow • Define the range of movement available prior to liquidity impact • Determine the cash reserve required to fund the COC	• Total investment size • Maximum financing needs • Depth of private-equity support • Free cash reserve availability

Assessing the revenue model of a new venture is really about validating the legitimacy of where revenue is going to come from and how it will be generated.

Cost structure and key driver assessment As also discussed in Chapter 13, understanding an organization's cost base is a fundamental managerial responsibility. So, too, is this need when assessing a new business venture. The core difference, however, is that in assessing existing businesses, managers have historical records to fall back on. In new ventures, particularly new business start-ups, such a history is not generally present. The end result is that cost estimates, like revenue estimates, are projected and/or anticipated. A number of key factors need to be reviewed by managers and entrepreneurs when assessing an organization's cost base (see Figure 15.8). These factors are as follows:

1 What does the overall cost structure look like? What is the relationship (to revenue) of product costs and operating expenses? What are the key cost centres that will ultimately drive a large percentage of the organization's cost base?

2 What costs are anticipated to be reoccurring versus those felt to be non-reoccurring?

3 What type of built-in expense creep do we anticipate within these cost areas?

4 Will market volatility, such as commodities, impact our expense lines? If so, by how much?

5 Do we feel that our cost base, as it is estimated, yields a competitive advantage?

Going back to our example of the ZOOM Corporation, let's assume that the organization estimates that product costs associated with building the Scorebook are estimated at 70% of the average selling price of $450. Fixed, semi-fixed, and committed costs are projected to be $378 million. Knowing this information, along with the various revenue ranges described above, now allows us to get a feel for the potential profitability of the Scorebook at the potential volume outcomes identified earlier. This is shown in Table 15.1.

ZOOM Corporation, based on revenue and cost estimates, is now able to determine that its upside operating profit potential (EBT) is $432 000 000, with its downside operating loss exposure being estimated at ($108 000 000). This pessimistic outcome of ($108 000 000) communicates to the management team that, should the pessimistic case outcome materialize, the organization will need to be prepared to spend an additional $108 000 000 to cover the operating loss associated with this

TABLE 15.1 ZOOM Corporation: Optimistic, Realistic, and Pessimistic Sales Forecasts

	2 Million Scorebooks Sold	4 Million Scorebooks Sold	6 Million Scorebooks Sold
Revenue @ ASP of $450	$900 000 000	$1 800 000 000	$2 700 000 000
Less Product Costs @70% of ASP	$630 000 000	$1 260 000 000	$1 890 000 000
Equals GPM	$ 270 000 000	$ 540 000 000	$ 810 000 000
Less Operating Expenses	$ 378 000 000	$ 378 000 000	$ 378 000 000
Equals EBT	($ 108 000 000)	$ 162 000 000	$ 432 000 000

weak market performance. This becomes part of the financial risk assessment and the decision-making process of whether to assign this project a "go" or a "no go" decision.

Assessing benchmark requirements Benchmark requirements focus on an assessment of key performance indicators that will assist us in better understanding the various outcomes that could materialize given the estimates we have made and the operational efficiencies that need to be achieved (see Figure 15.8). Two key benchmarks are understanding the point at which the organization becomes **cash flow positive**, and where the initial estimated breakeven point is anticipated to be. "Cash flow positive" is that point where cash inflows finally exceed cash outflows for the organization. This is an important first step in defining how long a new venture's burn rate will last. As long as cash outflows exceed cash inflows, additional capital will be needed to offset the burn rate occurring. Breakeven point, as defined in Chapter 13, is that point in time where total revenue = total expenses and, therefore, profit = $0. Using our ZOOM Corporation example, based on the information provided the breakeven point for the Scorebook for its first year of operation is as follows:

> **Cash Flow Positive** refers to that point in time when an organization is able to cover the actual cash expenses of an operation from the revenue it generates.

$$\text{BEP units} = \text{FC}/(\text{SP} - \text{VC})$$
$$\text{BEP units} = \$378\ 000\ 000/(\$450 - \$315)$$
$$\text{BEP units} = \$378\ 000\ 000/\$135$$
$$\text{BEP units} = 2.8 \text{ million}$$

Two key benchmarks are understanding the point at which the organization becomes cash flow positive, and where the initial estimated breakeven point is anticipated to be.

Other key benchmark requirements would be, for example, striving for a gross profit margin of 30%, or an operating margin of 9%. Table 15.2 illustrates the impact that margin erosion can have on operating results if cost creep or cost inefficiencies work their way into the operating processes of the Scorebook's first-year launch results at its anticipated sales volume of 4 million units.

Table 15.2 illustrates that even though 4 million units are expected to be sold, a potential rise in product costs (which negatively impacts GPM), which causes an erosion of GPM by −3%, and/or a rise in operating expenses (such as higher than expected marketing costs), will negatively impact operating profit. Just as managers and entrepreneurs need to be cognizant of ranges of outcomes in sales revenue,

TABLE 15.2   ZOOM Corporation Gross Profit Margin Erosion

	4 Million Units Sold GPM = 30% and OE = $378M (Benchmark)	4 Million Units Sold GPM Erodes to 27% and OE Remains at $378M	4 Million Units Sold GPM = 27% and OE Rises to $400M
Revenue	$1 800 000 000	$1 800 000 000	$1 800 000 000
GPM	$ 540 000 000	$ 486 000 000	$ 486 000 000
Operating Exp. (OE)	$ 378 000 000	$ 378 000 000	$ 400 000 000
Operating Profit (EBT)	$ 162 000 000	$ 108 000 000	$ 86 000 000

they must also recognize that cost estimates are just that, and that a range of potential outcomes can occur even if sales projections are made.

Anticipating initial cash flow projections As discussed in Chapters 12 and 13, the cash operating cycle defines the timing and size of cash inflows and outflows. By seeking to define and anticipate estimates associated with the movement of cash within a new business venture, managers and entrepreneurs are able to identify the key impact factors on cash flow and proactively plan for it. This important metric relating to liquidity assists in ensuring that developing and maintaining adequate capital reserves is factored into the financial risk assessment process (see Figure 15.8).

Defining the capitalization well Up to this point, our financial discussion has focused on assessing the financial risk associated with the new venture or new product launches operating framework. Our emphasis has been on ensuring that we understand our sales forecast and the corresponding revenue derived from it, our cost base and the key performance indicators around which we will benchmark, and the need to understand the estimated cash operating cycle of the new venture or product. This is, however, only one-half of the financial assessment equation and process. In addition to assessing the financial potential of the business, once it is operating we also need to assess the magnitude of capital asset investment and other pre-launch costs, often referred to as **start-up costs**, required to launch the new business venture and/or a new product line. In many situations, this can, and will, require a considerable capital commitment. Even for small business entities, start-up costs can run into the thousands of dollars. As an example, the start-up costs of an M&M Food Market are estimated to be $350 000 to $450 000. These start-up costs are needed to cover equipment, construction costs in customizing a location for the shop, legal and professional fees, grand-opening advertising, staff training, product initial inventory, and other costs associated with the use of the M&M Food Market name and its trademark.[3]

> In addition to assessing the financial potential of the business, once it is operating we also need to assess the magnitude of capital asset investment and other pre-launch costs, often referred to as start-up costs, required to launch the new business venture and/or a new product line.

To truly understand the magnitude of the total capital needed to launch and support a new business venture or product (start-up costs and initial operational costs), managers and entrepreneurs are advised to make use of a business model called the **capitalization well**. The idea behind the capitalization well (see Figure 15.9) is to provide a framework by which managers and entrepreneurs can assess the full capital requirements that will be needed to ensure the successful capitalization of a business venture. By doing so, managers and entrepreneurs can minimize one of the primary reasons for new venture failures, that being **undercapitalization**. Fully understanding the capitalization requirements of the organization also results in a much better outcome pertaining to "go and no go" decisions at the outset of a venture assessment process versus dealing with significant and unanticipated cash burns and cash deficiencies once a business or product launch is underway.

Start-up Costs are the initial capital investment required to launch a new business or product venture.

Capitalization Well refers to a framework for assessing the full capital requirements of a business venture.

Undercapitalization is the situation where a company lacks the required funding to continue business activities.

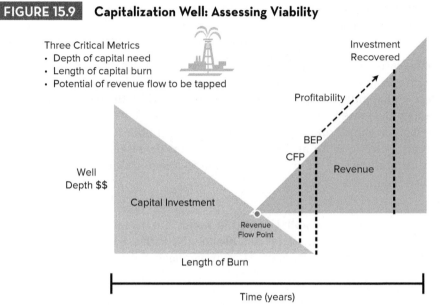

FIGURE 15.9   **Capitalization Well: Assessing Viability**

To fully understand the capitalization well concept, think of the process involved in drilling for oil. Our initial phase is exploring for oil. This research-based phase will require the organization to spend some capital in determining where, and with what process, we should drill for the oil we hope to find. Once a site and start date have been determined, the organization will then need to proceed with some fairly significant capital asset expenditures (start-up costs). This would entail purchasing and/or developing the oil rig or oil well components, shipping them, erecting them, and then testing the site and training staff to ensure that the rig or well is ready to go and that all pre-operational requirements are met. Following this start-up period is the commencement of operations. With our oil rig or oil well, this would be drilling for oil. Keep in mind that we may need to drill for a period of time before oil begins to flow. Assuming that all goes well, we will then begin to see oil pumping through our well. Again, we need to recognize that this may not be of sufficient quantity to cover our drilling costs. As our oil well continues to produce oil and we realize the revenue from it, we will eventually be able to cover our direct costs. This is where we finally become cash flow positive (CFP). This is then followed by a breakeven point (BEP) where we not only cover direct costs, but are now covering our total expense line, including non-cash transactions such as depreciation. Finally, assuming that revenue continues to grow, we begin earning profit, followed by reaching that point where our investment is fully recovered. Ideally, the well remains profitable long after the payback period is reached, and continues to generate profit for our oil company.

The same holds true for a business. We may need to spend a considerable amount of money prior to seeing any definitive revenue flow. A new business venture requires initial investment on determining the viability of the concept or idea. This could be spent on concept design and prototype development, market research such as surveys, focus groups, competitive analysis, and test marketing, to mention a few initiatives in this phase. This is then followed by investment in the capital asset base required to support the new venture. This could be a bricks and mortar location, manufacturing equipment, technology-based hardware and software, pre-launch marketing, recruitment, hiring and training of staff, and so on. With all of this in place, we then open our doors and commence business operations, striving to move to cash flow positive and breakeven point as quickly as possible in order to minimize our burn rate. With the burn rate eliminated, our focus is then placed on driving profitability to recoup our investment and to create long-term wealth for our stakeholders.

In assessing business plans and new ventures, managers and entrepreneurs need to define and understand three key fundamental points relating to the capitalization well:

1 What is the depth of the capital burn—in other words, how much money will we truly need?

2 What is the length of the capital burn—how long will it take to get to cash flow positive and then breakeven point?

3 What is the potential revenue that we believe can be realized? Will this enable us to achieve profitability and long-term business stability, return the investment made in the business, and contribute positively to stakeholder wealth?

In utilizing the capitalization well as a core element of the financial risk analysis of a new business venture, we are trying to conclude whether we have the financial capacity to create and support the business venture until such a time that its revenue stream is sufficient to ensure profit stability and long-term sustainability. Depending on the situation, this could take a number of months or even years (see Figure 15.10[4]). For example, Amazon.com, founded by Jeff Bezos in July 1994 and launched in 1995, did not generate an operating profit until it reached a sales volume in excess of $1 billion in the fourth quarter of 2001. Shopify, featured in a previous Business in Action in this chapter, had yet to make a profit as of December 31, 2018 despite generating over $1 billion in revenue (the company was generating a positive cash flow from operations). The same holds true for Salesforce.com. Established in 1999, Salesforce.com, as it pursued its rapid growth opportunities, did not become consistently profitable until 18 years later (2017).[5]

FIGURE 15.10   **New Venture Evolution**

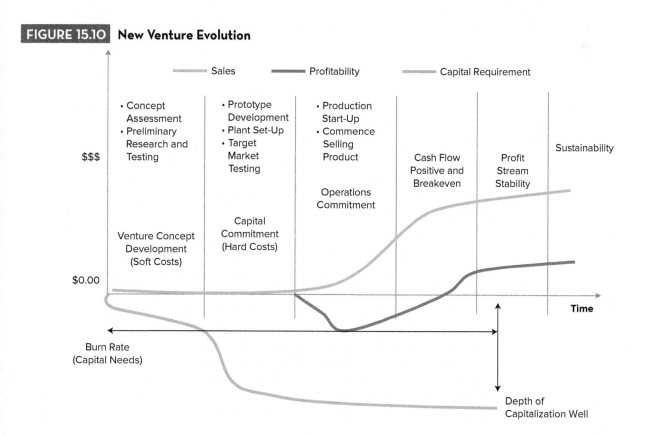

Business IN ACTION

Business Development Bank of Canada (BDC)

As many budding and experienced entrepreneurs understand, unimpeded access to capital and knowledge is essential in building a viable business. In order to fill that demand, the Business Development Bank of Canada (BDC) has defined itself as Canada's only financial institution dedicated exclusively to entrepreneurs.

A Crown corporation operating at arm's length from its sole shareholder, the Government of Canada, the BDC is a profitable organization that helps create and develop strong Canadian businesses by providing financing, consulting services, and securitization primarily to small and medium-sized enterprises (SME). Its network of more than 132 business centres (with 2200 employees) across Canada supports entrepreneurs in all industries and at all stages of development. Services include lending for a variety of projects and providing business advice relating to strategic planning, acquisitions, business transitions, human resources management, international growth, technology implementation, operational efficiency, and sales and marketing. In addition to these core services, BDC also conducts extensive research and analysis of economic trends and issues affecting small and medium-sized businesses. Reports and studies are available free of charge on BDC's website, bdc.ca.

A key component of BDC's value proposition to entrepreneurs is its ability to arrange an array of financing options complementary to those available from other financial institutions. For newer businesses or smaller projects, BDC can provide small business loans of up to $100 000 online in 2 to 5 business days. It also offers growth and transition capital to fund such projects as production expansions, new equipment purchases, or the exit of an entrepreneur from his or her business. An advantage of this financing is that it provides entrepreneurs with the necessary capital for growth or transition without diluting ownership. BDC supports its customers' financing needs through three major funding avenues: venture capital (providing start-up capital to fuel

Business Development Bank of Canada (BDC)

great ideas); growth and transition capital (supporting working capital, as well as transition and business acquisition needs); and growth equity capital (taking a minority stake in a business to assist it in accelerating its growth). A notable recipient of BDC venture capital funding is D-Wave Systems Inc., a quantum-computing firm based in British Columbia (highlighted in Chapter 7). Other companies that have recently (2018–19) benefited from BDC's support include Surrey, B.C.-based Kendrick Equipment, Halifax-based Sancton, Prince George, B.C.-based BID Group, Montreal-based Industries Polykar, and Ottawa-based Deslaurier Custom Cabinets.

A certified B Corp (Beneficial Corporation), BDC emphasizes corporate social responsibility (CSR) in every facet of its operations, and utilizes a transparent organizational structure that makes roles, decision making, and accountability clear. BDC has been profitable since 1998, paying over $500 million in dividends to the Government of Canada ($69.7 million in fiscal year 2018). Recognized consistently as one of Canada's top 100 employers, the BDC is proud to support the growth of over 56 000 SMEs in Canada. These businesses generate $251 billion annually and employ 900 000 people across the country.

As of this writing, the BDC is working closely with the Government of Canada to deploy $400 million in capital through Canada's Venture Capital Action Plan (VCAP). The BDC is also the proud recipient of the VCAP's coveted Deal of the Year award four times in six years (2012–18). The BDC has committed more than $31 billion in capital since its inception in support of small- and medium-sized businesses. The company has recently announced its commitment to deploy $700 million in support of Canadian clean technology firms, $200 million to its Women in Technology Fund (now the largest in the world), and $280 million in support of companies in Atlantic Canada.

Operations Analysis

Often overlooked in light of the emphasis on market analysis and financial assessment, a key analytical area in determining whether a business venture will be successful lies in a firm understanding of the infrastructure, equipment, and value chain flow that will be needed to effectively execute the business plan and the accompanying business strategy. A well-developed business plan will demonstrate just how the business and/or its products and services will be developed, communicated, and connected to customers. Think of this as a business schematic that details the framework around which the business plan will be executed.

As an example, consider McDonald's decision to develop and offer its Big Mac sandwich to its customers. The Big Mac consists of two beef patties, special sauce, lettuce, cheese, pickles, and onions on a sesame seed bun. For McDonald's, the operational analysis would entail how to fully integrate the creation of this sandwich in the back end (kitchen and food prep areas) of its quick-service restaurant locations, and deliver it to customers at the time of purchase. This would entail a full value chain development plan (see Figure 15.11). A business plan and the business venture assessment processes look at the legitimacy of an operation as well as the efficiency and effectiveness associated with it.

> A key analytical area in determining whether a business venture will be successful lies in a firm understanding of the infrastructure, equipment, and value chain flow that will be needed to effectively execute the business plan and the accompanying business strategy.

FIGURE 15.11   **Value Chain: McDonald's Big Mac**

Inbound Logistics	Operations	Outbound Logistics	Marketing and Sales	Customer Service
• Product procurement • Product storage • Inventory levels	• Product handling and preparation • Portion control • Big Mac assembly flow • Kitchen configuration • Quality C=control • Training	• Product packaging • Big Mac holding, pending sale • Quality control—shelf life	• Advertising and communication • Pricing • In-store promotions • Menu board set-up • Meal Deal packaging	• Staff delivery training • Warming bin management • Product quality assessment

Source: Value Chain adapted from Michael Porter—Value Chain Analysis.

The plan will also detail the expertise required to staff the proposed venture, the capacity that the operation possesses with respect to the design, development, and delivery of the products and/or services, and the supporting infrastructure needed to ensure that the operation can deliver on the vision and the communication strategy commitments being made. Using an additional example, assume that a business plan indicates a new restaurant venture is projecting sales of $2 million. An analysis of the menu indicates that an average cheque amount from its customers, based on menu item pricing, is estimated to be $15. The restaurant's seating capacity consists of 10 tables, each with 4 chairs. This means that the "per seating" capacity of the restaurant is 40 patrons. The restaurant plan calls for it to be open 350 days per year, serving lunch and evening diners. The question is whether the seating capacity of the restaurant can realistically deliver $2 million in sales given an average cheque size of $15 per diner. A quick operational analysis would yield the following:

1 $2 million in sales, at $15 per diner, requires 133 334 diners per year.

2 Dividing the 133 334 diners by 350 days results in 381 diners per day.

3 Assuming 40 seats, this means that we will need to serve approximately 10 diners per day, per chair, in order to achieve the estimated $2 million in sales. Is this possible?

To achieve the results noted above would require a very high-volume-based operation. Will market demand provide 381 diners per day? Can the kitchen and serving staff handle this volume? How many tables can a single server handle? If the average person sits in a seat for 45 minutes per meal, this means that the seat must be occupied for 7.5 hours per day with diners. Given that peak-period times are between 12 p.m. and 2 p.m. for lunch, and 4:30 p.m. and 7:30 p.m. for dinner, can we realistically expect to have all chairs fully occupied all the time? These are just some of the questions that need to be asked to determine the viability of the operation in order to yield the desired sales revenue figures, given the identified price point that the restaurant realistically can achieve.

Up to this point, our two examples have focused on base-level operational issues that need to be assessed as part of our operational analysis. Keep in mind that the situation is more complex than this in that technology decisions, environmental safety and compliance decisions, legal risk assessment, engineering and R&D decisions, and employee management decisions all form part of this analytical process as well. Using the value chain model identified in Chapter 12 and shown again in Figure 15.12 is an excellent way to assess the overall legitimacy of the operational model being proposed within the new venture.

FIGURE 15.12 **Value Chain: Support Activities**

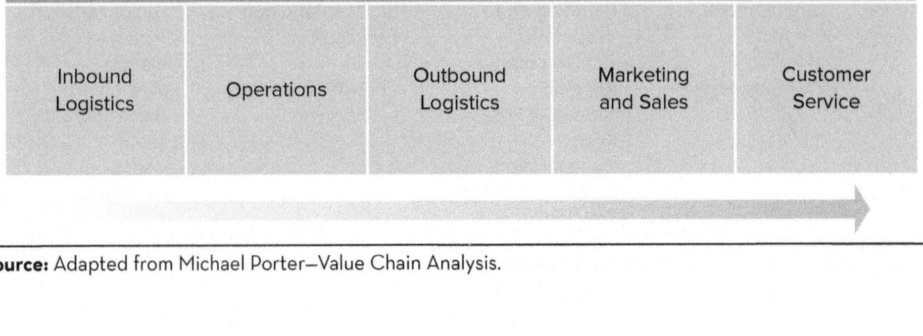

Source: Adapted from Michael Porter—Value Chain Analysis.

Management Competency Analysis

In the assessment of a business venture, the ability of the management team to illustrate its competencies to successfully execute the business plan and yield the intended financial results is paramount in the eyes of private-equity companies and investors considering bankrolling the new venture. In many cases, the final "go or no go" decision comes down to this management acumen analysis. Fully assessing the overall competencies and commitment of an entrepreneur and/or a management team is never an easy task. This becomes even more critical when specialized skills are required early on to ensure successful business and/or product development. Skill requirements also may change as the venture proceeds through the various stages of development noted in Figure 15.13. In summarizing this process, however, an assessment of the overall managerial acumen and the human resource talent base required can be framed around three fundamental questions:

1 What specific competencies, skills, experience, and expertise are essential to the effective execution of the business plan?

2 Do the individuals identified as key to the business start-up demonstrate a possession of such competencies, skills, experience, and expertise? In other words, can these individuals translate the vision and the near-term objectives into specific tactical and actionable plans?

3 In addition to the operating expertise requirements noted above, do these same individuals possess the required relationships and leadership skills to successfully execute the plan?

Looking for the answers to the three questions noted above results in the need to conduct an exhaustive evaluation of the key individuals and/or management team who represent the business venture. This evaluation requirement means assessing both objective and subjective success characteristics of these individuals in order to determine the probability that they can truly deliver the projected results identified within the business plan.[6] To ensure a thorough assessment of this individual and/or management acumen, prospective investors and/or business plan analysts will often focus on the metrics presented in the management acumen model illustrated in Figure 15.13 (originally presented in Chapter 7). Again, an easy way to remember these success-based evaluation metrics is by the acronym MERFS.

> In the assessment of a business venture, the ability of the management team to illustrate its competencies to successfully execute the business plan and yield the intended financial results is paramount in the eyes of private-equity companies and investors considering bankrolling the new venture.

FIGURE 15.13 **Management Acumen Assessment Model (MERFS)**

What management needs to demonstrate:

M = Motivation	E = Expertise	R = Risk Acceptance	F = Focus	S = Self-Belief
• Adaptability • Realism • Durability • Desire to excel • Bulldog mentality	• Skill • Knowledge • Direct experience • Willingness to make decisions • Customer contacts • Network with suppliers, channel partners • Access to specialized skills	• Perception of risk and underlying stresses • Ability to mitigate or control risk • Ability to balance the risk with the passion	• Strategic plan • Vision • Leadership • Rifle vs. shot-gun • Recognition of when to make changes	• Confidence • Time • Treasure • Talent • Commitment • Skin in the game

For a business venture to be given a "go" decision, investors and decision makers need to confirm that the individuals and/or management team possess solid assessment scores across all five of these areas. A deficiency in any one area can, and often will, result in an ineffective execution of a business plan.

Contingency Plans or Exit Options

Contingency plans or exit options refer to whether or not there is an intended back-up plan for the business and, if so, what type of conditions would trigger such a strategy. In some cases, contingency plans or exit options can be thought of as a "plan B" to be taken where anticipated revenue growth does not materialize. In other cases, as in an exit plan, options can be a formal intent of the entrepreneur to exit a business or venture via a planned sale of the business once a certain sales volume or level of profitability is achieved. Private-equity investors and stakeholders are interested in the overall long-term commitment that an entrepreneur or company has to a given product, service, or business entity. Equally important is the recognition by an entrepreneur or management team that a different skill set may be required once certain growth levels are realized. For some entrepreneurs, their focus is all about creating market space and establishing innovative solutions to new technology needs. Once a foothold has been established in a market, their interest then shifts toward moving away from the day-to-day management needs of the organization and focusing on the next new innovative ideas. In analyzing a business venture, the formal communication of an exit strategy signals to the financial supporters of the venture that the entrepreneur envisions a defined and limited involvement period. This should be assessed against the business and plan and the corresponding analysis across the other five areas mentioned in order to understand how identified contingency plans or an exit strategy integrates into the overall business model. Measuring these back-up plans against the findings resulting from a capitalization well analysis enables us to determine whether such a strategy, as communicated, significantly impacts the overall risk of the project. This is then incorporated into the "go or no go" decision process.

LO5   Reality Check—The Perils of Starting a New Business

Starting a new business can be one of the most exciting events in an individual's life. At the same time, the journey to a successful business is one fraught with perils and challenges. Yes, we hear of the success stories relating to Mark Zuckerberg, Steve Jobs, Sara Blakely, Elon Musk, and Jeff Bezos, to mention a few. But for each success story, there are a significantly greater number of stories where businesses fell short of the expectations of their would-be entrepreneurs. Take Mike Gozzo, as an example. In 2011 he and his cousin Steve Panetta started a software company called Appifier, which focused on the creation of a mobile app option for WordPress. Mike and Steve thought that they had created a unique business opportunity that would enable them to rocket to success. Backed by government grants and supported by Montreal-based start-up accelerator FounderFuel, the company appeared to be well capitalized out of the gate. Unfortunately, however, the burn rate (use/outflow of capital) exceeded the ability to generate revenue from their software product. Despite long hours at the office, undeniably relentless commitment, and a will to succeed, Appifier found itself in a downward spiral. Funding dried up, and staff began to leave. Shortly thereafter, Mike and Steve were forced to pull the plug, and close the company. The chapter-opening Business in Action (Vanhawks) provides additional insight into the challenges of getting a new business venture off the ground in today's increasingly hyper-competitive marketplace.[7]

Working long hours, the feeling of isolation, loneliness, poor diet, lack of sleep, and fear of failure have been acknowledged as common elements of an entrepreneur's life, particularly at the front end of a business start-up. Add to this the potential for bad investment advice, misreading the market in terms of demand and/or timing, the need to appease impatient investors, and the need to constantly sell, sell, sell, even when things don't seem to be clicking, and even the most mentally strong individuals can be challenged. Periods of depression, coupled with analysis/paralysis on what to do or where to go next, can add unimaginable levels of stress to individuals and their family life. Essential to managing this is the ability to find balance in one's life and to set limits around what is realistically possible.

It is also not just in the start-up phase where these pressures occur. As a company grows, sales accelerate, new employees are brought on, and the business's structure requires increasing attention, the time commitment from business owners accelerates as well. It is here that feelings associated with loss of control and heightened levels of anxiety continue to challenge the mental strength and durability of those involved. As one would-be entrepreneur noted, starting a business is a great way to go crazy.

Perhaps the most common comment from entrepreneurs is the fact that the business lives inside their head 24/7. There just never seems to be an opportunity to take a break. The mind is constantly swirling as to how to change this, tweak that, or maximize this new opportunity. Again, it comes back to balance, developing a support team to assist in moving things along when the challenges seem to become too difficult to handle. One also needs to recognize that the idea that failure is not an option is simply not reality. Failures occur, and will continue to do so. Entrepreneurs need to have around them a group of advisers who can maintain a logical and realistic view of the business's potential as it evolves, in order offset the passion and failure avoidance that exist within business owners and founders.

Having said all of this, starting a business or becoming a business owner can be, and is for many, one of the most enjoyable experiences an individual can experience. In developing your business plan and in launching your business, be sure to create a healthy work environment for you and your family. Even though this does not appear in the fishbone diagram relating to venture assessment (Figure 15.2), make it a conscious part of the planning and assessment process. In doing so, you will be better able to manage and balance the challenges business entrepreneurship places on all of us.

Acquiring an Existing Business

LO6

In many cases, the idea of developing a new business opportunity from the ground up **(organic growth)** represents significantly greater risk than a company or individual is willing to take on. This may be the result of an immediate need to gain access to a particular market, the length of time it may take to develop the competencies and/or capabilities internally to successfully compete, concerns over heightened competition and its potential for deteriorating margins and profitability, or the long-term capital commitment required to generate the scale needed to ensure profitability and sustainability. The alternative to growing organically is to consider the **acquisition** of an existing business that offers the entrepreneur and/or a company immediate access to a currently operating entity and, therefore, access to a desired market and an established customer base. Just as success in

Organic Growth refers to growth that comes from an organization's existing business portfolio.

Acquisition refers to the process of acquiring another company or operation.

FIGURE 15.14   **Acquisition Process**

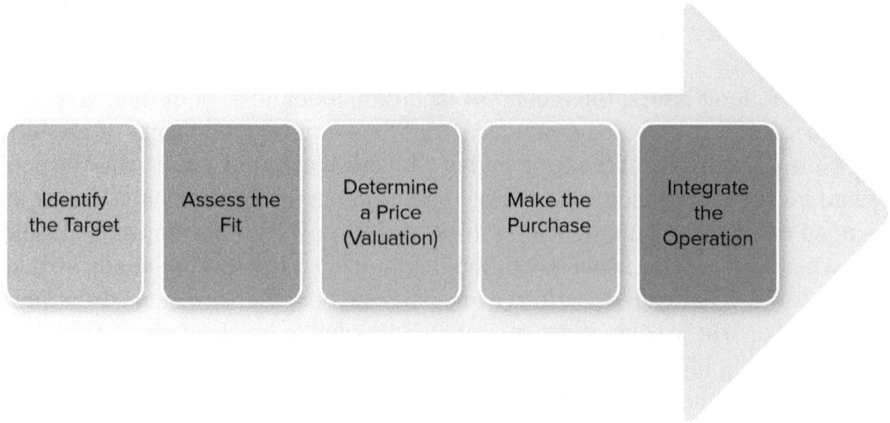

the start-up of a new business or business line is predicated on an organized and thorough assessment of a proposed business plan, so too is the case for acquiring a company. The venture assessment process identified in Figure 15.2 is still very much part of this process. Market risk and financial risk "due diligence" needs to be properly conducted. A determination of the value advantage that the acquisition needs to bring to the entrepreneur and/or the company must be recognized and validated. The efficiency and capacity of the operation needs to be assessed, not only in terms of current scale and market delivery but also in terms of the forward-looking objectives of the acquiring individual or organization. If the acquiring organization intends to keep all, or part, of the existing management team, then the level of managerial competency needs to be assessed as well. In addition to this process, an acquisition also presents some additional analysis on the part of the entrepreneur or the acquiring company. This entails identifying the potential target for acquisition, determining a price to offer for the company or operation to be purchased, arranging the financing for the acquisition, and then integrating the acquisition into the business portfolio. This process is shown, in a summary format, in Figure 15.14.

> The alternative to growing organically is to consider the acquisition of an existing business that offers immediate access to a currently operating entity and, therefore, access to a desired market and an established customer base.

- **Identify the Target** refers to conducting a search as to potential candidates for acquisition. Once found, preliminary negotiations will need to take place to determine whether the acquiring company should proceed with a formal "fit" analysis.

- **Assess the Fit** takes us back to Figure 15.2 and the due diligence associated with our six-phase venture assessment process. Given that we are purchasing a going concern, however, it also requires additional due diligence in a number of key areas. This additional due diligence will, most likely, focus around technology and intellectual property, product and/or service offerings, capital asset infrastructure and operational efficiencies, financial capacity and debt structure, HR policies and procedures, sales and marketing approaches, culture, and overall organizational practices. Key focal points of this analysis will be to determine **operational synergies** that can be realized, cost savings that can be achieved, and the cultural fit of the two organizations.

Operational Synergies refers to maximization of productivity and efficiency through the combining of resources.

FIGURE 15.15 **Acquisition Valuation Model**

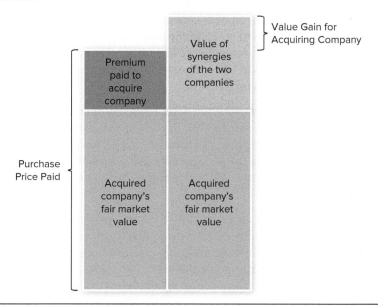

Source: "CEO's Guide to Corporate Finance, Corporate Finance Practice," Dobbs, Huyett, Koller, McKinsey & Company, McKinsey Quarterly, 2010, February 2011.

- **Determine a Price** focuses on business valuation. At some point in the process, an offer and acceptance need to be made. For the acquiring company, the price being paid for the acquisition must not exceed the current value of the company plus the anticipated synergies to be realized. In reality, the acquiring company will strive for an agreed-upon price below this point in order to realize an immediate value for the acquisition. For the selling company, the value must be sufficient to ensure that investors view the sale of the company as being in their best interests. This will generally mean striving for a value that exceeds the immediate market value of the organization (see Figure 15.15).

The price of the acquisition can be determined in a number of ways. Valuation methods can include P/E ratios, **EBITDA** calculations, gross profit margins, revenue forecasting, market capitalization analysis, total enterprise analysis modelling, cash flow analysis, and net present value calculations coupled with weighted cost of capital (WACC) calculations. The actual valuation process for medium and large company-based acquisitions is often developed by financial analysts on behalf of the companies involved in the acquisition and is beyond the scope of this textbook. In many cases, the valuation process will include a number of approaches in order to validate an acceptable purchase price range. The key point to remember in the setting of price is that the value being placed on the target should not be set too high, in that the cash flow benefits anticipated from the acquisition must exceed the cost of debt and other cash outflows required to make the purchase. Other factors that will have to be taken into consideration will be the cost of debt associated with the purchase and whether any, or all, of the target company's liabilities will also be assumed.

EBITDA is earnings before interest and taxes + depreciation expense + amortization expense.

> The key point to remember in the setting of price is that the value being placed on the target should not be set too high, in that the cash flow benefits anticipated from the acquisition must exceed the cost of debt and other cash outflows required to make the purchase.

- **Make the Purchase** involves the legal steps associated with the actual purchase of the target. A key component of this phase will be a finalization of how the acquisition will be financed. Will it be an all-cash purchase? Will it be a combination of cash and shares of stock in the acquiring company? Will it include substantial short and/or long-term debt? In addition, major acquisitions within an industry may result in regulatory review at multiple levels of government, including international regulatory review.

- **Integrate the Operation** implies the actual process of transitioning business processes and protocols to and through the acquired company once the actual purchase process is completed. In many ways, this is the most challenging aspect of the purchase. This is the execution of the tactics needed in order for the objectives for the acquisition and the achievement of the anticipated synergies to be realized.[8]

Although on a somewhat smaller scale, the same process holds true for small businesses. Entrepreneurs interested in acquiring an existing business must approach it in the same manner as large corporations approach an acquisition. Great care needs to be taken in valuing the existing business and in determining an acceptable price to pay, given the anticipated additional value that the entrepreneur feels he or she can create. Paying too high a price or taking on too much debt in the purchase of the business can result in most of the benefit of the acquisition accruing to the seller. The base principle of ensuring that inflows of cash exceed the anticipated (and possibly, higher) outflows of cash, once the acquisition takes place, is a core barometer for ensuring that the newly acquired company can remain liquid and solvent. The case study that follows offers an illustration of the thought process would-be entrepreneurs could consider in determining a purchase price for a small business.

Case Study—So You Want to Buy a Small Business

Potential valuation approaches You want to buy a small business. The problem is that you are uncertain as to how to value it. One of the biggest challenges for individuals looking to purchase a small business is the determination of a legitimate price for it. Unfortunately, there is no one-formula-fits-all when drawing conclusions as to whether the requested purchase price is appropriate. The type of business, the sector it is operating within, the current disruptions that might be occurring within it, and the future growth or decline trends existing within the geographic area where the business is located can and will impact the overall attractiveness of the business and, ultimately, its purchase price.

Having said this, four main factors can be taken into consideration when looking to determining the price for a small business. These four factors, if assessed accurately, should enable a would-be entrepreneur to reach a good understanding of the potential business's value and, as such, be in a position to make a purchase offer to the seller.

1 Asset valuation—this is drawing a conclusion as to the fair market value of the tangible (working) assets owned by the company. By **fair market value** we are referring to the cost of replacing the working assets of the business less an offset amount (think in terms of depreciation) for wear and tear, or the using up of the asset (reduced life expectancy due to usage). It may also include an amount for recent leasehold improvements made by the seller into the building where the business is located.

2 Intangible value (**goodwill**)—an easy way to think of this is the perceived value of the brand and/or the name of the business. A key component of this valuation would be an assessment of the strength of the customer base (going

Fair Market Value is the price that a tangible asset or property is worth in the marketplace.

Goodwill is the additional amount that a company or individual is willing to add to the value of a company it is acquiring, above the fair market value of its tangible assets.

forward) and the overall reputation of the company since it was established. This particular valuation is probably the most difficult to place a value on, as it is often subjective and, in many cases, is referred to as a psychological value versus a tangible value.

3 Percentage of current average sales revenue, or a multiple of current average earnings—a percentage of sales revenue valuation is just that. You would multiply the recent average sales by a specific percentage (say, 50%).

In using a multiple of the current average earnings, financial analysts typically utilize EBITDA (earnings before interest and taxes, plus depreciation and amortization). Depreciation and/or amortization amounts are non-cash items (a cheque is not written for these expenses). The use of EBITDA is thought to offer the best indication of the true earnings of the organization for valuation purposes.

In conducting the analysis for either approach, one would want to look at what are termed "normalized" earnings or sales revenue, which discounts any anomalies relating to earnings flow or sales revenue flow (such as one year of particularly high earnings or sales revenue which is determined to be an exception).

4 Future cash flow potential—this focuses on the value of future cash flows from operating activities, discounted by a risk rate, to determine a value for purchase price purposes. The intent of this approach is to base the valuation on the anticipated future cash potential the prospective owner could look to realize, at least in the short run, in assuming control of the business. The risk (or what is termed the discount) rate is usually related to, or based on, the desired return on investment that the prospective owner would have for the business. The idea is to sum the future cash flows, discounted at the defined risk rate, in order to determine the value of the company's operation as a going concern in the future.

The example (CRT Inc.) shown below will illustrate how these four factors work together to arrive at a potential value for a small business acquisition.

Example: CRT—The company being acquired Let's assume that CRT Inc. is a small technology-based company you are considering purchasing. Established in 2011, the company has shown fairly steady growth since its inception, and has generated a loyal customer base of small and medium-size businesses in need of expertise in network development and maintenance. What is particularly attractive to you about this market is the fact that technology is increasingly becoming a necessary cornerstone of business models for both large and small businesses. Having said this, many small and medium-size businesses simply do not have the resources to maintain a full-time information technology department. For you, this translates into a real business opportunity to further grow CRT Inc. and offer the expertise and support that is becoming more vital to the long-term success of all businesses.

The current owner of CRT Inc. has decided to retire and has approached you to take over the business. Financial information (summarized for simplicity purposes) relating to CRT Inc. is as follows:

	2018	2017	2016	2015	2014
Sales revenue	$822 000	$806 000	$775 000	$768 000	$760 000
EBITDA (Earnings before interest and taxes + depreciation and amortization)	$ 68 500	$ 44 200	$ 39 800	$ 37 700	$ 35 400

In addition to the above-summarized financial information, your analysis of CRT Inc.'s financial statements and support documentation determines the following:

- Tangible Working Assets of CRT Inc., which include a building and equipment, are currently valued at $500 000 (fair market value), and which the owner would like to add to the sale of the business.

Doing some preliminary analysis of the additional services that you would like to offer, as well as drawing conclusions relating to your ability to keep existing clients and add new clients to the business, you have developed the following sales revenue and cash flow from operating activities projections for the upcoming five years:

	2019	2020	2021	2022	2023
Projected sales revenue	$840 000	$855 000	$873 000	$890 000	$907 000
Projected cash flow from operating activities @ 15.6% of revenue*	$ 131 264	$ 133 608	$ 136 421	$ 139 077	$ 141 734

*For simplicity purposes, assume that your financial analysis has concluded that projected cash flow is anticipated to be 15.6% of revenue.

You are impressed with the way that the business has been run, the strength of the relationships CRT Inc. has with its customers, and the overall competitiveness the company has demonstrated against existing rivals. In addition, the current owner has agreed to stay on for a period of 12 months to ensure a smooth and healthy transition of the business, and its customers, to you. Given this, you are comfortable with valuing the CRT Inc.'s intangible asset (goodwill) at $100 000.

The projected valuation Given our analysis, we are now in a position to determine an initial potential purchase price for CRT Inc. Just a reminder: in developing this potential valuation, a number of the assumptions that will be used are subjective to the specific situation (business and market) being analyzed. Also, different individuals have different approaches to arriving at a purchase price. The intent here is simply to illustrate one potential approach, in order to provide you with a better understanding as to the valuation thought process associated with the purchase of a small business.

Here is what we know:

1. Tangible working assets have been valued at $500 000

2. Intangible assets (goodwill) have been valued at $100 000

These two give us an initial base valuation of $500 000 to $600 000 (depending whether you want to acknowledge the goodwill valuation in the purchase offer).

3. Sales revenue has increased steadily over the past couple of years, although it was relatively stagnant earlier on. Overall, sales have averaged $786 000 per year over the past five years.

4. EBITDA has also increased steadily over the past couple of years. The increase has been quite dramatic in the past year, indicating that some scale/volume advantages seem to be realized, due to the sales revenue increase being experienced. The most current two-year average is $56 350.

Additional Assumptions

Conducting some additional due diligence has resulted in the following conclusions:

1. Researching similar purchases in the small and medium-size technology segment has indicated that a standard valuation approach relating to earnings is to use a multiple of EBITDA of 6.5× the average of the most current two years.

2. Researching similar purchases in the small and medium-size technology segment has indicated that a standard valuation approach relating to sales revenue is to use a percentage of sales of 50% of the five-year average.

3. A risk assessment of the business, based on discussions with our bank's financial officer as well as looking at the overall competitive landscape, has led us to conclude that a risk rate of 12% would be appropriate. The discount factors (take from present value of $1 table) associated with a 12% discount rate are shown in the table below.

	2019	2020	2021	2022	2023
Discount rate at 12%	0.892857	0.797194	0.71178	0.635518	0.567427

The Calculation

	Valuation Approach #1: Using Percentage of Sales @ 50%	Valuation Approach #2: Multiple of 6.5× EBITDA	Valuation Approach #3: Future Value of Cash Flow Discounted at 12% Risk Rate*
Tangible asset value	$500 000	$500 000	$500 000
Intangible asset value (goodwill)	$100 000	$100 000	$100 000
EBITDA (2-year average) at 6.5×		$366 275	
Percentage of sales revenue (5-year average) at 50%	$393 000		
Future value of cash flow discounted at 12% risk rate*			$499 000
Estimated "high-end" value of business	$993 000	$966 275	$1 099 000
Estimated "low end of range"— assuming we do not include intangible asset value (goodwill)	$893 000	$866 275	$999 000

*For each year: annual projected cash flow from operating activities (over the upcoming five years) × discount rate. Sum for all five years.

This illustration shows that the value of this business (plus the purchase of the building and equipment), based on the assumptions used, would be between approximately $860 000 and $1 100 000, depending on the willingness to compensate the owner for the full value of the working assets, intangible asset (goodwill), and the valuation approach used. It is also appropriate to note that the percentage of sales approach is, in general, viewed as being the least accurate approach, as it does not reflect the profitability and operating efficiency of the business. Valuations based on future cash flows also need to be developed with caution, as overly optimistic forecasts relating to sales and customer retention will distort the results. In general, although not always the case, reliance on the multiple of EBITDA appears to be the most common initial approach.

Again, it is important to recognize that each individual may come up with a different purchase price. The purpose here is to illustrate one approach to the process (versus indicating that this is the only way that such a computation can be developed). Keep in mind as well that this is just a suggested price range based solely on financial conclusions. As noted at the onset of this example, we need to factor into this valuation any current disruptions that might be occurring within the industry, the future growth or decline trends existing within the geographic area where the business is located, our ability to retain the existing customer base and build upon it, and other factors specific to the marketplace at large.

Keep in mind that establishing a price for a potential business is just one of many steps a would-be entrepreneur needs to take in determining whether they should proceed with a business acquisition. Acquiring a business is a negotiated process. Legal proceedings, succession planning, business expectation assessment, client lists, supplier contracts, economic influences, intellectual capital (patents, trademarks, etc.) rights, business structure (sole proprietor, partnership, corporation), commitments and bylaws, and debt management covenants, to mention a few, all need to be fully assessed and understood as part of this process. Once in, you then need to make sure that you fully understand how the business truly operates and, following a solid assessment of the operation, determine what actions you can take to improve its overall performance. This requires the use of the concepts and models relating to business strategy development and execution and planning cycles discussed in Chapter 6.

A Note Pertaining to Not-for-Profits

Just as for-profit entities need to seek out new business opportunities in order to grow their companies, so too do not-for-profits. Historically, many not-for-profits have relied on external funding sources, such as government, foundations, and granting agencies, to cover their operating expenses. For foundations, reduced returns on principal invested have resulted in a reduction in the dollar amount of support that they, in turn, are able to provide. Faced with budgetary deficits coupled with taxpayers demanding minimal increases in taxes, governments are reducing or withdrawing support in many non–core service areas. Transfers to non-government granting agencies are also being reduced. The end result is that not-for-profits are being increasingly challenged to create new revenue streams and business opportunities. Management teams, largely focused on administrative efficiency and service delivery, now find themselves challenged to become increasingly entrepreneurial if they are to survive and grow. A good example of this entrepreneurial transition is a recent agreement between Sunnybrook Health Sciences Centre, located in Toronto, and Sanofi-aventis, a major pharmaceutical player. Researchers at Sunnybrook have created a breakthrough compound that could help millions of people afflicted with diabetes. The agreement provides Sanofi-aventis with exclusive rights to commercialize a compound, called Vasculotide, that is designed to treat chronic wounds, a major threat to diabetics. The licensing fee, paid in the form of royalties, will return to Sunnybrook Health Sciences Centre much-needed dollars to support continued research and to fund patient care.[9] Other not-for-profits, such as the Salvation Army, the March of Dimes, and the Cerebral Palsy Association of Canada, have developed retail thrift stores as a mechanism for generating revenues to support their organizational missions and financial requirements. The Business in Action feature on SolarShare illustrates the use of a cooperative business arrangement for the execution of a business opportunity.

As has been stated earlier, the balancing act for not-for-profits seeking additional revenue through the sale of products and/or services is to accomplish this without being perceived as abandoning their mission, and without causing the for-profit sector to challenge their not-for-profit status, and the tax shield that it provides, due to perceived unfair competitive practices. Absent the ability to seek private-equity investment, and challenged by heightened competition among NFPs for a dwindling pool of philanthropic dollars, not-for-profits increasingly need entrepreneurial ideas and concepts if they are to ensure the long-term sustainability of their organizations.

Business IN ACTION

SolarShare—Cooperatively Redefining Renewable Energy Investments

SolarShare is a cooperative, not-for-profit enterprise that purchases, owns, and operates solar photovoltaic (PV) installations in the province of Ontario. We are all familiar with the traditional organizational profit model highlighted in this text, but what is a cooperative? The International Co-operative Alliance (ICA) defines a cooperative as "an autonomous association of persons united voluntarily to meet their common economic, social, and cultural needs and aspirations through a jointly owned and democratically controlled enterprise." Cooperatives can be used as a corporate vehicle in almost all sectors of the economy, but they differ from traditional organizations in that most strive to operate in a manner that maintains a balance among people, planet, and profit, often referred to as the triple bottom line.

SolarShare's value proposition is based around providing Ontarians with triple-bottom-line benefits on their investments: a financial return, local community power and job creation, and environmentally friendly clean energy production. A unique business model is used to achieve this. First, SolarShare utilizes a bridge loan (currently at 10% interest) to fund the construction of an optimal solar PV site, which may be located on rooftops or exposed land areas. Once the solar PV site is operational, the bridge loan is then refinanced via the offering of SolarShare bonds to individuals and businesses residing in Ontario. By purchasing a Solar Bond, SolarShare members currently earn 5% simple interest annually on a 5-year bond and 6% on a 15-year bond. The revenue to pay bondholders their earned interest comes from the sale of the generated renewable energy into the electricity grid. To date, bondholders have received $4 million in energy returns while supporting the development of clean energy alternatives.

The Ontario Power Authority (OPA) has guaranteed the purchase price of SolarShare's power for 20 years through the establishment of feed-in-tariff (FIT) contracts. Successful in Europe, these contracts

(and overall approach) are designed to encourage investment in renewable energy sources, which generally have large initial capital investment requirements and long investment timelines. SolarShare achieves the triple bottom line by hiring local contractors to install the solar PV projects, using the guaranteed power prices to provide a low-risk, financially competitive return on the purchased bonds, and allocating any surplus to fund further renewable energy projects. A sample of how a SolarShare project is developed and its underlying benefits is provided in the image below.

Many private companies are vying for rooftops and land space in Ontario's solar PV industry, but they typically employ the traditional model of private finance. SolarShare's value proposition and use of the cooperative model, however, yield some unique competitive advantages when bidding for solar PV sites. For example, the OPA's FIT rules give priority to community-owned FIT projects, which allows SolarShare to quickly secure spaces and guaranteed prices for their upcoming solar PV projects. Having a cooperative designation also improves access to community-oriented roof hosts and developers, such as schools and municipalities, because of their aligned values. Furthermore, commercial properties that host a SolarShare solar PV project benefit from SolarShare branding through grassroots community engagement. Like any investment, there are potential risk factors to be considered. Solar energy production requires advanced equipment, and there is no

Courtesy of SolarShare, used with permission.

guarantee it will generate electricity and revenue as expected. However, SolarShare has a diverse portfolio of solar PV projects to disperse the risk across multiple projects, therefore reducing impact in the event that a project performs below expectations. Projects underwritten by SolarShare can be found across Ontario, including Brampton (6), Kingston (3), Markham, Aurora, Mississauga, Timiskaming (8), Kaladar, and Toronto, to name a few.

In order to purchase a Solar Bond, one must become a member of the SolarShare cooperative by paying a $40 lifetime fee, which offers privileges to members in addition to the bond investment opportunity. As a democratically controlled enterprise, SolarShare membership provides its members with a vote at SolarShare board meetings regardless of investment—as opposed to publicly traded companies, where you have as many votes as you do shares. Additionally, members may log in to their SolarShare account at any time to view how their projects are performing, with real-time updates. Solar Bonds are available to any individual or business of Ontario, but only individuals may become eligible voting members to preserve the cooperative designation.

A division of TREC Renewable Energy Co-operative, SolarShare's completed projects total 14 MW of installed capacity and carry a value in excess of $60 million. With their competitive "lower-risk" rates of return, Solar Bonds can be an impactful foundation of any investment package, including RRSPs. TREC also operates two wind-powered energy cooperatives, Lakewind and WindShare, which owns 50% of the wind turbine at the Canadian Exhibition Place in Toronto.

Web Integration

To learn more about Solar Share and TREC, visit **www.solarbonds.ca** and **www.trec.on.ca**.

Management Reflection—The "Go or No Go" Decision

As stated earlier in this chapter, the idea of starting one's own business has tremendous appeal to many individuals. The feeling of being your own boss can be second to none. Having said that, the physical, emotional, and financial stress that it places upon an individual, and his/her family, can be challenging to say the least. An important aspect of assessing a business opportunity is the understanding of the market risk and the level of financial commitment the new business will require. The use of the "capitalization well" (see Figure 15.9), developing a strong feeling for the initial capital requirements at the time of business inception, and the ongoing required cash infusions needed to become cash flow positive and reach the breakeven point are essential analytical elements to determining whether a business opportunity can attain the revenue levels required to sustain itself and whether its backers possess the capacity to provide the level of capitalization needed to ensure its formation and operational liquidity and solvency. Financial risk assessment alone, however, does not constitute a formal venture analysis. Investors and/or business analysts must look beyond the numbers and fully analyze other health and performance metrics. Reviewing the product development process, assessing customer connection tactics, critically evaluating the acumen of the management and/or entrepreneurial team, and identifying the specialized assets and employee skill sets needed for success are all fundamental to this analysis.[10] Analysts and investors also need to assess the operational capacity of the infrastructure being put into place in order to determine if the financials being projected can actually be realized via the value chain being developed. Venture analysis is all about validating the opportunity, placing this

FIGURE 15.16   **Market/Opportunity Pyramid**

opportunity in context with the external market dynamics within which it will operate, and assessing the people skills on board to seal the deal and drive its execution.
The core "go or no go" decision will, ultimately, come down to whether the idea being presented can achieve sufficient scale to ensure short-term initial success and
longer-term sustainability. A tool to assist in the conclusion of a "go or no go" decision is what is termed the market/opportunity pyramid (see Figure 15.16). If the response to the five questions posted in the pyramid is yes, then a "go" decision would
appear to be the likely conclusion reached.

Chapter Summary

The purpose of this chapter is to provide students with a base-level understanding of
the process required to competently assess a new business venture. This process,
which has been developed around six key phases, seeks to develop a systematic approach toward the analysis of the market risk and financial risk that the venture will
be exposed to. This analytical process also assesses the internal competencies present within the management team, the proposed business structure, and the vision of
the entrepreneurs behind the project in terms of sustainability and commitment,
thereby enabling the reviewer to draw conclusions relating to the viability and
potential success of the venture. The six phases that form this process are market
analysis, value analysis, financial analysis, operations analysis, management
competency analysis, and exit options. The discussion also recognizes that not all
business opportunities are created organically, but that opportunities for acquiring
a business form a key part of new business opportunity and growth plans. With this
in mind, a preliminary discussion of the approach that individuals and/or businesses
should consider when acquiring a business is also provided. The chapter closes with

a note pertaining to the role of venture analysis in the not-for-profit sector, and a closing management reflection on the key components that form the decision-making process leading up to a "go or no go" business venture decision.

Developing Business Knowledge and Skills

Key Terms

entrepreneur *p. 594*

litmus test *p. 599*

cash flow positive *p. 604*

start-up costs *p. 605*

capitalization well *p. 605*

undercapitalization *p. 605*

organic growth *p. 613*

acquisition *p. 613*

operational synergies *p. 614*

EBITDA *p. 615*

fair market value *p. 616*

goodwill *p. 616*

Questions for Discussion

1. What is meant by the term "fatal flaws"? Why is the identification of fatal flaws so important when assessing a business venture? (LO1)

2. Describe the "litmus test" approach to conducting a value analysis. Do you agree with this approach? Is there anything else that you would add to it? (LO3)

3. With respect to new ventures, what is the importance of conducting a sensitivity analysis when assessing revenue potential and projected cost estimates? (LO3, LO4)

4. What is the purpose of the capitalization well? Why is knowing this information so important to new venture analysis? (LO3, LO4)

5. What are the key perils that entrepreneurs need to recognize and plan for when launching a new business start-up or embarking upon an aggressive growth strategy? (LO5)

6. What additional factors need to be taken into consideration (beyond the six phases of business venture assessment) when considering an acquisition? (LO6)

Question for Individual Action

Assume that you are considering opening a College Pro painting franchise in your home town this summer. Using the six phases of new venture assessment as a guide, prepare a business plan for this potential new venture. Be sure to focus on both market risk and financial risk analysis.

Team Exercise

Choose a recent public corporate acquisition. Research both the acquiring company and the target company. What reasons were provided for the acquisition? What synergies were identified as key immediate benefits and communicated by the acquiring company to stakeholders at the time of the acquisition? What was the purchase price? How was the acquisition financed? Now, fast-forward to today. Have the synergies that were communicated at the time of the acquisition actually been realized? Is the acquisition believed to be successful in the eyes of the acquiring stakeholders? Prepare a presentation to your class summarizing your conclusions.

Case for Discussion 1

Financial Assessment of a Business Opportunity

New Venture Opportunity Analysis—Perfect Blend

Given your business background and acumen, a friend and her spouse have asked you to evaluate a potential business opportunity they have been researching. Having a strong love of coffee, ample savings, and some experience in the service industry sector, they have been searching for an opportunity that will enable them to test their entrepreneurial spirit and skills. After months of searching, they believe that they have stumbled upon the *perfect* opportunity for a café/bakery/deli-style business.

Perfect Blend Franchise Opportunity

The opportunity they are asking you to formally assess is an investment in a franchise called the Perfect Blend. Franchise marketing literature indicates that Perfect Blend franchisers can earn upward of an annual 15% return on investment (ROI) and achieve annual sales volumes as high as $1.5 million. Quick at math, your friend realizes that netting 15% of an estimated $200 000 to $250 000 equity investment is approximately $35 000. Not bad compared to the paltry interest rates on savings accounts being paid by banks today (1% range).

Discussions with the franchisor (Perfect Blend) have indicated the following franchise-based expenses.

- A one-time franchise fee of $40 000
- Annual franchise royalties of 6% of gross sales
- Annual marketing fund payments of 3% of gross sales

Perfect Blend

The Perfect Blend provides a complete line of coffee, specialty coffees, and food products. The Perfect Blend Café and Bakery franchise was started by two former executives with Tim Hortons, and now total 51 locations across Central and Western Canada. A product breakdown for the typical Perfect Blend Café and Bakery franchise would be as follows:

- A wide range of coffee and assorted beverages including lattés, cappuccinos, espressos, steamers, blended teas, frozen drinks, and smoothies.
- "Perfection" sandwiches featuring power breakfast bagel sandwiches, paninis, pitas, wraps, and deli sandwiches including the famous "Montreal smoked meat" sandwich
- Fresh-baked-daily breads, muffins, cookies, pastries, and sweets
- All natural and organically stocked soups, salads, and California nouvelle cuisine

Although it is recognized that the actual size of the Perfect Blend Café and Bakery franchise will vary by location, most stores are in the 2500-square-foot range.

As was indicated earlier, franchise store revenues for the 51 stores currently operating in Canada have hit as high as $1.5 million. Annual store revenue, on average, however, is generally around the $1.2 million level (in years two and beyond).

Your Task

Excited about the opportunity, your friend and her spouse are all set to write the $40 000 cheque necessary to get their franchise awarded and to begin making their dream of being in business for themselves a reality. An initial trip to the bank, however, has doused their enthusiasm a bit, as the lender is requiring that they create a business plan prior to agreeing to lend them a portion ($420 000) of the estimated dollars needed to buy the equipment and prepare the store for opening day.

Analytical Focus

Based on the expenses estimates provided by the couple (see appendix below), you are now ready to begin preparing for a more formal discussion and reaching some conclusions relating to whether they should pursue this opportunity. In this regard, look to assess the opportunity based on the following questions:

a. Given class discussion and your prior exposure to business:

- What initial questions would you pose to your friend and her spouse with respect to the venture?

- What would you identify as being your biggest concern in launching a Perfect Blend franchise?

b. Identify the estimated start up-costs (to the point of commercialization) associated with this investment.

c. Calculate the initial BEP (breakeven point) for this venture in $$$, as well as BEP+P, and BEP+P+DPR.

d. Conduct a sensitivity analysis associated with potential revenue outcomes (realistic, pessimistic, and optimistic). Given your anticipated revenue range, create a projected statement of comprehensive income (income statement) that captures this range of outcomes and identifies the estimated profit potential.

e. Create a projected year-one statement of cash flow for the organization. Based on this, provide a recommendation for an additional working capital allowance (if required) for the first year of operation.

f. Given the bank's limit of $420 000 in financing, how much money would you recommend that your friend and her spouse need to personally invest in order to properly finance this start-up?

g. What concerns (if any) do you have about this investment, given the financial analysis you have conducted?

Finally, although aggregate financial analysis is important, what key additional underlying information would you direct them to develop in order to fully assess this risk? This should include operational and/or market risk concerns.

Appendix: Financial Information
Financial Capacity

- Your friend and her spouse's pre-approved borrowing line from the bank (conditional upon an acceptable business plan) is $420 000. This would be repaid over 10 years* and carries an interest rate of 7.5% on the loan. Assuming approval, the first-year loan amortization schedule would be as follows:

  ○ Annual interest payments in year 1 = $31 200

  ○ Annual principal repayment in year 1 = $28 800

1st Year Estimated Sales

- Initial first-year sales for a Perfect Blend franchise are typically around $1 080 000. There have been a few stores recently, however, whose first-year sales revenues have reached $1 200 000. Having said this, some franchise store locations have failed to reach $1 000 000 in sales in year 1, with average sales revenue of $950 000.

- The average cheque size per visit per customer is $8.00.

---

*Amortization period for the loan cannot exceed the length of the franchise agreement (10 years)

Estimated Start-up Costs

- The initial investment for equipment, betterments and improvements is projected to be $500 000.

- Incorporation fees and related professional fees to start the business are estimated at $3500.

- Prepaid expenses (deposits, site reconfiguration, etc.) are $20 000, payable prior to the start of business operations.

- Owner training and pre-opening expenses (at the Winnipeg head office location) are estimated at $10 000.

- Pre-opening inventory, required to be purchased prior to the commencement of operations, would be 1/12th of the annual cost of goods sold.

Estimated Operating Expenses (based on average existing franchise performance)

- **Annual Direct Operating Expenses** (as a percentage of sales) are typically as shown:

  - Cost of Goods Sold   34%

  - Total Labour   32%

  - Royalties   6%

  - Perfect Blend Ad Fund   3%

  - Local Advertising Expenses   1%

  - Misc. Expenses   7%

- **Annual Indirect Operating Expenses**, based on local market conditions, are estimated to be:

  - Lease Costs $35.00 per square foot**

  - Utilities $3.50 per square foot**

  - Insurance $10 000

  - Professional Fees $1500

  - Depreciation*   10% of Total Value of Equipment (10-yr straight-line depreciation*** schedule)

  - Lease Costs $35.00 per square foot**

**Use average store square footage of 2500 sq. ft., noted above, to project these expenses

***Depreciation schedule cannot exceed franchise agreement period (10 years)

Case for Discussion 2

Entrepreneurship: Skills and Opportunity

Alexandra Greenhill and Careteam Technologies

Dr. Alexandra Greenhill is no stranger to Canada's new-venture community. A physician with a talent for tech, she spearheaded the development of myBestHelper, a digital marketplace that connects families and providers of child care, home care, and elder care services. The two-sided platform is free for helpers, with an easily navigable interface allowing them to create a profile and apply for jobs in minutes. Families can post jobs and search for helpers for free, and build an enhanced membership profile for a fee.

Greenhill also developed Littlecodr, a card game that teaches children to code. She and cofounder Nathan Slee began talking about teaching kids to code when they were attending the GROW conference in Whistler, B.C. Greenhill talked about a card game she had been using with her children and Slee quickly developed a Web site to promote the idea to other attendees.

"It resonated so much that before the tech conference wrapped up, the pair had sold 24 games and were committed to turning Greenhill's homemade game into Little Codr," the *Vancouver Sun* reported at the time.

She has gone on to advise numerous health and IT ventures, and has served as a mentor and a judge in numerous hackathons and start-up weekends.

"As an executive physician, I didn't know I was an entrepreneur until I met other entrepreneurs and realized my mindset is like theirs," Greenhill says. "I discovered that entrepreneurs are people who think 'hey, this can be made better!' and then go to make it happen."

She has received numerous awards for her achievements, including being recognized as one of WXN's Top 100 Most Powerful Women in Canada. She is also the only Canadian to be recognized as a Cartier Women's Initiative Award Laureate.

"You'd be hard pressed to find anybody in Vancouver who doesn't know who she is," says entrepreneur and investor David Tedman. Tedman was a founder at Vancouver-based Invoke, responsible for the acceleration of ventures including HootSuite, Foodee, and BrightKit.

Greenhill's latest venture is Careteam, where she is co-founder, CEO, and CMO (chief medical officer). A member of the Vancouver-based Digital Technology Supercluster, Careteam's mission is to defragment health care. Anyone who has ever cared for a seriously ill friend or family member knows exactly what problem Careteam is attempting to solve. While many services are provided by a range of formal health care providers, services are also provided by informal and "hidden" providers, including patients themselves.

"It's not just about coordinating between the formal health care physicians and the formal providers," says Careteam COO Rob Attwell. "It's also the family and a sprawling network of direct and indirect caregivers that play a critical role in mitigating the illness experience for complex patients."

Unfortunately, there is no platform on which the services of the myriad providers and all of the associated information can easily be reconciled.

Careteam aims to be that platform.

Its "AI-enabled, patient-first ecosystem"—a sort of "virtual binder"—provides for collaboration among health care professionals, friends and family members, and third-party app integration.

Careteam aims to deliver against the four elements of the quadruple bottom line advanced by the Institute for Healthcare Improvement (IHI): improving the health of the population, reducing the cost of providing health care, improving the care experience for individual patients, and increasing the satisfaction of health care providers. It is currently involved with several large-scale pilot projects, including one with the 23 organizations under the Champlain Dementia Network in Ottawa.

"Careteam unites the patient, family, personal caregivers and health care providers as one team around a shared, dynamic care plan," says Sheila Bauer, CEO of the Dementia Society.

The organization is also expanding into the U.S. and the U.K.

Questions

1. What business model elements do myBestHelper and Careteam have in common? How do they create value? Consider using the value analysis litmus test to support your answer. You might also visit https://www.mybesthelper.com /and https://careteam.tech/ to learn more about each venture.

2. In addition to Greenhill as CEO and Ivey grad Attwell as COO, the management team at Careteam comprises experienced health technology executive Jeremy Smith as CCO and experienced tech leader Kevin Lysyk as CTO. Using the Management Acumen Assessment Model (MERFS) and any other information you wish to gather, comment on whether you believe the Careteam passes the management competency analysis test as part of the venture analysis fishbone diagram.

Glossary

Accounts Payable   refers to money owed by an organization to its suppliers and other short-term service providers.

Accounts Receivable   refers to money owed by customers of the organization for products or services that the organization has delivered to such customers, but has not yet received payment for.

Acquisition   refers to the process of acquiring another company or operation.

Activities   refer to key processes an organization undertakes in order to deliver products and services to the marketplace.

Activity Ratios   assist managers in assessing the efficiency and effectiveness of key components of an organization's operations.

Arbitration   is the settling of a dispute by a third party, whose decision is considered to be binding on both parties to the dispute.

Assets   refers to (1) the infrastructure and resource base of the organization; (2) the resources that the organization has at its disposal and that it can utilize in the generation of business activity and, ultimately, profit.

Balance of Trade   is the relationship between imports and exports over a defined period of time. A positive balance (where exports exceed imports) is known as a trade surplus. A negative balance (where imports exceed exports) is known as a trade deficit.

Black Market   is the illegal market that arises within economies where goods are scarce, taxation on such goods is high, or the prices of legitimate goods are beyond the capacity of significant segments of the population to buy.

Board of Directors   is the term for the governing body of a corporation, comprising individuals chosen or elected to oversee the management of the organization; an appointed or elected body of a for-profit or not-for-profit corporation that oversees and advises management on issues challenging the organization on behalf of its stakeholders and shareholders.

Bond   refers to a credit facility with which an organization borrows money for a stipulated period of time. In return for the use of these funds, the organization promises to pay the holder of the bond an agreed-upon amount of interest at regular intervals (generally, semi-annually) during the period of time for which the funds are borrowed.

Breakeven Point (BEP)   refers to the point where total expenses = total revenue. The income statement, which takes into consideration actual cash expenses as well as non-cash expenses, results in profit = $0.

Business   refers to the mission-focused activities aimed at identifying the needs of a particular market or markets, and the development of a solution to such needs through the acquisition and transformation of resources into goods and services that can be delivered to the marketplace at a profit.

Business Models   can be best visualized as the underlying operational platform or structure which a business uses to position its approach to a given market and thereby generate its revenue and, most importantly, derive its profit.

Business-Level Strategy   outlines specific objectives the organization hopes to achieve for each of its identified business initiatives and/or business units.

Buy-Sell Agreement   is a written agreement among the partners that details the sale by one partner and the purchase by another of the business interest of the selling partner.

Cannibalism   is the reduction in sales of an existing product/service due to the launch of a new, similarly targeted product/service offering.

Capacity   refers to the maximum amount of product that can be produced, or services delivered, given facility, equipment, and process constraints.

Capital   refers to the money needed by an organization to support asset-based expenditures, meet operating cash requirements, and invest in the development of new products and/or services which the organization desires to introduce into the marketplace.

Capital Asset Evaluation and Acquisition   refers to an assessment by the operations management team of the state of current capital assets and a determination as to their applicability to meeting the needs of the organization.

Capital Asset Transactions   are the decisions managers make with respect to investment and divestment of capital assets (buildings, equipment, business subsidiaries) that may be needed, or are no longer needed, as part of the organization's business system.

Capital Structure   refers to an organization's mixture (use) of debt, internal cash reserves, and external equity-based investments in financial support of operational activities.

Capitalization Well   refers to a framework for assessing the full capital requirements of a business venture.

Cash Flow Positive   refers to that point in time when an organization is able to cover the actual cash expenses of an operation from the revenue it generates.

Cash Operating Cycle (COC)   refers to the amount of time it takes for an organization to recover the cash (product is sold and money is received) it has paid out for the development, production, and distribution of products.

Channel Intermediary   refers to an organization that assists a company in the distribution and delivery of goods or services to its customers.

Chartered Banks   are financial institutions regulated under the Canada Bank Act. Their primary responsibility is to bring together borrowers and lenders by accepting deposits and lending out money—all in a manner that safeguards the interests of their customers.

Code of Conduct   is the name for a statement that describes the required responsibilities, actions, and rules of behaviour of an organization's employees.

Collateral is an asset that an individual pledges as security toward a credit facility (loan); the individual agrees to forfeit the collateral in the event of an inability to repay the loan.

Collective Bargaining Agreement is a legally binding document that defines the policies, procedures, and protocols both the company and its union have agreed to with respect to the regulation of workplace conditions for a defined period of time.

Collective Entrepreneurship ensures that the involvement of the community where an organization is located and the population that it serves are reflected in the formulation and implementation of the strategy.

Commercial Endeavours refers to the markets the organization serves, the products and services it offers, and the needs it professes to meet in the marketplace.

Commoditization is the process by which products and/or services that have been considered unique and/or distinguishable in the past become similar, or non-differentiated in the eyes of the consumer.

Comparative Advantage refers to the ability of a country to produce or supply goods or services at a lower cost than other countries or to possess resources or unique services that are unavailable elsewhere.

Competitive Advantage occurs when a company possesses capabilities that enable it to perform critical activities better than its rivals; this advantage enables it to generate greater sales and/or margins and creates preference for its products and services in the minds of its customers.

Competitive Emphasis refers to the extent to which the organization rewards and reinforces goal achievement, emphasizes competitiveness (internal and external), and defines its success on the basis of market superiority.

Consumer Price Threshold refers to the maximum price point that the customer is willing to pay for a product or services.

Control Protocols refers to the rigidity or flexibility associated with the application of, and adherence to, rules, policies, and procedures within the organization.

Controlled Systems refers to economic systems where the fundamentals of the law of supply and demand, private ownership, entrepreneurship, and wealth creation are largely restricted or absent, and the government fully controls the economic direction and activity.

Convenience Goods are goods purchased by customers on a regular basis, with minimum effort and little emotional connection.

Coordination of the Work Effort is the organization and allocation of the HR complement, and the development of the structure surrounding it, in a manner that produces the most effective and efficient business system.

Corporate Social Responsibility (CSR) is the understanding that the purpose of an organization is to create shared value (business and society) by strategically integrating into its actions a partnership mentality with society where the objectives of both parties are met.

Corporate-Level Strategy defines what the organization intends to accomplish and where it plans to compete.

Corporation is a business entity that, legally, is separate and distinct from its owners.

Cost of Borrowing refers to the total sum of money over and above the principal borrowed paid by an organization as a result of incurring and repaying a debt obligation. This would include interest paid as well as costs incurred in setting up the credit facility.

Cost of Capital is the cost of company funds (both debt and equity).

Cost Structure the expenses that will be incurred as a result of offering products and/or delivering services to the marketplace.

Cradle-to-Cradle Sustainability Management is the process whereby organizations create production and distribution techniques that are not just more efficient but are truly waste free.

Credit Facilities is a general term that describes the variety of loans that could be offered to a business or a country.

Crowdfunding is the process of funding a project or business venture by raising money via an Internet-supported funding management system.

Culture defines how the individuals within the organization behave and how the organization as a whole will react to both internal and external challenges and stimuli.

Customer Desertion occurs when customers move to a competitive offering due to a change in brand or product communication message focus.

Customer Intimacy is the term for the interactions and connectivity that organizations seek to foster with their customers in order to meet their expectations for contact, service, and support.

Customer Service refers to the support provided to customers before, during, and following the purchase process.

Debt Leverage refers to the use of debt to finance an organization's capital asset base.

Debt Ratios focus on the amount of debt an organization has taken on, the relationship of this debt value against its total asset base, and the ability of the organization to meet its debt servicing (payments) obligations.

Decision-Making Control refers to the level of responsibility and decision-making authority that is actually transferred to each specific managerial position.

Deflation occurs when prices fall. The concern with deflation is that falling prices reduces revenue and income, which affects the ability to meet debt obligations as well as impacting government tax revenue.

Degradation is the deterioration of the environment through the depletion of resources and the destruction of ecosystems.

Departmentalization refers to the process of dividing the organization's work units into defined functional areas.

Designated Restricted Assets are assets that have been earmarked for a specific purpose and that are not available for managers to support organizational operating needs.

Direct Distribution refers to connecting directly with customers and handling the final sale of products and/or the delivery of services without the assistance of a channel intermediary.

Directional Lock-In is the level of financial and operational commitment an organization incurs as a result of implementing the organization's strategies.

EBITDA is earnings before interest and taxes + depreciation expense + amortization expense.

Eco-efficiency Management is the tactical shift required within our business operations to maximize the efficiency of our resource utilization and minimize or eliminate the resulting current degradation to the planet.

Economies of Scale are reductions in the cost base of an organization as a result of greater size, process standardization, or enhanced operational efficiencies.

Employee Interaction refers to the value-creating skills an organization's employees bring to the marketplace. The success of many businesses lies with the specialized skills that exist within its labour force.

Entrepreneur refers to a person who starts a business and is willing to accept the risk associated with investing money in order to make money.

Environmental Stewardship is the integration of sustainability values into the managing of environmental resources.

Ethics is a reflection of the moral principles or beliefs about what an individual views as being right or wrong.

Exchange is an organization that facilitates the trading of securities, stocks, commodities, and other financial instruments. Exchanges provide a platform for selling these financial instruments to the public at large.

Exclusive Distribution refers to a decision by an organization to offer its products and/or services through a single market representative.

Expense Creep refers to the tendency for expenses associated with the organization's various cost lines to rise due to inflationary pressures, union negotiated contracts, and so on.

Facility Design and Layout refers to infrastructure layout and related facility components that will be required to house and support the processes and materials used by the organization.

Fair Market Value is the price that a tangible asset or property is worth in the marketplace.

Feed-in Tariff refers to government payment subsidy arrangements whereby participants are paid a guaranteed premium for energy developed through the adoption of alternate energy sources.

Financial Protectionism refers to government actions or policies that restrict or restrain the outflow of funds from one economy to another.

Fixed Costs (Indirect Costs) are those costs that, although not directly tied to the manufacturing of a specific product or the delivery of a specified service, nonetheless exist as a result of conducting our business and operating our company.

Floating Exchange Rate is one whose value is allowed to move relative to other currencies. The value of the currency is set by foreign exchange market and is influenced by the demand for that currency via the forex market.

Forecasting and Budgeting refers to management's ability to project forward anticipated results for the upcoming quarter, year, or planning-cycle period.

Foreign Direct Investment (FDI) occurs when a company or individual from one country makes an investment into a business within another country. This investment can reflect the physical ownership of productive assets or the purchase of a significant interest in the operations of a business.

Forensic Accounting is the integration of accounting, auditing, and investigative skills.

For-Profit Companies are organizations whose overarching objective is profitability and wealth creation on behalf of their shareholders and stakeholders.

Free Trade Agreements facilitate international trade between companies that is not constrained or regulated by governments, and that is not impacted via the use of tariffs, duties, or other monetary restrictions.

G7/8 is a quasi-organization comprising the world's major fully developed economies. The G7 consists of the United States, Japan, Germany, Great Britain, France, Italy, and Canada. In 2006, the G7 transitioned to the G7/8 with the inclusion of Russia into its membership. Heads of the G7/8 countries meet at least once annually to discuss major economic, political, and societal issues challenging the global marketplace. Recent meeting trends have also resulted in representatives of major developing economies (such as China) attending at least part or all of such summit meetings. Although still relevant, the G7/8 is seeing its overall global economic influence diminishing, as the larger G20, consisting of the G7/8 countries as well as representatives from developing economies, is anticipated to become the more policy-influencing organization with respect to economic decisions globally.

Gantt Chart is a methodology used to schedule the steps associated with a project and the time required to complete each step.

GDP (Gross Domestic Product) refers to the total market value of the goods and services (economic output) a nation produces domestically over a period of time (generally one calendar year).

Goodwill is the additional amount that a company or individual is willing to add to the value of a company it is acquiring, above the fair market value of its tangible assets.

Grievances are complaints raised by an employee.

Gross Profit Margin is the portion of an organization's revenue that is left over after the organization has paid the direct costs (wages, components, materials, etc.) associated with its products or services.

Harvesting is a strategy that reflects a reduced commitment to a particular market given its perceived weak future growth or profitability potential.

Hostile Takeover refers to an attempt by a company to take over another company whose management and board of directors are unwilling to agree to the merger or takeover.

Inbound Logistics refers to the management of supplier relationships relating to those parts and/or components, or finished products, that are brought into the organization in order to produce finished products for delivery to the marketplace.

Incorporation is the legal process of setting up a corporation.

Indirect Distribution implies the use of a channel intermediary, such as a broker, wholesaler, or retailer, to facilitate the sales of a company's products and/or services to its customers.

Inflation   is a rise in the level of prices of goods and services within an economy over a period of time.

Inflection Points   are decision points where the current path a business is taking is assessed relative to where the company is and where it should be.

Information Technology–Based Operational Analytics   refers to the assessment of historical, as well as predictive data in a way that enables the operations management team to actively manage the organization's current and future operational needs.

Integrity   is honesty, reliability, ethics, moral judgment.

Intensive Distribution   is a decision by an organization to distribute the product and/or service through as many locations or channel outlets as is possible.

IPO (Initial Public Offering)   refers to the initial sale of stock, by a corporation, through a public exchange.

ISO (International Organization for Standardization)   is the world's largest developer and publisher of international standards.

Joint and Several Liability   refers to the liability obligation of partners as the result of a legal contract. Partners can be held individually liable for their share of the obligation (several), or fully liable for the full obligation (joint) in the event that the other parties to the agreement are unable to pay their obligations.

Labour   refers to the human resource (talent) requirements of the business.

Lagging Indicators   are outputs measured after the fact (such as revenue, profitability, net new customers, and sales lead conversion rate).

Law of Supply and Demand   refers to the ability of the market, independent of external influences, to determine the price for which a product or service will be bought and sold.

Leading Indicators   are activities and actions that can be tracked or measured at the front end, revealing almost instantaneously how well the organization is executing its strategy.

Lease Obligations   represent a legal obligation to pay a service provider with an agreed-upon amount of money, via a defined periodic payment schedule over an identified period, in return for the use of property, equipment, or some other service.

Leverage   refers to the amount of debt an organization uses in order to finance its asset base.

Liabilities   are the debts or financial obligations that an organization has incurred as a result of conducting its business.

Limited Liability Partnership (LLP)   is a partnership that is made up of both general partners (at least one) and limited (passive) partners.

Line of Credit   refers to an arrangement with a lending institution that provides an organization with a pre-arranged borrowing ceiling (maximum) that the organization can draw on at any time, and in any amount, up to the agreed-upon limit.

Liquidity   refers to the cash position of a company and its ability to meet its immediate debt and operational obligations. It also refers to the ability of the company to convert existing assets to cash in order to meet such obligations.

Litmus Test   refers to a process or something that is used to make a judgment or draw conclusions about the acceptability of an opinion.

Long-Term Credit Facilities   represent debt that an organization obligates itself to repay over a time frame that exceeds one year.

Long-Term Note   refers to a credit facility under which an organization borrows a stipulated amount of money for a defined period of time (which exceeds one year), and with a defined interest rate schedule (fixed or variable).

Managerial Acumen   refers to the foresight, drive, knowledge, ability, decision-making competency, and ingenuity of the organization's key individuals—its owners or top-level managers.

Managerial Hierarchy   refers to the number of levels of management deemed necessary to effectively manage the organization, and the sequential ranking of the managerial positions in relationship to one another.

Margin   represents the portion of an organization's revenue that is left over after paying for an identified level of costs.

Market Capitalization Value   refers to the current market value of an organization. It is calculated by taking the number of shares outstanding multiplied by the current value of its shares.

Marketing   is the process through which organizations design, develop, and communicate the value of their products and/or services.

Marketing and Sales   refers to those activities that create profile and awareness for the organization's products, services, or brand(s), and the benefits derived from the acquisition and use of such products or services.

Marketing Mix   refers to an organization's strategic and tactical decisions relating to its product/service offerings, pricing, distribution, and marketing communication efforts and approaches.

Mark-up Pricing   refers to the addition to the manufacturer's price that distributors add to the price of a product to ensure that their own direct and indirect costs are covered and that their profit margin is achieved.

Materials Management   refers to the management of the inputs required in order to develop the products or services that the organization is intent on delivering to the marketplace.

Mediation   is the process by which management and the union invite a third party to assist in the resolution of a dispute.

Message Rifling   is a focused message, driven by a well-defined and developed value proposition, that is targeted specifically at a defined audience.

Mission   defines an organization's purpose or reason for existence.

Mixed Distribution Systems   are distribution systems that incorporate both direct and indirect distribution options within their distribution strategy.

Mixed Economic System   refers to an economic system that contains components of both open and controlled systems. It includes the core principles of economic freedom, with some degree of centralized economic planning and government regulation and involvement.

Monopolistic Markets are markets that possess a number of different suppliers of products and services, but the nature of the product or service, along with the marketing effort initiated by businesses within the sector, has enabled true differentiation to set in.

Monopoly-based Markets are markets that are served by a single product/service supplier.

Mortgage refers to a credit facility that is backed by real estate collateral (generally, the real estate the mortgage underwrites), and that sets forth a defined schedule of periodic payments for the full repayment of the debt owed, plus interest, over a defined period of time.

Multi-Channel Distribution refers to the incorporation of a number of different channel connections through which customers can purchase a product and/or service.

Nature of the Work refers to the specific tasks that need to be accomplished at the individual job level within the organization.

Net Change in Cash Position refers to the net movement in the cash position of the organization based on operating, financing, and investing activities.

Not-for-Profit Organizations (NFPs) are organizations whose overarching objective is not profitability and wealth creation but to deliver services to the people, groups, and communities that they serve via a model of collective interest and social goal achievement.

Offshoring is transferring a component (operations, service, support) of a firm's business system to another country for the purpose of reducing costs, improving efficiency or effectiveness, or developing a competitive advantage.

Oligopoly-based Markets are markets that contain a small number of suppliers that control a large percentage of market share within the market, and that compete on the basis of products and/or services that have achieved success in distinguishing themselves from their competitors.

Open System refers to an economic system that adheres to the principles of economic freedom: the law of supply and demand, full and open access to the principles of private ownership, entrepreneurship, and wealth creation, and an absence of regulation on the part of government.

Operating Plan is a detailed, immediate-term set of objectives and corresponding tactics designed to achieve a specific business initiative.

Operating Profits equal total revenue minus total operating expenses.

Operational Synergies refers to maximization of productivity and efficiency through the combining of resources.

Operational Transactions represent the flow of money within the organization that is directly related to day-to-day business dealings.

Operations refers to the manufacturing and/or product change processes set up to ensure that the final product the organization is manufacturing or handling is ready for the marketplace.

Operations Cycle is the alignment of the operational tasks within an organization by its management team in order to meet the strategic outcomes defined in the organization's business strategy.

Operations Management is the effective design, development, and management of the processes, procedures, and practices embedded within an organization's business system for the purpose of achieving its strategic intent.

Opportunity Assessment is analyzing the marketplace in such a way (via marketing research and data analytics) that enables the organization to determine which segments are most likely to respond to its communication messages and purchase its products and/or services.

Organic Growth refers to growth that comes from an organization's existing business portfolio.

Organizational Culture and Decision-Making Structure is a reflection of the framework of the business activities and decision-making ecosystem that exists within an organization.

OTC (Over-the-Counter) refers to stocks being publicly traded through a dealer network versus an exchange.

Outbound Logistics refers to getting the finished product to the customer via a distribution channel that is accessible, convenient, and able to minimize stockouts and other sales impediment factors.

Outsourcing is contracting out a portion of, or a component of, a firm's business system for the purpose of reducing costs, improving efficiency or effectiveness, acquiring expertise, or developing a competitive advantage.

Owners' Equity represents the value of capital received from the owners of the business that is used to fund the start-up or ongoing operations of the business, as well as reflecting the value of the organization's retained earnings.

Paris Agreement has an overall objective to bind all nations to a "common cause" response to the emerging crisis associated with climate change.

Parity means being equal or equivalent to; specifically, the value of one currency being equal to that of another.

Partners refers to complementary dependencies and/or relationships we have with other organizations that are deemed essential to the design, development, and delivery of products and services to the marketplace.

Partnership is a business organization that is formed by two or more individuals.

Partnership Agreement is a written agreement among the partners that outlines the expectations of each partner and details how the partnership is going to work.

Payback Period represents the length of time required to recover, or earn back, the cost of an investment.

Peak Model Theories are based on the belief that resources are finite and that, at some point in time, the availability of such resources will pass their maximum production point and begin to decline.

Pegging is when the value of one country's currency remains constant against another currency. It is also referred to as a fixed exchange rate.

Personal Power is the power that a manager possesses as a result of his/her leadership competencies. It is the ability to motivate, facilitate, demonstrate empathy, and collaborate with staff in order to meet organizational expectations.

PERT Chart is a scheduling methodology that focuses on task sequencing and the identification of the critical path of steps that will most greatly impact the ability to complete a project, and the length of time needed for completion.

PESTEL Analysis refers to a macro-level assessment of the political, economic, social, technology, environmental, and legal trends that can or will impact the markets within which an organization competes.

Philanthropy refers to the receipt of funds from another person or organization for the purpose of using them to enhance the well-being of others.

Ponzi Scheme is a type of investment fraud that involves the payment of purported returns to existing investors from funds contributed by new investors.

Position Power is the power that a manager legitimately holds due to the title he/she has within an organization. This power is derived on the basis of expertise, legitimacy of rank, the ability to control rewards and resources, and the obligation to assess performance.

Positioning refers to our ability to develop a unique, credible, sustainable, and valued place in the minds of our customers for our brand, products, and/or services.

PPP (Purchasing Power Parity) a measure that takes into account the relative cost of living and the inflation rates of each country, and adjusts the total value of economic activity accordingly.

Predetermined Purchase List refers to the ranking of products/services that purchasers develop for all the options available when making a purchase decision.

Price Dilution means that the price of existing shares of stock will decline due to the fact that a larger number of shares (which represent ownership in the company) now exist.

Price Discounting is a reduction in the price of the product with the intent to stimulate the sale of the product over a defined period of time.

Price Elasticity is the change in demand that is anticipated to occur at the various price points the organization is considering for its product and/or service.

Price Skimming refers to the utilization of a premium price strategy in order to maximize the margin return on the sale of each individual unit of a particular product.

Primary Activities relate to the specific activities through which the development and transformation of a product or service occurs as it is produced and delivered to the marketplace.

Primary Sources of Information are those that an organization develops or utilizes to generate information specific to the organization and the products and services it offers.

Private Corporations are corporations whose ownership is private. The shares of stock of the corporation are not publicly traded.

Private Equity refers to equity capital that is obtained by an organization from private sources (not through one of the public exchanges).

Process Design, Layout, and Execution refers to the assessment and implementation of the tasks necessary to get the required work accomplished, and how such tasks will be grouped and sequenced to ensure that the most efficient and effective processes are utilized in the production of products and/or services.

Process Management is the design and development of the work flow and connectivity of the transformation requirements (processes) needed to ensure that an organization's products and services are efficiently produced and effectively delivered to the marketplace.

Process Simplification is the design and utilization of a minimum number of tasks when developing products and/or services.

Process Standardization is the design and utilization of common platforms and common task sequencing to produce/develop a variety of products or services.

Product/Service Management refers to the variety of activities that commence with the design and development of potential new products in R&D and extend to the post-purchase support of products/services now in the hands of customers.

Product/Service Portfolio refers to the different items, products, and/or services that a company offers for sale.

Productivity Cycle includes the processes involved in transforming materials into a product or service available for sale in the marketplace.

Profit is the "bottom line" result an organization has realized for an identified, immediate period of time. In simple terms, Total Revenue − Total Expenses = Profit.

Profit Leaks are inefficiencies within an organization's marketing mix that result in margin erosion and loss of profit.

Profitability measures how well a company is using its resources over a specific period of time to generate earnings relative to its competitors.

Profitability Margin is the portion of an organization's revenue that is left after all operating expenses associated with its products or services have been paid.

Profitability Ratios focus on assessing the amount of income the organization has earned in comparison to the operating activity that has taken place and the assets that have been used to support its generation.

Protectionism is the outcome of the intent of economic policies that are put in place to protect or improve the competitiveness of domestic industries via impeding or restricting the openness of a market or markets to foreign competitors through the use of tariffs, trade restrictions, quotas, artificial control of currency values, or other related activities.

Psychological Pricing is the utilization of pricing tactics that are designed to respond to the psychological tendencies of purchasers.

Public Corporations are corporations whose shares of stock are traded on at least one stock exchange or are publicly available in the over-the-counter market.

Public Equity refers to equity investments in an organization, by investors, as a result of the purchase of publicly traded shares (stock) due to an initial public offering (IPO) or an additional public offering (APO), also referred to as a secondary offering.

Purely Competitive Markets   are markets that are characterized by a number of similar (undifferentiated) products or services, the absence of a dominant market leader, and few barriers to entry.

Ratios   seek to define the relationship between critical components of information found on the financial statements.

Rebates   are a temporary price reduction offered on a product or service in order to stimulate sales. Rebates can be offered at the point of sale or on a deferred basis (example: mail-in).

Recession   is a period of time that marks a contraction in the overall economic activity within an economy. A recession is typically believed to occur when an economy experiences two or more quarters of negative GDP movement.

Resource Management   is the ability to actively manage existing supplies and regenerate new supplies of materials in such a way that we minimize resource depletion.

Resources   refers to four core areas: assets, labour, capital, and managerial acumen.

Restructuring   addresses the need to change an organization's business system or desired position in the marketplace, or to make fundamental changes to the way an organization does business.

Retained Earnings   refers to the dollar amount of net earnings accumulated over the history of an organization that it has chosen to hold within the organization.

Revenue Model   focuses on the relationship between the prices organizations are able to charge for their services, the volume of purchases they are able to generate, and the profitability derived from such activity.

Risk Allowance   refers to the degree of entrepreneurship that is embedded into the organization.

Rootedness   refers to the extent to which the NFP is interwoven into the fabric of the community that it serves and is supported by a broad representation of its organizations, businesses, and citizens.

Sales Revenue   = Per Unit Selling Price × Quantity Sold

Secondary Offering   refers to an additional public offering of an organization's stock for the purpose of raising new capital.

Secondary Sources of Information   are those that already exist and are available at no cost or on a fee basis; managers use these information sources to conduct research and draw conclusions.

Segmentation   refers to determining the best way to divide the market in a manner that will result in a better understanding of potential customer needs, interests, preferences, attitudes, and behaviours.

Segmentation Stretch   refers to expanding the focus of a product/service to similar and related market segments that share a positive affinity for the product/service offering.

Selective Distribution   refers to a decision by an organization to sell its products and/or services through a limited number of channel intermediaries.

Short-Term Credit Facilities   refers to debt obligations that an organization takes on for a short period of time, generally less than one year.

Silo Mentality   refers to managerial decisions that do not take into consideration the cross-organizational impact that such decisions will have.

Six Sigma   is a methodology that focuses on a philosophy of total improvement.

Sole Proprietorship   refers to a business that is owned by one person and that is initiated without a requirement to create a separate legal entity.

Solvency   refers to the long-term stability of the company and its ability to meet its ongoing debt and operational obligations, and to fund future growth.

Solvency and Liquidity Ratios   analyze the financial obligations that an organization has against its financial resources in order to determine whether the organization possesses sufficient capital to meet its upcoming needs.

Sovereign Debt   is debt issued or guaranteed by a national government.

Sovereign Wealth Funds   are country- or state-owned investment funds.

Span of Control   refers to the number of subordinates a manager has reporting to him or her.

Stakeholder   refers to individuals, groups, or organizations that have a direct or indirect relationship with an organization, and that can be impacted by its policies, actions, and decisions. Stakeholders could include customers, suppliers, government, employees, and so on.

Start-up Costs   are the initial capital investment required to launch a new business or product venture.

Statement of Cash Flows   provides managers with a full understanding of the total movement of cash (from all sources) into and out of the business.

Statement of Changes in Financial Position   refers to a financial statement that provides managers with an understanding of the resources the organization has at its disposal at a given point in time, and the financial obligations the business has incurred as a result of purchasing these resources.

Statement of Comprehensive Income   is the financial statement that responds to the question of whether our business is earning a profit as a result of the sales we have made versus the expenses we have incurred in developing our goods and services and delivering them to the marketplace.

Stock   is a security that represents a percentage of ownership in a corporation's assets, and entitlement to a pro-rata claim on earnings when released.

Stock Exchange   is an exchange that provides a variety of services to investors, brokers, and traders, in support of the trading of stocks and other investment-related products and services.

Stockholders   refers to any person, company, or organization that owns at least one share of stock in a specific company.

Strategy   refers to the development of plans and decisions that will guide the direction of the firm and determine its long-term performance.

Structure   is the formal framework around which tasks are organized and responsibilities allocated within an organization.

Supply Chain Management   is the management of the interdependencies among suppliers, manufacturers, and distributors; it seeks to develop the terms and conditions that will enable all parties to efficiently and effectively meet their obligations to one another due to their business relationships.

Supply Chain Operating Execution   refers to the execution of the specific tasks necessary to ensure that key performance results are achieved.

Supply Chain Performance Evaluation   refers to the critical outcomes that the supply chain must achieve in support of the organization's overall operating performance.

Support Activities   are those areas within the organization that are not directly associated with the actual processes the organization uses to produce products and/or deliver services but that are an integral part of the support structure the primary activities rely on to successfully execute strategy.

SWOT   stands for strengths, weaknesses, opportunities, and threats.

Tactics   refers to the immediate-term actions which a firm executes in order to meet the short-term objectives set forth in the current planning cycle.

Target Marketing   is the process whereby organizations determine which market segments represent the strongest clustering of potential customers who are most likely to purchase the product and who have the capacity to do so.

TQM (Total Quality Management)   is a broad-based approach to managing quality within the organization.

Undercapitalization   is the situation where a company lacks the required funding to continue business activities.

Union Steward (Shop Steward)   is a representative of the union who works in ensuring that employee interests, as outlined by the collective bargaining agreement, are respected by the company and its management team.

Value Chain   is the term for the processes and initiatives needed to support and direct the product/service transformation within the organization, the creation of the value proposition applicable to such products/services, and the distribution, marketing, sales, and service in support of these products/services.

Value Maximization   refers to maximizing the benefits (price/quality comparison) that an individual or set of customers will realize as a result of using a product or service.

Value Proposition   is a statement that summarizes whom a product or service is geared toward and the benefits the purchaser will realize as a result of using the product or service.

Variable Costs (Direct Costs)   are those costs that are directly tied to the manufacturing of a product or the delivery of a service depending on the type of business being assessed.

Venture Capitalist   refers to an individual who provides capital to a business venture for start-up or expansion purposes.

Vision   is a forward-thinking statement that defines what a company wants to become and where it is going.

Visionary Leadership   involves inspiring your workforce (talent) to pursue a shared goal, beyond ordinary expectations.

Vitality   refers to the ability of the NFP to grow and sustain its membership base and donor base.

Whistleblowing   is the process through which an individual informs someone in authority of a dishonest act or the dishonest behaviour of another person.

Work Efficiencies   refers to the alignment of the tasks required to support the design, development, marketing, distribution, and sale of an organization's products/services in the most efficient and effective manner possible.

Endnotes

Chapter 1

1. Adapted from Osterwalder and Pigneur, *Business Model Generation: A Handbook for Visionaries, Game Changers, and Challengers,* John Wiley & Sons, Inc., 2010.

2. Gareth R. Jones, *Introduction to Business: How Companies Create Value for People,* McGraw-Hill Irwin, 2007, pp. 4–33.

3. "Microsoft Recognizes Outstanding Contributions by Suppliers," Microsoft.com, May 2014.

4. "Microsoft Corporation, 10-K Filing, August 2018," Microsoft.com/investor/SECFilings.

5. "The Rise of Cheap Smartphones," *The Economist,* April 5, 2014, print edition.

6. "Microsoft Corporation, 10-K Filing, August 2018," Microsoft.com/investor/SECFilings.

7. Ibid.

8. "Amazon Go Could Open 'Thousands' of Stores Over Next Three Years," CSA staff, *Chain Store Age,* chainstoreage.com/technology/amazon-go-could -open-thousands-of-stores-over-next-three-years/#, September 19, 2018.

9. Shelley Kirkpatrick, "Visionary Leadership Theory," *Encyclopedia of Leadership, 2004,* Sage Publications, 2011.

10. Elspeth Murray and Peter Richardson, *Fast Forward: Organizational Change in 100 Days,* Oxford University Press, Inc., 2002.

11. http://www.fastcompany.com/1690654/blockbuster -bankruptcy-decade-decline, September 22, 2010, referenced October 2014.

12. QMI Agency, "Target Acquisition Highlights Canada's Allure for Foreign Retailers," *Toronto Sun,* January 14, 2011, www.torontosun.com; Strauss and McNish, "With Target, Canada's Retail Landscape Set for Massive Makeover," *The Globe and Mail,* January 13, 2011, www.theglobeandmail.com.

Chapter 2

1. G7/8, http://www.g7.utoronto.ca/what_is_g8.html, July 27, 2009.

2. Foreign Affairs and International Trade Canada, "State of Trade and Investment Update 2009," www .international.gc.ca/economist-economiste/performance, May 26, 2010; "Economic Research," BMO Capital Markets, June 22, 2007.

3. Trading Economics, https://tradingeconomics.com /canada, February 18, 2019.

4. Michael Porter, "Diamond Model, Competitive Advantage of Nations Diamond Model," http://www .valuebasedmanagement.net/methods_porter_diamond _model.html, referenced August 22, 2008.

5. "Foreign Direct Investment, 2017," Statistics Canada, https://tradingeconomics.com/canada/foreign-direct -investment, January 31, 2019.

6. Historical Price, Statistics Canada Charts, https:// www150.statcan.gc.ca/t1/tbl1/en/cv.action?pid=18100001 01#timeframe, January 31, 2019.

7. Statistics Canada, "Sales of Fuel," Statista.com, January 31, 2019.

8. Bannock, Baxter, and Davis, *Dictionary of Economics,* 7th edition, Penguin Books.

9. https://countryeconomy.com/gdp/canada, January 31, 2019.

10. Trading Economics, "Canada GDP," http://www .tradingeconomics.com/canada/gdp, referenced January 8, 2015.

11. https://www.statista.com/statistics/270001/distribution -of-gross-domestic-product-gdp-across-economic -sectors-in-the-us/, January 31, 2019.

12. The World Factbook—Central Intelligence Agency, https://www.cia.gov/library/publications/the-world -factbook/fields/2012.html, January 31, 2019.

13. https://tradingeconomics.com/canada/gdp-growth -annual, Statistics Canada, February 5, 2019.

14. T. Macklem and K. Lynch, "What Will It Take to Restore Canada's Potential Growth?" *The Globe and Mail,* January 31, 2018.

15. RBC Economics/Research, "Provincial Outlook, December 2014," http://www.rbc.com/economics /economic-reports/pdf/provincial-forecasts/provfcst -dec2014.pdf, referenced January 10, 2015.

16. BMO Financial Group, "BMO Annual Debt Report," August 5, 2014, http://newsroom.bmo.com/press-releases /bmo-annual-debt-report-household-debt-up-6-per-ce-tsx -bmo-201408050960770001, referenced January 11, 2015.

17. Gordon Isfeld, "Bank of Canada More Worried about Household Debt Than Falling Oil Prices," *Financial Post,* December 3, 2014, http://business.financialpost .com/2014/12/03/bank-of-canada-more-hawkish-on -economy-though-oil-price-plunge-household-debt-pose -risks/, referenced January 11, 2015.

18. RBC Economics, http://www.rbc.com/economics /economic-data/pdf/economy_can.pdf, January 2019.

19. Canadian Grocer, http://www.canadiangrocer.com/top -stories/headlines/food-prices-to-rise-1-5-to-3 -5-in-2019-84463, December 4, 2018.

20. Knoema, World GDP Ranking by Country, https:// knoema.com/nwnfkne/world-gdp-ranking-2017-gdp-by -country-data-and-charts, December 2018.

21. Peter Franklin, Osler, Hoskin & Hartcourt LLP, "Canada: Wilson Report Recommends Far-Reaching Changes to Canadian Investment and Competition Laws,"

July 17, 2008, Mondaq, http://www.mondaq.com/article.asp?articleid163368, referenced August 9, 2008.

22. History of Foreign Takeovers in Canada, https://www.toronto.com/news-story/8130901-a-history-of-foreign-takeovers-in-canada/, February 2018.

23. "Announced M&As from Canada to Abroad," IMAA, https://imaa-institute.org/m-and-a-canada/, February 7, 2019.

24. Conference Board of Canada, "Environment," http://www.conferenceboard.ca/hcp/details/environment.aspx, referenced January 21, 2015.

25. "Canadians Conflicted about 3Es: Environment, Energy and the Economy," CBC, https://www.cbc.ca/news/business/cbc-ekos-poll-energy-economy-country-conflicted-1.3483312, February 7, 2019.

26. Aging Workforce News, "Canada: Oil Industry Facing Skills Shortage," www.agingworkforcenews.com, March 29, 2011; David Friend, "Canadian Workforce Aging Rapidly," www.thestar.com, March 4, 2008.

27. "Canadian Business Counts," June 2018, Statistics Canada, https://www150.statcan.gc.ca/n1/daily-quotidien/180821/dq180821c-eng.htm, accessed February 7, 2019.

28. McInnes Cooper, "Digital Privacy Act, 5 FAQs About the New Mandatory Data Breach Response Obligations," https://www.mcinnescooper.com/publications/the-digital-privacy-act-5-faqs-about-the-new-mandatory-breach-response-obligations-effective-november-1-2018/, February 7, 2019.

29. "Canadian Retail Sales MOM," Trading Economics, http://www.tradingeconomics.com/canada/retail-sales, referenced January 2019.

30. "5-Year Potash Price," InvestmentMine, http://www.infomine.com/investment/metal-prices/potash/5-year/, referenced January 2019.

31. Michael Porter, "Five Competitive Forces Model," Value Based Management.net, http://www.valuebasedmanagement.net/methods_porter_five_forces.html, referenced August 22, 2008.

32. Digital Music News, "Music Downloads Are Nearing Extinction as Sales Tank 27.4%," https://www.digitalmusicnews.com/2018/07/10/music-downloads-extinct/, February 7, 2019.

33. McDonald's Revenue 2016–2018, https://www.macrotrends.net/stocks/charts/MCD/mcdonalds/revenue, February 7, 2019.

34. eMarketerRetail, https://retail-index.emarketer.com/company/data/53fb4e4eddb53b4f60ebedfa/53fb4f1eddb53d57b8093bc5/lfy/false/mcdonalds-store-productivity, February 11, 2019.

35. American Customer Satisfaction Index Scores, 2006 to 2018, https://www.statista.com/statistics/194988/customer-satisfaction-with-us-limited-service-restaurants-since-2006/, February 11, 2019.

36. "Fallen Arches: Can McDonald's Get Its Mojo Back?" *Fortune*, fortune.com/2014/11/12/can-mcdonalds-get-its-mojo-back/, referenced January 31, 2015.

37. McDonald's Net Income 2016–2018, https://www.macrotrends.net/stocks/charts/MCD/mcdonalds/net-income, February 11, 2019.

38. https://corporate.mcdonalds.com/corpmcd/investors-relations/financial-information/annual-reports.html, referenced 2018.

Chapter 3

1. Wal-Mart Stores Inc., 2018 Financial Factbook, Fiscal Year 2018, https://s2.q4cdn.com/056532643/files/doc_financials/2018/annual/FY18-Fact-Book.pdf, February 12, 2019.

2. "Lululemon: Store Locations," http://www.lululemon.com/stores/#show-location-list, referenced January 22, 2015.

3. "Magna: Facts & History," http://www.magna.com/about-magna/facts-history, referenced January 22, 2015.

4. Fortune Global 500, 2018, http://fortune.com/global500/list/filtered?searchByName=Magna%20International, February 12, 2019.

5. "Chinese Company, US Farm Coop to Build Milk-Powder Plant in Kansas," ChinaDaily USA, November 14, 2014, http://usa.chinadaily.com.cn/business/2014-11/14/content_18911802.htm, referenced January 22, 2015.

6. "Plant to Open in Kitchener Thanks to U.S. Duties on Chinese Steel Nails," The Record.com, December 11, 2014, http://www.therecord.com/news-story/5203581-plant-to-open-in-kitchener-thanks-to-u-s-duties-on-chinese-steels-nails/, referenced January 22, 2015.

7. "New Chinese Baby Formula Plant to Buy Canadian Milk," CBC News, https://www.cbc.ca/news/politics/feihe-plant-trade-1.4228502, August 3, 2017.

8. "For More Chinese Firms, It Pays to Make It in the U.S.A.," *Wall Street Journal*, https://www.wsj.com/articles/for-more-chinese-firms-it-pays-to-make-it-in-the-u-s-a-1488127931, February 26, 2017.

9. Sheridan Prasso, "American Made, Chinese Owned," *Fortune*, May 24, 2010.

10. "Alberta's Oil Sands, Economic Benefits," http://oilsands.alberta.ca/economicinvestment.html, referenced January 23, 2015.

11. "The Great Oil Sands Era Is Over," https://newsinteractives.cbc.ca/longform/the-great-oilsands-era-is-over, September 17, 2018; "$40B LNG Project in Northern B.C. Gets Go-Ahead," https://www.cbc.ca/news/canada/british-columbia/kitimat-lng-canada-1.4845831, October 2, 2018.

12. Vanderklippe and Hoffman, "China Makes Billion-Dollar Oil Patch Move," *The Globe and Mail Report on Business*, May 13, 2010.

13. Shawn McCarthy, "Canada a Quiet Powerhouse in Africa's Mining Sector," *The Globe and Mail*, May 10, 2010; Canadian Mining Assets, Natural Resources Canada, Informational Bulletin, http://www.nrcan.gc.ca/mining-materials/publications/15382, referenced January 15, 2015; https://www.newswire.ca/news-releases/enbridge-announces-definitive-agreement-to-acquire-all-public-equity-of-spectra-energy-partners-advances

-corporate-structure-simplification-691628621.html;
https://www.globenewswire.com/news-release/2016/11
/01/1300331/0/en/Columbia-Pipeline-Partners-LP
-Announces-Agreement-to-Purchase-its-Outstanding
-Common-Units-and-Declares-Quarterly-Distribution
.html.

14. *Global Metromonitor 2018*, Brookings Institution,
https://www.brookings.edu/wp-content/uploads/2018/06
/Brookings-Metro_Global-Metro-Monitor-2018.pdf,
referenced February 15, 2019.

15. Companies in Dublin, Ireland, https://www.glassdoor
.ca/Reviews/dublin-reviews-SRCH_IL.0,6_IM1052
.htm?countryRedirect=true, referenced February 15,
2019.

16. CAE Inc., https://www.cae.com, February 15, 2019.

17. Jeff Immelt, "Time to Re-embrace Globalisation," *The
Economist, The World in 2009*, print edition, Nov. 19,
2008.

18. "The World Trade Organization...Members and Observers,"
www.wto.org, referenced January 27, 2015.

19. "In Italy's Piracy Culture, Black Market Is Thriving,"
New York Times, www.nytimes.com.

20. "Judge in Massachusetts Download Case Rules for Music
Companies," *USA Today*, July 31, 2009, www.usatoday
.com.

21. "A Debt Crisis Seems to Have Come Out of Nowhere,"
NPR, https://www.npr.org/sections/goatsandsoda/2018/0
4/20/604169277/a-debt-crisis-seems-to-have
-come-out-of-nowhere, April 20, 2018.

22. "The US Debt and How It Got So Big," The Balance,
https://www.thebalance.com/the-u-s-debt-and-how-it-got
-so-big-3305778, February 13, 2019.

23. "What Is the Paris Agreement?" https://unfccc.int
/process-and-meetings/the-paris-agreement/what-is-the
-paris-agreement, referenced February 21, 2019.

24. Bank of Canada, https://www.bankofcanada.ca/,
February 24, 2019.

25. "How Do Exchange Rates Work?" Brightside, http://
www.brightknowledge.org/knowledge-bank/business
-and-finance/features-and-resources/how-do-exchange
-rates-work, referenced January 29, 2015.

26. Investor's List: Countries with Fixed Currency Exchange
Rates, http://www.investmentfrontier.com/2013/02/19
/investors-list-countries-with-fixed-currency-exchange
-rates/, referenced January 29, 2015.

27. "CIC, Sovereign Wealth Fund," *Globe and Mail Report on
Business*, August 12, 2009.

28. "China Is Hoops Country," https://www
.bloomberg.com/opinion/articles/2017-09-28
/basketball-not-soccer-is-china-s-game-of-choice.

29. "The NBA Is China's Most Popular League." CNBC,
https://www.cnbc.com/2018/11/20/the-nba-is-chinas-most
-popular-sports-league-heres-how-it-happened.html,
November 20, 2018; "The NBA's Hoop Dream: World
Domination," *Bloomberg Businessweek*, February 23,
2015, referenced May 23, 2015.

Chapter 4

1. The Sustainability Business Report, "Natural Capitalism,"
www.sustreport.org/business, March 2011; The
Sustainable Development Journey, BSD Global, www
.iisd.org/business/sd_journey.aspx, March 2011;
McDonough & Braungart, "The NEXT Industrial
Revolution," *The Atlantic Online*, www.theatlantic.com
/past/docs/issues/98oct/industry.htm, March 2011.

2. United Nations Department of Economic and Social
Affairs, Population Division (2017), *World Population
Prospects: The 2017 Revision*, New York: United Nations.

3. Ibid.

4. "One Degree Over: Climate Change on Crop Yields," *The
Economist*, Science and Technology, March 19, 2011.

5. Beinhocker and Oppenheim, "Building a Post-Carbon
Economy," McKinsey & Company, February 2009, http://
whatmatters.mckinseydigital.com/climate_change
/building-a-postcarbon-economy, March 2011.

6. International Agencies Promote Global Revolution in
Vehicle Fuel Economy, Global Fuel Economy Initiative
News Release, January 25, 2011.

7. "Impact of Deforestation, Atmospheric Role of Forests,"
Mongabay.com, http://rainforests.mongabay.com, March
2011; "Deforestation," National Geographic.com, http://
environmenta.nationalgeographic.com/environment
/globalwarming/deforestation/overview, March 2011;
"10 Countries with Highest Deforestation Rates in the
World," www.forestforclimate.org, September 2009.

8. Nasa Global Climate Change, https://climate.nasa.gov,
referenced February 27, 2019.

9. McCartor and Becker, *World's Worst Pollution Problems
2010: Top 6 Toxic Threats*, Blacksmith Institute, New
York, NY.

10. Andrea Thompson, "Pollution May Cause 40 Percent of
Global Deaths," www.lifescience.com, September 2007.

11. https://www.pureearth.org/, referenced June 29, 2019.

12. Enerdata, Global Energy Statistical Yearbook 2018,
https://yearbook.enerdata.net/total-energy/world
-consumption-statistics.html, referenced March 1, 2019.

13. Enerdata, Global Energy Statistical Yearbook 2018,
https://yearbook.enerdata.net/total-energy/world
-consumption-statistics.html, referenced March 1, 2019.

14. McKinsey's Global Energy Perspective 2019, https://
www.mckinsey.com/industries/oil-and-gas/our-insights
/global-energy-perspective-2019, referenced March 1, 2019.

15. "American Oil Is Coming to Flood the Market—Or Is
It?" *Forbes*, https://www.forbes.com/sites/ellenrwald
/2019/01/03/american-oil-is-coming-to-flood-the-market
-or-is-it/#6174a03232ec, January 3, 2019.

16. Alberta Energy, https://www.energy.alberta.ca/OS/AOS
/Pages/FAS.aspx, referenced March 1, 2019.

17. "Suncor Cuts $1B in Capital Spending, Plans to Chop
1000 Positions," *Calgary Herald*, January 14, 2015, http://
calgaryherald.com/business/energy/suncor-cuts-1b-in-capital
-plans-to-chop-1000-positions, referenced February 11, 2015.

18. "Averting the Next Energy Crisis: The Demand Challenge," McKinsey Global Institute, McKinsey & Company, March 2009.

19. World Economic Forum, "90% of Fish Stocks Are Used Up—Fisheries Subsidies Must Stop Emptying the Ocean," https://www.weforum.org/agenda/2018/07/fish-stocks-are-used-up-fisheries-subsidies-must-stop/, July 13, 2018.

20. Peter Goodchild, Depletion of Key Resources, Facts at your Fingertips, Culture of Change, January 2010

21. David Hopkins, "Depletion of Water Resources More Serious Than Oil Reserves," www.edie.net/news, February 18, 2005; Alex Hutchinson, "Las Vegas Tries to Prevent a Water Shortage," Popular Mechanics, www.popularmechanics.com/science/environment, October 1, 2009; Dan Shapley, "Natural Resources Being Depleted at Record Rates: Vital Signs Report," www.thedailygreen.com/environmental-news/laterst/6628, 2011; Southern Nevada Water Authority, www.snwa.com, referenced February 11, 2015.

22. "Water Deeply, Desalination in Las Vegas," https://www.newsdeeply.com/water/articles/2018/04/17/desalination-in-las-vegas-faraway-ocean-could-aid-future-water-needs, April 17, 2018; The Nevada Independent, "The Las Vegas Pipeline Is Dead, the Las Vegas Pipeline Is Alive," https://thenevadaindependent.com/article/the-las-vegas-pipeline-is-dead-the-las-vegas-pipeline-is-alive, referenced March 3, 2019.

23. Dobbs, Lund, and Schreiner, "How the Growth of Emerging Markets Will Strain Global Finance," McKinsey Quarterly, McKinsey & Company, December 2010.

24. Dobbs and Spence, "The Era of Cheap Capital Draws to a Close," McKinsey Quarterly, McKinsey & Company, February 2011.

25. Dictionary of Sustainable Management, http://www.sustainabilitydictionary.com/cradle-to-cradle/, referenced February 12, 2015.

26. Berns, Townend, Khayat, Balagopal, Reeves, Hopkins, and Kruschwitz, The Business of Sustainability, Imperatives, Advantages, and Actions, The Boston Consulting Group, September 2009.

27. "The Colour of Money: Wyoming Hot Springs Transformation from Coins Tossed by Tourists," Dreamstime, Toronto Star, April 9, 2011.

28. Joe Castaldo, "Special Report: Nuclear Options," Canadian Business, April 11, 2011.

29. Ibid, and CBC News, "Canada Narrows List of Possible Locations for Nuclear Waste Facility," https://www.cbc.ca/news/technology/canada-narrows-list-of-possible-locations-for-nuclear-waste-facility-1.2604160, April 9, 2014.

Chapter 5

1. David Voreacos, "Madoff Criminal Charges: Summary of the 11 Counts Against Him," Bloomberg, March 11, 2009; Diana B. Henriques, "Madoff Sentenced to 150 Years for Ponzi Scheme," New York Times, June 30, 2009; "Madoff's Victims," WSJ Reporting: The Associated Press, The Wall Street Journal, March 6, 2009; Anthony Destefano, "Prosecutors Reduce Madoff's Ponzi Scheme Total to $13B," Newsday.com, June 19, 2009.

2. The Guardian, "Apple and Samsung Fined for Deliberately Slowing Down Phones," https://www.theguardian.com/technology/2018/oct/24/apple-samsung-fined-for-slowing-down-phones, October 24, 2018.

3. "Biggest Scandals of 2017," Fortune, http://fortune.com/2017/12/31/biggest-corporate-scandals-misconduct-2017-pr/, December 31, 2017.

4. Ibid.

5. Ingrid Peritz, "Jones Enjoyed Lavish Lifestyle at Investors' Expense, Trustee Says," The Globe and Mail, August 19, 2009.

6. Oliver Moore, "Dozens of Charges Laid in Nova Scotia Legislature Expenses Scandal," The Globe and Mail, February 14, 2011; Leblanc and Sher, "Quebec Corruption Probe Reaches From Hard Hats to High Rise Offices," The Globe and Mail, December 3, 2010; Jordana Huber, "Integrity Czar to Review Agency Expenses, McGuinty," National Post, Canwest News Service, September 1, 2009; and Rod Mickleburgh, "Trial's End Lets Campbell Liberals Off the Hook," The Globe and Mail, October 18, 2010.

7. "What You Need to Know about the SNC-Lavalin Affair," CBC News, https://www.cbc.ca/news/politics/trudeau-wilson-raybould-attorney-general-snc-lavalin-1.5014271, February 13, 2019.

8. Supra note 6.

9. "When Your Calendar Is a Moral Document: A Conversation with Reverend Jim Wallis, CEO, Sojourners," McKinsey Quarterly, McKinsey & Company, January 2010.

10. Felton, Hudnut, and Witt, "Building a Stronger Board, Corporate Governance," McKinsey Quarterly, McKinsey & Company, 1995, Number 2; and Felton and Watson, "Change Across the Board," McKinsey Quarterly, McKinsey & Company, 2002, Number 4.

11. Donovan A. McFarlane, "The Importance of Business Ethics to Small Ventures," Entrepreneurship and Innovation Management Journal, Volume 1, Issue 1, pps. 50–59.

12. Barry Shaw, "Bill 198—Sarbanes-Oxley Comes to Canada," BRS Management Consulting, www.itprojecttemplates.com/WP_SEC_BillC198.htm, 2005; Stephanie Ben Ishai, Associate Professor, Osgoode Hall Law School, "Sarbanes-Oxley, Five Years Later: A Canadian Perspective," Loyola University Law Journal, June 2008, www.luc.edu.

13. News Release, Financial Accounting Standards Board, January 28, 2011, www.fasb.org/cs/; International Accounting Standards Board, ISAB and FASB update to G20 Leaders, June 2, 2010, www.ifrs.org.

14. 2017 Cone Communications CSR Study, http://www.conecomm.com/research-blog/2017-csr-study, referenced March 11, 2019.

15. Bonini, McKillop, and Mendonca, "What Consumers Expect from Companies," McKinsey Quarterly, McKinsey & Company, 2007.

16. Bonini, Brun, and Rosenthal, "Valuing Corporate Social Responsibility: McKinsey Global Survey Results," *McKinsey Quarterly,* McKinsey & Company, 2009; Bonini, McKillop, and Mendonca, "What Consumers Expect From Companies," *McKinsey Quarterly,* McKinsey & Company, 2007.

17. "Six Tiny Treasures: The McGhee Sextuplets," *The Oprah Winfrey Show,* February 21, 2011.

18. *Boulevard Magazine,* August/September 2016, https://issuu.com/boulevardlifestylesinc/docs/aug_sep_2016, referenced March 15, 2019.

19. Neil Edmunds, P. Eng., "Impacts and Mitigations of In Situ Bitumen Production from Alberta Oil Sands," Submission to XXIst World Energy Congress, Montreal 2010.

20. B. Ross and J. Rhee, "Are You Playing Rental Car Roulette? Federal Study: Major Rental Agencies Rent Out Cars That Have Been Recalled for Defects," ABC News, www.abcnews.com, February 25, 2011; Rental Car Recalls in the U.S.A.—How the Industry Responds, June 18, 2017.

21. Diane Jermyn, "The Top 50 Greenest Employers," *The Globe and Mail,* April 22, 2010; Keys, Malnight, and van der Graaf, "Making the Most of Corporate Social Responsibility," *McKinsey Quarterly,* McKinsey & Company, December 2009; and Bonini, Brun, and Rosenthal, "Valuing Corporate Social Responsibility: McKinsey Global Survey Results," *McKinsey Quarterly,* McKinsey & Company, 2009.

22. Gap, "Our P.A.C.E. Program," https://www.gap.com/browse/info.do?cid=91471, referenced March 15, 2019.

23. The Business of Giving, Special Advertising Section, *Fortune* magazine in partnership with CECP, *Fortune,* February 7, 2011.

24. David Bruser, "Game Over For Shady Charity," *Toronto Star,* March 8, 2011.

25. "The CRA Has Denied over $7 Billion in Tax Claims Due to This One Scam," Global News, https://globalnews.ca/news/4132157/canada-charity-tax-scams-tax-shelters/, April 2018.

26. Number of Canadians Concerned about Charity Fraud Up Considerably, www.newswire.ca, February 2011.

27. https://www.moneysense.ca/save/financial-planning/2017-charity-100-bonus-charity-grades/, referenced March 13, 2019.

28. https://www.bombardier.com/en/governance/code-of-ethics.html

29. Anna Mehler Paperny and Patrick Cain, "Chequed Out: Inside the Payday Loan Cycle," Global News, February 11, 2015, http://globalnews.ca/news/1797406/chequed-out-inside-the-payday-loan-cycle/, referenced February 27, 2015.

30. Canadian Payday Loan Association, http://www.cpla-acps.ca/english/aboutcpla.php, referenced February 27, 2015.

31. Strengthening Ontario's Payday Loans Act, Payday Lending Panel Findings and Recommendations Report, Prepared by Deloitte, May 2014, referenced February 27, 2015.

32. http://www.moneymart.ca/payday-loans/pricing/disclosure-ontario.aspx, referenced February 27, 2015.

33. Jerry Buckland, "Financial Exclusion: Fringe Banks, and Poverty in Urban Canada," University of Toronto Press, 2012, http://www.utppublishing.com/Hard-Choices-Financial-Exclusion-Fringe-Banks-and-Poverty-in-Urban-Canada.html, referenced February 27, 2015.

34. Government of Canada, https://www.canada.ca/en/financial-consumer-agency/programs/research/payday-loans-market-trends.html, referenced March 13, 2019.

35. *Supra* note 33.

36. "Vancity Fair and Fast Loan," https://www.vancity.com/Loans/TypesOfLoans/FairAndFastLoan/, referenced February 27, 2015.

37. "Payday Lenders Squeezed by New Legislation," https://www.theglobeandmail.com/report-on-business/small-business/payday-lenders-squeezed-by-new-regulations/article37361268/, December 17, 2017.

Chapter 6

1. Kevin P. Coyne, "Sustainable Competitive Advantage," McKinsey & Company, www.mckinseyquarterly.com, 2000.

2. "Vision and Values," RBC, http://www.rbc.com/aboutus/visionandvalues.html, referenced March 16, 2019.

3. Suncor, "Our Mission, Vision, and Values," https://www.suncor.com/about-us/our-mission-vision-and-values, referenced March 16, 2019.

4. https://www.blackberry.com/ca/en/company/overview, referenced July 30, 2019

5. http://www.rbc.com/aboutus/visionandvalues.html, referenced March 16, 2019.

6. Suncor, "Our Mission, Vision, and Values," referenced March 16, 2019.

7. http://www.bpincomefund.com/about-bp/mission/default.aspx, referenced March 16, 2019.

8. 9TO5Mac, "Apple Car: Everything We Know about Apple's Rumored Electric Car," https://9to5mac.com/guides/apple-car/, February 2019.

9. Apple Acquisitions, https://acquiredby.co/apple-acquisitions/, Crunchbase, https://www.crunchbase.com/organization/apple/acquisitions/acquisitions_list, referenced March 18, 2019.

10. "Target Corporation to Exit Canada after Racking Up Billions in Losses," *Financial Post,* January 15, 2015, http://business.financialpost.com/2015/01/15/target-corp-calls-it-quits-in-canada-plans-fair-and-orderly-exit/, referenced February 20, 2015.

11. McDonald's 2018 10K, http://d18rn0p25nwr6d.cloudfront.net/CIK-0000063908/94ad07bd-66c3-433c-a81e-94f1587b0ed8.pdf, referenced March 18, 2019.

12. "McDonald's Value Strategy Takes a Turn," QSR, https://www.qsrmagazine.com/finance/mcdonalds-value-strategy-takes-turn, July 2018; "Number of McDonald's Restaurants Worldwide," https://www.thoughtco.com

/number-of-mcdonalds-restaurants-worldwide-1435174, January 25, 2019; McDonald's 2018 10K, http://d18rn0p25nwr6d.cloudfront.net/CIK-0000063908/94ad07bd-66c3-433c-a81e-94f1587b0ed8.pdf, referenced March 18, 2019.

13. Kevin P. Coyne, "Sustainable Competitive Advantage"; Roberto Buaron, "New Game Strategies," McKinsey & Company, www.mckinseyquarterly.com, 2000; Richard N. Foster, "Attacking through Innovation," McKinsey & Company, www.mckinseyquarterly.com, 2000; Amar Bhide, "Hustle as Strategy," *Harvard Business Review*, McKinsey & Company, www.mckinseyquarterly.com, 1986.

14. "Apple Pay Now Available at Nearly 16,000 Cardless Chase ATMs," https://www.macrumors.com/2018/08/01/chase-cardless-atms-apple-pay/, August 1, 2018.

15. "Canada Post Segment Reports $94 Million Loss before Tax in Third Quarter," https://www.newswire.ca/news-releases/canada-post-segment-reports-94-million-loss-before-tax-in-third-quarter-701369381.html, November 27, 2018.

16. "Grocers Getting Squeezed for Market Share and Margins," *Montreal Gazette*, http://www.montrealgazette.com/business/Grocers1getting1squeezed1market1share1margins/9510713/story.html, referenced February 25, 2015.

17. "Apple Pay Gains Momentum with an Estimated 250 Million Users," https://www.macrumors.com/2018/08/09/apple-pay-250-million-users-estimated/, August 9, 2018.

18. "Apple Pay Users Are the Types of Customers Banks Like, Says Chase," The Verge, February 25, 2015, http://www.theverge.com/2015/2/25/8106341/apple-pay-users-are-the-types-of-customers-banks-like-says-chase, referenced February 25, 2015.

19. Mars, Mars.com, referenced February 25, 2015.

20. The following resources have influenced this section of the text: Kevin P. Coyne, "Sustainable Competitive Advantage," McKinsey & Company, www.mckinseyquarterly.com, 2000; Roberto Buaron, "New Game Strategies," McKinsey & Company, www.mckinseyquarterly.com, 2000; Richard N. Foster, "Attacking through Innovation," McKinsey & Company, www.mckinseyquarterly.com, 2000; Amar Bhide, "Hustle as Strategy," *Harvard Business Review*, McKinsey & Company, www.mckinseyquarterly.com, 1986.

21. Shaw Communications Inc., "Our Culture," http://www.shaw.ca/corporate/careers/our-culture/, referenced March 19, 2019.

22. Shaw Communications, Company Overview, https://www.shaw.ca/uploadedFiles/Corporate/Investors/Presentations_And_Meetings/Investor_Relations_Presentation_January_2019.pdf, January 2019.

23. Investor Relations Presentation, https://www.shaw.ca/uploadedFiles/Corporate/Investors/Presentations_And_Meetings/Investor_Relations_Presentation_January_2019.pdf, January 2019.

24. The work of Dr. Peter Richardson, Queen's University, with respect to planning cycles and strategic turnarounds was a general resource for the discussion in this section of the text.

25. "Nokia Shows There Is Life after Mobiles," *Financial Times*, FT.com, July 24, 2014, referenced February 27, 2015; "Nokia to Re-license Handset Brand," *Financial Times*, FT.com, November 14, 2014, referenced February 27, 2015; "Nokia Announces Plans to Accelerate Strategy Execution," Nokia Corporation, October 25, 2018.

26. Guide for Analysis of Social Economy Enterprises, Réseau d'investissement social du Québec, 2005, ISBN 2-923253-01-9.

27. Ibid.

28. https://www.agropur.com/en/our-cooperative/our-history

29. https://www.saputo.com/en/investors

30. https://www150.statcan.gc.ca/n1/pub/21-004-x/2017001/article/14786-eng.htm

31. Ibid.

32. Ibid.

33. Ibid.

34. https://www.cbc.ca/news/politics/canada-supply-management-explainer-1.4708341

35. https://www.cbc.ca/news/politics/tuesday-dairy-nafta-usmca-next-1.4845810

36. https://www.agropur.com/en/our-cooperative/finances

37. Francine Kopun, "Target's Failure Sends a Message to International Retailers," *The Toronto Star*, January 16, 2015, http://www.thestar.com/business/2015/01/16/targets-failure-sends-a-message-to-international-retailers.html, referenced January 18, 2015.

38. Jonathon Rivait/*National Post*, http://business.financialpost.com/2015/01/15/target-corps-spectacular-canada-flop-a-gold-standard-case-study-for-what-retailers-shouldnt-do/.

39. Hollie Shaw, "Target Corp's Spectacular Canada Flop: A Gold Standard Case Study for What Retailers Shouldn't Do," *Financial Post*, January 15, 2015, http://business.financialpost.com/2015/01/15/target-corps-spectacular-canada-flop-a-gold-standard-case-study-for-what-retailers-shouldnt-do/, referenced January 16, 2015.

40. "Brian Cornell Addresses Questions about Exiting Canada," A Bullseye View, January 15, 2015, http://www.abullseyeview.com/2015/01/qa-brian-cornell-target-exits-canada/#.VLfAqKqhrC4.twitter, referenced January 16, 2015.

Chapter 7

1. Adapted in part from "The 7 Traits of Successful Entrepreneurs," January 10, 2014, http://www.entrepreneur.com/article/230350, referenced March 10, 2015.

2. "50 Great Entrepreneurial Quotes," http://www.travismcashan.com/50-great-entrepreneurial-quotes/, referenced March 10, 2015.

3. Adventures in Business Ventures, BNN—Business Day, March 10, 2015.

4. "Entrepreneurship, Evaluating New Venture Opportunities, Conversations with Venture Capitalists," Harvard Business School, http://www.hbs.edu/entrepreneurship /newbusiness/2004fall_1.html, referenced March 12, 2015.

5. Fitbit Inc., CapitalIQ.com, https://www.capitaliq.com /CIQDotNet/Financial/KeyStats.aspx?CompanyId =49068649, referenced March 21, 2019; "The Story of Fitbit: How a Wooden Box Became a $4 Billion Company," Wareable.com, https://www.wareable.com /fitbit/youre-fitbit-and-you-know-it-how-a-wooden-box -became-a-dollar-4-billion-company, September 9, 2016.

6. "What Should Apple Do with Its Cash," https:// investorplace.com/2019/01/what-should-apple-cash-on -hand-simg/, January 30, 2019.

7. Richard Stutely, *The Definitive Business Plan*, revised 2nd edition, FT Prentice Hall, 2007.

8. A&W, Get Started, https://awfranchise.ca/urban/, referenced March 22, 2019.

9. Tim Hortons.com, Frequently Asked Questions, https:// www.timhortons.com/us/en/corporate/franchising -frequently-asked-questions.php, referenced March 22, 2019.

10. The A&W Franchise Opportunity, A&W Food Services of Canada Inc., www.awfranchise.ca, June 2011; Tim Hortons Canada Franchise Information, www .timhortons.com, June 2011.

11. NCFA, 2019 Canadian Fintech and Funding Directory, https://ncfacanada.org/canadian-crowdfunding -directory/, referenced March 22, 2019.

12. National Crowdfunding Association of Canada, http:// ncfacanada.org/canadian-crowdfunding-directory/, referenced March 13, 2015.

13. Fundica.com, referenced March 13, 2015.

14. Ontario Securities Commission, www.osc.gov.on.ca, June 15, 2010; Autorité des marchés financiers (AMF), www.lautorite.qc.ca/autorite/a-propos.en.html, June 15, 2010. In addition, the following resources have influenced this section of the text: Holly Crosgrey, "Registering a Sole Proprietorship in Canada," Resources for Canadian Business Owners, The Free Library, May 28, 2009; Partnerships FAQ, Leanlegal.com, www .leanlegal.com/faq_partnerships.asp, June 14, 2010; and Limited Partnerships & Limited Liability Partnerships, Lohn Caulder Chartered Accountants, Topical Library, www.lohncaulder.com, June 2010.

15. "Lululemon Athletica Inc.," Advent International, www .adventinternational.com/investmentdata, June 15, 2010; Lululemon Athletica Inc. IPO, www.123jump.com, Yordanka Bahchevanska, August 1, 2007; Lululemon Receives $195 Million Infusion, Sporting Goods Business, January 1, 2006, AllBusiness, a D&B Company, www .allbusiness.com, June 2010; and Lululemon Athletica Inc., SEC Filing, Form S-1A-EX 3.5, Amended and Restated Certificate of Incorporation, www.secinfo .com, June 30, 2010.

16. Lisa Priest, "Diabetes Discovery Brings Out Hospital's Entrepreneurial Side," *The Globe and Mail,* February 15, 2011.

17. Dobbs, Leslie, and Mendonca, "Building a Healthy Organization," *McKinsey Quarterly,* McKinsey & Company, 2005, Number 3, February 2011.

Chapter 8

1. George Ambler, "25 Lessons from Jack Welch," Practice of Leadership.net, www.thepracticeofleadership.net, May 14, 2010.

2. Notes from *Mission Critical Marketing,* Ken Wong, Queen's University School of Business, May 2010.

3. Organizational Structure, www.referenceforbusiness .com/ob-or/organizational-structure.html, May 10, 2010; and Organizational Structure, www.npd-solutions.com /orgstructure.html, May 10, 2010.

4. Geert Hofstede, *Hofstede's Cultural Dimensions Model,* www.geert-hofstede.com, May 2011.

5. "Organizational Culture," Mikander, Human Resource Development, www.mikander.fi/en/culture.php, May 2010.

6. The following resources have influenced this section of the text: Saxby, Parker, Nitse, and Dishman, "Environmental Scanning and Organizational Culture," *Market Intelligence & Planning,* Volume 20, MCB UP Ltd., 2002; and Mikander, "Organizational Culture, Human Resource Development," www .mikander.fi/en/culture.php, May 2010.

7. "The Chinese Plane on Boeing's Radar," *Bloomberg Businessweek,* March 1, 2019.

8. Stuart C. Gibson, "How to Make Restructuring Work for Your Company," 2001, HBS Working Knowledge, Harvard Business School, http://hbswk.hbs.edu/cgi -bin/print?id 5 2476, May 2010; Richard Heygate, "Immoderate Redesign," *McKinsey Quarterly,* February 1993, www.mckinseyquarterly.com, May 2010.

9. https://www.forbes.com/sites/bobevans1/2018/09/24 /microsoft-ceo-satya-nadella-unveils-new-customer -weapon-tech-intensity/#dc910d4d2f41

10. https://www.forbes.com/sites/bobevans1/2018/09/17 /how-1-microsoft-is-beating-amazon-google-and -everyone-else-in-the-cloud-the-strategic -breakdown/#50c9bf1795d4

11. Ibid.

12. Ibid.

13. https://www.vanityfair.com/news/business/2012/08 /microsoft-lost-mojo-steve-ballmer

14. https://qz.com/work/1539071/how-microsoft-ceo-satya -nadella-rebuilt-the-company-culture/

15. Ibid.

16. https://www.newswire.ca/news-releases/microsoft -announces-new-canadian-headquarters-in-downtown -toronto-692971421.html

Chapter 9

1. The following resources have influenced this section of the text: Matthew Guthridge, Asmus B. Komm, and Emily Lawson, "Making Talent a Strategic Priority," *McKinsey Quarterly*, 2008, Number 1; and Gurdjian, Triebel, "Identifying Employee Skill Gaps," *McKinsey Quarterly*, May 2009.

2. The following resources have influenced this section of the text: Matthew Guthridge, Asmus B. Komm, and Emily Lawson, "Making Talent a Strategic Priority," *McKinsey Quarterly*, 2008, Number 1; "Motivating Employees When Budgets Are Tight," *McKinsey Quarterly*, www.mckinseyquarterly.com, May 2010; and Dewhurst, Guthridge, and Mohr, "Motivating People: Getting Beyond Money," *McKinsey Quarterly*, November 2009.

3. Moskowitz, Levering, and Tkaczyk, "The 100 Best Companies to Work For," *Fortune*, February 8, 2010; "*Financial Post*'s Ten Best Companies to Work for in 2010," Yerema and Caballero, Mediacorp Inc. (staff editors), November 2009; www.eluta.ca/top-employer, April 2010; and Dewhurst, Guthridge, and Mohr, "Motivating People: Getting Beyond Money," *McKinsey Quarterly*, November 2009.

4. "Canada's 50 Best Employers," *Maclean's*, November 7, 2014, http://www.macleans.ca/work/bestcompanies /canadas-50-best-employers-of-2014/, referenced April 4, 2015.

5. Gurdjian, Triebel, "Identifying Employee Skill Gaps," *McKinsey Quarterly*, May 2009.

6. Where Are You on the Journey of Good to Great? Diagnostic Tool, Individual Worksheet Packet, Release Version 1.0, Jim Collins, www.jimcollins.com, April 30, 2010.

7. *Global Human Capital Trends 2015*, Deloitte University Press, Deloitte Touche Tohmatsu Limited, 2015.

8. "Managing Employee Relations in a Unionized Environment," MyHR, http://www2.gov.bc.ca/myhr/article. page?ContentID1974128f1-3350-5aca-426e -bd326890571b&PageNumber13, referenced April 5, 2015.

9. "Managing in a Unionized Workplace," MindTools, http:// www.mindtools.com/pages/article/managing-unionized .htm, referenced April 5, 2015.

10. Government of Canada, Federal Contractors Program, https://www.canada.ca/en/employment-social -development/programs/employment-equity/federal -contractor-program.html, referenced March 31, 2019.

11. Aboriginal Employment Preferences, Policy, https://www .chrc-ccdp.gc.ca/eng/content/aboriginal-employment -preferences-policy, referenced March 31, 2019.

12. Ambaile, Kramer, "How Leaders Kill Meaningful Work," *McKinsey Quarterly*, January 2012, referenced March 27, 2015.

13. Hsieh and Yuk, "Leadership as the Starting Point of Strategy," *McKinsey Quarterly*, 2005, Number 1, McKinsey & Company, www.mckinseyquarterly.com.

14. "CEO of the Year 2014," *Canadian Business*, December 2014, referenced March 26, 2015.

15. Barton, Grant, Horn, "Leading in the 21st Century," McKinsey & Company, June 2012, http://www.mckinsey .com/insights/leading_in_the_21st_century/leading_in _the_21st_century, referenced March 26, 2015.

16. Kmazur Kewich, "Goalposts Set for Success," *Financial Post*, May 3, 2010; Derek Sankey, "Managing Staff Gets Personal," *Financial Post*, May 3, 2010; "The Things That Keep Business Owners Awake," www.BizLaunch.ca, *Toronto Star*, April 24, 2010.

17. Derek Sankey, "Managing Staff Gets Personal," *Financial Post*, May 3, 2010.

18. https://www.sodexousa.com/home/about-us /fundamentals.html

19. https://www.sodexousa.com/home/corporate -responsibility.html

20. https://www.sodexo.com/home/about-us/what-we-do /awards.html

21. https://ca.sodexo.com/home/media/news-and-press -releases/newsListArea/news-and-press-releases/2018-top -diversity-employer.html

22. https://www.sodexo.com/home/inspired-thinking/case -studies/blogList-area/case-studies/2018-global-diversity -and-inclus.html

23. https://content.eluta.ca/top-employer-sodexo/

24. https://ca.sodexo.com/home/about-us.html

25. https://www.sodexousa.com/home/about-us /fundamentals.html

26. https://www.aramark.ca/about-us/m-kit

Chapter 10

1. Kenneth Wong, *Marketing for Profit: The Mission Critical Approach*, AMBA Mission Critical Marketing, Queen's University, 2007.

2. Francois Legarde, Social Marketer, Marketing and Positioning Presentation, YMCA of Ontario, CEO Conference, February 2006.

3. "Case Study: Porter Airlines," *Financial Times*, ft.com, http://www.ft.com/intl/cms/s/0/a26dfab8-6086-11e0-9fcb -00144feab49a.html#axzz3Wx36FIwX, referenced April 10, 2015.

4. Ansoff Matrix, QuickMBA Strategic Management, www .quickmba.com/strategy/matrix/ansoff, July 2010.

5. "Canadian Tire Retail, Facts and Stats," Canadian Tire Corporation, http://corp.canadiantire.ca/en/media /factsandstats/pages/canadiantireretail.aspx, July 2010; Canadian Tire Annual Report 2009, http://canadiantire .ca/en/investors/financialreports, July 2010.

6. Population by Year, Province, and Territory, Summary Table, Statistics Canada, www.statcan.gc.ca, April 2, 2019.

7. "Spotify's Podcast Play," *Fortune Magazine*, April 2019.

8. "What Does Facebook Own? Here's the Companies It Has Acquired and the Reasons Why," April 2014, http://www .pocket-lint.com/news/128617-what-does-facebook-own -here-s-the-companies-it-has-acquired-and-the-reasons -why, referenced April 10, 2015.

9. Tata, Leadership with Trust, www.tata.com, June 2011.

10. The following resource was a key contributor to the thoughts in this section of the text: Court, Elzinga, Mulder, and Vetvik, "The Consumer Decision Journey," *McKinsey Quarterly*, 2–9, Number 3, December 2010.

11. Ken Wong, Queen's University, Instructional Slides, MBUS 800, Role of the General Manager, 2006–2008.

12. Court, Elzinga, Mulder, and Vetvik, "The Consumer Decision Journey," *McKinsey Quarterly*, 2–9, Number 3, December 2010.

13. Humane Society of Canada, www.humanesociety.com, January 2011; and Kingston Humane Society, www.kingstonhumanesociety.com, January 2011.

14. Ibid.

15. Kenneth Wong, *Marketing for Profit: The Mission Critical Approach*, AMBA Mission Critical Marketing, Queen's University, 2007.

16. https://www.pg.com/annualreport2018/index.html#/Financial-Highlights

17. https://www.tidedrycleaners.com/services

18. https://www.cnn.com/2019/02/20/business/tide-cleaners-laundry-service/index.html

19. https://adage.com/article/cmo-strategy/tide-cleaners-launches-national-rollout-plan-2-000-locations/316677

20. Ibid.

21. Ibid.

Chapter 11

1. K. Allison and C. Nuttall, "Dell to Sell Computers through Walmart," FT.com (*Financial Times*), May 24, 2007.

2. https://www.axios.com/all-of-amazons-major-2018-acquisitions-f8d30e64-b05a-46a4-b79a-d3199bb22374.html, referenced April 5, 2019.

3. shopify.com/guides/ultimate-guide-to-pop-up-shops

4. Sofame Technologies Inc., www.sofame.com, August 2010; Sofame Technologies Inc.: Sparking Growth in a Mature Manufacturing Company, Case Study, Ken Mark, Ivey Publishing 9B09M070, 2009.

5. David Edelman, "Four Ways to Get More Value from Digital Marketing," *McKinsey Quarterly*, McKinsey & Company, March 2010.

6. https://www.internetworldstats.com/stats.htm, referenced April 5, 2019.

7. Zephoria Digital Marketing, https://zephoria.com/top-15-valuable-facebook-statistics/, March 2019; Statistics —YouTube, https://expandedramblings.com/index.php/youtube-statistics/, referenced April 5, 2019; https://www.omnicoreagency.com/twitter-statistics/, referenced April 5, 2019.

8. "Tim Hortons Tops Two Million 'Likes' on Facebook," November 2012, http://www.timhortons.com/ca/en/corporate/Tims-Tops-Two-Million-Facebook-Fans.php, referenced April 16, 2014.

9. http://www.facebook.com/timhortons, June 21, 2011; https://www.socialbakers.com/statistics/facebook/pages/detail/90790343096-tim-hortons, referenced April 5, 2019.

10. http://www.facebook.com/lululemon, April 16, 2015.

11. Full List of Brands, Frito Lay, www.fritolay.com/our-snacks/full-list-of-brands.html, accessed July 31, 2019.

12. "The BCG Growth-Share Matrix," NetMBA Business Knowledge Center, www.netmba.com/strategy/matrix/bcg/, January 2011.

13. Marn, Roegner, and Zawada, "Pricing New Products," *McKinsey Quarterly*, McKinsey & Company, 2003; and Dolan, Gourville, Principles of Pricing, Harvard Business School, 9-506-021, April 3, 2009.

Chapter 12

1. "Digital Business Initiatives Demand the Use of IT Operations Analytics to Spark Transformation," Gartner, March 2015, http://www.gartner.com/document/3015519?ref=lib, referenced May 17, 2015.

2. Hitt, Black, Porter, and Gaudes, *Management,* Canadian edition, Pearson Custom Publishing, 2009.

3. The iPhone X Costs $999.00. *Money*, http://money.com/money/5014941/iphone-x-cost-price/, November 8, 2017.

4. Michael Porter, "Value Chain Model Framework," Value Based Management.net, www.valuebasedmanagement.net, May 25, 2010; and Michael Porter, "The Value Chain," QuickMBA Strategic Management, www.quickmba.com/strategy/value-chain/, May 25, 2010.

5. Nickels, McHugh, McHugh, and Cosa, *Understanding Canadian Business*, 6th edition, McGraw-Hill Ryerson, 2007; Hitt, Black, Porter, and Gaudes, *Management*, Canadian edition, Pearson Custom Publishing, 2009.

6. Toyota Production System, Toyota Vision and Philosophy, www2.toyota.co/jp/en/vision/production_system/, 1995–2010 Toyota Motor Corporation.

7. "Walmart Corporate," www.walmart.com/aboutus, May 27, 2010.

8. Tony Van Alphen, "800 New Toyota Jobs for Ontario," *Toronto Star*, December 11, 2009; "Area Toyota Plants Will Lose about 10% of Production," *London Free Press*, https://lfpress.com/business/local-business/local-auto-jobs-stable-as-toyota-adjusts-vehicle-production-plans, March 17, 2019.

9. Demand Drives, Optimizing Inventory-to-Cash Conversion to Drive Financial Performance, Executive Report, SSA Global, January 2006; Constantine, Ruwadi, and Wine, "Management Practices That Drive Supply Chain Success," *McKinsey Quarterly*, McKinsey & Company, February 2009.

10. Putten and MacMillan, *Unlocking Opportunities for Growth*, Wharton School Publishing, July 2008.

11. "Tide Laundry Products and Accessories," www.tide.ca, June 2010.

12. "Introducing the Gartner Business Model Framework," Gartner, October 2011, http://www.gartner.com/documen t/1824717?ref=QuickSearch&sthkw=gartner%20business %20model&refval=151253928&qid=, referenced May 18, 2015.

13. "Big Data and Analytics," IBM, http://www.ibm.com /big-data/ca/en/big-data-and-analytics/operations -management.html, referenced May 18, 2015.

14. "About ISO," International Organization for Standardization, www.iso.org/iso/home, May 2010.

15. Six Sigma, Aveta Business Solutions, www.sixsigmaonline .org/six-sigma-training-certification-information, May 2010; and Lean Sigma Institute Six Sigma Methodology, www.sixsigmainstitute.com, May 2010.

16. "Total Quality Management," Business Excellence, www .beexcellence.org/Total-quality-management, May 2010.

17. www.economicdevelopmentwinnipeg.com/newsroom /read,post/755/10-things-you-should-know-about -winnipeg-s-price-industries; www.priceindustries.com /corporate/about-us

Chapter 13

1. Statista.com, Shipment Forecast Sales of Tablets, Laptops and Desktops Worldwide from 2010 to 2023, https://www.statista.com/statistics/272595/global -shipments-forecast-for-tablets-laptops-and-desktop -pcs/, referenced April 9, 2019.

2. CapitalIQ.com, Microsoft Corporation, https://www .capitaliq.com/CIQDotNet/Financial/IncomeStatement .aspx?CompanyId=21835, referenced April 9, 2019.

3. Wal-Mart Stores Inc., Financials, CapitalIQ.com, https:// www.capitaliq.com/CIQDotNet/Financial/IncomeStatement .aspx?CompanyId=313055, referenced April 10, 2019.

4. Investment and capital structure terms were validated via a check against the *Investment Dictionary*, www .investopedia.com, June 2010.

5. CNBC, https://www.cnbc.com/2017/03/02/snapchat-snap -open-trading-price-stock-ipo-first-day.html, March 2, 2017; USA Today, https://www.usatoday.com/story/money /business/2018/12/07/top-ipos-2018-26-biggest-companies -went-public-year/38611947/, referenced April 11, 2019.

6. Small Cap Power, https://smallcappower.com/top-stories /top-performing-canadian-ipos/, January 5, 2018; https:// www.thestar.com/business/personal_finance/investing /2018/01/02/canadian-ipos-rebound-in-2017-and-set-stage -for-blockbuster-2018-pwc-says.html, January 2, 2018; http://www.investcom.com/ipo/historical.htm, http:// www.marketwire.com, referenced April 11, 2019.

7. https://www.pehub.com/canada/2018/11/bain-to-sell -more-canada-goose-shares-in-secondary-deal/, November 22, 2018.

8. "National Bank of Canada and Fiera Capital Corporation Announce Secondary Offering of Class A Share," February 2015, https://ca.finance.yahoo.com/news /national-bank-canada-fiera-capital-122800341.html, referenced May 10, 2015.

9. Scott Deveau, "Porter Drops Plans for IPO," *Financial Post*, www.financialpost.com, June 1, 2010. BNN Bloomberg, https://www.bnnbloomberg.ca/porter -airlines-isn-t-for-sale-but-an-ipo-is-inevitable-ceo -deluce-1.526536, July 14, 2016.

10. Marn, Roegner, and Zawada, "Pricing New Products," *McKinsey Quarterly*, McKinsey & Company, 2003; Dolan and Gourville, Principles of Pricing, Harvard Business School, 9-506-021, April 3, 2009.

11. "Shaw Announces Acquisition of a Restructured Canwest for $2.0 Billion," Shaw News Release, Shaw Investor Relations, www.shaw.ca, June 2010; Dana Flavelle and John Spears, "Shaw Buys Control of Canwest Global," www.thestar.com, February 12, 2010; "Canwest Global Communications Corporation, Company History," www.canwestglobal.com, June 2010; Calvin Leung, "The Good, The Bad and the Ugly: Canwest Global Communications," *Canadian Business*, March 30, 2009; Dana Flavelle, "Canwest CEO Opposed Bankruptcy Decision," www.thestar.com, January 11, 2010; "Debt Tests Canadian Media Giant Canwest," *New York Times DealBook*, edited by Andrew Ross Sorkin, February 27, 2009; "Canwest's Dance with Debt," Business Canada, CBC News, www.cbc.ca/money /story/2009/02/24/f-canwest.html, April 23, 2009; and Susan Krashinsky, "Canwest Newspapers to Sport New Name," *The Globe and Mail Report on Business*, www.theglobeandmail.com, July 2, 2010.

Chapter 14

1. The following resource supports the commentary across this section of the text and was also used to check the accuracy of the formulas provided: *Introduction to Financial Ratios and Financial Statement Analysis*, William Bruns, Harvard Business School, rev. September 13, 2004. The following resource was also used to check the accuracy of formulas: Definitions Verification, www .investopedia.com, January 2010.

2. CapitalIQ.com, annual and quarterly financial statements, BlackBerry Ltd., Apple, Google, and Microsoft, referenced April 12, 2019.

3. Bennett Stewart, "EVA Momentum: One Ratio That Tells the Whole Story, EVA Dimensions," *Journal of Applied Corporate Finance: A Morgan Stanley Publication*, Spring 2009.

4. CapitalIQ.com, referenced April 12, 2019.

5. Guide for Analysis of Social Economy Enterprises, Réseau d'investissement social du Québec, 2005.

Chapter 15

1. Saras D. Sarasvathy, *New Venture Performance*, Darden Business Publishing, University of Virginia, UV0811, 2006.

2. The following resources provided a general reference to comments made throughout this chapter: Course Notes, MBUS 981, Management of New Ventures, Dr. Elspeth Murray, School of Business, Queen's University, February 2011; Richard Stutely, *The Definitive Business Plan*, revised 2nd edition, FT Prentice Hall, 2007; and

Peter J. Capezio, *Manager's Guide to Business Planning*, Briefcase Books, McGraw-Hill Ryerson, 2010.

3. Franchise Package, M&M Food Markets: https://www.mmfoodmarket.com/en/franchising/how-to-become-a-franchise-partner, referenced April 17, 2019.

4. The following resource was used as a general reference for the creation of Figure 15.10 and the discussion in this section of the text: *Milestones for Successful Venture Planning*, Block Macmillan Harvard Business Review, Reprint 85503.

5. 2003 Annual Report, Notes to Consolidated Financial Statements, p. 78, Amazon.com/investor relations/annual reports and proxies, February 2011; Shopify Financial Results, CapitalIQ.com, April 18, 2019, Salesforce.com; https://www.capitaliq.com/CIQDotNet/Financial /IncomeStatement.aspx?CompanyId=122917&statekey =78951c86ca4b4ccb842e41979ff9f68a

6. Hamermesh, Heskett, and Roberts, *A Note on Managing the Growing Venture*, Harvard Business School, 9-805 -092, August 2005.

7. Tracey Lindeman, "The Downside of Starting Up: Depression, Anxiety, Loneliness, Even Suicide—The Entrepreneurship Struggle Is Real," *Montreal Gazette*, May 15, 2015, http://montrealgazette.com /business/the-downside-of-starting-up-depression -anxiety-loneliness-even-suicide-the-entrepreneurship -struggle-is-real?__lsa16e4f-2003, referenced May 22, 2015.

8. The following resource was used as a general resource for the discussion in this section of the text: *Note on Valuation for Venture Capital*, Teddy Rosenberg, Richard Ivey School of Business, Ivey Management Services, 9B09N009, March 2009.

9. Lisa Priest, "Diabetes Discovery Brings Out Hospital's Entrepreneurial Side," *The Globe and Mail*, February 15, 2011.

10. Dobbs, Leslie, and Mendonca, "Building a Healthy Organization," *McKinsey Quarterly*, McKinsey & Company, 2005, Number 3, February 2011.

Chapter Sources

Chapter 1

Business In Action: Microsoft—Reinventing the Business Model Sources: Adapted from Richard Waters, "Risks High as Microsoft Passes Cloud Milestone," FT.com/companies/technologies, http://www.ft.com/intl/cms/s/0/1c149432-811a-11e4-b956-00144feabdc0.html?ftcamp1crm/email/_2014___12___20141211__/emailerts/Company_alert/product&siteedition1intl#axzz3OBLiq0OP, December 11, 2014; https://www.capitaliq.com/CIQDotNet/Charting4/ModernBuilder.aspx?CompanyId=21835&chkKeyDev=1&fromC3=1&fromC2=1; Microsoft 10-K filing, August 3, 2018.

Business In Action: Canadian Tire—Building Out the Business Model Source: http://corp.canadiantire.ca/EN/AboutUs/Pages/FastFacts.aspx, referenced October 2014.

Business In Action: BlackBerry—Reinventing the Business Model Sources: "BlackBerry Limited, Historical Prices," https://ca.finance.yahoo.com/q/hp?s=BBRY&a=01&b=4&c=1999&d=09&e=16&f=2014&g=m&z=66&y=66, referenced October 2014; http://www.theglobeandmail.com/report-on-business/who-is-john-chen-the-man-named-to-rescue-blackberry/article15240527/, referenced October 2014; Michael Lewis, "BlackBerry Planning More Devices," *Toronto Star*, September 27, 2014; BlackBerry Limited Fiscal Year Third Quarter Results, December 20, 2018.

Business In Action: Toyota Builds for a Greener Future Sources: Brenda Welch, "Toyota Builds for a Greener Future, Corporate Caring," *Montreal Gazette*, May 10, 2008, p. A17; Ma Jie and Naoko Fujimura, "Japan Inc. Cashes in on Abenomics as Toyota Profit to Rise," *Bloomberg*, July 29, 2013, referenced January 10, 2015; Sustainability Data Book 2018, Toyota Corporation, Toyota-global.com/sustainability/report/sr/, January 8, 2019.

Business In Action: Women—Visionary Leaders In Their Own Right Source: Money Crashers, "Top 10 Female CEOs and Influential Business Women of American Companies," moneycrashers.com/female-ceos-influential-women-business/, January 8, 2019; *Fortune Magazine*, "Most Powerful Women: Fortune's 2018 Women in Business to Watch," fortune.com/most-powerful-women, September 24, 2018; Doug Murray, "20 Canadian Companies with Female CEOs," slice.ca/money/photos/companies-with-female-ceos-canada, February 7, 2018.

Chapter 2

Business In Action: Canada—A "Petro Economy" Sources: Investopedia.com, https://www.investopedia.com/articles/investing/021315/how-why-oil-impacts-canadian-dollar-cad.asp, January 31, 2019; Google.com, https://www.google.com/search?q=us+canada+exchange+rate&rlz=1C1CHBF_enCA698CA698&oq=US+canada&aqs=chrome.0.0j69i57j0l4.3424j1j4&sourceid=chrome&ie=UTF-8, January 31, 2019; Crude and Commodity Prices, WIT Crude Oil, http://www.oil-price.net/, referenced January 21, 2015; Bank of Canada, Exchange Rate 10-Year Lookup, http://www.bankofcanada.ca/rates/exchange/10-year-lookup/, referenced January 27, 2015; Canada Balance of Trade, Trading Economics & Statistics Canada, http://www.tradingeconomics.com/canada/balance-of-trade, referenced January 8, 2015.

Business In Action: 2019 Index of Economic Freedom Source: Heritage Foundation, "2019 Index of Economic Freedom," http://www.heritage.org/index/country/canada#, referenced January 31, 2019.

Business In Action: Role of the Bank of Canada Source: Bank of Canada, "About the Bank," www.bankofcanada.ca, referenced August 6, 2008.

Business In Action: GDP—Shifting the GDP Emphasis Sources: Statistics Canada, Alberta Innovation and Advanced Education, "Alberta GDP, Economic Diversity 2013," http://albertacanada.com/business/overview/economic-results.aspx, referenced January 8, 2015; Alberta Government: Gross Domestic Product, https://economicdashboard.alberta.ca/GrossDomesticProduct, February 5, 2019; Government of Canada: Economic Overview, https://www.wd-deo.gc.ca/eng/243.asp?wbdisable=true, February 5, 2019.

Business In Action: The Canadian Banking System Sources: World Economic Forum, Soundness of Banks, http://reports.weforum.org/global-competitiveness-index-2017-2018/competitiveness-rankings/#series=EOSQ087, February 5, 2019; Canadian Bankers Association, "Fast Facts About the Canadian Banking System," https://cba.ca/fast-facts-the-canadian-banking-system, February 5, 2019.

Chapter 3

Business In Action: Can Canada Compete in Today's Global Marketplace? Sources: "Canada Faces a Serious Productivity Problem," https://www.theglobeandmail.com/business/commentary/article-canada-faces-a-serious-productivity-problem/, July 1, 2018; "Canadians Are Gaining on the Productivity Front," *Wall Street Journal*, September 5, 2014, http://blogs.wsj.com/canadarealtime/2014/09/05/canadians-are-gaining-on-the-productivity-front/, referenced January 23, 2015; "Canada Slips a Notch in Global Competitiveness Ranking," *The Globe and Mail*, September 2, 2014, http://www.theglobeandmail.com/report-on-business/economy/canada-slips-a-notch-in-global-competitiveness-ranking/article20313100/, referenced January 23, 2015.

Business In Action: Lululemon Athletica—From a Small Business to a Global Player Sources: Lululemon Athletica Inc., capitaliq.com, referenced February 11, 2019; http://investor.lululemon.com/events.cfm, referenced February 11, 2019; Our Company History, www.lululemon.com, referenced January 28, 2015.

Business In Action: Fortune Global 500 Sources: "Global 500 2018," *Fortune*, http://fortune.com/global500/#, referenced February 12, 2019.

Business In Action: Alimentation Couche-Tard—A Fortune 500 Company Sources: Alimentation Couche-Tard, Annual Report 2018 and Investor Presentation, November 2018, https://corpo.couche-tard.com/en/investor-relations, referenced February 14, 2019.

Business In Action: CAE—An Innovation and Technology Leader Source: CAE Inc., https://www.cae.com/about-cae/; CAE Investor Presentation, https://www.cae.com/media/documents/Corporate/CAE_Investor_presentation_FY18Q2.pdf, referenced February 15, 2019.

Figure 3.4: WTO: Key Services Sources: www.wto.org; Mohammad Zaheer, "Functions of WTO," TRCB.com, http://www.trcb.com/finance/economics/functions-of-wto-254.htm; WTO Agreement, Worldtradelaw.net, www.worldtradelaw.net/uragreements/wtoagreement.pdf.

Business In Action: Global Spotlight—International Monetary Fund Sources: IMF Website Annual Reports, imf.org; *The Guardian*, https://www.theguardian.com/world/2018/sep/26/argentina-imf-biggest-loan, September 27, 2018, referenced February 17, 2019.

Business In Action: Global Spotlight—World Bank Source: World Bank, www.worldbank.org, referenced February 17, 2019.

Business In Action: Global Spotlight—People's Republic of China Sources: The World Bank, referenced January 27, 2015; Trading Economics, www.tradingeconomics.com, February 20, 2019; "China Set to Lower GDP Growth Target in 2019," CNBC; "An

Overview of Chinese Debt," http://www.cadtm.org/An-Overview-of -Chinese-Debt, February 20, 2019; Trading Economics, "China Balance of Trade," http://www.tradingeconomics.com/china/balance -of-trade, referenced February 20, 2019; "The Reality of China's Economic Slowdown," https://www.forbes.com/sites /yuwahedrickwong/2018/08/23/the-reality-of-chinas-economic -slowdown/#147dac314d86, referenced February 20, 2019; "China's Second-in-Command: We're Facing Greater Difficulties in Keeping Economy Stable," https://www.cnbc.com/2018/09/19/chinas-li-keqiang -says-economic-challenges-are-increasing.html, September 19, 2018.

Business In Action: Global Spotlight—Emergence of the G20 Source: G20, www.g20.org, February 17, 2019.

Business In Action: Canada Goose Source: Canada Goose Fiscal Update 2018, https://s21.q4cdn.com/699882010/files/doc _presentations/2018/03/Canada-Goose-Investor-Handout-v2.pdf, February 24, 2019; "Canada Goose Sells a Majority Stake—With a Made-in-Canada Guarantee," *The Globe and Mail*, December 10, 2013, http://www.theglobeandmail.com/report-on-business/canada -goose-sells-majority-stake-to-us-private-equity-firm/article15848715/, referenced January 28, 2015; "Canada Plays Catch-up in Race for Trade with China," *The Globe and Mail*, August 10, 2009.

Business In Action: Export Development Canada (EDC) Sources: Economic Development Canada (EDC), 2017 Annual Report, https:// www.edc.ca/EN/About-Us/Corporate-Reports/Pages/default.aspx; Canadian Benefits Scorecard 2017, https://www.edc.ca/EN/Knowledge -Centre/Economic-Analysis-and-Research/Documents/canadian -benefits-scorecard.pdf, referenced February 21, 2019.

Chapter 4

Business In Action: Cascades—Green by Nature Sources: Cascades, http:/www.cascades.com/en/sustainable-development /overview/, referenced February 26, 2019; Cascades, http://www .cascades.com/en/sustainable-development/commitment/message -management/, referenced February 26, 2019; Corporate Knights 2018 Best 50, https://www.corporateknights.com/reports/2018-best-50/; and Investor Presentation, July 2018, https://www.cascades.com /media/multiuploader_images/47/92/49/ScotiamarketingEuropeFINAL _1.pdf, referenced February 26, 2019.

Business In Action: Canada and Water Consumption Sources: The Conference Board of Canada, Environment, Water Consumption, http://www.conferenceboard.ca/hcp/details /environment/water-consumption.aspx, referenced February 10, 2015; Program on Water Governance, Factsheet: Water Use and Consumption in Canada, www.watergovernance.ca/factsheet; Shrubsole and Draper, *Water (Ab)uses and Management in Canada*, UBC Press, 2007; Canada vs. the OECD: An Environmental Comparison, OECD Environmental Data 1999, March 2011, revisited February 2015; Global News, "This Is How Much Water Canadians Waste," https://globalnews.ca/news/3016754/this-is-how-much-water -canadians-waste/, October 30, 2016.

Business In Action: Canada and the Environment—Sounding the Alarm Source: *Climate Action in Ontario: What's Next?* 2018 Greenhouse Gas Progress Report, Dianne Saxe, Environmental Minister of Ontario, Kingston Climate Change Symposium, January 17, 2019.

Business In Action: The Paris Agreement—Canada Source: The Paris Agreement, https://unfccc.int/process-and-meetings/the-paris -agreement/what-is-the-paris-agreement, referenced February 27, 2019.

Business In Action: Alberta's Oil Sands Sources: "Canadian Economic Impacts of New and Existing Oil Sands Development in Alberta (2014–2018)," Canadian Research Energy Institute, November 2014, referenced February 14, 2015; "Oilsands Climate Impacts," Pembina Institute, referenced February 13, 2015; "Oil Sands Today: Canada's Oil Sands Producers," https://www .canadasoilsands.ca/topics/RestorLand/Pages/default.aspx, referenced February 14, 2015; Alberta Energy, Facts and Statistics,

https://open.alberta.ca/dataset/b3fd8657-f6ee-4883-afbc -1339e7b7f476/resource/856e78a2-4f4f-4557-9ef1-676648eb9c3d /download/2015-facts-stats-energy-alberta-quick-facts-2015-02.pdf, referenced February 28, 2019.

Business In Action: ExxonMobil and Algae Biofuels—Will the Research Effort Yield a Transportation Fuel Option? Sources: "ExxonMobil, Synthetic Genomics Ink New Pact for Algae Biofuels," *Biofuels Digest*, May 17, 2013, http://www .biofuelsdigest.com/bdigest/2013/05/17/exxonmobil-synthetic -genomics-ink-new-pact-for-algae-biofuels/, referenced February 12, 2015; "Exxon's $100M Algae Investment Falls Flat," Oil Price.com, May 28, 2013, http://oilprice.com/Alternative-Energy/Biofuels /Exxons-100m-Algae-Investment-Falls-Flat.html, referenced February 12, 2015; "ExxonMobil Algae Biofuels Research and Development Program," www.exxonmobil.com/corporate/files /news_pub_algae_factsheet.pdf; "ExxonMobil Plans $600M Investment in Biofuels," Environment News Service, www.ens -newswire.com/ens/jul2009; Katie Howell, "Exxon Sinks $600M into Algae-Based Biofuels in Major Strategy Shift," Greenwire, www .nytimes.com/gwire/2009/07/14; "Exxon Thinks It Can Create Biofuel from Algae at Massive Scale," Fast Company, https://www .fastcompany.com/40539606/exxon-thinks-it-can-create-biofuel-from -algae-at-massive-scale, March 6, 2018.

Business In Action: Canon—Managing Materiality and the Environment Source: Canon Global, https://global.canon/en/csr /environment/, referenced March 3, 2019.

Chapter 5

Business In Action: Josephson Institute's 12 Ethical Principles for Business Ethics Source: Josephson Institute's Exemplary Leadership & Business Ethics, http://josephsononbusinessethics.com /category/business-ethics/, referenced March 4, 2019.

Business In Action: Working Canadians and the Pressure of Ethical Standards Sources: "Canada's Business Ethics Under Scrutiny: 4 in 10 Have Witnessed Wrongdoing," Huffington Post Canada, http:// www.huffingtonpost.ca/2013/07/07/business-ethics_n_3558228.html, referenced February 16, 2015; Workers Feel Increasingly Pressured to Compromise Ethical Standards, Triple Pundit, https://www.triplepundit .com/story/2018/workers-feel-increasingly-pressured-compromise -ethical-standards-says-eci/12901.

Business In Action: The Concept of Fraud Sources: "Fraud," *The Free Dictionary* by Farlex, http://legal-dictionary .thefreedictionary.com/fraud, referenced February 16, 2015; Pamela Murphy, Queen's University, QSB Insight Talks, Fraud Myths, referenced February 16, 2015.

Business In Action: The Ethisphere Institute World's Most Ethical Companies Source: Ethisphere, "World's Most Ethical Companies," http://ethisphere.com/; Covenant Health, https://www .covenanthealth.ca/ethics-centre/business-ethics, referenced March, 13, 2019; BMO, https://newsroom.bmo.com/2018-03-14-BMO-Named -One-of-the-2018-Worlds-Most-Ethical-Companies-by-the-Ethisphere -Institute, referenced March 13, 2019.

Business In Action: Canada's Best Corporate Citizens, 2017 Sources: 2017 Best Corporate Citizens in Canada Ranking, Corporate Knights, https://www.newswire.ca/news-releases/2017-best -corporate-citizens-in-canada-ranking-reveals-progress-in-gender -diversity-and-linking-pay-to-corporate-sustainability-626712321 .html, June 6, 2017.

Business In Action: McDonald's Corporation Sources: L. Burkitt, "Companies' Good Deeds Resonate with Consumers," Forbes.com, May 27, 2010, http://www.forbes.com/2010/05/26/microsoft-google -apple-ford-cmo-network-most-inspiring-companies.html, referenced July 12, 2010; McDonald's Corporation, 2009, Worldwide Corporate Responsibility Online Report: The Values We Bring to the Table, referenced July 12, 2010; https://corporate.mcdonalds.com/corpmcd /scale-for-good/our-food/foodsafety.html#approach, referenced March 13, 2019.

Chapter 6

Business In Action: Scotiabank—Executing Strategy Globally Sources: Scotiabank, Corporate Profile, https://www.scotiabank.com/ca/en/about/inside-scotiabank/corporate-profile.html; Peru Reports, https://perureports.com/pacific-alliance/; https://www.theglobeandmail.com/business/article-scotiabank-strikes-26-billion-deal-for-md-financial/; https://www.thestar.com/business/2018/02/12/scotiabank-buying-investment-manager-jarislowsky-fraser-for-950-million.html; Scotiabank Investor Presentation, Q3, 2018, https://www.scotiabank.com/content/dam/scotiabank/corporate/quarterly-reports/2018/q3/2018Q3-Marketing-Presentation.pdf, referenced March 16, 2019.

Business In Action: HBC—Reinventing Itself in the Age of Digital Transformation Sources: eTail Canada, "Here's How Hudson's Bay Company Is Reinventing Itself as a Digital Institution," https://etailcanada.wbresearch.com/hudsons-bay-company-reinventing-digital-institution-strategy-ty-u; Global News, "All Home Outfitter Locations in Canada to Close, HBC Says," https://globalnews.ca/news/4987449/home-outfitters-closing-hbc/; BNN Bloomberg, "What's the Strategy Behind HBC's European Merger," https://www.bnnbloomberg.ca/video/what-s-the-strategy-behind-hbc-s-european-merger~1486266.

Figure 6.10: Competitive Advantage (VRIN) Equation Source: Adapted from Barney's VRIN Framework (1991).

Business In Action: What Makes for a Bad Strategy? Sources: Richard P. Rumelt, "Good Strategy/Bad Strategy: The Difference and Why It Matters," Crown Business Publishers, 2011; Richard P. Rumelt, "The Perils of Bad Strategy," *McKinsey Quarterly*, June 2011, referenced February 27, 2015.

Business In Action: Planning a Small Business Strategy Source: Interview, Elwin Derbyshire, Canadian Tire Centre—Cataraqui, Kingston, Ontario, September 3, 2009, revisited in March 2019.

Chapter 7

Business In Action: Saputo Inc.—A Case of Classic Entrepreneurship Sources: Saputo Fact Sheet, Q3-FY2019, https://www.saputo.com, referenced March 20, 2019; Company Profile, www.saputo.ca/investors/en/investors.com, March 20, 2019; Saputo Inc. Company History, www.fundinguniverse.com, March 20 2019; The Rich 100: Canada's Wealthiest People, https://www.canadianbusiness.com/lists-and-rankings/richest-people/top-25-richest-canadians-2018/image/22/, referenced March 20, 2019; Stade Saputo, Montreal Impact, https://www.impactmontreal.com/en/search/stadium%20expansion, referenced March 6, 2015.

Business In Action: Success Is in the Details Source: Richard Branson, "Good Delivery Relies on Attention to Detail," *Canadian Business*, February 28, 2011.

Business In Action: Payfirma (Merrco)—Making Payments Delightful, One Business at a Time Sources: Payfirma, https://www.payfirma.com/about-us/, referenced March 15, 2015; Crunchbase, https://www.crunchbase.com/organization/payfirma-corporation, referenced March 15, 2015; "Payfirma CEO Michael Gokturk Talks to Cantech Letter," February 19, 2015, http://www.cantechletter.com/2015/02/payfirma-ceo-michael-gokturk-talks-cantech-letter/, referenced March 15, 2015; Merrco Payments Inc. and HAW Capital Corp. Announce Amalgamation Agreement, https://www.payfirma.com/releases/merrco-payments-inc-haw-capital-corp-announce-amalgamation-agreement/, October 22, 2018; "Payfirma CEO Confirms Overwhelming Majority Support of Shareholders and Warns against False and Misleading Claims from Obstructing Directors," https://www.newswire.ca/news-releases/payfirma-ceo-confirms-overwhelming-majority-support-of-shareholders-and-warns-against-false-and-misleading-claims-from-obstructing-directors-650591123.html, October 12, 2017.

Business In Action: So, You Want to Start a Booster Juice Source: Booster Juice, www.boosterjuice.com, referenced March 22, 2019.

Business In Action: Kickstarter—Bring Your Creative Project to Life Sources: Kickstarter, https://www.kickstarter.com/help/stats?ref=press; ProductHype, https://blog.producthype.co/all-time-most-funded-kickstarter-projects/; Top Ten Most Crowd Funded Kickstarter Canadian Campaigns, PlanetWeb.ca, http://www.planetweb.ca/news/top-10-funded-canadian-campaigns-ever/, referenced March 22, 2019.

Business In Action: Sequoia Capital Sources: Sequoia Capital, www.sequoiacap.com; Sequoia Capital, Crunch Base Profile, www.crunchbase.com/financial-organization/sequoia-capital; Disrupt SF 2018, "Playing the Global Game, Sequoia Can Cut Checks for Up to $1 Billion," https://techcrunch.com/2018/09/06/playing-the-global-game-sequoia-can-cut-checks-for-up-to-1-billion/, referenced March 22, 2019.

Chapter 8

Business In Action: Inclusion and Diversity—It Does Make a Difference Source: Hunt, Yee, Prince, and Dixon-Fyle, McKinsey & Company, "Delivering Through Diversity," January 2018; Gurchiek, "Six Steps for Building an Inclusive Workplace," https://www.shrm.org/hr-today/news/hr-magazine/0418/pages/6-steps-for-building-an-inclusive-workplace.aspx, March 19, 2018.

Business In Action: Virtual Organizations Source: Advantages and Disadvantages of Virtual Teams, MSG Management Study Guide, http://www.managementstudyguide.com/virtual-teams-advantages-and-disadvantages.htm, referenced March 19, 2015.

Business In Action: The Importance of a Strong Corporate Culture Source: Jaruzelski, Loehr, Holman, Booz, and Company, "Why Culture Is Key," *Strategy+Business*, Reprint 11404, referenced March 18, 2015.

Business In Action: Tony Hsieh, CEO Zappos Source: Zappos.com, referenced March 22, 2015; "Tony Hsieh, Zappos, and the Art of Great Company Culture," https://blog.kissmetrics.com/zappos-art-of-culture/, referenced March 22, 2015; "Zappos Gives Up on Canada Due to Customs Problems," TechDirt, https://www.techdirt.com/articles/20110321/00490713569/zappos-gives-up-canada-due-to-customs-problems.shtml, referenced March 22, 2015.

Business In Action: Microsoft—Restructuring for the Future Source: "Microsoft Unveils Biggest Reorganization in Years," *Bloomberg Businessweek*, March 29, 2018; Laura Troyani, "3 Examples of Organizational Change Done Right," TinyPulse, https://www.tinypulse.com/blog/3-examples-of-organizational-change-and-why-they-got-it-right, May 25, 2017.

Chapter 9

Business In Action: The War for Talent Sources: "The Aging US Workforce," Stanford Centre on Longevity, July 2013, http://longevity.stanford.edu/2013/04/18/the-aging-u-s-workforce-a-chartbook-of-demographic-shifts/, referenced March 24, 2015; Elizabeth G. Chambers, Mark Foulon, Helen Handfield-Jones, Steven M. Hankin, Edward G. Michaels III, "The War for Talent," *McKinsey Quarterly*, 1998, Number 3; Elizabeth Axelrod, Helen Handfield-Jones, Tim Welsh, "War for Talent, Part II," *McKinsey & Company*, 2001; J. Morgan, "The War for Talent: It's Real and Here's Why It's Happening," *Inc.*, https://www.inc.com/jacob-morgan/the-war-for-talent-its-real-heres-why-its-happening.html, December 22, 2107.

Business In Action: Creating an Employer Brand Sources: "In the War for Talent, Your Best Weapon Is Your Current Talent," Forbes Coaches Council, https://www.forbes.com/sites/forbescoachescouncil/2018/07/17/in-the-war-for-talent-your-best-weapon-is-your-current-workforce/#72b804a5360e, July 17, 2018; "Three Strategies to Win the War for Talent," Vistage, https://www.vistage.com/research-center/talent-management/20180824-3-strategies-win-war-talent/, August 24, 2018; Gallup Workplace, "Dismal Employee Engagement a Sign of Global Mismanagement," https://www.gallup.com/workplace/231668/dismal-employee-engagement-sign-global-mismanagement.aspx, referenced March 27, 2019.

Business In Action: Gokhan Cifci—Rewarding Staff for a Job Well Done Source: "Restaurant Owner Rewards Staff with Trip to Cuba," *Niagara This Week, Kingston Heritage*, February 19, 2015, http://www.niagarathisweek.com/news-story/5346250-restaurant -owner-rewards-staff-with-trip-to-cuba/, referenced April 3, 2015.

Business In Action: Creative Ways to Reward Employees Sources: BDC, https://www.bdc.ca/en/articles-tools /employees/manage/pages/engaging-staff-low-cost-rewards.aspx; "20 Ways to Reward Your Employees without Spending a Dime," *Inc.*, https://www.inc.com/lolly-daskal/20-ways-to-reward-your-employees -without-spending-a-dime.html; The Keg, https://www.kegsteakhouse .com/keg-spirit-foundation/overview/, referenced March 28, 2019.

Business In Action: Evolution of Motivational Theory Source: ACCEL Team Development Practices, www.accel-team.com, April 23, 2010, Excerpts from a Supervisor's Guide to Employee Motivation.

Chapter 10

Business In Action: Facebook and YouTube: Still the Social Network Industry Leaders Sources: Zephoria Digital Marketing, https://zephoria.com/top-15-valuable-facebook-statistics/, March 2019; Digital Information World, https://www.digitalinfor, mationworld.com/2019/01/most-popular-global-social-networks-apps -infographic.html, January 1, 2019; B2C, 2019 Socia Media Trends and Statistics, https://www.business2community.com/social -media/2019-social-media-trends-statistics-02156179, January 2, 2019.

Business In Action: D-Wave Systems Inc.—Positioning within a Specialized Niche Sources: D-Wave Overview, D-Wave the Quantum Computing Company, Investor Presentation, www.dwavesys.com, referenced April 12, 2015; D-Wave Systems Inc., Brochure, www .dwavesys.com, referenced April 12, 2015; VB, "D-Wave Previews Quantum Computing Platform with Over 5,000 Qubits," https:// venturebeat.com/2019/02/27/d-wave-previews-quantum -computing-platform-with-over-5000-qubits/, February 27, 2019.

Business In Action: 3M Company Source: Marc Gunther, Marilyn Adamo, and Betsy Feldman, "3M's Innovation Revival," *Fortune*, September 2010, www.fortune.com, December 2010; 3M Investor Relations, https://investors.3m.com/financials/annual-reports-and -proxy-statements/default.aspx, referenced March 31, 2019; Environmental Leader, https://www.environmentalleader .com/2018/12/3m-requires-all-new-products-to-have-sustainability -value-commitment/, December 6, 2018.

Business In Action: Loblaw Companies Limited—Repositioning Its Brand Source: "Loblaw Targets Food-Savvy Canadians in Major Marketing Overhaul," *The Globe and Mail*, September 18, 2014, http:// www.theglobeandmail.com/report-on-business/industry-news /marketing/loblaw-targets-food-savvy-canadians-in-major-marketing -overhaul/article20647658/, referenced April 12, 2015; Canada's Most Innovative Companies 2015, "How Loblaws Stays on Cutting Edge after 96 Years," *Canadian Business*, http://www.canadianbusiness .com/innovation/most-innovative-companies-2015-loblaw/, referenced April 12, 2015; "Digital Strategy Paying Off for Loblaw," *Canadian Grocer*, http://www.canadiangrocer.com/top-stories/headlines/digital -strategy-paying-off-for-loblaw-85814, February 22, 2019.

Chapter 11

Business In Action: The Battle for Cloud-Based Gaming Heats Up Sources: "Tencent Follows Google into Cloud Gaming with 'Start' Pilot," FT.com, https://www.ft.com/content/4b7595ac-552b-11e9-a3db -1fe89bedc16e, April 2, 2019; "Price Tag for South Korea's Nexon Expected to Reach $15b," FT.com, https://www.ft.com/content /dafdca04-40b4-11e9-9bee-efab61506f44, April 1, 2019; Project xCloud, "Choice for How and When to Play," Microsoft, Xbox Wire, https://news.xbox.com/en-us/2019/03/12/project-xcloud-choice-for -how-and-when-you-play/, March 12, 2019; VB, "Cloud Gaming Has Potential, But Its Execution Isn't a Breeze," https://venturebeat .com/2018/06/23/cloud-gaming-has-potential-but-its-execution-isnt-a -breeze/view-all/, June 23, 2018.

Business In Action: Canada's Most Admired Brands Sources: Venture Vancouver, "These Are the Most Admired Companies in Canada in 2019," https://dailyhive.com/vancouver/most-admired -companies-canada-2019; "Canadian Tire Tops Google as Most Admired Company," *Strategy*, http://strategyonline.ca/2019/04/01 /canadian-tire-tops-google-as-most-admired-company/; "Tim Hortons Falls from 4th to 50th in Survey of Canadians' Most Admired Brands," *The Star*, https://www.thestar.com/business/2018/04/05/tim -hortons-falls-from-4th-to-50th-in-survey-of-canadians-most-admired -brands.html; Leger National 2018 Corporate Reputation Study, https://corporatereputationstudy.com/wp-content/uploads/2018/04 /NATIONAL_CorpRepSurvey_2018.pdf.

Business In Action: Business-to-Business (B2B) Sales Sources: Boaz, Murnane, and Nuffer, "The Basics of Business-to-Business Sales Success," *McKinsey Quarterly*, McKinsey & Company, May 2010; Davie, Stephenson, and Valdivieso de Uster, "Three Trends in Business-to-Business Sales," *McKinsey Quarterly*, McKinsey & Company, May 2010.

Business In Action: The Emergence of Omnichannel Marketing Sources: "The Shopping Decision Tree," *MIT Technology Review*, http://www.technologyreview.com/featuredstory/522706/the -shopping-decision-tree/, referenced April 16, 2015; "The Definition of Omni-Channel Marketing—Plus 7 Tips," http://blog.marketo .com/2014/04/the-definition-of-omni-channel-marketing-plus-7-tips .html, referenced April 16, 2015; "The Omni-Channel Experience: Marketing Meets Ubiquity," *Forbes*, http://www.forbes.com/sites /danielnewman/2014/07/22/the-omni-channel-experience-marketing -meets-ubiquity/, referenced April 16, 2015; "What Is OmniChannel?" http://omnichannel.me/what-is-omnichannel/, referenced April 16, 2015; "New Research Shows Growing Impact of Online Research on In-Store Purchases," *Forbes*, https://www.forbes.com/sites /johnellett/2018/02/08/new-research-shows-growing-impact-of-online -research-on-in-store-purchases/#5bb1eb7b16a0, February 8, 2018.

Business In Action: Transportation—Cost Implications (Global Reach) Sources: "Keep on Trucking," *Economist*, http://www .economist.com/node/16595179?story_id116595179, August 2010; S. McCarthy and N. Vanderklippe, "As Oil Nears $100 Mark, Threat to Recovery Grows," *The Globe and Mail*, www.globeandmail.com, January 18, 2011; J. Wohl and N. Zieminski, "Costs Put New Pressures on Manufacturers in 2011," www.nationalpost.com, January 13, 2011.

Business In Action: The Hospital for Sick Children—Marketing a Fundraising Campaign Source: SickKids Foundation, "SickKids Launches $1.3 Billion Fundraising Campaign to Build a New Hospital," https://www.sickkidsfoundation.com/aboutus/newsandmedia /news2017octsickkidscampaignbuildnewhospital; "SickKids Hospital Rallying 'Crews' around $1.3-Billion Fundraising Drive," https://www .ctvnews.ca/canada/sickkids-hospital-rallying-crews-around-1-3 -billion-fundraising-drive-1.4126468, referenced April 7, 2019.

Case for Discussion: Omnichannel—The New Normal at Nordstrom Sources: Nordstrom: About Us, https://shop.nordstrom .com/content/about-us; "The Integration Imperative at Nordstrom— Striking the Omni-channel Balance," Diginomica, https:// diginomica.com/integration-imperative-nordstrom-striking-omni -channel-balance/; Nordstrom Local, https://shop.nordstrom.com /content/nordstrom-local?breadcrumb=Home%2FServices%2FNordst rom+Local; "Why Nordstrom Is Beating All of Its Department Store Competitors," https://finance.yahoo.com/news/nordstrom-beating -department-store-competitors-125704786.html; "How Nordstrom and Macy's Are Tackling Today's Retail Challenges," *Forbes*, https://www .forbes.com/sites/walterloeb/2018/04/09/challenges-facing-retail-in -2018-how-nordstrom-and-macys-tackle-these-issues/#45c1b487219a; "How a Millennial Mindset Is Helping This 116-Year-Old Retailer," *Ad Age*, https://adage.com/article/cmo-strategy/a-millennial-mindset -helping-116-year-retailer/307734; "Nordstrom Hopes Technology Helps Pave a Path to Success," *Forbes*, http://fortune.com /longform/nordstrom-high-touch-tech-fortune-500/, referenced April 9, 2019.

Chapter 12

Business In Action: The Big Data Revolution Is Here Sources: Artificial Intelligence Innovation Report, 2018, Deloitte; Big Data Executive Survey 2018, Data and Innovation, How Big Data and AI Are Driving Business Innovation, New Vantage Partners, Big Data and Analytics in the Automotive Industry, 2018, Deloitte.

Business In Action: Walmart—A Lean, Keen Operating Machine Source: Fortune 500, *Fortune* and "Walmart Corporate," https://corporate.walmart.com/; Investopedia, https://www.investopedia.com/articles/personal-finance/011815/how-walmart-model-wins-everyday-low-prices.asp; https://corporate.walmart.com/our-story, referenced May 13, 2019.

Business In Action: AI—Assisting Our Response Capabilities in Emergency Situations Sources: "Officials: Camp Fire, Deadliest in California History, Was Caused by PG&E Electrical Transmission Lines," https://www.cnbc.com/2019/05/15/officials-camp-fire-deadliest-in-california-history-was-caused-by-pge-electrical-transmission-lines.html; "Two Years Later: 20 Percent of Homes Lost During Fort McMurray Wildfires Fully Rebuilt," https://www.ctvnews.ca/canada/two-years-later-20-per-cent-of-homes-lost-during-fort-mcmurray-wildfires-fully-rebuilt-1.3914654; "2017 Hurricane Season Was the Most Expensive in U.S. History," https://news.nationalgeographic.com/2017/11/2017-hurricane-season-most-expensive-us-history-spd; "AI to the Rescue: 5 Ways Machine Learning Can Assist during Emergency Situations," https://hub.packtpub.com/ai-rescue-5-ways-machine-learning-can-assist-emergency-situations/.

Business In Action: Desire2Learn—Pioneering Innovative Methods in eLearning Sources: Sarah Barmak, "How the 'Netflix of Education' Is Using Big Data in the Classroom," *Canadian Business*, March 19, 2015, http://www.canadianbusiness.com/innovation/most-innovative-2015-d2l-brightspace/, referenced April 24, 2015; "How We Started," Desire to Learn, d2l.com/about, referenced May 18, 2019; https://eliterate.us/state-higher-ed-lms-market-us-canada-end-2018/; https://www.insidehighered.com/digital-learning/article/2017/05/17/where-trends-are-going-lms-market; https://edutechnica.com/tag/market-share/, referenced May 18, 2019.

Chapter 13

Business In Action: Assent Compliance—Securing Equity Capital Funding Sources: https://www.cvca.ca/industry-data/; https://www.businesswire.com/news/home/20181023005316/en/Assent-Compliance-Receives-100-Million-CAD130-Million; https://ottawacitizen.com/business/local-business/assent-compliance-secures-20m-in-drive-to-accelerate-growth; https://obj.ca/article/ottawa-based-assent-compliance-raises-130m-venture-capital; https://techcrunch.com/2017/07/14/canadas-assent-compliance-raises-31-4m-series-b-round-to-help-businesses-stay-in-compliance/.

Business In Action: Apple—Where Does Its Revenue Come From? Sources: "Apple Reports Q1-2019 Results," https://www.apple.com/newsroom/2019/01/apple-reports-first-quarter-results/; MacRumors.com, https://www.macrumors.com/2019/01/29/apple-1q-2019-results/; "Apple Results: A Record September Quarter with $62.9B Revenue," https://sixcolors.com/post/2018/11/reminder-apple-financial-results-released-today/.

Business In Action: What Is the Best Way to Cut Costs? Sources: Layton and Penttinen, "A Better Way to Cut Costs," *McKinsey Quarterly*, McKinsey & Company, October 2009.

Business In Action: Dollar Stores—Rise of the Ultra-Low-Cost Player Sources: "The Dollar-Store Economy," *The New York Times*, August 18, 2011, http://www.nytimes.com/2011/08/21/magazine/the-dollar-store-economy.html?pagewanted=all&_r=1; "How the Dollar Store War Was Won," *Fortune*, May 1, 2015, http://fortune.com/how-dollar-store-war-was-won/; Press Release, "Dollar Tree, Inc. Reports Results for the Fourth Quarter and Full Year Fiscal 2014," February 25, 2015, http://www.dollartreeinfo.com/investors/global/releasedetail.cfm?ReleaseID=898208; "Dollar Tree to Buy Dollar Giant Stores for $52M," *Bloomberg Business*, October 11, 2010; "Dollar Stores in Expansion Mode as More Canadians Feel Cash Pinch," *Global News*, September 11, 2010, http://globalnews.ca/news/1558409/dollar-stores-in-expansion-mode-as-more-canadians-feel-cash-pinch/, referenced May 9, 2015; "When We Visited Family Dollar...," https://www.businessinsider.com/family-dollar-store-tour-2018-8; "Dollarama Officially Opens Online Store in Canada," https://www.ctvnews.ca/business/dollarama-officially-opens-an-online-store-in-canada-1.4262752; Dollar Tree, Dollar General and Dollarama Financial Results, capitaliq.com, referenced April 10, 2019.

Business In Action: What Is an IPO and How Does It Work? Sources: Raj Bhuptani, "How Does IPO Pricing Work?" *Forbes*, August 2013, http://www.forbes.com/sites/quora/2013/11/08/how-does-ipo-pricing-work/, referenced May 2015; https://finance.yahoo.com/quote/FB/history/ and https://finance.yahoo.com/quote/TWTR/history?p=TWTR&.tsrc=fin-srch, referenced April 2019.

Chapter 14

Business In Action: Tying Financial Results to Executive Compensation Sources: Dobbs, Leslie, and Mendonca, "Building the Healthy Corporation," *McKinsey Quarterly*, 2005; "Executive Compensation Is Out of Control. What Now?" *Forbes*, https://www.forbes.com/sites/shelliekarabell/2018/02/14/executive-compensation-is-out-of-control-what-now/#59ab1287431f, February 14, 2018.

Business In Action: The Vulnerability of Leverage Sources: "The Optimal Use of Financial Leverage in a Corporate Capital Structure," Investopedia, http://www.investopedia.com/articles/investing/111813/optimal-use-financial-leverage-corporate-capital-structure.asp, referenced May 14, 2015; https://www.retaildive.com/news/the-biggest-buyouts/541078/ and https://www.retaildive.com/news/the-money-explosion/540735/, referenced April 12, 2019.

Chapter 15

Business In Action: Vanhawks—The Challenges of Commercializing a Great Idea Sources: "Canadian Startup Raises $820,000 on Kickstarter," June 6, 2014, http://www.macleans.ca/work/entrepreneur/vanhawks-story/, referenced April 2015; "Vanhawks Raises $1.6M to Help Put the Valour Smartbike on the Road," March 4, 2015, http://techcrunch.com/2015/03/04/vanhawks-raises-1-6m-to-help-put-the-valour-smartbike-on-the-road/, referenced April 2015; Vanhawks Valour | First Ever Connected Carbon Fibre Bicycle, May 1, 2014, https://www.kickstarter.com/projects/19; Queen's School of Business, Master of Entrepreneurship and Innovation Homepage, referenced April 30, 2015; http://business.queensu.ca/grad_studies/mei/index.php 31822269/vanhawks-valour-first-ever-connected-carbon-fibre/description, referenced April 29, 2015; Vanhawks Website—About, Specs, FAQs, referenced April 29, 2015; Queen's School of Business, Master of Entrepreneurship and Innovation Homepage, referenced April 30, 2015; http://business.queensu.ca/grad_studies/mei/index.php, referenced April 29, 2015; Alex Choi, VanHawks, direct commentary, August 5, 2015; "Vanhawks Acquired by Ontario-based Automotive Parts Manufacturer Warren Industries," https://betakit.com/vanhawks-acquired-by-ontario-based-automotive-parts-manufacturer-warren-industries/, April 21, 2017.

Business In Action: Disney—Recognizing a Market Shift and Opportunity Sources: "Disney Unveils Price, Launch Date for Big Streaming Push," Reuters, https//reuters.com/article/us-walt-disney-streaming/disney, April 11, 2019; https://www.techradar.com/news/disney-streaming-service-disneys-all-inclusive-streaming-package-explained, April 15, 2019.

Business In Action: Shopify Inc.—A Canadian Tech Success Story Sources: "How Shopify Became the Go-To Ecommerce Platform for Startups," *Entrepreneur*, http://www.entrepreneur.com/article/222967, referenced May 20, 2015; "Shopify Features," http://www.shopify.ca/online/ecommerce-solutions, referenced May 20, 2015; "The Narwhal Club: Home to Canada's $1 Billion Dollar Tech

Startups," Visual Capitalist, http://www.visualcapitalist.com/narwhal-club-1-billion-dollar-canadian-tech-companies/, referenced May 20, 2015; "Shopify Hits Star Status with Sparkling IPO," *The Globe and Mail*, May 21, 2015; http://time.com/3893474/shopify-ipo-trading/, Yahoo Finance, https://finance.yahoo.com/quote/SHOP?p=SHOP&.tsrc=fin-srch, https://investors.shopify.com/Investor-News-Details/2018/Shopify-Completes-Offering-of-Class-A-Subordinate-Voting-Shares-55166507c/default.aspx, December 18, 2018.

Case for Discussion 2: Entrepreneurship: Skills and Opportunity Sources: Gillian Shaw, "Card Game Teaches Little Ones Computer Coding Basics," *Vancouver Sun*, http://www.vancouversun.com/business/Card+game+teaches+little+ones+computer+coding+basics/10461111/story.html; https://www.startupnews.ca/2018/11/alexandra-greenhill-one-of-canadas-top-100-most-powerful-women/; "The Nanny Connection: My Best Helper Allows Canadian Families to Vet Caretakers Online," *Financial Post*, https://business.financialpost.com/entrepreneur/fp-startups/the-nanny-connection-my-best-helper-allows-canadian-families-to-vet-caretakers-online; Alexandra Greenhill, "Healthcare Coordination—It Takes a Village, and a Tech Platform," https://www.linkedin.com/pulse/healthcare-coordination-takes-village-tech-platform-greenhill/; https://ottawacitizen.com/sponsored/health-sponsored/dementia-society-trying-out-a-new-app-with-the-potential-to-make-things-simpler-for-people-living-with-dementia.

Index

Note: Boldface indicates the page numbers on which key terms are defined.